The Vega Factor

The Vega Factor

Oil Volatility and the Next Global Crisis

Kent Moors

WILEY

John Wiley & Sons, Inc.

Published by John Wiley & Sons, Inc., Hoboken, New Jersey.
Published simultaneously in Canada.

For general information on our other products and services or for technical support, please contact our Customer Care Department within the United States at (800) 762–2974, outside the United States at (317) 572–3993 or fax (317) 572–4002.

Wiley also publishes its books in a variety of electronic formats. Some content that appears in print may not be available in electronic books. For more information about Wiley products, visit our web site at www.wiley.com.

Library of Congress Cataloging-in-Publication Data:

Moors, Kent, 1948-
    The Vega Factor : Oil Volatility and the Next Global Crisis / Kent Moors.
      p. cm
    Includes index.
    ISBN 978-0-470-60208-9 (cloth); ISBN 978-1-118-07707-8 (ebk);
    ISBN 978-1-118-07708-5 (ebk); ISBN 978-1-118-07708-5 (ebk);
      1. Petroleum products—Prices.   2. Petroleum industry and trade.
3. Petroleum reserves—Political aspects. I. Title.
  HD9560.4.M577 2011
  338.2'3282—dc22

                                     2010053515

Printed in the United States of America

10 9 8 7 6 5 4 3 2 1

To My Wife Marina:
The True Love of My Life—First, Last, and Always

Contents

Preface

Futures contracts in oil (as with other commodities) were introduced to stabilize trading in forward consignments, open the market to a broader sourcing of liquidity, and lessen the control exercised by major producers and distributors. From the standpoint of these considerations, their introduction was largely a beneficial development.

Less than 30 years later, however, the trading is giving way to pronounced volatility, shaking traditional market pricing mechanisms and threatening to destabilize large areas of both developed and developing economies. Such a result arises from the pervasive presence of energy. In turn, that energy presence remains predicated upon the positioning and pricing of oil.

I may well prefer some other fuel reliance: a low-carbon approach, one that emphasizes alternative and renewable sources. But that will not happen for several decades. Whether we like it or not, oil remains the mainstay of the energy mix. That means the volatility hitting crude has a widening economic impact. That effect is intensifying and the instability resulting is beginning to erode the dynamics of exchange. More established considerations such as supply, demand, currency valuations, stockpiles, production estimates, and a range of financial and support elements—the foundation on which the market has determined oil pricing until recently—will serve merely to accentuate this crisis.

This is not because peak oil is upon us (although it seems poised on the horizon), or that OPEC is using crude as a bargaining chip, or that rentier states have decided to magnify short-term immediate profits, or even that some major geopolitical event has radically changed the availability or distribution of oil. All of these could, of course, add to the volatility. Yet, the rapidly approaching crisis is emerging within the oil trading system itself.

The way the market trades oil is making it progressively more difficult to price it. The rise of crude as both a commodity and an asset has introduced a new and unsettling element into the pricing equation. The relationship between paper barrels (futures contracts) and wet barrels (actual oil consignments for delivery) results in two overarching developments: (1) profit from driving the "paper price" higher (not axiomatically a bad thing, since market are predicated upon the profit motive) in turn is creating a greater strain on the real market pricing of the underlying commodity; and (2) a rising inability to price options upon which futures contract traders rely to hedge their bets has already introduced new concerns over the use of collateralized and synthetic asset and debt obligations to bridge the difference between the paper and wet barrels.

This is not simply a new development in market pricing arising from the usual suspects (supply, demand, forex, etc.). It is something intensified by the process of futures contract trading itself. It is what I refer to as *oil vega*. And it threatens to produce a far more protracted crisis than the aftermath of the subprime mortgage mess.

There are two principal objectives to this book. The first considers how one approaches the structure of, and changes in, the oil market. The second involves the nature of this unfolding oil vega crisis. The combination of these two leads to one inescapable conclusion. Oil instability will intensify; more traditional concerns over supply, demand, currency values, and infrastructure will augment the volatility, but the trade in futures contracts will remain the primary driver.

Chapter 1 introduces the concept of oil vega, along with a general description of how I intend to approach and employ the concept. That brief overview is then followed by four chapters discussing basic market factors and the ways in which they are undergoing accelerated alteration in a rapidly changing environment. In each case, I demonstrate how traditional notions of how the market operates, or the way in which players position themselves within it, will no longer provide adequate offset to the crisis. Here, we consider the relationship between oil vega and elements of risk (Chapter 2); how oil pricing has been approached and why that is changing (Chapter 3); the impact of oil trading and its connection to the value of the dollar, credit, and liquidity (Chapter 4); as well as significant changes in the relationships among the production, processing, and distribution sectors of the oil market, the positioning of companies and their impact, or, as I call it, the upstream/downstream tradeoff (Chapter 5).

Chapter 6 addresses the impact of government action in attempts to combat oil vega. The conclusion here is rather direct—there is very little that the public sector can do to attenuate the crisis. It can, however, make matters much worse. The primary governmental approaches considered in this chapter will largely worsen an already deteriorating climate, Chapter 7 will advance an initial framework of how oil vega should be approached in an attempt to mollify its impact. But it is also a rather frank assessment on how difficult that process will be. This essentially follows from its origin. Oil vega does not result from fraud, illegal activity, or an onslaught from a foreign power. It results from the very process utilized in an attempt to introduce forward stability into the futures trading of oil.

I need also to make some comments on the structure of this book. Given that I intend this work to begin a serious discussion of an accelerating crisis, it is written to address two audiences. The first comprises general readers, while the second considers those interested in greater detail, along with an emphasis on the research, scholarly, and analytical dimensions. Therefore, I have attempted to make the text accessible, while reserving to the endnotes additional explanations and references to approaches that the researcher or specialist would find of interest. These sources have been selected with some care to provide a more complete and accessible introduction to the broader range of considerations emerging from a number of quarters. Wherever possible, I have indicated where works not generally available, especially unpublished papers and monographs, can be retrieved electronically. Each citation, therefore, provides an opportunity for the reader to engage herself with the fuller debates while not detracting from the argument advanced in the text.

I have benefited greatly from the professional expertise of the superb staff at John Wiley & Sons, especially Editorial Director Debra Englander, Senior Editorial Manager Emilie Herman, and Editorial Program Coordinator Adrianna Johnson. I also wish to thank Mike Ward, the Publisher of Money Map Press, who encouraged me to write the book, and for the support and encouragement of Alex Williams, the Editorial Director at my advisory publications *Oil and Energy Investor* and *Energy Advantage*. I also acknowledge with great appreciation the receipt of a Duquesne University Presidential Scholarship Award, providing some very welcome time to devote to writing.

As with all things in my life, however, I thank most of all my wife Marina, whose support and encouragement, along with the occasional strategic use of the verbal whip, made this book possible. My life would mean little without her.

Chapter 1

The Meaning of
Oil Vega

There is unprecedented volatility entering the oil market, transforming pricing and increasing instability. It will place a premium on setting prices via futures contracts without due regard for the actual market value of the underlying crude oil consignments. Increasing usage of synthetic derivatives will augment the problem in a manner reminiscent of the subprime mortgage disaster, but having an even more pronounced impact. Neither the way in which oil companies are structured or operate will temper this oncoming wave, while governmental action worldwide will only exacerbate the crisis.

In short, there is a perfect storm developing in the energy sector and it's going to be a nasty one.

The pages to follow detail what that storm looks like. This book results from years of analysis, consulting and practice in a very changing oil sector. Often such activity has ended being more about broader political, economic, or financial matters than directly related to the underlying raw material itself. Such a focus is hardly surprising, given the endemic position of crude oil, the impact its supply and pricing has on modern ideas of technology and lifestyle, and the new world of regarding oil as both a commodity and an asset. In addition, based on holding a doctorate in political science, having personally experienced the economic transitions in what suddenly became a post-Soviet area, and spending some three decades teaching about the relationships between theory and practice, my view is that the transitions may have come about more easily than I first realized.

One conclusion has clearly emerged from these experiences. The ongoing situation surrounding oil will encompass an increasingly volatile mixture (no pun intended) of market, investment, and political ramifications. For several years, it has been my intention to write down some extended thoughts about this tripartite connection and the volatility emerging as a consequence. I had always intended that the product would bring a broad variety of studies to bear on an accelerating problem in a way that would allow both the interested general reader and the specialist to gain some benefit from the treatment.

Such an idea has been an ongoing work in progress for the past five years. As both an academic and a consultant, I had observed the rising concerns on the oil question expressed by researchers and practitioners. The nature of oil volatility provided the focus for what I intended to write. Only recently, however, has my project also obtained an immediacy of purpose.

That immediacy resulted from two occasions some five weeks apart. Both confirmed my analysis but also telegraphed that the threat was advancing much faster than I had anticipated. The first was an early August 2009 meeting held in The City, London's financial center. In attendance was a select group of hedge-fund directors, investment bankers, market analysts, and risk managers, along with the usual support coterie of numbers crunchers and model builders. The subject was oil and the prognosis was both unanimous and extraordinary.

The assembled were not there to announce the demise of the oil age—at least, not yet. But they were holding a wake of sorts. Crude oil would remain a commodity bought and sold on exchanges worldwide, with the benchmark prices issued each trading day from

New York and London largely determining the price. The catch was this. Sketched in their facial expressions and couched in carefully chosen words that morning was a startling revelation. Nobody in the room still believed they could either control oil volatility or, for that matter, provide adequate estimates of it. Oil was their lifeblood, a main source of their revenue and influence, the asset around which they had constructed a mighty edifice of financial power. And they no longer had a clue where it was headed.

That the gathering occurred in London, rather than Vienna (where OPEC, the preeminent producers' group meets) or New York (the location of most daily trades in the product), tells one much about how oil investment has changed. More money is raised for international oil projects within a three-mile radius of the Liverpool Street rail station than any other single place on earth. Wells may be spud in the Saudi desert, the Russian tundra, the Nigerian delta, or the jungles of New Guinea. Futures may trade the extracted product on stock exchanges throughout the world. However, funding for the drilling, service, and wellhead operations, and the pipelines and processing facilities, progressively comes from the London Stock Exchange (LSE) or, in particular for the companies emerging in response to the rapidly changing market, the LSE's Alternative Investment Market (AIM).

In late September 2009, the second meeting took place. This time the location was the new convention center in Pittsburgh and the venue was a meeting of the G20 heads of state—the 19 dominant global economies with the European Union as an organizational entity thrown in for good measure. The public usually receives only two views of such meetings—the staged press conferences and the unrest in the streets. Neither actually says much about what is really going on. In far less public sessions agendas are set, consensus is forged, and common statements of purpose are developed. These may be multilateral exercises or bilateral agreements. Either way, the gathering facilitates, but hardly concludes, the process. The success of the meetings is determined at sessions taking place elsewhere after it has ended. The G20 in Pittsburgh followed such a format.

The formal proceedings in Pittsburgh lasted less than two days. The agenda-setting meetings away from public view, however, transpired over a five-day period. At one of those sessions, advisors attached to various national delegations discussed the state of the oil market. They reflected the same concerns addressed by the London bankers five weeks earlier. Only this time, in dialogue that intended to set an ongoing agenda for future meetings, they reached a quick agreement on two matters. First, they anticipated a return of the oil market volatility that resulted in a high of $147.27 a barrel by July 11, 2008, doubling prices in less than a year. Second, this time more pronounced international political consequences would emerge as a direct result of the oil swings.

These meetings in London and Pittsburgh are the most recent indications that we have a major problem developing, one involving financial and political consequences directly resulting from what takes place in the oil market. Volatility remains the catalyst. However, one aspect has changed. We can no longer regard it as something likely to occur in the remote future. It is fast approaching.

This book is not a call to arms on energy security, a demand for a renewed commitment to alternative energy, or an argument for resurgence in international oil dialogue. All of these are certainly necessary, but not the primary focus of this treatment. None of these will realize much success unless we come to grips with the underlying issue. As we progressively remove ourselves from the worst financial crisis in three generations, as this long slow process of recovery unfolds, a fundamentally different, less stable, and far less predictable oil market will be there to greet us. It is toward an understanding of this altered state of affairs that the following analysis directs attention. Make no mistake. While the changes will first manifest themselves in the trading markets, it will be the political playing field that will ultimately decide matters.

What I call *oil vega* will be the single most pervasive and disturbing element of the energy market moving forward. It speaks of rising volatility, an inability to predict pricing changes or impact, deteriorating policy alternatives, and the probable global political consequences. Instability in both the market and governmental responses to it will likely result in intensified and repetitive cycles of crises, producing increasingly dangerous political consequences.

I have borrowed the concept of *vega* from option[1] traders to label this new environment. As traders use it, vega relates to the way in which the price of an option changes with the change in volatility.

Of course, things are never quite that easy. Traders need to determine a value for the option and be able to revise their estimates on that value as market changes take place in the futures contract on which it is based. For that they need a pricing model. The volatility component in their pricing model, from which one determines a theoretical value for the option against which a trader calculates the option's market price, is called *implied volatility*. Vega represents the rate of change in the theoretical value of an option as it relates to a change in implied volatility.

Vega is, therefore, a "second order" or derivative concept to the actual change in the value of a security. It measures the amount by which the price of an option changes when volatility changes.[2] Volatility is simply the measurement of how often and by what amount a market factor revises. Usually, that factor is price, and is represented by another "Greek"—*delta*.[3] Now this translates into the presence of a higher vega, indicating greater fluctuations in the underlying prices of actual contracts.

Volatility is often regarded as a general measure of the risk in an option (or security, stock share, tradable asset, etc.). It measures anticipated fluctuations over a period of time. One expects that price will change more often for an instrument with higher volatility. The greater the price swing, the greater the volatility. Options for underlying securities having high volatility will cost more than those with low volatility. Several measures are used to gauge volatility. One of the most common is calculating a standard deviation. If the measurement is against a known common index, such as determining stock volatility against the S&P index, the result is a security's *beta*. While not included in the usual "Greeks" applied by option traders, beta obviously does have some use as a measure of the market (nondiversifiable) risk associated with any security. Options, however, do not have a readily available common index against which to gauge changes in price. Also, this may begin with a consideration of price changes, but notice that vega describes the *rate* of the change, not simply the change itself.

This will be important in our usage, since the essential thesis of this book is that the increasing rate (along with the range) of changes will generate instability. This will have a pervasive and serious impact. Simply put, *oil vega will result in the increasing inability to determine the genuine value of crude oil based on its market price.*

That inability will erode the ability to predict, plan and compensate. This will be problem enough for the market. However, given the interconnection between the public and private sectors when it comes to energy policy, the consequences of oil vega will impact most visibly and seriously on the global intergovernmental stage.

This new environment is certain to raise the political heat, shorten international tempers, and make global oil a much more volatile and less predictable commodity. Unless we come to grips with the changes now emerging, none of the moves to make nations more secure, uncover new energy sources, or bring about a global oil consensus will make much difference. A rising tide of uncertainty will engulf the first. The second, while certainly the essential solution in the long term, will not have time to develop before the crisis hits. The volatile nature of crude oil will already have significantly damaged the market well before a weaning from primary dependence upon oil is possible. The third will fall victim to the competing policies of rentier nations, transit states, and end-consuming countries.

We have developing market (dis)order—a pervasive and endemic disequilibrium masquerading as the "new order" in the oil market. It is not that we will suddenly run out of crude oil, although that day is approaching.[4] The gravamen of the situation involves the increasing inability to develop adequate market remedies for expanding volatility. An even more unsettling shortcoming will develop: It will become progressively more difficult to predict the volatility itself.

Supply meeting demand is, of course, a fundamental ingredient in the instability, especially in how participants regard the cycle of volatility as it unfolds. However, it is not the supply-demand relationship itself that causes the problem. Available supply is less the sole driving issue in this new (dis)order. Price fluctuations will result from more than simply the perception of how much crude oil is left.

A simple review of predictions presented prior to the (usually) Wednesday morning release of Energy Information Administration (EIA)[5] weekly figures on oil and oil product inventories indicates current predictive abilities are already suspect. The "actual"[6] figures provided are often quite at variance to the predictions. We also are becoming increasingly concerned about the ability of EIA or the International Energy Agency (IEA)[7] to provide meaningful worldwide demand figures.

Significant demand pressures are underestimated or not considered at all. The IEA has acknowledged this problem, essentially resulting from continued overreliance on demand from developed countries and selected developing markets (e.g., China, India, East Asia) and underestimation of significant demand pressures in producing countries and other less-developed regions of the world.[8]

A clear signal that what I call oil vega is becoming a rising concern was issued by the EIA on October 7, 2009. It has found it necessary to follow a new reporting format.

> Energy prices are volatile. They change as market participants adjust their expectations to new information from physical energy markets and markets for energy-related financial derivatives. Futures and options markets are a valuable source of information regarding these changing expectations.
>
> Starting with the October 2009 issue [released October 6, 2009], Energy Information Administration's (EIA) *Short-Term Energy Outlook (STEO)* began tracking crude oil and natural gas futures prices and the market's assessment of the range in which prices are expected to trade. We do this using a measure of risk derived from the New York Mercantile Exchange (NYMEX) Light Sweet Crude Oil Options and Natural Gas Options markets known as "implied volatility." Implied volatility is nothing more than a standard deviation for the expected futures returns embedded in the option's price.[9]

The commodity option–pricing model is derived directly from the Black-Scholes option pricing model, based upon the Black–Scholes equation—the most famous single formula ever articulated for trading options.[10]

The equation itself produces a model that is often quite restrictive in application, given that it involves six major assumptions: (1) there are no dividends on the underlying security during the life of the option, (2) European-style exercise (that is, only at expiry) is followed, (3) markets are efficient, (4) there are no commissions charged, (5) interest rates are constant and known, and (6) returns exhibit lognormal distribution (i.e., providing a normal distribution, allowing thereby the use of standard statistical techniques on the resulting data). This last assumption is very significant in the estimation of option premiums since a lognormal distribution is usually a better indication of anticipated price movements than the direct usage of variables because the log of returns is bounded downside at zero. Despite its shortcomings, however, the model still provides the ability to make approximations useful in a wide range of applications. As is often the case, the devil remains in the details!

In turn, the Black-Scholes option pricing model includes as variables the spot price (market price of the underlying asset on the valuation date), the strike price (the price at which the holder of the option has the right to buy or sell the underlying contract), the time until the option expires, the risk-free interest rate until expiry (typically a zero coupon government bond yield), volatility, and the average yield of the underlying asset for the life of the option.

The EIA goes on to explain:

The NYMEX employs Fischer Black's commodity option-pricing model,[11] to calculate the implied volatility, which the NYMEX publishes nightly. EIA recognizes some assumptions made for the model used by the Black model are controversial—e.g., futures prices are lognormally distributed with constant volatility—and will be conducting ongoing research into the price-formation process. However, EIA believes this approach—widely used by market participants, investment banks, and central banks—has been demonstrated to be sound. EIA uses the implied volatilities to create confidence intervals, which are forward-looking expected values resulting from the trading and risk transfer of market participants.[12]

The range of the confidence interval is determined by the *confidence level* specified for the interval. The confidence level represents the probability that the final market price for a particular futures contract, such as December 2010 crude oil, will fall somewhere within the lower and upper range of prices. For example, for a 95 percent confidence level, we calculate a range of prices within which there is a 95 percent likelihood the delivered price for the commodity will fall (for the month the commodity goes to physical delivery). In other words, there is a 5 percent chance the price for that specific month will fall outside of the 95 percent confidence interval. The higher the confidence level, the wider the range between lower and upper limits.[13]

Yet the problem is actually worse than currently recognized. As we shall see, neither oil vega nor, for that matter, the traditional oil pricing patterns, always follow normal market expectations. Oil is a commodity able to defy those expectations, a tendency accelerating over the past several years, despite the global economic downturn.

What makes it such a stubborn and resilient market deviant is its central position in economies. Energy usage is certainly the pervasive element in the structure of markets and, despite recent concerns to the contrary, crude oil remains the dominant energy source. It defines industrial and commercial development and productivity in a wide range of ways from transport to petrochemicals. It even largely determines the pricing of natural gas, its primary hydrocarbon energy exchange equivalent. As such, normal changes in usage in response to price fluctuations (price and demand elasticity/inelasticity) are not applied to oil as readily as to other market products.

A transition from oil to natural gas, or further on to genuine new sources of energy, is hampered by over a century of infrastructure development and, until recently, the belief that oil supply is plentiful and prices will remain low. The transition will occur only when two things happen: first, when average prices rise to levels at which economic expansion starts to contract and, second, when delivery and usage systems are no longer able to structure sufficient forward planning. Both of these trigger mechanisms are on the horizon. They are accentuating an already difficult market situation and intensifying the problems.

I have said on several occasions that we have about thirty years left of a sustainable crude-oil-based economy.[14] Crude oil will certainly remain an element in the energy mix well into the twenty-first century—extracted, sold, processed, and used. However, the levels of volatility experienced, spot shortages, the increasing cost of processing inferior grades of crude oil or of upgrading heavy oil, bitumen, and oil sands to synthetic oil, declines in supply, regional market imbalances, and a number of other problems will progressively render crude unacceptably costly, inefficient, and prone to accelerating instability. The dynamics of essential market expansion and diversification will necessitate a change.

This is especially significant for the U.S. market, where the economy base has historically depended upon the availability of cheap and plentiful energy (timber, then coal, and, until recently, oil). There were clear indications in the dramatic rise of oil prices through early July 2008 that the cost of resulting energy flows had become a major impediment to economic development and even market stability in developed economies. Similar restraining indicators resulted from the combined dramatic decline in oil prices and the credit crunch experienced in late 2008.[15] It is important to remember that the ultimate impact of oil vega results from the rate of volatility, not simply from price movements in only one direction.[16] The situation has been even more apparent (and immediate) in those nations where advancing industrialization holds the key to further economic expansion.[17]

Nonetheless, irrespective of price or ease of availability, crude will remain a primary energy source in parts of the developing world, where the absence of either a genuine alternative resource base or adequate levels of investment will require its continued use. In addition, the rising competition for available supply over the next decade will drive prices higher. This will increase political pressures in several vulnerable regions and contribute to the volatility in the market as a whole. A grand global zero-sum game is developing, where we are already witnessing diversions of supply to areas prepared to pay a higher premium for product.[18]

In response, the most developed states can hardly select a go-it-alone policy. This is especially true of the United States. It is important to emphasize at the outset that adopting a "fortress America" planning approach will avail the nation of little in this situation. The chimera of any argument to make the United States self-sufficient in oil is fallacious on its face value. The oil market has become globally integrated, with the United States dependent on imports for the bulk of what is used daily.[19] That import total includes a rising amount of imported refined oil products. Data and analysis supplement recent experience, indicating that domestic markets cannot insulate themselves from global energy volatility, whether those nations are net exporters or importers of oil. [20]

Much has been written about the cycles of oil pricing.[21] From early 2008 on, we have certainly experienced significant movement in both directions—to almost $150 a barrel in early July 2008 on the New York Mercantile Exchange (NYMEX)[22] and then down to a low of less than $33 in late December of the same year. However, while the upward pressure on prices through the midsummer resulted largely from concern over spikes in demand and trading fueled by the declining exchange value of the U.S. dollar,[23] the rapid decline in prices following the widening credit and liquidity drain-off experienced in the third quarter of 2008 did result in appreciable declines in demand, reflecting the result anticipated from a traditional market trigger—declining demand results in declining price, the reverse of the rise experienced six months earlier.[24]

The important point, however, is this. The pressures prompting a decline in oil prices were exogenous to the oil supply-demand cycle. Put simply—and we shall have much more to say on this subject later—the protracted credit-liquidity-finance crisis and the corresponding worldwide recession resulting from it has masked a continuing deterioration in the ability of oil supplies to meet demand. We have not seen that shortfall reemerge for the simple reason that there have been other economic matters that were even more pressing. The resurgence of that demand, which without doubt will quickly occur as overall financial equilibrium returns to the broader markets, will create another upward spiral in both prices and volatility. Once the "outside" factors are removed, oil vega will intensify along with the market instabilities associated with it. It is hardly a question of *whether*, but rather *when*.

Normally, cuts in oil prices will occasion a greater demand for crude and refined products. This has resulted in an ongoing debate over the actual meaning of efficiency and the nature of the relationship between cost and oil usage.[25] However, the declines in pricing on this occasion resulted from demand reductions for broader economic reasons. As productivity, consumption, real estate prices, and commercial investment declined, while unemployment, bankruptcies, and defaults increased, demand for oil products was cut appreciably. The destruction of wealth and purchasing power led to a concomitant destruction of oil demand.

Certainly by the first quarter of 2010, we were witnessing an initial stabilizing of oil pricing, along with signals that demand is returning. It is well known that increasing levels of energy demand regularly precede major upward corrections in markets as a whole. That does not happen merely because people wake up one morning feeling more confident about their consumption rates or lifestyles. It is because energy usage is a front-end support requirement for a rise in leading indicators,[26] with the recovery taking place well before it registers in lagging indicators.[27] In other words, energy in general and its dominant constituent—oil—in particular, will experience an increase in demand at an early stage of a recovery process, before that recovery is recognized in wider economic sectors.

As oil vega intensifies, increasing price instability (the assumption here is of *rising* prices, although rapid movements in either direction would be troubling), escalating supply-demand concerns, and a widening inability of markets to predict and compensate without engendering disproportionate consequences, the public sector will step in to deal with the problem. I shall suggest in the analysis to follow that oil vega will revise the playing field of world politics—threatening to add thereby another level of concern. This book will suggest that it will be the political arena, rather than the market, that will ultimately decide the matter. Unless there is a genuine global strategy in place, a protracted crisis will ensue. An extreme result would be conflict over resources, but the more likely outcome would be recurring oil-based domestic and regional legislative and regulatory decisions impeding free trade, cross-border capital flows, and access to assets. That could be as damaging and as disruptive.

This book is also not a history of either the oil market or the players within it. The academic within me is always tempted to explain the nuances of how we end up at a juncture at which significant policy decisions are required. In fact, my initial approach to this book attempted to do just that. Ultimately, the size of the resulting manuscript (about three times the current one), combined with the difficulty of unfolding a number of disparate "plot lines" in a single commentary, gravitated against that effort. I shall provide some of the historical writing originally intended for this work in other venues directed to audiences primarily interested in such matters. For those desiring to augment the treatment in the current volume with more historically oriented approaches, there are several works I would recommend.[28]

What results is a more focused and immediate emphasis upon the contemporary issues at hand: a rapidly accelerating crisis in the contemporary oil sector, resulting from rising volatility and the impact of the vega factor.

Finally, most treatments of oil spend considerable time discussing Middle Eastern instability, geopolitical concerns, and possible conflicts over available resources, along with national security considerations and related strategic applications. These are certainly major concerns. As a political scientist by training, having experience in global risk management policy development and execution, I recognize the importance of such matters.[29] We shall touch on some of them during the course of this book. However, this is neither the primary focus nor the intention of what follows.

I wish to emphasize at the outset that, while rising instability and uncertainty in such quarters will add to the acceleration of the vega factor, they are not the causes. Even if we should enter a period of expanding international good will and understanding, while experiencing a significant decline in geopolitical tensions (admittedly, an unlikely prospect), we shall still experience the crisis in oil. This is not one initiated by OPEC, Iran, Chavez, the European Union, Russia, resource nationalism, sovereign wealth funds, or a host of other political variables. These factors can only intensify the problems.

The oncoming crisis, the onset of oil vega, is a product of the oil market itself. It is not thrust upon it from the outside. It emerges from how oil is now extracted, processed, traded, priced, and hedged.

That makes it far more dangerous and difficult to control.

Chapter 2

How Oil Volatility Relates to Strategic Risk

Calgary, November 2008

Having finished a risk assessment workshop for the Canadian Oil Sands Conference, I am meeting over lunch with executives from Suncor Energy, a leading producer of synthetic crude from the fabled Athabasca basin. If developed (and the environmental impact controlled), the oil sands of Alberta could provide reserves equivalent to those of Saudi Arabia. But production is under intense pressure from dramatic declines in global oil prices, down 70 percent in barely four months (the collapse would reach 78 percent before the end of the year). By this point, not a single oil sands project development is profitable.

"This is all about figuring the market and we can't do that until prices bear some relationship to real demand," a veteran field manager points out. All agree that the low price reflects pressures of a broader financial constriction, not the oil sector itself. However, an oil company needs to structure policy based upon actual estimates of production capacity and end-user needs.

"We have to confront the volatility and work that into a focused production plan moving forward," a company financial officer finally suggests. Everybody nods in agreement . . . but the table then turns uncomfortably silent.

Volatility is the devil to put into a projection. It never plots well.

■ ■ ■

In the six months between the high summer of 2008 and January 2009, the bottom fell out of the global oil market. Every crude oil producer in the world was posing the same question as that raised in Calgary. Some regions—for example, Russia and the Caspian basin—experienced the credit collapse and financial meltdown after it had hit in Europe and North America, thereby assuring that their recovery would be more anemic and occur later than elsewhere. During the last six months of 2010, prices increased and indications emerged of renewed demand moving back into the market. That certainly served to spike prices further as supply concerns returned.

However, the essential problem already apparent with U.S. demand, and certain to accelerate moving forward, deals not simply with price levels. It addresses expanded volatility, producing an inability to provide estimates, and widening perceptions of a deepening breakdown. This is the oil vega mentioned in Chapter 1, and it will ultimately have an impact far more pervasive than its effect on oil sands producers in Canada or SUV owners in the United States.

Oil vega will directly damage markets, investment profiles, and production capabilities and generate both economic and political conflict. Ultimately, the preeminence of this volatility will focus upon the political players—nations and their policymakers—upon whom the full weight of the challenges and their consequences will come to rest.

Much of the general public still regards oil volatility as merely intermittent departures from some prevailing overall stability, preferring to regard it as an interruption from the normal activities of an otherwise predictable energy sector. This approach is likewise manifest in the way officials still address each crisis, providing "solutions" that are at best incomplete responses to the underlying situation.

This guarantees that, when decision makers finally abandon such a view and recognize the problem for what it is, there will be less flexibility in response and a higher likelihood of confrontation. The "crisis over the crisis," the realization that the increasing volatility of oil is not simply a product of ruthless speculators or rogue nations but endemic to the product and its availability, will be far worse than the sequence of problems giving rise to it. The sum will be far greater than its parts—and far more dangerous.

Markets may facilitate decisions on the usage of commodities, capital, assets, and supply, and provide a distribution mechanism for resources while making possible the addressing of wider demand considerations. However, markets do not make policy. That is a governmental responsibility. Some may still suggest that markets may make better social-wide decisions than elected officials. Yet to do so requires that one accept two premises. First, efficiency is the only acceptable measurement of policy. Second, markets are an optimization of rational choice. The first, while still espoused as desirable via the so-called efficient market hypothesis in a range of applications,[1] is nonetheless regularly undermined by the claims of rights, interests, duties, and obligations incumbent on any community exercise. The second is a highly dubious premise upon which to base anything beyond individual profit making.

Put succinctly, markets provide a common location for the pursuit of individual gain. In that sense, they are exercises in collective emotion not reason. Recently, they have exhibited a rather irrational character.[2] Some suggest that this reflects more the uncertainty of a financial crisis.[3] With markets at equilibrium existing only in the constricted confines of mathematical models and increasing volatility characterizing markets as a whole, greater utilization of public policy approaches has emerged. That means the days of expecting governments to keep hands off are over, as witnessed by the unparalleled global-wide government stimulus packages starting in 2008.

The precedents for significant government intervention are already present in the rescue of credit and in the funneling of liquidity into the market.[4] As the oil vega problem intensifies, we are likely to see it met by a heavier government response. One may well debate the advisability or the potential for success in such endeavors, but no longer their likelihood.

In coming to grips with this intensifying strain on the system, we need to recognize the several layers on which it is playing out. The political will be the ultimate level of decision making. However, in clarifying the nature of the unfolding crisis it is still advisable for the discussion to begin with the market. It is the market that accounts for the physical and financial exchange of oil. It is where the commodity is produced, financed, exchanged, processed, and sold. Therefore, the initial focus is how oil vega affects the market and our approach to it.

I need to start with a simple and troubling observation. The oil market I have wrestled with for the past several decades has ended. Replacing it is one fueled by instability, intense volatility in both pricing and trading, along with a level of uncertainty not witnessed since the late 1970s. The environment against which this new market (dis)order plays out, however, is very different from that experienced 30 years ago. Then I was still under the delusion that adequate supply was available to meet any expanding demand, a view still largely shared by analysts across the spectrum. It was thought merely a question of dealing with the regional and political differences that made it difficult to bring the crude to market. That is no longer the case.

What we are beginning to experience is not simply an aberrant cycle in oil usage or a short-term result of a slow emergence from the worst international financial crisis of the past 80 years. While both of these have been integrally related over the past two years, they have also been masking a deeper, more endemic, and far more disconcerting development. The underpinning dynamics of the oil chain will progressively be unable to meet the expectations of the market. And that, in turn, will intensify the volatility resulting.

The new (dis)order will threaten assumptions applied to the oil market for decades while at the same time introducing concerns that will require we abandon current thinking. A range of factors in this regard are quickly approaching. It remains to be seen how fast (not if) demand returns at higher levels than those experienced prior to the financial crisis and how soon the lack of requisite supply to meet this demand will become apparent.

To rising supply-demand pressures, must be added refinery capacity shortfalls, changes in market holding structures, new financing and trading approaches to crude oil and oil products, as well as the ever-present specter of geopolitical, climactic, and a range of other exogenous factors. As we shall see in the analysis to follow, all of this will make the continued reliance on a crude-oil-based economy unsustainable.

This book addresses how the accelerating volatility in the oil market (oil vega) will impact decision making worldwide. It is, therefore, about a wide array of applied risk considerations transforming the perspective, approach, and operations of policy makers. It is not primarily about the technical aspects of the oil market or trading in its products, although we shall need to establish some grounding in both—providing the rationale for the subject matter addressed in this and subsequent chapters.

The Meaning of Volatility

Oil vega initially manifests in market trade and our treatment will begin there. The impact of that volatility will extend well beyond the exchange. However, it makes sense to start with the commodity itself and the future contracts based upon it. We have become accustomed to measuring implied volatility[5] and reacting to its movement in estimating where entire markets are likely to go. Sometimes referred to as the "fear index," the Chicago Board Options Exchange (CBOE)[6] Volatility Index (VIX) measures implied volatility of S&P 500 index options.[7] VIX futures contracts began trading in 2004, followed by the trading of exchange-listed VIX options in February 2006 and VIX futures-based Exchange Traded Notes (ETNs),[8] launched by Barclays iPath in February 2009. A high VIX reading represents an investment opinion that the market will move sharply. It is, therefore, a registration of risk.[9] Figure 2.1 illustrates the rise in VIX trading corresponding to increases in volatility.

While a high VIX often translates into a downward equities market (risk leading to a bout of investor aversion), the figure is actually neutral on whether the deviation will be up or down. It is a measure of volatility in either direction. This is indicated by the way VIX is calculated. Usually, however, it translates into an equating of volatility

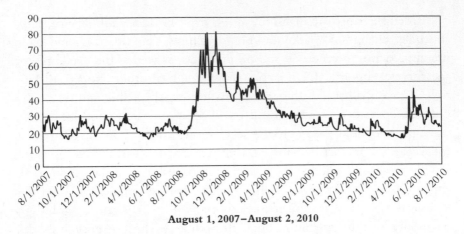

August 1, 2007–August 2, 2010

Figure 2.1 VIX Closing Prices

with instability, although that is not justified by the statistical exercise itself. However, that may be warranted, as I shall note, from an overall appraisal of the market environment. VIX does not create the market perception. It is a measure of perceptions held by market participants.

Technically, it is actually the square root of the par variance swap rate for a security over a 30-day period. In turn, the variance swap rate measures the average distance between each value observed and the mean of a data point set. It is equal to the sums of the squares of the deviations from the mean, while at the same time being the square of the standard deviation of the values in the observation sequence. It is very important to recognize that the VIX is the volatility of a variance swap, not the volatility of a volatility swap (since volatility here is the square root of the variance). For the analyst, this is quite significant because, while a variance swap can be perfectly reproduced by a series of vanilla (i.e., simple, usually American or European style, having a standard strike price and expiration date) put and call options, a volatility swap requires dynamic hedging (hedging for vega and gamma exposures).[10]

The success of the VIX led to the CBOE introducing other equity index volatility options: the DJIA [Dow Jones Industrial Average] Volatility Index (VXD), Nasdaq Volatility Index (VXN), the Russell 2000 Volatility Index (RXV), the S&P 100 Volatility Index (VXO), the S&P 500 3-Month Volatility Index (VXV), and the S&P 500 VARB-X Strategy Benchmark (VTY).

The process finally moved into commodities, and into our primary interest in this analysis. On July 15, 2008, the CBOE began publishing its Crude Oil Volatility Index (Oil VIX, ticker—OVX). As the CBOE notes:

> The CBOE Crude Oil Volatility Index ("Oil VIX," Ticker—OVX) measures the market's expectation of 30-day volatility of crude oil prices by applying the VIX methodology to United States Oil Fund, LP (Ticker—USO) options spanning a wide range of strike prices. With the introduction of the first commodity-based volatility index, CBOE embarks on the next generation of VIX benchmarks, extending the franchise to new asset classes. In the coming months, CBOE plans to develop volatility indexes based on other commodities (e.g., gold) and foreign currencies.[11]

OVX has quickly become the standard media measure of oil volatility. This applies the VIX methodology to options on the United Sates Oil Fund (USO),[12] providing a similar 30-day expectation of crude oil volatility. The CBOE had begun trading USO options on May 9, 2007, and now has a volume in excess of 50,000 contracts per day. The introduction of that trade was necessary because the CBOE could not introduce a volatility index without also trading in the underlying asset-based options.

With the real-time OVX updates flashing on trading screens and in view on the data bars of all business news channels, the market impact of crude oil volatility has arrived. Thus far, the analysis of OVX performance is still very provisional. One reason for this, of course, is the short time in which it has been available.

However, given that the methodology is the same as the VIX, researchers have already applied it to known data sets, providing a more extensive time line. Two provisional considerations are emerging. The first suggests that an index introduced in a rapidly constricting credit and liquidity market (i.e., the global financial crunch intensifying in earnest as the index was introduced) may have skewed what the index was reflecting from the market. In short, OVX may have been telling as much about the overall market decline as it was about the underlying commodity (remember, this is based upon traded securities: the USO).

Second, as a commodity, oil responds to pressures other than those occasioned by trading exchanges alone. When, added to this, the peculiarities of how crude oil responds to market supply and demand are considered, we should expect divergence from what the VIX tells the United States about stock shares.[13] Figure 2.2 shows us the spike in OVX during the decline experienced in crude oil prices during the second half of 2008 and the stagnant recovery that occurred through the first half of 2009. Notice that the highest OVX closing figures took place during December 2008, at the same time crude oil next-month futures prices were tanking to the low-$30s per barrel.

However, given the nature of the underlying volatility measured, it has already demonstrated one striking departure from VIX. Whereas a spike in VIX usually results in downward performance in equity markets, once the oil market was beyond the collapse of the fourth quarter in 2008, a similar result in OVX can just as easily result in an *increase* in crude oil prices.[14] This may well be a result of the index having as its underlying value a commodity, rather than securities.[15] That commodity also has an end use, and that use provides a direct economic consequence, unlike equity trades. If the actual volatility is accelerating in cycles extending for a shorter period than the 30-day tracking utilized by the methodology, OVX is not particularly successful in reflecting

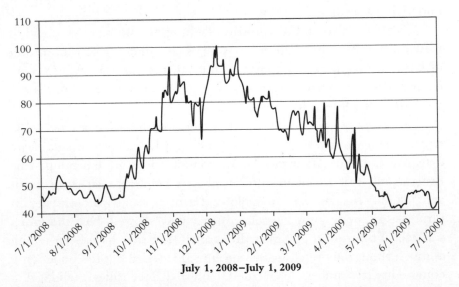

July 1, 2008–July 1, 2009

Figure 2.2   OVX Closing Prices

the actual dynamics of the underlying crude oil. The actual nature of oil vega, therefore, is hardly limited to what OVX tells us about USO (itself a security that does not always give us an accurate picture of crude oil in the market).[16] As a plotting of the two during the particularly volatile period of May 1, 2008, through May 1, 2009, tells us (see Figure 2.3), the trend lines indicate a divergence.

This is why oil vega is likely to exhibit greater swings than other measurements of volatility. Commodities have direct market uses and experience more immediate market pressures than do equities. Yet, in my judgment, the primary reason for the dramatic OVX results is more pervasive. It arises from a quite significant change in the position of crude oil. The underlying volatility reflects oil's new dual, almost schizophrenic, character. Given the relationships struck between crude oil and currency value on the one hand, and market energy needs and availability on the other, an oil contract represents both a commodity for delivery and a financial asset.

This dual nature has transformed crude oil contracts into a "swing" asset between traditional energy transactions and a much wider trading audience. It has also changed the nature of the distinction between the

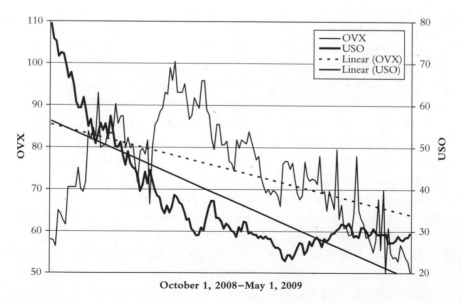

October 1, 2008–May 1, 2009

Figure 2.3   OVX versus USO

"wet barrel" (the actual crude or oil product) and the "paper barrel" (the future contract, and/or, by extension, the option on that crude or product). This, in itself, comprises a primary change in emphasis.

Not so long ago, both the wet and the paper barrel referred only to the time-sensitive relationship between crude oil production and transport. In this more-limited application of the terms, still used today, oil traders distinguish between consignments of crude oil already out of the ground and given a date for loading onto a tanker (wet), as contrasted to oil extracted but not yet given a date for loading (paper). "Physical oil" and "nonphysical oil" are also terms used to distinguish between the two. Once oil receives a loading date, it is considered to have "turned wet," becoming "dated cargo."

These were the only meanings associated with the terms until the advent of trading in futures contracts. The NYMEX introduced a futures contract for heating oil in 1978, a trading mechanism that languished for several years, followed by the WTI crude oil futures contract in 1983. In 1981, the International Petroleum Exchange (IPE) in London started futures trading in gasoil, subsequently initiating contracts in Brent crude beginning in 1988. The watershed event in bringing about the increase in future contract usage was the 1986 collapse in oil prices. This resulted in a rapid incorporation of futures into the mainstream of the oil industry. The monthly futures contract price became a standard for assessing the oil market as a whole, certainly from the standpoint of the media pundit or business data outlet. Figure 2.4 illustrates NYMEX July futures contract prices from 1983 to 2010. NYMEX and IPE introduced over 20 different oil and gas contract types through the early 2000s, but five carry the current load: NYMEX WTI, NYMEX Heating Oil, NYMEX Gasoline, IPE Brent, and IPE Gasoil.[17]

Trading traditionally was about the commodity itself and centered about the end-user of the wet barrel—the refiner in the case of crude, the distributor in the case of oil products. Now the terms are still used in this way, but they have been extended by a very different trading market. Today, the trade in paper barrels far outdistances the volume of trade in wet barrels.

However, the underlying value of the actual commodity requires that the pricing of a futures contract, and options applied to it, compensate for any disparity. This prompts the introduction of a *hedge ratio*.

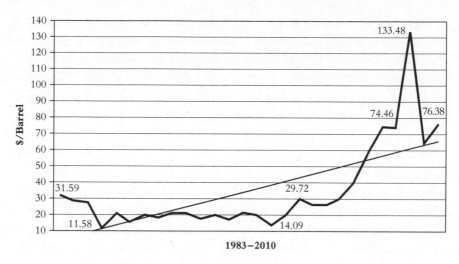

Figure 2.4 NYMEX Monthly July Contract Prices

This merely compares the value of a futures contract to the value of the underlying commodity being hedged. The trader wants to protect against *basis risk*—the discrepancy arising when investments in a hedging strategy meant to be offsetting do not result in price changes in exactly opposite directions from each other. To the extent that a transaction does not result in exact counter values, the risk of the position increases.

Basis risk results from such imperfect hedging. One of the most common manifestations of such risk arises in the use of several different assets underlying derivatives with the underlying cash assets being hedged, or a difference in the expiry of the futures and the selling date of the "wet asset." In such a situation, the asset spot price (i.e., the price for immediate sale of the underlying oil) and the price contained in the futures contract do not converge on the expiration date of the future. The discrepancy between the two prices is the value of the basis risk.[18]

Similar considerations come into play on the wet side as well. Both upstream (field production) and downstream (refining and distribution) entities must provide for basis risk.[19] As discussed later, a producing country faces the added problem of insulating its domestic currency from the destabilizing influences of hard-currency revenues. Hence, the introduction of an oil stabilization fund becomes a necessary corrective mechanism.

Trading markets are all about liquidity. Broadly speaking, the return on a trade, especially one involving a commodity such as oil, is a function of its anticipated liquidity as well as upon the covariance of its own return and liquidity with overall market return and liquidity.[20] The idea of covariance is important because it is a comment on how the change in the value or liquidity in an oil contract is supposed to parallel the change in these considerations for the market as a whole. That the vega of one or both of these may continue in one direction while the overall market indicators move in another, testifies to the increasing volatility in oil trading. That trade also reflects another interesting aspect of market liquidity. Research, and the modeling accompanying it, indicates that a continuing negative pressure on the value of a traded asset will result in lowering current returns expected while tending to increase returns predicted for a future date.[21] This relates to the well-known flight to liquidity phenomenon. Similar to flight to quality, flight to liquidity results when investors exchange lower liquidity (and thereby perceived to be higher risk) paper in favor of investments having higher liquidity (with U.S. treasuries heading up that list).[22] Put simply, pressure on the "wet barrel" makes the spot market less liquid while emphasizing the increased liquidity of the paper barrel.[23]

When this tendency becomes more apparent in a trading environment, requiring the injection of massive liquidity from the outside, the distortions in liquidity flow become a significant worry. That is certainly one of the possible negative consequences of large stimulus packages intent on kick-starting credit-starved financial markets. A persistent concern recently has been the extent to which government largess actually resulted in rescuing asset value. There may be a demonstrable relationship between rising liquidity and improving asset value in stable markets,[24] but the resulting increased liquidity experienced in the recent rescue efforts may end up only in expanding the spread between asset and derivative, thereby providing the next stage in the construction of financial bubbles.[25] This certainly has a direct application to oil and how it trades. I deal with this matter in Chapters 4 and 7. Recent commentary is beginning to focus on this issue.[26]

For some analysts, this has resulted in a "broken" market,[27] one in which the liquidity is moving from the asset that should have a ready cash value (the crude oil) to the derivative serving only as a trading tool (or hedge) for that asset. This, in turn, results in a further weakening of the ability to estimate the real value inherent in the connection between the actual commodity and the futures contract based upon it. A corresponding increase in oil vega necessarily results. This also helps to explain the apparent disconnect between rising oil prices as experienced on trading exchanges and the continuing claim by producers (particularly visible from OPEC) that there remains languishing demand for their "wet" product. For example, OPEC had regularly pointed to this problem from 2005 through 2008, despite dramatic price increases in the crude-oil futures contracts negotiated in New York and London.[28]

Progressively, the spot market is becoming less liquid while the futures market carries the brunt of oil liquidity without correspondingly improving the market value of the asset itself. Normally, one would expect that the price of crude oil would rise to the price of the futures contracts as those contracts reach expiry. Such a convergence, after all, is the basic assumption underlying the stability argument in favor of futures contracts. The merging of the two prices should occur if the underlying asset and the futures contract based upon it are governed by a normal supply/demand dynamic, allowing an easy transfer from paper to wet barrel.

That is becoming less the case because the two dominant futures markets trade derivatives off WTI (New York) and Brent (London) crude-oil delivery contracts, yet these two benchmark crude rates constitute a declining percentage of global world oil trade. This, in turn, provides difficulty in pricing mechanisms for much of the crude oil actually traded, and has led to the rise in attempts to establish new benchmark crude rates, exchanges, and contracts.

In this increasingly (dis)ordered environment, an acceleration in oil prices need not, and often does not, represent a shortage of wet barrels but, rather, rising estimated valuation in paper barrels. It is, therefore, a financial, not a commodity, and once again raises the risk of wet barrels chasing paper barrels—real assets chasing pricing levels resulting from trading considerations not actual market needs.[29]

Now there are also concerns on the wet barrel side of whether supply can meet demand. I shall consider these matters later. At this juncture, however, the question arises over what is actually the reason for the hedge in these transactions. If the changes in valuation on the futures contract and options upon it are not reflecting the actual asset contained in the underlying wet barrel, than what is pricing revisions in the trade really reflecting? Are we seeing concerns reflected over inflation, expectations of a genuine demand side change in the oil delivery market, or the oil vega? Once again, volatility emerges as a primary causal element, especially in light of the liquidity needs arising from the futures contract and the hedging of that paper.[30]

Oil volatility, the oil vega, is becoming an endemic market element. As the price instability intensifies, it will become the single most decisive factor in an environment of rising risk. The decisions required by a wide array of risk calculations will demand a fundamental revision in the way I approach the energy sector, consider some difficult choices, and introduce significant tradeoffs. These will progressively become less indicative of either the value of the underlying asset or the actual supply/demand projections. While both asset price and projections will certainly continue to be elements in the overall equation, the volatility factor will progressively take center stage as the driving force in the oil market, reflecting similar positions it already holds in other trading segments.[31]

I wish to emphasize again that, while the rising instability of oil vega will become visible in the trading environment, it will hardly remain there. The most pervasive and dangerous ramifications will unfold in broader market and political environments. I need, therefore, to adopt a much more expansive regard for risk for the simple reason that the most significant elements of that risk will play out in places other than a trading exchange.

The Meaning of Strategic Risk

The following is provided as a generic definition of risk: *An event or perceived probability that effects an environment, has implications that are unknown, provides a greater fluidity to determinations of value or result, and has a time horizon.*[32] This means that any notion of risk contains four elements: (1) the likelihood of providing future changes;[33] (2) the inability to provide, in any *a priori* fashion, a range of resolutions having a certain outcome; (3) an expected impact on the desirability of an asset, process, product, or result; and (4) a concern that tends to change over time.

Risk is used to designate a wide range of situations in which a return or outcome is unknown. The focus adopted by this book is to advance a *synthetic view of risk*, one that combines elements from the worlds of business, investment, and politics as they pertain to oil and its volatility.

I use the term synthetic risk merely to indicate that considerations are brought together from differing applications, but make no attempt to develop an analytical modeling technique. It is important to point out, however, that the term *synthetic risk* is already used in at least two ways. First, the synthetic nature of risk can refer to the assets upon which risk calculations are applied. In this case, reference is to a number of possible combinations of cash and derivative instruments intended to replicate the performance of another type of financial paper.

In this way, there emerges a range of hedging applications—synthetic puts and calls, bonds, convertibles, debt, futures, options, securities, and equities, among others. Such synthetic holdings share elements with collateralized debt obligations (CDOs), thereby assuming the same concern over usage as derivative issuances during the credit collapse beginning in 2008.[34]

Second, synthetic risk can also refer to an analytical process by which a connection is made between judgment and data. This approach is employed in political or societal applications of risk assessment, as well as in finance.[35]

However, the primary impact of risk so considered will be at the level of the policy maker. I refer to this as *strategic risk* to highlight three singularly important elements shared by the decision making addressing it. First, strategic risk involves those issues tending to have an impact upon the direction of an entire nation, organization, or corporation.[36]

Second, it involves a broader time frame. A time consideration is one of the main differentiations between the strategic and the tactical. Tactical decisions and risk involve choices affecting key elements in the overall strategy, but tend to impact on the day-to-day implementation of decision making.[37]

Third, strategic risk decisions always have as an objective the achievement of a competitive advantage.[38] This is adversarial:[39] it marshals resources within a changing environment,[40] while relating fundamentally to what stakeholders in a nation (citizens), organization (members), or corporation (shareholders) view as acceptable goals or aspirations.[41]

Strategic risk so considered can be applied to the decision-making process in each of the three major areas of interest related to oil vega—investment, market, and political. However, its normal usage in each of these tends to focus upon a particular threat—to portfolio balance in the first, corporate structure in the second, or national security in the third. I mean to use the term quite broadly, recognizing that it has a variety of meanings resulting from applications in differing contexts. Nonetheless, however we choose to cut it, a strategic implication or effect signifies a development believed to have the greatest significance and widest impact.

For present purposes, I shall define as strategic *any risk recognized as a threat to the priorities, security, or overall integrity of a system*. The more comprehensive the system—that is, the larger the aggregate comprising it—the greater the perceived strategic risk. Therefore, those situations considered examples of political strategic risk tend to be labeled as more serious than those regarded as threatening market exchange, business prospects, or investment return. Of course, such a ranking may turn out not to be justified when considering the actual nature of each occurrence.

The perception of threat, rather than the substantive character of that threat, usually determines the strength of the response. As such, we cannot limit the assignment of risk only to those situations resulting from the application of rational assumptions or models. In the real world of policy choices, especially those arising from volatile situations, the perceptions of decision-makers often become the driving influence.[42] The understanding of strategic risk as something measurable emerged a bit later than other risk categorizations, although, given its often highly subjective nature, such measurements have always been rather proximate.[43] The term, however, has been in usage for centuries.[44]

In addition to strategic risk, there are four other risk categories important to the understanding of oil volatility. Risk analysis, along the lines briefly summarized below, is a staple application in commodities markets, comprising a primary tool in the valuation of futures contracts and options. As such, it is perhaps the most visible evaluation of risk to oil vega. Yet this category extends no further than the exposure of paper barrels to the volatility of the exchange market. I shall refer to this as *investment risk*. It is certainly not the sole risk with which I am concerned, nor is it the degree of risk that is likely to have the greatest impact on policy makers. But it is the risk recognized first by traders.

Other primary categories contributing to the intensifying risk context surrounding oil vega I will label *availability risk*, *extraction risk*, and *conflict risk*. Availability risk considers wet-barrel volume in the market or the capacity to move product into the market to meet the perceived relationship between supply and demand, along with the market prices commanded for the processing use of crude oil and the consumption of refined oil products.

Extraction risk involves reactions to the expanding concerns about overall production levels, the ability to offset declining fields, the prevalence of lower quality crude, rising wellhead expenses, and the mix of conventional and unconventional sourcing. This risk addresses the composite of problems emerging at the wellhead level.

Finally, I distinguish conflict risk as a separate category. This considers the prospects for confrontation arising from the access to and distribution of crude. This may surface politically, as a manifestation of the broader idea of strategic risk. However, it generally emerges more quickly in the competition among companies in the market itself. This is not simply a private sector phenomenon. Because some of the companies involved in such competition are state-controlled or state-run, especially when it comes to the largest of the crude-oil producers worldwide, government priorities have an effect early on.

Investment, availability, extraction, and conflict risk are all components of, often regarded as precursors to, the recognition and assessment of strategic risk. However, we need to investigate further the underlying nature of risk and its applications before proceeding to a consideration of how these five categories help the United States deal with oil vega.

In the business world, risk denotes everything from production snafus, through operational problems, adverse environmental impacts, brand attacks, joint-venture partner problems, to direct threats upon a firm's overall plan. The term "business risk" is often applied to the likelihood that a company may have significant cash flow problems, have insufficient revenue to maintain operations or even go bankrupt. When used in this way, risk often becomes a gauge of a company's investment worth, its ability to maintain a current dividend or earnings level.

In the investment world, risk represents the uncertainty of an earned return and has a number of usages. More directly for our purposes is the application of risk factors to derivatives. There, the main concern is risk associated with imperfect hedging of options applied to futures contracts, otherwise known as basis risk.[45]

All risk includes elements shared commonly with a system as a whole and those that are unique to that occurrence. I shall have more to say about the systemic/unsystemic distinction in a moment, but it is important to understand that risk of either type hardly emerges in a vacuum. The environment in which risk is recognized and against which decision making must operate is a primary factor.[46] Political and market reactions have a decided tendency to overreact when that context is subject to accelerating volatility arising from an inability to determine a low-intensity approach[47] to questions of fair value, supply, or intent. All of these are certainly present with oil. Risk in such situations is perceived as having an escalating nature—namely, the presumption becomes one of the consequences of risk increasing in seriousness as the time frame moves forward. Trading overreactions to escalating crude oil prices are a clear example of this phenomenon. I have more to say about this in Chapter 4.

The basic concept of risk is employed in a wide range of applications, but it was an early-twentieth-century observation that introduced the belief that it could be measured and documented. In 1921, the economist Frank H. Knight[48] offered a famous distinction between risk and *uncertainty*, arguing that risk involved randomness with knowable probabilities, while uncertainty dealt with randomness having unknowable probabilities. Risk, therefore, could be measured, while uncertainty could not.

This approach to risk is also known as "Knightian uncertainty," which argues the distinction between making a decision having unknown outcomes but having a known *ex-ante* distribution of probability (risk) and those decisions facing an unknown probability distribution of random occurrences (uncertainty). In risk so understood, Knight argues, certain rules (e.g., maximizing expected utility) can be applied. It is, therefore, the applicability of one or more benchmarks that allow "randomness with known probabilities," according to Knight.

Despite the significant impact of Knight's contribution, there has been very little progress in articulating a more precise approach.[49]

Nonetheless, the distinction was quite useful in developing more rigorous analytical techniques to model ongoing production or related product exchange considerations.

Among the best known is the first version of the law of variable proportions in the theory of production, also referred to as the law of decreasing marginal returns. It states that output will increase if certain designated inputs relative to other fixed inputs increases. Over time, however, additional output will decline relative to the increase in the same inputs.[50] Risk analysis had emerged as a recognized tool in both economic studies and business.[51]

The application of risk analysis to investment management revolutionized its usage. This is largely the result of Nobel laureate Harry M. Markowitz.[52] His contributions to the development of Modern Portfolio Theory (MPT) most clearly emerged in the articulation of the "Markowitz Efficient Portfolio" and the "Markowitz Efficient Frontier."

The Markowitz Efficient Portfolio represents a portfolio having the highest aggregate rate of return consistent to a given accepted level of risk. An investor cannot further diversify in an attempt to increase an expected rate of return without accepting a greater degree of risk exposure. Correspondingly, one cannot decrease exposure to risk without proportionately decreasing the expected return.

Meanwhile, the Markowitz Efficient Frontier is the graphical expression of a set of all portfolios providing the highest expected rate of return at each level of risk accepted. Markowitz theorized that each level of risk contains one combination of assets giving the highest level of expected return. An efficient set of portfolios is represented as a line on a graph, with risk as the x-axis and expected return as the y-axis. The graphical depiction of the "frontier" represents the boundary of the set of feasible portfolios having the maximum return for a given level of risk. Any portfolios above the frontier cannot be achieved. Any below the frontier are dominated by the Markowitz Efficient Portfolio.

Both of these established major underpinnings for the capital asset pricing model (CAPM)[53] utilized to determine an asset's theoretically appropriate rate of return. CAPM, in turn, introduced the applied mathematical distinction between systematic (or market) risk and unsystemic risk, resulting in what is now a basic approach in financial theory.

The risk of any portfolio comprises systematic risk, also referred to as undiversifiable risk, and unsystemic risk, also called diversifiable or idiosyncratic risk. Systematic risk is that degree of risk shared by all securities in a market. On the other hand, unsystemic risk is that risk represented by individual assets. Such individual asset risk can be diversified to a lower level by incorporating a greater number of assets in the portfolio, thereby "averaging out" specific elements of risk.

However, this is not possible for the systematic risk resulting from portfolio trade in a single market. The number of assets required to accomplish a sufficient diversification of a portfolio is largely a function of asset volatility and would tend to be lower in developed markets and higher in developing or emerging markets.

It is important to note that only risk that is not diversified is rewarded in the CAPM model. As such, the return on an asset necessary to compensate for the risk taken must be viewed in terms of how it contributes to the overall risk position of the portfolio as a whole, not in terms of whatever individual isolated risk that asset may represent on its own. In the CAPM approach, portfolio risk is represented by higher variance,[54] and thereby less predictability. According to CAPM, a portfolio's beta[55] is the primary determinant of returns from an investor exposed to systematic risk.[56]

The distinction between systematic and unsystemic risk, although originating in investment analysis, has direct bearings upon estimating risk levels in each of the five analytical categories I propose to apply in the discussion of oil vega. Volatility may well result from factors that oil shares with other commodities, broader production and distribution concerns, the overall condition of exchange trading, conflict environments that oil shares with other segments, or decision-making perspectives on events including oil, but not limited to it. These would be examples of systematic risk in the application of availability, extraction, investment, conflict, and strategic risk considerations, respectively. Conversely, considering these analytical categories while regarding oil as an independent or unique exercise would comprise an examination of unsystemic risk.

While we shall have occasion to apply all of these risk categories to oil vega, several of the chapters are designed to focus discussion on particular applications of risk to volatility. The exercise is hardly intended to be exhaustive. In addition, I am primarily interested in outlining the emerging oil vega problem rather than developing a methodology for measuring risk. And while this book may succeed in providing some of the elements in an initial intuitive approach to formalizing how vega is regarded, it is likewise not an exercise in model building. There will be time enough for the development of formal analytical tools once the acceleration in oil vega hits in earnest. Rather, the categorization of risk presented here should be regarded as little more than several ways of regarding causal connections or providing a general way to provide preliminary ways of approaching oil vega.

Nonetheless, it seems appropriate to emphasize particular risk applications early, to give the discussion a sense of direction if nothing else. As such, the discussion of pricing in Chapter 3 introduces a number of the factors involved in applying notions of what I have termed availability risk to oil. Chapter 4 further focuses attention on dimensions of investment risk as contained in the relationship of oil to the intensifying contemporary trading pressure on paper barrels, as well as broader credit market and currency concerns. The upstream/downstream tradeoff considered in Chapter 5 addresses major elements associated with extraction risk. Chapter 6 discusses the governmental role and, thereby, introduces a conflict risk component. Chapter 7 sketches out the accelerating strategic risk and suggests some initial measures in response. The arrival of international financial stagnation, an associated reduction in overall aggregate demand levels, weakness in the euro, concerns over European debt, and the mother of all offshore platform blowouts (the Deepwater Horizon disaster) have impeded an otherwise more rapid arrival of the full crisis. None of these events, however, changes the endogenous dynamics of oil vega; each merely delays its arrival.

These types of risk are hardly mutually exclusive and this book will resist the temptation to provide abstract categories to enhance game theory or other similar exercises. Such approaches certainly have their place in analysis, but should never be allowed to prejudge the situation against which they are applied. The primary strength of theory is its ability to provide guidance to understand or explain, not to reshape events in its own likeness. We do not accomplish much by simply redefining.

The risk applications used here have a contributing explanative utility but are not meant to provide a formal structure. Nor are we endeavoring to take volatility, by nature unfolding in a very fluid and imprecise environment, and reduce it to "a few simple rules." It requires a rethinking of the market, the position of oil, and the consequences of that position. Oil vega cannot be resolved by an elegant formula or new combination of concepts. It obliges us to get our hands dirty and recognize that responding to the approaching danger lies not in the lack of methodology, but in the messy problems of the real world.

Chapter 3

Determining Oil Prices

New York City, February 2009

Psychology often determines more in a market than the actual underlying dynamics. This is a case in point. I am about to begin a briefing to Wall Street energy sector analysts. The subject is supposed to be a pending initial placement offer (IPO) in London for a state-run bank in Kazakhstan. The bank does oil project finance for the government in Astana, along with major Kazakh oil companies. The IPO could be a possible backdoor into the expected run-up in Caspian crude production.

However, this is also a depressed futures market (at the time). NYMEX contracts that morning are showing only modest improvement from the disastrous levels of late December and early January. The informal prebriefing conversation, therefore, turns to the broader market. It is clear that the real underlying asset value (for the wet barrels) would justify a price in the $45 range, yet the paper contract remains stubbornly south of $38.

Some of the group is clearly at a loss. But then looking around the room I can understand why. Nobody is older than 25. The last time anything like this happened, they were in grade school. "We have wet barrels depressed by paper barrels," one notes, "that makes no sense." I smile. "They should have seen the carnage in 1986," I mutter to myself.

"Well, gentlemen," I finally say out loud, "Welcome to the illogical world of oil pricing. Let's talk about more predictable matters . . . like Kazakh banking."

■ ■ ■

The most visible aspect of oil is its price. Following the level has become a part of daily life, with the NYMEX and Brent future prices a staple of the evening news. Public opinion equates the price of crude oil to that at the pump, with the resulting consumer cost providing the usual starting point for the political clamor over energy. Actually, while the cost of crude remains the single largest component in the retail price of gasoline, we see in Chapter 5 that the structure from wellhead to retail outlet also has its effect.

However, this is an unusual pricing dynamic, one that often stubbornly refuses to follow either normal market forces or expectations. The price collapse experienced between October 2008 and early March 2009 did not reflect the underlying oil market. Neither in some fundamental respects did the price spikes in June and July of 2008. Both mirrored other economic concerns, exogenous to the oil market itself. We can provide a rationale in retrospect for portions of these movements. Nonetheless, the way in which oil pricing plays out does not always reflect supply and demand, market forces, or even logic.

As Chapter 2 notes, the notion of availability risk addresses wet barrel volume, the capacity moved in to address dimensions of supply and demand. The prices experienced by a refinery for the crude oil processed and the end user for the retail oil products consumed are market consequences of such availability risk. Prices become the common yardstick by which that risk is perceived.

Pricing, Sourcing, and Peak Oil

Rising oil prices have resulted in renewed debates over priorities in U.S. energy policy. Some say the rising prices are realities of an economy dependent upon increasingly more expensive sources of crude oil. Others suggest the problem results primarily from monopolistic market controls exerted either by oil companies or the governments of producing nations. And still others claim that the rising societal dependence on certain categories of energy has built into the market a guaranteed upward price pressure, since demand cannot be offset easily or met by alternative sources.

Whatever is perceived as the cause, proponents of any rationale agree that the pricing mechanism is also sensitive to global political, climactic, or financial crises and events. A range of considerations are present for the analyst to consider in forecasting oil prices,[1] accentuated by the inability to control or even predict the impact of many of them.

A price is merely a market mechanism setting an exchange value for a given commodity. Price levels provide us with a way of comparing related products, or the same product over time, and it is the essential function of a price system to allow an economy to allocate available resources. As we shall observe further on in this chapter, however, oil prices have certain unusual (or, perhaps more accurately, atypical) elements separating them from pricing determinations for most other market commodities. Oil often may share some of these atypical elements with other natural resources—for example, minerals for which no realistic substitutes are available.[2] To the extent that oil prices cannot be offset by the short-term substitution of other energy sources, expansive conservation, or technological improvement, the price commanded by oil in the market has a basic impact extending well beyond the immediate cost to the consumer of the oil product itself.

This flows directly from its position. Oil remains the base of a modern society. As a source of energy, lubrication, or petrochemicals, oil has a fundamental impact on life as we have come know it. But it also is an essential commodity whose availability and affordability decisively impact security and expectations. From the standpoint of the United States, the relationship between oil and national security is a direct one. Strong arguments have arisen to urge new directions in energy, less reliance on fossil fuels, and greater concern over the environmental impacts of oil use, while emphasizing development of renewable energies that are more directly under national control.

I am personally sympathetic to many of these approaches. But the reality of the current situation is, to me at least, quite clear. We cannot reach any preferred energy option, regardless of the technology and money expended or the national commitment made, without several decades of continued reliance upon crude oil. Revisions in the current situation are necessary, but the time frame for significant change is seen in decades, not years. Even with a bold new direction in energy sources and usage, we will still rely upon an oil-based economy for some time to come.

And that means national energy security policy will remain a policy dominated by oil concerns. For American policy, this also results in a greater reliance on elements over which Washington has more problematic control. This has been a recent development, unfolding over only a few decades. At the beginning of the 1940s, the United States held over 60 percent of global crude oil productive capacity, was the source of the world's oil surplus (that excess capacity drawn upon to balance market pressures and/or support national policy objectives for countries around the globe), and was the largest net exporter of oil and oil products. Some 30 years later, the United States had become a net (and permanent) oil importer,[3] losing as well during the same period (beginning in the early 1970s) its position as international oil surplus provider. Today, despite oil recorded in almost 100 countries (see Appendix A: World Proved Oil Reserves), over 65 percent of the known[4] oil reserves worldwide are controlled by countries bordering upon the Persian Gulf.[5]

The changes occurring from 1970 forward were significant in several ways. As Daniel Yergin has observed:

> The 1970s also saw a dramatic shift in world oil. Demand was catching up to available supply. . . . The late 1960s and early 1970s were, for the most part, years of high economic growth for the industrialized world and, in some years, outright boom.

This growth was fueled by oil. . . . The late 1960s and early 1970s were the watershed years for the domestic U.S. oil industry. The United States ran out of surplus capacity.[6]

Sources are not the only troubling issue policy makers are facing. Continued availability at levels necessary to meet demand is also being questioned. Yet concerns have been expressed regarding the amount of crude oil remaining for extraction worldwide. Estimates vary, and the debate has become a protracted one.

This debate revolves about a famous, although often misunderstood, section of a 1956 paper by Marion King Hubbert.[7] According to the paper's thesis and later applications,[8] Hubbert estimated that the high point of U.S. domestic crude oil production would take place in the early 1970s (by 1972 in his later treatments). That turned out to be correct. The actual apogee took place in 1970–1971. Thereupon, a number of analysts applied Hubbert's reasoning to global crude oil production, concluding that the peak of production internationally would take place between 2004 and 2008.[9]

More recently, other estimates of the global high point have been pushed back as far as 2047, depending on the methodology and sources employed.[10] There are two primary points of contention in these discussions. The first considers the manner in which reserve estimates are calculated. The second posits a fundamental difference of perspective— the availability of fossil fuels is less a result of physical nature and more a result of market forces. The best-known supporter of the latter position is Morris A. Adelman.[11] We shall have more to say on both of these issues further on in this chapter.

Adherents to the idea of producing nonfossil energy sources as a means of reducing dependence upon crude oil have renewed the argument that reliance upon hydrocarbons is ill-warranted. It is an argument that has much force and considerable merit. Unfortunately, despite technological advances and a rising public (and political) chorus singing the praises of renewable energy, none of the proposed solutions is near-term. Certainly, scientific breakthroughs are possible and may well decrease crude oil dependence. But such developments are not imminent.[12] For the foreseeable future, contemporary life must rely upon the availability of fossil fuels.[13]

Oil and Market Forces

Oil policy is initially about satisfying physical needs. Such needs are registered in a market environment. One would anticipate that oil is subject to the same underlying forces as other elements in the market. That is, it follows the principles of supply and demand, registers the same predictable responses to changing market conditions, and is governed by exchange and transfer considerations similar to other products and services. However, crude oil supplies are not simply deposited into a neutral market mechanism. Few if any products ever are. But the perplexing realization has been this: hydrocarbons and other forms of energy have consistently frustrated analysts attempting to read into them the same kinds of behaviors recognized in other products. This has not been a problem for economists alone. As Øystein Noreng points out:

> No single theoretical discipline of the social sciences has been successful in analyzing the energy markets with results of a predictive value. Insight into oil and other energy issues is fragmented. Basic philosophical questions over energy are unsettled. There is no coherent general theory of energy that can be used to analyze the impact of increasing energy supplies on the political economy of different societies, such as that of the relationship between capital and labor.[14]

But the problems faced by economists in attempting to explain the workings of oil in particular and energy in general are more striking. In the classical political economic theories of Adam Smith, David Ricardo, and John Stuart Mill, those setting the stage for what remains the foundation for the dominant approach even today (now usually called neoliberalism), energy serves no function in the determination of value creation. It was one of those elements (technology being another) that did not constitute a factor of production.[15]

When analysts in the twentieth century set about to provide a more active position for energy in the creation of value—that is, decided to treat energy as a causative element—they were confronted with the question of how one determines oil prices under market conditions. Classical political economics placed great emphasis on explanations regarding the determination of price as essentially a result of the units of labor expended. Price, therefore, was a concomitant result of a broader labor theory of value, with the ever-present principle of scarcity as the bridge between determinations of value and determinations of price. What resulted was a domineering neoliberal theory of prices.[16] However, that theory provided little guidance when considering the position of energy in the determination of either direct or mediate pricing. To date, there has yet to emerge a consistent theory or applicable model fully explaining how oil prices operate.[17]

As Rognvaldur Hannesson observes, the normal expectations in calculating prices are framed by scarcity and rationing. "The implication is that resources in finite supply have a value over and above what it costs to produce them, owing to their scarcity. The role of the price is to ration the use of the resource over time."[18] That sounds very similar to how most products are expected to act in any organized exchange environment. However, that is not the case with oil. Oil does not respond as most other goods do to market factors. Oil is not price elastic.[19] Changes in the price of oil do not seem to have an impact on the supply of oil in the market.[20] Ultimately, one would expect that oil would follow basic principles of supply and demand, but, as we shall see later, that is also problematic.

Even the ability to estimate price is initially complicated by a number of factors. These include the lack of transparent data on basic necessary components in the calculation of cost—such as the actual state of field reserves,[21] the impact of technical improvements at the wellhead allowing for either an increase in extraction or a lowering of lifting costs, or the application of creative oil company approaches to the determination of a range of elements, including discount rates,[22] sliding scales,[23] and overhead costs, for example. All of these impact the actual cost of doing business but are not usually available to the economic analyst gauging their macroeconomic impact.

Reserve calculations have the most impact. There are a number of ways of estimating what is available for extraction, but the figures often do not translate into an easily determined causative factor bearing upon market price. Initially, this is a supply and demand issue, although, as we shall see in a moment, the demand inelasticity of oil does not conform well to expectations of supply/demand either. One would think that, if we know demand is X and there is Y amount of crude oil available, absent other considerations, price ranges ought to be determinable. Unfortunately, that is not how the process works. Given the various ways in which reserves are expressed, there is not a direct correlation between what is estimated to be in the ground and what can be cost-efficiently translated into market product.[24]

Reserves are not the same as oil-in-place. Oil-in-place is volume that can be readily determined, since it is a measurable existing quantity. Unfortunately, that does not automatically translate into extraction, since the oil may not be recoverable without exorbitant expense for a host of reasons—for example, difficulties occasioned by the geological configuration of the reservoir;[25] levels of impurities such as metallic, sulfur, or high wax content; gravity;[26] high viscosity;[27] or water coning.[28]

Most petroleum geologists will tell you that only about 3 percent of oil in place can be obtained by natural means without reducing the reservoir pressure to the point where no further extraction is forthcoming. The location of the oil within a reservoir may be a function of the geological configuration, but once extraction commences pressure is decreased uniformly throughout the structure. Absent the performance of extraction techniques, therefore, solely relying upon the natural pressure of the reservoir means leaving 97 percent of the oil in the ground. Of course, nobody these days does that.[29] But the cost of maintaining and increasing well production has a direct bearing upon the decision to increase extraction rates, and cost must calculate the intended return from an end market price for the refined product.

Such an observation is instructive when considering how reserves are calculated. Reserves also have a more direct corollary to market expectations than does any concept of oil-in-place. Stated simply, high probability reserves available at an affordable lifting cost plus downstream expense realizing an acceptable return from sale will produce additional extraction.

Sounds easy, right? Unfortunately, the dynamics of the market never allow such a straightforward approach. To begin with, the lag time between identification of fields and extraction has no relationship to market need or the price paid at the end of the process. No oil company wants to invest funds in a field that produces oil only after the market price has begun to decline. A field comprising step-out wells[30] located in an already logged[31] and developed region with known geological and chemical properties in existing producing reservoirs, with rigs available on site, can have initial bore holes spud quickly. Oil can be flowing in a matter of weeks if all goes well.

But this is also usage of proved, or at worst highly probable, reserves in a confined area, which may well impact overall reservoir pressure. Additionally, the determination of how far the reservoir extends may also be incorrect, leading to the drilling of a dry hole. The lag time is even more an issue with wells drilled in newer areas. And the development of a genuinely new field can easily take five years or longer. None of this is encouraging to the CFO or the head of marketing, both of whom need to have a more stable outlook of future relative demand requirements.

So some crude remains in the ground. Much of the determination of what volume will be extracted and sent to market centers about a calculation of current versus expected prices. If the current price is considered to be higher than what can be anticipated at some future date, then it is in the interest of the company to pump it. If prices are likely to be higher in the future, it is more profitable for the crude to remain in the reservoir. Now each extraction also brings into play other considerations, for example, maintenance of pressure and maintaining the integrity of the wells, but, most important, by drawing higher levels of extraction, the reservoir will be depleted more quickly. This may also cause an increase in overall operating expenses, should the remaining crude become more difficult to extract. If this is also a project under a production sharing agreement (PSA), in which royalties, taxes, and other tariffs and/or fees are paid, then the dynamics of government estimations may also mitigate appreciable changes in extraction rates. Most PSAs specify extraction levels, especially when sliding scales are involved, making it more difficult for the company unilaterally to change rates easily.

Hotelling, Adelman, and Scarcity

The theoretical justification for withholding production from the market belongs to Harold Hotelling and arises in what may be the most famous (and debated) single essay in oil production ever written.[32]

Hotelling argued that crude oil was a fixed asset. As Dag Harald Claes well puts it:

> [A]n exhaustible resource can be regarded as a fixed asset that the owner can either extract or leave in the ground. The problem for the owner is to maximize the profit over the total exhaustion time. If oil is extracted immediately, the value of it equals the interest rate (provided that the social discount rate equals the market interest rate.). The only reason to leave the oil in the ground is a perception of future price increase.[33]

From this follows the Hotelling rule, also referred to as the r principle: the annual growth rate of the net price[34] of the oil must equal the rise in the interest or discount rate to provide that profits realized by leaving oil in the ground match the profits from extracting and selling the oil.[35] The utilization of an interest or discount rate means that the profit calculation should exceed the expected return if funds were used in other investments.

The r principle has become a mainstay for two generations of oil analysts. In some cases, such as those arising from stable markets in which price swings are limited, the predictions made by applying the principle do largely conform to the practices actually realized in the market.[36] But there has often been a question of whether the approach actually tells us anything. In which direction does the causality actually flow in the cost-price relationship? Does the pricing decision really follow from the cost determinations? These questions are important because the determination of prices is not simply a reaction to market conditions when it comes to oil.

This introduces some of the significant problems arising from relying upon the r principle in determining prices. First, the rule does not seem to reflect how oil companies make decisions in other than stable situations.[37] An alternative view argues that development decisions (and hence the availability of additional market supply) are made on factors which have little to do with the primary hypothesis that "value in ground" must at least parallel forward value equal to interest or discount rate applications. Basic to this contrary approach is the argument that oil companies are primarily interested in increasing oil stocks (known reserves available for rather immediate commercial use), and that this issue has a more fundamental impact on determining development rates.

The r principle also anticipates that the market prices for oil and oil products should follow the level of *marginal cost*.[38] But this has often not been the case.[39] Given that field development requires a multiyear projection of expenses, the actual determination of acceptable price (upon which to base extraction) is not primarily a reaction to volatility in the market price. One would expect that the there would be a price convergence toward the lowest marginal cost, usually defined as the cost of the cheapest additional barrel.[40] But given the longer-term perspective applied to the oil process—in which expenses need to be broken down and estimated for each stage from field development, through extraction, transport, refining, distribution of oil product, and the like—fixed costs rather than variable costs are more significant.[41]

That means the overriding concept of marginal cost operates quite differently with oil than it does with other commodities in the market. The impact of a marginal change is applied over a broader time frame and tends to distort the actual relationship between price and costs. Recalling that oil is not price elastic, there is no immediate correlation between price and volume in the market at any given time.[42] Rather, given the longer-term approach dictated by the development-extraction-refining-retail process, available supplies are not subject to the variegations of current abrupt market changes, but driven by a need to level out expenses.[43]

Another criticism of the r principle has received much visibility in the literature. This is primarily associated with Adelman, arguably the most visible oil economist over the past several decades, and it constitutes a rejection of Hotelling's basic premise. Adelman argues that the very notion of a "fixed stock" of oil is not only an incorrect assumption; it is also of no practical market significance. It is not the amount of stock available but the dynamic of the market that determines price. Put succinctly, the total amount of oil "in the earth is an irrelevant nonbinding constraint. If expected finding-development costs exceed the expected net revenues, investment dries up, and the industry disappears. Whatever is left in the ground is unknown, probably unknowable, but surely unimportant: a geological fact of no economic interest."[44]

Instead, this line of reasoning espouses that the notion of a fixed stock is the wrong premise upon which to define an economic process (such as pricing) conducted under uncertainty. The level of production is determined by the market interplay between costs and prices played out into the future. "The estimated resource cannot be the starting point for estimating costs and prices."[45] If the price of oil increases, the impetus to develop new fields and drill new wells increases as well. For Adelman, Hotelling's overall approach (both the "rule" and the later application into the "valuation principle"[46]) have been "thoroughly discredited. A valid theory was joined to a wrong premise, the fixed stock. It gave results contrary to fact."[47]

A rather larger volume of studies give credence to Adelman's criticism. The *r* principle often does not provide a valid indicator of actual market price determinations.[48] Adelman does acknowledge that Hotelling provided a major contribution enabling the calculation of scarcity:

> Once we discard the false assumption of a limited stock, we can see Hotelling's great contribution: to reduce the vague notion of "resource scarcity" to an observable economic fact: the present value of a unit of inventory, subject to the same errors as any other asset values. When over a long period there is no up-creep in the market values there is no increase in scarcity.[49]

But scarcity cannot be measured *a priori*. If there is no starting point constituting a fixed amount of natural resources, there can be no automatic increase in price resulting from an anticipated draw down of reserves. Adelman suggests that the actual cost of replacing reserves is a better gauge of scarcity, and further acknowledges at this point that the *r* principle has something to say of value. *"The early-warning signal of scarcity is a persistent rise in development cost and in the in-ground value of oil reserves."*[50]

In other words, if the cost of replacing expended reserves rises, resulting in a corresponding rise in the market value of reserves, then there is a scarcity curve developing. In such a situation, the reasoning of both Adelman and Hotelling converge. Yet, for Adelman, that convergence is a function of market forces, not the siphoning off of a portion from some hypothetical fixed asset. The function of a rising price is to encourage more development investment, resulting in the bringing on line of more oil, and hence an eventual equilibrium in the market place, constraining further price increases. Similarly, a decline in price would constrain further development, causing field projects to be delayed and wells to be capped. In this scenario oil stays in the ground, but as a result of market dynamics, not as a cause of them.[51]

This sounds much like the traditional interplay between supply and demand, the effects of which impact most products in a market. Oil also feels the effects of the interchange between the two, but in a different, more staggered manner. It takes a large movement in price before the demand for oil is cut. Oil, in other words, exhibits inelasticity of demand[52] in all but the most drastic upward price scenarios.[53] As clearly indicated by the dramatic declines paralleling the credit crisis in 2008 and 2009, however, a demand decline is not simply a function of price. It is also a result of public assumptions. And such assumptions often result in oil confounding the expectations resulting from market supply and demand dynamics.

For example, in the aftermath of the 1973 to 1974 Arab oil embargo, the moves both to conserve energy and to exchange energy supplies resulted more from public perceptions of the market than the actual availability of oil products.[54] In such a "pre-futures" market trading environment, panic buying was a major fuel for the price hike,[55] resulting in calls for lowering speed limits and thermostats, increasing the efficiency of automobiles and appliances, and renewed interest in solar, thermal, wind, and biomass alternative energy sources.[56]

On the supply side, the relationship between available crude-in-place and market price is a closely guarded industry estimate. A number of *ex post facto* determinations of that relationship can be suggested, but the identification of some trigger mechanism is almost impossible to arrive at before the fact. Nonetheless, one would expect that a decline in the overall supply of crude would pressure prices to rise until such time as the price justifies the provision of additional stock, either from crude-in-place or as a result of expanded exploration and development programs.

Yet the interesting manifestations of the price spikes of late appear to be on the demand side of this equation.[57] It is the coincidence of genuine increases in demand for oil products and the psychology of perceptions about the market that are underpinning current price movements. This is quite a departure from previous price increases. With the exception of the East Asian financial crisis, which exploded in October of 1997 with the Hong Kong stock market meltdown after simmering since late 1995,[58] all major crude oil pricing swings of the past 30 years[59] were results of supply-side considerations, either actual or perceived. That is, changes in supplies, or a belief that such changes were imminent, fueled changes in price.

In the price increases occurring from 2004 through 2008, however, consistently robust demand for oil has supported rising prices, despite increases in supply, with future contracts extending the upper level of the pricing curve well beyond what market dynamics themselves would seem to warrant.[60] Additionally, indications are that high taxes imposed in Europe,[61] usage of subsidies and price controls in emerging markets, and the lessening of oil-first energy policies in more developed countries, are serving to slow the growth of demand, but not the over-all level of the demand itself.[62] Such developments are accentuated by the differential between demand for the crude oil at the source (the "wellhead") and demand for selected refined products. To the extent that the demand for selected products increases while the demand for crude oil remains constant, the demand curve reflects more the avail-ability of certain refinery capacities rather than a more general market demand for the base crude.

The Question of Reserves

Pricing also has something to say about expected availability of crude oil reserves. It is correct to say that the immediate goal of any field development is the addition of reserves capable of being brought to market in short order. In fact, it is the desire to add to known reserves that constitutes the reason any new field is developed. Oil companies, therefore, do not enter into exploration and development projects to satisfy current market demand. That demand is met with existing stock, replaced by more newly identified reserves. Such a relationship between oil-in-place and reserves has a direct impact upon market pricing, given the overall influence of scarcity calculations previously discussed.

However, the determination of reserves is itself open to interpretation. There are a number of ways to calculate and categorize reserves. But the majority of analysts use the following criteria, or categories similar to them.[63] Reserves are initially divided between provable and unproved. Both represent crude oil that somebody believes is present in a field, but are subject to the following distinctions:

Proved Reserves[64]

- Can be estimated with reasonable certainty.
- Generally must be supported by actual production or formation tests. Indirect indications like electric logs[65] are usually not adequate.
- Include both drilled locations and the undrilled locations that directly offset commercially producing locations.
- Must have operational facilities to process and transport the reserves to market.
- Have publicly quoted company reserve statistics.[66]

Unproved Reserves

- Are less certain than proved reserves.
- May require future economic conditions different from current conditions.
- Are estimated for internal planning or special evaluations, but not routinely compiled.
- May be divided into two risk classifications: probable[67] and possible.[68]

A provisional identification that something is "recoverable," however, is of little real use. To say that reserves are recoverable addresses only the physical ability to extract the crude. The most important determinant is whether reserves of a certain classification are *economically* or *commercially* recoverable. It is the market, via the interplay between the cost of producing the crude and the price at which derived oil products can be sold, that determines whether the oil that can be lifted is actually taken out of the ground. Most oil field analysts, therefore, utilize a combination of "proved plus probable"[69] in attempting to arrive at a realistic estimate of field production.

Unfortunately the proliferation of reserve definitions, combined with the ways in which those reserves are folded into occasionally creative auditing practices, contributes to what are often arbitrary book values.[70] "At times, book values are contradictory even inside a company, not to mention the reporting problems that exist between governments and countries"[71] when such diverging book values are used to determine profits, taxes, royalties, or other fees.

As a result, the contribution of reserve value to any calculation of operational return is always suspect. And that, in turn, has a direct impact on more fundamental decisions. This is because the overall cost of a field is largely determined by the proceeds of oil sales minus development costs, operational expenses, taxes, royalties, and the like. The field manager needs to be particularly cognizant of the extraction flow, while the general manager needs to have a more comprehensive view of the wholesale and retail market conditions, especially so in the case of refinery capacity. Consumers, after all, do not buy crude oil. They buy the refined product.

What price, then, is necessary before a field development project is justified? Or conversely, at what point do rising lifting costs, or the increasingly expensive recourse to secondary recovery methods, dictate that a well should be capped? Neither of these decisions has an immediate impact; each is felt only much later in the market process. Yet the analyst is required to make a determination well before the results of that decision are experienced. We are speaking here of cost and price considerations emerging throughout the process—from crude oil exploration to oil product retail sale.

The foregoing discussion of market factors also has a major limitation. Unlike the models employed by neoclassical economists, where the market provides access and information to all participants, market control when it comes to oil is highly restricted. Stated simply, this is a noncompetitive sector. There is insufficient competition in four essential respects, each of which reduces the usage of alternatives as a way of restraining prices. First, there are too few crude oil producers (the *oligarchic* element). Second, there are too few primary refining customers to process the crude into commercial products (the *oligopsonistic* element). Third, there are too few purveyors of finished products to retail consumers (the *oligopolistic* element). Fourth, there remain too few placements for the revenues realized (the *hegemonic* element).

The first three of these aspects are often viewed as examples of monopolistic practices in international oil. The equivalence may be present in those domestic production markets where only a single government-controlled company operates. But in all other cases it is the presence of too few alternative sources or venues, rather than the total lack of other participants, that determines the dynamics.

Even in the case of the single dominant state oil company monopolizing supplies of crude oil in an emerging market country, access to, and sales within, global markets are hardly controlled by such a company. It is that access which determines return on the commodity. Such a company may act like a monopoly in access to the crude sources back home, but not beyond.

Still, the advantages provided by being a supplier of hydrocarbons as contrasted to being a customer can have a significant impact upon translating raw material strength into political and diplomatic leverage. As contemporary history well documents, having the ability to influence the trade direction and pricing of crude oil placements can be an offsetting factor to lack of development. The distinction between being a price maker and a price taker is fundamental in the oil market.

The fourth, the hegemonic element, considers control over the investment of, and return from, oil sale proceeds. Despite significant changes in the world oil market, that hegemony has remained American. The recognition of this financial reality may be the single most important factor in explaining the endemic American presence in global oil affairs. It is not because the United States consumes more energy products than any other nation. It does, but that is not the point. It is because the United States provides most of the financial intermediation.

Finally, there is a major impact on oil pricing which will be a backdrop for most of what will be said in this book. The introduction of political factors extraneous to straight market driven elements may well have a decisive effect on the relationship between rising oil prices faced by consumers and the rise in marginal cost confronting oil producers. Governments, and the politicians, political parties, social forces and traditions informing them, play a permeating role in oil production and trade. Despite the preference to separate politics and economics, governments and trade, we are well counseled by Robert Gilpin that "international political economy assumes that the interests and policies of states are determined by the governing political elite, the pressures of powerful groups within a national society, and the nature of the 'national system of political economy.'"[72] Gilpin adds that ". . . national security is and always will be the principal concern of states. In a 'self-help' international system[73]. . . states must constantly guard against actual or potential threats to their political and economic independence."[74]

Price, while discussed independently as a thematic element in any oil discussion, is not actually determined by market forces operating in a vacuum. Political decisions rarely provide the most efficient remedy to a public problem, certainly so when energy is the subject matter. A straight market approach to oil pricing would use the price level as a way of limiting demand, thereby making supply considerations dependent upon what the market can extract from end users. In short, raise the price to a level which equalizes the "demand gap" between the supply available and what primary (i.e., large volume) customers are prepared to pay for it, and then pass on as much of the additional expense to end users of lubricant, refined product and electricity as the market will allow.

In so doing, the market is obliged to provide what the normal exchange of oil products usually does not—demand elasticity. Now, apart from exercises in pure economic theory, there are no serious suggestions advocating such a Draconian approach. Nonetheless, a significant corollary from the "market only" perspective emerges. What is contested by those who put forward the market as the proper mediator of price is the intervention of exogenous factors, such as governments, in the process.

The market, Adelman and others contend, places two limitations on how far oil prices can rise. Aside from the amount of oil usage curtailed by more marginal users of the products, there are two overall considerations at play. The first stipulates that the higher the rise in oil prices, the greater the reward from substituting alternative sources of energy. The second holds that rising prices stimulate additional short-term competition, thereby bringing down the overall price.

The normal provisions of demand inelasticity provide that demand remains relatively constant regardless of price. However, the durability of demand inelasticity tends to erode as prices rise beyond a certain point, since it is forward expectations that translate into either sub-stitution or cutbacks by consumers and/or increased production by competitors. It is, therefore, how sustainable the price increases appear that remains the crucial factor in whether market-dependent factors actually influence demand.

Demand elasticity (or inelasticity) is not a constant, but fluctuates, even in more moderate pricing environments. It is axiomatic that rising prices tend to suppress demand only when a threshold is reached—one where the combination of rising price levels and expectations about the future direction of prices begin to suppress the forward usage of oil products. Given what transpired following the oil pricing shocks of the 1970s or following the historic rise to almost $150 a barrel in July 2008, one might suggest that the decline in demand tends to occur only after considerations of supply have begun to affect adversely parts of the economy that are not within the energy sector (e.g., extraction, petrochemicals, and power generation), or heavily dependent upon it (e.g., transportation, mining, and most areas of agriculture).

A threshold price would then become that price for oil beyond which, for example, industrial production, manufacturing, consumer products, or housing begins to contract. The introduction of tradable future contracts for oil and oil products and the advent of tradable options may be the single most important mitigating elements in the determi-nation of such threshold pricing.

Any government able to influence its domestic market, especially one in which the officials are accountable to voters, will intervene to prevent such a straight correlation between rising prices and lowered demand. Economic ideologies aside, unencumbered market forces, especially when oil and oil products are involved, run the genuine risk of widespread dislocation and human suffering. In some market sectors, a temporary disequilibrium can be allowed to stabilize on its own. Substitutions of one product for another, short-term changes in lifestyle, or individual decisions to forego something will serve to bring supply and demand back into focus with a corresponding adjustment in prices.

But such is not the case with oil. This is not a sector in which theories of laissez-faire and economic liberalism, invisible hands, and enlightened self-interest, can guarantee security. There are, as we shall see, insufficient competition and a genuine inability to substitute for the increasing expense of energy.

All of which means governments will intervene, providing artificially determined price levels, quotas, supply and source considerations, tariffs, pipeline and retail regulations, as well as a myriad of secondary applications to influence energy consumption, all under the guise of the public good. This book will not discuss the merits of such approaches. But they are reflections of a more fundamental concern with which we do have an interest: as volatility, the oil vega, becomes more pronounced, governments will intervene under the guise of national security.

These considerations of price and security comprise the poles within which most of the oil debate is playing out. It is where the tradeoffs are constructed contributing to the rise and fall of government policies. Those tradeoffs may also determine the rise and fall of governments. Oil is the pervasive energy source for modern society. And that assures its central position in any debate of national security—certainly now, in the post 9/11 period, more than ever.

Chapter 4

Dollars, Credit, Financial Crises, . . . and the Oil Connection

Moscow, July 2009

I have come to Moscow, a location where I have spent much time over the past two decades, to meet with an oil trading company on a diesel deal. The project will import the fuel into West Africa. When listing those regions of the globe having the greatest need for oil products, Nigeria rarely comes to mind. The country is a global top-five extractor and one of the last remaining sources for light sweet crude, the low weight and low sulfur oil most prized by refineries. However, it has insufficient processing capacity and exports most of its crude. It also manages to generate only 15 percent of the electricity needed domestically. That means two things. First, private generators must produce virtually all of the power needed. Second, those generators run on imported diesel.

But why have a meeting about this project in Moscow? The trading market in wet barrels has changed dramatically over the past year. The international financial crisis has affected all segments of the oil sector, but it has hit traders the worst. A large number of them worldwide have been unable to secure credit. Normally, these firms would trade in the volume remaining after large houses satisfied their biggest global clients. However, they need to float the consignment until a purchaser transfers funds. For that, they need access to lines of credit.

My medium-sized project would be of no interest to the few huge houses now coming to control most of the oil product flow. I need to find an intermediary with access to both product and credit. That has taken several months longer than anticipated since the houses I had worked with over the years have suspended business. The trader selected must be directly connected to a refinery and have both the requisite export approvals and experience moving consignments in the credit freeze.

I finally found one. They have been trading for a decade, based in Moscow, exporting crude and products for a major Russian vertically integrated oil company having its own major bank. The trader has even successfully moved volume within the last two weeks. In addition, the house and oil company have offices on the same block.

I arrive for the meeting to find only two employees in the office. "Where is Sergei?" I asked one of them, referring to the export director. "Looking for a job, like the rest of us," he responded, adding, "We are closing operations tomorrow morning."

The crisis is quickly making this market an impossible place to do business.

■ ■ ■

There is a temptation, a strong one judging by the best-sellers list, to hold greedy Wall Street bankers and their progeny responsible for the mortgage and real estate financial crisis. Make no mistake, there is plenty of blame to go around: the unbridled pursuit of profit, cutting corners with inadequate disclosures, lending of money to those who really could not afford to take it (subprime mortgages, non-creditworthy investment holdings, collaterally deficient derivative offerings, and so on), with a con man thrown in here and there for good measure.[1] Profit and bonuses fueled the spiral, with the pursuit of self-interest becoming virtually the only justification of the free-market ideology—what John Cassidy succinctly calls "rational irrationality"[2]—fund managers, brokers, and individual investors coming up with very rational reasons for opting into what are essentially irrational market moves.

One disquieting result of the recent meltdown is its broader scope. Earlier crises have tended to focus on a particular market sector. This one may have appeared to start that way—clothed as a subprime mortgage collapse. However, the impact has been far more expansive, affecting financial, credit, and asset markets well beyond real estate. It is also a harbinger of things to come. The real estate bubble at the core of the problem was extended, disfigured, and prolonged by a wave of increasing profitability resulting from the milking of the spread between asset values (actual real estate) and paper values (mortgages on that real estate).

This was accomplished by interjecting between the two a novel way of providing for additional revenue streams while at the same time apparently reducing risk. Once securitizing future payments on mortgages became the norm, and an entirely new avenue for generating returns emerged (one that did not add anything to the actual overall real market value of the underlying assets), the way was open for an increasingly artificial view of the actual strength of the market. To put it simply, primary return no longer came from the mortgages themselves. It came from the intermediary securitizing of those mortgages.

It is indicative of the blind rush to profits that market drivers ignored clear, emerging evidence of accelerating credit instability. It appears in hindsight obvious that weaker paper (subprime mortgages, or mortgage clones emphasizing interest-only payments, along with the reduced requirements for debtors to demonstrate assets actually held or income actually earned) increases the risk of default. Rather than tighten the process to control the risk, the injection of securitization approaches allowed those who issued the mortgages to extract additional profit up front while at the same time extracting themselves from holding the risk on a rising inability to pay.

It also dramatically increases the damage. Collateralized suspect mortgages bundled with stronger paper, subject to cross-uses of collateral, and serving as underlying assets themselves in the issuance of entirely new generations of derivative paper place entire ranges of financial holdings under suspicion. A massive credit crunch is the result.

Everybody knows a fund manager, broker, or investment head who now says she recognized what was happening, but was unable to get out. Removing oneself from the feeding frenzy would mean sacrificing returns, bonuses, and in all likelihood one's job. Investors, oblivious to the real fundamentals, would vacate funds not involved in such securitized debt obligations for those that were. The performance was just too good. That meant keeping up with the other guys on the Street even when that went against what one's own analysis could readily demonstrate.

I say more on this in a moment. It is important, however, to emphasize the bottom line up front. Extorting paper profits from securitizing the difference between assets and future returns on those assets initially will increase the apparent market value of the underlying asset itself. That was certainly the case with real estate for well more than a decade.

But this is not sustainable. Two elements come into play, both reflective of the underlying fallacy predicating the process. First, to keep the increasingly artificial securitization sequence going, the price for the actual asset subject to physical exchange in the market (the residential or commercial property) becomes dependent upon the need to extract continuing levels of return from paper issued not to reflect that asset value but dictated by profit requirements. When that no longer can occur, a credit retrenchment follows.

Second, in what follows the pattern of a genuine Ponzi scheme, new and more inventive paper must emerge. This starts as a further relaxing of initial mortgage requirements to continue the flow of new debt, thereby further weakening the overall mortgage pool. This is now well recognized, comprising one of the staple elements in any criticism of the entire mortgage securitization environment. However, another parallel development also emerges. The market is just coming to grips with this one. How bad the results are going to be with the addition of this dimension remains unknown. And that uncertainty will further erode confidence in a much broader array of debt paper generally considered secure. Additional derivative paper, tying the weakening securitized mortgage paper to usually unrelated collateralized debt, emerges. This intensifies concerns over the creditworthiness of wider swaths of the market.

This is a very succinct prologue to what is coming. Unfortunately, the next crisis will be much worse. It is already taking shape in the oil market. While that market is reflecting elements perceived in real estate, this oncoming crisis is not simply going to be a transition of the asset price bubble from one sector of the economy to another. What we are about to experience will constitute a more extensive credit crunch occasioned by the increasing inability to value a fundamental asset.

Few if any corners of the international markets will escape the carnage. What we have experienced in the subprime mortgage securitization debacle is the first credit collapse resulting from a prolonged inability to see adequate market-sustaining asset values translated into the value of future paper. More to the point, the return demand of the paper drove the price requirements of the underlying asset to unsustainable levels. We are approaching that point in the oil market, where the fallout is likely to be worse.

The only reason oil pricing has not already begun unraveling results from extended reductions in demand occasioned by the subprime-induced financial mess. Economists and other social scientists would call this an exogenous factor. The demand decline is not a result of any dynamics occasioned within the oil market itself, but rather because of pressures exerted upon that sector from the outside. As the demand returns, as it must if economic recovery is to take place, oil volatility will usher in a far more serious credit constriction. This will also happen well before we have completely left the current financial problems. Mark well how the subprime mortgage crisis unfolded. It is a dress rehearsal for the next.

Even if legal, much of what the market experienced in 2002 to 2009 in the real state implosion was due to practitioners who knew that Rome was about to burn. They just thought the really nasty outcomes would not happen on their watch. Perhaps more accurately, they believed that there was always somebody else prepared to buy Rome, thereby delaying the conflagration indefinitely.

How the market articulated such a "principle," the belief that massive amounts of risk could be offloaded without jeopardizing the cash cow as a whole, makes this financial collapse fundamentally different from others. What places it apart, and forms the focus of both this chapter and, in a broader sense, this book as a whole, was the belief that a mechanism had emerged to relegate such crises to the pages of history. Simply put, practitioners had succumbed to the idea that new break-throughs would allow the market to continue expanding risk without a corresponding bubble burst.

All market dives have had their share of greedy, unprincipled, and even criminal participants. I propose, however, to dispense with the finger pointing, with laying blame or criticizing actions by individuals or entities. There is certainly enough of that deserved and currently underway in other venues. For the purposes of this book, who did what and when makes far less difference than why the system in place facilitated it and what that means for oil vega and the increasing volatility moving into oil trade.

Even if all participants had the best of motives (a notion, I admit, that strains both credulity and logic), the result would have been essentially the same. This was a systemic failure, an endemic collapse so engrained in the fabric of the financial world that there is nothing of substance to prevent it from happening again.

The classic, and still widely accepted, explanation of financial crises is to regard them as resulting from excesses (usually monetary), leading to a cycle of booms and busts. Analysts initially concluded that this is what began in 2005, becoming widespread by 2007, and demonstrated most emphatically in a volatile cycle in real estate prices.[3] However, this crisis was markedly different. We do not have an example here of typical cycles operating in a way to confirm any traditional understanding of the general equilibrium theory; its origins actually began with a fundamental departure from the idea that markets react to changes in supply and demand, replacing one level of market equilibrium with another.[4] In the past, the dominant thinking assumed (and virtually always required) an appreciable restructuring and downsizing of return expectations before the correction took hold. That is, profits would take a hit before the market could return to positive territory.

This time, purveyors of the new financial sleight of hand challenged one of the major premises upon which markets had traditionally operated. They came to the unsettling conclusion that the market could now effectively ignore the relationship between the extension of credit and the assumption of risk. Such a judgment ushers in one of the most serious and questionable introductions of moral hazard.[5] Undercutting one of the fundamental restraints relied upon to limit market overextensions, they believed (and in several quarters still do) that it was possible to continue the profit-making exercise without having to shoulder the risk attendant to the securitized assets in question. Despite the initial provision of, and subsequent crunch in, credit as a central element in previous financial crises,[6] this time around practitioners believed they had found a way to evade the downside in the expanding pursuit of return.

As I will note in a moment, asset securitization[7] introduced the belief that risk could be repackaged, sold, and cleared in such a way as to: (1) reduce the corresponding downside to manageable terms, (2) generate additional asset (and collateral) value, and (3) remove the traditional market impediment to expanding such value. This last aspect is the real culprit. It removes the essential ingredient that had served essentially to cap earlier attempts to play musical chairs with the world of finance. The original issuer of subprime loans no longer carried the risk of the creditor's performance moving forward. The original mortgage had been bundled with others, divided into parcels, and sold as new investment instruments.

Therein lies the quintessential "bubble accelerator." The mortgage-backed security (MBS) along with its cousins—the collateral debt obligation (CDO) and a myriad asset-backed security (ASB) clones—hardly ushered in the real estate collapse. However, the approach certainly did inflate the problem out of all proportion. It likewise illustrated the very myopic view prompted by a mainstay in traditional free-market thinking. The tacit expression of this view surfaced shortly before the real estate bubble had burst,[8] but the inability of market supporters to accept it indicated the size of the blinders.

While recognizing that real estate was subject to cycles, the new free market apologists believed that it comprised an overall low-risk investment prospect. That is because it reflects the overall size, economic mobility, and income prospects of an aggregate population, viewed as a whole (not as an assemblage of individuals). In short, it regards the commercial relationships among otherwise quite separate people as sufficient to provide equilibrium. So long as one coordinates the availability of both new and existing housing on the market with the number of new buyers, the system is at parity. After all, as a colleague once pointed out, "People prefer to buy homes, rather than rent. But if that home is an existing residence, whoever lives there is moving out and also needs someplace to live."[9] In short, while aberrations exist, the market should be self-perpetuating.

The one fatal flaw in this logic is the same shortcoming I see all the time in my public sector advising. It views only one half of what is required to make the transaction work. With the real estate market, as with the problem of unfunded mandates in government circles, players have managed to emphasize widely shared desires to own property (policy outcomes in public decision making) while avoiding the question of how to finance it. The real estate bubble provided clear indications that the desire to own a house is widely shared by all. Unfortunately, the ability to finance this desire is not.[10] Seen in their best light, subprime mortgages provided the opportunity to own a home, but increasingly were being promoted to a segment of the population having little realistic chance of pulling it off.

The securitization schemes also introduced two major roadblocks preventing the market from easily correcting the overheating spiral. First, since the "toxic"[11] assets in question had been parceled out into so many derivative issuances (both the initial MBS offerings and secondary/tertiary papers based upon them), a relatively insignificant percentage of overall debt outstanding[12] caused a significant constriction in liquidity.[13] The subprime loans were now so thoroughly intermixed with other debt holdings, themselves representing paper asset and collateral value for an even greater range of investments, that they prompted wide areas of the market to come under suspicion, brought into question huge holdings by major banks worldwide, and ushered in a cataclysmic credit freeze. This was accentuated by the fact that securitization by its very nature decreases transparency. Therefore, once there is a question about the structural integrity of asset-backed securities, the loss of confidence or trust becomes more difficult to attenuate.

Second, this is a classic example of moral hazard,[14] since those who are responsible for issuing the loan to begin with are no longer the parties shouldering the risk if the creditor defaults. That bifurcation of responsibility is not axiomatically a problem. Nor for that matter does it explode automatically into a significant moral hazard concern—unless the advantage from exporting the risk entices an overextension in the issuance of credit. After all, as I indicate, securitizing debt, utilizing assets as collateral for additional applications and the spreading out of risk are not bad ideas per se. In fact, I have personally designed securitization programs in the past for oil projects, pipeline capacity, refinery crude oil cuts, surplus electricity, discounted sovereign defaulted debt, and even the financing of first-run Hollywood films that achieved their purposes without engendering a run on banks or an epileptic seizure of credit.

As such, we need to avoid rejecting securitization altogether. It remains a very useful, sometimes essential, tool. Correctly structured and employed, it succeeds in lessening risk for projects or transactions unlikely to move forward by traditional financing methods. Securitization is also very successful at allocating capital, and does so very efficiently.

The moral hazard problem emerges when the primary source of profit becomes the securitization itself, while the underlying revenue stream becomes increasingly dependent upon the expansion of the securitizing network. In such an environment, at some point there is little structural difference between a mortgage-backed security and a chain letter or a Ponzi scheme.

You may ask, if this subprime problem was essentially confined to unwarranted mortgages extended in only certain markets—primarily in the United States—how could it have had a global impact, and so quickly? The answer involves the lifeblood of the global market itself.

The realities of international finance dictate that credit extended in one nation easily end up on the books of banks, holdings, hedge funds, pensions, insurance reserves, and portfolio investors in others. Crises in the Mexican peso (1995), Thai assets and banks (1997), Russian T-bills (1998), the Argentinean peso (2001), and more recently Dubai's indebtedness (2009) are all recent examples of this cross-border effect.

Normally, the market can at least partially stop the bleeding by trying to isolate the cause. Segregate the weak institutions, currency or paper, strengthen the defenses and advance selective credit to banks still liquid. The pain may go on for some time, but the principal damage remains localized.

The present crisis, however, is not susceptible to such fiscal triage. While nations throughout the world continue to administer their own home remedies in the form of bailouts, stimulus packages, and, in some cases, effective nationalization, the problem persists. There are a number of reasons for this, but one is paramount. This is a dollar-driven crisis in an international market that needs to hold and trade in dollar-denominated debt.

Here is where the oil connection emerges. While we were laboring under the crushing weight of a drying-up of credit, collapsing commercial paper markets, and interbank problems, all reflecting the preeminence of the dollar and tied to it for underlying value, oil has become the primary bridge in escaping from the first and solidifying the second. As such, however, oil also becomes a primary ingredient in the crisis itself. The mass media, and more knowledgeable analysts, have in the past referred to an oil bubble (the price hikes through the spring and summer of 2008, for example) and will certainly be doing so again. However, this is hardly an independent phenomenon.

The oil market is rapidly becoming a major barometer of the overall international financial crisis. Given the central position occupied by oil vega within that market, volatility will likewise occupy a central position in the ongoing crisis itself. Oil has not been the sole cause of the constrictions. However, how the pricing of oil plays out will be one of the primary ingredients in determining in what way the global market morphs moving forward. There are significant changes taking place in the international flows of capital, credit, and investment. Oil is becoming the lightning rod attracting all of them.

I propose in this chapter to sketch the relationship between crude oil on the one hand and the current financial crisis on the other. This obliges that we focus attention upon how the emergence of oil's schizophrenic nature as both a commodity and a financial asset has served to concentrate the broader realities of a global investment market forced to navigate amidst significant uncertainties involving credit availability, currency valuations, and psychology.

This is a limited view by intention. There are other recent works devoted to the wider understanding of how the global market arrived at this point.[15] Causality, while certainly an important explanatory factor, belies the real significance of what will happen next. A number of elements came together to produce this "perfect storm," but it is oil that has risen to serve as a primary clearinghouse for the consequences.

This chapter considers what I referr to as investment risk in Chapter 2. I will argue that the relationship between wet and paper barrels in the current market reflects more than just the availability of crude oil and the ability to trade it. Oil vega becomes a central concern because it both reflects and embodies four distinguishable ingredients in the crisis—*dollarization, securitization,* the availability of *liquidity* and the collapse in *confidence/trust*. These constitute the engines that drove the meltdown.

All of them directly relate to the way in which oil is valued and traded. The first three are financial matters; the last is psychological. While the first three may be more familiar to the traditional way economists view markets, it is the fourth—garnered from a social sciences approach to the situation—that may be the most decisive.

The interchange among these four comprises the bridge between market matters in general and the conditions surrounding oil in particular. That bridge assures oil vega will progressively reflect the rising instability in the wider market, augmented by developments endemic to oil itself, and provide additional difficulties in estimating where both oil and that broader market are going.

The confidence/trust factor is both the easiest to understand and the most difficult to quantify. While dollarization, securitization, and liquidity each lend themselves to detailed economic analysis, confidence/trust does not. It is a staple of the developing discipline of behavioral economics that it considers driving forces in market activity that are not susceptible to empirical analysis much beyond either opinion surveys or game theory. As such, I end this chapter with a few concluding comments on the confidence/trust dimension, devoting the body of this chapter to the impact of dollarization, securitization, and liquidity.

This may be a classic example of the chicken and the egg syndrome. As the new cycles of volatility kick in, there will be an escalating inability to determine causality. At an early point in the progression, it will be difficult to say whether the market as a whole or oil in particular is the culprit. Shortly thereafter, distinguishing the genuine cause from the effect will be impossible. Repetitive waves of instability will ensue. At that point, the ability to lay blame will be the least of concerns. More significantly, however, developments will test our ability to predict forward market movements in any genuine sense. The volatility itself will have acquired a life of its own.

The specific characteristics remain to be determined. However, in my judgment, one conclusion is already clear. Matters will be getting much worse. The fundamental deficiency remains. It is reminiscent of the traditional "inner-tube problem." For those of us old enough to remember having to pump up these things, we also recall what happens when an air bubble appears. Push it down in one place and it just pops up somewhere else. The entire range of government stimulus plans, dramatic interest rate cuts, expanded discount operations, and incentive programs introduced to combat the crisis merely rearrange the location of the bubble. Recent events remind us of what happens next. Bubbles burst. To extend the metaphor to its conclusion: This just happens to be one of those inner tubes with multiple bubbles.

Oil and Global Dollarization

There has been much written about the dollarization of the global market.[16] The generation of petrodollar revenues worldwide has demanded dollar-denominated investment instruments and assets in which to place those revenues. Investment flows and return requirements gravitate to those segments of the market that have the most efficient exchange potential. Given the predominance of the dollar in global trade over the past several decades, that means the exchange preference favors the greenback as the currency of choice.

Now that preference has come under increasing pressure of late, given the sliding exchange value of the dollar *vis-à-vis* the euro, British pound sterling, Chinese yuan, and even the yen, among others. However, the euro remains the only serious alternative. Investment holdings worldwide require a sufficiently large asset base denominated in a currency before there is any serious move to exchange one hegemonic currency with another. The euro is the only real contender to the dollar, but presents so many problems in its own right that any dislodging of the dollar in the near to medium term is highly unlikely.

At stake is seigniorage, the advantages accruing to a nation whenever others are obliged to use its currency.[17] This is what provides a decisive benefit for the dollar. As more greenbacks are required abroad, to service trade and capital flows, the United States benefits from what is essentially an interest-free loan. It allows Washington to print money that remains in foreign banks to support ongoing cross-border financial and fiduciary requirements.

To the extent that recipient banks do not repatriate this excess currency, it does not contribute to domestic inflation in the American market (although it does contribute to inflationary pressures in the national economies retaining the dollars). Additionally, even when repatriated, to the extent that these dollars are invested in sovereign debt (U.S. treasuries) or dollar-denominated commercial paper or corporate debt, it also does not contribute to American market inflation. The key is keeping the dollars out of circulation back home. Of course, dollar-denominated investment instruments and paper are available in other markets worldwide. Placing dollar proceeds in this paper abroad accomplishes the same purpose as not repatriating it back to the United States.

Collectively, these dollars abroad—either resulting from trade or deposits to effect later transactions—are usually referred to as petrodollars. This is because virtually all cross-border transactions in oil or natural gas are denominated in dollars and, over time, this has become the groundsel of the expatriated dollar holdings. The dollar-denomination of hydrocarbon trade results from a famous (and at the time quite secret) agreement engineered in 1974 by then–U.S. Secretary of State Henry Kissinger and the Saudi Arabian Monetary Agency (SAMA, the equivalent of a Saudi central bank). Riyadh agreed to denominate its crude oil sales in dollars,[18] with the rest of OPEC production following suit. That effectively required all oil (and natural gas) transactions globally to do the same.

The Soviet Union was the world's leading oil producer at the time. However, with the exception of some banks in Finland,[19] the ruble was not a convertible currency. Even Moscow had to use the dollar. As prices of crude oil began to rise, a U.S. market increasingly reliant on foreign oil sources began to experience a rapidly rising balance of payments deficit. Subsequent displacement of domestic-based manufacturing with product from Japan, China, East Asia, and elsewhere also contributed to the widening current account gap.

Yet the seiniorage conferred by the foreign use of dollars allows the financing of those widening trade deficits without undergoing what would otherwise be the normal expectation: domestic inflation.[20] A number of analysts have suggested that globalization in general, based as it is upon dollar reliance, similarly allows the United States to deal with its rising budget deficit as well as trade imbalances.[21]

For the nations obtaining the dollars in payment, however, the situation is quite different. Assuming initially that the overall exchange value of the dollars remains constant against other major currencies, the receiving market has only two alternatives. The first is to absorb the proceeds into domestic use; the second is to segregate the dollars from the local market (and home currency). Now in either case there will certainly be the desire to utilize the revenue in some way. Otherwise obtaining it has been of no advantage. Yet the receiving country has to consider effects that are in large measure the opposite of those facing the United States.

The recognition is as old as David Hume, who suggested the price-specie flow mechanism in the latter eighteenth century. He observed that a rising inflow of specie (gold or silver) into an economy as a result of trade (or payment) surpluses increases the domestic money supply, stimulates inflation, and thereby increases the prices of exports. Over time, that decreases the trade/payment surplus.

Applying this to our present purposes means the following. If left alone, the dollars coming into the recipient economy, for example resulting from international crude oil sales, will increase the value of the domestic currency for which they exchange. That will raise domestic prices and generate inflation.[22] It likewise will lessen the overall trading advantage of that economy. By raising domestic prices (and costs), it will lessen the positive trading differential between the sale of raw material abroad and the price of importing necessary technology, supplies and manufactured goods. This produces a double whammy: inflation at home and rising effective trading costs for necessary imports. It is for this reason that oil-producing countries have introduced oil funds or equivalent sovereign wealth funds to invest sale proceeds abroad.

These funds insulate the oil revenue from the domestic economy, thereby attempting to minimize the inflationary impact, by investing internationally. Yet, upon the repatriation of the international investment returns, there will be an inflationary impact. The degree of that impact depends on where the government injects the proceeds back home. If, for example, the use is to supplement pensions throughout the general population—a usually laudable social objective—it will have an immediate, direct, and compounding contribution to inflation. Raising pensions will stimulate greater expenditures for food, shelter, clothing, and medicine. In short, we can reasonably anticipate pensioners to buy articles of genuine need. Unfortunately, that means directly increasing the circulating currency in the economy and the velocity of the currency exchanges that are made—a textbook example of the generic formula for a rise in inflation.

Other expenditures required for improvements in the domestic economy could provide less immediate or pronounced inflation, such as certain infrastructure development projects for which the government purchases most of the required goods, technical expertise, or services abroad.[23] Employing local labor would still be inflationary, as would sourcing goods and services from local providers. The key to offsetting the inflationary impact involves an expansion and diversification of what is done in the domestic economy, improving the volume of finished product and non-raw material commodities as a percentage of aggregate exports, while at the same time purchasing more imported needs abroad with the initial investment proceeds.

Perhaps the least inflationary acquisition of equipment and technology for domestic use results from the foreign purchasing of military arms and weapons systems. Of course, that also occasions other disturbing policy concerns, both internally and externally.

The Norwegian example, both the first oil fund and the model relied upon by producing nations in designing their own approaches,

has the most limited usage. It is also illustrative of an element contained in all other funds globally. Here, the government primarily
makes use of fund proceeds only to supplement central budgetary
expenditures when revenues from sales decline. The fund, therefore,
serves as a supplement to tax revenues applied only to cover a collapse
in market pricing. Oslo discourages initiating new programs or budget
lines from proceeds and requires that state-controlled StatoilHydro[24]
finance its expansion requirements via the more traditional routes of
sale revenues, international syndicated bank credits, and/or securitization
of future production (more on this approach further on).

In applying trading proceeds to international investment, which is
the sole reason for oil funds, countries are primarily concerned with
three factors: (1) a guaranteed return (low risk), (2) the available volume
of investment paper (liquidity), and (3) ease of access (size of market).
Interestingly, not on the list is the level of return. A producing nation
will accept a lower rate so long as the market guarantees that return.

Given the forward nature of the proceeds generated—officials often
refer to the funds as necessary to provide security for future generations—
there is also the added ingredient that the overriding assumption views
the returns as not usually available for immediate use.

Exceptions (i.e., contemporary spending) involve capital expenditure-
intensive major infrastructure commitments for ongoing hydrocarbon
development or transport projects, less frequently domestic investment
projects, or unusual needs.[25] In these cases, the determination is that
such sector-specific expenditures will provide for additional accretions
to the fund in the future, a kind of "priming the pump" approach.
If the expense results from addressing needs widely supported at home,
despite the inflationary or even destabilizing impact, local consensus
has more of an impact than longer-term economic considerations.

Almost invariably, these examples are the result of significant dis-
locations and/or ethnic and cultural conflicts. The Azerbaijani decision
to use oil fund proceeds to assist internally displaced persons (IDPs)
from the Nagorno-Karabakh conflict with Armenia is such a case, as is
the Iranian decision to provide assistance for those injured or families
impacted during both the 1979 revolution and the Iran-Iraq War of
1982–1988.[26] Both have widespread local approval and reflect strongly
held social commitments.

Upon occasion, especially in the Russian experience,[27] politics intrudes to compel injections of fund proceeds directly into the local economy. Officials well recognize that this is inflationary, but the political benefits outweigh the drawbacks, especially in the run up to an election. Establishing fund proceeds as a direct channel to central budgets is a significant problem. Aside from the inflationary impact, the political enticement legislatures obtain from providing short-term remedies for social needs structures a dangerous dependency moving forward. In addition to the Russian example, in which the question remains of who has the *de facto* control over the fund, similar problems have been experienced, for example, in the Alaskan and Venezuelan oil funds.[28]

It remains, however, the usage of fund proceeds rather than the process that determines the extent of domestic problems. In this regard, the Venezuelan example is least commendatory. There, massive mismanagement of the domestic budget has obliged the government to subsidize ongoing expenditure lines, provide direct subsidies to the population and pay for daily imported needs. All of these are certainly necessary and make for very successful populist political agendas. But they are directly inflationary and provide widening disruptive results for the domestic market.

However, quite apart from how proceeds are used domestically, what is important for our purposes at this point is how the dollarization of the trade in oil contributes to a widening financial crisis. Given the need to put oil sale proceeds to work as engines for investment return in the international market, producing nations will require increasingly available dollar-denominated investment instruments. The traditional usage of proceeds to buy U.S. sovereign debt has had a declining advantage for most of the past decade. With the expanding weakness of the dollar's exchange rate *vis-à-vis* other currencies, its purchasing power has plummeted in the international market. This becomes a major concern for producing countries having undiversified economies (and that includes most of them), given their need to import the bulk of nonenergy goods.[29] What results is a two fold problem. Oil-producing countries realize less effective purchasing power with the petrodollars gained, while the corresponding exchange rate results in added cost for the imports of virtually everything else.

By 2005–2006, therefore, some OPEC members started looking into alternative dollar-denominated investments, those that could offer better returns, thereby offsetting the declining purchasing power of the dollar. Foreign exchange rate analysis indicates that, during the six-year period between 2003 and 2009, the overall Saudi external purchasing power resulting from crude sales effectively declined by 62 percent.

Saudi officials had expressed publicly their unease over this state of affairs,[30] but those statements hardly expressed the anxiety at SMSA. It was clear by 2005 that petrodollar proceeds were not matching the rise in import costs. The subsequent crude oil price spike occurring into the summer of 2008 helped matters, but not as much as the casual observer might think. The attending inflation occasioned created problems, both in the domestic markets of OPEC producers and in the price hikes demanded by European providers of required imported goods. The net advantage to Saudi Arabia or Kuwait, and certainly even more so to other OPEC members such as Venezuela or Nigeria, was considerably less than a simple calculation of sales price minus extraction costs might have indicated.

Therefore, officials in several producing countries moved dollar-denominated investments in an attempt to counter declining purchasing power. SAMA does not provide published (or for that matter transparent) figures on how it invests petrodollars. However, according to European banking sources, declines in Saudi purchasing of U.S. treasuries, along with anecdotal information provided by Saudi contacts, indicated that Riyadh initiated the investment transition, certainly by 2005. Every indication points to a massive movement of investments out of U.S. sovereign debt into higher-yield paper—with a weighting to mortgage-backed securities and a range of collateralized debt obligations. In short, SAMA, with in all likelihood other OPEC national monetary authorities following its lead, invested right into the mortgage-securitization–led financial crisis.

The Saudi economy will certainly not collapse because of this adventure, but it has been shaken. Other OPEC members more reliant on crude sale proceeds are in deeper problems. There are indications emerging that the decline in effective returns is putting significant pressure on budget balances in Caracas—a not unexpected result, given the Venezuelan usage of oil fund proceeds noted above.

This assures a renewed emphasis on extracting more reliable returns from dollar-denominated investments and a rising push to decrease the dollar portion of foreign exchange currency baskets, experiments with new benchmark crude rates, and even more usage of non-dollar-denominated contracts. That means the contagion issuing from the subprime mortgage crisis has hardly stopped. In a very real sense, it is only beginning.

Securitization and Oil

Public investment agencies, oil funds, banks, hedge fund managers and private investors in the global securitization market need to rely on ratings agencies. The structured debt involved comprises a complex bundling of paper from a number of sources. While they all may be, for example, retail mortgages, they hardly come from the same geographic area, mortgage type, or credit rating. Now subprime or alternate income or asset-based paper should have been bundled together. That largely occurred, at least initially; otherwise the ability to rate the paper would decline precipitously. Between 2004 and 2006, and the real ratcheting up of the securitizing curve, Wall Street had issued at least $1.3 trillion in subprime-asset-backed mortgage securities, representing about 75 percent of all subprime mortgages issued and more than 40 percent of all mortgages regardless of type.[31] By 2008 and the genuine beginning of the meltdown, the market in subprime mortgage debt paper clearly exceeded $2 trillion,[32] or well over 60 percent of all the subprime mortgages issued. That figure mushrooms to over $3 trillion by August of 2009. There was a clear indication that default rates in the underlying mortgages upon which the paper was based, which had been running at rates much higher than the mortgage market as a whole, were intensifying. Precise estimates are difficult to arrive at by the late summer of 2009, but market sources indicate that at least 90 percent of subprime and other high-risk suspect mortgages by that point had already passed into the rapidly weakening collateralized debt market.

Two safeguards had failed by this point. The first resulted from the nature of the collateralization utilized. The second amounted to a wholesale capitulation of the ratings services to the avalanche of paper. In the first case, concerns emerged over whether the bundling of debt

had put mortgages of the same type together. That certainly took place
with the initial introduction of the paper as it had during the run-
up of usage in the early 2000s. However, the market was now rapidly
changing—driven by extremely attractive returns, rapidly escalating
demand, and intense pressure on paper cutters to meet quotas. A more
liberal interpretation intervened, with a widening differential in paper
quality ending up in the same collateralized parcels. Now the rating
agencies should have provided a protective wall against this happening.
However, as we see in a moment, that did not happen.

In addition to the rising suspicions surrounding the quality of the
paper included, a second development relating to the overall categorization and quality of debt emerged with the expansion of the derivatives
based upon mortgages and other debt. This is where the real crisis
took off. As the demand for derivatives increased, the types circulated
became far more complex. We can actually label much of these new
issuances as "derivative derivatives." These tertiary and later generations are much higher risk. Initial-level collateralized debt at least has
an underlying asset in view (or at least discernible somewhere on the
horizon). As the leveraged asset moves through additional layers of
collateralization, the ability to provide it with a confident value declines.
This paper comprises exotic, discounted, and highly volatile securities.
These are derivatives whose underlying "asset" is actually another derivative. As the crisis affecting the underlying mortgage-backed securities
and related paper intensified, therefore, it had an impact well beyond the
dollar-value of the initial securitizations.

Utilizing the original MBOs as collateral for later issuances magnified
the problem considerably. Firm estimates of these later issuances, often
used to underwrite a range of transactions between banks and investment houses, are difficult to make. However, market sources suggest
an increasing of the overall volume of debt derivatives circulating by
several hundred percent. Both the suspicions arising from the actual
condition of the mortgages included in the initial securitizations and the
usage of those MBOs as the collateral for tertiary securities resulted in
a full-blown attack on the confidence held in the paper itself—and a
corresponding constriction in credit.

The second safeguard failure involved the ratings agencies, primarily Fitch, Moody's, and Standard & Poor's, by far the dominant.

The securitization of mortgages is a more complex exercise to value than other collateralized debt obligations. The very nature of the paper makes it less transparent with a higher degree of difficulty in determining the overall quality of mortgages and likelihood of default. That allows the agencies to charge more for their services; on average four times as much as more conventional collateralized assets. This is essentially high-risk paper, but it also provides greater returns, guaranteeing an increasing demand. The ratings agencies, in turn, would find themselves in competition for this rising and lucrative business. Issuers would often be in the position of being able to shop around for a favorable rating, with the agencies facing the prospect of losing a significant and expanding new revenue line if they did not provide the desired rating—a certain recipe for disaster.[33]

What followed roiled all financial markets. It made no difference whether or not there was any direct connection to the high-risk mortgages or the debt paper issuing from them. The intensifying default rate among suspect mortgages, an attendant collapse in the value of MBOs and the constriction of credit that followed paralyzed global capital flow. Toxic paper permeated primary asset classifications worldwide, given the widespread use of securitized debt obligations either directly or partially based upon the paper. The creditworthiness of major banks, trading houses, investment and hedge funds, as well as the expected holdings in sovereign wealth and private equity funds, came into question.

Given the widespread need for lines of credit and forward financing in the oil industry, the crisis would have a heavy impact on funding requirements for ongoing and new projects. Taken alone, the subprime mess would have had an adverse impact on its own for oil financing needs. As noted in the next section, liquidity considerations in oil, as with most other sectors of the market, translate into a need for access to credit. As we shall also observe, oil's dual nature—serving as both a commodity for delivery and a financial asset—will accentuate the problems from dollar-denominated contracts. That will also translate into a serious liquidity concern.

However, there is another dimension to the securitization issue arising when one considers the oil sector. Quite apart from the effect of MBOs on credit availability for oil, there is the added dimension of securitization in oil itself. This happens in several ways. Most new exploration and production (E&P) projects are too expensive to fund from petty cash. Capital expenditure needs can be met by additional issues of company shares. Ultimately, of course, IPOs become options of declining utility. What companies will rely upon are syndicated bank credit lines, the collateral for which being the market value of the crude oil not yet extracted.[34]

Such an approach has been of increasing use in the last several decades, as overall project expenses increase.[35] It also introduces the wider financing application of securitization. Once a company has begun utilizing what amounts to the future-flow of volume as a contemporary revenue source, the way is open to treat later production as a source of collateral to meet current or ongoing financing needs. In short, future consignments of crude oil or oil products become securitized assets in a manner similar to mortgages or debt.[36]

Initially, these applications extend little further than hedging on future market pricing, acting largely in place of or in addition to futures contracts and options. Providing a floor for the sale of crude or refined oil products is as essential for wet barrel sellers and buyers as it is for traders focused upon gaining profit from the paper barrels based upon the asset. In practice, however, the derivatives employed have evolved into a way of bridging various debt and financing considerations quite beyond the collateralizing of the asset in the ground or the refinery itself.

What we have here is a rapidly developing, but exceptionally opaque, world of oil securitization. This is the movement from project finance, through structured finance, to a combination of the two best referred to as structured project finance. This is injecting the possibilities and problems of credit debt obligations (CDOs) and related synthetic[37] finance squarely into the production of oil.

Project finance is merely the raising of capital for ongoing operational needs utilizing either company assets or (as is more often the case with oil) future cash flow as collateral. On the other hand, structured finance involves raising capital (and/or managing risk) by issuing securities tailored to the particular needs of issuers or investors. Structured project finance, therefore, becomes the use of such issuances to fund projects. CDOs and related paper will become the method of choice.

Given that oil is a commodity with known end-uses, it is certainly true that acting as the underlying asset in such transactions has a value dependent primarily on its future expected market price. In the case of oil still in the ground or refinery volume not yet processed, the corresponding securitized paper (or, for that matter, syndicated bank credit) will always carry a value discounted to expected future market levels. Accomplishing that end requires the employment of a range of structured intermediary derivatives.

This has given rise to new generations of paper, having as well structured applications to other approaches already summarized.[38] This begins with CDOs and collateralized loan obligations (CLOs). Neither of these first emerged in the oil sector, but both have become convenient mechanisms for producers, providing what amounts to venues for ongoing project finance and/or operational protection. They are appealing as a way lenders can synthetically refinance project-financing portfolios.

Usually the availability of CDOs in issued tranches should allow an investor (in theory at least) to tailor holdings to her level of risk tolerance. With the exception of junior tranches, each has a seniority (subordination) over those tranches below it.[39] Subordinating (higher-level) issues also carries tighter tests of collateral quality and integrity. These tests trigger a flow of either interest or principal (or both) to senior paper from lower paper, thereby providing for the retirement of the more senior tranches. Junior tranche subordination provides the necessary credit enhancements for senior tranches, providing CDOs issued on the senior tranches to receive a credit rating reflecting their priority status in the overall structured financing program. The junior tranches, therefore, allow an investor to acquire a more leveraged exposure to the underlying CDO portfolio itself, thereby providing a greater return potential for the decision to tolerate a greater level of risk.[40]

The instrument also (once again in theory) allows an exposure to a diversified range of debt obligations. In fact, it is this prospect of diversification that provides the primary advantage to project borrowers, lenders, and investors. However, this also becomes an essential element often more difficult to determine in practice.

Trading requirements expect underlying CDO assets to meet a range of eligibility criteria, including diversity, weighted average rating, weighted average maturity, and weighted average spread or coupon.[41]

These are supposed to be in accordance with the methodologies applied by the major ratings agencies.

However, ratings agencies are not passing judgment on each asset in the portfolio. Rather, in the case of synthetic issues, they provide judgments on classes of paper. Such an approach has proven adequate for a number of CDOs in various market sectors. Unfortunately, one of the major shortcomings in agency approaches in the subprime mortgage crisis was a series of diversification assumptions that turned out to be fundamentally incorrect. Diversification should lower the overall risk in a portfolio, the idea being that weak debt assets are offset by stronger examples elsewhere. That did not happen with the subprime crisis.

The key to making diversification work is a CDO or equivalent instrument actually combining underling paper that represents a genuine combination of risk elements. Standard & Poor's, Moody's, Fitch, or some other lower-positioned agency would then assign a rating reflecting the overall risk incorporated in the pool of assets underlying the issuance. Given that the crisis CMOs in question overwhelmingly contained subprime and other suspect mortgages—in other words they combined debt of the same class—some other factor had to provide the diversification element. In traditional synthetic mortgage obligations, that element is geographic, and it has worked out rather well in distributing risk. Unfortunately, that turned out not to be the case this time. Suspect mortgages combined from places like Los Angeles, Las Vegas, Miami, and Phoenix merely magnified rather than discounted the risk. They all tended to act in the same way, default at the same rate (much higher than other classes of mortgages), and provided the same, rather than diversified, risk characteristics.

The same problem may well emerge in oil CDOs and clone paper. As we move into the genuine oil vega crisis cycle, classes *of oil* (largely determined by benchmark rates), geographic locations, and liquidity of finance options, among a number of other factors, will need to be offset by rating procedures adequately balancing actual market risk factors. Unfortunately, many of the oil CDOs currently available would not provide sufficient protection from a multiplication of risk similar to subprime MDOs. That means a more careful inspection of the debt and a concerted focus on real diversification. Of concern, however, is the fact that there has not been any move to remedy the shortcomings illustrated by rating agency performance, nor is there any likelihood that the appetite for synthetic finance will abate anytime soon.

Still, while recognizing the endemic problems remaining, we want to avoid throwing the proverbial baby out with the bathwater. Synthetic issuances in general have proven successful in both raising finance and spreading out risk. Remember that the global investment community is constantly in pursuit of increasing profitability, and that carries a recognized assumption of risk.

CDOs in a wide range of applications beyond the oil and gas sector have demonstrated that it is easier to sell packaged debt obligations than it is to attempt the refinancing, sale, or swap of each credit exposure individually. This has certainly been the case with hydrocarbons as well.

As an added attraction—and much prized in the current market, which is constantly on the lookout for new securitization opportunities— the CDOs and CLOs make possible an expansion of the paper seller's ability to enter into additional structured finance. They should also allow financial institutions to manage exposure to regions, crude oil types, national markets, and production locations in a better way than if a bank attempted to address each in a separate transaction.

The underlying premise of CDOs and related paper states that a pool of defined debt instruments will perform in a predictable manner, allowing reliable estimates, thereby, of default rates, ranges of loss and recovery, time frames, and the like, and the corollary assumptions about them. During times of relative market stability, as Culp and Forrester put it, "With appropriate levels of credit enhancement, CDOs can be financed in a cost-efficient manner that reveals and captures the 'arbitrage' between the interest and yield return received on the CDO's assets, and the interest and yield expense of the CDO securities issued to finance them."[42]

It is important to understand that the assets "beneath" have a primary affect upon a CDO's capital structure. This certainly should extend to matching the characteristics of the debt obligation itself—e.g., underlying floating rate assets should result in CDO tranches that have a floating interest rate (or a swap allowance to offset interest incompatibilities). In addition, a matter having a direct connection to oil project CDOs, if the underlying assets oblige subsequent capital commitments, infrastructure construction, working-capital arrangements, or post-completion finance, the CDO tranches should provide additional access to lines of credit.

Given the myriad possible variations of debt and loan obligations, structured finance options, derivative paper, and the like, it is not unusual for commercial paper intermediaries to hold the CDOs, almost without exception in the case of those issuances requiring ongoing access to additional finance. The intermediaries then provide a range of pricing and funding options to the wider market. This, in turn, introduces a need for ratings of both the CDO and the intermediary and a rather involved structure of corresponding procedures and structural requirements. Obviously, those CDOs requiring the greatest level of additional finance will have the narrowest independent flexibility.

Conversely, CDOs containing fully funded debt obligations can largely avoid most, if not all, of the need to use intermediaries and should constitute the most appealing investment targets. Therefore, the most attractive assets for inclusion into CDOs include project finance loans, especially those relating to extracted raw materials or products having known market value and demand, along with the leasing, operational, secondary, and service contracts; transport; and processing needs related to such loans.

Oil-project CDOs carry all of these positive assumptions and are primed to expand significantly in the near-term, especially as we move into the cycles of oil vega and the volatility they will trigger both in the financial markets and in those sectors servicing or relying upon crude oil extractions and processing.

There are several major reasons why this is so. Investors regard the types of project finance loans and accompanying debt provided by the oil sector as attractive assets for the issuance of CDOs because they have higher expected recovery rates and shorter recovery periods than equivalently rated corporate debt obligations,[43] along with a known, established, and intensifying end-user market demand. As a result, CDOs containing project finance debt as their underlying asset base tend to issue at lower cost with a higher arbitrage utility than equivalent paper.[44]

However, there are two important caveats as we move forward into the next crisis. First, several of the primary assumptions upon which rating agencies act in determining overall security of project debt versus corporate debt are essentially without sufficient statistical support. In short, there have been few studies conducted. More to the point, there have been no studies subjecting this assumption to CDO performance during times of high oil volatility. What we have, therefore, are assumptions garnered during a period of debt usage in a market environment that is not likely to reflect what is coming.

Second, it will hardly be smooth sailing for agencies in determining ratings for oil CDOs. One of the main challenges remains diversification. As noted above, inadequate diversification, or more properly the incorrect assumption that a geographic differentiation of mortgage sourcing represented genuine diversity, comprised a main failure in the subprime MBO collapse. I have briefly noted a similar problem could emerge in oil-asset-based synthetic debt issuances.

The main problem is the difficulty of determining whether one has diversity or only a semblance of it. For example, including only European or Chinese or North American natural gas shale plays may run the risk of too narrowly confining a geographic and/or source matrix. Despite having a number of distinct projects, they may still include common undiversified problems and, therefore, provide no risk offset. Including project finance debt from different geographic locations and energy types may still not be enough to provide a genuine risk distribution. Exposure could remain to the same endemic weakness. For example, Arctic Circle–offshore Russian natural gas, continental Chinese coal-bed methane, and Venezuelan Orinoco Belt heavy-oil production certainly would appear to provide both a geographic and energy difference. Yet all three suffer from technology and infrastructure needs that domestic sources cannot provide (to this point anyway). Therefore, the risk profile appears disturbingly similar.

As a result, project-funded CDOs currently available usually do not contain debt assets consisting solely of projects from within a single industrial sector. Until the CMO debacle, rating agencies would often penalize CDOs coming from a single industry. At the same time, however, the instruments would still rate highly enough to allow sales.

I must emphasize that CDOs including only oil-project-funded debt as assets are currently infrequent. However, the increasing use of derivative paper already issued to hedge crude and oil product sales combined with the rising volatility about to hit the overall sector will oblige the rapid expansion of all manner of synthetic structures.

This means that the industry diversification standards applied by agencies will in all probability morph into regarding distinct elements in the upstream/downstream sequence as diversity. Whether considering exploration, production, field development, refining, storage, shipping, distribution, or retail sales, along with a range of service and secondary providers, constitutes sufficient diversification within oil or natural gas remains to be determined. A parallel attempt to cross-securitize different types of energy (crude oil, natural gas, electricity) or types of the same energy—light and heavy oil, along with bitumen and oil sands, for example, or conventional free standing natural gas with shale, coal bed methane, tight gas, and gas hydrates—may not actually distribute risk sufficiently, either.

There is no question that the oil sector will experience a significant increase in securitization schemes. The sector, however, has not witnessed a rapid rise in synthetic financing while at the same time undergoing significant volatility. Neither historical experience in the sector nor the use of debt obligations in other applications provides much guidance. Fundamental to the use of CDOs and equivalent schemes is a need for increasing access to credit and liquidity. Unfortunately, that leads us to consider a second problem area.

Oil and Liquidity

Liquidity merely refers to the ability to translate an asset into cash. Money, therefore, is the most liquid, while an asset that can only be transferred after a prolonged search for a buyer would be considered illiquid. Liquidity is essential for continuing market operations in any sector and credit is the primary vehicle by which that liquidity flows. The current credit constriction in global banking, therefore, indicates that a wide portion of the interbank market remains effectively illiquid. Only a portion of the credit market is operating more than two years after the full fury of the CMO crisis hit.

Oil activity (either production or trade) requires liquidity as much as market applications in any other sector. Therefore, continuing access to lines of credit are also necessary. Given the market value of the underlying asset (the crude oil or oil product itself), liquidity in oil trade is represented by the interchange between the underlying asset and the futures contracts and options based upon the asset. Liquidity in trade, therefore, represents the relationship between wet and paper barrels.

The reliance upon derivatives for increasing access to liquidity in trading operations parallels the rising interest in CDOs for the funding of projects. We should anticipate, therefore, that liquidity considerations—in the form of trading spreads or structured project funding—will rise relative to the perceived condition of credit markets.

The actual condition of market liquidity, however, is another matter. Here, oil transactions certainly influence and are influenced by U.S. dollar global liquidity, as graphically illustrated by Figure 4.1. As a result, a brief discussion of what is meant by such liquidity is in order. Recall that despite pressures building to the contrary, the trade remains dollar-denominated. The preferred way of calculating U.S. dollar global liquidity has been one developed by Merrill Lynch and now in wide use by others. Until recently, it was a reliable predictive indicator

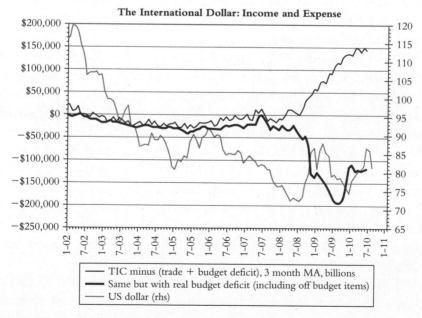

Figure 4.1   Global Dollarization
SOURCES: International Monetary Fund; Federal Reserve.

and had been for almost three decades. This approach essentially says that the liquidity level equals the U.S. monetary base plus reserves held in custody by the Federal Reserve on behalf of foreign interests— primarily central banks and primarily Asian.

Accordingly, the conventional wisdom held that a rise in the U.S. current account deficit,[45] certainly a very visible aspect now for several years, would result in a corresponding enhancement of global liquidity. Such a result would follow from countries (i.e., their central banks or monetary authorities) having a current account surplus with the U.S. offsetting that surplus by investing dollar proceeds in U.S. sovereign debt. Recall that until the subprime meltdown such investments also included a rising interest in CMOs and other synthetic paper in preference to corporate debt, the other standard dollar-denominated target.

As I have also observed earlier in this chapter, this provided the U.S. economy with the advantage of seiniorage while also allowing the dollar recipient countries to utilize the proceeds without incurring domestic inflation. The United States could tolerate rising balance of payments problems without the deficit resulting in domestic dislocation (and a heavy dose of inflation), while the global economy in general, and dollar holders in particular, could experience genuine stimulus to expansion and investment.

Or so the mantra proclaimed. Beginning in the fourth quarter of 2005, however, matters began to change. The traditional way of gauging global liquidity was clearly showing a slowdown, but it was incapable of indicating the degree of what was to come. As happens so often with predictive measures, based on historical data, trends, and assumptions, they are incapable of signaling the truly atypical market development. Market equilibrium theories may postulate a bell-shaped-curve view of excessive swings up or down. Unfortunately, markets hardly provide such symmetry. Rather, "outlier" events are more dramatic and frequent than the academic theories express (a point I return to in Chapter 7). The corresponding relationship between global liquidity (denominated in dollars) and the dollar index is provided in Figure 4.2.

This started in earnest by the time we had moved into 2006. Liquidity growth had begun to decelerate, as gauged by the traditional measure. What that measure picked up was a slowdown in both of its major indicators. It found a slower growth forecast for the U.S. monetary base,

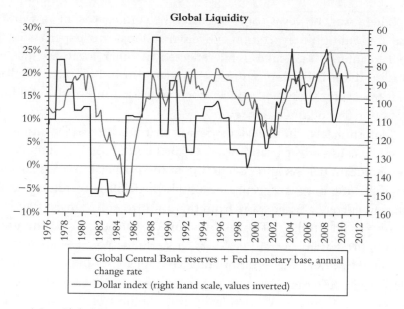

Figure 4.2   Global Liquidity versus Dollar Index
SOURCES: International Monetary Fund (www.imf.org/external/np/sta/cofer/eng); Federal Reserve (quarterly report).

a development that proponents wrote off as a short-term reaction to the Federal Reserve raising interest rates. Similarly, there emerged a lower amount of foreign reserves deposited with the Fed, its other indicator. That, in turn, was explained by the preponderance of Asian central banks in the calculations and the need by those countries to offset rising oil prices.

Both of these had been taking place for at least six months, but the approach regarded them as market adjustments, not signals of the collapse coming. The initial estimates—still seeing growth in both the U.S. and global markets, albeit at a slower pace—resulted from the reliance on past trends and market moves. There was no way to extrapolate from such data a genuine *contraction* in global liquidity. The primary indicators, therefore, were commenting on a market likened to moving downstream in a fog without a paddle. Unfortunately, that stream was the financial equivalent of the Niagara River moving rapidly toward a precipice of the same name.

There was, however, one salient point coming out of this otherwise misleading interpretation. Given the slowdown experienced by the Fed interest rate hikes, and reflected in other locations internationally, there had been a decline in speculators borrowing dollars. Even the overly simplified conventional approach in estimating global liquidity rates could see this result.

Unfortunately, the prevalent view at that juncture badly misunderstood the cause-effect relationship revealed by the data.[46] Failing to see any significant deleveraging occurring in the financial markets, analysts concluded the drop in speculation employing dollars merely indicated a shift in currency usage away from the dollar to euros, Swiss francs, or British pounds sterling. The last was unlikely at best, given the parallel indicators of an overall weakness in sterling-based speculative borrowing. However, the position received apparent support from the ongoing double-digit rise in the euro monetary base throughout the period. Figure 4.3 provides a basic indication of the broader money supply during the period, while Figure 4.4 provides a general picture of the new structure of global liquidity.

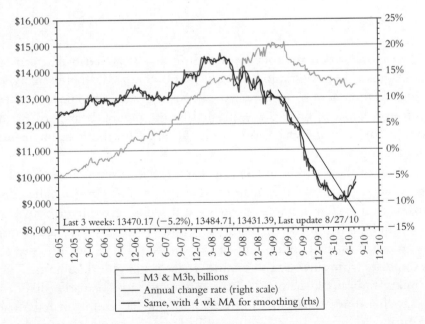

Figure 4.3   Broader-Based Money Supply
SOURCE: http://nowandfutures.com/key_stats.html#global_liquidity.

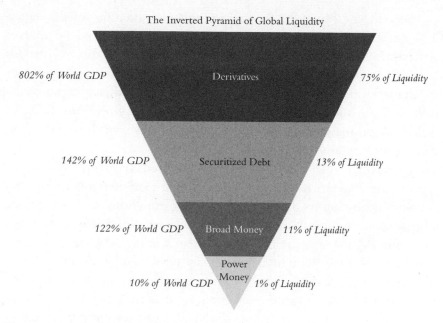

Figure 4.4   Liquidity Breakdown
SOURCE: Bank for International Settlements; Independent Strategy.

Here is what the approach either missed or misinterpreted. First, as we now know only too well, the leveraging (i.e., the utilization of debt) was not primarily a result of diversification in holdings from dollars but an entrenchment in dollar-denominated holdings through increasing dependence on CDOs, CMOs, CLOs, and other structured (and synthetic) alternatives. In other words, this was not a diversification of currency risk. Rather, it was actually reflecting a deeper reliance on dollars, even in the face of rising exchange rate concerns. In a fundamental sense, this should have been anticipated. The dollar overhang implicit in global liquidity needs to be collateralized to avoid a genuine free fall. I would maintain the market ultimately was able to combat this result only because of massive, and unprecedented, injections of liquidity into domestic markets by public agencies. Of course, we now await the dropping of the other shoe as a consequence of such governmental decisions, as any recovery will bring with it significant inflationary pressures.

Second, the concerted flow of liquidity into commodities emerged in earnest. A coincidence had emerged, well recognized by market analysts, between global liquidity and oil values from the early 1980s onward. A similar relationship existed between liquidity and aggregate Asian stock market indices over the same period. Both are hardly unexpected, given the connection between U.S. dollar global liquidity and dollar-denominated oil sales on one hand, and liquidity and Asian central bank reserve usage on the other.

However, other relationships also surfaced. Volatility indicators, namely the VIX discussed in Chapter 2, have exhibited a negative correlation against global liquidity measures throughout the first decade of this century. Global liquidity levels also have an inverse relationship to credit spreads—a significant increase in the spread usually means a significant drop in liquidity. Further, in what is a pronounced commentary on the past decade, a significant decline in global liquidity has *always* indicated a crisis—reflecting its existence or telegraphing its arrival, depending on the length of the decline and the perspective of the analyst. Such declines occurred in 1981 to 1982 (Mexico, Brazil), 1985 (Venezuela, Peru), 1989 to 1990 (U.S. Savings & Loan), 1995 (Mexico, Russia), 1997 to 1998 (Asia, Russia), 2001 (Argentina), and 2005 to 2006 (subprime mortgages).

The historical record indicates that a steep decline in liquidity will precipitate a crisis somewhere in the global market. The results are straight from Global Econ 101. An erosion of liquidity will result in a slowing (or absolute contraction) of gross domestic product (GDP) growth and/or a hit to financial markets. In retrospect, on each of those occasions listed since 1990, the relationship was a direct one.

Unfortunately, once again the judgments expressed drew the wrong conclusions, drawing from prior experience rather than being able to explain a decidedly more extreme decline underway. Each of the previous declines had global implications but was primarily local in nature. Each allowed dollar-denominated assets held elsewhere to serve as a counterweight to the decline, with rapid rises taking place once each situation stabilized. Yet a fixated focus on the overall foreign reserves held at the Fed—which increased from less than $100 billion in 1980 to almost $1.5 trillion by the first quarter of 2006—belied a continuing decline in percentage growth year-on-year. A rising aggregate foreign dollar total overshadowed a lagging growth rate in liquidity. In the somewhat constricted analytical environment created by the Merrill Lynch approach and those following it, the two primary statistical references seemed to be portending a crisis, but one similar to those previously experienced—damaging, but manageable.

The overall positive conclusions for the U.S. economy drawn from nearly three decades of global dollar liquidity build up were gaining confidence: (1) given the global appetite for dollars, the United States could sustain a large current account deficit indefinitely; and (2) the dollar acting as the world's primary reserve currency made that deficit seem almost irrelevant. It certainly did not create the kinds of problems a persistent deficit of that size would have posed for other economies. In addition, also predicated upon the basic two fold liquidity analysis, several studies emerged indicating there was a very low correlation between the global usage of the dollar and the American current account deficit.[47] In fact, some have suggested that the distribution among major global trading currencies would provide an adequate buffer, as at least partially suggested by the data summarized in Figure 4.5.

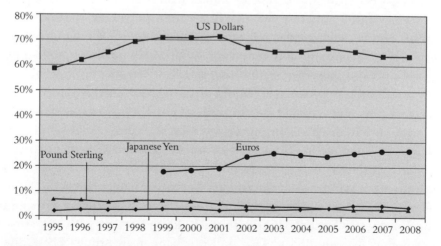

Figure 4.5 Global Reserve Composite

SOURCE: International Monetary Fund, Currency Composition of Official Foreign Exchange Reserves (COFER).

Yet overemphasizing foreign dollar reserves, which is where the conventional thinking progressively moves every time the global liquidity rate dips, is only viewing part of the picture. While central banks may adjust the distribution of currencies held in reserve, including the changes in ratios of currencies to each other in a "basket" used to determine exchange rates for a local currency, it is trade flows that ultimately dictate the foreign currencies held in reserve. With oil dollar-denominated, and other cross-border trade increasingly priced against the dollar as well, central banks have no recourse but to retain and increase dollar holdings (whether or not those same banks decrease the dollar effect on foreign exchange). Absent replacing the dollar with, say, the euro as the global liquidity base, dollar seiniorage would continue.

The caveat is this. Dollar strength for some time has exhibited an inverse relationship to the growth in global liquidity.[48] As overall liquidity increases, the dollar declines. As liquidity growth slows, the dollar improves. Obviously, interest rates are a major component, with periods in which the Fed increased rates showing a strengthening dollar, while the current environment of dramatic rate cuts as part of the stimulus arsenal contributes to dollar weakness.

The only reason the greenback is not significantly weaker than it is against other major currencies results from central banks having to introduce similar interest rate cuts in an attempt to kick-start a frozen credit sector. Such moves increase global liquidity. With the recovery slowly beginning and renewing inflationary pressures following closely behind, however, central banks are entering into a monetary game of chicken to see who blinks first. A coordinated approach to interest-rate hikes should be the result, but these joint exercises in money-supply management never produce the same results to all participants. Then again, as the rates rise, the advantage returns to the dollar, although overall currency strength would not approach the situation witnessed in the foreign exchange market by early 2006. Then, the Fed increased rates while the Bank of England cut rates and the European Central Bank was in a holding pattern with the euro, producing a strong dollar. That will not happen this time. These rate revisions will need careful coordination to avoid significant foreign exchange volatility.

However, one significant change has emerged. The movement of liquidity into commodities in general, but oil in particular, will intensify. Between the early 1980s and the mid-1990s, a body of research had emerged indicating a relationship between oil prices and exchange rates.[49] These studies, however, considered only the trading implications of the oil-currency exchange situation with primary focus on the 1974, 1979, and 1982 oil shocks. It was only in the later 1990s that the actual movement into crude oil and oil product futures contracts as a flight to liquidity begins seriously.

This move will have decisive implications for oil volatility moving forward. Studies of trading market liquidity have emphasized returns on stocks and bonds, along with the attendant traditional risk concerns associated with portfolio development. Themes in such research, however, are applicable to the transition of liquidity concerns to oil trading.[50]

It is now a daily staple in the media to focus on the relationship between the price of oil and the dollar's exchange rate. Commentators regularly declare a decline in the dollar (primarily against the euro) as one of the major reasons for the rise in oil prices. It is even normal to include a reference to a flight to liquidity or a flight to value.

The dual nature of crude oil and oil products—acing as both a commodity and a financial asset—has allowed this transition. Oil becomes a source or store of liquidity, preferred to the still globally dominant dollar because oil's market value allows a better hedge against the loss in dollar value in foreign exchange. Essentially, this results from oil having an ongoing end-user value (at refineries in the case of crude, and at the pump in the case of oil products).

Yet, we still witness the appreciation of oil prices with a decline in the dollar. The market calculates oil as more valuable when the dollar becomes less so. Recalling that the degree of liquidity is essentially the ease with which an asset can translate into cash, those assets having a high degree of transferability, trading in a high-volume market, and having a range of available derivative and securitization vehicles will become preferred investment targets. Oil possesses all of these elements.

In any trading scenario, usually the best indicator of liquidity is the bid and offer spread. Normally, the narrower the spread, the greater the liquidity. Recently, the rush to interest rate cuts by regulatory authorities throughout the world and the injection of massive amounts of stimulus by governments has produced a tidal wave of liquidity in a short time period resulting in significant movement in that spread beyond the actual increase in market demand for oil. Absent anything else transpiring in the market, this development in itself increases the price of oil futures contracts (as it does for many other commodities). However, it does nothing to increase the real market value of the underlying crude oil or oil products. Liquidity surpluses (I resist the temptation to call it yet another "bubble") are an inevitable result of such actions and have a direct effect on stimulating the further rise in oil prices.

The slow return of market demand for crude and oil products, given the protracted financial crisis, complicates the current situation. That prices have been rising as a reaction to rising liquidity and trading interest, but not as a result of genuine demand increases, tells us two things. First, there is a trading expectation that prices will continue to rise once the demand does return. Second, each pronounced rise (i.e., a jump of 5 percent or more rise in daily prices with the market in the $70 to $80 range) inflates the price even further, as the price of options become more difficult to determine. That will translate into broader swings as the market attempts to compensate. All of this is a result of a liquidity rush manifesting as a protracted rise in oil vega.[51]

Yet, the lack of liquidity globally was never really the issue, certainly not in oil trading. The problem was not the lack of liquidity but the constriction in credit providing access to the liquidity for trading purposes (the structure for releasing liquidity for working capital and operational purposes was another matter). Therefore, the way in which banks and other financial institutions served an intermediary position in the oil sector,[52] while freezing the credit markets in response to the CMO crisis, assured that even more liquidity would be required.

It did not take observers long to understand that any concerted move to get the credit markets up and operating would require the creation of an even greater liquidity overhang. When this occurs, traditionally the excess liquidity moves to those sectors having the greatest potential for ease of asset transfer. That almost always means commodities in general and raw materials (especially oil) in particular.

Yet, while policy officials in several major capitals worldwide avoided a global economy laboring under excessive unproductive liquidity (known as a liquidity trap),[53] signs emerged by the end of 2009 that sustainable recovery was still elusive. The liquidity injected is fueling an increase in commodity prices, but that is not translating into signs of a sustainable recovery. In fact, excess liquidity may not be moving into the kinds of productive assets needed for a recovery.

The strong rebound in oil prices in particular signals an unusual price spike in an initial cycle of a recovery, especially given that demand remains weak and additional supply to meet any demand increase is likewise suspect. Normally, the price of oil and other rapidly consumed commodities tend to experience accelerated increases during the late stages of an expansion, when supply becomes tight following strong demand over a period of time. That, after all, was the result in both recoveries of pricing in the 1980s, and the later more significant price increase in 2005 to 2008.

Absent any hard data to the contrary, the primary market-based rationale does not explain the rise. This rationale (actually, rationalization would be a better term) claims the price acceleration results from a return of growth (and supposedly, therefore, demand) in China, East Asia, and India. Yet, this growth has resulted in additional stockpiles of energy and raw materials, but not in any significant improvement in demand.

What has returned, a result of a marked recognition of the massive flow of cheap money combining with a renewed interest in positioning against the dollar, are moves using oil and other commodities as an asset of choice. That, in turn, increases speculative interest in oil futures, a matter I return to further on.

Of course, renewed speculation also increases the number of players. That is expected because, for oil, more potential trading participants are always an indicator of expanded liquidity (or at least the availability of it). According to the classifications used by the U.S. Commodities Futures Trading Commission (CFTC), there are four primary categories of participants in oil trade—each contributing to the liquidity environment but also having differing objectives. That makes overall estimates of liquidity difficult, given that the existence of a liquid asset does not mean all participants utilize or apply it in the same way.[54]

First are the producers and commodity consumers—those selling crude (operators) and oil products (refineries), along with those buying crude (refineries) and product (distributors). This is the category most directly related to the wet barrels, the actual underlying assets. However, it is now necessary that all stages in the oil sector (upstream through downstream) hedge sales and deliveries. Wet barrel parties, therefore, are also trading paper barrels, introducing a broader application liquidity transfer from oil assets to futures contracts.

The second category includes what the CFTC refers to as broker (or swap) dealers, primarily investment banks, who are issuing the derivative paper and facilitating the deals upon which much of the current oil-based liquidity depends.[55] The market transition is dramatic here. Prior to the onslaught of the global credit constriction (essentially before August 2007) producers and consumers (the first CFTC class) accounted for almost 30 percent of oil trading (by nominal value). Before the third quarter of 2007 ended, that figure had collapsed to less than 13 percent, while the dealers saw their market control grow to over 45 percent.[56] Much of this liquidity was effectively "locked into" the paper from that point on. There simply were not any other similarly attractive options. The leverage required demanded it.[57] The provision of securitized access to what is actually a commodity-based liquidity intensified.

The final two CFTC classes—money managers and other investors— occupy the demand end of the securitization chain. Here, the rapidly expanding appetite for new paper prompted the move in liquidity from producers/consumers to broker dealers. This is not a short-term phenomenon.[58] The massive liquidity additions intended to fuel recovery are making money cheaper (thereby enticing leverage) while also requiring the translation into assets easily moved into the market.[59] We will see this playing out for years. In my judgment, the attendant relationship between crude oil price increases and intensifying inflationary pressures is likely to follow the projection put forward by James Hamilton.[60]

Pricing in the crude oil futures market continues to reflect changes in volume, indicating that the market is not yet overheating— approximating the approach laid out by Moosa and Silvapulle a decade ago.[61] However, the market environment is undergoing considerable change. While liquidity increases, promoting its usage on oil derivatives and related securitized paper, the volatility in the futures contract prices will not find a counterbalance in an equivalent rise in demand for the underlying asset. The increase in demand for crude oil and oil products will lag behind the price acceleration in futures contracts fueled by the liquidity overhang and attendant concerns about a weakening dollar exchange rate. As liquidity continues to move into oil contracts, volatility will rise significantly—reinforcing the other sector elements stimulating oil vega.

It is tempting to view the widening spread between paper and wet barrels, along with the increasing volume in futures contract volume and the accompanying rise in volatility, as the result of speculation. Public opinion, frequently encouraged by the media, often charges speculators with causing most of the problems in the oil trading market, especially since there is a clear relationship between increasing futures contract volume and a rise in speculative activity.[62]

Speculation is really nothing other than an attempt to maximize a return from financial activity (usually investments, issuing loans, buying and selling assets, or acquiring low-rated paper) by increasing risk beyond the level at which the security of the initial principal sum is guaranteed. The overall margin of safety is significantly less than conventional investment. Speculators tend to take shorter-term positions, react to current events in a market rather than subject them to analysis, and typically utilize a higher degree of leveraging.

Given the shorter time frame involved and the need to have a sufficiently liquid market in which to act, commodities tend to attract such actions. Commodities also attract speculation because the action usually prefers the buying and selling of an asset, for which the speculator expects the futures contract or other derivative price to change irrespective of the actual market value provided by the underlying asset. Usually, speculators will prefer a market in which the future price is appreciating,[63] although an environment in which prices are falling will also attract speculators to short the market.

Other market participants generally prefer to have the participation of speculators because they provide two desirable factors. First, they add liquidity, and second, given their interest in acquiring a quick and maximum return, they tend to cover the more extreme positions. After all, if I want to conduct a trade, I need somebody on the other side prepared to take a financial risk. If there are no speculators present, only producers and end-consumers control the transactions. The oil sector went through a period in which the large international oil companies set prices (the so-called "Seven Sisters"[64]), followed by OPEC and other producers exercising similar control. Neither provided a market where the equilibrium had anything to do with a setting of genuine market prices. That changed with the introduction of crude oil futures contracts in the 1980s.[65] I return to the position occupied by the speculator in Chapters 6 and 7.

However, the futures market only took off, providing a modicum of predictability and broader investor ownership, once the actual buying and selling moved from the initial controlling buyers (major international oil companies) and sellers (producing countries). That required both formal and informal sources of liquidity—institutional investors in the former case, speculators in the latter.

The current situation, already providing a surfeit of liquidity from other sources, does call into question the position of speculators moving forward. One of the primary justifications for speculation has been its ability to add needed liquidity to the market. However, liquidity is not the current market problem, given the excess cash injection from the government. Yet, anecdotal analysis (amounting to what I would label "speculation on speculation") claims that upward to 60 percent of the volume in the crude oil futures market is actually coming from speculators.[66] That should mean additional speculation would run the risk of overheating the market.

Recent data indicate that is not taking place. Following the new transparency rules established by the CFTC, we should anticipate an improved ability to analyze speculative cash flows. In November 2009, Hilary Till concluded that:

> As long as one includes options positions, the T indices[67] for the NYMEX oil futures markets are not excessive, again, provided that it is acceptable to use the historical agricultural futures markets as a guide to the adequacy (or excess) of speculation.[68]

It is also noteworthy that from the summer of 2007 to the summer of 2008, the NYMEX WTI oil futures market did become more speculative (relative to hedging), even if the data for futures and options combined showed that the peak T index would not be regarded as excessive, using our historical benchmarks.[69]

In addition, while there is a liquidity surplus at the moment, additional infusions of public funds is hardly either a favorable answer or even a realistic prospect. That means, given the ongoing medium-term market requirements, speculative liquidity is still required. Despite the level of liquidity present at any given time, analysts have recognized, following upon the work of Holbrook Working,[70] that "what may be technically an excess of speculation is economically necessary for a well functioning market."[71]

The real unknown for the oil market, however, is the effect of increasing speculation in an extended volatile market—that is, with the intensification of oil vega. There is evidence from a range of trade in securities markets that rising volatility tends to result in an increase in both hedging and speculative activity.[72] We should expect this, since each either seeks to protect a position or profit from maximizing the spread between futures prices and the actual value of the underlying asset.

There are two things to keep in mind as the market moves into this extended volatility. First, there is no equivalent trading period to which we can turn for comparison. The previous bouts of instability since the mid-1980s (and the rise of crude oil futures trading) faced a market having far less volume, in which the pricing of crude was not as dependent upon the corresponding pricing of derivatives as it is now. Second, trading in the past was not as dependent on the level of liquidity. Such considerations may mean we are emerging into a rapidly changing market environment.

Oil and the Confidence / Trust Factor

As noted at the outset, I am ending this chapter with a few brief comments on the confidence/trust factor in the oil market. The herd mentality exhibited by commentators and the media in both the lead up to $147.27 oil in early July 2008 and the decline to $32.60 by the end of that year, had a clear connection to levels of confidence or trust held in oil market operations. They portrayed the rise up as favoring the investor (or speculator) and the oil companies (or OPEC), while the decline was thought to benefit the end consumer. Of course, the former also exhibited expectations of economic expansion while the latter was primarily a result of a financial crisis having a significant downward pressure on economic activity throughout the market. As a result, a consumer may finally have been able to afford gasoline for her SUV, but unfortunately no longer had a job to drive it to.

Concerns over the intentions of Iran—or OPEC or China or Russia or Venezuela or a multitude of other geopolitical actors—affect the confidence/trust factor, as do "peak oil" arguments, environmental concerns, opinions on the intentions of "big oil," or attitudes about Wall Street. Thus far, aside from comments about investment vehicles in general, or speculators in particular, common opinion has formed little in the way of dominant views on the oil market.

The same, however, cannot be said for those who trade in it. Here, the degree to which an investor has confidence/trust in the market as a whole clearly comprises a main factor in the decisions she makes. Usually, those decisions take their primary readings from how the dominant themes among the participants play out. As a result, market moves generally overreact to actual market developments. The trust/confidence collapse following the subprime mortgage crisis and related market problems is perhaps an example of this, but investors this time around had very good reasons for mistrusting the system.[73]

That means the approaching acceleration of oil vega is likely to have an even greater impact on market participant attitudes, magnified into unstable and dangerous ramifications for market performance as a whole.

Chapter 5

Oil Companies and the Upstream/Downstream Tradeoff

Gdansk, February 2010

I am in Gdansk to address a forum sponsored by European Parliament President Jerzy Buzek. Grupa LOTOS S.A. is the primary convener of the meeting and that gives me an opportunity to tour their operations.

LOTOS, a dominant Polish refinery, has one of the largest Baltic processing facilities located here in Gdansk. It also runs a network of some 500 Polish and Czech gasoline stations and has more recently moved into upstream, or crude oil production, projects. It is, therefore, a rising vertically integrated oil company (VIOC).

As with other VIOCs in the West, LOTOS focuses on the downstream sector—from refinery to retail distribution. That is where the profit is in free market oil activity. The group now includes some 18 divisions, but the refinery is still its center. And the extensive series of structures and pipelines located there is well into an ambitious expansion by the time of my visit. When all is done in 2015, the 10+ Program will move LOTOS from processing 6.2 million tons (45.5 million barrels) of crude oil annually, the 2008 total when work began, to over 10.5 million tons. The program requires a huge capital investment but will result in a considerably improved production rate of high-end (and profitable value-added) oil products.

CEO and president Pawel Olechnowicz is proud of the company's accomplishments and speaks glowingly about the future. Still, there is one overarching concern: the reason LOTOS has belatedly moved into acquiring positions in upstream production fields. It may have a dominant refinery operation, but it does not control its own crude.

The new production effort will help, but it not enough. The real reason a major upgrading was decided speaks to the way this refinery was developed. It was built during the Soviet period and still primarily refines Russian heavy sulfur content crude. It needs to spend a great deal of money to expand what crude flows it can process. The dynamics of Polish-Russian relations, therefore, have an immediate impact on whether LOTOS can continue expanding its refining presence. Pawel acknowledges the problem, but expects to weather it. Poles, after all, for centuries have done just that with neighboring Russia.

The day after my tour, however, the tension has increased. The LOTOS CEO is more somber at breakfast. Moscow that morning announced it may reevaluate its crude delivery commitments to Poland, both by sea and by pipeline. A curtailment of deliveries by sea would cripple the Gdansk refinery.

Welcome to the world of the upstream/downstream tradeoff. These days, a company's positioning in the overall oil sequence is determined by where its profit center is. That means greater vulnerability to outside pressure and an entire sector increasingly unable to handle what is coming next.

■ ■ ■

The current corporate structure in the oil sector obliges companies to concentrate on what each does most competitively, despite the continued existence of some firms that still try to cut across the major segments from production through refining to retail sales. This chapter explores why the current structure will have great difficulty in combating the rise of oil vega. The way companies are put together these days may even make the situation worse.

Recall that oil vega refers to the accelerating inability to determine a genuine value of crude oil based on its market price. The rise in market volatility makes it progressively more difficult to predict either revisions in oil pricing or its genuine impact on both the market and the policymaking apparatus. That rising volatility, the overall failure in predicting pricing changes or impact, and the ensuing deterioration in policy alternatives will result in more radical global politicizing of the situation. Instability in both the market and governmental responses to it will result in the likelihood of intensified and repetitive crises cycles, generating the increasing possibility of dangerous consequences.

Volatility can certainly reflect price movements in either direction, but the preponderance of the impact upon the market will be to move the prices up. This is almost certainly the result of the inability to peg what the underlying crude oil is actually worth in real terms. As we have already seen, the emerging environment will oblige traders to put price spreads (and options) for the futures contracts at a level to discount the implied risk of accelerating volatility.

One would expect that the traditional market supply and demand dynamics would intervene to address the situation. Therefore, should we not expect additional investment forthcoming to induce additional production, thereby increasing supply to meet the uncertainty? After all, previous cycles in the oil market resulted in the investment level moving up or down to compensate for supply requirements.

Unfortunately, the increasing problem with oil vega refers to the lack of an adequate market price peg, and that would make it more difficult to employ traditional mechanisms to even out crude oil pricing by providing additional supply. This is not simply a supply problem. The extent to which the instability results from the failure of the trading market to set the price reduces the ability of increasing supply to solve the problem. The only guaranteed success here in combating volatility would involve injecting such a significant increase in volume into the market that pricing would collapse.

The situation attendant from the fourth quarter of 2008 into the fourth quarter of 2010 has restrained the full exercise of oil vega because of a range of exogenous pressures on demand: a prolonged credit crunch, high unemployment, a sluggish industrial recovery, double-dip stock market concerns, euro zone default worries, and the threat that first Greece and then Ireland would disappear from the map, among others. An improvement in this environment will prompt the return of the very accelerating volatility that will spark the crisis. We cannot expect external problems to restrain the underlying oil market situation forever. For that matter, even with all of the accompanying restraining influences, crude oil prices are still rising.

This chapter indicates how the traditional supply-side solution for oil market pricing imbalances will not offset the emerging volatility. Simply put, companies cannot use market volume to offset oil vega. This is not primarily a volume deficiency, a concern over peak oil, or the usual bout of geopolitical handwringing. Oil vega is not about supply but about pricing. The production companies are structured to enhance bottom-line considerations reflecting one market view, a view predicated upon overarching supply-demand considerations. The problem, on the other hand, is arising elsewhere.

However, even if we were to accept the traditional view of petroleum economics, discount the added dimensions of volatility, oil vega, and paper barrel–wet barrel pricing spreads, and concentrate only on a "supply meeting known demand" approach, extraction risk will progressively render the current production structure insufficient. It is not likely, therefore, to meet either the actual problem or the one it was traditionally designed to meet.

The discussion in Chapter 2 introduces extraction risk as involving how the market has reacted to intensifying concerns about aggregate lifting volumes, declining field and crude quality concerns, as well as rising wellhead expenses and the changing mix of sourcing. To the extent that this is acknowledged (and it is the essential basis for the supply-demand approach in the market for the past century), it explains how operating companies approach the market.[1]

As I shall observe presently, oil companies throughout the world have been busy restructuring to emphasize booked reserves or profit margins. However, the future stability of the oil market no longer rests upon the revenues of the major international companies. In fact, the production sector will be incapable of preventing the next global crisis.

So that there is no misunderstanding about what I am stating, let me express it as succinctly as possible. *The direction of oil company structure will make it impossible for crude oil production to offset the inevitable accelerating volatility.* Majors emphasizing their primary profit centers—which are rapidly moving from field production—will only extend oil vega.

In support of this fundamental observation, the present chapter addresses primary elements on the supply side of the equation—overall field exploration, development, and production considerations. Operating companies' activities will comprise the focus. As such, I intend to sketch the most likely parameters of how producers will structure themselves and their projects moving forward.

Such dimensions are already coming into play. In the process, as the title of this chapter suggests, there is a change taking place in the way the largest oil companies both position themselves in the market and anticipate the changing dynamics of that market moving forward. I contend that primary company decisions involve a choice between focusing upon the upstream production or downstream (refining and distribution) segments. Even in the case of a vertically integrated oil company (VIOC)—a company positioned in both the upstream and downstream markets—its focus must reflect both market realities and genuine near- to medium-term competitive positioning.

There is no question that the realities of the oil market have obliged companies to change their footprint. In the process, the structural form of companies controlling the oil available has changed considerably. While VIOCs still conduct operations in both the upstream and downstream segments,[2] the overall market has become increasingly multifaceted.

The Rise of National Oil Companies (NOCs)

As indicated by Table 5.1, the actual control over global production volume has gravitated decisively away from privately held VIOCs and IOCs (international oil companies—highlighting both their reach and their multinational presence[3]) toward national oil companies (NOCs)—either owned outright or effectively controlled by the state. For 2007, the U.S. Department of Energy's Energy Information Administration (EIA) estimated that NOCs accounted for 52 percent of the global production and 88 percent of proven reserves.[4] The EIA estimates that 2009 global production came in at an average of 84,158,559 barrels per day (bpd).[5] Combining OPEC production with that of other state-controlled extraction volumes from China, Indonesia, Malaysia, Mexico, Norway, and Russia, indicates the NOC portion for 2009 approached 58 percent.[6]

Table 5.1 Top 50 Global Producers as of January 1, 2008

Rank by Oil Equivalent Reserves (OER)	Company	Liquids (million barrels)	Natural Gas (billion cubic feet)	Total OER Reserves (million barrels)
1	Saudi Aramco	259,900	253,800	303,285
2	National Iranian	138,400	948,200	300,485
3	Qatar General Petroleum	15,207	905,300	169,959
4	Iraq National Oil	115,000	119.9640	134,135
5	Petroleos de Venezuela (PDVSA)	99,377	170,920	128,594
6	Abu Dhabi National Oil	92,200	198,500	126,132
7	Kuwait Petroleum	101,500	55,215	110,990
8	Nigerian National Petroleum	36,220	183,990	67,671
9	National Oil (Libya)	41,624	50,100	50,028
10	Sonatrach (Algeria)	12,200	159,000	39,179
11	Gazprom (Russia)	0[1]	171,176	29,261
12	Rosneft (Russia)	17,513	25,108	21,805
13	PetroChina	11,706	57,111	21,469
14	Petronas (Malaysia)	5,360	82,992	19,547

Table 5.1   (Continued)

Rank by Oil Equivalent Reserves (OER)	Company	Liquids (million barrels)	Natural Gas (billion cubic feet)	Total OER Reserves (million barrels)
15	LUKOIL (Russia)	15,715	28	15,720
16	Egyptian General Petroleum	3,700	58,500	13,700
17	ExxonMobil (United States)	7,744	32,610	13,318
18	Petroleos Mexicanos (PEMEX)	11,048	12,57	13,198
19	BP (UK)	5,492	41,130	12,523
20	Petroleo Brasilerio (Petrobras)	9,613	12,547	11,578
21	Chevron (United States)	7,087	22,140	10,870
22	Royal Dutch/Shell	3,776	40,895	10,767
23	ConocoPhillips (United States)	6,320	25,438	10,668
24	Sonangol (Angola)	9,035	9,530	10,664
25	Petroleum Development Oman	5,500	30,000	10,628
26	Total (France)	5,778	25,730	10,176
27	Statoil Hydro (Norway)	2,389	20,319	5,862
28	ENI (Italy)	3,925	11,204	5,840
29	Dubai Petroleum	4,000	4,000	4,684
30	Petroleos de Ecuador	4,517	N/A	4,517
31	Pertamina (Indonesia)	903	20,538	4,414
32	EnCana (Canada)	927	13,300	3,201
33	Occidental Petroleum (United States)	2,228	3,843	2,883
34	China National Offshore Oil (CNOOC)	1,490	6,232	2,555
35	Devon Energy (United States)	998	8,994	2,535
36	Anadarko Petroleum (United States)	1,014	8,504	2,468
37	Repsol YPF (Spain)	952	8,137	2,343
38	Canadian Natural Resources	1,358	3,666	1,985
39	XTO Energy (United States)[2]	308	9,441	1,922

(continued)

Table 5.1 (Continued)

Rank by Oil Equivalent Reserves (OER)	Company	Liquids (million barrels)	Natural Gas (billion cubic feet)	Total OER Reserves (million barrels)
40	Ecopetrol (Columbia)	1,450	2,439	1,867
41	Chesapeake Energy (United States)	124	10,137	1,856
42	Talisman Energy (Canada)	749	5,464	1,683
43	Apache (United States)	1,134	2,446	1,552
44	EOG Resources (United States)	179	7,745	1,503
45	Romanian National Oil	863	3,550	1,470
46	BHP Billiton (Australia)	565	4,727	1,373
47	BG Group (UK)	393	5,572	1,345
48	Hess (United States)	885	2,668	1,341
49	Marathon Oil (United States)	650	3,450	1,240
50	Shell Canada	808	1,400	1,047

[1]Gazprom oil reserves are technically held by Gazprom Neft, now considered a separate entity by most commentators.

[2]ExxonMobil is finalizing the process of acquiring XTO.

SOURCE: www.petrostrategies.org/Links/worlds_largest_oil_and_gas_companies.htm.

The VIOCs, on the other hand, have moved their primary profit centers downstream—to emphasize the processing and distribution of oil products. Such companies are still involved in production joint ventures, and they remain important members of ventures developing new fields or, especially in the case of Libya a few years ago or Iraq today, reworking existing fields to increase productivity. Yet the primary generation of revenue for a VIOC is progressively moving to the refining and distribution of processed oil product.

This should not be surprising, given two factors. First, a VIOC of its very nature will gravitate to primary bottom-line considerations closer to the consumption end of the spectrum (refineries comprise the almost-exclusive major consumers of crude oil, while distribution and retail outlets provide oil products released by the refineries to the ultimate consumer).

Second, the decline in VIOC control over aggregate production is noticeable when comparing overall extraction volumes and reserves.[7] Put simply, there has been a significant shift in the control of both global reserves and lifting from privately held VIOCs to the state-held NOCs.[8]

Nonetheless—and this is the greatest indication that VIOCs are moving downstream in their emphasis, despite controlling less of the raw material—they dominate when it comes to revenue. According to the *Forbes* annual top "Global 500" companies, VIOCs hold 6 of the top 10 slots. The highest ranked NOC is Chinese state-controlled Sinopec at number 9, while China National Petroleum Corp. (CNPC) is number 13.[9] The initial conclusion is inescapable. NOCs dominate in the extraction and sale of raw material crude oil, but international VIOCs concentrate their activities in the production and sale of more profitable value-added products—gasoline, diesel, low-sulfur heating oil, jet fuel, and petrochemical feeder lines. That translates into higher revenue and larger profit margins.[10] The 20 highest ranking oil companies in the *Forbes* survey are listed in Table 5.2.

Concentration of production is one matter, sufficient supply to meet demand is quite another. Now demand with regard to oil (and energy in general) refers to the amount of product actually consumed, rather than a figure resulting from a demand curve.[11] That means oil demand has a greater sensitivity to actual market exchanges than does the demand calculation for other products. However, it also makes it more difficult to estimate forward-looking projections with any certainty.[12]

Despite recent declines in that demand, resulting from exogenous factors to the oil market itself,[13] the trend moving forward is for a rising constriction in the availability of wet barrels—that is, the actual crude oil and oil products. Paper barrels (the futures contracts) may drive the price of oil, but they are of little consequence if there is not actually sufficient crude oil to satisfy the volume of contracts needed to meet demand requirements.

Traditionally, securing supply in a rising demand scenario was regarded as a purely market-driven exercise. Rising prices for the product, prompted by increasing demand, would encourage additional investment in new drilling. That, in turn, would yield the additional supply necessary.[14] It is one of the essential arguments of this book that oil

Table 5.2   Top 20 Oil Companies in the 2009 Fortune 500

Overall Fortune 500 Rank	Company	Revenues ($ millions)	Profits ($ millions)
1	Royal Dutch/Shell	458,361	26,277
2	ExxonMobil (United States)	442,851	45,220
4	BP (UK)	367.053	21,157
5	Chevron (United States)	263,159	23,931
6	Total (France)	234,674	15,550
7	ConocoPhillips (United States)	230,764	−16,998[1]
9	Sinopec (China)	207,814	1,961
13	China National Petroleum (CNPC)	181,123	10,271
17	ENI (Italy)	159,348	12,917
22	Gazprom (Russia)	141,455	29,864
27	Petroleos de Venezuela (PDVSA)	126,364	7,451
31	Petroleos Mexicanos (PEMEX)	119,235	−10,056
33	Valero Energy (United States)	118,298	−1,131
34	Petroleo Brasilerio (Petrobras)	118,257	18.879
36	Statoil Hydro (Norway)	116,211	7,664
65	LUKOIL (Russia)	86.340	9.144
76	Repsol YPF (Spain)	79,177	3,968
80	Petronas (Malaysia)	76,965	15,309
86	Marathon Oil (United States)	73,504	3,528
101	Nippon Oil (Japan)	64,198	−2,505

[1]$35 billion write-off 4Q 2008; $34 billion for acquisition of Burlington Resources
SOURCE: http://money.cnn.com/magazines/fortune/global500/2009/full_list/.

vega, the rising volatility resulting from an inability of determining an actual market price for the wet barrel-paper barrel spread, has rendered this traditional approach untenable. Demand can be calculated, but the ability to price supply to meet it is becoming more a function of trading paper barrels as a new asset class than it is applying any conventional formula to determine price.

Now this "market determines supply" approach has several short-comings in the current environment of more rapid change in oil trading and contract structure. For one thing, it presupposes sufficient lead time. Aside from putting on line the few million barrels of excess daily capacity currently available (largely Saudi, with the remainder exclusively OPEC-based),[15] meeting any additional demand requires field development. Lead time needed for operations to begin at a brown field having any significant volume could average two years; a new green field may easily extend to seven or more years.[16]

Second, development expenses have skyrocketed. Whereas a spike above $100 a barrel would have generated considerable influx in 2007, it is sustainably high prices that are required today. Given that the new fields being discovered are considerably more expensive to develop, are located in less accessible or unstable locations, encompass inferior oil (with high sulfur or other impediments or heavier in weight or more viscous), and/or introduce significant geological and reservoir complexities, the nominal price of crude oil by itself is no longer the sole deciding factor.

Once OPEC emerged as a force of consequence in determining global oil prices, the continued use of long-term contracts could no longer insulate the VIOCs from market volatility, itself often more a result of OPEC member actions than actual market manifestations. Reducing their position in upstream operations, and thereby in the actual production of crude, made the international majors more dependent upon what the real producers were charging.[17] The immediate solution to this was the rise of the futures contracts market.

The Changing Nature of VIOCs

However, while allowing refinery arms of VIOCs to purchase crude wherever in the world a move would improve their bottom lines,[18] the futures market also introduced a number of other participants into the bidding process. The contracts emerging did address the main concerns majors had about the pricing process (a process they had once dictated by their dominant control over posted field prices, but had since relinquished to the rise of OPEC and other primary crude producers) and served, at least initially, to remove concerns about securing adequate supply. They also moved more of the control over the contracting future allotments to parties more interested in the return on the investment, rather than the delivery of oil consignments.[19] The attempt by VIOCs to stabilize positioning and returns resulted in their advancing new structures for their activities and new rounds of volatility emerged as a result.[20]

That introduced the need for majors to emphasize specialization. Of course, the specialization emerging did not result in VIOCs ending their positioning of operations throughout the upstream-downstream flow. It did mean, however, that each company would accentuate those aspects in which it had a competitive edge. The same driving force would unleash several periods of mergers and acquisitions (M&A). In fact, the move toward establishing competitive advantage provides for the environment in which mergers become a major tool.[21]

Mergers have reduced the number of larger players in the global market. The M&A market has also served as the primary tool for companies to augment reserves, and thereby improve the attractiveness of equity shares, without actually finding any new sources of supply.

By absorbing other companies, a surviving VIOC also acquires the target company's booked reserves. Those now are part of the VIOC's reserves and, while enhancing the attractiveness of the major's stock attractiveness to potential investors and contributing to a more robust market cap, the acquisition has contributed nothing to improving the supply side of the global supply-demand equation.

It is for this reason that the nature of acquisition is cyclical: It tends to be the preferable approach by majors in periods of sluggish market prices for oil. According to the dominant approach to market cycles practiced by the majors, lower oil prices depress the value of smaller companies below the level at which they can continue normal operations, compress their access to credit (even in normal, i.e., noncrisis environments), and correspondingly lower the real purchase price of reserves.

Given that the actual market value of the reserves emerges only when the crude is lifted, retaining the oil in the ground maximizes the return potential for the major. Unlike a smaller company, whose leverage becomes limited during times of lower prices, a VIOC can withhold the crude from the market longer. It also has the distinct advantage of acquiring a known quantity of established oil, in the process paying for only a portion of the overall expenses incurred in exploration and development. The principle has been understood for some time.[22]

However, it may actually accentuate the problem of oil vega. The approach continues to regard the focus as one of supply, but only addresses market price by applying the conventional supply-demand dynamic. Of course it does so solely from the supply side, relying upon the traditional notion that pricing is dependent upon the availability of product, with demand a factor largely determined by the resulting market price.

The advantage to the acquiring company is usually measured by an addition to its reserves-to-production (R/P) ratio—a measurement of proven reserves to annual production, measured in years. The figure ends up for majors somewhere between 20 and 40, although it is lower, 10 to 15 on average, in more mature production markets such as the United States. While it has been a standard yardstick for some time, there has been a debate over whether it actually tells us anything.[23]

In addition, growing larger may also have some pronounced disadvantages. Expenses associated with ongoing coordination increase, as does the cost accompanying a decline in overall efficiency. Despite the absorption of additional booked reserves (usually regarded as a good thing in enhancing equity share value), the acquisition cycle may also generate a number of downside considerations—duplication of facilities, increasing management costs, overstaffing, new field technical challenges, logistical and planning problems, and a host of others—all of which negatively affect the bottom line (and, thereby, detract from the market attractiveness of company shares). What is viewed as a positive acquisition of reserves, therefore, may not end up being a positive in practice,[24] producing in the more serious examples a pressure in the opposite direction—beyond vertical diversification or deintegration toward divestiture.[25]

One of the recurring problems emerging from the acquisition of assets is the continuing need for specific investments. In fact, this is an ongoing concern resulting from vertical integration. While assets can be acquired individually, a VIOC must incorporate them into a vertically run enterprise. That usually requires additional expenditures beyond those necessary to run the absorbed individual unit. In the case of downstream additions, this becomes a more serious consideration, given: (1) the competitive advantage of a refinery being regional in nature, not company-wide, and (2) the attempt to increase the market share for oil products obliging infrastructure improvements. On occasion, such integration requirements can dramatically increase the actual cost of an acquisition.[26]

One thing is quite clear. An acquisition strategy cannot address the essential problem in oil vega, accentuated by the rise in volatility. Relying upon supply as leverage in maintaining market prices actually anticipates that a company retaining reserves would release them when the price increases, thereby placing as the main focus one of maintaining supply equilibrium. However, as price volatility intensifies, VIOCs will restrain refinery capacity utilization and retain in-place reserves, at least until the prospect of spot shortages and expanded regional price differentiations move to require additional product. The balance advanced is one that addresses the bottom line of the companies more than the actual requirements of the market.

The process whereby majors acquire smaller companies does not, in itself, say anything about providing additional supply to the market or addressing shortages. What it does do, on the other hand, is place an emphasis on book reserves when the main market problem lies elsewhere. It is no longer true to say that either the supply or the demand side will dominate market considerations moving forward. That position is reserved for volatility.

Nonetheless, the current situation is introducing an intriguing departure from the conventional approach to company size and positioning. At the same time that we are continuing to witness periods of acquisition followed by periods of consolidation, rising opportunities highlighting focused field developments in many parts of the world have actually increased the desirability of emphasizing small (or at least medium-sized) operators. This move to smaller companies possessing a size advantage when it comes to developing smaller fields is upon occasion likewise reflected in investor preferences for equity shares of such companies over larger, multifaceted players.[27]

The fastest growing upstream sector involves development of fields considered too low in extractable volume to justify the attention of a major. One of the results of big companies getting bigger—at least ostensibly the reason for M&A activity—is a concomitant narrowing of the types of fields these companies can work profitably. More fields are falling below the threshold at which the major can realistically develop them. Often called *materiality, financial volume*, or *critical mass*, the approach holds that projects need to be above a certain size (from the standpoint of after-tax net present value) for an IOC or VIOC to have an interest. Simply guaranteeing a high internal rate of return on a project investment is not sufficient.

Upon occasion, this has been advanced by the very nature of an IOC or NOC. An IOC needs to generate returns on projects sufficient to support a wide range of activities. Such effective structural and organizational overhead requires large fields with greater extraction potential. While state companies can often offset such costs with state subsidies, they are also subject to serving as implementing agents for public policy. Given the need to retain the largest, or most strategic fields, for national control, NOCs are dictated by government policy to direct attention toward those largest fields, a direction mirrored by other domestic and foreign majors in those markets.[28] As a result of both government policy and the economies necessitated by the size of the operating company, a widening number of medium- to lower-sized fields become available to smaller companies.[29]

The objectives placed upon majors by the dictates of either organizational considerations or government policy are providing greater incentive for medium- and smaller-sized companies to specialize in developing fields with resources that come in below the level at which VIOCs or NOCs can operate effectively. This development is clear in a number of producing countries: Russia (below the 70-million-ton strategic level mandated by current statute, for which a Russian company must be the majority owner, or on the continental shelf, required to be operated by only Russian state-owned NOCs), Kazakhstan, and Peru, to provide three of the clearer examples. This is a rapidly growing sector of the industry. The bulk of production will remain with "Big Oil," but the greatest return on investment is increasingly found elsewhere. This is not simply a consideration of size, but more of fitting a company to a project.[30]

These developments challenge the conventional wisdom that the bigger the company, the greater the profits. That is still the case if one only considers aggregate profit levels, such as those provided by

ExxonMobil or Royal Dutch/Shell. However, the biggest companies are not realizing the greatest return on investment when compared to a number of smaller, focused, companies.[31] In these cases, leaner is better.

The profitability of such focused companies is also increasing. For the 12-month period ending July 1, 2010, 37 traded companies in this category posted returns on investment between 90 and 567 percent. Meanwhile, ExxonMobil reported a 17 percent decline for the same period, while Shell had an anemic gain of slightly more than 2 percent.

Obviously, a number of wildcatters—those independents drilling wells in unproven territory, usually having limited capital backing and involved in high-risk drilling—are always on the verge of going under. Nonetheless, the success of drillers having limited objectives in carefully designated fields has reached the point where there now exists a reasonably liquid exchange traded fund (ETF), the Wildcatters E&P ETF (WCAT), to index their activities.[32]

The observation that the dominant companies are compelled to pursue development of the largest fields is unsettling, given the rising need experienced by the market to obtain the bulk of available volume from fields of all sizes. Aside from deepwater drilling and the possibility that Arctic offshore drilling may yield promise, the likelihood is low that there are significantly large fields still awaiting discovery. The consensus is growing that the remaining deposits in excess of one billion barrels of extractable crude are primarily deepwater.[33] Unfortunately, the Gulf of Mexico Macondo-1 blowout on April 20, 2010 (otherwise known as the Deepwater Horizon disaster), has added new concerns over drilling in depths of more than 1,000 feet.[34] That well was over 5,000 feet deep.

Another Look at Supply and Reserve Estimates

Combined with renewed efforts to extend a deepwater drilling moratorium or severely restricting activities, these concerns are prompting recalculations of the available supply in the U.S. market. A recent report concluded that expectations put *all* net growth in American oil supply as coming from deepwater drilling through at least 2015, with that total accounting for over 4 percent of worldwide production.[35]

Overall, however, the impact may be more pronounced. Deutsche Bank has estimated that during the period of 1995 to 2010 deepwater drilling resulted in the addition of about 60 billion barrels of P2 reserves (those for which there is about a 50 percent chance of extraction at a cost consistent with market conditions). In addition, the bank's analysis concludes that deepwater drilling will account for some 10 percent of 2008 to 2015 global production and will be central to any ability to meet expected increases in world demand.[36]

In any event, the ability to predict actual production from reserve figures has become very problematic. Quite simply, availability of reserves does not seem to bear any direct relationship to the volume actually lifted.[37] Actual ratios of oil reserves to production vary greatly from region to region and from company to company. This results in renewed debate over the ability of the sector to provide adequate supply once precrisis demand returns to the market.

And concerns are intensifying. Several recent studies have concluded that overoptimistic reserve figures, and the inclination to regard available production levels as automatically following from them, are going to result in shortfalls.[38] Of course, I need once again to note that so long as aggregate demand levels remain unusually low, the full market impact of this problem remains delayed. However, indications are building that those levels are beginning to rise. The artificially depressed demand levels are a factor of the global financial crisis and that cycle is slowly drawing to a close.

This reserves-production observation introduces one of the most significant, and disquieting, of recent developments. The dominant producers are drawing out more extractable crude than they are replacing.[39] What type of reserves we are actually addressing is particularly important in this regard. As it happens, this single factor renders most reserve replacement figures offered by companies almost meaningless. Placing reserves on the company books is largely an exercise meant to improve the pricing of equity shares. As already observed, there is little direct correlation between those reserves and actual production rates. For example, with NYMEX crude oil prices approaching $150 a barrel in July of 2008, there remained over 300,000 orphan wells in West Texas containing millions of barrels in known reserves sitting idle. Even at the high price, it was still too expensive to lift the crude.

I regard extractable crude as referring to that volume whose production is justified for both technical and economic reasons. Merely labeling a category of reserves as having a certain percentage of production potential (50 percent, for example, or 30 percent) says nothing about whether the market and/or field conditions justify that production. This remains one of the major shortcomings of current replacement reserve usage. Much of what is contained in a company's annual report encompasses "discovered reserves" that will only become extractable under unusually high market prices and supply constraint conditions.

The decline in available volume at commercially acceptable rates is moving the market from one led by demand to one that is supply-constrained. This deserves some additional explanation. Most demand-driven approaches assume that supply will be provided to meet demand as it develops, but not beforehand. Such an approach, therefore, does not view stockpiling product as an efficient way to regulate trade. Given that the calculation of oil demand results from actual usage, rather than a demand curve,[40] a stable market would provide the supply as needed. If demand increases, there would be more production of raw material and refining of finished product. If demand declines, less supply of crude and oil product would result. Both analysts and practitioners regard a demand-driven market as preferable[41]—lowering both inventory costs (which can be significant in the case of oil and oil products) and expenses associated with the wholesale/retail network, as well as improving the optimum usage of field and wellhead equipment and technology.

There is considerable information emerging that the preferred demand-driven model will not remain viable when it comes to oil. Moving new oil volume onto the market takes time. The demand-driven model cannot restrain prices in the case of the market facing a rapid return (or net increase) in usage. Ultimately, where supply is not a concern (though the time frame of bringing it to market may be), demand will still determine matters, despite some rather excessive swings in the range of the market pricing realized. These are essentially the moves witnessed in the market over the past three decades. Even allowing for the occasional price hike resulting from a geopolitical flap, hurricane, refinery fire, pipeline leak, or similar short-term event, traders (and for that matter market participants as a whole) would regard the demand-driven approach as governing market exchanges. Prices would often be set higher than the actual wet barrel trade would justify, owing to the penchant for the paper barrel trading market to accelerate more quickly, but the availability of crude and product would not be the issue.

Some analysts have suggested that the speculative nature of futures contract trading itself is the primary reason market prices increase more than the actual value of the underlying commodity would justify. Daniel O'Sullivan has called this phenomenon *petromania*.[42] Regarding speculators as the culprits responsible for the price spike in the first half of 2008 has been a main staple in some approaches to oil prices, especially those seeking a simplistic solution to use politically in an ongoing tug-of-war with Wall Street. As Chapter 3 notes, however, the speculation itself is a by-product of the fundamental way in which trading takes place. Recall that speculators are usually very useful in injecting liquidity into a market and thereby providing a means to translate paper into wet barrel asset holdings.[43] I return to this matter in Chapters 6 and 7.

However, the prevailing view would still expect physical supply to meet demand. Ultimately, according to this approach, prices would reach a level at which demand would taper off,[44] resulting in a continuing cycle of price increases and declines.

That allows the observer to regard the oil market in much the same way as she would any other sector. Unfortunately, that is developing into a less-accurate perspective moving forward. Normally, the cost of the next available barrel of crude oil would determine contract pricing. However, in a supply-constrained view, that would translate into the *most expensive* next available barrel. Some of this follows from the market psychology in setting futures contract and option prices. Yet, this also arises from an increasingly expressed opinion that supply constriction is actually emerging.[45]

While the structure of oil company practice is well-suited to deal with either the demand-driven or supply-constrained model (although the demand-driven usually results in a greater efficiency and therefore a more positive bottom-line impact), it is not as effective in dealing with the emerging environment emerging—one in which volatility drives the operations, which is not the traditional movement of supply and demand. If the assumption is that a supply-constrained environment

is developing, companies would normally gear up for increasing production. If, on the other hand, that production requires repositioning
of trade in anticipation of oil vega, the current structure of vertical
integration among the largest companies accentuates the instability.

As observed above, vertical integration emphasizes the downstream segment from refinery to retail distribution. This is where the primary profit
rests; it further allows the VIOC to utilize volume from various sourcing,
both inside and outside its own corporate structure. That should provide
for a further leveraging of crude quality and production regions. Yet, the
resulting structure has not proven as convincing in the current situation.

This is because the essential underpinning of the vertical integration
defense has become a matter of dispute. There is evidence to conclude
that the advantage arising from integration has declined. It may have
been of benefit during a particular period in the oil market on efficiency
grounds but that no longer seems the case. One reason results from the
concentration of global production in fewer hands. OPEC may control
about 40 percent of worldwide volume, but the current structure of the
market disposes non-OPEC major producers (such as Russia, Canada,
Norway, and, until recently, Mexico[46]) to parallel OPEC moves.[47] This
is even relevant to unconventional production.[48]

The main factors that had prompted vertical integration are not the
same as those driving the current cycles of M&A. The latter is driven
by a move to increase proven reserves by acquiring other companies'
book reserves rather than locating new ones via exploration. Even the
last wave of mega mergers that profoundly changed the landscape of
the oil sector and produced the likes of ExxonMobil, ConocoPhillips,
ChevronTexaco (now known once again simply as Chevron), along
with the BP absorption of Amoco and Arco, is primarily a move to
concentrate control over the downstream sector.[49]

The historical argument posits that vertical integration was of benefit during the 1960s and 1970s for a number of reasons, led by reduction of transaction costs,[50] but the increasing complexity and expense
of downstream assets have resulted in a less cost-effective environment
in upstream holdings.[51] Data show that by 1979 to 1980, negative correlations had emerged between vertical integration and profitability.[52]

The driving force had become the refinery to distribution segment,
offsetting the earlier advantage of possessing large and internationally

dispersed field projects. The rationale for field access developed into having "swing" volume to use in attending variations of market need. Simply put, while the VIOC could acquire volume from any source, and had introduced deintegration as a way to accomplish that,[53] there remains a value within the overall corporate structure to have one's own sources to use in balancing internal refinery demand, for use in buttressing booked reserve figures (and thereby equity share value), while providing some bottom-line advantages from transfer pricing.

Transfer pricing comprises the cost to one unit of a corporation for goods or services provided by another unit. This is distinguished from a transaction between otherwise unrelated or unaffiliated companies—usually called an arm's-length transaction. An internal transfer pricing calculation is necessary to determine the profit/loss of each unit for accounting and tax purposes. However, and this is the point for our purposes, transfer pricing is less expensive than the market price that an arm's-length transaction would command.

A VIOC, therefore, stands to maximize return on processed oil products by effectively receiving crude oil from its own upstream projects at discount. Similarly, the provision of such other components as field services, oil trading, distribution, power, and chemicals would also benefit a VIOC's bottom lines through transfer pricing. In each of these transactions, the VIOC can structure the exchange to maximize profit for the corporation or project as a whole.[54] The practice has generated increasing opposition in producing countries, where it is regarded as a primary tool for multinational corporations avoiding local taxes.[55]

Swing volume, however, will not prove very beneficial in addressing a situation of rising volatility. Coming out of the worst international financial situation since the Great Depression, all eyes have been fixed on the demand levels. Each further indication of market sluggishness or sign of slow recovery is met with a projection of what that may mean for an overall level of oil demand. The pervasive assumption continues to be that the traditional way of looking at the market—one calling upon producers to provide the level of supply dictated by the level of demand—still governs both what we see and how we react.

Despite the arrival of oil vega, the oil market will still operate on the principle of supply meeting demand. Markets cannot be structured in any other way. The problem results from the ascendance of paper over wet barrels in determining the price. In effect, the strike price (at which the option for the futures contract is exercised) progressively determines the market (or spot) price.[56]

Unfortunately, we end up being unable to determine an actual price upon which the two factors can converge. In such an environment, the one into which I am suggesting we are moving and fast, oversupply—the most likely response by producers in the face of rising prices—will ultimately collapse the real market price of the commodity. As with most bubbles, however, that point will not be known until it is reached. Like the operation of some market-wide Ponzi scheme, oil vega will force the direction of pricing changes. That change will usually push prices up, although it will also have a similar effect coercing them down once the then current bubble bursts.

The move to maximize profits from the downstream segment of company activity has made it less likely that VIOCs can effectively serve as market definers in an age of oil vega. As I have observed above, the division between NOCs progressively controlling the bulk of the production while multinational VIOCs move downstream to emphasize bottom-line profitability will make it less likely that the companies can regulate a volatile market. For the past several years OPEC members, along with other major crude producers on one hand and crude-acquiring-dependent IOCs on the other, have bemoaned their lack of market control. In truth, neither any longer dictates market behavior. Oil vega is not a supply-demand manifestation. As such, the aspects against which companies are currently structured have little genuine impact on the rising volatility.

Put succinctly, supply and demand considerations are less driving the oil vega than they are created by it. Of course, the actual supply of crude oil and the demand exhibited for it still exist. Yet, aside from the myopic view of some analysts during brief periods of demand reduction or supply interruptions, the volatility does not come from the interaction between the traditional market measures. This is because the direction of that dynamic is no longer in doubt.

Once it becomes apparent that, aside from the occasional exogenously-induced movement in the market (e.g., credit constriction, geopolitical crisis, financial meltdown, rise in unemployment, or natural disaster) resulting in demand destruction, the conventional assumption that sufficient supply will rise up to meet demand is no longer tenable. For the past several years, apologists for the conventional way of viewing the supply-demand relationship have almost without fail considered such outside events as axiomatically a natural consequence of the oil market itself. This has morphed into a hydrocarbon regard reminiscent of the pattern recognition applications of fractal theory to epidemics, earthquakes, weather patterns, human life, and even Jackson Pollock paintings.[57] External pressures somehow become integrated elements within the overall "natural cycle" of oil . . . in a fractal sort of way![58]

Now I must admit a certain amount of personal fascination with the permutations, especially as they apply to market matters in general and oil in particular. Yet here is the nub of the matter. Their presence, even those elements exhibiting a fundamental character, does not really allow us to say anything timely about the underlying activities. In short, they cannot provide a tool for predicting where the pricing of oil or the market dynamics surrounding it would be going.

The reason fractals were introduced into this discussion in the first place is that, despite the recurrence of mathematical patterns that may well illustrate causality (hardly a surprise), exogenous causes are not part of the oil market itself. This is the case regardless of the facile attempts to make them so by the commentator or the pundit in the now-familiar exercise of "explaining" in detached, almost-certain language why crude oil does or does not do something in apparent disregard for the normal rules of the market. What cannot be adequately explained or correctly predicted is accorded a natural presence not justified, meant to reflect operations upon an underlying commodity by factors from outside the market system. The approach has also permeated analysis of market trade in what is often described as an application of chaos theory, or a chaos-fractal hybrid, to investment behavior.[59]

What cannot be adequately predicted or controlled is reified, or at least defined into submission. That does not make it natural and it does not make it endemic to the market. Oil is a natural product. Our use of it is not. Neither is the futures trading in it, the options obliged by that trade, or the oil vega resulting from it. There is simply nothing "natural" about this—either in the sense of utility or from the standpoint of what is indispensable to the commodity itself.

The inescapable conclusion is that the market cannot expect outside factors to temper oil demand forever. Exogenous factors are hardly permanent. We are already experiencing a rising recovery on the demand side, one that is fueled by a much greater expansion in developing markets than in developed ones.[60] That is triggering a price expansion as supply concerns emerge and regions such as Asia continue to pay a "premium" to secure adequate imports.[61] Even in the U.S. and European markets—despite recurring sluggishness in an economic recovery, persistently high unemployment, and sporadic industrial capital expenditure commitments all tempering the rise in demand—average spot crude pricing has increased some 260 percent in the United States[62] and over 228 percent in London[63] since lows registered at the end of 2008, as indicated by Figure 5.3.

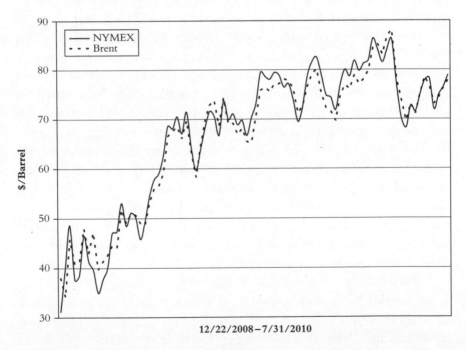

Figure 5.3   NYMEX and Brent Spot Prices

SOURCE: Energy Information Administration (EIA),at http://tonto.eia.doe.gov/dnav/pet/hist/ LeafHandler.ashx?n=PET&s=RWTC&f=D and http://tonto.eia.doe.gov/dnav/pet/hist/LeafHandler .ashx?n=PET&s=RBRTE&f=D.

The supply–demand difficulties emerging merely accentuate the oil vega problem, as we have already observed. Volatility feeds on perceptions of inadequate supply or mushrooming demand. And here the structure of major companies hardly helps. Rather than addressing the volatility, VIOCs and IOCs are now designed to make the largest profit possible from the instability. It is little wonder, therefore, that most of the majors have found an increasing percentage of their bottom line coming from oil trading—that component of the market where volatility provides the greatest opportunity to maximize returns. Until the Deepwater Horizon disaster in the Gulf of Mexico dramatically changed perspective at BP, the company was the leader in taking bold chances to capture returns from the trading markets,[64] a move duplicated by all of its competitors.[65]

VIOC Trading, Refinery Margins, and Profits

All of the majors have upgraded their trading arms, as volatility requires that they lock in as high a spread for crude and oil product prices as possible. The move is reflected in the percentage of reported profits that come from VIOC trading divisions. A contango market is one in which daily prices for crude oil futures rise in each subsequent month moving forward along the futures curve (also called the futures "strip," when referring to the actual contracts entered into by traders), which intensifies trading activity by oil majors. When the curve reverses, a quarterly report can tell you a great deal about how much a company had relied on trading to buttress profits.[66] Overall, anecdotal evidence suggests that oil majors may gain from 8 to more than 15 percent of overall profits from trading.[67] The trend is increasing with companies not previously involved in significant trading operations moving in that direction.[68]

The increasing reliance on trading futures contracts in crude oil consignments gives rise to active trading in the contracts for various refined oil products from the crude. Of particular interest here is the rapidly rising usage of a special trading instrument, one certainly to expand even further with the intensification of oil vega. A greater profit margin in instable markets will come from an ability to play crack spreads—the differentials between the prices of crude oil and various processed oil products.[69] If trading in general has intensified as an element of VIOC bottom lines, the application of futures interest to crack spreads has increased even faster.

Crack spreads provide VIOCs considerable leverage by affording a very useful hedge against unexpected or adverse market pricing movements. All refiners, both integrated and independent processing facilities, are vulnerable to unexpected market swings. With any refinery that must purchase some or all of its crude flow on the open market, and that applies to virtually all including those controlled by VIOCs, a rapid rise in the price of that crude constitutes a very significant economic risk. That risk could effectively (and quickly) run the plant into the red. Given that each refinery has a targeted optimal production mix,[70] it can apply a hedge against market pricing by buying futures of crude oil supply and selling futures contracts for its refined products according to the overall cuts (or component portions) of its anticipated production mix.

For this, refiners will hedge against price exposure by using a *crack ratio*. While this ratio is often the result of a more complicated mathematical exercise, we can for our purposes simplify it in the following shorthand way (which actually reflects how refinery managers summarize the result of their calculations). Assuming the usual crack spread between crude oil on the one hand and gasoline and heating oil on the other, the crack ratio can be expressed as C:G:H. C here refers to the barrels of crude oil, G the barrels of gasoline, and H the barrels of heating oil. This ratio is subject to the limitation that $C = G + H$. The refinery would then hedge by buying C barrels of crude oil and selling G barrels of gasoline and H barrels of heating oil in the futures contract market. The crack spread C:G:H would therefore correspond to the spread obtained by trading oil, gasoline, and heating oil according to this ratio. Widely used crack spreads reflect a 3:2:1, 5:3:2 and 2:1:1 ratio breakdown. Given that the 3:2:1 crack spread is the most utilized, widely quoted crack spread benchmarks are the "Gulf Coast 3:2:1" and the "Chicago 3:2:1," reflecting the ratio and point of delivery.[71]

Broader access to trading contracts is made available by the commodity markets. Tailored products have emerged to facilitate the trading of crack spreads. NYMEX provides what amounts to virtual crack spread futures contracts by treating a basket of underlying NYMEX futures contracts corresponding to a crack spread as a single transaction, with OTC (over-the-counter) transactions providing a range of more creative alternatives.

Treating crack spread futures baskets as a single transaction has the advantage of reducing the margin requirements for a crack spread futures position. And, of course, if there is a futures contract market in anything, there is also an options market in the same instruments.[72]

Traders anticipating an expansion in refinery profits (i.e., increasing crack spreads) will usually sell crude oil futures and simultaneously purchase heating oil and gasoline contracts. This is what is meant by *buying the crack* (less often called *buying into the crack*). If the assumption is correct, the trade will always be profitable. This is because crude oil costs lag behind increases in the prices of refined products. On the contrary, shrinking refiner margins (in the case of an expected rise of crude oil prices) can be traded profitably by *selling the crack*. That involves the opposite trading move—going long (buying) crude oil while going short (selling) gasoline and heating oil contracts.

The primary reason the 3:2:1 crack spread is preferred is the simple fact that it "double weights" gasoline, thereby outperforming a 2:1:1 spread when gasoline prices rise more than heating oil. Of course, if the opposite pressure is occurring, a declining demand for gasoline could push the 3:2:1 spread into trading at a discount. For much of the United States, this obliges that the trader also take into account seasonal adjustments in the demand for gasoline and heating oil. For that reason, 2:1:1 crack spreads are more evident from October through February.[73]

Notice, however, the entire market system for trading crack spreads remains based upon refineries being able to deliver distilled products and position those products against consignments of crude oil. Otherwise, the futures contracts actually traded would not be possible. Paper barrels may be driving the market pricing but it is still the availability of the wet barrels that makes the futures trading possible.

Nonetheless, refinery utilization rates ought to provide us with a standard rule of thumb in estimating aggregate performance reflecting both supply and demand. Unfortunately, the approach seems to reveal more about the manipulation of refinery capacity as a primary method for maximizing profit. The monthly aggregate U.S. refinery operable utilization rate[74] had not been above 90 percent since August 2007 and averaged only 84.5 percent for the entire period between January 2007 and May 2010. Of particular note is an average monthly rate of only 83.7 percent for the thirteen months between July 2007 and July 2008—the period resulting in a per barrel high of $147.27.[75] Only in July 2010 did the capacity rate exceed 90 percent for five out of the six weeks between July 9 and August 13.

These figures are accentuated by the rising concentration in fewer refineries[76] of an otherwise increasing crude oil input[77] and rising operable refining capacity.[78] The concentration implies a greater control over the distribution of retail commodities by fewer providers, especially in the U.S. market.[79] There is considerable anecdotal evidence that this is occurring. In stable market environments, the rationale for managing refining capacity is to maximize efficient usage. During times of price volatility, the practice is largely to maximize profit. It happens with overall prices moving in either direction. Much of the criticism lodged against speculators in the push up of crude oil prices culminating in July 2008 would have been better directed against VIOCs combining refinery capacity manipulation and their own trading desks to maximize the bottom line.[80]

The definitive differentials during periods of either rising or falling gasoline prices are only partly determined by the price of crude oil. It is true that crude oil pricing remains the single largest component in the ultimate price of refined retail product. However, the primary profit derives from the refinery margin.[81] Now that margin can be influenced by a number of factors, but, if a refinery experiences a loss, its primary solution is to cut the run, that is, to reduce the operable refinery capacity. That will almost always result in the eventual[82] rise in retail product prices (even more so for those distillates provided insufficient refinery capacity to begin with—diesel, for example) by a greater percentage than the aggregate rise in crude costs.

That spread turns out to be quite significant. My detailed analysis of the relationship between what I refer to as the *cost adjusted refinery margin* (CARM) and the *actual refinery margin* (ARM),[83] the difference between traditional company operations and recent approaches introduced to maximize refinery margin from the control of retail products, results in substantial additions to profit.

Companies do not provide their actual refinery margins, since the figures are considered proprietary. Therefore, I developed an alternative methodology to approximate actual refining costs (from which the ARM calculations were determined), applied known wholesale and distribution costs and related them to retail pricing. The requirement here was to equate actual retail proceeds for the five companies analyzed and compare them to a realistic estimate of costs.

Three regionally distinct and substantial refineries were studied for each of the five companies, with each facility weighted to reflect its actual contribution to the company's available oil product runs.[84] The weighting simply reflects the estimated average daily portion of total crude volume reflected by each refinery. Costs were compiled from refinery intake reports and verified by sources at the processing plants, managing tanker hauling and/or pipeline volume, and compared to figures provided by the company in quarterly filings.

On the retail side, 50 service stations, representing a national and market distribution, were utilized for each company. Those stations are listed in Table 5.4. Retail pricing was collected for each station from the *Oil Price Information Service* (OPIS)[85] for each of the 418 daily "snapshot" readings utilized in the study over an eight-year period.[86] The summary figure for each set of retail locations for each of the five companies was entered into the data survey. The wholesale price was obtained via the same data bank, since the OPIS figures also provide the DTW ("dealer tank wagon"—wholesale gasoline on a delivered basis to a retail location) and rack (wholesale gasoline sold at a terminal) prices for the same locations.

Additional components of the methodology included 42 gallons per barrel on average for CARM figures (the traditional base), while employing 47.5 gallons per barrel for the ARM figures. This provides for a determination of the net additional volume from the "crack yield" utilized by several state regulatory agencies, for example, the California Energy Commission, to determine a more accurate processing result. This figure utilizes an average 13 percent volume increase resulting from the cracking process[87] (with results extending to 118 percent aggregate volume for certain processes). A 42-gallon barrel of crude at intake when "cracked" resulting in the 13 percent average volume increase would yield 47.46 gallons. Also, a flat average of 12 percent

Table 5.4 Stations Surveyed by OPIS: ID Number and Location

EXXON		SHELL		BP		CITGO		MARATHON	
ID	Location	ID	Location	ID	Location	ID	Location	ID	Location
1297	New York, NY	1171	Farmingdale, ME	1261	Randolph, NJ	1186	St. Albans, VT	2007	Shelby, NC
1908	Chapel Hill, NC	1514	Troy, PA	2766	Naples, FL	1208	New Haven, CT	3209	Columbus, OH
2068	Leland, NC	1920	Henderson, NC	3455	Madison, IN	2061	Rockingham, NC	3757	Cottage Grove, MN
2191	Charleston, SC	2474	Valdosta, GA	4252	Crossville, TN	2594	Sanford, FL	6376	South Bend, IN
2388	Atlanta, GA	2710	Lake Worth, FL	4272	Backus, MN	3956	Hillside, IL	6755	East Lake, OH
2807	Port Saint Lucie, FL	2843	Birmingham, AL	5509	Milwaukee, WI	4113	High Ridge, MO	8680	Clover, SC
2940	Murfreesboro, TN	3463	Jasper, IN	5829	North Augusta, SC	4763	Houston, TX	13901	Utica, MI
4416	Bossier City, LA	4329	North Platte, NE	6031	Magnolia, MS	7489	Commerce, GA	14647	Orlando, FL
4470	Wolverine, MI	4811	Porter, TX	6068	Lees Summit, MO	13359	Michigan City, IN	14786	Lima, OH
7044	Saugerties, NY	5627	Clearlake, CA	6177	Southgate, MI	13536	Olean, NY	15322	Indianapolis, IN
8142	Portland, ME	5709	Roseburg, OR	6461	Kansas City, KS	14064	Elizabeth, NJ	16777	High Point, NC
11173	Chandler, AZ	6161	Sumner, WA	6572	Independence, KY	14169	Southfield, MI	20121	Greeneville, TN
14561	Minneapolis, MN	6195	Chattanooga, TN	6782	Philadelphia, PA	14253	Indianapolis, IN	20837	Louisville, KY

15299	Decatur, GA	6343	Southgate, MI	6817	Baltimore, MD	14304	Amityville, NY	21458	Decatur, IL
19244	New Market, VA	6462	Lake Charles, LA	6917	Louisville, KY	15090	Pittsburgh, PA	26936	Stockbridge, GA
20007	Lincoln, NE	6853	Derby, CT	7318	Elmhurst, NY	18968	Chattanooga, TN	40179	New Kensington, PA
21251	Newark, NJ	12538	Rancho Cucamonga, CA	7408	Glen Ellyn, IL	19176	Ladys Island, SC	49769	Minneapolis, MN
23058	Columbus, OH	13526	Brooklyn, NY	7529	Raleigh, NC	19909	Big Stone Gap, VA	107044	Detroit, MI
24114	Weirton, WV	13822	Aberdeen, OH	8060	Hollywood, FL	19950	Memphis, TN	150975	Chicago, IL
26543	Springfield, OR	14136	Chesapeake, VA	9660	Scott Depot, WV	20684	Aurora, IL	234305	Tampa, FL
32365	Bridgeport, CT	14547	Minneapolis, MN	10976	Myrtle Beach, SC	21278	Baltimore, MD	262565	Cleveland, OH
32424	Albany, NY	15042	Hackensack, NJ	12099	St. Louis, MO	24174	Kalamazoo, MI	291981	Milwaukee, WI
37577	Philadelphia, PA	15095	Pittsburgh, PA	13393	Chicago, IL	37140	Deep River, CT	327112	Silver Lake, MN
119687	Baltimore, MD	18467	Nashville, TN	13557	Detroit, MI	42157	Elkins, WV	327120	West Palm Beach, FL
119784	Washington, DC	18663	Red Oak, IA	13828	Atlanta, GA	44575	Philadelphia, PA	337467	Monroe, MI
119837	Newark, DE	39300	Philadelphia, PA	13945	Rocky Point, NY	46436	Mobile, AL	337126	Lexington, KY

(continued)

131

Table 5.4 (Continued)

EXXON ID	Location	SHELL ID	Location	BP ID	Location	CITGO ID	Location	MARATHON ID	Location
127202	Los Angeles, CA	39381	Stone Mountain, GA	14009	Indianapolis, IN	87635	Seattle, WA	337443	Highlands, NC
127203	Beaumont, TX	39467	Melbourne, FL	14014	Richmond, VA	88817	Colombia, SC	337461	Tarpon Springs, FL
132596	Detroit, MI	39663	Covington, LA	14154	Piscataway, NJ	106802	Detroit, MI	338391	Fort Wayne, IN
136619	Perry, MI	39712	Berkeley Springs, WV	14178	Miami, FL	258103	Milwaukee, WI	338675	Grand Rapids, MI
139101	Miami, FL	96990	Baltimore, MD	14990	St. Paul, MN	289137	Bedias, TX	338678	Malvern, OH
139121	Chicago, IL	130575	Los Angeles, CA	14524	Davenport, IA	289679	Laredo, TX	339276	Danville, KY
141365	Escondido, CA	131726	Chicago, IL	14662	Memphis, TN	291003	Cleveland, OH	401956	Morton, IL
263551	Milwaukee, WI	157651	Detroit, MI	14772	Washington, DC	313030	Springfield, MA	402141	West Lafayette, IN
263693	Orange, CT	158718	Tampa, FL	14786	Lima, OH	405254	Bronx, NY	476098	Miami, FL
263986	Tampa, FL	281232	Shrewsbury, MA	15090	Pittsburgh, PA	462646	Dallas, TX	493911	Bradford, OH
290148	San Marcos, TX	288732	San Antonio, TX	15178	Denver, CO	466205	Fort Meyers, FL	493945	Lisbon, OH
310356	San Diego, CA	476091	Miami, FL	15402	Brooklyn, NY	476169	Miami, FL	493987	Manitowoc, WI
402797	Boston, MA	441281	Dallas, TX	170802	Tampa, FL	489986	Washington, DC	494504	Crystal Lake, IL

Number	City
494973	San Francisco, CA
498533	Tyler, TX
505902	Augusta, GA
512437	Niagara Falls, NY
521385	Albany, LA
522699	El Cajon, CA
554059	Dallas, TX
554249	Seattle, WA
608883	St. Louis, MO
614012	Houston, TX
619265	Little Rock, AR
448730	Santa Fe, NM
449421	Cameron, AZ
461016	Cleveland, OH
483841	San Francisco, CA
484905	San Diego, CA
502971	Atlanta, GA
533290	Denver, CO
539846	Washington, DC
544594	St. Louis, MO
570926	Seattle, WA
570966	Houston, TX
271005	Columbus, OH
271008	Cleveland, OH
292661	Shelbyville, KY
440434	Dallas, TX
441300	Norfolk, VA
561771	Los Angeles, CA
570492	San Francisco, CA
610092	Seattle, WA
615688	Arlington, TX
618098	Omaha, NE
619715	Lake Havasu City, AZ
485546	Scott, LA
498329	Atlanta, GA
603558	Houston, TX
617045	St. Louis, MO
619132	Corpus Christi, TX
619180	Chicago, IL
620128	Raleigh, NC
620206	Boston, MA
620551	Fall River, MA
620740	Tampa, FL
620799	Utica, NY
494536	Cincinnati, OH
591252	New Richmond, WI
591283	Olivia, MN
592345	Lucasville, OH
592412	Asheboro, NC
592511	Linton, IN
592495	Warsaw, KY
592684	Franklin, OH
599571	Dayton, OH
600464	Fairfield, OH
602494	Chesterton, IN

against crude oil cost comprises an estimated average of returns realized for company trading in oil and oil product futures.

The complete data for three of the five companies studied—ExxonMobil, Shell, and BP—are shown in Appendices B-G.

As indicated in Table 5.5, for the period between January 1, 2000, and December 31, 2007, the study concluded that ExxonMobil, Shell, BP, CITGO, and Marathon collectively acquired a total of $82.14 billion in excess profits, comprising 18.1 percent of total aggregate company profits. Of great interest was the finding that over $73 billion of the total was gained from 2005 to 2007, with $22.92 billion (or 23.8 percent of all combined profits) represented by 2007 during the run-up of both crude oil and gasoline prices.[88]

There is a different dynamic for the consumer, however, when prices are collapsing. This was markedly so in the fall of 2008. The percentage decline in the pump price was much less dramatic than the corresponding decline in the costs of crude. According to EIA figures, near-month NYMEX WTI contracts declined in price from $141.37 per barrel on July 7, 2008, to $39.91 on December 22. That is a decline of 72 percent in the cost of crude oil. However, during the same period, the average price for all grades of gasoline in the U.S. market declined from $4.17 per gallon to $1.71, a drop of only 59 percent.[89] Company profits improve faster than the rise in crude prices when those prices are going up and retain an improved margin over any retail price benefit to consumers when the price of gasoline is going down.

Traditionally, the availability of supply—procured at adequate operating cost and production rates—sufficient to meet demand would allow such machinations to continue under the general rubric of a free-market economy. The ability of companies to meet market needs while maintaining robust profit margins beneath incremental pricing changes has until recently masked the rising concentration of operable refinery capacity.

That appears to be ending. The rise in overall refining capacity despite the reduced number of processing plants on line has brought about its own problem. With less than half of the refineries that existed in the United States less than 30 years ago still operating,[90] the concentration of production capacity in markedly fewer companies lessens the ability of smaller refiners to temper the market fluctuations or, for

Table 5.5 Excess Profits 2001 to 2007 ($ billions)

Year	EXXON	SHELL	BP	CITGO	MARATHON	Totals	CARM	ARM	Excess Profit	Excess Profit (as % of total profit)
2007	38.80	27.90	22.50	1.70	5.40	96.30	14.16	37.08	22.92	23.8%
2006	39.50	25.40	22.34	1.5	5.23	93.97	11.84	32.23	20.39	21.7%
2005	36.10	24.20	18.96	1.20	3.03	83.49	10.35	27.05	16.70	20.0%
2004	25.30	17.59	17.08	0.63	1.32	61.92	7.24	17.71	10.46	16.9%
2003	21.54	12.50	10.46	0.44	0.52	45.46	5.05	11.91	6.86	15.1%
2002	11.50	10.00	8.40	0.18	0.16	30.24	2.57	5.68	3.11	10.3%
2001	15.30	13.20	11.98	0.32	0.41	41.21	4.62	6.30	1.69	4.1%
Totals	188.04	130.79	111.72	5.96	16.07	452.58	52.95	137.97	82.14	18.1%

SOURCE: Author's calculations.

that matter, the interregional variations in capacity usage or pricing. Despite the mantra that consolidation increases efficiency, the concentration of sourcing and control in the distribution of retail product will serve merely to accentuate the instability endemic in oil vega.

The issue here is not ownership or branding but control over distribution. That ExxonMobil has decided to sell all its service stations in the United States[91] or that majors can point to more lease arrangements, convenience/warehouse store gasoline locations, and stations under "independent" management means little if the resulting retailer is required to sign an exclusive multiyear gasoline and oil product purchase agreement with the same company that used to own the outlet or has a preemptive control over market share. The same holds true for the few independent refiners left. They need access to the distribution infrastructure, given the decline in the role of the jobber (independent wholesalers who would purchase product and then distribute among its clients). There are considerable data emerging that the control over distribution, the current strategy of the VIOCs, has a direct causal relationship to major elements such as pricing, profits, and constriction in competition.[92]

While this may augment the bottom lines of oil majors, as with the developments upstream, it does little to offset the oil vega problem. We are left with the conclusion that the way companies are structured will accomplish little in offsetting the accelerating uncertainty. The companies are structured to return profit from the market, not to clarify the pricing quandary.

Neither are the traditional mechanisms for determining the market supply side balance and dynamics likely to be of much help. Even from a traditional perspective, one that approaches these elements from the standpoint of securing sufficient supply to meet demand, the indicators are troubling. However, they have no effect upon the volatility coming, since the problem is not fundamentally about having sufficient volume to meet market requirements.

This is also not simply a reflection of peak oil.[93] Few energy issues have so enthralled the general audience as the debate over peak oil, whether we have already used more than 50 percent of the extractable oil available. It is hardly as important a matter as the market once thought it was. That results as much as anything else from the now widespread acceptance of the need for society to wean itself from reliance on crude oil. It is also not the same as oil vega—a volatility, not a supply-side, concern. Still, increases in price and pricing instability will prompt a return to this discussion and the corresponding confusion of peak oil with oil vega. Yes, there are connections, and yes, supply/demand remains a concern. But peak oil addresses how much oil can still enter the market. Oil vega refers to the inability to set transparent and stable market prices once it gets there.

Additionally, there are indications that the increasing separation of production from processing will have an unwelcome additional pressure on the emerging volatility. There is also no correlation between accelerated merger and acquisition activity and lessening oil vega. Even if the M&A is successful, it succeeds only in retiring other players from the fields, not in lowering volatility. Neither does increasing the profitability of those remaining. The design and practice of the oil companies bear little connection to lessening volatility. It simply is not their purpose.

Volatility does not measure the direction of pricing—only its dispersion.[94] Additionally, the very nature of volatility runs at cross-purposes with any attempt to provide price stability. Recall that one of the problems in determining the relationship between oil volatility and price arises because, while pricing objectives seek constancy (or at least the projection of a constant rate against which market variations in price can be assessed), volatility of its very nature is not constant.[95]

All oil company financial models have volatility components built into them.[96] The problem is that such components do not actually measure volatility beyond using it in a generic sense to refer to swings in pricing or profitability. Upon occasion, they even compound the situation by confusing generic ideas of volatility with a skewed view of risk.[97] With luck, volatility ends up being an unknown variable canceling out from both sides of an equation and, therefore, not something that needs to be measured against the bottom line. In common practice, price is supposed to be that plotted point at the intersection of supply and demand, an illusory certainty apparently found only in textbooks. Price is not supposed to have a volatility component that rises above the relationship among supply, demand and price.

Oil companies base operations on such assumptions. However, the volatility I have been addressing in this book is not fundamentally such a market-generated fluctuation. Rather, it comes from the uncertain relationship between paper and wet barrels, not simply the availability of wet barrels in a demand-for-commodity market. And that means, with the possible exception of what its trading unit does, that a VIOC is not equipped to mitigate oil vega. The company cannot deal with it by manipulating supply levels. And that is its only real skill. The environment in which the company's bottom line dominates is not the environment from which oil vega is emerging. Both paper and wet barrels serve as assets, both are directed toward making profit, but the lynchpin here is not field production, refinery runs, or retail sales.

It is as if two participants have arrived for an athletic event, but one expected to play baseball and the other was prepared for fencing. They do not share the same idea of what constitutes the contest and are not even able to agree upon common rules to determine who is winning. But this is not a sport we are talking about. Energy is a pervasive, market-wide requirement. Making profit for one (the oil company) represents selling a product somebody else consumes. For the other (the trader), profit accrues from maximizing a spread on the buying and selling of a future concession. Futures may have begun as a way to even out the sale of oil and enhance the overall predictability of consignments. They have ended up creating a new assets class and an environment akin to two ships passing in the night, each bound for a different port with pilots speaking different languages.

The example of a sporting event is apt in another respect. Regardless of the contest, there must be an umpire or referee, somebody who applies and interprets rules, while preventing miscarriages. Sometimes, as with several pivotal moments during the 2010 World Cup matches, the referees come up short. Yet nobody expects them to participate in the contest, change the field of play, or invent a new way of playing the sport.

When the contest is one played out in a competitive market—among producers, traders, processors, and customers—and the contest is over the availability, pricing, and distribution of something as basic as energy, the referees are regulators and the public officials who oversee them. A certain amount of detachment from these folks is anticipated, especially in what passes for free markets. These umpires apply the rules and punish transgressors (usually with something worse than a yellow or red card), but all participants presume they would be objective and interject themselves into the fray only when a redress is warranted.

Unfortunately, this is not the case with a subject as vital as energy and it will become less so as we collide with rising oil vega. Government is already stepping in to change the playing field and has interjected itself as a participant. It no longer occupies a passive position, nor is it a disinterested observer from the sidelines.

Some of this is justified. Oil serves a social-wide need and government has a responsibility as large in scope. Upon occasion, that responsibility obliges intervention. What have changed, however, are the presumption and the urgency taking hold. Rather than being the infrequent occurrence, governments are now involved as a matter of course, fundamentally changing the markets and the outcomes.

As oil vega intensifies, the pressure for governments to intervene will increase as well. As with the problems arising from the very different objectives brought by companies and traders, governments have distinct views and goals. Public officials cannot take the chance that volatility will subside. Given that it will be a recurring difficulty, affording all manner of prospective economic and financial crisis scenarios, there will be more reliance placed upon public sector measures. Political agendas will coexist unevenly with market objectives. By the very nature of its legal position as overseer and protector of the commonwealth, government will find it hard to resist taking center stage as oil vega intensifies.

After all, the power to do so is concentrated in its hands . . . and this makes what comes next both inescapable and dangerous.

Chapter 6

How Government Action Increases Volatility

Kampala, June 2010

    I am in the capital of Uganda at the request of the U.S. Department of State to advise the government, parliament, and civic groups on the Lake Albert deposits. The oil found close by the border with the Democratic Republic of the Congo is going to change this country. Unfortunately, not all of that change will be welcome.

    The situation here is unusual. By finding a considerable amount of crude but deciding not to allow full development for two years, the government has bought itself some time. Unlike other developing economies, where field expansion takes place before the statutory and regulatory frameworks are in place—resulting in significant oversight, financial, environmental, and infrastructure problems—Uganda may be able to avoid the usual shortfalls associated with the rapid introduction of natural resource extraction.

That is, if the government can avoid the significant economic imbalance that will result. Massive injections of export revenue, proceeds as hard currency coming into a less stable currency zone, are certain to create a pronounced dislocation. That dislocation, in turn, is accentuated in economies that have a disproportionately large agricultural base—which is certainly true in Uganda.

In this case, the concern is heightened even more by the objective set out in the "National Oil and Gas Policy for Uganda." The document sets out the major dimensions of how the newfound natural resources will be overseen and developed. It also provides that the primary usage of proceeds will be for the early eradication of poverty.

As objectives go, this is a particularly laudable one. Unfortunately, providing funds to the poor is usually very inflationary for a nation. Assuming that they do the right thing for themselves and their families, they will buy food, clothing, and shelter. That quickly increases the amount of currency in the economy (the value of which has already been increased by the pressure of outside hard currency—the dollars resulting from oil sales) and the velocity of the exchange. That is the classic formula for inflation.

The heating up of the economy will take place in different ways in different sectors, but it will hit agriculture hardest. The very people the policy wants to help most, the rural poor, will be hurt most by an unregulated introduction of massive amounts of currency. The prices of consumer goods and material needed for sowing and harvesting crops will rise faster than the return from selling produce. Even staple existence loses out. While the crops grown are consumed on site, everything else necessary to live must still be purchased on the open (or sometimes black) market. There, prices will continue to rise.

The government, therefore, will have limited options, even in the face of a significant windfall.

In addition, the ability to budget and provide for needed development depends on the global price for crude and the ability of Uganda to provide it. Infrastructure has to be built: pipelines, pumping stations, separators, and treatment facilities, along with a refinery base to service local oil product needs.

In my meetings with Ministry of Energy and Mineral Development officials and standing parliamentary committees, the issue of how to provide sufficient predictability comes up frequently. Everybody recognizes the problem. It will take some time to establish a "wet barrel" benchmark crude rate for the production and then determine swap and pricing arrangements *vis-à-vis* other traded oil.

And that introduces what is a major concern in Kampala, one officials here share with other emerging market producers worldwide. Uganda may be producing the oil but it will be traders sitting in foreign exchanges determining the price through an array of futures contracts, options, and derivatives. That translates into the accelerating oil vega, the market volatility decreasing ability to determine realistic market prices for the "wet" barrels, the actual commodity.

It is this market oil that will be the lifeblood of Uganda. The emerging largess is coming from the ground in product, not from a trading exchange in futures contracts. As a result, a move is intensifying within the government and the legislature to establish an exchange in Kampala to require the trade of contracts inside Uganda. Members of the ministry and the parliament also regard this as a way to regulate the trade and the pricing.

Similar approaches are underway elsewhere. The home country would benefit from certain elements in the trading sequence by having a local exchange, for example, providing for a more efficient coordination of supply on the domestic market, or allowing for forward planning by producers and distributors.

However, officials also have the belief (widely shared in other capitals) that having a local exchange will allow for a regulation of the trades that actually end up pricing the oil. As already witnessed throughout the world, this is hardly the case. The one advantage from the standpoint of a domestic trading floor in an emerging country is the development of a home-based brokerage industry and some consequent taxing and fiduciary advantages.

But it will not determine the price for Ugandan oil in the international market because it will have no effect on oil vega. In fact, the more a home government attempts to regulate stability into the trade, the more that trade will go elsewhere.

Oil vega cannot be countered by unilateral government action. This will be a difficult lesson the government needs to learn in Kampala . . . and in London . . . and in Washington . . . and in . . . .

■ ■ ■

I usually consider my views eclectic, with a dislike for the need to pigeonhole ideas into one school of thought or another. But if obliged to make choices in the matters addressed in this book, I would probably come down on the side of neorealism,[1] with a further nod to the state-centric realism approach of Robert Gulpin,[2] especially when addressing the subject of the present chapter.

That means I regard the exchange among nations as being essentially self-serving in motivation, survivalist in intent, and taking place within a system lacking any centralized power to restrain the actions of individual states (i.e., as neorealism puts it, exhibiting anarchy). Those actions are offset only by the contrary moves of other nations. The individual state remains the central actor. When that action has an international economic impact, the essential motive is to achieve some cross-border advantage for a *domestic* economic or market reason.

This approach is important for present purposes. The primary reactions to oil vega will play out on the political stage and, while projected onto an international oil market, they will be introduced for decidedly internal purposes. With the possible exception of oil being used as a blatant political weapon in international competition, an eventuality often mentioned but having a low probability subsequent to the oil embargoes of 1973–1974,[3] the intent will be to stabilize the domestic pricing, distribution, and cost of oil and processed oil products.

The comments in this chapter will upon occasion consider the impact in other countries, especially those producing crude oil. Yet the primary focus will be on what occurs in the United States as a response to oil vega. The United States remains the largest importer of crude oil in the world, although China is poised to occupy that position shortly. However, regardless of whether it is number one or two, the combination of American consumption and financial centers will guarantee the reaction coming from Washington will have a disproportionate effect on the broader global market. It will be replicated, opposed, and evaded elsewhere. But it cannot be ignored.

Historically, the United States has had a spotty record when it comes to regulating the domestic oil market.[4] After several bouts with overly aggressive government interference—a reaction to World War II, the Cold War, changes in global sourcing, the rise of OPEC, concerns over the domestic economic and productivity base, attempts to protect local producers, and a range of other considerations—Washington decided to drop restrictions on imported crude. Thereupon emerged the straight line to today's reliance on foreign producers for two out of every three barrels used.

Traders will accentuate the volatility, synthetic debt will distort the actual paper-wet barrel relationships, and oil companies will emphasize the traditional supply-side solution for what is not a supply/demand problem, at least in its initial stages. But it will be governments—via legislation, regulations, cross-border and international policies—that will proceed to expand the difficulty and protract the crisis. This is not because public officials are callous, indifferent, misinformed, or stupid. It is because the public sector decision-making process is not set up to handle such matters.

There is no doubt that the decisions of governments will be decisive, especially in a market only now emerging from the financial turmoil that began in earnest in 2008 and still holding sway as I write this in late 2010. As the International Energy Agency (IEA) noted in its *World Energy Outlook 2010* (WEO2010)[5] demand is no longer likely to be tempered by rising prices or supply concerns. Insulation from the tendencies of the past market is developing as the matrix of sourcing and usage changes. Unconventional sourcing (heavy oil, bitumen, shale oil, and especially oil sands) will be increasingly relied upon, while the demand volume curve driver is moving fast to developing and emerging markets. Over the next 25 years, the IEA estimates that 93 percent of the increase in demand will come from non-OECD[6] countries, over half of the increase from China alone.

WEO2010 is only the latest report indicating the central position of governments in addressing the energy problems oncoming in everything from carbon capture and storage through energy transfers to support of new technology. Unfortunately, no amount of public sector involvement will adequately address the real problem in the sector, no matter how extensive or well-intentioned. Governments will be unable to temper the volatility implicit in oil vega.

The government approach to oil vega will prevent any win–win approaches. There will be rhetoric in support of multilateral approaches, perhaps some parallel discussion of application possibilities for Basel III-like accords,[7] and increased emphasis on alternative energy research, but this will be a protracted zero-sum conflict. The November 11–12, 2010, failure of the G20 meetings in Seoul to reach any resolution of currency valuation tensions is a precursor to what will happen when oil vega really digs in. There will be recriminations of a system denominating oil sales in dollars, another round of developing state suspicion about the intentions of the developed world, conspiracy theories lodged against OPEC, American financial institutions, or IOCs—and no move by any nation to relinquish leverage on any of the essential elements.

There are still some government approaches that can be introduced to mitigate the impact and I shall present them in Chapter 7. However, I need to make one thing clear at the outset of this chapter. There is no deliverance from oil vega. There is nothing government effectively can do to prevent it and much of what it will try is unfortunately only likely to make matters worse. The objective, as I briefly discuss in Chapter 7, needs to be an overall approach to contain the damage. Some sandbags can be put down when the water is low. But there will be a flood and there will be damage.

Governmental actions are domestic in nature, issuing from political decision makers exercising sovereign jurisdiction over a specific area. The oil market, however, is a decidedly integrated worldwide network. A decision made in Washington on oil matters for an avowed domestic reason has an impact around the globe. Yet the United States, importing the majority of its crude oil from elsewhere in the world, will be affected by similar decisions made in other capitals on other continents. The domestic government decisions, therefore, which will become more frequent as the oil vega intensifies, will be felt across borders. Proponents of a "Fortress America" approach are whistling the wrong tune. An insulated America will still feel the effects of decisions made elsewhere. For that matter, somehow becoming self-sufficient (a blatant political red herring) would still make the pricing in the United States subject to the decisions and events occurring elsewhere.

And a government will approach the crisis from the view of protecting its domestic economy, industries, currency, and employment. There will be considerable lip service to multilateral remedies and mutually beneficial solutions. But the decisions will be nationalistic and the benefits pursued country-specific. As such, a very cosmopolitan market crisis problem will be approached in a decidedly parochial way.

This chapter indicates how the political dimension will intensify, not remedy, the problem. As with our discussion on the structure of oil companies in Chapter 5, governments are not designed to offset oil volatility. Even if oil vega could be contained through unilateral political remedies, even if the problem were one of only domestic markets, the approach usually available to government will not do the job. The crisis is not one of inadequate supply (at least in the initial stages), or of oil being employed as a global political weapon, and does not occur because OPEC restricts volume or because the futures contract markets are insufficiently regulated. These and other speculations will be offered as scapegoats while governments seek political resolutions for a nonpolitical problem.

Despite intensifying calls for expanded regulatory and legal networks, greater oversight of company activity and enhanced control over exchanges and traders, governments will have little effect on the problem. The market may well experience manipulation, Ponzi schemes, criminal activity, and conspiracies. But these are not the causes of oil vega. This volatility arises from the way the market trades and the hedging requirements placed upon that trade. In applying political solutions to what is essentially indigenous market volatility, governments will succeed largely in distorting the battlefield without attending to the actual crisis.

Then why will governments act at all? They have no choice. Given the pervasive effect oil pricing has on the full range of economic activities, the public sector cannot allow the oil vega crisis to run unattended. This is not simply a matter of whether the free market system of trade in a basic commodity will remain. Governments will regard oil vega as an aberration, as an imbalance that needs redressing, with the accompanying rhetoric often couching actions taken as in defense of the free market, at least in developed countries. That will prompt decisions that accentuate rather than reduce the crisis.

Elsewhere, in the world of developing nations, the result will be much worse. Responses there will involve more heavy-handed government intervention, especially in those countries where there is little indigenous oil and a dependence on imported sources of energy. In some of these countries, where the current governments are weak to begin with or are approaching failed-state status,[8] we will witness accelerating internal political instability, with some effects flowing across borders and endangering intra- and interregional balances.

This will get ugly because of oil's central position in modern markets and economies. But it will also emerge as a result of the way energy deficiencies and pricing tend to pressure already vulnerable sectors in developing countries. Justifications for government action will include conspiracy theories and a renewal of the nastier side of the North/South debate,[9] along with calls from some of the more populous leaders to scrap the free-market system altogether.

What will result is less the defense of an ideological position on markets as an *ad hoc* reaction to something regarded as a departure from how oil is supposed to operate normally. As such, the public sector will incorrectly analyze the problem and pursue the wrong remedies. The problem is twofold, as should be emphasized here at the outset. First, "normal oil" is becoming progressively a relic (if it ever actually existed). Second, government attempts in the past to regulate oil volatility have been particularly unsuccessful.

Oil does not operate the way other commodities do in the marketplace (I discuss this in Chapter 3). Recall that oil vega is not primarily a result of supply/demand factors. Rather, as oil occupies a position in which it is both a commodity for use and an asset in which to store value, it is the uncertainty over how market price adequately reflects the dual nature of oil that drives the volatility. Now adjustments in supply have been able to offset volatility in the past because availability was regarded as providing product to meet a certain level of demand. Such a traditional approach makes two assumptions: (1) demand is the only primary driver of oil-volume requirements, and (2) there is no likelihood of a constriction in the market; that is, both adequate supply exists and access to it remains unimpeded.

However, as I observe in Chapter 7, the "traditional" approach has less genuine relevance to what is actually happening as the oil vega crisis begins to intensify. One example is particularly instructive in this regard—the performance of equity trading markets as a surrogate for the actual performance of oil. I have written before that this does not translate well in volatile markets, especially those in which the price is pressured upward—the environment into which we are now quickly moving.

Two years ago, the bottom was falling out of oil prices. That's when investors renewed the habit of using equity market performance as a barometer to gauge oil and oil product demand—an approach often adopted as a shorthand during times of oil market contraction. The approach has remained, though, buttressed by overgeneralized comments from on-air commentators and in-print pundits. Such an "equity proxy" may serve as an approximate read during periods of decline. But it becomes a dangerous placebo when matters begin experiencing accelerated upward change.

The next cycle of such change has already begun.

The use of stocks as a surrogate for oil prices tends to be valuable to the extent that oil acts the way equities do. That, in turn, depends on whether the stock market reflects five traditional underlying factors in oil pricing: the value of the dollar, refinery inventories, supply constrictions, M&A [mergers and acquisitions] activity, and industrial performance as an adequate measure of returning demand. However, a disconnect has emerged . . . indicating that there is actually a sixth factor at work—an upward bias developing in pricing volatility.

This volatility, in turn, does not simply reflect supply and demand. It primarily results from the widening spread between the pricing of futures contracts and the underlying effective market value of the actual crude oil—the "paper" barrel to "wet" barrel spread.

When this happens, equity performance has a reduced ability to predict oil performance. There is an oft-recognized (but just as often forgotten) recognition that oil does not always act the way market-driven considerations of supply and demand would prescribe. The OIL VIX, a measure of the market volatility in oil prices,[10] is another case in point. As occurring currently, it attests to accelerating volatility by often moving in the same direction as oil prices—reflecting price changes occurring more quickly than the 30-day average upon which the measure is based.

Volatility will drive oil prices moving forward.[11]

This means that the yardsticks generally applied are going to be of declining explanatory value as we move into the approaching cycle of oil vega. Governments, on the other hand, will continue to regard the situation as one in which the supply of oil remains the cardinal consideration. *This is not the problem.* Oil vega is not peak oil; it not a crisis of volume.

However, given the response available to governments, as the crisis intensifies the approach of government will guarantee that energy will play out as a zero-sum game, with political reactions to it as part of the accelerating problem, not a remedy. This will be experienced especially in those systems where leaders are held popularly responsible. However, democratic or autocratic, the result is going to be the same.[12]

Now there are a number of aspects to how and why the governmental reaction takes place. I intend in this chapter to pursue a very limited focus. We shall not discuss a range of admittedly important dimensions to governmental energy perceptions. These include a number of matters, from cross-border incursions and concerted warfare to usage of oil (or investment in, access to, transport, and distribution of oil), which will negotiate leverage in a wide range of applications. We are concerned only with the governmental response to oil vega.

And then there is also the relationship between the governmental apparatus and the producing companies themselves—whether those companies are national oil companies (NOCs), or private entities— either vertically integrated oil companies (VIOCs) or international oil companies (IOCs). Corporate structure makes a company either an arm of or a potential competitor to government policy objectives. I shall limit what could easily be a much broader discussion to how the public sector is likely to view both domestic and foreign oil companies. The companies, I suggest, will be seen as a threat to national stability and an adversary to national policy. This refrain is already being heard in public opinion,[13] especially so when the company in question is foreign.[14] This adversarial relationship also extends to NOCs or nationally registered oil companies that have an impact on policy, especially in foreign circles.[15]

Oil remains essential to domestic economic stability and development. Yet it is important to note that virtually all countries find their approaches to oil set by what occurs internationally. Trade in physical oil produces different expectations based on whether a nation exports or imports,[16] without regard to where the contract is settled or the oil exchanges hands. Exporters seek the highest sustainable prices for raw materials in the international market and the setting of a price that maximizes economic rent while still discouraging recourse to alternative energy development or long-term conservation in recipient countries.

From a policy standpoint, the trade is regarded as a by-product of international politics and markets. Yet, as I shall discuss later in this chapter, it is important to realize that domestic considerations in general and the type of political regime in particular, are not the decisive variables in setting the approach a nation takes in the pursuit of oil. Stated simply, whether a nation encourages popular participation or, for that matter, whether it is a democracy has little effect on that approach.

Nations may introduce a wide range of internal policies to restrict, expand, subsidize, or prioritize the distribution of oil products to the population. These policies may encourage or limit the development of private companies, or may facilitate or discourage the issuance of shares or financing or the use of land for exploration and production, among other considerations. When confronting the dynamics of oil vega, however, none of these is of much help.

It makes no difference where a nation figures in the global oil sector. Producing countries are as dependent upon the revenue generated from sales to other countries, or on the rent they exact from oil production,[17] as consuming nations are dependent upon securing sufficient volume at prices their economies can sustain. OPEC and Russia are as shackled by their need to sell oil internationally as are the United States and the European Union (EU) in their dependence upon buying it from others. Given the aggregate impact on domestic market performance, countries with undiversified economics relying upon the foreign sale of raw materials are usually in an even worse situation than diversified economies relying upon others for their energy.[18]

In cross-border policy, governments will usually regard oil as exercising one of two roles. First, it is treated as a commodity upon which foreign policies and goals are applied in a detached manner to further national interest priorities. That is, oil merely comprises another element in the "great game" of diplomacy, the application or reception of pressure in international affairs. Oil as a diplomatic tool is considered one of a number of aspects serving about the same function in furthering foreign policy objectives or views of national security. In this sense, it has little function apart from its utility as a furtherance of other objectives, existing as a way of enhancing national priorities in global politics.

The second view, in large measure a polar opposite, holds oil to be a strategic object, the acquisition and control of which serves as a direct tool (or weapon) in international affairs. Whereas its usage is paramount in the first case, here control of oil becomes the decisive element. It is this second approach that will become the dominant perspective as oil vega intensifies.

The approach will be tempered by whether the nation is a price maker or a price taker;[19] that is, whether it provides volume to the market or is dependent upon that market for its energy needs. Much of the commentary often begins with this distinction and assumes that it ultimately places nations in one of two camps—those that export oil or those that import it—with that position, therefore, determining fundamentally distinct and irreconcilable approaches.[20] While the points of departure may be different, I shall suggest that the ultimate result will be the same. Neither producing nor consuming nations will be able to attenuate the volatility. They both have interests in maximizing national position, but cannot provide a genuine market-wide solution.

And that will oblige each government to play the general market vulnerability for national advantage, even in those cases where a producer may provide additional volume or a consumer may introduce moves to conserve usage by the introduction of either taxation or incentive measures. In neither case is the condition of the overall aggregate market the consideration. Rather, the focus remains upon the impact on a domestic economy, a domestic market balance, or a domestic political consequence. These will not only fail to address the more expansive issue; they will often end up being counterproductive.[21]

This is not an indictment of political systems but merely an acknowledgement of what they are intended to accomplish. Despite the rise in internationalization, functional encomiums to combined global effort,[22] or the occasional multinational agreement "for the common good," one overarching reality has not changed. Borders still mean something, especially in a crisis environment where essential threatening factors extend beyond those borders.

Now a crisis environment is generally perceived as one in which there is acceleration in tension to a level considered unsustainable, requiring thereby a resolution.[23] All crises share the presence of instability that either produces or augurs an abrupt change. When applying this to economies and markets, the period of uncertainty can be quite protracted, appear in cycles, or return to test fundamental assumptions about systems or response, as Charles Kindleberger famously indicated.[24] In his approach, the overall crisis period actually encompassed over 250 years (from 1719 through the 1980s) and served to provide perspective for his cogent analysis on the Great Depression.[25] I continue to have the same fascination with his work I had as an undergraduate far too many years ago. Clarity of vision is rare among scholars, especially in the field of economics. But there are some striking parallels in what Kindleberger called the "taxonomy" of the subject[26] and the situation confronting us now.

The securing of sufficient oil supplies or, conversely, the selling of adequate volume at an acceptable price—each put in the context of sustaining a national economy—is certainly among the seminal issues precipitating crisis. Access to the oil market from the direction of the buyer or that of the seller has a pervasive consequence in perceptions of instability. And that will prompt a nationalistic and reactionary response by governments for one simple underlying reason.

There are a number of underlying reasons for this, but one permeates all such decision making. *Governments are fundamentally parochial when it comes to matters of preservation.* And that is how the oil vega crisis will be perceived.

This is not going to be the end of civilization as we know it, but it will lay to rest the political fiction that the crisis is avoidable or can be delayed until some other time in the future. As with all such matters, there were will be cycles, periods of stagnation, and counterbalances. Yet one matter seems certain. So long as we remain dependent upon crude oil, the oil vega problem will intensify.

Recall that this is essentially endemic to how oil is traded. Just as oil companies are not structured to lessen the impact of oil vega, neither are governments. That means, when public officials nonetheless attempt to mitigate what is more accurately an exogenous problem, the exercise almost always ends up as reactive and providing little in the way of resolution. The approach usually ends up one in which it is hoped that regulation will serve to stabilize a worsening situation.

Unfortunately, this is not the sort of problem that is self-correcting— until, of course, the next major bubble bursts and the market sweats the crisis out the hard way. There remain purists who resist any government involvement. They suggest these cycles are natural and cannot be avoided. Their argument is of interest academically. But a government will be unable to avoid interfering because of the pervasive position that oil occupies in the economy. This will not be perceived in the same ways as decisions to bailout banks, or homeowners who hold mortgages they cannot afford, or domestic automakers who are unable to compete. Those decisions were widely perceived as primarily impacting individual sectors. By contrast, oil vega will hit across the board in its impact.

Based upon the discussion in Chapter 4, *securitizing* the transactions, the debt resulting from those transactions, or the collateral base itself propels what begins as an intensifying sector-specific instability into a much broader crisis. In the case of subprime mortgages, the usage of the collateralized mortgage obligations and related synthetic paper infected the creditworthiness of a wide array of asset classes.

In the case of oil, the situation is patently worse almost from the outset. This is not a sector problem but one felt market-wide and pervasively. Oil touches everything. The impact of oil vega will demand government intervention. And that intervention will be of limited impact in controlling the volatility. It will, however, further destabilize the situation—and for one fundamental structural reason.

A government has as its primary objective the improvement of a domestic, not an international market; the preservation of a particular matrix of supply, demand, and distribution considerations. The extent to which officials address global concerns is the extent to which those concerns adversely impact upon national security, national economic stability, or the competitiveness of national trade.

In theory, of course, we could sketch the policy parameters of an altruistic state. However in practice, aside from a small number of humanitarian issues—those that do not bring into question fundamental assumptions about a nation's domestic society or contest a nation's objectives or needs—governments are neither equipped for nor prepared to provide a balanced energy market to others.

There are two overarching reasons for this. First, a government exercises sovereignty[27] over a delimited geographic area; any attempt to secure policy objectives in a wider orbit amounts to the use of power,[28] which is always a relative concept.[29] The oil market, however, is neither delimited by national boundaries nor subject to a unitary system of legislation and regulations. To put the matter simply, it does not answer to any particular set of laws or edicts. It does, however, become a ready focus for cross-border politics and conflict. Even primary producers such as Saudi Arabia and Russia are as dependent upon the global market as are nations such as the United States and China that rely upon others to supply the volume that their populations require.

Second, even if somehow a particular national or multinational governmental approach could come to grips with regulating the amount of crude oil available in the market—that is, decisions made actually controlling the flow of wet barrels—the essential problem is not addressed. In all likelihood, regulating the commodity would only make the matter worse. Remember, this is not a problem initially occasioned by supply/demand considerations. Oil vega results from an inability to determine proper pricing levels between wet and paper barrels, between the consignments and futures contracts based upon them. *Anything done by a government on this score will likely only make the problem worse because it will frame it in the wrong context.* This will be perceived as the defense of one nation's interests against the interests of others. When it comes to the availability and use of a raw material needed by all nations, the controlling and driving governmental view ends at its borders.

There is no doubt, however, that governments will intervene. In sketching their more likely reactions, I will note four elements. There are, of course, many more. But the following considerations will emerge in most, reflecting a government's perception or rationale or both. Nations will have varying degrees of leverage. Recall, however, that they are all going to be unsuccessful in challenging oil vega. This is neither a policy nor a domestic market issue. It does not result from a tangible supply/demand situation, from illegal or unfair trading, from a collapse in a domestic market, or from aspects relating only to an internal exchange platform. There is, in short, little a government can do about it.

The Price Maker/Price Taker Tradeoff and Supply

In the early stages, governments will rely on the market to temper volatility. Only when it becomes clear that the trading pits would be exacerbating rather than reducing volatility will governments initiate their own approaches.

Oil vega will affect both net producing and net consuming countries. However, the official response is going to be very different in each. The initial response from a producer is to maintain control over crude supplies, followed by intensifying the opportunity cost of producing now, rather than waiting for additional pricing data.[30] This acceleration of production results in a price maker country generating a larger production surplus. The government in this case would accelerate the depletion of oil reserves, accumulate a savings fund, and push forward with spending while increasing taxation.[31] The more primary the price maker—that is, the more significant is a country's position among the main producers—the greater is the tendency to manage oil vega in this manner.

Most top oil-producing countries do not have diversified economies. That means they are dependent on oil exports for the bulk of their revenue and must further rely on oil sales to fund needed imports. Therefore, the increasing depletion of oil reserves must be balanced with increasing exports and the minimizing of discount sales abroad to prevent the rising volatility from adversely impacting the domestic economy.[32] All countries will initially approach oil vega as a price volatility problem, one found in the relationship between supply and demand.[33] Neither price makers nor price takers have sufficient tools to offset it.

One should expect that a major producer would want to temper the market moves by balancing supply to a perceived demand.[34] This is, after all, the approach used by the cartel in determining the "call on OPEC."[35] However, given that oil vega arises from neither a demand nor a supply change, but the volatility in the trading itself, such conventional approaches will be of no help in offsetting the crisis. Aside from raising prices to a level that obliges further conservation (and thereby a destruction of demand[36]), producers' actions can directly impact only the supply side of the relationship.

However, when supply is increased (the primary result during the volatility associated with the oncoming oil vega[37]), the market instability will simply intensify. In the absence of a more traditional increase in demand levels, raising supply accomplishes little more than a heating of the market even further. Remember, this is not about product sales. This is about trading uncertainty. Even then, given the actual source of the instability, the rising supply will result in an upward pressure on options and further upward price volatility.[38]

In the case of a price taker, or country dependent upon imports, the situation is largely the reverse. Here, the primary emphasis needs to be on suppressing (or at least stabilizing) prices while continuing to secure adequate supply. Given that crude oil pricing remains the single most influential element in determining oil product pricing levels for domestic distribution and sale,[39] policy decisions in a price taker will target methods to offset rises in market pricing. Aside from direct

subsidies or tax incentives, both resulting in unsustainable and counterproductive results, the governmental action here would initially fall
into three categories: conservation; pressure on producers to increase
supplies; and/or fuel replacement. The first, while always an immediate possibility, is a limited recourse. The past several decades indicate
conservation is a valuable tool, but only when it is able to result in
significant changes on the level of discretionary usage. Cuts beyond
that point have a negative impact on economic production and overall
market performance.[40]

In traditional price or supply shocks (and remember oil vega as
detailed here is not a traditional shock), to the extent that the moves
toward conservation, with or without additional measures, are successful and the prices retreat, the decline in prices will generate greater
usage.[41] Once a crisis has passed, demand moves back up to or beyond
the level experienced prior to the price rises. The essential reason
why this did not happen after the 2008–2009 price retreat was its
cause. It resulted from a more pervasive financial meltdown, as I note
in Chapter 4, initiated by the subprime mortgage collapse, the implosion of
synthetic debt values, a constriction in credit, and a genuine retrenchment in industrial activity.

All larger end users will provide incentives of one sort or another,
as positive pressure to oblige availability of additional supply from producers. If the crisis extends for any length of time, there will emerge a
more concerted competition for those resources. Traditionally, this has
meant, at least short-term, a heightened position for producers over
consumers. Yet in the pricing problems experienced over the past three
decades, the market has readjusted supply and demand levels to compensate for movements up or down in overall pricing.

Developed countries would rely upon emerging markets to curb
demand first in accelerating pricing environments, given the attendant
inflationary pressures resulting. Stated simply, the developed world
could tolerate a price shock better than the developing world. Given
the need to use dollars in oil trade, emerging markets with weaker
domestic currencies would usually put the brakes on domestic usage
first. The inflation resulting from the rise in oil prices would result in
greater economic instability in the developing world,[42] obliging more
rapid government intervention to suppress domestic demand.

Now, however, two factors have intervened to change that scenario. First, the exchange rate value of the dollar has weakened significantly, improving the position of currencies such as the yuan and rupee. That means the inflationary impact of transferring dollars to the local currency has become less an issue as the dollar's value has declined.[43] Second, developing countries such as China and India require continued oil imports to maintain rising industrialization. The self-imposed curb on imports, therefore, is counterproductive in ways that simply were not as evident a decade ago.[44] In short, Washington can no longer expect Beijing, New Delhi, or other developing economies to run the kind of interference that they did earlier.

That translates into increasing competition for oil and declining leverage for the United States, which remains dependent upon imports for upwards to two-thirds of daily crude oil needs. The American market also must negotiate adequate imports while competing with other global regions prepared to pay much more. Even then, circumstances are working in favor of those traditionally paying such premiums.[45]

The supply of crude oil notwithstanding, neither price making or price taking countries will be able to use devices geared to supply and demand in the attempt to deal with oil vega. In an environment of rising crude oil volatility brought about by an inability to determine the effective market price, supply injections will exacerbate the problem.

National Security and the Nature of Speculation

Undiversified oil-producing countries view national *survival* as directly associated to the sale of crude oil. But it is in the developed West that the security issue will play itself out most visibly. This will be the justification for most of the governmental initiatives, especially in the United States, where the argument has found considerable support. For the medium term at least, gross domestic product (GDP) and economic performance are tied to energy in the form of crude oil.[46] That makes its availability and price matters of national significance. In the United States, the energy security debate continued almost unabated despite a significant fall in oil prices beginning in late 2008, with levels remaining subdued well into 2009. Now that we are in another upward cycle, the rhetoric will once again intensify on this issue.

This is certainly both a significant and, in some quarters, fervently held debate. On the one side are those contending that dependence upon foreign sources of crude oil makes the United States vulnerable. On the other side is the argument that, while such vulnerability may well be a concern, the availability of lower-priced volume requires the continuation (and even expansion) of imports.[47] The security versus price debate will continue, absent a pervasive, scalable, and affordable break-through in genuine alternative technology or the accelerated usage of natural gas to power transport needs[48] in the country.

Oil vega will be regarded as a combination of two factors. The first views it as merely an extension of the crude oil availability issue, much as is the case of the supply concerns addressed directly above. Here, the argument will again be made in the United States (and the EU) that, unless decreasing reliance is placed on importing supplies, external pro-viders will continue to hold the country (or the union) hostage. This is a very attractive position for candidates to hold during elections or for talking heads to make in a brief "debate" on some discussion show.

Yet the truth lies somewhere else. Neither the American or European markets can become self-sufficient in oil, even with a concerted conservation strategy.[49] Demand is too great, while the domestic pro-duction base is declining significantly in the United States,[50] and the brief respite in Europe provide by North Sea production is already nearing an end.[51] The substitution of unconventional sourcing[52]—Canadian oil sands, oil shale from Colorado, the Bakken or the Monterey Basin in California, heavy oil, or bitumen—may improve the situation somewhat, but will be much more expansive and create significant adverse environmental impact. Coal-to-liquid technologies are touted by some while others champion biofuels such as ethanol.[53] All of these will prove more expensive, imports will still be necessary, and even then neither the sourcing nor the volume of supply is the problem.

The second factor is one closer to the actual cause, but will be folded into a broader and equally unsuccessful attempt to regulate trading markets, as I shall summarize below. This factor would involve trad-ers, referred to as *speculators* in the political use of the term, and the rhetoric would be certain to elicit the requisite condemnation among the population. Here, the connection between regulating speculation and national security will be strained, at best. If the consideration of security includes the protection of a free-market economy, the ability of those prepared to take a risk must be secured. Speculators are actually necessary for the efficient operation of trading markets.[54] Without those prepared to occupy the more extreme positions in a transaction, utilization of liquidity become more problematic.[55]

The problem emerges when the intended causality is reversed. Speculation in the service of advancing genuine business is a driver of the market and provider of liquidity. However, when the speculation is itself the primary engine of advance, the situation becomes untenable quickly. We are well advised to heed Keynes's caution, which was written more than seven decades ago: "Speculators may do no harm as bubbles on a steady stream of enterprise. But the position is serious when enterprise becomes the bubble on a whirlpool of speculation."[56]

Of course, a market that has *only* speculation as its primary source of liquidity would fall prey to the same reasoning that brought us the mortgage-backed synthetic debt-obligation bubble. This is where I believe we are going to end up anyway: it is the essential result of oil vega and the synthetic debt approaches are necessary to bridge paper and wet-barrel values. But exclusive reliance on speculative finance produces an exchange environment requiring a continuous rolling over of maturing debt, given the likelihood that speculation results in cash flows from operating units amounting to less than cash payment commitments, usually over short-term periods.

According to Hyman Minsky:

[I]f cash receipts and payments are separated into income and a return of principal component (as, for example, monthly payments on a fully amortized home mortgage are separated), then the expected income receipts exceed the income (interest) payments on existing commitments in every period. Cash-flow deficiencies arise because there are commitments to pay cash on the account of the principal that are greater than the receipts on principal account during these periods. Speculative financing involves the rolling over of maturing debt.[57]

Focusing upon the source of liquidity, while instructive in estimating overall trends in trade, has a more central interest for our purposes.

The employment of synthetic derivatives is more pronounced with the rise of speculative finance. According to the distribution of assets versus cash obligations noted by Minsky, "Speculative finance involves the short financing of long positions."[58] When Minsky wrote that, the vehicles he had in mind were commercial banks. The rise in the use of synthetic debt and asset-backed obligations has expanded that notion considerably.[59]

It is in the approach to this new shadowy world of securitization that governments will make a major miscalculation. At this point, I want to confine my remarks to the relationship between speculation and liquidity. Because it is here that governmental action is almost certain to confuse cause and effect.

Speculative bubbles are considered as rapidly accelerating deviations of commodity prices—such as a barrel of oil—from a level considered their real market value level.[60] The "real value" is usually defined by technicals and fundamentals. Yet oil vega adds the additional impediment of preventing such traditional standards from determining such a price. The limitation in estimation occasioned by the rising volatility associated with oil vega is already becoming recognized as one of the primary problems in analysis.[61]

Speculative bubbles are usually identified only after the fact. As such, since they are not easily distinguishable from other market machinations in the initial stages, there is always the temptation to regard them as the causes of pricing movements that cannot be explained by traditional factors, rather than as the product of such movements.[62] This is a fundamental consideration in approaching speculation in oil.[63] Whereas a "normal" speculative bubble, once burst, will result in the real exchange commodity price falling to a level supported by market fundamentals, the problem with oil vega when related to speculation is the connection between the level of that speculation and the inability to determine a proper option price.

While there are a number of aspects in the oil pricing process that may be subject to regulatory pressure, a government cannot set an option price or dictate the spread between paper and wet barrels. The authorities can increase or decrease import/export considerations, lay out pricing caps or ranges for the sale of oil products, intervene in forex markets to influence the local currency valuation against the dollar (and, thereby, the price of crude oil exchange), or, in the case of the

United States, to stimulate (by increasing the export of manufactured goods) or discourage (by rendering imports more expensive) trade by attempting to influence the market value of the dollar itself.

All of this comments on the major problem with governmental action under the guise of national security considerations attempting to regulate speculation. But governments have no direct means (except possibly one, discussed in Chapter 7) to combat the speculation. Discouraging speculation is tantamount to ending the free exchange that prompted it. One could, of course, argue that excessive speculation comprises unfair competition or market manipulation, thereby justifying regulation. This is an approach that had been suggested following the 2008 upward spike in oil prices.[64] Yet, as we shall see in a moment, clearly fraudulent or restraint of competition activities, there is little the government could do that would provide any tangible oil vega offset, unless the objective is to determine where to remove genuine open access to trade in futures contracts.

The only caveat here, the sole instance in which a natural security argument would merge with a move to regulate speculation, would be in those cases where a foreign-based trader would be suspected of manipulating the U.S. crude oil or oil products market.[65] Even in this case, however, the rationale for the intervention is animated by the wrong objective. Regulating foreign involvement in trading having an impact on the U.S. market may placate some xenophobic view of national security. However, aside from the unlikely occasion of oil vega being deliberately perpetrated as a weapon against the American market from abroad, the approach has the wrong focus.

Despite some conclusions drawn from common perceptions or populist political rhetoric, the integral volatility inherent in oil vega is not a deliberate device introduced with the specific intention of making a fortune or undermining a nation. The first is part of the lure of Wall Street, the pursuit of the perfect deal. That latter is something more appropriate for potboiler fiction or Hollywood script writers. There are those who may attempt to do either once the crisis deepens. Yet such actions are not the cause of oil vega. They emerge once the Keynesian "whirlpool" has already developed. [66]

Why will governments nonetheless link the two? Actually, in a certain fundamental sense, oil vega *is* a national security issue. Not from the standpoint of an intentional offensive from a foreign adversary or even folded into the broader concern over the sourcing of America's needed crude oil supply. Given the pervasive impact oil has on the domestic economy, maintaining economic strength, employment, income generation, and a way of life are national security issues.

Then, there is the application of a corollary to Murphy's Law, stating "The administrator smiling during a time of crisis has figured out somebody to blame it on." If the real cause is beyond the reach of a governmental remedy, save for killing the patient (the free market), there is the ever-present temptation to find any culprit. There are some who will convince themselves this is actually the cause, perhaps more to find somebody to target than for any other reason. Finally, there is the clear recognition that what is happening in the trading of futures contracts is both a required element for the smooth running of the market in normal times and the occasion for the rise of oil vega. From a national security standpoint, however, decision makers may not have the luxury of adequately distinguishing the real problem from the trading environment in which it arises.

In each case, therefore, speculation will be portrayed as the threat. But speculation is not the cause of oil vega as much as it is a product. If the futures contract exchange market had not been created, the trading in oil would have remained cumbersome, oligopolistic, and inefficient.[67] The absence of futures contracts would not have alleviated the problem. It would have simply moved it even more decidedly into the political arena. Remember, futures were introduced to combat the broader volatility experienced in the 1970s. That volatility, in turn, resulted from the effective decision-making power being concentrated initially in the hands of a few IOCs, and then the transfer of that leverage to NOCs. Forward contracts were still being drawn up, but the overall financial market impact was more subdued, given that these were paper barrels representing near-term actual crude-oil barrel transfers.[68]

Governments, therefore, will have little success in combating oil vega by legislating in the traditional sense. Neither a view of national security nor the connection of it to a negative regard for speculation will prove of much help. Oil vega emerges from within the futures trading system, not as a result of some exogenous influence.

Sovereign Wealth Funds and the
Reaction of the West

The emergence of sovereign wealth funds (SWFs) may be the most significant outcome from the redistribution of oil sale proceeds and the advent of new global trading patterns. An SWF is a state-owned fund comprising an asset range that is acquired internationally.[69] It emerges when a country has a prolonged budgetary surplus augmented by little international debt. While the funds may be difficult to separate in practical terms, there have nonetheless been attempts to separate SWF proceeds per se from central bank holdings. An SWF has as its primary objective long-term return, while the foreign exchange holdings of a central bank are for short-term currency stabilization.[70]

There are two essential reasons for an SWF. One is to serve as savings for future generations. The second acts as stabilization to offset the adverse impact of a considerable influx of currency (or in some cases a rapid decline in oil prices). This latter aspect has been well understood since the eighteenth century and David Hume's introduction of the price-specie flow mechanism.[71] The movement of hard currency proceeds can create significant cross-sector destabilizing effects, often these days termed *the Dutch disease*.[72]

While SWF assets can come from a number of sources, raw material export revenue predominates. Of those, the main source for most of the assets is oil and gas proceeds. The SWF Institute calculates over 58 percent of the total comes from oil and gas (primarily, crude oil sales). As the institute notes in Table 6.1, 29 of the 50 top SWFs listed gain funds from oil or gas.

And that is of concern to Western governments. The proceeds from oil sales have become a potentially significant investment weapon. Traditional investment outlets can be dealt with (or not) by mechanisms already in place. A responding government can utilize its existing statutory and regulatory arsenal to encourage or discourage SWF-sourced investment within its domestic economy.[73]

Admittedly, the stated purpose of the SWF is to secure either current financial balance (stabilization) or the future prosperity of a population (savings). These may have policy implications for Western countries, but are not likely to contribute heightened concerns on

Table 6.1   Sovereign Wealth Fund Rankings by Assets under Management

Country	Fund Name	Assets ($ billions)	Began	Fund Source
UAE−Abu Dhabi	Abu Dhabi Investment Authority	627	1976	Oil
Norway	Government Pension Fund−Global	512	1990	Oil
Saudi Arabia	SAMA Foreign Holdings	415	N/A	Oil
China	SAFE Investment Company	347.1**	1997	Noncommodity
China	China Investment Corporation	332.4	2007	Noncommodity
Singapore	Government of Singapore Investment Corporation	247.5	1981	Noncommodity
China−Hong Kong	Hong Kong Monetary Authority Investment Portfolio	227.6	1993	Noncommodity
Kuwait	Kuwait Investment Authority	202.8	1953	Oil
China	National Social Security Fund	146.5	2000	Noncommodity
Russia	National Welfare Fund	142.5*	2008	Oil
Singapore	Ternasek Holdings	133	1974	Noncommodity
Qatar	Qatar Investment Authority	85	2005	Oil
Libya	Libyan Investment Authority	70	2006	Oil
Australia	Australian Future Fund	59.1	2004	Noncommodity
Algeria	Revenue Regulation Fund	56.7	2000	Oil
Kazakhstan	Kazakhstan National Fund	38	2000	Oil
U.S.−Alaska	Alaska Permanent Fund	35.5	1976	Oil
Ireland	National Pensions Reserve Fund	33	2001	Noncommodity
South Korea	Korea Investment Corporation	30.3	2005	Noncommodity
Brunei	Brunei Investment Agency	30	1983	Oil

Table 6.1   (Continued)

Country	Fund Name	Assets ($ billions)	Began	Fund Source
France	Strategic Investment Fund	28	2008	Noncommodity
Malaysia	Khazanah Nasional	25	1993	Noncommodity
Iran	Oil Stabilization Fund	23	1999	Oil
Chile	Social and Economic Stabilization Fund	21.8	1985	Copper
Azerbaijan	State Oil Fund	21.7	1999	Oil
UAE–Dubai	Investment Corporation of Dubai	19.6	2006	Oil
UAE–Abu Dhabi	International Petroleum Investment Company	14	1984	Oil
Canada	Alberta's Heritage Fund	13.8	1976	Oil
UAE–Abu Dhabi	Mubadala Development Company	13.3	2002	Oil
U.S.–New Mexico	New Mexico State Investment Council	12.9	1958	Noncommodity
New Zealand	New Zealand Superannuation Fund	12.1	2003	Noncommodity
Bahrain	Mumtalakat Holding Company	9.1	2006	Oil
Brazil	Sovereign Fund of Brazil	8.6	2009	Noncommodity
Oman	State General Reserve Fund	8.2	1980	Oil and gas
Botswana	Pula Fund	6.9	1994	Diamonds and minerals
East Timor	Timor–Leste Petroleum Fund	6.3	2005	Oil and gas
Saudi Arabia	Public Investment Fund	5.3	2008	Oil
China	China–Africa Development Fund	5.0	2007	Noncommodity
U.S.–Wyoming	Permanent Wyoming Mineral Trust Fund	3.6	1974	Minerals
Trinidad & Tobago	Heritage and Stabilization Fund	2.9	2000	Oil
UAE- Ras Al Khaimah	RAK Investment Authority	1.2	2005	Oil

(continued)

Table 6.1   (Continued)

Country	Fund Name	Assets ($ billions)	Began	Fund Source
Venezuela	FEM	0.8	1998	Oil
Vietnam	State Capital Investment Corporation	0.5	2006	Noncommodity
Nigeria	Excess Crude Account	0.5	2004	Oil
Kiribati	Revenue Equalization Reserve Fund	0.4	1956	Phosphates
Indonesia	Government Investment Unit	0.3	2006	Noncommodity
Mauritania	National Fund for Hydrocarbon Reserves	0.3	2006	Oil and gas
UAE–Federal	Emirates Investment Authority	N/A	2007	Oil
Oman	Oman Investment Fund	N/A	2006	Oil
UAE–Abu Dhabi	Abu Dhabi Investment Council	N/A	2007	Oil
Total Oil & Gas Related	2354.5			
Total Other	1681.6			
TOTAL	4036.1			

*This includes the Oil Stabilization Fund of Russia.

**Best guess estimation.

Note: All figures quoted are from official sources, or, where the institutions concerned do not issue statistics of their assets, from other publicly available sources. Some of these figures are best estimates as market values change day to day. Updated September 2010.

SOURCE: SWF Institute, available at www.swfinstitute.org/fund-rankings/.

their face. Then again, given that rentier countries usually have an undiversified economic base, especially in the range of manufacturing required, the SWF may serve as a ready source for import subsidies. Again, capital infrastructure projects necessary for domestic market development— for example, roads, housing, communications, water purification, and construction—are also likely recipients. And then there are the higher-visibility SWF attempts to purchase property, equity, and financial assets abroad. While each has trading and domestic consequences, none of these extends directly to the problem of oil volatility or oil vega.[74]

The SWF problem that does concern us here, and becomes recognized as such by importing countries, considers the relationship between the SWFs and the oil trading market. Now in point of fact, the SWF at issue need not have its funds obtained from the oil market at all to have an effect on the trade in oil. China, for example, has four of the nine largest SWFs, accounting in the aggregate for more than $1.05 trillion (exceeding 26 percent of the top-50 totals). These are not sourced from oil or gas. Yet China is itself a major importer of oil and gas. While its huge SWF assets may pose problems in other areas, therefore, they are not likely to pose one here.

However, there are specific ways in which the usage and movement of SWF funding volume will intensify oil vega. This can happen in one of three ways. First, the funds can affect the financing, production, and transport of product, either directly (serving as investment for project and/or infrastructure) or indirectly (facilitating the financing or collateralization of exports). The SWF-supported actions can then either benefit or penalize particular regions, countries, or markers.

Second, the funds could be used to establish holding companies for the purpose of acquiring future access to wet barrels in broader producing basins than those directly controlled by the SWF-sponsoring country. Here, the strategy may look like a parallel diversification of crude oil sourcing,[75] but the intention could well be one of advancing a political agenda.[76] Whether there is an ulterior motive or not, the interjection of SWF assets poses the possibility of markedly changing the dynamics of oil trade. Volume may still be present for purchase,[77] but pricing and availability may not be the result purely of market forces.

It is the third way, however, that carries the greatest danger from the point of view of oil vega. This involves the movement of SWF assets into the futures contract market, accentuating in the process both pricing instability and the very uncertainty that fuels oil vega. Now in one sense, this has been taking place all along. Producers as well as end-users need to hedge contracts to provide some balance in their forward exchanges. But I am talking here about the movement of significant funds into the transactions in futures contracts, into paper barrel transactions.

Discounting such movements for political or nonmarket reasons, SWF countries could certainly regard this as an opportunity to increase pricing artificially, and sustain spreads between paper and wet barrels, thereby extending margins and generating a greater return. Anecdotal evidence points toward Caracas[78] and Tehran[79] having attempted such moves in the past. In both cases, however, the attempt failed because neither country could muster a sufficient penetration. The liquidity brought to bear was insufficient (give the effective size of the Venezuelan and Iranian SWFs involved) and the move could not have been sustained for very long anyway. The level of liquidity injected into the futures market must be sufficient to control the outcome. That could not be expected with two countries having a combined SWF volume of less than $25 billion.

With a range of more pressing problems, manipulating the futures market would not seem to be a top priority for SWF nations. In addition, Saudi Arabia (clearly a major SWF player) has shown noticeable restraint in that direction in the past.[80] Nonetheless, the Venezuelan and Iranian economies are more dependent upon the price of oil than other OPEC members, especially in the case of Iran, as the combination of U.S., EU, and UN sanctions has resulted in a serious increase in the cost of transacting crude-oil sales.[81]

Still, the SWFs could be used for such a purpose, a realization creating some angst in Western capitals. In response (once again operating on the quite-warranted assumption that Western governments would continue to defend the free-exchange market), there are only two tangible responses. The first is to offset the outside liquidity flow with stimulus from the Bank of England or the Fed. The New York and London exchanges are the targets for a SWF attack, although entry into another European bourse would complicate matters a bit and put some added indirect pressure on the NYMEX and ICE benchmark crude prices. The SWF strategy cannot work, however, unless the liquidity brought in is sufficient to determine contract flow. The liquidity tit-for-tat, however, will still have an upward pressure on prices. And in any event, it is a defensive measure only by the primary Western exchanges. It may intensify oil vega, but it will have no success in attenuating the volatility.

The second will be to limit access by foreign-sourced funds to the trading pits. Two likely results would flow from such a move—some futures contract trading would move to other global locations and liquidity levels would have some balancing problems (since foreign investment moves are hardly in oil futures alone). The move would also tend to weaken the repatriation of dollars *qua* investment, since the oil trades are denominated in dollars and require dollar reserves in banks around the world for that purpose (the petrodollars discussed in Chapter 4). To the extent that the dollars are not used in futures contract transactions, there is less need for the petrodollars being held aboard. More will simply be repatriated, to add to U.S. inflationary pressures at home,[82] and the essential advantage of seigniorage[83] provided to the dollar will erode.

There is nonetheless some possibility that the effect of SWF moves could be offset, but it would be at a price. The market left behind after heavy injections of stimulus or concerted restriction of foreign funds would be less stable and prone to greater cycles of instability. More to the point, however, given that SWFs are not the cause of oil vega, but would only be employed as a device to ride the volatility to greater short-term returns, the problem is not solved. Here, government efforts will significantly damage market balance and not succeed in moving a nation closer to solving the underlying problem.

Regulating the Futures Market: The OTC Problem

The primary government response to oil vega will be an increasing regulation of the trading market. We have already witnessed calls for regulations in the wake of the 2008 oil-pricing spike. Yet, as I have already observed, the primary condemnation of speculators misses the point. Three elements already considered in this book are converging to make the impending bout with oil vega a vicious one—resulting in a pronounced contraction of asset value and another severe test of the interbank credit system.

First, the rising difficulty of equating paper barrel prices with an actual market value of the underlying consignments of crude oil is creating problems in determining proper option prices on futures contracts. That serves to increase the trading price but not the market value of the crude itself. It also serves to increase the uncertainty in the process by reducing the convergence between known wet barrels for delivery and the profit margins required by the futures trader.

Second, the problem is complicated by the now–traditionally regarded factors influencing crude oil pricing—currency exchange rates against the dollar, supply and demand, inventories, production costs, and geopolitical events, among others, and the rising political responses to them. As already noted, the problem here is that an ability to compensate (or at least to account for) all of these still does not get to the root of the oil vega problem. What these factors do accomplish, on the other hand, is provide targets that neither address the instability nor offer a remedy.

Third, the expanding usage of synthetic debt and securitized paper to make the process fit is placing the futures trading in oil within the crosshairs of regulators. Not all of this, of course, is unwarranted.[84] After all, it is the derivatives market that bears the brunt of the criticism for the subprime mortgage crisis. And the approach used to secure futures contract profits in oil operates in the same way. This is where regulators must focus their attention.

Now it is not the derivatives *per se* that are the problem. It has long been recognized that futures contracts traded on an exchange (with the NYMEX being the most important example) stabilize the overall trade in commodities, provided that trade does not have as its primary objective the willful manipulation of the process. Exchange-traded futures are the most visible target for regulation. However, the largely unregulated over-the-counter (OTC) market is the location for a rising amount of trade related to oil futures,[85] both contracts and swaps.[86] Unlike the exchange-based trade, which offers standardized contracts, OTC action can be on any structured product, exercised over any time period, and involving any number of elements. Usually, the OTC trades end up being made either (1) on an electronic basis whereby any number of parties may place bids and offers (contracts here usually end up looking like the more standardized versions available on an exchange), or (2) via two-party dealer markets, in which the contract may be custom-fitted to the trading requirements. The leading dealers

here are the very big boys, and it was this kind of exercise that aggra-
vated the collapse of the collateral mortgage obligation in the subprime
meltdown.

From a practical standpoint, exchange-traded futures and OTC swaps,
options, or swaptions[87] are close surrogates and a number of traders—
whether hedging actual positions or speculating—are active in both.
However, the unregulated OTC market remains a major concern. It is
of little comfort that the primary dealers in OTC paper related to oil
options and swaps are the same houses that brought us the mortgage
collapse. Where custom-designed instruments are involved, exotic synthetic debt paper is never far behind. Yet there is little data available on this
shadowy world of finance, either openly or to the regulatory agencies.

And that brings us to the matter of how to regulate this financial
swamp. The Commodity Exchange Act (CEA)[88] passed in 1936 provides for the oversight of derivatives markets. While regulations emerged
earlier in the twentieth century, a genuine regulatory position began
with the Commodity Futures Trading Commission (CFTC)[89] in 1974.
The CFTC is an independent agency and has its operations modeled
on those of the Securities and Exchange Commission (SEC).[90] Both
the CFTC and the SEC operate on the same assumption that trading
involving the public should take place on regulated exchanges, an
assumption shared by the bulk of securities and commodities law on
the books. However, neither has specific authority over OTC dealings
and neither has the power to collect the necessary information to
regulate the bilateral exchanges anyway.

What appears to be the primary source of problems in trades, options,
and the synthetic paper structuring them, therefore, remains outside the
purview of regulators. The CFTC does have a duty to prevent excessive
speculation.[91] Unfortunately, there are no standards or criteria established
to determine what "excessive" means. In addition, such provisions are
introduced to protect the small investor, not deal with the problem
of significant volume being moved by large institutional players. The
approach is paternalistic, maybe even justifiably so, but does not focus
upon the real problem.

Neither the statute giving it rise nor CFTC procedure is designed
to curb speculation per se, for the reasons I have discussed earlier. It is not
the existence of speculation that is the problem. Nor, for that matter,

does excessive trading volume automatically equal excessive speculation. Rather than a cause of pricing volatility, spiking volumes may also be the result. Both speculators and hedgers have been known to follow the herd mentality when it comes to perceiving market direction and practice irrational exuberance.[92]

Remember, however, that it is not the speculation itself that creates the oil vega problem. The volatility is built into the system. Speculators are merely attempting to profit from it, while hedgers are attempting to deal with increasing price risk. If it results that speculators are manipulating the market to gain that profit, then existing regulations will have something to say about it. This is also extending to the OTC market with each raid on a downtown Manhattan or southern Connecticut hedge fund or financing house (those involved in the private network cutting the paper for customized deals) alleged to have illegally gamed the system. Yet, oil vega is not a result of manipulation or illegal activity. What the regulations are focusing upon, therefore, is not the problem we are addressing.

Nonetheless, the rapid rise in the OTC market posed a serious challenge to regulators. The legislation, especially the CEA, anticipated (and in some cases seemed to require) that futures trading would occur only on a CFTC-regulated exchange.[93] In 2000, Congress introduced the Commodity Futures Modernization Act,[94] in part to address this question of whether OTC market trading could continue without CFTC oversight. The legislation posited three separate categories of commodity derivatives: financial commodities, agricultural commodities, and exempt commodities.

The first includes interest rate, currency price, or stock index trades, defined as excluded commodities. These are allowed on the OTC with little CFTC oversight, as long as small individual investors are excluded. Due to concerns over price manipulation, the second category, agricultural commodities, must be traded on a CFTC-regulated futures exchange, provided that they are derivatives of farm production contracts.[95] The third, the catch-all exempt commodities category, is everything that is not either a financial or an agricultural commodity. These days that means either metals or energy.

And herein lies the problem. This exemption from regulation was referred to as the "Enron loophole," allowing energy OTC trades to be conducted without CFTC supervision. The Wall Street Reform and Consumer Protection Act (Dodd-Frank) signed into law in July of 2010 has begun closing the loophole, and the extensions into OTC activities are expanding.[96] But genuine concerns remain.[97] To declare by fiat that no OTC energy trading would be allowed is not the intention. Rather, the object is to allow CFTC oversight, not to end speculation. The oversight may well be of some help, but it is not going to have an impact in curbing oil vega.

There has yet to emerge a report indicating that speculation has had a manipulative impact on oil pricing. A series of government reports indicated that no data existed to conclude manipulation had occurred[98] but these have been hotly contested. One prime basis for dismissing the reports is the CFTC distinction between commercial and noncommercial trading, one that upon occasion merely obfuscates the actual trading occurring. It creates what is known as the swap dealer loophole. As Daniel O'Sullivan succinctly puts it:

> *A priori*, any statistical study attempting to measure specula-
> tive influence on the oil price by using simply the traditional
> CFTC split between its own definitions of "commercial" and
> "non-commercial" market participation is invalid—simply
> and obviously because of the swap dealer loophole that allows
> speculative financial interest in the oil price to be hedged on
> NYMEX under the "commercial" cover.[99]

An attempt, therefore, to determine if speculation has unfairly moved price must first be able to determine the noncommercial nature of the transactions. If the contracts are actually to hedge a wet-barrel position, they are commercial, despite the result. If they were not for receipt but are nonetheless taking place on a regulated exchange, they would be considered commercial transactions on their face. A considerable amount of speculative movement can be hidden from regulators in this way, whether or not Dodd-Frank achieves its objectives.

There is another danger from attempts to regulate the futures and derivative trading in oil. It constitutes a regulatory tightrope that U.S. policymakers need to walk. Increasing oversight of oil trading on American exchanges may simply move the action abroad, beyond the reach of U.S. regulators. With reliance upon foreign oil for two-thirds of daily crude intake, moving a widening number of foreign contracts for that crude to foreign bourses could well compound the difficulty of preventing manipulation in pricing.

This is perhaps the greatest irony of all. By obliging that oil be denominated in dollars, Washington received seigniorage, an ability to export its inflation abroad, while receiving for the domestic economy what amounts to an interest-free loan. However, it also allows that trade in dollars to occur anywhere. The petrodollars remaining in foreign banks allow the United States to run a widening current-accounts deficit without generating the normally accompanying inflation. But they also can fund trade, futures, derivatives, and synthetic debt based upon them anywhere. The tools are already there. Populist rhetoric aside, coming down too heavily on both exchange and OTC futures may move the trade to Dubai, Singapore, or even the nascent St. Petersburg exchange in Russia.

There are other factors that would reinforce such a move. Weaning more oil trade from dollar-denomination requires a greater control over the contracts by local exchanges. Movement of futures contract traffic to Dubai, for example, would buttress the rise in importance of other crude benchmarks. That is already happening. West Texas Intermediate (WTI, the benchmark for NYMEX contracts in New York) and Dated Brent (accomplishing the same in London) remain the dominant benchmarks in daily trade, despite the fact that they together actually represent less than 15 percent of the contracts worldwide. The absolute majority of consignments are for sourer (higher sulfur content) and heavier-weighted oil than either WTI or Brent.

Early in 2010, a new sour crude rate emerged, the Argus Sour Crude Index (ASCI) benchmark.[100] Saudi Arabia has already moved to it and so have other OPEC producers. Similar rates are being developed for delivery to the Gulf Coast of the United States. The days of WTI as the dominant rate are rapidly drawing to a close. Can the contracts based on that benchmark be far behind? If regulatory pressure increases, the futures contract trade may just start moving to where the oil is produced. We still need that oil, but the trade in it would progressively end up beyond the reach of any American regulations. In addition to having a significant and negative impact on NYMEX, it would also add another dimension to the already-disconcerting energy security debate.

And, oh yes, after all has been discussed and debated, nothing actually takes on the real culprit in oil instability, the volatility incumbent in oil vega. This remains endemic to the market. It is not the result of manipulating speculators, foreign adversaries, fraudulent behavior, or illegal activity.

Is there anything that can help us to address the rapidly approaching crisis? This is the subject of the last chapter.

Chapter 7

Is There a Response?

London, October 2010

A meeting is taking place between a medium-sized company that is producing oil in several emerging countries and the bank expected to serve as lead book-runner on a syndicated loan to finance a new project. In such an arrangement, an operating company secures a loan to develop its field, essentially using the value of the oil to be extracted as collateral. That value is conservatively set by both the company and the financial institution by deliberately underestimating the volume of oil to be produced and the price for which it will be sold at the wellhead.[1] Both parties fully expect the actual result will be better, providing thereby an amount of protection against unexpected market turbulence. The bank then lessens its exposure by syndicating the finance to other banks—both reducing its risk by sharing it and picking up syndication fees in the process.

I have known the company's management for some time and they have asked my advice on structuring the deal. This would mark the third time the company and bank have worked together on the same type of syndication. The company is well regarded by the bank, coming in under budget and over projected production on both previous occasions. Each provided the bank with nice syndicating fees in addition to a return on its money.

However, this time around the bank vice president in charge of the negotiations offers three-year, six-month, LIBOR[2] plus 1,295 basis points. This amounts to an annualized interest rate of about 13.5 percent—and this is for what the VP admits is a known and "valued" customer!

The offer is significantly worse than either of the previous two times these parties have conducted business. My recommendation is for the company to break off negotiations. I also may have said something about getting better rates from Tony Soprano.

The credit constriction remains from the financial crisis, augmented by the severe downward spiral in oil prices leveling off only in the summer of 2009. But the underlying reason emerging from the abortive meeting in London speaks of something more sinister. As with another meeting in the same city a year earlier,[3] oil volatility moving forward is a matter of rising concern. The banks no longer have confidence in what the proper rate should be—because they no longer can determine an effective market value for the underlying crude oil. In such a situation, the bank is doing what participants in the futures trading market are doing. They raise the bar.

Oil vega is changing how projects are negotiated moving forward.

■ ■ ■

At the outset of this final chapter, I need to be frank. There are no easy answers here. Either suggested reforms miss the oil vega problem in the pursuit of malfeasance or they are so severe that the disease is countered only by killing the patient. The trade in oil requires a series of balances—between paper barrel and wet barrel, buyer and seller, supply and demand. I have argued that the advent of oil vega has disrupted those balances and that the problem will become more severe. The solution is not to be found in punitive regulations that succeed only in confusing the manipulator (speculator or government) with the trader who is attempting to set an option price in an unstable environment. All market participants attempt to make the trade into their own image and likeness anyway. What is one person's hedge is another person's manipulation.

In Chapter 6, I discuss various approaches governments are likely to take in combating oil vega. These attempts, however, will constitute more exercises in finding manipulation by speculators, fraud, sinister foreign motives and other illegal or security matters. While these are valid on a number of counts, they have nothing fundamentally to do with meeting the oil volatility crisis. Oil vega is the result of how the market operates, not an attempt by a trader to circumvent it or an enemy to undermine it. The culprit here is the trading system itself, not the criminal or agent provocateur.

The market will be unable to offset the volatility because its function is to serve as an exchange mechanism, not as an impediment to pricing volatility. It is a place buyers and sellers gather; it is not a policeman. Given the profit motive in running futures contracts on the deliveries of oil consignments, the pressure is always there to maximize return. This is the case whether that futures contract is used by a speculator to make a profit off paper barrels or by either a producer or end-user to hedge on a wet-barrel transaction. Normally, one expects that the counterparty element in trading will offset the excessive potential of any swing in one direction or another. The assumption remains that the market will return to some form of structural equilibrium after each aberration. Yet the present experience is one noting a higher degree of "fat tails" than predicted.

You need to stay with me on this. Fat tails are variations in probability distributions that exhibit an unusually large kurtosis (more of the variance is a result of extremely large but infrequent deviations from the mean, as opposed to more frequent but smaller deviations[4]). Now a normal distribution would suggest that results in excess of five standard deviations,[5] a "sigma 5 event," would be exceptionally rare, while a sigma 10 event would be mathematically impossible.

With fat tails, however, there are no limits to how large the deviation may be. When this is applied to investment markets, utilizing normal distribution curves (so that the resulting visual portrayal looks like a bell-shaped curve, with a distribution as pictured in Figure 7.1) significantly underestimates the actual risk. The "tail risk" is markedly higher.[6] This is because a normal distribution approach would posit that "large sigma" events would be rare outliers, while very large ones would simply never happen, period.

Actually, however, fat tails provide for more frequent "high kurtosis" events. If investment markets are experiencing these episodes, that is, if highly volatile situations are recurring more frequently, normal distributional approaches will not provide for an adequate explanation. The way most investors approach the market most of the time will decidedly underestimate the range and degree of variation in market reaction. This is the current condition of the market.[7]

The extreme variations do not have to happen often for there to be a destabilizing impact. In fact, the fat tails approach suggests more that the extremity of the variation, how far from the mean the event extends rather than its frequency, is the determining factor. Now the relationship between extreme variations and volatility in market performance is clear.[8] Additionally, the effectiveness of oil futures hedging in the face of extreme volatility is also problematic.[9] Basic to this difficulty is the ability to price options. And that leads us to a major problem in the way futures contract trade approaches volatility.

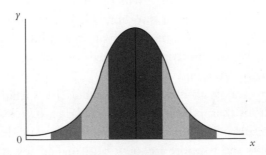

Figure 7.1   Normal Distribution Curve Standard Deviation

The very basis for setting options does not perform well in situations of high volatility. Put another way, the reason for the current discussion of fat tails and variance is to lead up to one important understanding of why pricing options under oil vega will be difficult, with those cases of high volatility making it virtually impossible. As I discuss in Chapter 1, the Black-Scholes option pricing model is the basis for determining option prices and, thereby, the use of oil futures contracts as a hedge. However, that model is predicated upon a *normal distribution*. If a fat-tail distribution emerges, Black-Scholes will underprice options appearing out of the money.[10] This flows from the fact that the normal distribution presumption would hold that such extreme variations would not occur. Yet it is what will result as volatility increases.

The limitation of the Black-Scholes model has been well understood. Until recently, the emergence of a sigma 5, 7, or higher event was considered a rarity. When it arrived, of course, significant damage was done and value destroyed. But the intervals existing between such occurrences were considered long enough to discount the impact and render the results tolerable as a necessary cost of trading.

Not any longer. Fat tails, and the volatility associated with them, are taking place more frequently.[11] As statisticians scurry to amend the model, providing a Rube Goldberg mixture of inefficient new ad hoc revisions and wishful thinking, the process itself is becoming driven by a singular, seminal, and chronic shortcoming.

The defect is tantamount to placing the determination of options using the formula in doubt during periods of high volatility. In other words, the Black-Scholes model, and the approach based upon it, cannot provide pricing guidance in the face of oil vega. Unfortunately, that is where we are heading, and fast. As a result, lacking a firm basis for setting an option price, traders will opt for the higher end of a pricing range, thereby further aggravating the situation.

The pricing that results will not simply lead to a series of options expiring without application, since the rise itself will tend to raise the price of futures. That will, in turn, heighten the spread between the paper and wet barrels, requiring the pricing of actual consignments to rise.

The pricing uncertainty is the first of two stages resulting from oil vega. The second emerges in the attempt to bring wet barrels in line with where the futures contracts are demanding pricing be pegged.

This requires the use of synthetic paper, swaps, and other derivatives to cover the actual differential as futures contracts approach expiration. Convergence becomes more difficult where the market value demanded by the paper barrel cannot be justified, according to the dynamics in the physical delivery market.

At some point, both the paper- and wet-barrel trading markets cannot sustain the increasingly artificial pricing maintenance, and another bubble bursts. However, given the pressures inherent in the futures trading system, the pursuit of profits will begin the process all over again. The cycles of boom and bust will compress, with the oil vega–destabilizing volatility occurring more frequently and with greater intensity. The new order will have its own "normal" distribution. Unfortunately, that distribution will contain more spikes of extreme variations. This is not simply volatility. This is volatility that intensifies with the ratcheting rise and ebb of oil vega. One feeds upon the other.[12]

There is no remedy for the problem of oil vega; the need is to control its effects. Even doing away with futures trading altogether would not solve the problem because some other form of derivative paper would be cut on the crude, anyway. In any event, the trade in futures contracts has provided tangible advantages in balancing out wet-barrel consignments.[13] However, the advent of crude-oil futures contracts as an asset holder per se, with the corresponding enticement to profit off the paper, has disproportionately moved the trading focus to the spread,[14] rather than the product.[15]

This is the actual target of calls to control speculation. Speculators make money (most of the time) off the paper, not the oil. If the across-the-board explosion in the derivatives markets has told us anything, it is this: leveraging, synthesizing, spreading risk, and collateralizing assets are all profitable. In normal environments, they are also useful as a liquidity management approach.[16]

To put this point in deeper relief, I will go one step further. If the attempt is to prevent (or significantly reduce) speculation, price volatility would not be offset. In some cases, it might even become more pronounced. A speculator is in this for a profit off the spread and has no interest in the underlying crude oil. She will, therefore, tend to take a position more extreme than a hedger. Taking such a position accomplishes two things: (1) facilitates trading within ranges more acceptable to those actually hedging wet product, and (2) maintains the liquidity flow necessary to accomplish the deal. This allows hedgers (those actually having an interest in the underlying crude oil) to execute trades without directly inducing upward or downward price pressure on the commodity. Otherwise, the lack of speculation could directly contribute to the increase in volatility. Removing speculators from the market would virtually guarantee that oil vega results in what those hedging wet-barrel contracts would have to do anyway.[17]

The primary reason for this is one of timing. Buy and sell orders from hedgers do not arrive on the market at the same time, nor are they usually specifying the same consignment size. In aggregate data, they appear to balance. But they do not offset each other in practice. Without a third-party source of liquidity to serve as the counterparty in a number of different transactions, interested in profiting from the deal but not interested in possessing the crude oil, market imbalances would have a far greater, and destabilizing, impact on oil prices. Speculators absorb excess demand on either side of the market.[18]

Ultimately, the key concepts involve risk—counterparty and systemic. Counterparty risk[19] relates to the effective balancing of hedged positions, the matter with which we are currently interested, while systemic risk[20] impacts upon the trading system as a whole. The latter is the primary concern of regulators, worried that speculation or rising derivative usage or both will destabilize and undermine the trading structure. The former concerns the balancing of buyer, median, and seller interests in forging contracts. There may be a way of bridging between the two in a package of regulatory changes, and I address that possibility further on in this chapter.

Normally, the standard applied in estimating counterparty risk is the degree to which each party has exposure to default, manifested by the likelihood of a counterparty's inability to meet obligations. Partially to offset this (and partially to bring under the same tent a number of related swap and derivative agreements involving the same parties), the individual arrangements between counterparties are legally combined under a master swap agreement between them.[21]

One of the key features of master swap agreements is the netting of exposures and of collateral requirements across different derivatives positions involving the same counterparties.

The volume of forward obligations required to keep the system operating will assure the continuance of futures contracts, while the addition of enhanced synthetic derivatives will progressively define the genuine spreads (and problems) of the trade. The only alternative here would be to return to the days of field-posted prices determining the contracts with a few IOCs dictating the price.

Where then are we to go? Let me dispense with the most obvious remedy first. One ultimate suggestion advanced by some pundits[22] is a significant curtailing of crude-oil use. I am personally in favor of weaning ourselves from oil, but there is also the need to be at least somewhat realistic about the immediate prospects. So let me advance two responses. First, this will not happen in the next decade and probably not for at least a decade beyond that, unless we are prepared to accept a pronounced contraction of the economy.[23] There are economic sectors where that move is advancing a bit more quickly, but the transport and petrochemical requirements preclude ending the trade any time in the near future. And then there are the expensive and enormous processing and delivery infrastructure changes to consider. This does not mean, of course, that we should avoid taking the opportunities where they exist and running with them,[24] only that we must be cognizant of the real limits involved.

Second, even in the unlikely event that futures trading would end in oil because of the reduced use of it, the energy sources utilized would develop their own trading instruments. Large futures contract markets already exist for natural gas and electricity (along with the "spark spread" bridging them), as well as thinly traded futures in a number of other alternative and renewable energy sources. Getting rid of oil, therefore, hardly gets rid of the vega problem.

We are, therefore, largely stuck with the way volatility plays in the market of futures contracts. Yet that does not mean nothing can be done about it. There are two categories of actions that can be taken in an attempt to limit the excess of the vega and try to mitigate the impact. Once again, they do not end, eliminate, or solve the problem. They do, however, provide some opportunity to attenuate it.

However, and this is important, *I do not believe either category alone will be sufficient to make much of a difference.* They need to be used in conjunction. Both in my judgment are necessary for the simple reason that the changes must revise some practices while retaining a liquidity inducement to arrest accelerating pricing volatility. These recommendations also intend to retain the position of futures contracts, maintain, with caveats, the usage of other derivatives, and resist the outright ban on speculators. The rationale for the latter is given in Chapters 5 and 6. The concern about speculative injections into the oil futures market for the purpose of manipulation has never been demonstrated, although there have been criticisms that how the studies were conducted had significant defects.[25] However, the natural gas market has had at least two instances in which suspicions ran high. One was the Enron scandal, in which the government specifically charged the company with market manipulation. Another was the Amaranth collapse.[26]

The first suggested category of action involves the federal regulatory changes likely to be coming on line to curb speculation. There was a noticeable decline in interest over such regulations when the price of oil tanked in the last quarter of 2008, indicating the connection was always with the visibility of high prices and the political pressure generated because of them. In any event, as noted already, these regulations are primarily to discourage manipulation, not to harness the volatility.

Chapter 6 discusses the essential shortcomings of government attempts to confront oil vega. Nonetheless, I propose to utilize several of the reform suggestions as a separate category to refine practice. Government regulation affords the most direct path to at least truncate the effect. Oil vega will still hit. Absent folding up the free market and having a dictation of prices from on high (and the U.S. system has never been particularly supportive of centrally controlled market planning), vega can only be channeled, not eliminated.

That being said, there is, in my judgment, a need for the following. All of these remedies are already present in one or more of the reform measures pending on Capitol Hill.

Raising Margins

The intent here is to confine the role of speculation on the market by requiring traders to put down a larger amount of money before they are allowed to engage in oil-futures contracts. A margin represents the sum a trader must deposit with an exchange to buy or sell a single futures contract. Multiple contracts require multiple deposits. The initial margin for a NYMEX contract is $9,788. Each contract is for 1,000 barrels. That means if the price is put at $85 a barrel, the contract is worth $85,000, but the trader need put down only 11.5 percent. Obviously, the higher is the level of the margin, the higher is the cost of trading.

According to views supporting this option, it would reduce the number involved, perhaps compel players to take reduced positions, and exclude altogether some of the smaller participants. Of course, it will do nothing to prevent the deeper pocketed funds from participating. Still, having fewer large participants would make more pervasive oversight more likely. The raising of margins could also be enhanced by requiring reserve accounts before a speculator could participate.

Unlike some of the Congressional approaches, this one is not designed to prevent speculation. However, it is one way to begin focusing that participation on serving as counterparty to hedging contracts, rather than operating on both sides of extended tree transactions to maximize profit.

Yet it is quite important not to move too far in this regard. One proposal in the House of Representatives, for example, prohibited anyone not having the ability to accept a wet-barrel contract (an actual delivery of crude) from being permitted to acquire futures contracts on an OTC derivatives market. One may have a dislike for the swap dealer loophole, but it does serve a purpose in stabilizing the futures trade. The requirement that a trader actually deal in crude oil consignments before she could deal with the paper barrels of future contracts essentially eliminates speculation and the advantages noted earlier.

All manner of swaps are necessary to realize a successful futures contract on an underlying shipment of oil. Proposals such as this one remove participation by all parties not intending to hold the oil. That reverts the trading system to one of hedgers on both sides, operating without an intermediary source of liquidity or incentive to see the deal work. Without speculation, the pricing dynamic would become less stable, and price volatility would be an issue every time a contract was under design.

Speculation Limits and Reducing Positions

This remedy is a corollary position to the first. Once again these suggestions in proposed legislation are attempts to curb manipulation. While I may sympathize, this is neither the problem confronted with oil vega nor the intention I have in advancing them. Quite apart from the heightened level of risk associated with accumulating large positions—the Amaranth example in future contracts or the more famous and spectacular Long-Term Capital Management (LTCM) collapse[27] coming readily to mind—accumulating large positions and/or assuming more extreme ends of a pricing or rating curve carries the danger of misestimating the pricing dynamics of the hedging contract. To accomplish a speculative move in this fashion requires multiple contracts in which the speculator needs to hold positions on both sides, peg adequate options, utilize several swaps, and (for the larger ones) enter into securitizations via synthetic paper. In short, this is no longer an exercise in establishing a position off a hedge. It is generating profit from a transaction made in the image and likeness of the speculator's profit motives.

Moving Oil Futures and Related Derivatives onto an Exchange

Allowing these instruments to remain OTC continues the problems in lack of transparency. It also perpetuates the swap dealer loophole. Now the Commodity Futures Trading Commission (CFTC)[28] has been gaining greater control over OTC transactions, but wants them moved to an exchange where the self-regulating rule of the exchange itself can take over.

One of the primary advantages of the movement to an exchange (certainly NYMEX, in the case of oil futures) is the ability to balance counterparty risk. But it would be a mistake to move all of the derivatives currently involved in futures contract transactions to the NYMEX. The primary exception here is the full range of credit swaps.

This is a problem in the House of Representatives approved Waxman-Markey bill. As it currently stands, the legislation would prevent an investor from entering into a credit default swap (CDS) unless the investor has an associated commercial business exposure to the borrower named in the CDS. That prevents third parties that do not have a commercial interest in the swap from participating in the transaction (a so-called "naked CDS").

Here is the problem: Under such a provision, a party having a commercial hedging need for CDS protection would often face difficulty finding a suitable counterparty. To add to the difficulty, the counterparty would apparently also be required to need commercial justification to hedge against a default by the same borrower.

But it hardly ends here. As Darrell Duffie observes:[29]

> Dealers themselves frequently trade with other dealers. Further, when offsetting a prior OTC derivatives position, it is common for market participants to avoid negotiating the cancellation of the original derivatives contract. Instead, a new derivatives contract that offsets the bulk of the risk of the original position is frequently arranged with the same or another dealer. As a result, dealers accumulate large OTC derivatives exposures, often with other dealers.
>
> Dealers are especially likely to be counterparties to other dealers in the case of credit default swaps (CDS), which are in essence insurance against the default of a named borrower. When a hedge fund decides to reduce a CDS position, a typical step in executing this offset is to have its original CDS position "novated" to another dealer, which then stands between the hedge fund and the original dealer by entering new back-to-back CDS positions with each. In this fashion, dealer-to-dealer CDS positions grew rapidly over the years.
>
> Based on data provided by the Depository Trust and Clearing Corporation (DTCC) in April 2009, of the current aggregate notional of about $28 trillion in credit default swaps whose terms are collected by DTCC's DerivServ Trade Information Warehouse, over $23 trillion are in the form of dealer-to-dealer positions.

These bear a familiarity with the collateralized debt obligations (CDOs) that I discuss in Chapter 4. These and other asset-backed securities may or may not be considered derivatives, according to this approach. As also previously noted, clones of these instruments are already being employed in smoothing out the edges of the paper-/wet-barrel spread in oil transactions. However, these structured approaches are not considered in the legislative proposals because they are covered by other regulations, and because they are not held under ISDA master-swap agreements.[30]

As Figure 7.2 indicates, the CDS spreads are one of the prime indicators of how serious the European debt crisis has become. As also indicated by the chart, however, the problem is also found in the United States. California, Illinois, and Michigan are slightly less likely to default than Portugal, but more likely than Italy.

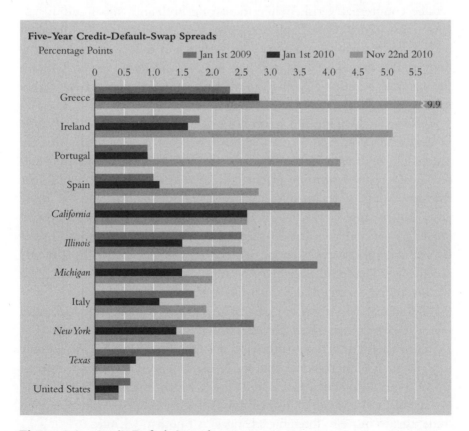

Figure 7.2 Credit Default Spreads

SOURCE: Obtained from "Not Greek Yet," *The Economist Online* (November 24, 2010), available at www.economist.com/blogs/dailychart/2010/11/credit-default-swaps_spreads.

Centralized Clearing

Several moves are underway to establish a centralized clearing system of OTC derivatives. A contract is cleared when a central "clearinghouse," operating as a clearing counterparty, steps in as a buyer positioned across from the original seller, and likewise becomes the seller to the original buyer. The original counterparties post an initial performance margin with the clearinghouse. As the position is marked to market each day, they pay or receive "variation" margin, reflecting any change in the market values of their positions.

Clearing insulates counterparties from each other, assuming that the clearinghouses are adequately structured and capitalized, and reduce counterparty risk, while increasing both individual and aggregate transparency. One could see how their usage would be preferred by legislative attempts to control derivatives and reduce market manipulation. But they would also serve in the control of oil vega by limiting the access to additional synthetic derivatives in OTC transactions determining the effective structure of the oil contract.

However, clearing is a relatively expensive process. For each type of derivatives contract, a clearinghouse must set up standard terms for acceptable contracts, determine how to calculate initial margins and set up a way to determine pricing for cleared derivatives. Systems for the processing of trades and collateral are needed. Because of these costs and because of the requirement for daily or even more frequent pricing, it only makes sense to clear types of derivatives that are relatively "commoditized," that is, widely and heavily traded in a standard form.[31] That could certainly be done with oil futures, although it would still take some doing to structure the required plumbing.

Additional provisions are part of the primary approaches currently under discussion that either concern matters divorced from oil trading or are approaches I would not support in the case of oil futures. One of these is a persistent Congressional attempt to limit or prohibit foreign traders. This is both detrimental to the trade itself, which is genuinely global and not specific to New York, and will run the decided risk of prompting the trade itself to move to foreign exchanges, as I note in Chapter 6.

In addition to this category of reform proposals coming from current legislation, there is a second category. This considers the sourcing for liquidity allowing the trades to take place. By introducing sources other than speculators or wet-barrel parties, and having that liquidity base serve to temper volatility, here is an opportunity to channel oil vega and lessen its impact.

I have in mind two such sources.

Using the SPR as Collateral in Securitizing Paper

The first involves using the U.S. Strategic Petroleum Reserve (SPR) as collateral to temper high volatility swings reflected in particularly viscous oil vega swings. The SPR[32] was set up after the Arab oil embargo of 1973–1974 and has a capacity of 727 million barrels, all but a few million barrels being used. There will never again be an embargo, meaning the rationale is no longer relevant. Nonetheless, there are a number of national security reasons why the SPR is still a valid idea.

Upon occasion, presidents have released volume from the SPR to relieve pricing pressure on the domestic market (with mixed results). The advantage of a national reserve would obviously disappear if the volume contained within it were released on the market. But that volume could be used as discounted collateral for securitized paper used in trade without the oil ever actually being put on the market.

In principle, this would be no different from the collateralization valuing process used in developing syndicated loan packages for oil projects.[33] There as well, oil in the ground is used to structure finance. And, as we know from the discussion in Chapter 3, that oil can provide greater value in certain situations if it is not extracted. A discounted estimation is employed to determine the forward value of the oil in reserve to determine the profitability of drilling now or drilling later.

The SPR can be applied on the same principle. This does mean government involvement in the oil market as a third-party source of credit to facilitate deals at more transparent and stable prices. Serving as a counterparty to both buyer and seller, perhaps associated with clearinghouse procedures, what amounts to a U.S. Oil Stabilization Fund could offset some of oil vega. The premise here is the same as sovereign wealth funds (SWFs), as Table 6.1 outlines, along with the corresponding discussion in Chapter 6. As I have already noted, those

SWFs that are essentially oil funds serve two purposes—either as stabilization funds or as savings funds. The United States would use the SPF as our example of a stabilization fund.

As rentier countries use their proceeds from extraction to offset problems in their domestic budgets, so we should use our oil in the ground to do the same. One again, this is not going to eliminate oil vega. But it might allow the American market to mitigate its impact.

For those purists out there who would claim this is a government involvement in private market matters, I would agree . . . if we were having this discussion several years ago. But after bailouts, and the attendant government ownership of banks, insurance companies, and, for a time, even General Motors, I would suggest that the question has already been put and answered.

Retail Investors

Liquidity to offset oil vega can also be provided in another way. Hundreds of thousands of individual investors provide liquidity to markets every trading day. Unlike the perspective of the speculator of the hedger, private retail investors have a fundamentally different view. That view is longer term, seeking profit but also stability. Most sectors of the stock market rely upon the retail investor to even out trading volatility. The oil futures upon which oil vega is predicated have only recently begun to feel the effect of private, small volume, aggregate retail investment. There needed to be a vehicle for this to increase.

That vehicle emerged with the introduction of exchange traded funds (ETFs) allowing individuals to invest in the spot price of crude oil as well as the movement in futures contracts, a move advanced in closed-ended funds also targeting the spread between paper and wet barrels. Retail investment is beginning to move more aggregate liquidity into the oil market. There are now dozens of ETFs available, with the United States Oil Fund (USO) the best known and most liquid.[34] Figure 7.3 depicts USO 2010 performance. However, the rising sophistication of both avenues and investors will increase the access.

This can temper volatility. But the volume would need to increase well beyond current levels. Nonetheless, I believe that this is an underappreciated dimension to what ETFs and exchange traded notes

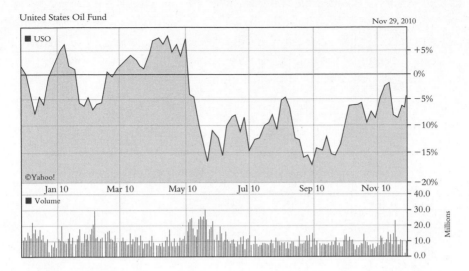

Figure 7.3 USO 2010 Performance

SOURCE: http://finance.yahoo.com/q/bc?t=1y&s=USO&l=on&z=l&q=l&c=&c=%5EGSPC; retrieved November 24, 2010.

(ETNs) bring to the party. My three investment services—*Oil and Energy Investor, Energy Advantage,* and *The Energy Inner Circle*—are premised on the rising impact of private investors in moving liquidity into the oil markets.[35]

One thing is certain. It is going to be a bumpy ride, as oil vega continues to pressure the market and negotiating around spiking volatility becomes a more common and necessary development.

This is a competition that pervades virtually everything else. And it levels both the large and the small. It is the energy equivalent of the African proverb that Thomas Friedman likes so much.

> Every morning in Africa, a gazelle wakes up.
> It knows it must run faster than the fastest lion or it will be killed.
> Every morning a lion wakes up.
> It knows it must outrun the slowest gazelle or it will starve to death.
> It doesn't matter whether you are a lion or a gazelle.
> When the sun comes up, you better start running.[36]

Appendix A

World Proved Oil Reserves (Billion Barrels)

Country/Region	BP Statistical Review	Oil & Gas Journal	World Oil
	12/31/2007	1/1/2009	12/31/2007
Bermuda	0	0	0
Canada	27.664	178.092	25.157
Greenland	0	0	0
Mexico	12.187	10.501	11.061
Saint Pierre and Miquelon	0	0	0
United States	30.460	21.317	21.317
North America	70.311	209.910	57.535
Antarctica	0	0	0
Antigua and Barbuda	0	0	0
Argentina	2.587	2.616	2.650
Aruba	0	0	0
Bahamas, The	0	0	0
Barbados	Not Separately Reported	0.002	Not Separately Reported
Belize	0	0.007	0
Bolivia	Not Separately Reported	0.465	0.459
Brazil	12.624	12.624	12.539
Cayman Islands	0	0	0
Chile	Not Separately Reported	0.150	0.009
Colombia	1.510	1.355	1.450
Costa Rica	0	0	0
Cuba	Not Separately Reported	0.124	0.712
Dominica	0	0	0
Dominican Republic	0	0	0
Ecuador	4.269	4.660	4.780
El Salvador	0	0	0

Country/Region	BP Statistical Review	Oil & Gas Journal	World Oil
Falkland Islands (Islas Malvinas)	0	0	0
French Guiana	0	0	0
Grenada	0	0	0
Guadeloupe	0	0	0
Guatemala	Not Separately Reported	0.083	Not Separately Reported
Guyana	0	0	0
Haiti	0	0	0
Honduras	0	0	0
Jamaica	0	0	0
Martinique	0	0	0
Montserrat	0	0	0
Netherlands Antilles	0	0	0
Nicaragua	0	0	0
Panama	0	0	0
Paraguay	0	0	0
Peru	1.097	0.416	0.419
Puerto Rico	0	0	0
Saint Kitts and Nevis	0	0	0
Saint Lucia	0	0	0
Saint Vincent/Grenadines	0	0	0
Suriname	Not Separately Reported	0.080	Not Separately Reported
Trinidad and Tobago	0.794	0.728	0.595
Turks and Caicos Islands	0	0	0
Uruguay	0	0	0
Venezuela	87.035	99.377	81.000
Virgin Islands, U.S.	0	0	0
Virgin Islands, British	0	0	0
Other—Country Not Specified	1.295	—	0.180

(continued)

Country/Region	BP Statistical Review	Oil & Gas Journal	World Oil
Central & South America	111.211	122.687	104.793
Albania	Not Separately Reported	0.199	0.200
Austria	Not Separately Reported	0.050	0.079
Belgium	0	0	0
Bosnia and Herzegovina	0	0	0
Bulgaria	Not Separately Reported	0.015	0.002
Croatia	Not Separately Reported	0.079	0.079
Cyprus	0	0	0
Czech Republic	Not Separately Reported	0.015	0.022
Denmark	1.113	1.060	1.114
Faroe Islands	0	0	0
Finland	0	0	0
Former Czechoslovakia	—	—	—
Former Serbia and Montenegro	—	—	—
Former Yugoslavia	—	—	—
France	Not Separately Reported	0.103	0.119
Germany	Not Separately Reported	0.276	0.150
Germany, East	—	—	—
Germany, West	—	—	—
Gibraltar	0	0	0
Greece	Not Separately Reported	0.010	Not Separately Reported
Hungary	Not Separately Reported	0.020	0.057

Country/Region	BP Statistical Review	Oil & Gas Journal	World Oil
Iceland	0	0	0
Ireland	Not Separately Reported	0	Not Separately Reported
Italy	0.781	0.407	0.442
Luxembourg	0	0	0
Macedonia	0	0	0
Malta	0	0	0
Netherlands	Not Separately Reported	0.100	0.230
Norway	8.172	6.680	6.693
Poland	Not Separately Reported	0.096	0.155
Portugal	0	0	0
Romania	0.478	0.600	0.480
Serbia	Not Separately Reported	0.078	Not Separately Reported
Slovakia	Not Separately Reported	0.009	Not Separately Reported
Slovenia	0	0	0
Spain	Not Separately Reported	0.150	Not Separately Reported
Sweden	0	0	0
Switzerland	0	0	0
Turkey	Not Separately Reported	0.300	0.261
United Kingdom	3.593	3.410	3.592
Other—Country Not Specified	1.434	—	0.126
Europe	15.570	13.657	13.801
Armenia	0	0	Not Separately Reported

(continued)

Country/Region	BP Statistical Review	Oil & Gas Journal	World Oil
Azerbaijan	7.000	7.000	Not Separately Reported
Belarus	Not Separately Reported	0.198	Not Separately Reported
Estonia	Not Separately Reported	Not Separately Reported	Not Separately Reported
Former U.S.S.R.	—	—	—
Georgia	Not Separately Reported	0.035	Not Separately Reported
Kazakhstan	39.828	30.000	Not Separately Reported
Kyrgyzstan	Not Separately Reported	0.040	Not Separately Reported
Latvia	Not Separately Reported	Not Separately Reported	Not Separately Reported
Lithuania	Not Separately Reported	0.012	Not Separately Reported
Moldova	Not Separately Reported	Not Separately Reported	Not Separately Reported
Russia	79.432	60.000	76.000
Tajikistan	Not Separately Reported	0.012	Not Separately Reported
Turkmenistan	0.600	0.600	Not Separately Reported
Ukraine	Not Separately Reported	0.395	Not Separately Reported
Uzbekistan	0.594	0.594	Not Separately Reported
Other—Country Not Specified	0.692	—	50.000
Eurasia	128.146	98.886	126.000
Bahrain	Not Separately Reported	0.125	Not Separately Reported

Country/Region	BP Statistical Review	Oil & Gas Journal	World Oil
Iran	138.400	136.150	137.000
Iraq	115.000	115.000	126.000
Israel	Not Separately Reported	0.002	Not Separately Reported
Jordan	Not Separately Reported	0.001	Not Separately Reported
Kuwait[6]	101.500	104.000	99.425
Lebanon	0	0	0
Oman	5.572	5.500	5.700
Qatar	27.436	15.210	20.000
Saudi Arabia[6]	264.209	266.710	264.825
Syria	2.500	2.500	2.900
United Arab Emirates	97.800	97.800	68.105
Yemen	2.780	3.000	2.670
Other—Country Not Specified	0.128	—	0.689
Middle East	755.325	745.998	727.314
Algeria	12.270	12.200	11.900
Angola	9.035	9.040	9.500
Benin	Not Separately Reported	0.008	Not Separately Reported
Botswana	0	0	0
Burkina Faso	0	0	0
Burundi	0	0	0
Cameroon	Not Separately Reported	0.200	Not Separately Reported
Cape Verde	0	0	0
Central African Republic	0	0	0
Chad	0.900	1.500	0
Comoros	0	0	0
Congo (Brazzaville)	1.940	1.600	1.940

(continued)

Country/Region	BP Statistical Review	Oil & Gas Journal	World Oil
Congo (Kinshasa)	Not Separately Reported	0.180	Not Separately Reported
Cote d'Ivoire (Ivory Coast)	Not Separately Reported	0.100	Not Separately Reported
Djibouti	0	0	0
Egypt	4.070	3.700	3.700
Equatorial Guinea	1.755	1.100	1.705
Eritrea	0	0	0
Ethiopia	Not Separately Reported	0.0004	Not Separately Reported
Gabon	1.995	2.000	3.184
Gambia, The	0	0	0
Ghana	Not Separately Reported	0.015	Not Separately Reported
Guinea	0	0	0
Guinea-Bissau	0	0	0
Kenya	0	0	0
Lesotho	0	0	0
Liberia	0	0	0
Libya	41.464	43.660	36.500
Madagascar	0	0	Not Separately Reported
Malawi	0	0	0
Mali	0	0	0
Mauritania	0	0.100	0
Mauritius	0	0	0
Morocco	Not Separately Reported	0.001	Not Separately Reported
Mozambique	0	0	0
Namibia	0	0	0
Niger	0	0	0
Nigeria	36.220	36.220	37.200

Country/Region	BP Statistical Review	Oil & Gas Journal	World Oil
Reunion	0	0	0
Rwanda	0	0	Not Separately Reported
Saint Helena	0	0	0
Sao Tome and Principe	0	0	0
Senegal	0	0	0
Seychelles	0	0	0
Sierra Leone	0	0	0
Somalia	0	0	Not Separately Reported
South Africa	Not Separately Reported	0.015	Not Separately Reported
Sudan	6.615	5.000	6.700
Swaziland	0	0	0
Tanzania	0	0	Not Separately Reported
Togo	0	0	0
Tunisia	0.596	0.425	0.601
Uganda	0	0	0
Western Sahara	0	0	0
Zambia	0	0	0
Zimbabwe	0	0	0
Other—Country Not Specified	0.622	—	1.786
Africa	117.482	117.064	114.716
Afghanistan	0	0	Not Separately Reported
American Samoa	0	0	0
Australia	4.158	1.500	4.150
Bangladesh	Not Separately Reported	0.028	Not Separately Reported

(continued)

Country/Region	BP Statistical Review	Oil & Gas Journal	World Oil
Bhutan	0	0	0
Brunei	1.200	1.100	1.078
Burma (Myanmar)	Not Separately Reported	0.050	0.188
Cambodia	0	0	0
China	15.493	16.000	18.052
Cook Islands	0	0	0
Fiji	0	0	0
French Polynesia	0	0	0
Guam	0	0	0
Hawaiian Trade Zone	—	—	—
Hong Kong	0	0	0
India	5.459	5.625	4.042
Indonesia	4.370	3.990	4.509
Japan	Not Separately Reported	0.044	Not Separately Reported
Kiribati	0	0	0
Korea, North	0	0	0
Korea, South	0	0	0
Laos	0	0	0
Macau	0	0	0
Malaysia	5.357	4.000	5.458
Maldives	0	0	0
Mongolia	0	0	0
Nauru	0	0	0
Nepal	0	0	0
New Caledonia	0	0	0
New Zealand	Not Separately Reported	0.060	0.148
Niue	0	0	0

Country/Region	BP Statistical Review	Oil & Gas Journal	World Oil
Pakistan	Not Separately Reported	0.339	0.310
Papua New Guinea	Not Separately Reported	0.088	0.200
Philippines	Not Separately Reported	0.139	0.118
Samoa	0	0	0
Singapore	0	0	0
Solomon Islands	0	0	0
Sri Lanka	0	0	0
Taiwan	Not Separately Reported	0.002	Not Separately Reported
Thailand	0.461	0.441	0.440
Timor-Leste (East Timor)	0	0	0
Tonga	0	0	0
U.S. Pacific Islands	0	0	0
Vanuatu	0	0	0
Vietnam	3.410	0.600	1.250
Wake Island	0	0	0
Other—Country Not Specified	0.939	—	0.106
Asia and Oceania	40.847	34.006	40.049
World Total	*1,238.892*	*1,342.207*	*1,184.208*

SOURCE: Energy Information Administration, posted March 3, 2009; available at www.eia.doe.gov/emeu/international/reserves.html.

Appendix B

Exxon CARM per Gallon (January 3, 2000 to December 31, 2007)

Date	Distribution Margin	Crude Oil Cost	Processing Margin	State/ Local Sales Tax	State Excise Tax	Federal Excise Tax	Retail Price
1/3/2000	$0.08	$0.58	$0.24	$0.10	$0.18	$0.18	$1.36
1/10/2000	$0.07	$0.59	$0.23	$0.10	$0.18	$0.18	$1.35
1/17/2000	$0.08	$0.62	$0.18	$0.10	$0.18	$0.18	$1.35
1/24/2000	$0.07	$0.66	$0.15	$0.10	$0.18	$0.18	$1.35
1/31/2000	$0.06	$0.62	$0.23	$0.10	$0.18	$0.18	$1.38
2/7/2000	$0.06	$0.62	$0.24	$0.10	$0.18	$0.18	$1.36
2/14/2000	$0.04	$0.68	$0.21	$0.10	$0.18	$0.18	$1.40
2/21/2000	$0.00	$0.66	$0.31	$0.11	$0.18	$0.18	$1.44
2/28/2000	−$0.04	$0.68	$0.40	$0.11	$0.18	$0.18	$1.52
3/6/2000	−$0.04	$0.71	$0.47	$0.12	$0.18	$0.18	$1.63
3/13/2000	−$0.02	$0.72	$0.55	$0.13	$0.18	$0.18	$1.74
3/20/2000	$0.02	$0.62	$0.66	$0.13	$0.18	$0.18	$1.79
3/27/2000	$0.17	$0.62	$0.50	$0.13	$0.18	$0.18	$1.79
4/3/2000	$0.17	$0.58	$0.52	$0.13	$0.18	$0.18	$1.77
4/10/2000	$0.25	$0.55	$0.45	$0.13	$0.18	$0.18	$1.75
4/17/2000	$0.32	$0.57	$0.35	$0.13	$0.18	$0.18	$1.74
4/24/2000	$0.30	$0.58	$0.32	$0.13	$0.18	$0.18	$1.70
5/1/2000	$0.23	$0.58	$0.38	$0.12	$0.18	$0.18	$1.67
5/8/2000	$0.15	$0.63	$0.40	$0.12	$0.18	$0.18	$1.66
5/15/2000	$0.14	$0.67	$0.33	$0.12	$0.18	$0.18	$1.63
5/22/2000	$0.10	$0.64	$0.39	$0.12	$0.18	$0.18	$1.61
5/29/2000	$0.08	$0.67	$0.38	$0.12	$0.18	$0.18	$1.61
6/5/2000	$0.08	$0.65	$0.40	$0.12	$0.18	$0.18	$1.61
6/12/2000	$0.07	$0.70	$0.38	$0.12	$0.18	$0.18	$1.61
6/19/2000	$0.06	$0.70	$0.37	$0.12	$0.18	$0.18	$1.62
6/26/2000	$0.02	$0.77	$0.36	$0.12	$0.18	$0.18	$1.64
7/3/2000	−$0.02	$0.68	$0.57	$0.13	$0.18	$0.18	$1.71
7/10/2000	$0.00	$0.66	$0.58	$0.13	$0.18	$0.18	$1.73
7/17/2000	$0.07	$0.69	$0.47	$0.13	$0.18	$0.18	$1.72
7/24/2000	$0.12	$0.62	$0.49	$0.13	$0.18	$0.18	$1.71
7/31/2000	$0.11	$0.60	$0.48	$0.12	$0.18	$0.18	$1.68
8/7/2000	$0.05	$0.64	$0.49	$0.12	$0.18	$0.18	$1.67
8/14/2000	−$0.05	$0.72	$0.51	$0.12	$0.18	$0.18	$1.67
8/21/2000	−$0.03	$0.72	$0.49	$0.12	$0.18	$0.18	$1.67
8/28/2000	−$0.07	$0.74	$0.54	$0.13	$0.18	$0.18	$1.70
9/5/2000	−$0.15	$0.77	$0.67	$0.13	$0.18	$0.18	$1.79
9/11/2000	−$0.11	$0.80	$0.66	$0.14	$0.18	$0.18	$1.85
9/18/2000	$0.05	$0.84	$0.44	$0.14	$0.18	$0.18	$1.83
9/25/2000	$0.08	$0.70	$0.58	$0.14	$0.18	$0.18	$1.83
10/2/2000	$0.09	$0.73	$0.52	$0.14	$0.18	$0.18	$1.83

Date	Distribution Margin	Crude Oil Cost	Processing Margin	State/ Local Sales Tax	State Excise Tax	Federal Excise Tax	Retail Price
10/9/2000	$0.14	$0.72	$0.46	$0.14	$0.18	$0.18	$1.83
10/16/2000	$0.07	$0.75	$0.49	$0.13	$0.18	$0.18	$1.81
10/23/2000	$0.06	$0.77	$0.47	$0.13	$0.18	$0.18	$1.80
10/30/2000	$0.01	$0.75	$0.54	$0.13	$0.18	$0.18	$1.80
11/6/2000	−$0.02	$0.74	$0.57	$0.13	$0.18	$0.18	$1.79
11/13/2000	$0.10	$0.78	$0.40	$0.13	$0.18	$0.18	$1.78
11/20/2000	$0.17	$0.81	$0.28	$0.13	$0.18	$0.18	$1.75
11/27/2000	$0.15	$0.80	$0.30	$0.13	$0.18	$0.18	$1.74
12/4/2000	$0.16	$0.67	$0.40	$0.13	$0.18	$0.18	$1.72
12/11/2000	$0.28	$0.59	$0.36	$0.13	$0.18	$0.18	$1.69
12/18/2000	$0.26	$0.59	$0.33	$0.12	$0.18	$0.18	$1.68
12/26/2000	$0.23	$0.59	$0.44	$0.12	$0.18	$0.18	$1.65
1/2/2001	$0.17	$0.51	$0.46	$0.12	$0.18	$0.18	$1.63
1/8/2001	$0.15	$0.52	$0.47	$0.12	$0.18	$0.18	$1.63
1/15/2001	$0.18	$0.60	$0.34	$0.12	$0.18	$0.18	$1.60
1/22/2001	$0.14	$0.65	$0.31	$0.12	$0.18	$0.18	$1.58
1/29/2001	$0.12	$0.59	$0.38	$0.12	$0.18	$0.18	$1.57
2/5/2001	$0.08	$0.64	$0.39	$0.12	$0.18	$0.18	$1.59
2/12/2001	$0.03	$0.65	$0.48	$0.12	$0.18	$0.18	$1.64
2/19/2001	$0.03	$0.61	$0.53	$0.12	$0.18	$0.18	$1.66
2/26/2001	$0.00	$0.60	$0.57	$0.12	$0.18	$0.18	$1.66
3/5/2001	$0.01	$0.62	$0.58	$0.13	$0.18	$0.18	$1.70
3/12/2001	$0.01	$0.54	$0.67	$0.13	$0.18	$0.18	$1.70
3/19/2001	$0.03	$0.56	$0.61	$0.13	$0.18	$0.18	$1.70
3/26/2001	−$0.01	$0.59	$0.61	$0.12	$0.18	$0.18	$1.68
4/2/2001	−$0.05	$0.55	$0.72	$0.13	$0.18	$0.18	$1.72
4/9/2001	−$0.09	$0.61	$0.75	$0.13	$0.18	$0.18	$1.75
4/16/2001	−$0.09	$0.64	$0.75	$0.13	$0.18	$0.18	$1.80
4/23/2001	−$0.03	$0.60	$0.76	$0.14	$0.18	$0.18	$1.83
4/30/2001	−$0.02	$0.63	$0.75	$0.14	$0.18	$0.18	$1.87
5/7/2001	$0.08	$0.62	$0.74	$0.14	$0.18	$0.18	$1.94
5/14/2001	$0.16	$0.64	$0.65	$0.14	$0.18	$0.18	$1.95
5/21/2001	$0.16	$0.64	$0.65	$0.14	$0.18	$0.18	$1.95
5/28/2001	$0.20	$0.64	$0.60	$0.14	$0.18	$0.18	$1.95
6/4/2001	$0.20	$0.63	$0.60	$0.14	$0.18	$0.18	$1.93
6/11/2011	$0.32	$0.65	$0.47	$0.14	$0.18	$0.18	$1.95
6/18/2001	$0.35	$0.62	$0.46	$0.14	$0.18	$0.18	$1.93
6/25/2001	$0.38	$0.60	$0.42	$0.14	$0.18	$0.18	$1.90
7/2/2001	$0.41	$0.58	$0.37	$0.14	$0.18	$0.18	$1.86

(continued)

Date	Distribution Margin	Crude Oil Cost	Processing Margin	State / Local Sales Tax	State Excise Tax	Federal Excise Tax	Retail Price
7/9/2001	$0.42	$0.62	$0.29	$0.14	$0.18	$0.18	$1.82
7/16/2001	$0.44	$0.57	$0.26	$0.13	$0.18	$0.18	$1.78
7/23/2001	$0.51	$0.57	$0.15	$0.13	$0.18	$0.18	$1.72
7/30/2001	$0.34	$0.57	$0.27	$0.12	$0.18	$0.18	$1.67
8/6/2001	$0.27	$0.58	$0.28	$0.12	$0.18	$0.18	$1.62
8/13/2001	$0.19	$0.59	$0.31	$0.12	$0.18	$0.18	$1.56
8/20/2001	$0.08	$0.57	$0.40	$0.11	$0.18	$0.18	$1.52
8/27/2001	$0.06	$0.56	$0.35	$0.11	$0.18	$0.18	$1.51
9/3/2001	−$0.12	$0.57	$0.71	$0.12	$0.18	$0.18	$1.64
9/10/2001	−$0.02	$0.59	$0.62	$0.12	$0.18	$0.18	$1.68
9/17/2001	$0.00	$0.61	$0.57	$0.12	$0.18	$0.18	$1.67
9/24/2001	$0.09	$0.44	$0.64	$0.12	$0.18	$0.18	$1.66
10/1/2001	$0.19	$0.49	$0.46	$0.12	$0.18	$0.18	$1.62
10/8/2001	$0.18	$0.47	$0.44	$0.12	$0.18	$0.18	$1.56
10/15/2001	$0.19	$0.47	$0.41	$0.11	$0.18	$0.18	$1.55
10/22/2001	$0.12	$0.46	$0.45	$0.11	$0.18	$0.18	$1.51
10/29/2001	$0.06	$0.47	$0.47	$0.11	$0.18	$0.18	$1.47
11/5/2001	$0.09	$0.43	$0.45	$0.11	$0.18	$0.18	$1.42
11/12/2001	$0.14	$0.45	$0.33	$0.10	$0.18	$0.18	$1.38
11/19/2001	$0.18	$0.37	$0.33	$0.10	$0.18	$0.18	$1.34
11/26/2001	$0.17	$0.39	$0.27	$0.10	$0.18	$0.18	$1.29
12/3/2001	$0.14	$0.42	$0.23	$0.08	$0.18	$0.18	$1.24
12/10/2001	$0.14	$0.38	$0.23	$0.09	$0.18	$0.18	$1.20
12/17/2001	$0.08	$0.39	$0.22	$0.08	$0.18	$0.18	$1.14
12/24/2001	$0.00	$0.44	$0.23	$0.08	$0.18	$0.18	$1.11
12/31/2001	−$0.07	$0.41	$0.31	$0.08	$0.18	$0.18	$1.10
1/7/2002	−$0.05	$0.45	$0.28	$0.08	$0.18	$0.18	$1.13
1/14/2002	$0.03	$0.40	$0.30	$0.09	$0.18	$0.18	$1.18
1/21/2002	$0.08	$0.39	$0.30	$0.09	$0.18	$0.18	$1.21
1/28/2002	$0.00	$0.43	$0.34	$0.09	$0.18	$0.18	$1.22
2/4/2002	$0.01	$0.43	$0.35	$0.09	$0.18	$0.18	$1.25
2/11/2002	$0.01	$0.48	$0.31	$0.09	$0.18	$0.18	$1.25
2/19/2002	$0.01	$0.45	$0.38	$0.10	$0.18	$0.18	$1.29
2/25/2002	$0.02	$0.45	$0.37	$0.10	$0.18	$0.18	$1.30
3/4/2002	$0.00	$0.50	$0.37	$0.10	$0.18	$0.18	$1.33
3/11/2002	−$0.02	$0.54	$0.47	$0.11	$0.18	$0.18	$1.45
3/18/2002	−$0.03	$0.58	$0.50	$0.11	$0.18	$0.18	$1.50
3/25/2002	$0.01	$0.55	$0.53	$0.12	$0.18	$0.18	$1.56
4/1/2002	$0.05	$0.61	$0.45	$0.12	$0.18	$0.18	$1.59
4/8/2002	$0.07	$0.60	$0.47	$0.12	$0.18	$0.18	$1.62

Date	Distribution Margin	Crude Oil Cost	Processing Margin	State/ Local Sales Tax	State Excise Tax	Federal Excise Tax	Retail Price
4/15/2002	$0.13	$0.56	$0.45	$0.12	$0.18	$0.18	$1.62
4/22/2002	$0.10	$0.62	$0.40	$0.12	$0.18	$0.18	$1.61
4/29/2002	$0.11	$0.63	$0.39	$0.12	$0.18	$0.18	$1.61
5/6/2002	$0.12	$0.60	$0.39	$0.12	$0.18	$0.18	$1.59
5/13/2002	$0.11	$0.65	$0.32	$0.12	$0.18	$0.18	$1.57
5/20/2002	$0.09	$0.64	$0.35	$0.12	$0.18	$0.18	$1.56
5/27/2002	$0.06	$0.57	$0.44	$0.12	$0.18	$0.18	$1.55
6/3/2002	$0.17	$0.56	$0.45	$0.12	$0.18	$0.18	$1.56
6/10/2002	$0.04	$0.54	$0.50	$0.12	$0.18	$0.18	$1.56
6/17/2002	$0.01	$0.59	$0.51	$0.12	$0.18	$0.18	$1.60
6/24/2002	$0.08	$0.60	$0.45	$0.12	$0.18	$0.18	$1.62
7/1/2002	$0.08	$0.61	$0.44	$0.12	$0.18	$0.18	$1.62
7/8/2002	$0.07	$0.60	$0.46	$0.12	$0.18	$0.18	$1.61
7/15/2002	$0.07	$0.62	$0.43	$0.12	$0.18	$0.18	$1.60
7/22/2002	$0.06	$0.61	$0.44	$0.12	$0.18	$0.18	$1.59
7/29/2002	$0.04	$0.61	$0.45	$0.12	$0.18	$0.18	$1.58
8/5/2002	$0.06	$0.61	$0.45	$0.12	$0.18	$0.18	$1.59
8/12/2002	$0.04	$0.64	$0.43	$0.12	$0.18	$0.18	$1.59
8/19/2002	$0.02	$0.69	$0.39	$0.12	$0.18	$0.18	$1.58
8/26/2002	$0.04	$0.67	$0.40	$0.12	$0.18	$0.18	$1.59
9/2/2002	$0.03	$0.64	$0.45	$0.12	$0.18	$0.18	$1.60
9/9/2002	$0.01	$0.69	$0.42	$0.12	$0.18	$0.18	$1.59
9/16/2002	$0.00	$0.68	$0.42	$0.12	$0.18	$0.18	$1.58
9/23/2002	$0.00	$0.71	$0.39	$0.12	$0.18	$0.18	$1.57
9/30/2002	−$0.01	$0.70	$0.39	$0.12	$0.18	$0.18	$1.56
10/7/2002	−$0.02	$0.68	$0.40	$0.11	$0.18	$0.18	$1.55
10/14/2002	−$0.03	$0.68	$0.41	$0.11	$0.18	$0.18	$1.53
10/21/2002	−$0.04	$0.64	$0.45	$0.11	$0.18	$0.18	$1.52
10/28/2002	−$0.05	$0.81	$0.49	$0.11	$0.18	$0.18	$1.52
11/4/2002	−$0.01	$0.60	$0.49	$0.12	$0.18	$0.18	$1.56
11/11/2002	$0.02	$0.58	$0.51	$0.12	$0.18	$0.18	$1.59
11/18/2002	$0.04	$0.60	$0.47	$0.12	$0.18	$0.18	$1.59
11/25/2002	$0.08	$0.61	$0.40	$0.12	$0.18	$0.18	$1.57
12/2/2002	$0.13	$0.61	$0.34	$0.12	$0.18	$0.18	$1.56
12/9/2002	$0.15	$0.61	$0.30	$0.11	$0.18	$0.18	$1.54
12/16/2002	$0.10	$0.66	$0.26	$0.11	$0.18	$0.18	$1.53
12/23/2002	$0.09	$0.73	$0.23	$0.11	$0.18	$0.18	$1.52
12/30/2002	$0.06	$0.72	$0.28	$0.11	$0.18	$0.18	$1.53
1/6/2003	$0.09	$0.73	$0.27	$0.12	$0.18	$0.18	$1.58

(continued)

Date	Distribution Margin	Crude Oil Cost	Processing Margin	State/Local Sales Tax	State Excise Tax	Federal Excise Tax	Retail Price
1/13/2003	$0.09	$0.74	$0.28	$0.12	$0.18	$0.18	$1.59
1/20/2003	$0.10	$0.80	$0.25	$0.12	$0.18	$0.18	$1.63
1/27/2003	$0.10	$0.74	$0.32	$0.12	$0.18	$0.18	$1.65
2/3/2003	$0.09	$0.76	$0.35	$0.12	$0.18	$0.18	$1.68
2/10/2003	$0.07	$0.81	$0.38	$0.13	$0.18	$0.18	$1.75
2/17/2003	$0.16	$0.87	$0.33	$0.14	$0.18	$0.18	$1.86
2/24/2003	$0.18	$0.88	$0.36	$0.14	$0.18	$0.18	$1.92
3/3/2003	$0.14	$0.85	$0.51	$0.15	$0.18	$0.18	$2.01
3/10/2003	$0.13	$0.88	$0.55	$0.15	$0.18	$0.18	$2.08
3/17/2003	$0.15	$0.82	$0.65	$0.16	$0.18	$0.18	$2.14
3/24/2003	$0.20	$0.63	$0.79	$0.16	$0.18	$0.18	$2.14
3/31/2003	$0.26	$0.69	$0.66	$0.16	$0.18	$0.18	$2.13
4/7/2003	$0.29	$0.60	$0.70	$0.16	$0.18	$0.18	$2.11
4/14/2003	$0.29	$0.62	$0.66	$0.15	$0.18	$0.18	$2.08
4/21/2003	$0.29	$0.67	$0.57	$0.15	$0.18	$0.18	$2.01
4/28/2003	$0.25	$0.54	$0.67	$0.15	$0.18	$0.18	$1.98
5/5/2003	$0.26	$0.58	$0.57	$0.14	$0.18	$0.18	$1.93
5/12/2003	$0.33	$0.60	$0.43	$0.14	$0.18	$0.18	$1.87
5/19/2003	$0.28	$0.64	$0.39	$0.13	$0.18	$0.18	$1.81
5/28/2003	$0.23	$0.66	$0.38	$0.13	$0.18	$0.18	$1.76
6/2/2003	$0.20	$0.70	$0.34	$0.13	$0.18	$0.18	$1.73
6/9/2003	$0.14	$0.72	$0.34	$0.13	$0.18	$0.18	$1.70
6/16/2003	$0.05	$0.71	$0.53	$0.13	$0.18	$0.18	$1.79
6/23/2003	$0.03	$0.71	$0.57	$0.13	$0.18	$0.18	$1.80
6/30/2003	$0.05	$0.88	$0.57	$0.13	$0.18	$0.18	$1.80
7/7/2003	$0.08	$0.68	$0.53	$0.13	$0.18	$0.18	$1.79
7/14/2003	$0.11	$0.71	$0.44	$0.13	$0.18	$0.18	$1.76
7/21/2003	$0.11	$0.72	$0.40	$0.13	$0.18	$0.18	$1.73
7/28/2003	$0.11	$0.68	$0.43	$0.13	$0.18	$0.18	$1.71
8/4/2003	$0.08	$0.72	$0.41	$0.13	$0.18	$0.18	$1.70
8/11/2003	$0.07	$0.73	$0.45	$0.13	$0.18	$0.18	$1.74
8/18/2003	$0.00	$0.70	$0.71	$0.14	$0.18	$0.18	$1.92
8/25/2003	$0.05	$0.72	$0.81	$0.16	$0.18	$0.18	$2.10
9/1/2003	$0.16	$0.72	$0.71	$0.16	$0.18	$0.18	$2.10
9/8/2003	$0.22	$0.66	$0.69	$0.15	$0.18	$0.18	$2.08
9/15/2003	$0.26	$0.64	$0.58	$0.15	$0.18	$0.18	$2.03
9/22/2003	$0.33	$0.62	$0.52	$0.15	$0.18	$0.18	$1.98
9/29/2003	$0.33	$0.65	$0.43	$0.14	$0.18	$0.18	$1.91
10/6/2003	$0.26	$0.69	$0.41	$0.14	$0.18	$0.18	$1.85
10/13/2003	$0.19	$0.72	$0.40	$0.13	$0.18	$0.18	$1.81

Date	Distribution Margin	Crude Oil Cost	Processing Margin	State / Local Sales Tax	State Excise Tax	Federal Excise Tax	Retail Price
10/20/2003	$0.19	$0.68	$0.40	$0.13	$0.18	$0.18	$1.81
10/27/2003	$0.15	$0.67	$0.42	$0.13	$0.18	$0.18	$1.74
11/3/2003	$0.13	$0.65	$0.44	$0.13	$0.18	$0.18	$1.71
11/10/2003	$0.11	$0.69	$0.40	$0.13	$0.18	$0.18	$1.69
11/17/2003	$0.07	$0.71	$0.42	$0.12	$0.18	$0.18	$1.68
11/24/2003	$0.13	$0.67	$0.40	$0.13	$0.18	$0.18	$1.69
12/1/2003	$0.14	$0.67	$0.39	$0.12	$0.18	$0.18	$1.68
12/8/2003	$0.14	$0.72	$0.31	$0.12	$0.18	$0.18	$1.65
12/15/2003	$0.13	$0.76	$0.25	$0.12	$0.18	$0.18	$1.62
12/22/2003	$0.12	$0.73	$0.28	$0.12	$0.18	$0.18	$1.61
12/29/2003	$0.08	$0.74	$0.29	$0.12	$0.18	$0.18	$1.59
1/5/2004	$0.13	$0.78	$0.28	$0.12	$0.18	$0.15	$1.62
1/12/2004	$0.17	$0.80	$0.25	$0.12	$0.18	$0.15	$1.67
1/19/2004	$0.10	$0.84	$0.29	$0.13	$0.18	$0.15	$1.69
1/26/2004	$0.13	$0.79	$0.35	$0.13	$0.18	$0.15	$1.73
2/2/2004	$0.12	$0.81	$0.36	$0.13	$0.18	$0.15	$1.75
2/9/2004	$0.14	$0.76	$0.46	$0.13	$0.18	$0.15	$1.82
2/16/2004	$0.15	$0.80	$0.45	$0.14	$0.18	$0.15	$1.87
2/23/2004	$0.09	$0.79	$0.67	$0.15	$0.18	$0.15	$2.03
3/1/2004	$0.14	$0.85	$0.63	$0.16	$0.18	$0.15	$2.11
3/8/2004	$0.16	$0.84	$0.62	$0.16	$0.18	$0.15	$2.11
3/15/2004	$0.19	$0.86	$0.56	$0.16	$0.18	$0.15	$2.10
3/22/2004	$0.18	$0.85	$0.57	$0.15	$0.18	$0.15	$2.08
3/29/2004	$0.16	$0.81	$0.63	$0.15	$0.18	$0.15	$2.08
4/5/2004	$0.12	$0.79	$0.73	$0.16	$0.18	$0.15	$2.13
4/12/2004	$0.16	$0.87	$0.64	$0.16	$0.18	$0.15	$2.16
4/19/2004	$0.16	$0.86	$0.64	$0.16	$0.18	$0.15	$2.15
4/26/2004	$0.15	$0.85	$0.63	$0.16	$0.18	$0.15	$2.12
5/3/2004	$0.10	$0.88	$0.64	$0.16	$0.18	$0.15	$2.11
5/10/2004	$0.09	$0.90	$0.74	$0.16	$0.18	$0.15	$2.22
5/17/2004	$0.11	$0.96	$0.70	$0.17	$0.18	$0.15	$2.27
5/24/2004	$0.13	$0.97	$0.72	$0.17	$0.18	$0.15	$2.32
5/31/2004	$0.18	$0.99	$0.66	$0.17	$0.18	$0.15	$2.33
6/7/2004	$0.19	$0.89	$0.74	$0.17	$0.18	$0.15	$2.32
6/14/2004	$0.20	$0.86	$0.73	$0.17	$0.18	$0.15	$2.29
6/21/2004	$0.25	$0.86	$0.85	$0.17	$0.18	$0.15	$2.26
6/28/2004	$0.21	$0.83	$0.70	$0.17	$0.18	$0.15	$2.24
7/5/2004	$0.20	$0.88	$0.63	$0.16	$0.18	$0.15	$2.20
7/12/2004	$0.17	$0.91	$0.62	$0.16	$0.18	$0.15	$2.19

(continued)

Date	Distribution Margin	Crude Oil Cost	Processing Margin	State / Local Sales Tax	State Excise Tax	Federal Excise Tax	Retail Price
7/19/2004	$0.16	$0.95	$0.59	$0.16	$0.18	$0.15	$2.19
7/26/2004	$0.18	$0.96	$0.53	$0.16	$0.18	$0.15	$2.16
8/2/2004	$0.18	$1.01	$0.45	$0.16	$0.18	$0.15	$2.13
8/9/2004	$0.18	$1.04	$0.39	$0.15	$0.18	$0.15	$2.09
8/16/2004	$0.12	$1.06	$0.39	$0.15	$0.18	$0.15	$2.05
8/23/2004	$0.10	$1.06	$0.41	$0.15	$0.18	$0.15	$2.05
8/30/2004	$0.18	$0.94	$0.49	$0.15	$0.18	$0.15	$2.10
9/6/2004	$0.16	$0.97	$0.46	$0.15	$0.18	$0.15	$2.07
9/13/2004	$0.15	$0.97	$0.47	$0.15	$0.18	$0.15	$2.05
9/21/2004	$0.11	$1.03	$0.44	$0.15	$0.18	$0.15	$2.05
9/27/2004	$0.06	$1.10	$0.44	$0.16	$0.18	$0.15	$2.09
10/4/2004	$0.09	$1.11	$0.51	$0.16	$0.18	$0.15	$2.20
10/11/2004	$0.08	$1.17	$0.58	$0.17	$0.18	$0.15	$2.33
10/18/2004	$0.09	$1.18	$0.62	$0.18	$0.18	$0.15	$2.40
10/25/2004	$0.14	$1.16	$0.58	$0.18	$0.18	$0.15	$2.39
11/1/2004	$0.17	$1.09	$0.60	$0.18	$0.18	$0.15	$2.37
11/8/2004	$0.22	$1.02	$0.60	$0.17	$0.18	$0.15	$2.34
11/15/2004	$0.22	$0.98	$0.61	$0.17	$0.18	$0.15	$2.31
11/22/2004	$0.25	$1.00	$0.51	$0.17	$0.18	$0.15	$2.26
11/29/2004	$0.24	$1.18	$0.32	$0.17	$0.18	$0.15	$2.24
12/6/2004	$0.32	$0.86	$0.52	$0.16	$0.18	$0.15	$2.19
12/13/2004	$0.46	$0.81	$0.38	$0.16	$0.18	$0.15	$2.14
12/20/2004	$0.32	$0.93	$0.32	$0.15	$0.18	$0.15	$2.05
12/27/2004	$0.27	$0.82	$0.44	$0.15	$0.18	$0.15	$2.01
1/3/2005	$0.22	$0.84	$0.41	$0.15	$0.18	$0.18	$1.98
1/10/2005	$0.17	$0.93	$0.33	$0.14	$0.18	$0.18	$1.93
1/17/2005	$0.13	$1.04	$0.26	$0.14	$0.18	$0.18	$1.93
1/24/2005	$0.08	$1.03	$0.34	$0.15	$0.18	$0.18	$1.96
1/31/2005	$0.12	$1.04	$0.36	$0.15	$0.18	$0.18	$2.03
2/7/2005	$0.11	$1.00	$0.43	$0.15	$0.18	$0.18	$2.05
2/14/2005	$0.09	$1.02	$0.47	$0.15	$0.18	$0.18	$2.09
2/21/2005	$0.11	$1.12	$0.40	$0.16	$0.18	$0.18	$2.15
2/28/2005	$0.07	$1.12	$0.47	$0.16	$0.18	$0.18	$2.18
3/7/2005	$0.07	$1.19	$0.44	$0.17	$0.18	$0.18	$2.23
3/14/2005	$0.08	$1.21	$0.47	$0.17	$0.18	$0.18	$2.29
3/21/2005	$0.09	$1.26	$0.43	$0.17	$0.18	$0.18	$2.10
3/28/2005	$0.06	$1.21	$0.57	$0.18	$0.18	$0.18	$2.38
4/4/2005	$0.00	$1.28	$0.64	$0.18	$0.18	$0.18	$2.46
4/11/2005	$0.04	$1.20	$0.80	$0.19	$0.18	$0.18	$2.59
4/18/2005	$0.04	$1.12	$0.87	$0.19	$0.18	$0.18	$2.58

Date	Distribution Margin	Crude Oil Cost	Processing Margin	State/ Local Sales Tax	State Excise Tax	Federal Excise Tax	Retail Price
4/25/2005	$0.09	$1.22	$0.71	$0.19	$0.18	$0.18	$2.57
5/2/2005	$0.15	$1.14	$0.72	$0.19	$0.18	$0.18	$2.56
5/9/2005	$0.19	$1.17	$0.61	$0.19	$0.18	$0.18	$2.52
5/16/2005	$0.30	$1.08	$0.55	$0.18	$0.18	$0.18	$2.47
5/23/2005	$0.29	$1.12	$0.48	$0.18	$0.18	$0.18	$2.43
5/30/2005	$0.27	$1.17	$0.41	$0.18	$0.18	$0.18	$2.39
6/6/2005	$0.21	$1.31	$0.31	$0.17	$0.18	$0.18	$2.36
6/13/2005	$0.14	$1.26	$0.40	$0.17	$0.18	$0.18	$2.33
6/20/2005	$0.10	$1.35	$0.37	$0.17	$0.18	$0.18	$2.35
6/27/2005	$0.06	$1.38	$0.43	$0.18	$0.18	$0.18	$2.41
7/4/2005	$0.07	$1.34	$0.51	$0.18	$0.18	$0.18	$2.46
7/11/2005	$0.10	$1.35	$0.53	$0.19	$0.18	$0.18	$2.53
7/18/2005	$0.22	$1.32	$0.45	$0.19	$0.18	$0.18	$2.54
7/25/2005	$0.12	$1.31	$0.56	$0.19	$0.18	$0.18	$2.54
8/1/2005	$0.07	$1.42	$0.51	$0.19	$0.18	$0.18	$2.55
8/8/2005	−$0.03	$1.47	$0.61	$0.19	$0.18	$0.18	$2.60
8/15/2005	$0.04	$1.51	$0.61	$0.20	$0.18	$0.18	$2.72
8/22/2005	$0.14	$1.49	$0.56	$0.20	$0.18	$0.18	$2.75
8/29/2005	−$0.15	$1.53	$0.82	$0.21	$0.18	$0.18	$2.77
9/5/2005	−$0.10	$1.54	$1.03	$0.23	$0.18	$0.18	$3.06
9/15/2005	$0.26	$1.46	$0.70	$0.22	$0.18	$0.18	$3.00
9/19/2005	$0.18	$1.56	$0.63	$0.22	$0.18	$0.18	$2.95
9/26/2005	$0.16	$1.52	$0.69	$0.22	$0.18	$0.18	$2.95
10/3/2005	$0.04	$1.51	$0.84	$0.22	$0.18	$0.18	$2.97
10/10/2005	$0.37	$1.43	$0.58	$0.22	$0.18	$0.18	$2.96
10/17/2005	$0.40	$1.49	$0.44	$0.21	$0.18	$0.18	$2.90
10/24/2005	$0.45	$1.41	$0.40	$0.21	$0.18	$0.18	$2.83
10/31/2005	$0.39	$1.38	$0.42	$0.20	$0.18	$0.18	$2.75
11/7/2005	$0.29	$1.35	$0.46	$0.20	$0.18	$0.18	$2.66
11/14/2005	$0.30	$1.32	$0.41	$0.19	$0.18	$0.18	$2.58
11/21/2005	$0.19	$1.32	$0.40	$0.18	$0.18	$0.18	$2.45
11/28/2005	$0.16	$1.32	$0.39	$0.18	$0.18	$0.18	$2.41
12/5/2005	$0.15	$1.32	$0.28	$0.17	$0.18	$0.18	$2.34
12/12/2005	$0.12	$1.41	$0.22	$0.17	$0.18	$0.18	$2.27
12/19/2005	$0.04	$1.31	$0.36	$0.17	$0.18	$0.18	$2.25
12/26/2005	$0.04	$1.33	$0.33	$0.17	$0.18	$0.18	$2.23
1/2/2006	−$0.04	$1.43	$0.30	$0.16	$0.18	$0.18	$2.21
1/9/2006	−$0.03	$1.45	$0.37	$0.17	$0.18	$0.18	$2.33
1/16/2006	$0.05	$1.51	$0.31	$0.18	$0.18	$0.18	$2.42

(*continued*)

Date	Distribution Margin	Crude Oil Cost	Processing Margin	State/Local Sales Tax	State Excise Tax	Federal Excise Tax	Retail Price
1/26/2006	−$0.03	$1.58	$0.33	$0.18	$0.18	$0.18	$2.42
1/30/2006	$0.03	$1.56	$0.47	$0.19	$0.18	$0.18	$2.51
2/6/2006	$0.02	$1.50	$0.47	$0.19	$0.18	$0.18	$2.54
2/13/2006	$0.15	$1.40	$0.41	$0.19	$0.18	$0.18	$2.52
2/20/2006	$0.12	$1.40	$0.40	$0.18	$0.18	$0.18	$2.47
2/27/2006	$0.09	$1.40	$0.41	$0.18	$0.18	$0.18	$2.44
3/6/2006	−$0.03	$1.43	$0.54	$0.18	$0.18	$0.18	$2.48
3/13/2006	$0.05	$1.42	$0.51	$0.19	$0.18	$0.18	$2.53
3/20/2006	$0.04	$1.39	$0.64	$0.20	$0.18	$0.18	$2.64
3/27/2006	$0.03	$1.48	$0.59	$0.20	$0.18	$0.18	$2.67
4/3/2006	$0.02	$1.54	$0.62	$0.20	$0.18	$0.18	$2.74
4/10/2006	−$0.03	$1.59	$0.67	$0.21	$0.18	$0.18	$2.81
4/17/2006	−$0.07	$1.63	$0.76	$0.21	$0.18	$0.18	$2.90
4/24/2006	−$0.07	$1.65	$0.90	$0.23	$0.18	$0.18	$3.07
5/1/2006	$0.02	$1.71	$0.87	$0.24	$0.18	$0.18	$3.20
5/8/2006	$0.04	$1.62	$1.06	$0.25	$0.18	$0.18	$3.33
5/15/2006	$0.02	$1.61	$1.08	$0.25	$0.18	$0.18	$3.33
5/22/2006	$0.02	$1.61	$1.02	$0.24	$0.18	$0.18	$3.25
5/29/2006	$0.04	$1.68	$0.94	$0.24	$0.18	$0.18	$3.27
6/5/2006	$0.04	$1.69	$0.92	$0.24	$0.18	$0.18	$3.27
6/12/2006	$0.15	$1.64	$0.82	$0.24	$0.18	$0.18	$3.23
6/19/2006	$0.19	$1.61	$0.78	$0.24	$0.18	$0.18	$3.20
6/26/2006	$0.16	$1.68	$0.71	$0.24	$0.18	$0.18	$3.16
7/3/2006	$0.07	$1.73	$0.77	$0.24	$0.18	$0.18	$3.19
7/10/2006	$0.09	$1.72	$0.80	$0.24	$0.18	$0.18	$3.19
7/17/2006	$0.11	$1.76	$0.76	$0.24	$0.18	$0.18	$3.24
7/24/2006	$0.10	$1.75	$0.76	$0.24	$0.18	$0.18	$3.22
7/31/2006	$0.10	$1.74	$0.74	$0.24	$0.18	$0.18	$3.20
8/7/2006	$0.09	$1.80	$0.68	$0.24	$0.18	$0.18	$3.19
8/14/2006	$0.14	$1.72	$0.73	$0.24	$0.18	$0.18	$3.21
8/21/2006	$0.20	$1.69	$0.66	$0.23	$0.18	$0.18	$3.16
8/28/2006	$0.25	$1.65	$0.59	$0.23	$0.18	$0.18	$3.10
9/4/2006	$0.23	$1.60	$0.59	$0.22	$0.18	$0.18	$3.01
9/11/2006	$0.26	$1.53	$0.57	$0.22	$0.18	$0.18	$2.95
9/18/2006	$0.31	$1.49	$0.46	$0.21	$0.18	$0.18	$2.85
9/25/2006	$0.31	$1.41	$0.46	$0.20	$0.18	$0.18	$2.76
10/2/2006	$0.25	$1.42	$0.43	$0.20	$0.18	$0.18	$2.68
10/9/2006	$0.22	$1.30	$0.51	$0.19	$0.18	$0.18	$2.60
10/16/2006	$0.20	$1.29	$0.48	$0.19	$0.18	$0.18	$2.54
10/23/2006	$0.16	$1.25	$0.51	$0.18	$0.18	$0.18	$2.48

Date	Distribution Margin	Crude Oil Cost	Processing Margin	State/ Local Sales Tax	State Excise Tax	Federal Excise Tax	Retail Price
10/30/2006	$0.15	$1.27	$0.46	$0.18	$0.18	$0.18	$2.43
11/6/2006	$0.06	$1.32	$0.46	$0.18	$0.18	$0.18	$2.40
11/13/2006	$0.05	$1.28	$0.58	$0.18	$0.18	$0.18	$2.46
11/20/2006	$0.06	$1.23	$0.65	$0.18	$0.18	$0.18	$2.50
11/27/2006	$0.06	$1.32	$0.55	$0.18	$0.18	$0.18	$2.49
12/4/2006	$0.05	$1.37	$0.52	$0.18	$0.18	$0.18	$2.50
12/11/2006	$0.06	$1.37	$0.50	$0.19	$0.18	$0.18	$2.50
12/18/2006	$0.09	$1.39	$0.51	$0.19	$0.18	$0.18	$2.56
12/25/2006	$0.14	$1.40	$0.51	$0.19	$0.18	$0.18	$2.61
1/1/2007	$0.13	$1.32	$0.59	$0.19	$0.18	$0.18	$2.61
1/8/2007	$0.17	$1.27	$0.62	$0.19	$0.18	$0.18	$2.63
1/15/2007	$0.17	$1.15	$0.69	$0.19	$0.18	$0.18	$2.58
1/22/2007	$0.19	$1.19	$0.59	$0.19	$0.18	$0.18	$2.54
1/29/2007	$0.12	$1.22	$0.60	$0.18	$0.18	$0.18	$2.49
2/5/2007	$0.07	$1.35	$0.54	$0.19	$0.18	$0.18	$2.54
2/12/2007	$0.03	$1.32	$0.71	$0.19	$0.18	$0.18	$2.63
2/19/2007	$0.07	$1.36	$0.70	$0.20	$0.18	$0.18	$2.71
2/26/2007	$0.05	$1.41	$0.75	$0.21	$0.18	$0.18	$2.80
3/5/2007	$0.07	$1.38	$0.86	$0.21	$0.18	$0.18	$2.90
3/12/2007	$0.06	$1.36	$1.04	$0.23	$0.18	$0.18	$3.07
3/19/2007	$0.03	$1.32	$1.12	$0.23	$0.18	$0.18	$3.08
3/26/2007	$0.07	$1.47	$1.00	$0.23	$0.18	$0.18	$3.15
4/2/2007	$0.06	$1.55	$1.00	$0.24	$0.18	$0.18	$3.23
4/9/2007	$0.08	$1.40	$1.11	$0.24	$0.18	$0.18	$3.25
4/16/2007	$0.03	$1.52	$1.14	$0.24	$0.18	$0.18	$3.31
4/23/2007	$0.09	$1.56	$1.04	$0.25	$0.18	$0.18	$3.32
4/30/2007	$0.03	$1.59	$1.11	$0.25	$0.18	$0.18	$3.36
5/7/2007	$0.06	$1.50	$1.26	$0.26	$0.18	$0.18	$3.46
5/14/2007	$0.13	$1.52	$1.17	$0.26	$0.18	$0.18	$3.45
5/21/2007	$0.17	$1.61	$1.03	$0.25	$0.18	$0.18	$3.44
5/28/2007	$0.21	$1.58	$0.99	$0.25	$0.18	$0.18	$3.41
6/4/2007	$0.31	$1.61	$0.82	$0.25	$0.18	$0.18	$3.37
6/11/2007	$0.35	$1.61	$0.74	$0.25	$0.18	$0.18	$3.32
6/18/2007	$0.25	$1.68	$0.69	$0.24	$0.18	$0.18	$3.24
6/25/2007	$0.14	$1.69	$0.74	$0.24	$0.18	$0.18	$3.19
7/2/2007	$0.07	$1.73	$0.77	$0.24	$0.18	$0.18	$3.19
7/9/2007	$0.12	$1.76	$0.65	$0.23	$0.18	$0.18	$3.14
7/16/2007	$0.14	$1.81	$0.60	$0.23	$0.18	$0.18	$3.16
7/23/2007	$0.21	$1.82	$0.48	$0.23	$0.18	$0.18	$3.12

(*continued*)

Date	Distribution Margin	Crude Oil Cost	Processing Margin	State/ Local Sales Tax	State Excise Tax	Federal Excise Tax	Retail Price
7/30/2007	$0.23	$1.87	$0.35	$0.23	$0.18	$0.18	$3.06
8/6/2007	$0.27	$1.76	$0.39	$0.22	$0.18	$0.18	$3.02
8/13/2007	$0.24	$1.74	$0.35	$0.22	$0.18	$0.18	$2.93
8/20/2007	$0.17	$1.73	$0.37	$0.21	$0.18	$0.18	$2.86
8/27/2007	$0.14	$1.75	$0.31	$0.21	$0.18	$0.18	$2.79
9/3/2007	$0.10	$1.80	$0.30	$0.21	$0.18	$0.18	$2.79
9/10/2007	$0.10	$1.86	$0.30	$0.21	$0.18	$0.18	$2.84
9/17/2007	$0.08	$1.91	$0.32	$0.22	$0.18	$0.18	$2.90
9/24/2007	$0.08	$1.96	$0.34	$0.22	$0.18	$0.18	$2.96
10/1/2007	$0.06	$1.89	$0.43	$0.22	$0.18	$0.18	$2.97
10/8/2007	$0.07	$1.86	$0.47	$0.22	$0.18	$0.18	$3.00
10/15/2007	$0.05	$2.03	$0.37	$0.23	$0.18	$0.18	$3.05
10/22/2007	$0.09	$2.05	$0.40	$0.23	$0.18	$0.18	$3.14
10/29/2007	$0.06	$2.20	$0.29	$0.23	$0.18	$0.18	$3.16
11/5/2007	$0.03	$2.20	$0.39	$0.24	$0.18	$0.18	$3.23
11/12/2007	$0.09	$2.22	$0.43	$0.25	$0.18	$0.18	$3.37
11/19/2007	$0.14	$2.21	$0.42	$0.25	$0.18	$0.18	$3.40
11/26/2007	$0.15	$2.28	$0.34	$0.25	$0.18	$0.18	$3.40
12/3/2007	$0.21	$2.07	$0.45	$0.25	$0.18	$0.18	$3.36
12/10/2007	$0.23	$2.01	$0.47	$0.25	$0.18	$0.18	$3.33
12/17/2007	$0.17	$2.09	$0.41	$0.24	$0.18	$0.18	$3.29
12/24/2007	$0.14	$2.16	$0.34	$0.24	$0.18	$0.18	$3.26
12/31/2007	$0.11	$2.23	$0.34	$0.24	$0.18	$0.18	$3.30

SOURCE: Author's calculations.

Appendix C

Exxon ARM per Gallon (January 3, 2000 to December 31, 2007)

Date	Distribution Margin	Crude Oil Cost	Discount to CARM Crude Oil Cost	Processing Margin	Premium to CARM Proc. Margin	Swap/ Hedge Spread	State/ Local Sales Tax	State Excise Tax	Federal Excise Tax	Excess Profit	Excess Profit %
1/3/2000	$0.09	$0.56	96.6%	$0.26	108.3%	$0.07	$0.10	$0.18	$0.18	−$0.12	8.8%
1/10/2000	$0.08	$0.57	96.6%	$0.25	108.7%	$0.07	$0.10	$0.18	$0.18	$0.12	8.9%
1/17/2000	$0.09	$0.60	96.8%	$0.20	111.1%	$0.07	$0.10	$0.18	$0.18	$0.12	9.2%
1/24/2000	$0.01	$0.64	97.0%	$0.17	113.3%	$0.08	$0.10	$0.18	$0.18	$0.06	4.2%
1/31/2000	$0.07	$0.60	96.8%	$0.25	108.7%	$0.07	$0.10	$0.18	$0.18	$0.12	9.0%
2/7/2000	$0.07	$0.60	96.8%	$0.26	108.3%	$0.07	$0.10	$0.18	$0.18	$0.12	9.1%
2/14/2000	$0.04	$0.66	97.1%	$0.23	109.5%	$0.08	$0.10	$0.18	$0.18	$0.12	8.7%
2/21/2000	$0.01	$0.64	97.0%	$0.32	103.2%	$0.08	$0.11	$0.18	$0.18	$0.12	8.3%
2/28/2000	$0.00	$0.66	97.1%	$0.42	105.0%	$0.08	$0.11	$0.18	$0.18	$0.16	10.6%
3/6/2000	−$0.01	$0.69	97.2%	$0.50	106.4%	$0.09	$0.12	$0.18	$0.18	$0.17	10.1%
3/13/2000	$0.01	$0.69	95.8%	$0.58	105.5%	$0.09	$0.13	$0.18	$0.18	$0.18	10.1%
3/20/2000	$0.02	$0.60	96.8%	$0.69	104.5%	$0.07	$0.13	$0.18	$0.18	$0.12	6.9%
3/27/2000	$0.19	$0.60	96.8%	$0.53	106.0%	$0.07	$0.13	$0.18	$0.18	$0.14	8.1%
4/3/2000	$0.19	$0.56	96.6%	$0.55	105.8%	$0.07	$0.13	$0.18	$0.18	$0.14	7.9%
4/10/2000	$0.28	$0.53	96.4%	$0.48	106.7%	$0.07	$0.13	$0.18	$0.18	$0.15	8.3%
4/17/2000	$0.36	$0.55	96.5%	$0.37	105.7%	$0.07	$0.13	$0.18	$0.18	$0.15	8.5%
4/24/2000	$0.34	$0.56	96.6%	$0.34	106.3%	$0.07	$0.13	$0.18	$0.18	$0.15	8.8%
5/1/2000	$0.26	$0.56	96.6%	$0.40	105.3%	$0.07	$0.12	$0.18	$0.18	$0.14	8.4%
5/8/2000	$0.17	$0.61	96.8%	$0.41	102.5%	$0.08	$0.12	$0.18	$0.18	$0.13	7.6%
5/15/2000	$0.16	$0.65	97.0%	$0.35	106.1%	$0.08	$0.12	$0.18	$0.18	$0.14	8.6%
5/22/2000	$0.11	$0.62	96.9%	$0.35	89.7%	$0.08	$0.12	$0.18	$0.18	$0.07	4.1%
5/29/2000	$0.09	$0.65	97.0%	$0.39	102.6%	$0.08	$0.12	$0.18	$0.18	$0.12	7.5%
6/5/2000	$0.09	$0.63	96.9%	$0.42	105.0%	$0.08	$0.12	$0.18	$0.18	$0.13	8.0%
6/12/2000	$0.08	$0.68	97.1%	$0.40	105.3%	$0.08	$0.12	$0.18	$0.18	$0.13	8.3%

Date	Distribution Margin	Crude Oil Cost	Discount to CARM Crude Oil Cost	Processing Margin	Premium to CARM Proc. Margin	Swap/ Hedge Spread	State/ Local Sales Tax	State Excise Tax	Federal Excise Tax	Excess Profit	Excess Profit %
6/19/2000	$0.07	$0.68	97.1%	$0.39	105.4%	$0.08	$0.12	$0.18	$0.18	$0.13	8.3%
6/26/2000	$0.02	$0.74	96.1%	$0.39	108.3%	$0.09	$0.12	$0.18	$0.18	$0.15	9.3%
7/3/2000	–$0.01	$0.66	97.1%	$0.60	105.3%	$0.08	$0.13	$0.18	$0.18	$0.14	8.3%
7/10/2000	$0.00	$0.64	97.0%	$0.61	105.2%	$0.08	$0.13	$0.18	$0.18	$0.13	7.5%
7/17/2000	–$0.08	$0.67	97.1%	$0.51	108.5%	$0.08	$0.13	$0.18	$0.18	–$0.01	–0.4%
7/24/2000	$0.13	$0.60	96.8%	$0.52	106.1%	$0.07	$0.13	$0.18	$0.18	$0.13	7.9%
7/31/2000	$0.12	$0.58	96.7%	$0.52	108.3%	$0.07	$0.12	$0.18	$0.18	$0.14	8.5%
8/7/2000	$0.06	$0.62	96.9%	$0.51	104.1%	$0.08	$0.12	$0.18	$0.18	$0.13	7.6%
8/14/2000	–$0.02	$0.69	95.8%	$0.53	103.9%	$0.09	$0.12	$0.18	$0.18	$0.17	10.0%
8/21/2000	–$0.02	$0.69	95.8%	$0.52	106.1%	$0.09	$0.12	$0.18	$0.18	$0.16	9.4%
8/28/2000	–$0.04	$0.71	95.9%	$0.57	105.6%	$0.09	$0.13	$0.18	$0.18	$0.18	10.5%
9/5/2000	–$0.08	$0.74	96.1%	$0.69	103.0%	$0.09	$0.13	$0.18	$0.18	$0.21	11.9%
9/11/2000	–$0.09	$0.77	96.3%	$0.68	103.0%	$0.10	$0.14	$0.18	$0.18	$0.17	9.0%
9/18/2000	$0.06	$0.81	96.4%	$0.46	104.5%	$0.10	$0.14	$0.18	$0.18	$0.16	8.8%
9/25/2000	$0.09	$0.68	97.1%	$0.60	103.4%	$0.08	$0.14	$0.18	$0.18	$0.13	7.3%
10/2/2000	$0.10	$0.70	95.9%	$0.54	103.8%	$0.09	$0.14	$0.18	$0.18	$0.15	8.1%
10/9/2000	$0.16	$0.69	95.8%	$0.48	104.3%	$0.09	$0.14	$0.18	$0.18	$0.16	8.5%
10/16/2000	$0.08	$0.72	96.0%	$0.51	104.1%	$0.09	$0.13	$0.18	$0.18	$0.15	8.3%
10/23/2000	$0.01	$0.74	96.1%	$0.49	104.3%	$0.09	$0.13	$0.18	$0.18	$0.09	5.0%
10/30/2000	$0.01	$0.72	96.0%	$0.56	103.7%	$0.09	$0.13	$0.18	$0.18	$0.14	7.8%
11/6/2000	$0.01	$0.71	95.9%	$0.59	103.5%	$0.09	$0.13	$0.18	$0.18	$0.17	9.4%
11/13/2000	$0.11	$0.75	96.2%	$0.41	102.5%	$0.09	$0.13	$0.18	$0.18	$0.14	8.1%
11/20/2000	$0.19	$0.78	96.3%	$0.29	103.6%	$0.10	$0.13	$0.18	$0.18	$0.16	9.0%

(continued)

Date	Distribution Margin	Crude Oil Cost	Discount to CARM Crude Oil Cost	Processing Margin	Premium to CARM Proc. Margin	Swap/Hedge Spread	State/Local Sales Tax	State Excise Tax	Federal Excise Tax	Excess Profit	Excess Profit %
11/27/2000	$0.17	$0.77	96.3%	$0.31	103.3%	$0.10	$0.13	$0.18	$0.18	$0.16	9.0%
12/4/2000	$0.18	$0.65	97.0%	$0.41	102.5%	$0.08	$0.13	$0.18	$0.18	$0.13	7.6%
12/11/2000	$0.31	$0.57	96.6%	$0.38	105.6%	$0.07	$0.13	$0.18	$0.18	$0.14	8.3%
12/18/2000	$0.29	$0.57	96.6%	$0.35	106.1%	$0.07	$0.12	$0.18	$0.18	$0.14	8.4%
12/26/2000	$0.26	$0.57	96.6%	$0.47	106.8%	$0.07	$0.12	$0.18	$0.18	$0.15	9.1%
1/2/2001	$0.19	$0.47	92.2%	$0.51	110.9%	$0.06	$0.12	$0.18	$0.18	$0.17	10.5%
1/8/2001	$0.17	$0.47	90.4%	$0.52	110.6%	$0.06	$0.12	$0.18	$0.18	$0.18	11.2%
1/15/2001	$0.20	$0.54	90.0%	$0.38	111.8%	$0.07	$0.12	$0.18	$0.18	$0.19	12.0%
1/22/2001	$0.16	$0.58	89.2%	$0.35	112.9%	$0.08	$0.12	$0.18	$0.18	$0.21	13.2%
1/29/2001	$0.13	$0.53	89.8%	$0.43	113.2%	$0.07	$0.12	$0.18	$0.18	$0.19	12.2%
2/5/2001	$0.09	$0.58	90.6%	$0.44	112.8%	$0.08	$0.12	$0.18	$0.18	$0.20	12.4%
2/12/2001	$0.03	$0.59	90.8%	$0.55	114.6%	$0.08	$0.12	$0.18	$0.18	$0.21	12.7%
2/19/2001	$0.03	$0.56	91.8%	$0.59	111.3%	$0.07	$0.12	$0.18	$0.18	$0.18	11.0%
2/26/2001	$0.01	$0.53	88.3%	$0.63	110.5%	$0.07	$0.12	$0.18	$0.18	$0.21	12.8%
3/5/2001	$0.01	$0.58	93.5%	$0.64	110.3%	$0.07	$0.13	$0.18	$0.18	$0.17	10.3%
3/12/2001	$0.01	$0.48	88.9%	$0.74	110.4%	$0.06	$0.13	$0.18	$0.18	$0.19	11.5%
3/19/2001	$0.03	$0.51	91.1%	$0.68	111.5%	$0.07	$0.13	$0.18	$0.18	$0.19	11.0%
3/26/2001	$0.00	$0.55	93.2%	$0.69	113.1%	$0.07	$0.12	$0.18	$0.18	$0.20	12.0%
4/2/2001	-$0.04	$0.48	87.3%	$0.80	111.1%	$0.07	$0.13	$0.18	$0.18	$0.23	13.1%
4/9/2001	-$0.06	$0.55	90.2%	$0.83	110.7%	$0.07	$0.13	$0.18	$0.18	$0.24	13.9%
4/16/2001	-$0.07	$0.58	90.6%	$0.83	110.7%	$0.08	$0.13	$0.18	$0.18	$0.24	13.2%
4/23/2001	-$0.01	$0.55	91.7%	$0.85	111.8%	$0.07	$0.14	$0.18	$0.18	$0.23	12.7%
4/30/2001	$0.01	$0.56	88.9%	$0.81	108.0%	$0.08	$0.14	$0.18	$0.18	$0.24	12.6%
5/7/2001	$0.09	$0.58	93.5%	$0.84	113.5%	$0.07	$0.14	$0.18	$0.18	$0.22	11.6%

Date	Distribution Margin	Crude Oil Cost	Discount to CARM Crude Oil Cost	Processing Margin	Premium to CARM Proc. Margin	Swap/ Hedge Spread	State/ Local Sales Tax	State Excise Tax	Federal Excise Tax	Excess Profit	Excess Profit %
5/14/2001	$0.18	$0.58	90.6%	$0.74	113.8%	$0.08	$0.14	$0.18	$0.18	$0.25	12.7%
5/21/2001	$0.18	$0.58	90.6%	$0.73	112.3%	$0.08	$0.14	$0.18	$0.18	$0.24	12.1%
5/28/2001	$0.22	$0.59	92.2%	$0.67	111.7%	$0.08	$0.14	$0.18	$0.18	$0.22	11.1%
6/4/2001	$0.22	$0.55	87.3%	$0.68	113.3%	$0.08	$0.14	$0.18	$0.18	$0.26	13.2%
6/11/2011	$0.36	$0.56	86.2%	$0.54	114.9%	$0.08	$0.14	$0.18	$0.18	$0.28	14.3%
6/18/2001	$0.39	$0.57	91.9%	$0.53	115.2%	$0.07	$0.14	$0.18	$0.18	$0.23	12.1%
6/25/2001	$0.43	$0.54	90.0%	$0.47	111.9%	$0.07	$0.14	$0.18	$0.18	$0.23	12.2%
7/2/2001	$0.46	$0.53	91.4%	$0.44	118.9%	$0.07	$0.14	$0.18	$0.18	$0.24	12.9%
7/9/2001	$0.47	$0.55	88.7%	$0.33	113.8%	$0.07	$0.14	$0.18	$0.18	$0.23	12.9%
7/16/2001	$0.49	$0.51	89.5%	$0.29	111.5%	$0.07	$0.13	$0.18	$0.18	$0.21	11.7%
7/23/2001	$0.57	$0.50	87.7%	$0.16	106.7%	$0.07	$0.13	$0.18	$0.18	$0.21	12.1%
7/30/2001	$0.38	$0.50	87.7%	$0.31	114.8%	$0.07	$0.12	$0.18	$0.18	$0.22	13.1%
8/6/2001	$0.30	$0.54	93.1%	$0.32	114.3%	$0.07	$0.12	$0.18	$0.18	$0.18	11.1%
8/13/2001	$0.21	$0.53	89.8%	$0.35	112.9%	$0.07	$0.12	$0.18	$0.18	$0.19	12.2%
8/20/2001	$0.09	$0.52	91.2%	$0.45	112.5%	$0.07	$0.11	$0.18	$0.18	$0.18	11.7%
8/27/2001	$0.07	$0.51	91.1%	$0.39	111.4%	$0.07	$0.11	$0.18	$0.18	$0.17	11.1%
9/3/2001	−$0.08	$0.52	91.2%	$0.79	111.3%	$0.07	$0.12	$0.18	$0.18	$0.24	14.5%
9/10/2001	$0.01	$0.54	91.5%	$0.69	111.3%	$0.07	$0.12	$0.18	$0.18	$0.22	13.1%
9/17/2001	$0.01	$0.56	91.8%	$0.63	110.5%	$0.07	$0.12	$0.18	$0.18	$0.19	11.6%
9/24/2001	$0.10	$0.39	88.6%	$0.71	110.9%	$0.05	$0.12	$0.18	$0.18	$0.18	11.0%
10/1/2001	$0.21	$0.42	85.7%	$0.51	110.9%	$0.06	$0.12	$0.18	$0.18	$0.20	12.3%
10/8/2001	$0.20	$0.41	87.2%	$0.49	111.4%	$0.06	$0.12	$0.18	$0.18	$0.19	11.9%
10/15/2001	$0.21	$0.44	93.6%	$0.45	109.8%	$0.06	$0.11	$0.18	$0.18	$0.15	9.4%

(continued)

Date	Distribution Margin	Crude Oil Cost	Discount to CARM Crude Oil Cost	Processing Margin	Premium to CARM Proc. Margin	Swap/ Hedge Spread	State/ Local Sales Tax	State Excise Tax	Federal Excise Tax	Excess Profit	Excess Profit %
10/22/2001	$0.13	$0.41	89.1%	$0.51	113.3%	$0.06	$0.11	$0.18	$0.18	$0.18	11.6%
10/29/2001	$0.07	$0.42	89.4%	$0.53	112.8%	$0.06	$0.11	$0.18	$0.18	$0.18	12.0%
11/5/2001	$0.10	$0.37	87.1%	$0.51	113.3%	$0.05	$0.11	$0.18	$0.18	$0.18	12.4%
11/12/2001	$0.16	$0.40	88.9%	$0.39	118.2%	$0.05	$0.10	$0.18	$0.18	$0.18	13.3%
11/19/2001	$0.20	$0.33	89.2%	$0.38	115.2%	$0.04	$0.10	$0.18	$0.18	$0.15	11.5%
11/26/2001	$0.19	$0.35	89.7%	$0.33	122.2%	$0.05	$0.10	$0.18	$0.18	$0.17	12.9%
12/3/2001	$0.16	$0.37	88.1%	$0.29	126.1%	$0.05	$0.08	$0.18	$0.18	$0.18	14.5%
12/10/2001	$0.16	$0.34	89.5%	$0.28	121.7%	$0.05	$0.09	$0.18	$0.18	$0.16	13.0%
12/17/2001	$0.09	$0.35	89.7%	$0.26	118.2%	$0.05	$0.08	$0.18	$0.18	$0.14	12.0%
12/24/2001	$0.01	$0.41	93.2%	$0.27	117.4%	$0.05	$0.08	$0.18	$0.18	$0.13	12.0%
12/31/2001	-$0.04	$0.36	87.8%	$0.35	112.9%	$0.05	$0.08	$0.18	$0.18	$0.17	15.4%
1/7/2002	-$0.03	$0.39	86.7%	$0.32	114.3%	$0.05	$0.08	$0.18	$0.18	$0.17	15.4%
1/14/2002	$0.03	$0.35	87.5%	$0.34	113.3%	$0.05	$0.09	$0.18	$0.18	$0.14	11.7%
1/21/2002	$0.09	$0.34	87.2%	$0.34	113.3%	$0.05	$0.09	$0.18	$0.18	$0.15	12.1%
1/28/2002	$0.01	$0.37	86.0%	$0.39	114.7%	$0.05	$0.09	$0.18	$0.18	$0.17	14.1%
2/4/2002	$0.02	$0.38	88.4%	$0.41	117.1%	$0.05	$0.09	$0.18	$0.18	$0.17	13.7%
2/11/2002	$0.02	$0.43	89.6%	$0.36	116.1%	$0.06	$0.09	$0.18	$0.18	$0.17	13.4%
2/19/2002	$0.01	$0.40	88.9%	$0.43	113.2%	$0.05	$0.10	$0.18	$0.18	$0.15	11.9%
2/25/2002	$0.02	$0.38	84.4%	$0.42	113.5%	$0.05	$0.10	$0.18	$0.18	$0.17	13.4%
3/4/2002	$0.01	$0.43	86.0%	$0.43	116.2%	$0.06	$0.10	$0.18	$0.18	$0.20	15.0%
3/11/2002	$0.00	$0.46	85.2%	$0.54	114.9%	$0.06	$0.11	$0.18	$0.18	$0.23	16.2%
3/18/2002	$0.01	$0.51	87.9%	$0.57	114.0%	$0.07	$0.11	$0.18	$0.18	$0.25	16.6%
3/25/2002	$0.01	$0.44	80.0%	$0.61	115.1%	$0.07	$0.12	$0.18	$0.18	$0.26	16.4%
4/1/2002	$0.06	$0.53	86.9%	$0.52	115.6%	$0.07	$0.12	$0.18	$0.18	$0.23	14.7%

Date	Distribution Margin	Crude Oil Cost	Discount to CARM Crude Oil Cost	Processing Margin	Premium to CARM Proc. Margin	Swap/ Hedge Spread	State/ Local Sales Tax	State Excise Tax	Federal Excise Tax	Excess Profit	Excess Profit %
4/8/2002	$0.08	$0.52	86.7%	$0.53	112.8%	$0.07	$0.12	$0.18	$0.18	$0.22	13.7%
4/15/2002	$0.15	$0.49	87.5%	$0.54	120.0%	$0.07	$0.12	$0.18	$0.18	$0.25	15.3%
4/22/2002	$0.11	$0.44	71.0%	$0.46	115.0%	$0.07	$0.12	$0.18	$0.18	$0.32	20.1%
4/29/2002	$0.12	$0.55	87.3%	$0.45	115.4%	$0.08	$0.12	$0.18	$0.18	$0.23	14.0%
5/6/2002	$0.13	$0.52	86.7%	$0.44	112.8%	$0.07	$0.12	$0.18	$0.18	$0.21	13.3%
5/13/2002	$0.12	$0.59	90.8%	$0.38	118.8%	$0.08	$0.12	$0.18	$0.18	$0.21	13.2%
5/20/2002	$0.10	$0.58	90.6%	$0.41	117.1%	$0.08	$0.12	$0.18	$0.18	$0.21	13.3%
5/27/2002	$0.07	$0.50	87.7%	$0.50	113.6%	$0.07	$0.12	$0.18	$0.18	$0.21	13.4%
6/3/2002	$0.19	$0.48	85.7%	$0.52	115.6%	$0.07	$0.12	$0.18	$0.18	$0.24	15.2%
6/10/2002	$0.04	$0.47	87.0%	$0.57	114.0%	$0.06	$0.12	$0.18	$0.18	$0.20	13.1%
6/17/2002	$0.01	$0.52	88.1%	$0.59	115.7%	$0.07	$0.12	$0.18	$0.18	$0.22	13.8%
6/24/2002	$0.09	$0.52	86.7%	$0.52	115.6%	$0.07	$0.12	$0.18	$0.18	$0.23	14.3%
7/1/2002	$0.09	$0.54	87.7%	$0.51	115.9%	$0.07	$0.12	$0.18	$0.18	$0.23	14.1%
7/8/2002	$0.08	$0.52	86.7%	$0.53	115.2%	$0.07	$0.12	$0.18	$0.18	$0.23	14.4%
7/15/2002	$0.01	$0.55	88.7%	$0.49	114.0%	$0.07	$0.12	$0.18	$0.18	$0.14	8.9%
7/22/2002	$0.07	$0.54	88.5%	$0.51	115.9%	$0.07	$0.12	$0.18	$0.18	$0.22	14.0%
7/29/2002	$0.04	$0.54	88.5%	$0.51	113.3%	$0.07	$0.12	$0.18	$0.18	$0.20	12.9%
8/5/2002	$0.07	$0.53	86.9%	$0.52	115.6%	$0.07	$0.12	$0.18	$0.18	$0.23	14.7%
8/12/2002	$0.04	$0.56	87.5%	$0.49	114.0%	$0.08	$0.12	$0.18	$0.18	$0.22	13.6%
8/19/2002	$0.02	$0.60	87.0%	$0.45	115.4%	$0.08	$0.12	$0.18	$0.18	$0.23	14.7%
8/26/2002	$0.04	$0.59	88.1%	$0.46	115.0%	$0.08	$0.12	$0.18	$0.18	$0.22	13.9%
9/2/2002	$0.03	$0.58	90.6%	$0.52	115.6%	$0.08	$0.12	$0.18	$0.18	$0.21	12.9%
9/9/2002	$0.01	$0.60	87.0%	$0.49	116.7%	$0.08	$0.12	$0.18	$0.18	$0.24	15.3%

(continued)

Date	Distribution Margin	Crude Oil Cost	Discount to CARM Crude Oil Cost	Processing Margin	Premium to CARM Proc. Margin	Swap/ Hedge Spread	State/ Local Sales Tax	State Excise Tax	Federal Excise Tax	Excess Profit	Excess Profit %
9/16/2002	$0.01	$0.60	88.2%	$0.49	116.7%	$0.08	$0.12	$0.18	$0.18	$0.24	15.3%
9/23/2002	$0.01	$0.62	87.3%	$0.44	112.8%	$0.09	$0.12	$0.18	$0.18	$0.24	15.0%
9/30/2002	$0.00	$0.61	87.1%	$0.45	115.4%	$0.08	$0.12	$0.18	$0.18	$0.24	15.6%
10/7/2002	$0.00	$0.61	89.7%	$0.46	115.0%	$0.08	$0.11	$0.18	$0.18	$0.23	14.9%
10/14/2002	–$0.01	$0.61	89.7%	$0.47	114.6%	$0.08	$0.11	$0.18	$0.18	$0.23	15.1%
10/21/2002	–$0.02	$0.56	87.5%	$0.51	113.3%	$0.08	$0.11	$0.18	$0.18	$0.24	15.6%
10/28/2002	–$0.03	$0.70	86.4%	$0.56	114.3%	$0.10	$0.11	$0.18	$0.18	$0.30	19.6%
11/4/2002	$0.00	$0.52	86.7%	$0.57	116.3%	$0.07	$0.12	$0.18	$0.18	$0.24	15.5%
11/11/2002	$0.02	$0.52	89.7%	$0.59	115.7%	$0.07	$0.12	$0.18	$0.18	$0.21	13.2%
11/18/2002	$0.04	$0.52	86.7%	$0.53	112.8%	$0.07	$0.12	$0.18	$0.18	$0.21	13.3%
11/25/2002	$0.09	$0.53	86.9%	$0.46	115.0%	$0.07	$0.12	$0.18	$0.18	$0.22	14.2%
12/2/2002	$0.15	$0.52	85.2%	$0.41	120.6%	$0.07	$0.12	$0.18	$0.18	$0.25	16.2%
12/9/2002	$0.17	$0.54	88.5%	$0.35	116.7%	$0.07	$0.11	$0.18	$0.18	$0.21	13.8%
12/16/2002	$0.11	$0.58	87.9%	$0.31	119.2%	$0.08	$0.11	$0.18	$0.18	$0.22	14.3%
12/23/2002	$0.10	$0.63	86.3%	$0.30	130.4%	$0.09	$0.11	$0.18	$0.18	$0.27	17.6%
12/30/2002	$0.07	$0.64	88.9%	$0.33	117.9%	$0.09	$0.11	$0.18	$0.18	$0.23	14.8%
1/6/2003	$0.10	$0.61	83.6%	$0.34	125.9%	$0.09	$0.12	$0.18	$0.18	$0.29	18.2%
1/13/2003	$0.10	$0.62	83.8%	$0.35	125.0%	$0.09	$0.12	$0.18	$0.18	$0.29	18.2%
1/20/2003	$0.11	$0.67	83.8%	$0.31	124.0%	$0.10	$0.12	$0.18	$0.18	$0.30	18.2%
1/27/2003	$0.11	$0.61	82.4%	$0.39	121.9%	$0.09	$0.12	$0.18	$0.18	$0.30	18.1%
2/3/2003	$0.10	$0.63	82.9%	$0.40	114.3%	$0.09	$0.12	$0.18	$0.18	$0.28	16.7%
2/10/2003	$0.08	$0.67	82.7%	$0.43	113.2%	$0.10	$0.13	$0.18	$0.18	$0.30	17.0%
2/17/2003	$0.18	$0.71	81.6%	$0.44	133.3%	$0.10	$0.14	$0.18	$0.18	$0.39	21.2%
2/24/2003	$0.20	$0.72	81.8%	$0.45	125.0%	$0.11	$0.14	$0.18	$0.18	$0.38	19.6%

Date	Distribution Margin	Crude Oil Cost	Discount to CARM Crude Oil Cost	Processing Margin	Premium to CARM Proc. Margin	Swap/ Hedge Spread	State/ Local Sales Tax	State Excise Tax	Federal Excise Tax	Excess Profit	Excess Profit %
3/3/2003	$0.16	$0.69	81.2%	$0.62	121.6%	$0.10	$0.15	$0.18	$0.18	$0.39	19.5%
3/10/2003	$0.15	$0.71	80.7%	$0.66	120.0%	$0.11	$0.15	$0.18	$0.18	$0.41	19.5%
3/17/2003	$0.17	$0.67	81.7%	$0.79	121.5%	$0.10	$0.16	$0.18	$0.18	$0.41	19.1%
3/24/2003	$0.22	$0.52	82.5%	$0.94	119.0%	$0.08	$0.16	$0.18	$0.18	$0.36	16.6%
3/31/2003	$0.29	$0.57	82.6%	$0.79	119.7%	$0.08	$0.16	$0.18	$0.18	$0.36	17.0%
4/7/2003	$0.32	$0.49	81.7%	$0.84	120.0%	$0.07	$0.16	$0.18	$0.18	$0.35	16.7%
4/14/2003	$0.32	$0.51	82.3%	$0.79	119.7%	$0.07	$0.15	$0.18	$0.18	$0.34	16.6%
4/21/2003	$0.32	$0.56	83.6%	$0.68	119.3%	$0.08	$0.15	$0.18	$0.18	$0.33	16.4%
4/28/2003	$0.28	$0.45	83.3%	$0.82	122.4%	$0.06	$0.15	$0.18	$0.18	$0.33	16.9%
5/5/2003	$0.29	$0.48	82.8%	$0.71	124.6%	$0.07	$0.14	$0.18	$0.18	$0.34	17.6%
5/12/2003	$0.37	$0.49	81.7%	$0.54	125.6%	$0.07	$0.14	$0.18	$0.18	$0.33	17.8%
5/19/2003	$0.31	$0.53	82.8%	$0.49	125.6%	$0.08	$0.13	$0.18	$0.18	$0.32	17.5%
5/28/2003	$0.26	$0.56	84.8%	$0.45	118.4%	$0.08	$0.13	$0.18	$0.18	$0.28	15.9%
6/2/2003	$0.22	$0.58	82.9%	$0.42	123.5%	$0.08	$0.13	$0.18	$0.18	$0.30	17.6%
6/9/2003	$0.16	$0.59	81.9%	$0.43	126.5%	$0.09	$0.13	$0.18	$0.18	$0.33	19.2%
6/16/2003	$0.06	$0.58	81.7%	$0.64	120.8%	$0.09	$0.13	$0.18	$0.18	$0.34	18.7%
6/23/2003	$0.04	$0.60	84.5%	$0.68	119.3%	$0.09	$0.13	$0.18	$0.18	$0.32	17.5%
6/30/2003	$0.06	$0.59	67.0%	$0.69	121.1%	$0.11	$0.13	$0.18	$0.18	$0.53	29.2%
7/7/2003	$0.09	$0.58	85.3%	$0.64	120.8%	$0.08	$0.13	$0.18	$0.18	$0.30	16.8%
7/14/2003	$0.12	$0.59	83.1%	$0.54	122.7%	$0.09	$0.13	$0.18	$0.18	$0.32	17.9%
7/21/2003	$0.12	$0.60	83.3%	$0.49	122.5%	$0.09	$0.13	$0.18	$0.18	$0.31	17.7%
7/28/2003	$0.12	$0.56	82.4%	$0.52	120.9%	$0.08	$0.13	$0.18	$0.18	$0.30	17.6%
8/4/2003	$0.09	$0.61	84.7%	$0.49	119.5%	$0.09	$0.13	$0.18	$0.18	$0.29	16.8%

(continued)

Date	Distribution Margin	Crude Oil Cost	Discount to CARM Crude Oil Cost	Processing Margin	Premium to CARM Proc. Margin	Swap/ Hedge Spread	State/ Local Sales Tax	State Excise Tax	Federal Excise Tax	Excess Profit	Excess Profit %
8/11/2003	$0.08	$0.60	82.2%	$0.54	120.0%	$0.09	$0.13	$0.18	$0.18	$0.32	18.3%
8/18/2003	$0.00	$0.58	82.9%	$0.85	119.7%	$0.08	$0.14	$0.18	$0.18	$0.34	17.9%
8/25/2003	$0.06	$0.61	84.7%	$0.96	118.5%	$0.09	$0.16	$0.18	$0.18	$0.36	17.0%
9/1/2003	$0.18	$0.61	84.7%	$0.87	122.5%	$0.09	$0.16	$0.18	$0.18	$0.38	17.9%
9/8/2003	$0.25	$0.55	83.3%	$0.94	136.2%	$0.08	$0.15	$0.18	$0.18	$0.47	22.6%
9/15/2003	$0.29	$0.53	82.8%	$0.71	122.4%	$0.08	$0.15	$0.18	$0.18	$0.35	17.1%
9/22/2003	$0.37	$0.51	82.3%	$0.62	119.2%	$0.07	$0.15	$0.18	$0.18	$0.32	16.4%
9/29/2003	$0.37	$0.55	84.6%	$0.55	127.9%	$0.08	$0.14	$0.18	$0.18	$0.34	17.7%
10/6/2003	$0.29	$0.56	81.2%	$0.51	124.4%	$0.08	$0.14	$0.18	$0.18	$0.34	18.5%
10/13/2003	$0.21	$0.60	83.3%	$0.52	130.0%	$0.09	$0.13	$0.18	$0.18	$0.35	19.1%
10/20/2003	$0.21	$0.56	82.4%	$0.50	125.0%	$0.08	$0.13	$0.18	$0.18	$0.32	17.8%
10/27/2003	$0.17	$0.56	83.6%	$0.51	121.4%	$0.08	$0.13	$0.18	$0.18	$0.30	17.3%
11/3/2003	$0.15	$0.54	83.1%	$0.53	120.5%	$0.08	$0.13	$0.18	$0.18	$0.30	17.4%
11/10/2003	$0.12	$0.59	85.5%	$0.49	122.5%	$0.08	$0.13	$0.18	$0.18	$0.28	16.7%
11/17/2003	$0.08	$0.58	81.7%	$0.51	121.4%	$0.09	$0.12	$0.18	$0.18	$0.32	18.8%
11/24/2003	$0.15	$0.56	83.6%	$0.49	122.5%	$0.08	$0.13	$0.18	$0.18	$0.30	17.8%
12/1/2003	$0.16	$0.59	88.1%	$0.49	125.6%	$0.08	$0.12	$0.18	$0.18	$0.28	16.7%
12/8/2003	$0.16	$0.60	83.3%	$0.39	125.8%	$0.09	$0.12	$0.18	$0.18	$0.31	18.6%
12/15/2003	$0.15	$0.64	84.2%	$0.33	132.0%	$0.09	$0.12	$0.18	$0.18	$0.31	19.2%
12/22/2003	$0.13	$0.61	83.6%	$0.35	125.0%	$0.09	$0.12	$0.18	$0.18	$0.29	17.9%
12/29/2003	$0.09	$0.62	83.8%	$0.36	124.1%	$0.09	$0.12	$0.18	$0.18	$0.29	18.2%
1/5/2004	$0.15	$0.65	83.3%	$0.36	128.6%	$0.09	$0.12	$0.18	$0.15	$0.32	20.0%
1/12/2004	$0.19	$0.66	82.5%	$0.33	132.0%	$0.10	$0.12	$0.18	$0.15	$0.34	20.1%
1/19/2004	$0.11	$0.69	82.1%	$0.34	117.2%	$0.10	$0.13	$0.18	$0.15	$0.31	18.4%

Date	Distribution Margin	Crude Oil Cost	Discount to CARM Crude Oil Cost	Processing Margin	Premium to CARM Proc. Margin	Swap / Hedge Spread	State / Local Sales Tax	State Excise Tax	Federal Excise Tax	Excess Profit	Excess Profit %
1/26/2004	$0.15	$0.65	82.3%	$0.44	125.7%	$0.09	$0.13	$0.18	$0.15	$0.34	19.9%
2/2/2004	$0.13	$0.68	84.0%	$0.45	125.0%	$0.10	$0.13	$0.18	$0.15	$0.33	18.7%
2/9/2004	$0.16	$0.64	84.2%	$0.56	121.7%	$0.09	$0.13	$0.18	$0.15	$0.33	18.2%
2/16/2004	$0.17	$0.63	78.8%	$0.55	122.2%	$0.10	$0.14	$0.18	$0.15	$0.39	20.6%
2/23/2004	$0.10	$0.63	79.7%	$0.82	122.4%	$0.09	$0.15	$0.18	$0.15	$0.41	20.4%
3/1/2004	$0.16	$0.69	81.2%	$0.75	119.0%	$0.10	$0.16	$0.18	$0.15	$0.40	19.1%
3/8/2004	$0.18	$0.69	82.1%	$0.76	122.6%	$0.10	$0.16	$0.18	$0.15	$0.41	19.5%
3/15/2004	$0.21	$0.70	81.4%	$0.69	123.2%	$0.10	$0.16	$0.18	$0.15	$0.41	19.7%
3/22/2004	$0.20	$0.69	81.2%	$0.68	119.3%	$0.10	$0.15	$0.18	$0.15	$0.39	18.8%
3/29/2004	$0.18	$0.65	80.2%	$0.76	120.6%	$0.10	$0.15	$0.18	$0.15	$0.41	19.6%
4/5/2004	$0.13	$0.64	81.0%	$0.88	120.5%	$0.09	$0.16	$0.18	$0.15	$0.40	19.0%
4/12/2004	$0.18	$0.71	81.6%	$0.78	121.9%	$0.10	$0.16	$0.18	$0.15	$0.42	19.6%
4/19/2004	$0.18	$0.70	81.4%	$0.79	123.4%	$0.10	$0.16	$0.18	$0.15	$0.43	20.1%
4/26/2004	$0.17	$0.70	82.4%	$0.75	119.0%	$0.10	$0.16	$0.18	$0.15	$0.39	18.5%
5/3/2004	$0.11	$0.72	81.8%	$0.76	118.8%	$0.11	$0.16	$0.18	$0.15	$0.40	18.7%
5/10/2004	$0.10	$0.74	82.2%	$0.88	118.9%	$0.11	$0.16	$0.18	$0.15	$0.42	18.8%
5/17/2004	$0.12	$0.79	82.3%	$0.83	118.6%	$0.12	$0.17	$0.18	$0.15	$0.43	18.7%
5/24/2004	$0.15	$0.80	82.5%	$0.86	119.4%	$0.12	$0.17	$0.18	$0.15	$0.45	19.2%
5/31/2004	$0.20	$0.82	82.8%	$0.79	119.7%	$0.12	$0.17	$0.18	$0.15	$0.44	18.8%
6/7/2004	$0.21	$0.82	92.1%	$0.88	118.9%	$0.11	$0.17	$0.18	$0.15	$0.34	14.5%
6/14/2004	$0.22	$0.70	81.4%	$0.87	119.2%	$0.10	$0.17	$0.18	$0.15	$0.42	18.5%
6/21/2004	$0.28	$0.69	80.2%	$1.01	118.8%	$0.10	$0.17	$0.18	$0.15	$0.46	20.5%
6/28/2004	$0.24	$0.68	81.9%	$0.83	118.6%	$0.10	$0.17	$0.18	$0.15	$0.41	18.3%

(continued)

Date	Distribution Margin	Crude Oil Cost	Discount to CARM Crude Oil Cost	Processing Margin	Premium to CARM Proc. Margin	Swap/ Hedge Spread	State/ Local Sales Tax	State Excise Tax	Federal Excise Tax	Excess Profit	Excess Profit %
7/5/2004	$0.22	$0.72	81.8%	$0.75	119.0%	$0.11	$0.16	$0.18	$0.15	$0.41	18.4%
7/12/2004	$0.19	$0.75	82.4%	$0.74	119.4%	$0.11	$0.16	$0.18	$0.15	$0.41	18.7%
7/19/2004	$0.18	$0.77	81.1%	$0.71	120.3%	$0.11	$0.16	$0.18	$0.15	$0.43	19.8%
7/26/2004	$0.20	$0.78	81.3%	$0.63	118.9%	$0.12	$0.16	$0.18	$0.15	$0.42	19.2%
8/2/2004	$0.20	$0.82	81.2%	$0.54	120.0%	$0.12	$0.16	$0.18	$0.15	$0.42	19.8%
8/9/2004	$0.20	$0.85	81.7%	$0.47	120.5%	$0.12	$0.15	$0.18	$0.15	$0.41	19.8%
8/16/2004	$0.13	$0.86	81.1%	$0.47	120.5%	$0.13	$0.15	$0.18	$0.15	$0.42	20.4%
8/23/2004	$0.11	$0.85	80.2%	$0.49	119.5%	$0.13	$0.15	$0.18	$0.15	$0.43	20.8%
8/30/2004	$0.20	$0.79	84.0%	$0.59	120.4%	$0.11	$0.15	$0.18	$0.15	$0.38	18.2%
9/6/2004	$0.18	$0.79	81.4%	$0.55	119.6%	$0.12	$0.15	$0.18	$0.15	$0.41	19.6%
9/13/2004	$0.17	$0.80	82.5%	$0.56	119.1%	$0.12	$0.15	$0.18	$0.15	$0.40	19.3%
9/21/2004	$0.12	$0.84	81.6%	$0.54	122.7%	$0.12	$0.15	$0.18	$0.15	$0.42	20.7%
9/27/2004	$0.07	$0.90	81.8%	$0.53	120.5%	$0.13	$0.16	$0.18	$0.15	$0.43	20.7%
10/4/2004	$0.10	$0.91	82.0%	$0.61	119.6%	$0.13	$0.16	$0.18	$0.15	$0.44	20.1%
10/11/2004	$0.09	$0.96	82.1%	$0.69	119.0%	$0.14	$0.17	$0.18	$0.15	$0.47	20.2%
10/18/2004	$0.10	$0.97	82.2%	$0.74	119.4%	$0.14	$0.18	$0.18	$0.15	$0.48	20.1%
10/25/2004	$0.16	$0.96	82.8%	$0.69	119.0%	$0.14	$0.18	$0.18	$0.15	$0.47	19.6%
11/1/2004	$0.19	$0.90	82.6%	$0.72	120.0%	$0.13	$0.18	$0.18	$0.15	$0.46	19.4%
11/8/2004	$0.25	$0.85	83.3%	$0.73	121.7%	$0.12	$0.17	$0.18	$0.15	$0.45	19.3%
11/15/2004	$0.25	$0.80	81.6%	$0.74	121.3%	$0.12	$0.17	$0.18	$0.15	$0.46	19.8%
11/22/2004	$0.28	$0.83	83.0%	$0.61	119.6%	$0.12	$0.17	$0.18	$0.15	$0.42	18.6%
11/29/2004	$0.27	$0.97	82.2%	$0.40	125.0%	$0.14	$0.17	$0.18	$0.15	$0.46	20.6%
12/6/2004	$0.36	$0.69	80.2%	$0.71	136.5%	$0.10	$0.16	$0.18	$0.15	$0.50	23.0%
12/13/2004	$0.52	$0.66	81.5%	$0.68	178.9%	$0.10	$0.16	$0.18	$0.15	$0.61	28.4%

Date	Distribution Margin	Crude Oil Cost	Discount to CARM Crude Oil Cost	Processing Margin	Premium to CARM Proc. Margin	Swap/ Hedge Spread	State/ Local Sales Tax	State Excise Tax	Federal Excise Tax	Excess Profit	Excess Profit %
12/20/2004	$0.36	$0.75	80.6%	$0.37	115.6%	$0.11	$0.15	$0.18	$0.15	$0.38	18.6%
12/27/2004	$0.30	$0.68	82.9%	$0.54	122.7%	$0.10	$0.15	$0.18	$0.15	$0.37	18.3%
1/3/2005	$0.25	$0.68	81.0%	$0.52	126.8%	$0.10	$0.15	$0.18	$0.18	$0.40	20.2%
1/10/2005	$0.19	$0.75	80.6%	$0.42	127.3%	$0.11	$0.14	$0.18	$0.18	$0.40	20.8%
1/17/2005	$0.15	$0.84	80.8%	$0.33	126.9%	$0.12	$0.14	$0.18	$0.18	$0.41	21.5%
1/24/2005	$0.09	$0.83	80.6%	$0.43	126.5%	$0.12	$0.15	$0.18	$0.18	$0.42	21.6%
1/31/2005	$0.13	$0.83	79.8%	$0.45	125.0%	$0.12	$0.15	$0.18	$0.18	$0.43	21.4%
2/7/2005	$0.12	$0.80	80.0%	$0.54	125.6%	$0.12	$0.15	$0.18	$0.18	$0.44	21.5%
2/14/2005	$0.10	$0.82	80.4%	$0.58	123.4%	$0.12	$0.15	$0.18	$0.18	$0.44	21.2%
2/21/2005	$0.12	$0.90	80.4%	$0.51	127.5%	$0.13	$0.16	$0.18	$0.18	$0.47	22.1%
2/28/2005	$0.08	$0.89	79.5%	$0.58	123.4%	$0.13	$0.16	$0.18	$0.18	$0.48	22.2%
3/7/2005	$0.08	$0.95	79.8%	$0.54	122.7%	$0.14	$0.17	$0.18	$0.18	$0.49	22.1%
3/14/2005	$0.09	$0.97	80.2%	$0.58	123.4%	$0.15	$0.17	$0.18	$0.18	$0.51	22.1%
3/21/2005	$0.10	$1.01	80.2%	$0.53	123.3%	$0.15	$0.17	$0.18	$0.18	$0.51	24.3%
3/28/2005	$0.07	$0.98	81.0%	$0.71	124.6%	$0.15	$0.18	$0.18	$0.18	$0.53	22.1%
4/4/2005	$0.01	$1.03	80.5%	$0.79	123.4%	$0.15	$0.18	$0.18	$0.18	$0.56	22.9%
4/11/2005	$0.04	$0.97	80.8%	$0.99	123.8%	$0.14	$0.19	$0.18	$0.18	$0.56	21.8%
4/18/2005	$0.04	$0.91	81.3%	$1.07	123.0%	$0.13	$0.19	$0.18	$0.18	$0.54	21.1%
4/25/2005	$0.10	$0.98	80.3%	$0.88	123.9%	$0.15	$0.19	$0.18	$0.18	$0.57	22.0%
5/2/2005	$0.17	$0.91	79.8%	$0.89	123.6%	$0.14	$0.19	$0.18	$0.18	$0.56	21.8%
5/9/2005	$0.21	$0.95	81.2%	$0.75	123.0%	$0.14	$0.19	$0.18	$0.18	$0.52	20.7%
5/16/2005	$0.34	$0.87	80.6%	$0.68	123.6%	$0.13	$0.18	$0.18	$0.18	$0.51	20.6%
5/23/2005	$0.32	$0.91	81.3%	$0.59	122.9%	$0.13	$0.18	$0.18	$0.18	$0.48	19.9%

(continued)

Date	Distribution Margin	Crude Oil Cost	Discount to CARM Crude Oil Cost	Processing Margin	Premium to CARM Proc. Margin	Swap/ Hedge Spread	State/ Local Sales Tax	State Excise Tax	Federal Excise Tax	Excess Profit	Excess Profit %
5/30/2005	$0.30	$0.95	81.2%	$0.51	124.4%	$0.14	$0.18	$0.18	$0.18	$0.49	20.5%
6/6/2005	$0.24	$1.05	80.2%	$0.39	125.8%	$0.16	$0.17	$0.18	$0.18	$0.53	22.3%
6/13/2005	$0.16	$1.01	80.2%	$0.51	127.5%	$0.15	$0.17	$0.18	$0.18	$0.53	22.8%
6/20/2005	$0.11	$1.08	80.0%	$0.46	124.3%	$0.16	$0.17	$0.18	$0.18	$0.53	22.6%
6/27/2005	$0.07	$1.11	80.4%	$0.53	123.3%	$0.17	$0.18	$0.18	$0.18	$0.55	22.6%
7/4/2005	$0.08	$1.08	80.6%	$0.63	123.5%	$0.16	$0.18	$0.18	$0.18	$0.55	22.4%
7/11/2005	$0.11	$1.09	80.7%	$0.65	122.6%	$0.16	$0.19	$0.18	$0.18	$0.55	21.8%
7/18/2005	$0.25	$1.06	80.3%	$0.56	124.4%	$0.16	$0.19	$0.18	$0.18	$0.56	22.0%
7/25/2005	$0.13	$1.06	80.9%	$0.69	123.2%	$0.16	$0.19	$0.18	$0.18	$0.55	21.5%
8/1/2005	$0.08	$1.14	80.3%	$0.63	123.5%	$0.17	$0.19	$0.18	$0.18	$0.58	22.8%
8/8/2005	$0.00	$1.18	80.3%	$0.75	123.0%	$0.18	$0.19	$0.18	$0.18	$0.64	24.5%
8/15/2005	$0.04	$1.21	80.1%	$0.75	123.0%	$0.18	$0.20	$0.18	$0.18	$0.62	22.8%
8/22/2005	$0.16	$1.20	80.5%	$0.69	123.2%	$0.18	$0.20	$0.18	$0.18	$0.62	22.5%
8/29/2005	–$0.08	$1.23	80.4%	$1.01	123.2%	$0.18	$0.21	$0.18	$0.18	$0.74	26.8%
9/5/2005	–$0.06	$1.25	81.2%	$1.00	97.1%	$0.18	$0.23	$0.18	$0.18	$0.48	15.8%
9/15/2005	$0.29	$1.26	86.3%	$1.26	180.0%	$0.18	$0.22	$0.18	$0.18	$0.97	32.2%
9/19/2005	$0.20	$1.25	80.1%	$0.77	122.2%	$0.19	$0.22	$0.18	$0.18	$0.66	22.3%
9/26/2005	$0.18	$1.22	80.3%	$0.85	123.2%	$0.18	$0.22	$0.18	$0.18	$0.66	22.5%
10/3/2005	$0.04	$1.23	81.5%	$1.03	122.6%	$0.18	$0.22	$0.18	$0.18	$0.65	21.9%
10/10/2005	$0.41	$1.15	80.4%	$0.71	122.4%	$0.17	$0.22	$0.18	$0.18	$0.62	21.0%
10/17/2005	$0.45	$1.21	81.2%	$0.54	122.7%	$0.18	$0.21	$0.18	$0.18	$0.61	21.0%
10/24/2005	$0.50	$1.15	81.6%	$0.53	132.5%	$0.17	$0.21	$0.18	$0.18	$0.61	21.5%
10/31/2005	$0.44	$1.10	79.7%	$0.53	126.2%	$0.17	$0.20	$0.18	$0.18	$0.61	22.0%
11/7/2005	$0.32	$1.07	79.3%	$0.57	123.9%	$0.16	$0.20	$0.18	$0.18	$0.58	21.9%

Date	Distribution Margin	Crude Oil Cost	Discount to CARM Crude Oil Cost	Processing Margin	Premium to CARM Proc. Margin	Swap/Hedge Spread	State/Local Sales Tax	State Excise Tax	Federal Excise Tax	Excess Profit	Excess Profit %
11/14/2005	$0.34	$1.07	81.1%	$0.51	124.4%	$0.16	$0.19	$0.18	$0.18	$0.55	21.3%
11/21/2005	$0.21	$1.05	79.5%	$0.51	127.5%	$0.16	$0.18	$0.18	$0.18	$0.56	22.8%
11/28/2005	$0.18	$1.05	79.5%	$0.49	125.6%	$0.16	$0.18	$0.18	$0.18	$0.55	22.8%
12/5/2005	$0.17	$1.07	81.1%	$0.36	128.6%	$0.16	$0.17	$0.18	$0.18	$0.51	21.7%
12/12/2005	$0.13	$1.14	80.9%	$0.29	131.8%	$0.17	$0.17	$0.18	$0.18	$0.52	22.9%
12/19/2005	$0.04	$1.06	80.9%	$0.46	127.8%	$0.16	$0.17	$0.18	$0.18	$0.51	22.5%
12/26/2005	$0.04	$1.07	80.5%	$0.41	124.2%	$0.16	$0.16	$0.18	$0.18	$0.50	22.4%
1/2/2006	–$0.02	$1.23	86.0%	$0.38	126.7%	$0.17	$0.17	$0.18	$0.18	$0.47	21.3%
1/9/2006	–$0.01	$1.26	86.9%	$0.38	102.7%	$0.17	$0.17	$0.18	$0.18	$0.39	16.9%
1/16/2006	$0.06	$1.31	86.8%	$0.39	125.8%	$0.18	$0.18	$0.18	$0.18	$0.47	19.5%
1/26/2006	$0.00	$1.37	86.7%	$0.41	124.2%	$0.19	$0.18	$0.18	$0.18	$0.51	21.1%
1/30/2006	$0.03	$1.36	87.2%	$0.58	123.4%	$0.19	$0.19	$0.18	$0.18	$0.50	19.8%
2/6/2006	$0.02	$1.30	86.7%	$0.59	125.5%	$0.18	$0.19	$0.18	$0.18	$0.50	19.7%
2/13/2006	$0.17	$1.22	87.1%	$0.51	124.4%	$0.17	$0.19	$0.18	$0.18	$0.47	18.6%
2/20/2006	$0.13	$1.22	87.1%	$0.49	122.5%	$0.17	$0.18	$0.18	$0.18	$0.45	18.1%
2/27/2006	$0.10	$1.21	86.4%	$0.50	122.0%	$0.17	$0.18	$0.18	$0.18	$0.46	18.8%
3/6/2006	–$0.01	$1.24	86.7%	$0.67	124.1%	$0.17	$0.18	$0.18	$0.18	$0.51	20.6%
3/13/2006	$0.06	$1.23	86.6%	$0.63	123.5%	$0.17	$0.19	$0.18	$0.18	$0.49	19.4%
3/20/2006	$0.04	$1.21	87.1%	$0.79	123.4%	$0.17	$0.20	$0.18	$0.18	$0.50	18.8%
3/27/2006	$0.03	$1.29	87.2%	$0.73	123.7%	$0.18	$0.20	$0.18	$0.18	$0.51	19.0%
4/3/2006	$0.02	$1.34	87.0%	$0.76	122.6%	$0.18	$0.20	$0.18	$0.18	$0.52	19.2%
4/10/2006	–$0.01	$1.39	87.4%	$0.83	123.9%	$0.19	$0.21	$0.18	$0.18	$0.57	20.3%
4/17/2006	–$0.04	$1.43	87.7%	$0.94	123.7%	$0.20	$0.21	$0.18	$0.18	$0.61	20.9%

(continued)

235

Date	Distribution Margin	Crude Oil Cost	Discount to CARM Crude Oil Cost	Processing Margin	Premium to CARM Proc. Margin	Swap/ Hedge Spread	State/ Local Sales Tax	State Excise Tax	Federal Excise Tax	Excess Profit	Excess Profit %
4/24/2006	–$0.05	$1.44	87.3%	$1.12	124.4%	$0.20	$0.23	$0.18	$0.18	$0.65	21.1%
5/1/2006	$0.02	$1.50	87.7%	$1.07	123.0%	$0.21	$0.24	$0.18	$0.18	$0.62	19.2%
5/8/2006	$0.04	$1.41	87.0%	$1.31	123.6%	$0.19	$0.25	$0.18	$0.18	$0.65	19.7%
5/15/2006	$0.02	$1.41	87.6%	$1.32	122.2%	$0.19	$0.25	$0.18	$0.18	$0.63	19.0%
5/22/2006	$0.02	$1.40	87.0%	$1.26	123.5%	$0.19	$0.24	$0.18	$0.18	$0.64	19.8%
5/29/2006	$0.04	$1.46	86.9%	$1.17	124.5%	$0.20	$0.24	$0.18	$0.18	$0.65	19.9%
6/5/2006	$0.04	$1.47	87.0%	$1.14	123.9%	$0.20	$0.24	$0.18	$0.18	$0.64	19.7%
6/12/2006	$0.17	$1.43	87.2%	$1.02	124.4%	$0.20	$0.24	$0.18	$0.18	$0.63	19.4%
6/19/2006	$0.21	$1.41	87.6%	$1.06	135.9%	$0.19	$0.24	$0.18	$0.18	$0.69	21.7%
6/26/2006	$0.18	$1.47	87.5%	$0.91	128.2%	$0.20	$0.24	$0.18	$0.18	$0.63	20.0%
7/3/2006	$0.08	$1.49	86.1%	$0.96	124.7%	$0.21	$0.24	$0.18	$0.18	$0.65	20.3%
7/10/2006	$0.10	$1.48	86.0%	$0.99	123.8%	$0.21	$0.24	$0.18	$0.18	$0.65	20.3%
7/17/2006	$0.12	$1.53	86.9%	$0.95	125.0%	$0.21	$0.24	$0.18	$0.18	$0.64	19.8%
7/24/2006	$0.11	$1.52	86.9%	$0.96	126.3%	$0.21	$0.24	$0.18	$0.18	$0.65	20.2%
7/31/2006	$0.11	$1.51	86.8%	$0.93	125.7%	$0.21	$0.24	$0.18	$0.18	$0.64	20.0%
8/7/2006	$0.10	$1.57	87.2%	$0.84	123.5%	$0.22	$0.24	$0.18	$0.18	$0.62	19.3%
8/14/2006	$0.16	$1.50	87.2%	$0.91	124.7%	$0.21	$0.24	$0.18	$0.18	$0.63	19.5%
8/21/2006	$0.22	$1.48	87.6%	$0.83	125.8%	$0.20	$0.23	$0.18	$0.18	$0.60	19.1%
8/28/2006	$0.28	$1.43	86.7%	$0.74	125.4%	$0.20	$0.23	$0.18	$0.18	$0.60	19.3%
9/4/2006	$0.26	$1.39	86.9%	$0.73	123.7%	$0.19	$0.22	$0.18	$0.18	$0.57	19.0%
9/11/2006	$0.29	$1.34	87.6%	$0.71	124.6%	$0.18	$0.22	$0.18	$0.18	$0.54	18.4%
9/18/2006	$0.35	$1.29	86.6%	$0.58	126.1%	$0.18	$0.21	$0.18	$0.18	$0.54	18.9%
9/25/2006	$0.35	$1.22	86.5%	$0.59	128.3%	$0.17	$0.20	$0.18	$0.18	$0.53	19.2%
10/2/2006	$0.28	$1.23	86.6%	$0.54	125.6%	$0.17	$0.20	$0.18	$0.18	$0.50	18.7%

Date	Distribution Margin	Crude Oil Cost	Discount to CARM Crude Oil Cost	Processing Margin	Premium to CARM Proc. Margin	Swap/ Hedge Spread	State/ Local Sales Tax	State Excise Tax	Federal Excise Tax	Excess Profit	Excess Profit %
10/9/2006	$0.25	$1.13	86.9%	$0.63	123.5%	$0.16	$0.19	$0.18	$0.18	$0.48	18.3%
10/16/2006	$0.22	$1.12	86.8%	$0.61	127.1%	$0.15	$0.19	$0.18	$0.18	$0.47	18.7%
10/23/2006	$0.18	$1.08	86.4%	$0.63	123.5%	$0.15	$0.18	$0.18	$0.18	$0.46	18.5%
10/30/2006	$0.17	$1.10	86.6%	$0.57	123.9%	$0.15	$0.18	$0.18	$0.18	$0.45	18.6%
11/6/2006	$0.07	$1.15	87.1%	$0.58	126.1%	$0.16	$0.18	$0.18	$0.18	$0.46	19.1%
11/13/2006	$0.07	$1.11	86.7%	$0.71	122.4%	$0.15	$0.18	$0.18	$0.18	$0.47	19.3%
11/20/2006	$0.07	$1.07	87.0%	$0.81	124.6%	$0.15	$0.18	$0.18	$0.18	$0.48	19.1%
11/27/2006	$0.07	$1.15	87.1%	$0.69	125.5%	$0.16	$0.18	$0.18	$0.18	$0.48	19.2%
12/4/2006	$0.06	$1.19	86.9%	$0.65	125.0%	$0.16	$0.18	$0.18	$0.18	$0.48	19.4%
12/11/2006	$0.07	$1.19	86.9%	$0.62	124.0%	$0.16	$0.19	$0.18	$0.18	$0.47	19.0%
12/18/2006	$0.10	$1.20	86.3%	$0.63	123.5%	$0.17	$0.19	$0.18	$0.18	$0.49	19.0%
12/25/2006	$0.10	$1.21	86.4%	$0.64	125.5%	$0.17	$0.19	$0.18	$0.18	$0.45	17.2%
1/1/2007	$0.15	$1.16	87.9%	$0.74	125.4%	$0.16	$0.19	$0.18	$0.18	$0.49	18.7%
1/8/2007	$0.19	$1.12	88.2%	$0.78	125.8%	$0.15	$0.19	$0.18	$0.18	$0.48	18.3%
1/15/2007	$0.19	$1.01	87.8%	$0.87	126.1%	$0.14	$0.19	$0.18	$0.18	$0.48	18.5%
1/22/2007	$0.21	$1.06	89.1%	$0.75	127.1%	$0.14	$0.19	$0.18	$0.18	$0.45	17.8%
1/29/2007	$0.13	$1.08	88.5%	$0.76	126.7%	$0.15	$0.18	$0.18	$0.18	$0.46	18.3%
2/5/2007	$0.08	$1.19	88.1%	$0.69	127.8%	$0.16	$0.19	$0.18	$0.18	$0.48	19.0%
2/12/2007	$0.08	$1.16	87.9%	$0.91	128.2%	$0.16	$0.19	$0.18	$0.18	$0.57	21.6%
2/19/2007	$0.08	$1.20	88.2%	$0.88	125.7%	$0.16	$0.20	$0.18	$0.18	$0.51	18.9%
2/26/2007	$0.06	$1.24	87.9%	$0.95	126.7%	$0.17	$0.21	$0.18	$0.18	$0.55	19.6%
3/5/2007	$0.08	$1.22	88.4%	$1.07	124.4%	$0.17	$0.21	$0.18	$0.18	$0.55	18.8%
3/12/2007	$0.07	$1.21	89.0%	$1.31	126.0%	$0.16	$0.23	$0.18	$0.18	$0.59	19.3%

(continued)

Date	Distribution Margin	Crude Oil Cost	Discount to CARM Crude Oil Cost	Processing Margin	Premium to CARM Proc. Margin	Swap/ Hedge Spread	State/ Local Sales Tax	State Excise Tax	Federal Excise Tax	Excess Profit	Excess Profit %
3/19/2007	$0.07	$1.17	88.6%	$1.41	125.9%	$0.16	$0.23	$0.18	$0.18	$0.64	20.7%
3/26/2007	$0.08	$1.31	89.1%	$1.27	127.0%	$0.18	$0.23	$0.18	$0.18	$0.62	19.6%
4/2/2007	$0.07	$1.38	89.0%	$1.28	128.0%	$0.19	$0.24	$0.18	$0.18	$0.65	20.0%
4/9/2007	$0.09	$1.22	87.1%	$1.39	125.2%	$0.17	$0.24	$0.18	$0.18	$0.64	19.6%
4/16/2007	$0.03	$1.34	88.2%	$1.43	125.4%	$0.18	$0.24	$0.18	$0.18	$0.65	19.7%
4/23/2007	$0.10	$1.37	87.8%	$1.32	126.9%	$0.19	$0.25	$0.18	$0.18	$0.67	20.1%
4/30/2007	$0.03	$1.42	89.3%	$1.39	125.2%	$0.19	$0.25	$0.18	$0.18	$0.64	19.1%
5/7/2007	$0.07	$1.33	88.7%	$1.59	126.2%	$0.18	$0.26	$0.18	$0.18	$0.69	19.9%
5/14/2007	$0.15	$1.32	86.8%	$1.47	125.6%	$0.18	$0.26	$0.18	$0.18	$0.70	20.4%
5/21/2007	$0.15	$1.41	87.6%	$1.29	125.2%	$0.19	$0.25	$0.18	$0.18	$0.63	18.4%
5/28/2007	$0.24	$1.40	88.6%	$1.25	126.3%	$0.19	$0.25	$0.18	$0.18	$0.66	19.3%
6/4/2007	$0.35	$1.42	88.2%	$1.03	125.6%	$0.19	$0.25	$0.18	$0.18	$0.63	18.8%
6/11/2007	$0.39	$1.42	88.2%	$0.95	129.1%	$0.19	$0.25	$0.18	$0.18	$0.64	19.2%
6/18/2007	$0.28	$1.48	88.1%	$0.87	126.1%	$0.20	$0.25	$0.18	$0.18	$0.61	18.9%
6/25/2007	$0.16	$1.48	87.6%	$0.93	125.7%	$0.20	$0.24	$0.18	$0.18	$0.62	19.5%
7/2/2007	$0.01	$1.54	89.0%	$0.97	126.0%	$0.21	$0.24	$0.18	$0.18	$0.54	16.8%
7/9/2007	$0.13	$1.56	88.6%	$0.82	126.2%	$0.21	$0.24	$0.18	$0.18	$0.59	18.8%
7/16/2007	$0.16	$1.60	88.4%	$0.75	125.0%	$0.22	$0.23	$0.18	$0.18	$0.60	18.9%
7/23/2007	$0.24	$1.61	88.5%	$0.61	127.1%	$0.22	$0.23	$0.18	$0.18	$0.59	18.9%
7/30/2007	$0.26	$1.64	87.7%	$0.45	128.6%	$0.22	$0.23	$0.18	$0.18	$0.58	19.1%
8/6/2007	$0.30	$1.56	88.6%	$0.51	130.8%	$0.21	$0.22	$0.18	$0.18	$0.56	18.6%
8/13/2007	$0.27	$1.54	88.5%	$0.45	128.6%	$0.21	$0.22	$0.18	$0.18	$0.54	18.5%
8/20/2007	$0.19	$1.53	88.4%	$0.46	124.3%	$0.21	$0.21	$0.18	$0.18	$0.52	18.1%
8/27/2007	$0.16	$1.55	88.6%	$0.47	151.6%	$0.21	$0.21	$0.18	$0.18	$0.59	21.1%

Date	Distribution Margin	Crude Oil Cost	Discount to CARM Crude Oil Cost	Processing Margin	Premium to CARM Proc. Margin	Swap/ Hedge Spread	State/ Local Sales Tax	State Excise Tax	Federal Excise Tax	Excess Profit	Excess Profit %
9/3/2007	$0.11	$1.59	88.3%	$0.38	126.7%	$0.22	$0.21	$0.18	$0.18	$0.52	18.5%
9/10/2007	$0.11	$1.64	88.2%	$0.38	126.7%	$0.22	$0.21	$0.18	$0.18	$0.53	18.8%
9/17/2007	$0.09	$1.68	88.0%	$0.41	128.1%	$0.23	$0.22	$0.18	$0.18	$0.56	19.3%
9/24/2007	$0.09	$1.72	87.8%	$0.43	126.5%	$0.24	$0.22	$0.18	$0.18	$0.58	19.4%
10/1/2007	$0.07	$1.67	88.4%	$0.55	127.9%	$0.23	$0.22	$0.18	$0.18	$0.58	19.4%
10/8/2007	$0.08	$1.65	88.7%	$0.61	129.8%	$0.22	$0.22	$0.18	$0.18	$0.58	19.4%
10/15/2007	$0.06	$1.79	88.2%	$0.47	127.0%	$0.24	$0.23	$0.18	$0.18	$0.59	19.5%
10/22/2007	$0.10	$1.80	87.8%	$0.51	127.5%	$0.25	$0.23	$0.18	$0.18	$0.62	19.6%
10/29/2007	$0.07	$1.94	88.2%	$0.37	127.6%	$0.26	$0.23	$0.18	$0.18	$0.61	19.4%
11/5/2007	$0.03	$1.93	87.7%	$0.49	125.6%	$0.26	$0.24	$0.18	$0.18	$0.63	19.6%
11/12/2007	$0.10	$1.96	88.3%	$0.51	118.6%	$0.27	$0.25	$0.18	$0.18	$0.62	18.3%
11/19/2007	$0.16	$1.97	89.1%	$0.53	126.2%	$0.27	$0.25	$0.18	$0.18	$0.64	18.7%
11/26/2007	$0.17	$1.99	87.3%	$0.44	129.4%	$0.27	$0.25	$0.18	$0.18	$0.68	20.1%
12/3/2007	$0.24	$1.81	87.4%	$0.57	126.7%	$0.25	$0.25	$0.18	$0.18	$0.66	19.6%
12/10/2007	$0.26	$1.69	84.1%	$0.61	129.8%	$0.24	$0.25	$0.18	$0.18	$0.73	22.0%
12/17/2007	$0.19	$1.84	88.0%	$0.52	126.8%	$0.25	$0.24	$0.18	$0.18	$0.63	19.2%
12/24/2007	$0.19	$1.88	87.0%	$0.44	129.4%	$0.26	$0.24	$0.18	$0.18	$0.69	21.1%
12/31/2007	$0.12	$1.92	86.1%	$0.45	132.4%	$0.27	$0.24	$0.18	$0.18	$0.70	21.1%

SOURCE: Author's calculations.

Appendix D

Shell CARM per Gallon (January 3, 2000 to December 31, 2007)

Date	Distribution Margin	Crude Oil Cost	Processing Margin	State/ Local Sales Tax	State Excise Tax	Federal Excise Tax	Retail Price
1/3/2000	$0.08	$0.58	$0.24	$0.10	$0.18	$0.18	$1.36
1/10/2000	$0.07	$0.59	$0.23	$0.10	$0.18	$0.18	$1.35
1/17/2000	$0.08	$0.62	$0.18	$0.10	$0.18	$0.18	$1.35
1/24/2000	$0.07	$0.66	$0.15	$0.10	$0.18	$0.18	$1.35
1/31/2000	$0.06	$0.62	$0.23	$0.10	$0.18	$0.18	$1.38
2/7/2000	$0.06	$0.62	$0.24	$0.10	$0.18	$0.18	$1.36
2/14/2000	$0.04	$0.68	$0.21	$0.10	$0.18	$0.18	$1.40
2/21/2000	$0.00	$0.66	$0.31	$0.11	$0.18	$0.18	$1.44
2/28/2000	−$0.04	$0.68	$0.40	$0.11	$0.18	$0.18	$1.52
3/6/2000	−$0.04	$0.71	$0.47	$0.12	$0.18	$0.18	$1.63
3/13/2000	−$0.02	$0.72	$0.55	$0.13	$0.18	$0.18	$1.74
3/20/2000	$0.02	$0.62	$0.66	$0.13	$0.18	$0.18	$1.79
3/27/2000	$0.17	$0.62	$0.50	$0.13	$0.18	$0.18	$1.79
4/3/2000	$0.17	$0.58	$0.52	$0.13	$0.18	$0.18	$1.77
4/10/2000	$0.25	$0.55	$0.45	$0.13	$0.18	$0.18	$1.75
4/17/2000	$0.32	$0.57	$0.35	$0.13	$0.18	$0.18	$1.74
4/24/2000	$0.30	$0.58	$0.32	$0.13	$0.18	$0.18	$1.70
5/1/2000	$0.23	$0.58	$0.38	$0.12	$0.18	$0.18	$1.67
5/8/2000	$0.15	$0.63	$0.40	$0.12	$0.18	$0.18	$1.66
5/15/2000	$0.14	$0.67	$0.33	$0.12	$0.18	$0.18	$1.63
5/22/2000	$0.10	$0.64	$0.39	$0.12	$0.18	$0.18	$1.61
5/29/2000	$0.08	$0.67	$0.38	$0.12	$0.18	$0.18	$1.61
6/5/2000	$0.08	$0.65	$0.40	$0.12	$0.18	$0.18	$1.61
6/12/2000	$0.07	$0.70	$0.38	$0.12	$0.18	$0.18	$1.61
6/19/2000	$0.06	$0.70	$0.37	$0.12	$0.18	$0.18	$1.62
6/26/2000	$0.02	$0.77	$0.36	$0.12	$0.18	$0.18	$1.64
7/3/2000	−$0.02	$0.68	$0.57	$0.13	$0.18	$0.18	$1.71
7/10/2000	$0.00	$0.66	$0.58	$0.13	$0.18	$0.18	$1.73
7/17/2000	$0.07	$0.69	$0.47	$0.13	$0.18	$0.18	$1.72
7/24/2000	$0.12	$0.62	$0.49	$0.13	$0.18	$0.18	$1.71
7/31/2000	$0.11	$0.60	$0.48	$0.12	$0.18	$0.18	$1.68
8/7/2000	$0.05	$0.64	$0.49	$0.12	$0.18	$0.18	$1.67
8/14/2000	−$0.05	$0.72	$0.51	$0.12	$0.18	$0.18	$1.67
8/21/2000	−$0.03	$0.72	$0.49	$0.12	$0.18	$0.18	$1.67
8/28/2000	−$0.07	$0.74	$0.54	$0.13	$0.18	$0.18	$1.70
9/5/2000	−$0.15	$0.77	$0.67	$0.13	$0.18	$0.18	$1.79
9/11/2000	−$0.11	$0.80	$0.66	$0.14	$0.18	$0.18	$1.85
9/18/2000	$0.05	$0.84	$0.44	$0.14	$0.18	$0.18	$1.83
9/25/2000	$0.08	$0.70	$0.58	$0.14	$0.18	$0.18	$1.83
10/2/2000	$0.09	$0.73	$0.52	$0.14	$0.18	$0.18	$1.83

Date	Distribution Margin	Crude Oil Cost	Processing Margin	State/ Local Sales Tax	State Excise Tax	Federal Excise Tax	Retail Price
10/9/2000	$0.14	$0.72	$0.46	$0.14	$0.18	$0.18	$1.83
10/16/2000	$0.07	$0.75	$0.49	$0.13	$0.18	$0.18	$1.81
10/23/2000	$0.06	$0.77	$0.47	$0.13	$0.18	$0.18	$1.80
10/30/2000	$0.01	$0.75	$0.54	$0.13	$0.18	$0.18	$1.80
11/6/2000	−$0.02	$0.74	$0.57	$0.13	$0.18	$0.18	$1.79
11/13/2000	$0.10	$0.78	$0.40	$0.13	$0.18	$0.18	$1.78
11/20/2000	$0.17	$0.81	$0.28	$0.13	$0.18	$0.18	$1.75
11/27/2000	$0.15	$0.80	$0.30	$0.13	$0.18	$0.18	$1.74
12/4/2000	$0.16	$0.67	$0.40	$0.13	$0.18	$0.18	$1.72
12/11/2000	$0.28	$0.59	$0.36	$0.13	$0.18	$0.18	$1.69
12/18/2000	$0.26	$0.59	$0.33	$0.12	$0.18	$0.18	$1.68
12/26/2000	$0.23	$0.59	$0.44	$0.12	$0.18	$0.18	$1.65
1/2/2001	$0.17	$0.51	$0.46	$0.12	$0.18	$0.18	$1.63
1/8/2001	$0.15	$0.52	$0.47	$0.12	$0.18	$0.18	$1.63
1/15/2001	$0.18	$0.60	$0.34	$0.12	$0.18	$0.18	$1.60
1/22/2001	$0.14	$0.65	$0.31	$0.12	$0.18	$0.18	$1.58
1/29/2001	$0.12	$0.59	$0.38	$0.12	$0.18	$0.18	$1.57
2/5/2001	$0.08	$0.64	$0.39	$0.12	$0.18	$0.18	$1.59
2/12/2001	$0.03	$0.65	$0.48	$0.12	$0.18	$0.18	$1.64
2/19/2001	$0.03	$0.61	$0.53	$0.12	$0.18	$0.18	$1.66
2/26/2001	$0.00	$0.60	$0.57	$0.12	$0.18	$0.18	$1.66
3/5/2001	$0.01	$0.62	$0.58	$0.13	$0.18	$0.18	$1.70
3/12/2001	$0.01	$0.54	$0.67	$0.13	$0.18	$0.18	$1.70
3/12/2001	$0.03	$0.56	$0.61	$0.13	$0.18	$0.18	$1.70
3/26/2001	−$0.01	$0.59	$0.61	$0.12	$0.18	$0.18	$1.68
4/2/2001	−$0.05	$0.55	$0.72	$0.13	$0.18	$0.18	$1.72
4/9/2001	−$0.09	$0.61	$0.75	$0.13	$0.18	$0.18	$1.75
4/16/2001	−$0.09	$0.64	$0.75	$0.13	$0.18	$0.18	$1.80
4/23/2001	−$0.03	$0.60	$0.76	$0.14	$0.18	$0.18	$1.83
4/30/2001	−$0.02	$0.63	$0.75	$0.14	$0.18	$0.18	$1.87
5/7/2001	$0.08	$0.62	$0.74	$0.14	$0.18	$0.18	$1.94
5/14/2001	$0.16	$0.64	$0.65	$0.14	$0.18	$0.18	$1.95
5/21/2001	$0.16	$0.64	$0.65	$0.14	$0.18	$0.18	$1.95
5/28/2001	$0.20	$0.64	$0.60	$0.14	$0.18	$0.18	$1.95
6/4/2001	$0.20	$0.63	$0.60	$0.14	$0.18	$0.18	$1.93
6/11/2011	$0.32	$0.65	$0.47	$0.14	$0.18	$0.18	$1.95
6/18/2001	$0.35	$0.62	$0.46	$0.14	$0.18	$0.18	$1.93
6/25/2001	$0.38	$0.60	$0.42	$0.14	$0.18	$0.18	$1.90
7/2/2001	$0.41	$0.58	$0.37	$0.14	$0.18	$0.18	$1.86

(*continued*)

Date	Distribution Margin	Crude Oil Cost	Processing Margin	State/Local Sales Tax	State Excise Tax	Federal Excise Tax	Retail Price
7/9/2001	$0.42	$0.62	$0.29	$0.14	$0.18	$0.18	$1.82
7/16/2001	$0.44	$0.57	$0.26	$0.13	$0.18	$0.18	$1.78
7/23/2001	$0.51	$0.57	$0.15	$0.13	$0.18	$0.18	$1.72
7/30/2001	$0.34	$0.57	$0.27	$0.12	$0.18	$0.18	$1.67
8/6/2001	$0.27	$0.58	$0.28	$0.12	$0.18	$0.18	$1.62
8/13/2001	$0.19	$0.59	$0.31	$0.12	$0.18	$0.18	$1.56
8/20/2001	$0.08	$0.57	$0.40	$0.11	$0.18	$0.18	$1.52
8/27/2001	$0.06	$0.56	$0.35	$0.11	$0.18	$0.18	$1.51
9/3/2001	−$0.12	$0.57	$0.71	$0.12	$0.18	$0.18	$1.64
9/10/2001	−$0.02	$0.59	$0.62	$0.12	$0.18	$0.18	$1.68
9/17/2001	$0.00	$0.61	$0.57	$0.12	$0.18	$0.18	$1.67
9/24/2001	$0.09	$0.44	$0.64	$0.12	$0.18	$0.18	$1.66
10/1/2001	$0.19	$0.49	$0.46	$0.12	$0.18	$0.18	$1.62
10/8/2001	$0.18	$0.47	$0.44	$0.12	$0.18	$0.18	$1.56
10/15/2001	$0.19	$0.47	$0.41	$0.11	$0.18	$0.18	$1.55
10/22/2001	$0.12	$0.46	$0.45	$0.11	$0.18	$0.18	$1.51
10/29/2001	$0.06	$0.47	$0.47	$0.11	$0.18	$0.18	$1.47
11/5/2001	$0.09	$0.43	$0.45	$0.11	$0.18	$0.18	$1.42
11/12/2001	$0.14	$0.45	$0.33	$0.10	$0.18	$0.18	$1.38
11/19/2001	$0.18	$0.37	$0.33	$0.10	$0.18	$0.18	$1.34
11/26/2001	$0.17	$0.39	$0.27	$0.10	$0.18	$0.18	$1.29
12/3/2001	$0.14	$0.42	$0.23	$0.08	$0.18	$0.18	$1.24
12/10/2001	$0.14	$0.38	$0.23	$0.09	$0.18	$0.18	$1.20
12/17/2001	$0.08	$0.39	$0.22	$0.08	$0.18	$0.18	$1.14
12/24/2001	$0.00	$0.44	$0.23	$0.08	$0.18	$0.18	$1.11
12/31/2001	−$0.07	$0.41	$0.31	$0.08	$0.18	$0.18	$1.10
1/7/2002	−$0.05	$0.45	$0.28	$0.08	$0.18	$0.18	$1.13
1/14/2002	$0.03	$0.40	$0.30	$0.09	$0.18	$0.18	$1.18
1/21/2002	$0.08	$0.39	$0.30	$0.09	$0.18	$0.18	$1.21
1/28/2002	$0.00	$0.43	$0.34	$0.09	$0.18	$0.18	$1.22
2/4/2002	$0.01	$0.43	$0.35	$0.09	$0.18	$0.18	$1.25
2/11/2002	$0.01	$0.48	$0.31	$0.09	$0.18	$0.18	$1.25
2/19/2002	$0.01	$0.45	$0.38	$0.10	$0.18	$0.18	$1.29
2/25/2002	$0.02	$0.45	$0.37	$0.10	$0.18	$0.18	$1.30
3/4/2002	$0.00	$0.50	$0.37	$0.10	$0.18	$0.18	$1.33
3/11/2002	−$0.02	$0.54	$0.47	$0.11	$0.18	$0.18	$1.45
3/18/2002	−$0.03	$0.58	$0.50	$0.11	$0.18	$0.18	$1.50
3/25/2002	$0.01	$0.55	$0.53	$0.12	$0.18	$0.18	$1.56
4/1/2002	$0.05	$0.61	$0.45	$0.12	$0.18	$0.18	$1.59
4/8/2002	$0.07	$0.60	$0.47	$0.12	$0.18	$0.18	$1.62

Date	Distribution Margin	Crude Oil Cost	Processing Margin	State/ Local Sales Tax	State Excise Tax	Federal Excise Tax	Retail Price
4/15/2002	$0.13	$0.56	$0.45	$0.12	$0.18	$0.18	$1.62
4/22/2002	$0.10	$0.62	$0.40	$0.12	$0.18	$0.18	$1.61
4/29/2002	$0.11	$0.63	$0.39	$0.12	$0.18	$0.18	$1.61
5/6/2002	$0.12	$0.60	$0.39	$0.12	$0.18	$0.18	$1.59
5/13/2002	$0.11	$0.65	$0.32	$0.12	$0.18	$0.18	$1.57
5/20/2002	$0.09	$0.64	$0.35	$0.12	$0.18	$0.18	$1.56
5/27/2002	$0.06	$0.57	$0.44	$0.12	$0.18	$0.18	$1.55
6/3/2002	$0.17	$0.56	$0.45	$0.12	$0.18	$0.18	$1.56
6/10/2002	$0.04	$0.54	$0.50	$0.12	$0.18	$0.18	$1.56
6/17/2002	$0.01	$0.59	$0.51	$0.12	$0.18	$0.18	$1.60
6/24/2002	$0.08	$0.60	$0.45	$0.12	$0.18	$0.18	$1.62
7/1/2002	$0.08	$0.61	$0.44	$0.12	$0.18	$0.18	$1.62
7/8/2002	$0.07	$0.60	$0.46	$0.12	$0.18	$0.18	$1.61
7/15/2002	$0.07	$0.62	$0.43	$0.12	$0.18	$0.18	$1.60
7/22/2002	$0.06	$0.61	$0.44	$0.12	$0.18	$0.18	$1.59
7/29/2002	$0.04	$0.61	$0.45	$0.12	$0.18	$0.18	$1.58
8/5/2002	$0.06	$0.61	$0.45	$0.12	$0.18	$0.18	$1.59
8/12/2002	$0.04	$0.64	$0.43	$0.12	$0.18	$0.18	$1.59
8/19/2002	$0.02	$0.69	$0.39	$0.12	$0.18	$0.18	$1.58
8/26/2002	$0.04	$0.67	$0.40	$0.12	$0.18	$0.18	$1.59
9/2/2002	$0.03	$0.64	$0.45	$0.12	$0.18	$0.18	$1.60
9/9/2002	$0.01	$0.69	$0.42	$0.12	$0.18	$0.18	$1.59
9/16/2002	$0.00	$0.68	$0.42	$0.12	$0.18	$0.18	$1.58
9/23/2002	$0.00	$0.71	$0.39	$0.12	$0.18	$0.18	$1.57
9/30/2002	−$0.01	$0.70	$0.39	$0.12	$0.18	$0.18	$1.56
10/7/2002	−$0.02	$0.68	$0.40	$0.11	$0.18	$0.18	$1.55
10/14/2002	−$0.03	$0.68	$0.41	$0.11	$0.18	$0.18	$1.53
10/21/2002	−$0.04	$0.64	$0.45	$0.11	$0.18	$0.18	$1.52
10/28/2002	−$0.05	$0.81	$0.49	$0.11	$0.18	$0.18	$1.52
11/4/2002	−$0.01	$0.60	$0.49	$0.12	$0.18	$0.18	$1.56
11/11/2002	$0.02	$0.58	$0.51	$0.12	$0.18	$0.18	$1.59
11/18/2002	$0.04	$0.60	$0.47	$0.12	$0.18	$0.18	$1.59
11/25/2002	$0.08	$0.61	$0.40	$0.12	$0.18	$0.18	$1.57
12/2/2002	$0.13	$0.61	$0.34	$0.12	$0.18	$0.18	$1.56
12/9/2002	$0.15	$0.61	$0.30	$0.11	$0.18	$0.18	$1.54
12/16/2002	$0.10	$0.66	$0.26	$0.11	$0.18	$0.18	$1.53
12/23/2002	$0.09	$0.73	$0.23	$0.11	$0.18	$0.18	$1.52
12/30/2002	$0.06	$0.72	$0.28	$0.11	$0.18	$0.18	$1.53
12/6/2003	$0.09	$0.73	$0.27	$0.12	$0.18	$0.18	$1.58

(continued)

Date	Distribution Margin	Crude Oil Cost	Processing Margin	State/Local Sales Tax	State Excise Tax	Federal Excise Tax	Retail Price
12/13/2003	$0.09	$0.74	$0.28	$0.12	$0.18	$0.18	$1.59
12/20/2003	$0.10	$0.80	$0.25	$0.12	$0.18	$0.18	$1.63
12/27/2003	$0.10	$0.74	$0.32	$0.12	$0.18	$0.18	$1.65
2/3/2003	$0.09	$0.76	$0.35	$0.12	$0.18	$0.18	$1.68
2/10/2003	$0.07	$0.81	$0.38	$0.13	$0.18	$0.18	$1.75
2/17/2003	$0.16	$0.87	$0.33	$0.14	$0.18	$0.18	$1.86
2/24/2003	$0.18	$0.88	$0.36	$0.14	$0.18	$0.18	$1.92
3/3/2003	$0.14	$0.85	$0.51	$0.15	$0.18	$0.18	$2.01
3/10/2003	$0.13	$0.88	$0.55	$0.15	$0.18	$0.18	$2.08
3/17/2003	$0.15	$0.82	$0.65	$0.16	$0.18	$0.18	$2.14
3/24/2003	$0.20	$0.63	$0.79	$0.16	$0.18	$0.18	$2.14
3/31/2003	$0.26	$0.69	$0.66	$0.16	$0.18	$0.18	$2.13
4/7/2003	$0.29	$0.60	$0.70	$0.16	$0.18	$0.18	$2.11
4/14/2003	$0.29	$0.62	$0.66	$0.15	$0.18	$0.18	$2.08
4/21/2003	$0.29	$0.67	$0.57	$0.15	$0.18	$0.18	$2.01
4/28/2003	$0.25	$0.54	$0.67	$0.15	$0.18	$0.18	$1.98
5/5/2003	$0.26	$0.58	$0.57	$0.14	$0.18	$0.18	$1.93
5/12/2003	$0.33	$0.60	$0.43	$0.14	$0.18	$0.18	$1.87
5/19/2003	$0.28	$0.64	$0.39	$0.13	$0.18	$0.18	$1.81
5/28/2003	$0.23	$0.66	$0.38	$0.13	$0.18	$0.18	$1.76
6/2/2003	$0.20	$0.70	$0.34	$0.13	$0.18	$0.18	$1.73
6/9/2003	$0.14	$0.72	$0.34	$0.13	$0.18	$0.18	$1.70
6/16/2003	$0.05	$0.71	$0.53	$0.13	$0.18	$0.18	$1.79
6/23/2003	$0.03	$0.71	$0.57	$0.13	$0.18	$0.18	$1.80
6/30/2003	$0.05	$0.88	$0.57	$0.13	$0.18	$0.18	$1.80
7/7/2003	$0.08	$0.68	$0.53	$0.13	$0.18	$0.18	$1.79
7/14/2003	$0.11	$0.71	$0.44	$0.13	$0.18	$0.18	$1.76
7/21/2003	$0.11	$0.72	$0.40	$0.13	$0.18	$0.18	$1.73
7/28/2003	$0.11	$0.68	$0.43	$0.13	$0.18	$0.18	$1.71
8/4/2003	$0.08	$0.72	$0.41	$0.13	$0.18	$0.18	$1.70
8/11/2003	$0.07	$0.73	$0.45	$0.13	$0.18	$0.18	$1.74
8/18/2003	$0.00	$0.70	$0.71	$0.14	$0.18	$0.18	$1.92
8/25/2003	$0.05	$0.72	$0.81	$0.16	$0.18	$0.18	$2.10
9/1/2003	$0.16	$0.72	$0.71	$0.16	State Excise	Federal Excise	$2.10
9/8/2003	$0.22	$0.66	$0.69	$0.15	$0.18	$0.18	$2.08
9/15/2003	$0.26	$0.64	$0.58	$0.15	$0.18	$0.18	$2.03
9/22/2003	$0.33	$0.62	$0.52	$0.15	$0.18	$0.18	$1.98
9/29/2003	$0.33	$0.65	$0.43	$0.14	$0.18	$0.18	$1.91
10/6/2003	$0.26	$0.69	$0.41	$0.14	$0.18	$0.18	$1.85
10/13/2003	$0.19	$0.72	$0.40	$0.13	$0.18	$0.18	$1.81

Date	Distribution Margin	Crude Oil Cost	Processing Margin	State/Local Sales Tax	State Excise Tax	Federal Excise Tax	Retail Price
10/20/2003	$0.19	$0.68	$0.40	$0.13	$0.18	$0.18	$1.81
10/27/2003	$0.15	$0.67	$0.42	$0.13	$0.18	$0.18	$1.74
11/3/2003	$0.13	$0.65	$0.44	$0.13	$0.18	$0.18	$1.71
11/10/2003	$0.11	$0.69	$0.40	$0.13	$0.18	$0.18	$1.69
11/17/2003	$0.07	$0.71	$0.42	$0.12	$0.18	$0.18	$1.68
11/24/2003	$0.13	$0.67	$0.40	$0.13	$0.18	$0.18	$1.69
12/1/2003	$0.14	$0.67	$0.39	$0.12	$0.18	$0.18	$1.68
12/8/2003	$0.14	$0.72	$0.31	$0.12	$0.18	$0.18	$1.65
12/15/2003	$0.13	$0.76	$0.25	$0.12	$0.18	$0.18	$1.62
12/22/2003	$0.12	$0.73	$0.28	$0.12	$0.18	$0.18	$1.61
12/29/2003	$0.08	$0.74	$0.29	$0.12	$0.18	$0.18	$1.59
1/5/2004	$0.13	$0.78	$0.28	$0.12	$0.18	$0.15	$1.62
1/12/2004	$0.17	$0.80	$0.25	$0.12	$0.18	$0.15	$1.67
1/19/2004	$0.10	$0.84	$0.29	$0.13	$0.18	$0.15	$1.69
1/26/2004	$0.13	$0.79	$0.35	$0.13	$0.18	$0.15	$1.73
2/2/2004	$0.12	$0.81	$0.36	$0.13	$0.18	$0.15	$1.75
2/9/2004	$0.14	$0.76	$0.46	$0.13	$0.18	$0.15	$1.82
2/16/2004	$0.15	$0.80	$0.45	$0.14	$0.18	$0.15	$1.87
2/23/2004	$0.09	$0.79	$0.67	$0.15	$0.18	$0.15	$2.03
3/1/2004	$0.14	$0.85	$0.63	$0.16	$0.18	$0.15	$2.11
3/8/2004	$0.16	$0.84	$0.62	$0.16	$0.18	$0.15	$2.11
3/15/2004	$0.19	$0.86	$0.56	$0.16	$0.18	$0.15	$2.10
3/22/2004	$0.18	$0.85	$0.57	$0.15	$0.18	$0.15	$2.08
3/29/2004	$0.16	$0.81	$0.63	$0.15	$0.18	$0.15	$2.08
4/5/2004	$0.12	$0.79	$0.73	$0.16	$0.18	$0.15	$2.13
4/12/2004	$0.16	$0.87	$0.64	$0.16	$0.18	$0.15	$2.16
4/19/2004	$0.16	$0.86	$0.64	$0.16	$0.18	$0.15	$2.15
4/26/2004	$0.15	$0.85	$0.63	$0.16	$0.18	$0.15	$2.12
5/3/2004	$0.10	$0.88	$0.64	$0.16	$0.18	$0.15	$2.11
5/10/2004	$0.09	$0.90	$0.74	$0.16	$0.18	$0.15	$2.22
5/17/2004	$0.11	$0.96	$0.70	$0.17	$0.18	$0.15	$2.27
5/24/2004	$0.13	$0.97	$0.72	$0.17	$0.18	$0.15	$2.32
5/31/2004	$0.18	$0.99	$0.66	$0.17	$0.18	$0.15	$2.33
6/7/2004	$0.19	$0.89	$0.74	$0.17	$0.18	$0.15	$2.32
6/14/2004	$0.20	$0.86	$0.73	$0.17	$0.18	$0.15	$2.29
6/21/2004	$0.25	$0.86	$0.85	$0.17	$0.18	$0.15	$2.26
6/28/2004	$0.21	$0.83	$0.70	$0.17	$0.18	$0.15	$2.24
7/5/2004	$0.20	$0.88	$0.63	$0.16	$0.18	$0.15	$2.20
7/12/2004	$0.17	$0.91	$0.62	$0.16	$0.18	$0.15	$2.19

(continued)

Date	Distribution Margin	Crude Oil Cost	Processing Margin	State/ Local Sales Tax	State Excise Tax	Federal Excise Tax	Retail Price
7/19/2004	$0.16	$0.95	$0.59	$0.16	$0.18	$0.15	$2.19
7/26/2004	$0.18	$0.96	$0.53	$0.16	$0.18	$0.15	$2.16
8/2/2004	$0.18	$1.01	$0.45	$0.16	$0.18	$0.15	$2.13
8/9/2004	$0.18	$1.04	$0.39	$0.15	$0.18	$0.15	$2.09
8/16/2004	$0.12	$1.06	$0.39	$0.15	$0.18	$0.15	$2.05
8/23/2004	$0.10	$1.06	$0.41	$0.15	$0.18	$0.15	$2.05
8/30/2004	$0.18	$0.94	$0.49	$0.15	$0.18	$0.15	$2.10
9/6/2004	$0.16	$0.97	$0.46	$0.15	$0.18	$0.15	$207.00
9/13/2004	$0.15	$0.97	$0.47	$0.15	$0.18	$0.15	$2.05
9/21/2004	$0.11	$1.03	$0.44	$0.15	$0.18	$0.15	$2.05
9/27/2004	$0.06	$1.10	$0.44	$0.16	$0.18	$0.15	$2.09
10/4/2004	$0.09	$1.11	$0.51	$0.16	$0.18	$0.15	$2.20
10/11/2004	$0.08	$1.17	$0.58	$0.17	$0.18	$0.15	$2.33
10/18/2004	$0.09	$1.18	$0.62	$0.18	$0.18	$0.15	$2.40
10/25/2004	$0.14	$1.16	$0.58	$0.18	$0.18	$0.15	$2.39
11/1/2004	$0.17	$1.09	$0.60	$0.18	$0.18	$0.15	$2.37
11/8/2004	$0.22	$1.02	$0.60	$0.17	$0.18	$0.15	$2.34
11/15/2004	$0.22	$0.98	$0.61	$0.17	$0.18	$0.15	$2.31
11/22/2004	$0.25	$1.00	$0.51	$0.17	$0.18	$0.15	$2.26
11/29/2004	$0.24	$1.18	$0.32	$0.17	$0.18	$0.15	$2.24
12/6/2004	$0.32	$0.86	$0.52	$0.16	$0.18	$0.15	$2.19
12/13/2004	$0.46	$0.81	$0.38	$0.16	$0.18	$0.15	$2.14
12/20/2004	$0.32	$0.93	$0.32	$0.15	$0.18	$0.15	$2.05
12/27/2004	$0.27	$0.82	$0.44	$0.15	$0.18	$0.15	$2.01
1/3/2005	$0.22	$0.84	$0.41	$0.15	$0.18	$0.18	$1.98
1/10/2005	$0.17	$0.93	$0.33	$0.14	$0.18	$0.18	$1.93
1/17/2005	$0.13	$1.04	$0.26	$0.14	$0.18	$0.18	$1.93
1/24/2005	$0.08	$1.03	$0.34	$0.15	$0.18	$0.18	$1.96
1/31/2005	$0.12	$1.04	$0.36	$0.15	$0.18	$0.18	$2.03
2/7/2005	$0.11	$1.00	$0.43	$0.15	$0.18	$0.18	$2.05
2/14/2005	$0.09	$1.02	$0.47	$0.15	$0.18	$0.18	$2.09
2/21/2005	$0.11	$1.12	$0.40	$0.16	$0.18	$0.18	$2.15
2/28/2005	$0.07	$1.12	$0.47	$0.16	$0.18	$0.18	$2.18
3/7/2005	$0.07	$1.19	$0.44	$0.17	$0.18	$0.18	$2.23
3/14/2005	$0.08	$1.21	$0.47	$0.17	$0.18	$0.18	$2.29
3/21/2005	$0.09	$1.26	$0.43	$0.17	$0.18	$0.18	$2.10
3/28/2005	$0.06	$1.21	$0.57	$0.18	$0.18	$0.18	$2.38
4/4/2005	$0.00	$1.28	$0.64	$0.18	$0.18	$0.18	$2.46
4/11/2005	$0.04	$1.20	$0.80	$0.19	$0.18	$0.18	$2.59
4/18/2005	$0.04	$1.12	$0.87	$0.19	$0.18	$0.18	$2.58

Date	Distribution Margin	Crude Oil Cost	Processing Margin	State/Local Sales Tax	State Excise Tax	Federal Excise Tax	Retail Price
4/25/2005	$0.09	$1.22	$0.71	$0.19	$0.18	$0.18	$2.57
5/2/2005	$0.15	$1.14	$0.72	$0.19	$0.18	$0.18	$2.56
5/9/2005	$0.19	$1.17	$0.61	$0.19	$0.18	$0.18	$2.52
5/16/2005	$0.30	$1.08	$0.55	$0.18	$0.18	$0.18	$2.47
5/23/2005	$0.29	$1.12	$0.48	$0.18	$0.18	$0.18	$2.43
5/30/2005	$0.27	$1.17	$0.41	$0.18	$0.18	$0.18	$2.39
6/6/2005	$0.21	$1.31	$0.31	$0.17	$0.18	$0.18	$2.36
6/13/2005	$0.14	$1.26	$0.40	$0.17	$0.18	$0.18	$2.33
6/20/2005	$0.10	$1.35	$0.37	$0.17	$0.18	$0.18	$2.35
6/27/2005	$0.06	$1.38	$0.43	$0.18	$0.18	$0.18	$2.41
7/4/2005	$0.07	$1.34	$0.51	$0.18	$0.18	$0.18	$2.46
7/11/2005	$0.10	$1.35	$0.53	$0.19	$0.18	$0.18	$2.53
7/18/2005	$0.22	$1.32	$0.45	$0.19	$0.18	$0.18	$2.54
7/25/2005	$0.12	$1.31	$0.56	$0.19	$0.18	$0.18	$2.54
8/1/2005	$0.07	$1.42	$0.51	$0.19	$0.18	$0.18	$2.55
8/8/2005	−$0.03	$1.47	$0.61	$0.19	$0.18	$0.18	$2.60
8/15/2005	$0.04	$1.51	$0.61	$0.20	$0.18	$0.18	$2.72
8/22/2005	$0.14	$1.49	$0.56	$0.20	$0.18	$0.18	$2.75
8/29/2005	−$0.15	$1.53	$0.82	$0.21	$0.18	$0.18	$2.77
9/5/2005	−$0.10	$1.54	$1.03	$0.23	$0.18	$0.18	$3.06
9/15/2005	$0.26	$1.46	$0.70	$0.22	$0.18	$0.18	$3.00
9/19/2005	$0.18	$1.56	$0.63	$0.22	$0.18	$0.18	$2.95
9/26/2005	$0.16	$1.52	$0.69	$0.22	$0.18	$0.18	$2.95
10/3/2005	$0.04	$1.51	$0.84	$0.22	$0.18	$0.18	$2.97
10/10/2005	$0.37	$1.43	$0.58	$0.22	$0.18	$0.18	$2.96
10/17/2005	$0.40	$1.49	$0.44	$0.21	$0.18	$0.18	$2.90
10/24/2005	$0.45	$1.41	$0.40	$0.21	$0.18	$0.18	$2.83
10/31/2005	$0.39	$1.38	$0.42	$0.20	$0.18	$0.18	$2.75
11/7/2005	$0.29	$1.35	$0.46	$0.20	$0.18	$0.18	$2.66
11/14/2005	$0.30	$1.32	$0.41	$0.19	$0.18	$0.18	$2.58
11/21/2005	$0.19	$1.32	$0.40	$0.18	$0.18	$0.18	$2.45
11/28/2005	$0.16	$1.32	$0.39	$0.18	$0.18	$0.18	$2.41
12/5/2005	$0.15	$1.32	$0.28	$0.17	$0.18	$0.18	$2.34
12/12/2005	$0.12	$1.41	$0.22	$0.17	$0.18	$0.18	$2.27
12/19/2005	$0.04	$1.31	$0.36	$0.17	$0.18	$0.18	$2.25
12/26/2005	$0.04	$1.33	$0.33	$0.17	$0.18	$0.18	$2.23
1/2/2006	−$0.04	$1.43	$0.30	$0.16	$0.18	$0.18	$2.21
1/9/2006	−$0.03	$1.45	$0.37	$0.17	$0.18	$0.18	$2.33
1/16/2006	$0.05	$1.51	$0.31	$0.18	$0.18	$0.18	$2.42

(continued)

Date	Distribution Margin	Crude Oil Cost	Processing Margin	State/ Local Sales Tax	State Excise Tax	Federal Excise Tax	Retail Price
1/26/2006	−$0.03	$1.58	$0.33	$0.18	$0.18	$0.18	$2.42
1/30/2006	$0.03	$1.56	$0.47	$0.19	$0.18	$0.18	$2.51
2/6/2006	$0.02	$1.50	$0.47	$0.19	$0.18	$0.18	$2.54
2/13/2006	$0.15	$1.40	$0.41	$0.19	$0.18	$0.18	$2.52
2/20/2006	$0.12	$1.40	$0.40	$0.18	$0.18	$0.18	$2.47
2/27/2006	$0.09	$1.40	$0.41	$0.18	$0.18	$0.18	$2.44
3/6/2006	−$0.03	$1.43	$0.54	$0.18	$0.18	$0.18	$2.48
3/13/2006	$0.05	$1.42	$0.51	$0.19	$0.18	$0.18	$2.53
3/20/2006	$0.04	$1.39	$0.64	$0.20	$0.18	$0.18	$2.64
3/27/2006	$0.03	$1.48	$0.59	$0.20	$0.18	$0.18	$2.67
4/3/2006	$0.02	$1.54	$0.62	$0.20	$0.18	$0.18	$2.74
4/10/2006	−$0.03	$1.59	$0.67	$0.21	$0.18	$0.18	$2.81
4/17/2006	−$0.07	$1.63	$0.76	$0.21	$0.18	$0.18	$2.90
4/24/2006	−$0.07	$1.65	$0.90	$0.23	$0.18	$0.18	$3.07
5/1/2006	$0.02	$1.71	$0.87	$0.24	$0.18	$0.18	$3.20
5/8/2006	$0.04	$1.62	$1.06	$0.25	$0.18	$0.18	$3.33
5/15/2006	$0.02	$1.61	$1.08	$0.25	$0.18	$0.18	$3.33
5/22/2006	$0.02	$1.61	$1.02	$0.24	$0.18	$0.18	$3.25
5/29/2006	$0.04	$1.68	$0.94	$0.24	$0.18	$0.18	$3.27
6/5/2006	$0.04	$1.69	$0.92	$0.24	$0.18	$0.18	$3.27
6/12/2006	$0.15	$1.64	$0.82	$0.24	$0.18	$0.18	$3.23
6/19/2006	$0.19	$1.61	$0.78	$0.24	$0.18	$0.18	$3.20
6/26/2006	$0.16	$1.68	$0.71	$0.24	$0.18	$0.18	$3.16
7/3/2006	$0.07	$1.73	$0.77	$0.24	$0.18	$0.18	$3.19
7/10/2006	$0.09	$1.72	$0.80	$0.24	$0.18	$0.18	$3.19
7/17/2006	$0.11	$1.76	$0.76	$0.24	$0.18	$0.18	$3.24
7/24/2006	$0.10	$1.75	$0.76	$0.24	$0.18	$0.18	$3.22
7/31/2006	$0.10	$1.74	$0.74	$0.24	$0.18	$0.18	$3.20
8/7/2006	$0.09	$1.80	$0.68	$0.24	$0.18	$0.18	$3.19
8/14/2006	$0.14	$1.72	$0.73	$0.24	$0.18	$0.18	$3.21
8/21/2006	$0.20	$1.69	$0.66	$0.23	$0.18	$0.18	$3.16
8/28/2006	$0.25	$1.65	$0.59	$0.23	$0.18	$0.18	$3.10
9/4/2006	$0.23	$1.60	$0.59	$0.22	$0.18	$0.18	$3.01
9/11/2006	$0.26	$1.53	$0.57	$0.22	$0.18	$0.18	$2.95
9/18/2006	$0.31	$1.49	$0.46	$0.21	Excise	Excise	Retail
9/25/2006	$0.31	$1.41	$0.46	$0.20	$0.18	$0.18	$2.76
10/2/2006	$0.25	$1.42	$0.43	$0.20	$0.18	$0.18	$2.68
10/9/2006	$0.22	$1.30	$0.51	$0.19	$0.18	$0.18	$2.60
10/16/2006	$0.20	$1.29	$0.48	$0.19	$0.18	$0.18	$2.54
10/23/2006	$0.16	$1.25	$0.51	$0.18	$0.18	$0.18	$2.48

Date	Distribution Margin	Crude Oil Cost	Processing Margin	State/ Local Sales Tax	State Excise Tax	Federal Excise Tax	Retail Price
10/30/2006	$0.15	$1.27	$0.46	$0.18	$0.18	$0.18	$2.43
11/6/2006	$0.06	$1.32	$0.46	$0.18	$0.18	$0.18	$2.40
11/13/2006	$0.05	$1.28	$0.58	$0.18	$0.18	$0.18	$2.46
11/20/2006	$0.06	$1.23	$0.65	$0.18	$0.18	$0.18	$2.50
11/27/2006	$0.06	$1.32	$0.55	$0.18	$0.18	$0.18	$2.49
12/4/2006	$0.05	$1.37	$0.52	$0.18	$0.18	$0.18	$2.50
12/11/2006	$0.06	$1.37	$0.50	$0.19	$0.18	$0.18	$2.50
12/18/2006	$0.09	$1.39	$0.51	$0.19	$0.18	$0.18	$2.56
12/25/2006	$0.14	$1.40	$0.51	$0.19	$0.18	$0.18	$2.61
1/1/2007	$0.13	$1.32	$0.59	$0.19	$0.18	$0.18	$2.61
1/8/2007	$0.17	$1.27	$0.62	$0.19	$0.18	$0.18	$2.63
1/15/2007	$0.17	$1.15	$0.69	$0.19	$0.18	$0.18	$2.58
1/22/2007	$0.19	$1.19	$0.59	$0.19	$0.18	$0.18	$2.54
1/29/2007	$0.12	$1.22	$0.60	$0.18	$0.18	$0.18	$2.49
2/5/2007	$0.07	$1.35	$0.54	$0.19	$0.18	$0.18	$2.54
2/12/2007	$0.03	$1.32	$0.71	$0.19	$0.18	$0.18	$2.63
2/19/2007	$0.07	$1.36	$0.70	$0.20	$0.18	$0.18	$2.71
2/26/2007	$0.05	$1.41	$0.75	$0.21	$0.18	$0.18	$2.80
3/5/2007	$0,07	$1.38	$0.86	$0.21	$0.18	$0.18	$2.90
3/12/2007	$0.06	$1.36	$1.04	$0.23	$0.18	$0.18	$3.07
3/19/2007	$0.03	$1.32	$1.12	$0.23	$0.18	$0.18	$3.08
3/26/2007	$0.07	$1.47	$1.00	$0.23	$0.18	$0.18	$3.15
4/2/2007	$0.06	$1.55	$1.00	$0.24	$0.18	$0.18	$3.23
4/9/2007	$0.08	$1.40	$1.11	$0.24	$0.18	$0.18	$3.25
4/16/2007	$0.03	$1.52	$1.14	$0.24	$0.18	$0.18	$3.31
4/23/2007	$0.09	$1.56	$1.04	$0.25	$0.18	$0.18	$3.32
4/30/2007	$0.03	$1.59	$1.11	$0.25	$0.18	$0.18	$3.36
5/7/2007	$0.06	$1.50	$1.26	$0.26	$0.18	$0.18	$3.46
5/14/2007	$0.13	$1.52	$1.17	$0.26	$0.18	$0.18	$3.45
5/21/2007	$0.17	$1.61	$1.03	$0.25	$0.18	$0.18	$3.44
5/28/2007	$0.21	$1.58	$0.99	$0.25	$0.18	$0.18	$3.41
6/4/2007	$0.31	$1.61	$0.82	$0.25	$0.18	$0.18	$3.37
6/11/2007	$0.35	$1.61	$0.74	$0.25	$0.18	$0.18	$3.32
6/18/2007	$0.25	$1.68	$0.69	$0.24	$0.18	$0.18	$3.24
6/25/2007	$0.14	$1.69	$0.74	$0.24	$0.18	$0.18	$3.19
7/2/2007	$0.07	$1.73	$0.77	$0.24	$0.18	$0.18	$3.19
7/9/2007	$0.12	$1.76	$0.65	$0.23	$0.18	$0.18	$3.14
7/16/2007	$0.14	$1.81	$0.60	$0.23	$0.18	$0.18	$3.16
7/23/2007	$0.21	$1.82	$0.48	$0.23	$0.18	$0.18	$3.12

(continued)

Date	Distribution Margin	Crude Oil Cost	Processing Margin	State/ Local Sales Tax	State Excise Tax	Federal Excise Tax	Retail Price
7/30/2007	$0.23	$1.87	$0.35	$0.23	$0.18	$0.18	$3.06
8/6/2007	$0.27	$1.76	$0.39	$0.22	$0.18	$0.18	$3.02
8/13/2007	$0.24	$1.74	$0.35	$0.22	$0.18	$0.18	$2.93
8/20/2007	$0.17	$1.73	$0.37	$0.21	$0.18	$0.18	$2.86
8/27/2007	$0.14	$1.75	$0.31	$0.21	$0.18	$0.18	$2.79
9/3/2007	$0.10	$1.80	$0.30	$0.21	$0.18	$0.18	$2.79
9/10/2007	$0.10	$1.86	$0.30	$0.21	$0.18	$0.18	$2.84
9/17/2007	$0.08	$1.91	$0.32	$0.22	$0.18	$0.18	$2.90
9/24/2007	$0.08	$1.96	$0.34	$0.22	$0.18	$0.18	$2.96
10/1/2007	$0.06	$1.89	$0.43	$0.22	$0.18	$0.18	$2.97
10/8/2007	$0.07	$1.86	$0.47	$0.22	$0.18	$0.18	$3.00
10/15/2007	$0.05	$2.03	$0.37	$0.23	$0.18	$0.18	$3.05
10/22/2007	$0.09	$2.05	$0.40	$0.23	$0.18	$0.18	$3.14
10/29/2007	$0.06	$2.20	$0.29	$0.23	$0.18	$0.18	$3.16
11/5/2007	$0.03	$2.20	$0.39	$0.24	$0.18	$0.18	$3.23
11/12/2007	$0.09	$2.22	$0.43	$0.25	$0.18	$0.18	$3.37
11/19/2007	$0.14	$2.21	$0.42	$0.25	$0.18	$0.18	$3.40
11/26/2007	$0.15	$2.28	$0.34	$0.25	$0.18	$0.18	$3.40
12/3/2007	$0.21	$2.07	$0.45	$0.25	$0.18	$0.18	$3.36
12/10/2007	$0.23	$2.01	$0.47	$0.25	$0.18	$0.18	$3.33
12/17/2007	$0.17	$2.09	$0.41	$0.24	$0.18	$0.18	$3.29
12/24/2007	$0.14	$2.16	$0.34	$0.24	$0.18	$0.18	$3.26
12/31/2007	$0.11	$2.23	$0.34	$0.24	$0.18	$0.18	$3.30

SOURCE: Author's calculations.

Appendix E

Shell ARM per Gallon (January 3, 2000 to December 31, 2007)

Date	Distribution Margin	Crude Oil Cost	Discount to CARM Crude Oil Cost	Processing Margin	Premium to CARM Proc. Margin	Swap/ Hedge Spread	State/ Local Sales Tax	State Excise Tax	Federal Excise Tax	Excess Profit	Profit %
1/3/2000	0.084	0.56	96.6%	$0.25	104.2%	$0.07	$0.10	$0.18	$0.18	$0.10	7.4%
1/10/2000	0.071	0.58	98.3%	$0.24	104.3%	$0.07	$0.10	$0.18	$0.18	$0.09	6.8%
1/17/2000	0.081	0.59	95.2%	$0.18	100.0%	$0.07	$0.10	$0.18	$0.18	$0.11	7.8%
1/24/2000	0.071	0.62	93.9%	$0.16	106.7%	$0.08	$0.10	$0.18	$0.18	$0.13	9.6%
1/31/2000	0.061	0.60	96.8%	$0.24	104.3%	$0.07	$0.10	$0.18	$0.18	$0.11	7.6%
2/7/2000	0.061	0.59	95.2%	$0.26	108.3%	$0.07	$0.10	$0.18	$0.18	$0.13	9.2%
2/14/2000	0.040	0.67	98.5%	$0.22	104.8%	$0.08	$0.10	$0.18	$0.18	$0.10	7.3%
2/21/2000	0.000	0.65	98.5%	$0.33	106.5%	$0.08	$0.11	$0.18	$0.18	$0.11	7.6%
2/28/2000	−0.040	0.68	100.0%	$0.41	102.5%	$0.08	$0.11	$0.18	$0.18	$0.09	6.0%
3/6/2000	−0.040	0.69	97.2%	$0.48	102.1%	$0.09	$0.12	$0.18	$0.18	$0.11	7.0%
3/13/2000	−0.020	0.67	93.1%	$0.57	103.6%	$0.09	$0.13	$0.18	$0.18	$0.16	9.0%
3/20/2000	0.020	0.60	96.8%	$0.69	104.5%	$0.07	$0.13	$0.18	$0.18	$0.12	7.0%
3/27/2000	0.172	0.59	95.2%	$0.53	106.0%	$0.07	$0.13	$0.18	$0.18	$0.14	7.6%
4/3/2000	0.172	0.56	96.6%	$0.54	103.8%	$0.07	$0.13	$0.18	$0.18	$0.11	6.3%
4/10/2000	0.253	0.51	92.7%	$0.49	108.9%	$0.07	$0.13	$0.18	$0.18	$0.15	8.5%
4/17/2000	0.324	0.55	96.5%	$0.37	105.7%	$0.07	$0.13	$0.18	$0.18	$0.11	6.5%
4/24/2000	0.303	0.54	93.1%	$0.34	106.3%	$0.07	$0.13	$0.18	$0.18	$0.13	7.8%
5/1/2000	0.233	0.56	96.6%	$0.40	105.3%	$0.07	$0.12	$0.18	$0.18	$0.11	6.7%
5/8/2000	0.152	0.62	98.4%	$0.42	105.0%	$0.08	$0.12	$0.18	$0.18	$0.11	6.5%
5/15/2000	0.142	0.64	95.5%	$0.35	106.1%	$0.08	$0.12	$0.18	$0.18	$0.13	8.1%
5/22/2000	0.101	0.61	95.3%	$0.41	105.1%	$0.08	$0.12	$0.18	$0.18	$0.13	7.9%
5/29/2000	0.081	0.66	98.5%	$0.40	105.3%	$0.08	$0.12	$0.18	$0.18	$0.11	6.9%
6/5/2000	0.081	0.65	100.0%	$0.41	102.5%	$0.08	$0.12	$0.18	$0.18	$0.09	5.5%
6/12/2000	0.071	0.67	95.7%	$0.42	110.5%	$0.08	$0.12	$0.18	$0.18	$0.15	9.6%

Date	Distribution Margin	Crude Oil Cost	Discount to CARM Crude Oil Cost	Processing Margin	Premium to CARM Proc. Margin	Swap/ Hedge Spread	State/ Local Sales Tax	State Excise Tax	Federal Excise Tax	Excess Profit	Profit %
6/19/2000	0.061	0.66	94.3%	$0.40	108.1%	$0.08	$0.12	$0.18	$0.18	$0.15	9.5%
6/26/2000	0.020	0.74	96.1%	$0.38	105.6%	$0.09	$0.12	$0.18	$0.18	$0.14	8.7%
7/3/2000	−0.020	0.66	97.1%	$0.61	107.0%	$0.08	$0.13	$0.18	$0.18	$0.14	8.3%
7/10/2000	0.000	0.64	97.0%	$0.62	106.9%	$0.08	$0.13	$0.18	$0.18	$0.14	8.0%
7/17/2000	0.071	0.66	95.7%	$0.52	110.6%	$0.08	$0.13	$0.18	$0.18	$0.16	9.5%
7/24/2000	0.121	0.58	93.5%	$0.54	110.2%	$0.07	$0.13	$0.18	$0.18	$0.17	9.7%
7/31/2000	0.111	0.56	93.3%	$0.51	106.3%	$0.07	$0.12	$0.18	$0.18	$0.14	8.5%
8/7/2000	0.051	0.60	93.8%	$0.52	106.1%	$0.08	$0.12	$0.18	$0.18	$0.15	8.8%
8/14/2000	−0.051	0.68	94.4%	$0.54	105.9%	$0.09	$0.12	$0.18	$0.18	$0.16	9.3%
8/21/2000	−0.030	0.70	97.2%	$0.52	106.1%	$0.09	$0.12	$0.18	$0.18	$0.14	8.1%
8/28/2000	−0.071	0.72	97.3%	$0.57	105.6%	$0.09	$0.13	$0.18	$0.18	$0.14	8.1%
9/5/2000	−0.152	0.73	94.8%	$0.70	104.5%	$0.09	$0.13	$0.18	$0.18	$0.16	9.0%
9/11/2000	−0.111	0.77	96.3%	$0.71	107.6%	$0.10	$0.14	$0.18	$0.18	$0.17	9.4%
9/18/2000	0.051	0.81	96.4%	$0.46	104.5%	$0.10	$0.14	$0.18	$0.18	$0.15	8.3%
9/25/2000	0.081	0.69	98.6%	$0.49	84.5%	$0.08	$0.14	$0.18	$0.18	$0.00	0.3%
10/2/2000	0.091	0.69	94.5%	$0.55	105.8%	$0.09	$0.14	$0.18	$0.18	$0.16	8.7%
10/9/2000	0.142	0.70	97.2%	$0.49	106.5%	$0.09	$0.14	$0.18	$0.18	$0.14	7.5%
10/16/2000	0.071	0.70	93.3%	$0.52	106.1%	$0.09	$0.13	$0.18	$0.18	$0.17	9.4%
10/23/2000	0.061	0.74	96.1%	$0.50	106.4%	$0.09	$0.13	$0.18	$0.18	$0.15	8.5%
10/30/2000	0.010	0.73	97.3%	$0.57	105.6%	$0.09	$0.13	$0.18	$0.18	$0.14	7.8%
11/6/2000	−0.020	0.66	89.2%	$0.60	105.3%	$0.09	$0.13	$0.18	$0.18	$0.20	11.1%
11/13/2000	0.101	0.68	87.2%	$0.42	105.0%	$0.09	$0.13	$0.18	$0.18	$0.21	12.1%
11/20/2000	0.172	0.78	96.3%	$0.31	110.7%	$0.10	$0.13	$0.18	$0.18	$0.16	9.1%

(continued)

255

Date	Distribution Margin	Crude Oil Cost	Discount to CARM Crude Oil Cost	Processing Margin	Premium to CARM Proc. Margin	Swap/ Hedge Spread	State/ Local Sales Tax	State Excise Tax	Federal Excise Tax	Excess Profit	Profit %
11/27/2000	0.152	0.74	92.5%	$0.32	106.7%	$0.10	$0.13	$0.18	$0.18	$0.18	10.2%
12/4/2000	0.162	0.66	98.5%	$0.42	105.0%	$0.08	$0.13	$0.18	$0.18	$0.11	6.5%
12/11/2000	0.283	0.55	93.2%	$0.38	105.6%	$0.07	$0.13	$0.18	$0.18	$0.13	7.9%
12/18/2000	0.263	0.54	91.5%	$0.35	106.1%	$0.07	$0.12	$0.18	$0.18	$0.14	8.6%
12/26/2000	0.233	0.55	93.2%	$0.47	106.8%	$0.07	$0.12	$0.18	$0.18	$0.14	8.7%
1/2/2001	0.176	0.49	96.1%	$0.49	106.5%	$0.06	$0.12	$0.18	$0.18	$0.12	7.2%
1/8/2001	0.156	0.51	98.1%	$0.50	106.4%	$0.06	$0.12	$0.18	$0.18	$0.11	6.6%
1/15/2001	0.187	0.58	96.7%	$0.37	108.8%	$0.07	$0.12	$0.18	$0.18	$0.13	8.1%
1/22/2001	0.145	0.64	98.5%	$0.33	106.5%	$0.08	$0.12	$0.18	$0.18	$0.11	7.2%
1/29/2001	0.125	0.59	100.0%	$0.42	110.5%	$0.07	$0.12	$0.18	$0.18	$0.12	7.3%
2/5/2001	0.083	0.64	100.0%	$0.42	107.7%	$0.08	$0.12	$0.18	$0.18	$0.11	6.9%
2/12/2001	0.031	0.66	101.5%	$0.51	106.3%	$0.08	$0.12	$0.18	$0.18	$0.10	6.0%
2/19/2001	0.031	0.60	98.4%	$0.56	105.7%	$0.07	$0.12	$0.18	$0.18	$0.11	6.9%
2/26/2001	0.000	0.59	98.3%	$0.61	107.0%	$0.07	$0.12	$0.18	$0.18	$0.12	7.3%
3/5/2001	0.010	0.60	96.8%	$0.62	106.9%	$0.07	$0.13	$0.18	$0.18	$0.13	7.9%
3/12/2001	0.010	0.50	92.6%	$0.71	106.0%	$0.06	$0.13	$0.18	$0.18	$0.15	8.5%
3/12/2001	0.031	0.54	96.4%	$0.65	106.6%	$0.07	$0.13	$0.18	$0.18	$0.13	7.5%
3/26/2001	-0.010	0.56	94.9%	$0.65	106.6%	$0.07	$0.12	$0.18	$0.18	$0.14	8.4%
4/2/2001	-0.052	0.52	94.5%	$0.76	105.6%	$0.07	$0.13	$0.18	$0.18	$0.13	7.8%
4/9/2001	-0.093	0.58	95.1%	$0.79	105.3%	$0.07	$0.13	$0.18	$0.18	$0.14	8.0%
4/16/2001	-0.093	0.62	96.9%	$0.79	105.3%	$0.08	$0.13	$0.18	$0.18	$0.13	7.4%
4/23/2001	-0.031	0.56	93.3%	$0.80	105.3%	$0.07	$0.14	$0.18	$0.18	$0.15	8.2%
4/30/2001	-0.021	0.58	92.1%	$0.81	108.0%	$0.08	$0.14	$0.18	$0.18	$0.18	9.9%
5/7/2001	0.083	0.62	100.0%	$0.79	106.8%	$0.07	$0.14	$0.18	$0.18	$0.13	6.6%

Date	Distribution Margin	Crude Oil Cost	Discount to CARM Crude Oil Cost	Processing Margin	Premium to CARM Proc. Margin	Swap/ Hedge Spread	State/ Local Sales Tax	State Excise Tax	Federal Excise Tax	Excess Profit	Profit %
5/14/2001	0.166	0.61	95.3%	$0.69	106.2%	$0.08	$0.14	$0.18	$0.18	$0.15	7.8%
5/21/2001	0.166	0.61	95.3%	$0.69	106.2%	$0.08	$0.14	$0.18	$0.18	$0.15	7.8%
5/28/2001	0.208	0.57	89.1%	$0.65	108.3%	$0.08	$0.14	$0.18	$0.18	$0.20	10.5%
6/4/2001	0.208	0.59	93.7%	$0.64	106.7%	$0.08	$0.14	$0.18	$0.18	$0.16	8.5%
6/11/2011	0.332	0.62	95.4%	$0.51	108.5%	$0.08	$0.14	$0.18	$0.18	$0.16	8.2%
6/18/2001	0.363	0.61	98.4%	$0.49	106.5%	$0.07	$0.14	$0.18	$0.18	$0.13	6.6%
6/25/2001	0.394	0.55	91.7%	$0.45	107.1%	$0.07	$0.14	$0.18	$0.18	$0.17	8.8%
7/2/2001	0.426	0.56	96.6%	$0.41	110.8%	$0.07	$0.14	$0.18	$0.18	$0.15	7.8%
7/9/2001	0.436	0.60	96.8%	$0.31	106.9%	$0.07	$0.14	$0.18	$0.18	$0.13	7.2%
7/16/2001	0.457	0.55	96.5%	$0.29	111.5%	$0.07	$0.13	$0.18	$0.18	$0.14	7.6%
7/23/2001	0.529	0.54	94.7%	$0.18	120.0%	$0.07	$0.13	$0.18	$0.18	$0.15	8.6%
7/30/2001	0.353	0.51	89.5%	$0.29	107.4%	$0.07	$0.12	$0.18	$0.18	$0.16	9.7%
8/6/2001	0.280	0.54	93.1%	$0.31	110.7%	$0.07	$0.12	$0.18	$0.18	$0.15	9.2%
8/13/2001	0.197	0.52	88.1%	$0.33	106.5%	$0.07	$0.12	$0.18	$0.18	$0.17	10.8%
8/20/2001	0.083	0.50	87.7%	$0.44	110.0%	$0.07	$0.11	$0.18	$0.18	$0.18	11.9%
8/27/2001	0.062	0.51	91.1%	$0.37	105.7%	$0.07	$0.11	$0.18	$0.18	$0.14	9.2%
9/3/2001	−0.125	0.54	94.7%	$0.75	105.6%	$0.07	$0.12	$0.18	$0.18	$0.13	8.2%
9/10/2001	−0.021	0.52	88.1%	$0.66	106.5%	$0.07	$0.12	$0.18	$0.18	$0.18	10.7%
9/17/2001	0.000	0.55	90.2%	$0.61	107.0%	$0.07	$0.12	$0.18	$0.18	$0.17	10.4%
9/24/2001	0.093	0.39	88.6%	$0.68	106.3%	$0.05	$0.12	$0.18	$0.18	$0.15	8.8%
10/1/2001	0.197	0.36	73.5%	$0.49	106.5%	$0.06	$0.12	$0.18	$0.18	$0.23	14.0%
10/8/2001	0.187	0.35	74.5%	$0.48	109.1%	$0.06	$0.12	$0.18	$0.18	$0.22	14.3%
10/15/2001	0.197	0.36	76.6%	$0.45	109.8%	$0.06	$0.11	$0.18	$0.18	$0.21	13.8%

(continued)

Date	Distribution Margin	Crude Oil Cost	Discount to CARM Crude Oil Cost	Processing Margin	Premium to CARM Proc. Margin	Swap/ Hedge Spread	State/ Local Sales Tax	State Excise Tax	Federal Excise Tax	Excess Profit	Profit %
10/22/2001	0.125	0.39	84.8%	$0.48	106.7%	$0.06	$0.11	$0.18	$0.18	$0.16	10.6%
10/29/2001	0.062	0.38	80.9%	$0.51	108.5%	$0.06	$0.11	$0.18	$0.18	$0.19	12.8%
11/5/2001	0.093	0.40	94.1%	$0.48	106.7%	$0.05	$0.11	$0.18	$0.18	$0.11	7.7%
11/12/2001	0.145	0.39	86.7%	$0.35	106.1%	$0.05	$0.10	$0.18	$0.18	$0.14	10.1%
11/19/2001	0.187	0.32	86.5%	$0.36	109.1%	$0.04	$0.10	$0.18	$0.18	$0.13	9.8%
11/26/2001	0.176	0.33	84.6%	$0.31	114.8%	$0.05	$0.10	$0.18	$0.18	$0.15	11.9%
12/3/2001	0.145	0.31	73.8%	$0.26	113.0%	$0.05	$0.08	$0.18	$0.18	$0.20	15.8%
12/10/2001	0.145	0.32	84.2%	$0.25	108.7%	$0.05	$0.09	$0.18	$0.18	$0.13	10.9%
12/17/2001	0.083	0.32	82.1%	$0.24	109.1%	$0.05	$0.08	$0.18	$0.18	$0.14	12.3%
12/24/2001	0.000	0.38	86.4%	$0.25	108.7%	$0.05	$0.08	$0.18	$0.18	$0.13	12.0%
12/31/2001	−0.073	0.38	92.7%	$0.33	106.5%	$0.05	$0.08	$0.18	$0.18	$0.10	8.8%
1/7/2002	−0.055	0.41	91.1%	$0.32	114.3%	$0.05	$0.08	$0.18	$0.18	$0.13	11.4%
1/14/2002	0.033	0.36	90.0%	$0.34	113.3%	$0.05	$0.09	$0.18	$0.18	$0.13	11.1%
1/21/2002	0.087	0.35	89.7%	$0.35	116.7%	$0.05	$0.09	$0.18	$0.18	$0.14	11.9%
1/28/2002	0.000	0.38	88.4%	$0.38	111.8%	$0.05	$0.09	$0.18	$0.18	$0.14	11.6%
2/4/2002	0.011	0.41	95.3%	$0.39	111.4%	$0.05	$0.09	$0.18	$0.18	$0.11	9.0%
2/11/2002	0.011	0.46	95.8%	$0.36	116.1%	$0.06	$0.09	$0.18	$0.18	$0.13	10.3%
2/19/2002	0.011	0.42	93.3%	$0.44	115.8%	$0.05	$0.10	$0.18	$0.18	$0.14	11.2%
2/25/2002	0.022	0.42	93.3%	$0.44	117.8%	$0.05	$0.10	$0.18	$0.18	$0.15	11.7%
3/4/2002	0.000	0.45	90.0%	$0.44	118.9%	$0.06	$0.10	$0.18	$0.18	$0.18	13.5%
3/11/2002	−0.022	0.51	94.4%	$0.53	112.8%	$0.06	$0.11	$0.18	$0.18	$0.15	10.5%
3/18/2002	−0.033	0.55	94.8%	$0.56	112.0%	$0.07	$0.11	$0.18	$0.18	$0.16	10.5%
3/25/2002	0.011	0.52	94.5%	$0.57	107.5%	$0.07	$0.12	$0.18	$0.18	$0.14	8.8%
4/1/2002	0.055	0.61	100.0%	$0.51	113.3%	$0.07	$0.12	$0.18	$0.18	$0.14	8.7%

Date	Distribution Margin	Crude Oil Cost	Discount to CARM Crude Oil Cost	Processing Margin	Premium to CARM Proc. Margin	Swap/ Hedge Spread	State/ Local Sales Tax	State Excise Tax	Federal Excise Tax	Excess Profit	Profit %
4/8/2002	0.077	0.62	103.3%	$0.50	106.4%	$0.07	$0.12	$0.18	$0.18	$0.09	5.5%
4/15/2002	0.142	0.56	100.0%	$0.53	117.8%	$0.07	$0.12	$0.18	$0.18	$0.16	9.8%
4/22/2002	0.109	0.60	96.8%	$0.46	115.0%	$0.07	$0.12	$0.18	$0.18	$0.16	10.2%
4/29/2002	0.120	0.58	92.1%	$0.44	112.8%	$0.08	$0.12	$0.18	$0.18	$0.19	11.5%
5/6/2002	0.131	0.55	91.7%	$0.44	112.8%	$0.07	$0.12	$0.18	$0.18	$0.18	11.5%
5/13/2002	0.120	0.61	93.8%	$0.37	115.6%	$0.08	$0.12	$0.18	$0.18	$0.18	11.4%
5/20/2002	0.098	0.62	96.9%	$0.41	117.1%	$0.08	$0.12	$0.18	$0.18	$0.17	10.6%
5/27/2002	0.066	0.54	94.7%	$0.50	113.6%	$0.07	$0.12	$0.18	$0.18	$0.16	10.6%
6/3/2002	0.186	0.51	91.1%	$0.51	113.3%	$0.07	$0.12	$0.18	$0.18	$0.19	12.4%
6/10/2002	0.044	0.49	90.7%	$0.57	114.0%	$0.06	$0.12	$0.18	$0.18	$0.19	12.1%
6/17/2002	0.011	0.53	89.8%	$0.58	113.7%	$0.07	$0.12	$0.18	$0.18	$0.20	12.6%
6/24/2002	0.087	0.54	90.0%	$0.51	113.3%	$0.07	$0.12	$0.18	$0.18	$0.20	12.3%
7/1/2002	0.087	0.58	95.1%	$0.50	113.6%	$0.07	$0.12	$0.18	$0.18	$0.17	10.5%
7/8/2002	0.077	0.56	93.3%	$0.52	113.0%	$0.07	$0.12	$0.18	$0.18	$0.18	11.1%
7/15/2002	0.077	0.56	90.3%	$0.49	114.0%	$0.07	$0.12	$0.18	$0.18	$0.20	12.6%
7/22/2002	0.066	0.56	91.8%	$0.50	113.6%	$0.07	$0.12	$0.18	$0.18	$0.19	11.9%
7/29/2002	0.044	0.58	95.1%	$0.51	113.3%	$0.07	$0.12	$0.18	$0.18	$0.17	10.6%
8/5/2002	0.066	0.60	98.4%	$0.51	113.3%	$0.07	$0.12	$0.18	$0.18	$0.15	9.4%
8/12/2002	0.044	0.62	96.9%	$0.49	114.0%	$0.08	$0.12	$0.18	$0.18	$0.16	10.1%
8/19/2002	0.022	0.65	94.2%	$0.44	112.8%	$0.08	$0.12	$0.18	$0.18	$0.17	11.1%
8/26/2002	0.044	0.66	98.5%	$0.46	115.0%	$0.08	$0.12	$0.18	$0.18	$0.15	9.7%
9/2/2002	0.033	0.62	96.9%	$0.51	113.3%	$0.08	$0.12	$0.18	$0.18	$0.16	10.0%
9/9/2002	0.011	0.62	89.9%	$0.46	109.5%	$0.08	$0.12	$0.18	$0.18	$0.19	12.2%

(continued)

Date	Distribution Margin	Crude Oil Cost	Discount to CARM Crude Oil Cost	Processing Margin	Premium to CARM Proc. Margin	Swap/ Hedge Spread	State/ Local Sales Tax	State Excise Tax	Federal Excise Tax	Excess Profit	Profit %
9/16/2002	0.000	0.64	94.1%	$0.48	114.3%	$0.08	$0.12	$0.18	$0.18	$0.18	11.5%
9/23/2002	0.000	0.65	91.5%	$0.42	107.7%	$0.09	$0.12	$0.18	$0.18	$0.18	11.2%
9/30/2002	-0.011	0.67	95.7%	$0.44	112.8%	$0.08	$0.12	$0.18	$0.18	$0.16	10.5%
10/7/2002	-0.022	0.66	97.1%	$0.46	115.0%	$0.08	$0.11	$0.18	$0.18	$0.16	10.3%
10/14/2002	-0.033	0.62	91.2%	$0.47	114.6%	$0.08	$0.11	$0.18	$0.18	$0.20	13.0%
10/21/2002	-0.044	0.58	90.6%	$0.51	113.3%	$0.08	$0.11	$0.18	$0.18	$0.19	12.7%
10/28/2002	-0.055	0.77	95.1%	$0.56	114.3%	$0.10	$0.11	$0.18	$0.18	$0.20	13.3%
11/4/2002	-0.011	0.56	93.3%	$0.57	116.3%	$0.07	$0.12	$0.18	$0.18	$0.19	12.2%
11/11/2002	0.022	0.55	94.8%	$0.58	113.7%	$0.07	$0.12	$0.18	$0.18	$0.17	10.8%
11/18/2002	0.044	0.54	90.0%	$0.53	112.8%	$0.07	$0.12	$0.18	$0.18	$0.20	12.3%
11/25/2002	0.087	0.57	93.4%	$0.46	115.0%	$0.07	$0.12	$0.18	$0.18	$0.18	11.5%
12/2/2002	0.142	0.56	91.8%	$0.39	114.7%	$0.07	$0.12	$0.18	$0.18	$0.19	11.9%
12/9/2002	0.164	0.54	88.5%	$0.34	113.3%	$0.07	$0.11	$0.18	$0.18	$0.20	12.8%
12/16/2002	0.109	0.61	92.4%	$0.31	119.2%	$0.08	$0.11	$0.18	$0.18	$0.19	12.3%
12/23/2002	0.098	0.66	90.4%	$0.27	117.4%	$0.09	$0.11	$0.18	$0.18	$0.21	13.6%
12/30/2002	0.066	0.68	94.4%	$0.32	114.3%	$0.09	$0.11	$0.18	$0.18	$0.17	11.2%
12/6/2003	0.105	0.67	91.8%	$0.33	122.2%	$0.09	$0.12	$0.18	$0.18	$0.22	14.1%
12/13/2003	0.105	0.66	89.2%	$0.34	121.4%	$0.09	$0.12	$0.18	$0.18	$0.24	15.3%
12/20/2003	0.116	0.72	90.0%	$0.31	124.0%	$0.10	$0.12	$0.18	$0.18	$0.25	15.5%
12/27/2003	0.116	0.65	87.8%	$0.38	118.8%	$0.09	$0.12	$0.18	$0.18	$0.26	15.5%
2/3/2003	0.105	0.67	88.2%	$0.38	108.6%	$0.09	$0.12	$0.18	$0.18	$0.23	13.4%
2/10/2003	0.081	0.70	86.4%	$0.42	110.5%	$0.10	$0.13	$0.18	$0.18	$0.26	14.8%
2/17/2003	0.186	0.81	93.1%	$0.39	118.2%	$0.10	$0.14	$0.18	$0.18	$0.25	13.5%
2/24/2003	0.209	0.80	90.9%	$0.41	113.9%	$0.11	$0.14	$0.18	$0.18	$0.26	13.8%

Date	Distribution Margin	Crude Oil Cost	Discount to CARM Crude Oil Cost	Processing Margin	Premium to CARM Proc. Margin	Swap/ Hedge Spread	State/ Local Sales Tax	State Excise Tax	Federal Excise Tax	Excess Profit	Profit %
3/3/2003	0.163	0.78	91.8%	$0.58	113.7%	$0.10	$0.15	$0.18	$0.18	$0.26	13.2%
3/10/2003	0.151	0.79	89.8%	$0.62	112.7%	$0.11	$0.15	$0.18	$0.18	$0.29	13.8%
3/17/2003	0.174	0.74	90.2%	$0.74	113.8%	$0.10	$0.16	$0.18	$0.18	$0.29	13.7%
3/24/2003	0.232	0.56	88.9%	$0.92	116.5%	$0.08	$0.16	$0.18	$0.18	$0.31	14.4%
3/31/2003	0.302	0.62	89.9%	$0.77	116.7%	$0.08	$0.16	$0.18	$0.18	$0.30	14.3%
4/7/2003	0.337	0.53	88.3%	$0.81	115.7%	$0.07	$0.16	$0.18	$0.18	$0.30	14.2%
4/14/2003	0.337	0.54	87.1%	$0.82	124.2%	$0.07	$0.15	$0.18	$0.18	$0.36	17.4%
4/21/2003	0.337	0.59	88.1%	$0.65	114.0%	$0.08	$0.15	$0.18	$0.18	$0.29	14.3%
4/28/2003	0.291	0.47	87.0%	$0.78	116.4%	$0.06	$0.15	$0.18	$0.18	$0.29	14.4%
5/5/2003	0.302	0.51	87.9%	$0.67	117.5%	$0.07	$0.14	$0.18	$0.18	$0.28	14.6%
5/12/2003	0.383	0.53	88.3%	$0.51	118.6%	$0.07	$0.14	$0.18	$0.18	$0.28	14.7%
5/19/2003	0.325	0.56	87.5%	$0.46	117.9%	$0.08	$0.13	$0.18	$0.18	$0.27	15.0%
5/28/2003	0.267	0.58	87.9%	$0.45	118.4%	$0.08	$0.13	$0.18	$0.18	$0.27	15.1%
6/2/2003	0.232	0.62	88.6%	$0.40	117.6%	$0.08	$0.13	$0.18	$0.18	$0.26	14.8%
6/9/2003	0.163	0.65	90.3%	$0.37	108.8%	$0.09	$0.13	$0.18	$0.18	$0.21	12.3%
6/16/2003	0.058	0.63	88.7%	$0.60	113.2%	$0.09	$0.13	$0.18	$0.18	$0.24	13.6%
6/23/2003	0.035	0.63	88.7%	$0.67	117.5%	$0.09	$0.13	$0.18	$0.18	$0.27	15.0%
6/30/2003	0.058	0.78	88.6%	$0.65	114.0%	$0.11	$0.13	$0.18	$0.18	$0.29	16.3%
7/7/2003	0.093	0.62	91.2%	$0.62	117.0%	$0.08	$0.13	$0.18	$0.18	$0.24	13.7%
7/14/2003	0.128	0.62	87.3%	$0.52	118.2%	$0.09	$0.13	$0.18	$0.18	$0.27	15.5%
7/21/2003	0.128	0.63	87.5%	$0.47	117.5%	$0.09	$0.13	$0.18	$0.18	$0.26	15.3%
7/28/2003	0.128	0.60	88.2%	$0.51	118.6%	$0.08	$0.13	$0.18	$0.18	$0.26	15.2%
8/4/2003	0.093	0.63	87.5%	$0.48	117.1%	$0.09	$0.13	$0.18	$0.18	$0.26	15.3%

(continued)

261

Date	Distribution Margin	Crude Oil Cost	Discount to CARM Crude Oil Cost	Processing Margin	Premium to CARM Proc. Margin	Swap/ Hedge Spread	State/ Local Sales Tax	State Excise Tax	Federal Excise Tax	Excess Profit	Profit %
8/11/2003	0.081	0.62	84.9%	$0.53	117.8%	$0.09	$0.13	$0.18	$0.18	$0.29	16.6%
8/18/2003	0.000	0.62	88.6%	$0.83	116.9%	$0.08	$0.14	$0.18	$0.18	$0.28	14.8%
8/25/2003	0.058	0.63	87.5%	$0.94	116.0%	$0.09	$0.16	$0.18	$0.18	$0.31	15.0%
9/1/2003	0.186	0.62	86.1%	$0.83	116.9%	$0.09	$0.16	$0.18	$0.18	$0.33	15.8%
9/8/2003	0.256	0.58	87.9%	$0.81	117.4%	$0.08	$0.15	$0.18	$0.18	$0.31	15.1%
9/15/2003	0.302	0.56	87.5%	$0.68	117.2%	$0.08	$0.15	$0.18	$0.18	$0.30	14.7%
9/22/2003	0.383	0.54	87.1%	$0.61	117.3%	$0.07	$0.15	$0.18	$0.18	$0.30	15.0%
9/29/2003	0.383	0.57	87.7%	$0.51	118.6%	$0.08	$0.14	$0.18	$0.18	$0.29	15.3%
10/6/2003	0.302	0.61	88.4%	$0.48	117.1%	$0.08	$0.14	$0.18	$0.18	$0.27	14.9%
10/13/2003	0.221	0.63	87.5%	$0.47	117.5%	$0.09	$0.13	$0.18	$0.18	$0.28	15.3%
10/20/2003	0.221	0.60	88.2%	$0.47	117.5%	$0.08	$0.13	$0.18	$0.18	$0.26	14.5%
10/27/2003	0.174	0.59	88.1%	$0.49	116.7%	$0.08	$0.13	$0.18	$0.18	$0.25	14.6%
11/3/2003	0.151	0.57	87.7%	$0.52	118.2%	$0.08	$0.13	$0.18	$0.18	$0.26	15.1%
11/10/2003	0.128	0.61	88.4%	$0.47	117.5%	$0.08	$0.13	$0.18	$0.18	$0.25	14.8%
11/17/2003	0.081	0.63	88.7%	$0.49	116.7%	$0.09	$0.12	$0.18	$0.18	$0.25	14.7%
11/24/2003	0.151	0.59	88.1%	$0.47	117.5%	$0.08	$0.13	$0.18	$0.18	$0.25	14.9%
12/1/2003	0.163	0.59	88.1%	$0.46	117.9%	$0.08	$0.12	$0.18	$0.18	$0.25	15.1%
12/8/2003	0.163	0.63	87.5%	$0.37	119.4%	$0.09	$0.12	$0.18	$0.18	$0.26	15.7%
12/15/2003	0.151	0.67	88.2%	$0.30	120.0%	$0.09	$0.12	$0.18	$0.18	$0.25	15.6%
12/22/2003	0.139	0.64	87.7%	$0.33	117.9%	$0.09	$0.12	$0.18	$0.18	$0.25	15.3%
12/29/2003	0.093	0.65	87.8%	$0.34	117.2%	$0.09	$0.12	$0.18	$0.18	$0.24	15.2%
1/5/2004	0.151	0.68	87.2%	$0.34	121.4%	$0.09	$0.12	$0.18	$0.15	$0.28	17.0%
1/12/2004	0.198	0.70	87.5%	$0.31	124.0%	$0.10	$0.12	$0.18	$0.15	$0.28	17.0%
1/19/2004	0.117	0.74	88.1%	$0.35	120.7%	$0.10	$0.13	$0.18	$0.15	$0.28	16.4%

Date	Distribution Margin	Crude Oil Cost	Discount to CARM Crude Oil Cost	Processing Margin	Premium to CARM Proc. Margin	Swap/ Hedge Spread	State/ Local Sales Tax	State Excise Tax	Federal Excise Tax	Excess Profit	Profit %
1/26/2004	0.151	0.67	84.8%	$0.42	120.0%	$0.09	$0.13	$0.18	$0.15	$0.31	17.7%
2/2/2004	0.140	0.69	85.2%	$0.43	119.4%	$0.10	$0.13	$0.18	$0.15	$0.31	17.5%
2/9/2004	0.163	0.65	85.5%	$0.55	119.6%	$0.09	$0.13	$0.18	$0.15	$0.31	17.3%
2/16/2004	0.175	0.68	85.0%	$0.54	120.0%	$0.10	$0.14	$0.18	$0.15	$0.33	17.7%
2/23/2004	0.105	0.65	82.3%	$0.80	119.4%	$0.09	$0.15	$0.18	$0.15	$0.38	18.7%
3/1/2004	0.163	0.73	85.9%	$0.75	119.0%	$0.10	$0.16	$0.18	$0.15	$0.37	17.3%
3/8/2004	0.186	0.72	85.7%	$0.74	119.4%	$0.10	$0.16	$0.18	$0.15	$0.37	17.4%
3/15/2004	0.221	0.72	83.7%	$0.67	119.6%	$0.10	$0.16	$0.18	$0.15	$0.38	18.3%
3/22/2004	0.210	0.71	83.5%	$0.68	119.3%	$0.10	$0.15	$0.18	$0.15	$0.38	18.4%
3/29/2004	0.186	0.68	84.0%	$0.75	119.0%	$0.10	$0.15	$0.18	$0.15	$0.37	18.0%
4/5/2004	0.140	0.69	87.3%	$0.87	119.2%	$0.09	$0.16	$0.18	$0.15	$0.35	16.6%
4/12/2004	0.186	0.76	87.4%	$0.76	118.8%	$0.10	$0.16	$0.18	$0.15	$0.36	16.7%
4/19/2004	0.186	0.77	89.5%	$0.77	120.3%	$0.10	$0.16	$0.18	$0.15	$0.35	16.3%
4/26/2004	0.175	0.73	85.9%	$0.75	119.0%	$0.10	$0.16	$0.18	$0.15	$0.37	17.3%
5/3/2004	0.117	0.77	87.5%	$0.76	118.8%	$0.11	$0.16	$0.18	$0.15	$0.35	16.7%
5/10/2004	0.105	0.79	87.8%	$0.88	118.9%	$0.11	$0.16	$0.18	$0.15	$0.37	16.8%
5/17/2004	0.128	0.81	84.4%	$0.83	118.6%	$0.12	$0.17	$0.18	$0.15	$0.41	18.2%
5/24/2004	0.151	0.83	85.6%	$0.85	118.1%	$0.12	$0.17	$0.18	$0.15	$0.41	17.6%
5/31/2004	0.210	0.85	85.9%	$0.78	118.2%	$0.12	$0.17	$0.18	$0.15	$0.41	17.5%
6/7/2004	0.221	0.78	87.6%	$0.88	118.9%	$0.11	$0.17	$0.18	$0.15	$0.39	16.7%
6/14/2004	0.233	0.73	84.9%	$0.87	119.2%	$0.10	$0.17	$0.18	$0.15	$0.41	17.7%
6/21/2004	0.291	0.75	87.2%	$1.02	120.0%	$0.10	$0.17	$0.18	$0.15	$0.42	18.8%
6/28/2004	0.245	0.71	85.5%	$0.84	120.0%	$0.10	$0.17	$0.18	$0.15	$0.39	17.6%

(continued)

Date	Distribution Margin	Crude Oil Cost	Discount to CARM Crude Oil Cost	Processing Margin	Premium to CARM Proc. Margin	Swap/Hedge Spread	State/Local Sales Tax	State Excise Tax	Federal Excise Tax	Excess Profit	Profit %
7/5/2004	0.233	0.75	85.2%	$0.75	119.0%	$0.11	$0.16	$0.18	$0.15	$0.39	17.7%
7/12/2004	0.198	0.78	85.7%	$0.74	119.4%	$0.11	$0.16	$0.18	$0.15	$0.39	17.7%
7/19/2004	0.186	0.81	85.3%	$0.70	118.6%	$0.11	$0.16	$0.18	$0.15	$0.39	17.8%
7/26/2004	0.210	0.82	85.4%	$0.63	118.9%	$0.12	$0.16	$0.18	$0.15	$0.38	17.8%
8/2/2004	0.210	0.89	88.1%	$0.54	120.0%	$0.12	$0.16	$0.18	$0.15	$0.36	16.9%
8/9/2004	0.210	0.91	87.5%	$0.47	120.5%	$0.12	$0.15	$0.18	$0.15	$0.36	17.4%
8/16/2004	0.140	0.93	87.7%	$0.47	120.5%	$0.13	$0.15	$0.18	$0.15	$0.36	17.4%
8/23/2004	0.117	0.94	88.7%	$0.49	119.5%	$0.13	$0.15	$0.18	$0.15	$0.34	16.8%
8/30/2004	0.210	0.80	85.1%	$0.58	118.4%	$0.11	$0.15	$0.18	$0.15	$0.37	17.7%
9/6/2004	0.186	0.83	85.6%	$0.55	119.6%	$0.12	$0.15	$0.18	$0.15	$0.37	0.2%
9/13/2004	0.175	0.82	84.5%	$0.56	119.1%	$0.12	$0.15	$0.18	$0.15	$0.38	18.6%
9/21/2004	0.128	0.88	85.4%	$0.53	120.5%	$0.12	$0.15	$0.18	$0.15	$0.38	18.6%
9/27/2004	0.070	0.94	85.5%	$0.53	120.5%	$0.13	$0.16	$0.18	$0.15	$0.39	18.8%
10/4/2004	0.105	0.96	86.5%	$0.61	119.6%	$0.13	$0.16	$0.18	$0.15	$0.40	18.1%
10/11/2004	0.093	0.10	8.5%	$0.69	119.0%	$0.14	$0.17	$0.18	$0.15	$1.33	57.2%
10/18/2004	0.105	1.01	85.6%	$0.74	119.4%	$0.14	$0.18	$0.18	$0.15	$0.45	18.6%
10/25/2004	0.163	0.98	84.5%	$0.69	119.0%	$0.14	$0.18	$0.18	$0.15	$0.45	18.9%
11/1/2004	0.198	0.93	85.3%	$0.71	118.3%	$0.13	$0.18	$0.18	$0.15	$0.43	18.1%
11/8/2004	0.256	0.87	85.3%	$0.72	120.0%	$0.12	$0.17	$0.18	$0.15	$0.43	18.3%
11/15/2004	0.256	0.84	85.7%	$0.73	119.7%	$0.12	$0.17	$0.18	$0.15	$0.41	17.9%
11/22/2004	0.291	0.86	86.0%	$0.61	119.6%	$0.12	$0.17	$0.18	$0.15	$0.40	17.8%
11/29/2004	0.280	1.01	85.6%	$0.39	121.9%	$0.14	$0.17	$0.18	$0.15	$0.42	18.8%
12/6/2004	0.373	0.74	86.0%	$0.62	119.2%	$0.10	$0.16	$0.18	$0.15	$0.38	17.2%
12/13/2004	0.536	0.69	85.2%	$0.46	121.1%	$0.10	$0.16	$0.18	$0.15	$0.37	17.4%

Date	Distribution Margin	Crude Oil Cost	Discount to CARM Crude Oil Cost	Processing Margin	Premium to CARM Proc. Margin	Swap/ Hedge Spread	State/ Local Sales Tax	State Excise Tax	Federal Excise Tax	Excess Profit	Profit %
12/20/2004	0.373	0.79	84.9%	$0.39	121.9%	$0.11	$0.15	$0.18	$0.15	$0.37	18.3%
12/27/2004	0.315	0.70	85.4%	$0.53	120.5%	$0.10	$0.15	$0.18	$0.15	$0.35	17.6%
1/3/2005	0.265	0.71	84.5%	$0.51	124.4%	$0.10	$0.15	$0.18	$0.18	$0.38	19.0%
1/10/2005	0.205	0.69	74.2%	$0.41	124.2%	$0.11	$0.14	$0.18	$0.18	$0.47	24.2%
1/17/2005	0.157	0.86	82.7%	$0.33	126.9%	$0.12	$0.14	$0.18	$0.18	$0.40	20.8%
1/24/2005	0.096	0.84	81.6%	$0.43	126.5%	$0.12	$0.15	$0.18	$0.18	$0.42	21.4%
1/31/2005	0.145	0.86	82.7%	$0.45	125.0%	$0.12	$0.15	$0.18	$0.18	$0.42	20.7%
2/7/2005	0.133	0.83	83.0%	$0.54	125.6%	$0.12	$0.15	$0.18	$0.18	$0.42	20.6%
2/14/2005	0.108	0.85	83.3%	$0.58	123.4%	$0.12	$0.15	$0.18	$0.18	$0.42	20.1%
2/21/2005	0.133	0.94	83.9%	$0.50	125.0%	$0.13	$0.16	$0.18	$0.18	$0.44	20.3%
2/28/2005	0.084	0.93	83.0%	$0.58	123.4%	$0.13	$0.16	$0.18	$0.18	$0.45	20.6%
3/7/2005	0.084	1.01	84.9%	$0.55	125.0%	$0.14	$0.17	$0.18	$0.18	$0.45	20.1%
3/14/2005	0.096	1.03	85.1%	$0.58	123.4%	$0.15	$0.17	$0.18	$0.18	$0.45	19.7%
3/21/2005	0.108	1.04	82.5%	$0.54	125.6%	$0.15	$0.17	$0.18	$0.18	$0.50	23.8%
3/28/2005	0.072	1.03	85.1%	$0.71	124.6%	$0.15	$0.18	$0.18	$0.18	$0.48	20.1%
4/4/2005	0.000	1.07	83.6%	$0.78	121.9%	$0.15	$0.18	$0.18	$0.18	$0.50	20.5%
4/11/2005	0.048	0.98	81.7%	$0.99	123.8%	$0.14	$0.19	$0.18	$0.18	$0.56	21.7%
4/18/2005	0.048	0.94	83.9%	$1.07	123.0%	$0.13	$0.19	$0.18	$0.18	$0.52	20.3%
4/25/2005	0.108	1.01	82.8%	$0.88	123.9%	$0.15	$0.19	$0.18	$0.18	$0.54	21.2%
5/2/2005	0.181	0.97	85.1%	$0.89	123.6%	$0.14	$0.19	$0.18	$0.18	$0.51	19.8%
5/9/2005	0.229	0.98	83.8%	$0.76	124.6%	$0.14	$0.19	$0.18	$0.18	$0.52	20.6%
5/16/2005	0.362	0.92	85.2%	$0.68	123.6%	$0.13	$0.18	$0.18	$0.18	$0.48	19.5%
5/23/2005	0.349	0.94	83.9%	$0.62	129.2%	$0.13	$0.18	$0.18	$0.18	$0.51	21.1%

(continued)

Date	Distribution Margin	Crude Oil Cost	Discount to CARM Crude Oil Cost	Processing Margin	Premium to CARM Proc. Margin	Swap/ Hedge Spread	State/ Local Sales Tax	State Excise Tax	Federal Excise Tax	Excess Profit	Profit %
5/30/2005	0.325	0.98	83.8%	$0.52	126.8%	$0.14	$0.18	$0.18	$0.18	$0.50	20.7%
6/6/2005	0.253	1.12	85.5%	$0.39	125.8%	$0.16	$0.17	$0.18	$0.18	$0.47	19.9%
6/13/2005	0.169	1.05	83.3%	$0.50	125.0%	$0.15	$0.17	$0.18	$0.18	$0.49	21.0%
6/20/2005	0.121	1.13	83.7%	$0.46	124.3%	$0.16	$0.17	$0.18	$0.18	$0.49	21.0%
6/27/2005	0.072	1.15	83.3%	$0.54	125.6%	$0.17	$0.18	$0.18	$0.18	$0.52	21.5%
7/4/2005	0.084	1.12	83.6%	$0.63	123.5%	$0.16	$0.18	$0.18	$0.18	$0.52	20.9%
7/11/2005	0.121	1.13	83.7%	$0.65	122.6%	$0.16	$0.19	$0.18	$0.18	$0.52	20.7%
7/18/2005	0.265	1.11	84.1%	$0.56	124.4%	$0.16	$0.19	$0.18	$0.18	$0.52	20.6%
7/25/2005	0.145	1.09	83.2%	$0.69	123.2%	$0.16	$0.19	$0.18	$0.18	$0.53	20.9%
8/1/2005	0.084	1.12	78.9%	$0.63	123.5%	$0.17	$0.19	$0.18	$0.18	$0.60	23.7%
8/8/2005	−0.036	1.19	81.0%	$0.76	124.6%	$0.18	$0.19	$0.18	$0.18	$0.60	23.1%
8/15/2005	0.048	1.24	82.1%	$0.77	126.2%	$0.18	$0.20	$0.18	$0.18	$0.62	22.8%
8/22/2005	0.169	1.25	83.9%	$0.69	123.2%	$0.18	$0.20	$0.18	$0.18	$0.58	21.0%
8/29/2005	−0.181	1.28	83.7%	$1.01	123.2%	$0.18	$0.21	$0.18	$0.18	$0.59	21.4%
9/5/2005	−0.121	1.29	83.8%	$1.27	123.3%	$0.18	$0.23	$0.18	$0.18	$0.65	21.4%
9/15/2005	0.313	1.22	83.6%	$0.87	124.3%	$0.18	$0.22	$0.18	$0.18	$0.64	21.3%
9/19/2005	0.217	1.31	84.0%	$0.78	123.8%	$0.19	$0.22	$0.18	$0.18	$0.62	21.2%
9/26/2005	0.193	1.27	83.6%	$0.85	123.2%	$0.18	$0.22	$0.18	$0.18	$0.63	21.2%
10/3/2005	0.048	1.28	84.8%	$1.02	121.4%	$0.18	$0.22	$0.18	$0.18	$0.60	20.2%
10/10/2005	0.446	1.21	84.6%	$0.73	125.9%	$0.17	$0.22	$0.18	$0.18	$0.62	20.9%
10/17/2005	0.482	1.25	83.9%	$0.56	127.3%	$0.18	$0.21	$0.18	$0.18	$0.62	21.4%
10/24/2005	0.542	1.18	83.7%	$0.51	127.5%	$0.17	$0.21	$0.18	$0.18	$0.60	21.3%
10/31/2005	0.470	1.16	84.1%	$0.52	123.8%	$0.17	$0.20	$0.18	$0.18	$0.57	20.6%
11/7/2005	0.349	1.13	83.7%	$0.57	123.9%	$0.16	$0.20	$0.18	$0.18	$0.55	20.7%

Date	Distribution Margin	Crude Oil Cost	Discount to CARM Crude Oil Cost	Processing Margin	Premium to CARM Proc. Margin	Swap/ Hedge Spread	State/ Local Sales Tax	State Excise Tax	Federal Excise Tax	Excess Profit	Profit %
11/14/2005	0.362	1.11	84.1%	$0.54	131.7%	$0.16	$0.19	$0.18	$0.18	$0.56	21.7%
11/21/2005	0.229	1.11	84.1%	$0.50	125.0%	$0.16	$0.18	$0.18	$0.18	$0.51	20.7%
11/28/2005	0.193	1.09	82.6%	$0.49	125.6%	$0.16	$0.18	$0.18	$0.18	$0.52	21.6%
12/5/2005	0.181	1.10	83.3%	$0.35	125.0%	$0.16	$0.17	$0.18	$0.18	$0.48	20.5%
12/12/2005	0.145	1.18	83.7%	$0.28	127.3%	$0.17	$0.17	$0.18	$0.18	$0.48	21.3%
12/19/2005	0.048	1.09	83.2%	$0.43	119.4%	$0.16	$0.17	$0.18	$0.18	$0.46	20.2%
12/26/2005	0.048	1.11	83.5%	$0.39	118.2%	$0.16	$0.17	$0.18	$0.18	$0.45	20.1%
1/2/2006	−0.045	1.16	81.1%	$0.37	123.3%	$0.17	$0.16	$0.18	$0.18	$0.51	22.9%
1/9/2006	−0.034	1.18	81.4%	$0.46	124.3%	$0.17	$0.17	$0.18	$0.18	$0.53	22.8%
1/16/2006	0.056	1.23	81.5%	$0.39	125.8%	$0.18	$0.18	$0.18	$0.18	$0.55	22.6%
1/26/2006	−0.034	1.29	81.6%	$0.41	124.2%	$0.19	$0.18	$0.18	$0.18	$0.56	23.0%
1/30/2006	0.034	1.27	81.4%	$0.58	123.4%	$0.19	$0.19	$0.18	$0.18	$0.59	23.5%
2/6/2006	0.022	1.22	81.3%	$0.59	125.5%	$0.18	$0.19	$0.18	$0.18	$0.58	22.9%
2/13/2006	0.168	1.14	81.4%	$0.51	124.4%	$0.17	$0.19	$0.18	$0.18	$0.55	21.7%
2/20/2006	0.135	1.14	81.4%	$0.50	125.0%	$0.17	$0.18	$0.18	$0.18	$0.54	22.0%
2/27/2006	0.101	1.13	80.7%	$0.51	124.4%	$0.17	$0.18	$0.18	$0.18	$0.55	22.5%
3/6/2006	−0.034	1.16	81.1%	$0.67	124.1%	$0.17	$0.18	$0.18	$0.18	$0.57	22.9%
3/13/2006	0.056	1.15	81.0%	$0.64	125.5%	$0.17	$0.19	$0.18	$0.18	$0.58	22.8%
3/20/2006	0.045	1.13	81.3%	$0.79	123.4%	$0.17	$0.20	$0.18	$0.18	$0.58	22.0%
3/27/2006	0.034	1.20	81.1%	$0.73	123.7%	$0.18	$0.20	$0.18	$0.18	$0.60	22.5%
4/3/2006	0.022	1.25	81.2%	$0.77	124.2%	$0.18	$0.20	$0.18	$0.18	$0.63	22.9%
4/10/2006	−0.034	1.29	81.1%	$0.83	123.9%	$0.19	$0.21	$0.18	$0.18	$0.65	23.0%
4/17/2006	−0.079	1.33	81.6%	$0.94	123.7%	$0.20	$0.21	$0.18	$0.18	$0.67	23.0%

(continued)

Date	Distribution Margin	Crude Oil Cost	Discount to CARM Crude Oil Cost	Processing Margin	Premium to CARM Proc. Margin	Swap/ Hedge Spread	State/ Local Sales Tax	State Excise Tax	Federal Excise Tax	Excess Profit	Profit %
4/24/2006	−0.079	1.35	81.8%	$1.12	124.4%	$0.20	$0.23	$0.18	$0.18	$0.71	23.1%
5/1/2006	0.022	1.40	81.9%	$1.08	124.1%	$0.21	$0.24	$0.18	$0.18	$0.73	22.7%
5/8/2006	0.045	1.35	83.3%	$1.31	123.6%	$0.19	$0.25	$0.18	$0.18	$0.72	21.6%
5/15/2006	0.022	1.31	81.4%	$1.34	124.1%	$0.19	$0.25	$0.18	$0.18	$0.76	22.7%
5/22/2006	0.022	1.30	80.7%	$1.27	124.5%	$0.19	$0.24	$0.18	$0.18	$0.76	23.3%
5/29/2006	0.045	1.36	81.0%	$1.18	125.5%	$0.20	$0.24	$0.18	$0.18	$0.77	23.4%
6/5/2006	0.045	1.35	79.9%	$1.15	125.0%	$0.20	$0.24	$0.18	$0.18	$0.78	23.8%
6/12/2006	0.168	1.30	79.3%	$1.04	126.8%	$0.20	$0.24	$0.18	$0.18	$0.78	24.0%
6/19/2006	0.213	1.31	81.4%	$0.99	126.9%	$0.19	$0.24	$0.18	$0.18	$0.73	22.7%
6/26/2006	0.180	1.37	81.5%	$0.91	128.2%	$0.20	$0.24	$0.18	$0.18	$0.73	23.1%
7/3/2006	0.079	1.41	81.5%	$0.96	124.7%	$0.21	$0.24	$0.18	$0.18	$0.73	22.8%
7/10/2006	0.101	1.42	82.6%	$0.99	123.8%	$0.21	$0.24	$0.18	$0.18	$0.71	22.2%
7/17/2006	0.123	1.43	81.3%	$0.96	126.3%	$0.21	$0.24	$0.18	$0.18	$0.75	23.3%
7/24/2006	0.112	1.44	82.3%	$0.97	127.6%	$0.21	$0.24	$0.18	$0.18	$0.74	23.0%
7/31/2006	0.112	1.42	81.6%	$0.95	128.4%	$0.21	$0.24	$0.18	$0.18	$0.75	23.5%
8/7/2006	0.101	1.47	81.7%	$0.86	126.5%	$0.22	$0.24	$0.18	$0.18	$0.74	23.1%
8/14/2006	0.157	1.49	86.6%	$0.92	126.0%	$0.21	$0.24	$0.18	$0.18	$0.64	20.0%
8/21/2006	0.224	1.39	82.2%	$0.84	127.3%	$0.20	$0.23	$0.18	$0.18	$0.71	22.4%
8/28/2006	0.281	1.34	81.2%	$0.75	127.1%	$0.20	$0.23	$0.18	$0.18	$0.70	22.5%
9/4/2006	0.258	1.30	81.3%	$0.74	125.4%	$0.19	$0.22	$0.18	$0.18	$0.67	22.3%
9/11/2006	0.292	1.24	81.0%	$0.72	126.3%	$0.18	$0.22	$0.18	$0.18	$0.66	22.2%
9/18/2006	0.348	1.21	81.2%	$0.59	128.3%	$0.18	$0.21	$0.18	$0.18	$0.63	22.0%
9/25/2006	0.348	1.15	81.6%	$0.61	132.6%	$0.17	$0.20	$0.18	$0.18	$0.62	22.4%
10/2/2006	0.281	1.15	81.0%	$0.56	130.2%	$0.17	$0.20	$0.18	$0.18	$0.60	22.4%

Date	Distribution Margin	Crude Oil Cost	Discount to CARM Crude Oil Cost	Processing Margin	Premium to CARM Proc. Margin	Swap/ Hedge Spread	State/ Local Sales Tax	State Excise Tax	Federal Excise Tax	Excess Profit	Profit %
10/9/2006	0.247	1.06	81.5%	$0.63	123.5%	$0.16	$0.19	$0.18	$0.18	$0.54	20.9%
10/16/2006	0.224	1.05	81.4%	$0.61	127.1%	$0.15	$0.19	$0.18	$0.18	$0.55	21.6%
10/23/2006	0.180	1.00	80.0%	$0.63	123.5%	$0.15	$0.18	$0.18	$0.18	$0.54	21.8%
10/30/2006	0.168	1.03	81.1%	$0.57	123.9%	$0.15	$0.18	$0.18	$0.18	$0.52	21.4%
11/6/2006	0.067	1.07	81.1%	$0.57	123.9%	$0.16	$0.18	$0.18	$0.18	$0.53	21.9%
11/13/2006	0.056	1.04	81.3%	$0.72	124.1%	$0.15	$0.18	$0.18	$0.18	$0.54	21.9%
11/20/2006	0.067	1.02	82.9%	$0.81	124.6%	$0.15	$0.18	$0.18	$0.18	$0.52	21.0%
11/27/2006	0.067	1.06	80.3%	$0.69	125.5%	$0.16	$0.18	$0.18	$0.18	$0.57	22.7%
12/4/2006	0.056	1.13	82.5%	$0.66	126.9%	$0.16	$0.18	$0.18	$0.18	$0.55	22.0%
12/11/2006	0.067	1.10	80.3%	$0.62	124.0%	$0.16	$0.19	$0.18	$0.18	$0.56	22.5%
12/18/2006	0.101	1.09	78.4%	$0.64	125.5%	$0.17	$0.19	$0.18	$0.18	$0.61	23.7%
12/25/2006	0.157	1.13	80.7%	$0.64	125.5%	$0.17	$0.19	$0.18	$0.18	$0.59	22.4%
1/1/2007	0.161	1.11	84.1%	$0.74	125.4%	$0.16	$0.19	$0.18	$0.18	$0.55	21.0%
1/8/2007	0.210	1.05	82.7%	$0.78	125.8%	$0.15	$0.19	$0.18	$0.18	$0.57	21.8%
1/15/2007	0.210	0.95	82.6%	$0.86	124.6%	$0.14	$0.19	$0.18	$0.18	$0.55	21.2%
1/22/2007	0.235	0.99	83.2%	$0.74	125.4%	$0.14	$0.19	$0.18	$0.18	$0.54	21.2%
1/29/2007	0.148	1.02	83.6%	$0.75	125.0%	$0.15	$0.18	$0.18	$0.18	$0.52	21.1%
2/5/2007	0.086	1.12	83.0%	$0.68	125.9%	$0.16	$0.19	$0.18	$0.18	$0.55	21.6%
2/12/2007	0.037	1.09	82.6%	$0.89	125.4%	$0.16	$0.19	$0.18	$0.18	$0.58	21.9%
2/19/2007	0.086	1.14	83.8%	$0.88	125.7%	$0.16	$0.20	$0.18	$0.18	$0.58	21.4%
2/26/2007	0.062	1.18	83.7%	$0.95	126.7%	$0.17	$0.21	$0.18	$0.18	$0.61	21.8%
3/5/2007	0.086	1.17	84.8%	$1.08	125.6%	$0.17	$0.21	$0.18	$0.18	$0.61	21.1%
3/12/2007	0.074	1.14	83.8%	$1.29	124.0%	$0.16	$0.23	$0.18	$0.18	$0.65	21.1%

(continued)

Date	Distribution Margin	Crude Oil Cost	Discount to CARM Crude Oil Cost	Processing Margin	Premium to CARM Proc. Margin	Swap/ Hedge Spread	State/ Local Sales Tax	State Excise Tax	Federal Excise Tax	Excess Profit	Profit %
3/19/2007	0.037	1.10	83.3%	$1.39	124.1%	$0.16	$0.23	$0.18	$0.18	$0.66	21.3%
3/26/2007	0.086	1.21	82.3%	$1.26	126.0%	$0.18	$0.23	$0.18	$0.18	$0.71	22.6%
4/2/2007	0.074	1.30	83.9%	$1.27	127.0%	$0.19	$0.24	$0.18	$0.18	$0.72	22.3%
4/9/2007	0.099	1.17	83.6%	$1.38	124.3%	$0.17	$0.24	$0.18	$0.18	$0.69	21.1%
4/16/2007	0.037	1.28	84.2%	$1.42	124.6%	$0.18	$0.24	$0.18	$0.18	$0.71	21.4%
4/23/2007	0.111	1.30	83.3%	$1.29	124.0%	$0.19	$0.25	$0.18	$0.18	$0.72	21.6%
4/30/2007	0.037	1.35	84.9%	$1.38	124.3%	$0.19	$0.25	$0.18	$0.18	$0.71	21.1%
5/7/2007	0.074	1.26	84.0%	$1.58	125.4%	$0.18	$0.26	$0.18	$0.18	$0.75	21.8%
5/14/2007	0.161	1.28	84.2%	$1.46	124.8%	$0.18	$0.26	$0.18	$0.18	$0.74	21.5%
5/21/2007	0.210	1.34	83.2%	$1.31	127.2%	$0.19	$0.25	$0.18	$0.18	$0.78	22.8%
5/28/2007	0.259	1.33	84.2%	$1.26	127.3%	$0.19	$0.25	$0.18	$0.18	$0.76	22.3%
6/4/2007	0.383	1.35	83.9%	$1.05	128.0%	$0.19	$0.25	$0.18	$0.18	$0.76	22.4%
6/11/2007	0.432	1.34	83.2%	$0.98	133.2%	$0.19	$0.25	$0.18	$0.18	$0.79	23.8%
6/18/2007	0.309	1.40	83.3%	$0.95	137.7%	$0.20	$0.24	$0.18	$0.18	$0.80	24.7%
6/25/2007	0.173	1.40	82.8%	$0.92	124.3%	$0.20	$0.24	$0.18	$0.18	$0.71	22.1%
7/2/2007	0.086	1.45	83.8%	$0.97	126.0%	$0.21	$0.24	$0.18	$0.18	$0.70	22.1%
7/9/2007	0.148	1.48	84.1%	$0.81	124.6%	$0.21	$0.23	$0.18	$0.18	$0.68	21.6%
7/16/2007	0.173	1.50	82.9%	$0.75	125.0%	$0.22	$0.23	$0.18	$0.18	$0.71	22.5%
7/23/2007	0.259	1.51	83.0%	$0.60	125.0%	$0.22	$0.23	$0.18	$0.18	$0.70	22.4%
7/30/2007	0.284	1.55	82.9%	$0.44	125.7%	$0.22	$0.23	$0.18	$0.18	$0.69	22.5%
8/6/2007	0.333	1.47	83.5%	$0.49	125.6%	$0.21	$0.22	$0.18	$0.18	$0.66	22.0%
8/13/2007	0.296	1.45	83.3%	$0.44	125.7%	$0.21	$0.22	$0.18	$0.18	$0.65	22.0%
8/20/2007	0.210	1.47	85.0%	$0.48	129.7%	$0.21	$0.21	$0.18	$0.18	$0.62	21.6%
8/27/2007	0.173	1.46	83.4%	$0.39	125.8%	$0.21	$0.21	$0.18	$0.18	$0.61	22.0%

Date	Distribution Margin	Crude Oil Cost	Discount to CARM Crude Oil Cost	Processing Margin	Premium to CARM Proc. Margin	Swap/ Hedge Spread	State/ Local Sales Tax	State Excise Tax	Federal Excise Tax	Excess Profit	Profit %
9/3/2007	0.124	1.51	83.9%	$0.41	136.7%	$0.22	$0.21	$0.18	$0.18	$0.64	22.9%
9/10/2007	0.124	1.56	83.9%	$0.38	126.7%	$0.22	$0.21	$0.18	$0.18	$0.63	22.1%
9/17/2007	0.099	1.60	83.8%	$0.41	128.1%	$0.23	$0.22	$0.18	$0.18	$0.65	22.3%
9/24/2007	0.099	1.65	84.2%	$0.42	123.5%	$0.24	$0.22	$0.18	$0.18	$0.64	21.8%
10/1/2007	0.074	1.59	84.1%	$0.43	100.0%	$0.23	$0.22	$0.18	$0.18	$0.54	18.2%
10/8/2007	0.086	1.55	83.3%	$0.59	125.5%	$0.22	$0.22	$0.18	$0.18	$0.67	22.3%
10/15/2007	0.062	1.70	83.7%	$0.47	127.0%	$0.24	$0.23	$0.18	$0.18	$0.69	22.5%
10/22/2007	0.111	1.71	83.4%	$0.50	125.0%	$0.25	$0.23	$0.18	$0.18	$0.71	22.5%
10/29/2007	0.074	1.79	81.4%	$0.37	127.6%	$0.26	$0.23	$0.18	$0.18	$0.77	24.3%
11/5/2007	0.037	1.82	82.7%	$0.49	125.6%	$0.26	$0.24	$0.18	$0.18	$0.75	23.3%
11/12/2007	0.111	1.86	83.8%	$0.54	125.6%	$0.27	$0.25	$0.18	$0.18	$0.76	22.5%
11/19/2007	0.173	1.86	84.2%	$0.53	126.2%	$0.27	$0.25	$0.18	$0.18	$0.76	22.3%
11/26/2007	0.185	1.89	82.9%	$0.43	126.5%	$0.27	$0.25	$0.18	$0.18	$0.79	23.2%
12/3/2007	0.259	1.72	83.1%	$0.57	126.7%	$0.25	$0.25	$0.18	$0.18	$0.77	22.8%
12/10/2007	0.284	1.69	84.1%	$0.59	125.5%	$0.24	$0.25	$0.18	$0.18	$0.74	22.1%
12/17/2007	0.210	1.75	83.7%	$0.52	126.8%	$0.25	$0.24	$0.18	$0.18	$0.74	22.5%
12/24/2007	0.173	1.80	83.3%	$0.43	126.5%	$0.26	$0.24	$0.18	$0.18	$0.74	22.8%
12/31/2007	0.136	1.87	83.9%	$0.44	129.4%	$0.27	$0.24	$0.18	$0.18	$0.75	22.8%

SOURCE: Author's calculations.

Appendix F

BP CARM per Gallon (January 3, 2000 to December 31, 2007)

Date	Distribution Margin	Crude Oil Cost	Processing Margin	State / Local Sales Tax	State Excise Tax	Federal Excise Tax	Retail Price
1/3/2000	$0.08	$0.58	$0.24	$0.10	$0.18	$0.18	$1.36
1/10/2000	$0.07	$0.59	$0.23	$0.10	$0.18	$0.18	$1.35
1/17/2000	$0.08	$0.62	$0.18	$0.10	$0.18	$0.18	$1.35
1/24/2000	$0.07	$0.66	$0.15	$0.10	$0.18	$0.18	$1.35
1/31/2000	$0.06	$0.62	$0.23	$0.10	$0.18	$0.18	$1.38
2/7/2000	$0.06	$0.62	$0.24	$0.10	$0.18	$0.18	$1.36
2/14/2000	$0.04	$0.68	$0.21	$0.10	$0.18	$0.18	$1.40
2/21/2000	$0.00	$0.66	$0.31	$0.11	$0.18	$0.18	$1.44
2/28/2000	−$0.04	$0.68	$0.40	$0.11	$0.18	$0.18	$1.52
3/6/2000	−$0.04	$0.71	$0.47	$0.12	$0.18	$0.18	$1.63
3/13/2000	−$0.02	$0.72	$0.55	$0.13	$0.18	$0.18	$1.74
3/20/2000	$0.02	$0.62	$0.66	$0.13	$0.18	$0.18	$1.79
3/27/2000	$0.17	$0.62	$0.50	$0.13	$0.18	$0.18	$1.79
4/3/2000	$0.17	$0.58	$0.52	$0.13	$0.18	$0.18	$1.77
4/10/2000	$0.25	$0.55	$0.45	$0.13	$0.18	$0.18	$1.75
4/17/2000	$0.32	$0.57	$0.35	$0.13	$0.18	$0.18	$1.74
4/24/2000	$0.30	$0.58	$0.32	$0.13	$0.18	$0.18	$1.70
5/1/2000	$0.23	$0.58	$0.38	$0.12	$0.18	$0.18	$1.67
5/8/2000	$0.15	$0.63	$0.40	$0.12	$0.18	$0.18	$1.66
5/15/2000	$0.14	$0.67	$0.33	$0.12	$0.18	$0.18	$1.63
5/22/2000	$0.10	$0.64	$0.39	$0.12	$0.18	$0.18	$1.61
5/29/2000	$0.08	$0.67	$0.38	$0.12	$0.18	$0.18	$1.61
6/5/2000	$0.08	$0.65	$0.40	$0.12	$0.18	$0.18	$1.61
6/12/2000	$0.07	$0.70	$0.38	$0.12	$0.18	$0.18	$1.61
6/19/2000	$0.06	$0.70	$0.37	$0.12	$0.18	$0.18	$1.62
6/26/2000	$0.02	$0.77	$0.36	$0.12	$0.18	$0.18	$1.64
7/3/2000	−$0.02	$0.68	$0.57	$0.13	$0.18	$0.18	$1.71
7/10/2000	$0.00	$0.66	$0.58	$0.13	$0.18	$0.18	$1.73
7/17/2000	$0.07	$0.69	$0.47	$0.13	$0.18	$0.18	$1.72
7/24/2000	$0.12	$0.62	$0.49	$0.13	$0.18	$0.18	$1.71
7/31/2000	$0.11	$0.60	$0.48	$0.12	$0.18	$0.18	$1.68
8/7/2000	$0.05	$0.64	$0.49	$0.12	$0.18	$0.18	$1.67
8/14/2000	−$0.05	$0.72	$0.51	$0.12	$0.18	$0.18	$1.67
8/21/2000	−$0.03	$0.72	$0.49	$0.12	$0.18	$0.18	$1.67
8/28/2000	−$0.07	$0.74	$0.54	$0.13	$0.18	$0.18	$1.70
9/5/2000	−$0.15	$0.77	$0.67	$0.13	$0.18	$0.18	$1.79
9/11/2000	−$0.11	$0.80	$0.66	$0.14	$0.18	$0.18	$1.85
9/18/2000	$0.05	$0.84	$0.44	$0.14	$0.18	$0.18	$1.83
9/25/2000	$0.08	$0.70	$0.58	$0.14	$0.18	$0.18	$1.83
10/2/2000	$0.09	$0.73	$0.52	$0.14	$0.18	$0.18	$1.83

Date	Distribution Margin	Crude Oil Cost	Processing Margin	State/ Local Sales Tax	State Excise Tax	Federal Excise Tax	Retail Price
10/9/2000	$0.14	$0.72	$0.46	$0.14	$0.18	$0.18	$1.83
10/16/2000	$0.07	$0.75	$0.49	$0.13	$0.18	$0.18	$1.81
10/23/2000	$0.06	$0.77	$0.47	$0.13	$0.18	$0.18	$1.80
10/30/2000	$0.01	$0.75	$0.54	$0.13	$0.18	$0.18	$1.80
11/6/2000	−$0.02	$0.74	$0.57	$0.13	$0.18	$0.18	$1.79
11/13/2000	$0.10	$0.78	$0.40	$0.13	$0.18	$0.18	$1.78
11/20/2000	$0.17	$0.81	$0.28	$0.13	$0.18	$0.18	$1.75
11/27/2000	$0.15	$0.80	$0.30	$0.13	$0.18	$0.18	$1.74
12/4/2000	$0.16	$0.67	$0.40	$0.13	$0.18	$0.18	$1.72
12/11/2000	$0.28	$0.59	$0.36	$0.13	$0.18	$0.18	$1.69
12/18/2000	$0.26	$0.59	$0.33	$0.12	$0.18	$0.18	$1.68
12/26/2000	$0.23	$0.59	$0.44	$0.12	$0.18	$0.18	$1.65
1/2/2001	$0.17	$0.51	$0.46	$0.12	$0.18	$0.18	$1.63
1/8/2001	$0.15	$0.52	$0.47	$0.12	$0.18	$0.18	$1.63
1/15/2001	$0.18	$0.60	$0.34	$0.12	$0.18	$0.18	$1.60
1/22/2001	$0.14	$0.65	$0.31	$0.12	$0.18	$0.18	$1.58
1/29/2001	$0.12	$0.59	$0.38	$0.12	$0.18	$0.18	$1.57
2/5/2001	$0.08	$0.64	$0.39	$0.12	$0.18	$0.18	$1.59
2/12/2001	$0.03	$0.65	$0.48	$0.12	$0.18	$0.18	$1.64
2/19/2001	$0.03	$0.61	$0.53	$0.12	$0.18	$0.18	$1.66
2/26/2001	$0.00	$0.60	$0.57	$0.12	$0.18	$0.18	$1.66
3/5/2001	$0.01	$0.62	$0.58	$0.13	$0.18	$0.18	$1.70
3/12/2001	$0.01	$0.54	$0.67	$0.13	$0.18	$0.18	$1.70
3/19/2001	$0.03	$0.56	$0.61	$0.13	$0.18	$0.18	$1.70
3/26/2001	−$0.01	$0.59	$0.61	$0.12	$0.18	$0.18	$1.68
4/2/2001	−$0.05	$0.55	$0.72	$0.13	$0.18	$0.18	$1.72
4/9/2001	−$0.09	$0.61	$0.75	$0.13	$0.18	$0.18	$1.75
4/16/2001	−$0.09	$0.64	$0.75	$0.13	$0.18	$0.18	$1.80
4/23/2001	−$0.03	$0.60	$0.76	$0.14	$0.18	$0.18	$1.83
4/30/2001	−$0.02	$0.63	$0.75	$0.14	$0.18	$0.18	$1.87
5/7/2001	$0.08	$0.62	$0.74	$0.14	$0.18	$0.18	$1.94
5/14/2001	$0.16	$0.64	$0.65	$0.14	$0.18	$0.18	$1.95
5/21/2001	$0.16	$0.64	$0.65	$0.14	$0.18	$0.18	$1.95
5/28/2001	$0.20	$0.64	$0.60	$0.14	$0.18	$0.18	$1.95
6/4/2001	$0.20	$0.63	$0.60	$0.14	$0.18	$0.18	$1.93
6/11/2011	$0.32	$0.65	$0.47	$0.14	$0.18	$0.18	$1.95
6/18/2001	$0.35	$0.62	$0.46	$0.14	$0.18	$0.18	$1.93
6/25/2001	$0.38	$0.60	$0.42	$0.14	$0.18	$0.18	$1.90
7/2/2001	$0.41	$0.58	$0.37	$0.14	$0.18	$0.18	$1.86
7/9/2001	$0.42	$0.62	$0.29	$0.14	$0.18	$0.18	$1.82

(*continued*)

Date	Distribution Margin	Crude Oil Cost	Processing Margin	State/ Local Sales Tax	State Excise Tax	Federal Excise Tax	Retail Price
7/16/2001	$0.44	$0.57	$0.26	$0.13	$0.18	$0.18	$1.78
7/23/2001	$0.51	$0.57	$0.15	$0.13	$0.18	$0.18	$1.72
7/30/2001	$0.34	$0.57	$0.27	$0.12	$0.18	$0.18	$1.67
8/6/2001	$0.27	$0.58	$0.28	$0.12	$0.18	$0.18	$1.62
8/13/2001	$0.19	$0.59	$0.31	$0.12	$0.18	$0.18	$1.56
8/20/2001	$0.08	$0.57	$0.40	$0.11	$0.18	$0.18	$1.52
8/27/2001	$0.06	$0.56	$0.35	$0.11	$0.18	$0.18	$1.51
9/3/2001	−$0.12	$0.57	$0.71	$0.12	$0.18	$0.18	$1.64
9/10/2001	−$0.02	$0.59	$0.62	$0.12	$0.18	$0.18	$1.68
9/17/2001	$0.00	$0.61	$0.57	$0.12	$0.18	$0.18	$1.67
9/24/2001	$0.09	$0.44	$0.64	$0.12	$0.18	$0.18	$1.66
10/1/2001	$0.19	$0.49	$0.46	$0.12	$0.18	$0.18	$1.62
10/8/2001	$0.18	$0.47	$0.44	$0.12	$0.18	$0.18	$1.56
10/15/2001	$0.19	$0.47	$0.41	$0.11	$0.18	$0.18	$1.55
10/22/2001	$0.12	$0.46	$0.45	$0.11	$0.18	$0.18	$1.51
10/29/2001	$0.06	$0.47	$0.47	$0.11	$0.18	$0.18	$1.47
11/5/2001	$0.09	$0.43	$0.45	$0.11	$0.18	$0.18	$1.42
11/12/2001	$0.14	$0.45	$0.33	$0.10	$0.18	$0.18	$1.38
11/19/2001	$0.18	$0.37	$0.33	$0.10	$0.18	$0.18	$1.34
11/26/2001	$0.17	$0.39	$0.27	$0.10	$0.18	$0.18	$1.29
12/3/2001	$0.14	$0.42	$0.23	$0.08	$0.18	$0.18	$1.24
12/10/2001	$0.14	$0.38	$0.23	$0.09	$0.18	$0.18	$1.20
12/17/2001	$0.08	$0.39	$0.22	$0.08	$0.18	$0.18	$1.14
12/24/2001	$0.00	$0.44	$0.23	$0.08	$0.18	$0.18	$1.11
12/31/2001	−$0.07	$0.41	$0.31	$0.08	$0.18	$0.18	$1.10
1/7/2002	−$0.05	$0.45	$0.28	$0.08	$0.18	$0.18	$1.13
1/14/2002	$0.03	$0.40	$0.30	$0.09	$0.18	$0.18	$1.18
1/21/2002	$0.08	$0.39	$0.30	$0.09	$0.18	$0.18	$1.21
1/28/2002	$0.00	$0.43	$0.34	$0.09	$0.18	$0.18	$1.22
2/4/2002	$0.01	$0.43	$0.35	$0.09	$0.18	$0.18	$1.25
2/11/2002	$0.01	$0.48	$0.31	$0.09	$0.18	$0.18	$1.25
2/19/2002	$0.01	$0.45	$0.38	$0.10	$0.18	$0.18	$1.29
2/25/2002	$0.02	$0.45	$0.37	$0.10	$0.18	$0.18	$1.30
3/4/2002	$0.00	$0.50	$0.37	$0.10	$0.18	$0.18	$1.33
3/11/2002	−$0.02	$0.54	$0.47	$0.11	Excise	$0.18	$1.45
3/18/2002	−$0.03	$0.58	$0.50	$0.11	$0.18	$0.18	$1.50
3/25/2002	$0.01	$0.55	$0.53	$0.12	$0.18	$0.18	$1.56
4/1/2002	$0.05	$0.61	$0.45	$0.12	$0.18	$0.18	$1.59
4/8/2002	$0.07	$0.60	$0.47	$0.12	$0.18	$0.18	$1.62
4/15/2002	$0.13	$0.56	$0.45	$0.12	$0.18	$0.18	$1.62

Date	Distribution Margin	Crude Oil Cost	Processing Margin	State/ Local Sales Tax	State Excise Tax	Federal Excise Tax	Retail Price
4/22/2002	$0.10	$0.62	$0.40	$0.12	$0.18	$0.18	$1.61
4/29/2002	$0.11	$0.63	$0.39	$0.12	$0.18	$0.18	$1.61
5/6/2002	$0.12	$0.60	$0.39	$0.12	$0.18	$0.18	$1.59
5/13/2002	$0.11	$0.65	$0.32	$0.12	$0.18	$0.18	$1.57
5/20/2002	$0.09	$0.64	$0.35	$0.12	$0.18	$0.18	$1.56
5/27/2002	$0.06	$0.57	$0.44	$0.12	$0.18	$0.18	$1.55
6/3/2002	$0.17	$0.56	$0.45	$0.12	$0.18	$0.18	$1.56
6/10/2002	$0.04	$0.54	$0.50	$0.12	$0.18	$0.18	$1.56
6/17/2002	$0.01	$0.59	$0.51	$0.12	$0.18	$0.18	$1.60
6/24/2002	$0.08	$0.60	$0.45	$0.12	$0.18	$0.18	$1.62
7/1/2002	$0.08	$0.61	$0.44	$0.12	$0.18	$0.18	$1.62
7/8/2002	$0.07	$0.60	$0.46	$0.12	$0.18	$0.18	$1.61
7/15/2002	$0.07	$0.62	$0.43	$0.12	$0.18	$0.18	$1.60
7/22/2002	$0.06	$0.61	$0.44	$0.12	$0.18	$0.18	$1.59
7/29/2002	$0.04	$0.61	$0.45	$0.12	$0.18	$0.18	$1.58
8/5/2002	$0.06	$0.61	$0.45	$0.12	$0.18	$0.18	$1.59
8/12/2002	$0.04	$0.64	$0.43	$0.12	$0.18	$0.18	$1.59
8/19/2002	$0.02	$0.69	$0.39	$0.12	$0.18	$0.18	$1.58
8/26/2002	$0.04	$0.67	$0.40	$0.12	$0.18	$0.18	$1.59
9/2/2002	$0.03	$0.64	$0.45	$0.12	$0.18	$0.18	$1.60
9/9/2002	$0.01	$0.69	$0.42	$0.12	$0.18	$0.18	$1.59
9/16/2002	$0.00	$0.68	$0.42	$0.12	$0.18	$0.18	$1.58
9/23/2002	$0.00	$0.71	$0.39	$0.12	$0.18	$0.18	$1.57
9/30/2002	−$0.01	$0.70	$0.39	$0.12	$0.18	$0.18	$1.56
10/7/2002	−$0.02	$0.68	$0.40	$0.11	$0.18	$0.18	$1.55
10/14/2002	−$0.03	$0.68	$0.41	$0.11	$0.18	$0.18	$1.53
10/21/2002	−$0.04	$0.64	$0.45	$0.11	$0.18	$0.18	$1.52
10/28/2002	−$0.05	$0.81	$0.49	$0.11	$0.18	$0.18	$1.52
11/4/2002	−$0.01	$0.60	$0.49	$0.12	$0.18	$0.18	$1.56
11/11/2002	$0.02	$0.58	$0.51	$0.12	$0.18	$0.18	$1.59
11/18/2002	$0.04	$0.60	$0.47	$0.12	$0.18	$0.18	$1.59
11/25/2002	$0.08	$0.61	$0.40	$0.12	$0.18	$0.18	$1.57
12/2/2002	$0.13	$0.61	$0.34	$0.12	$0.18	$0.18	$1.56
12/9/2002	$0.15	$0.61	$0.30	$0.11	$0.18	$0.18	$1.54
12/16/2002	$0.10	$0.66	$0.26	$0.11	$0.18	$0.18	$1.53
12/23/2002	$0.09	$0.73	$0.23	$0.11	$0.18	$0.18	$1.52
12/30/2002	$0.06	$0.72	$0.28	$0.11	$0.18	$0.18	$1.53
1/6/2003	$0.09	$0.73	$0.27	$0.12	$0.18	$0.18	$1.58
1/13/2003	$0.09	$0.74	$0.28	$0.12	$0.18	$0.18	$1.59
1/20/2003	$0.10	$0.80	$0.25	$0.12	$0.18	$0.18	$1.63

(*continued*)

Date	Distribution Margin	Crude Oil Cost	Processing Margin	State/ Local Sales Tax	State Excise Tax	Federal Excise Tax	Retail Price
1/27/2003	$0.10	$0.74	$0.32	$0.12	$0.18	$0.18	$1.65
2/3/2003	$0.09	$0.76	$0.35	$0.12	$0.18	$0.18	$1.68
2/10/2003	$0.07	$0.81	$0.38	$0.13	$0.18	$0.18	$1.75
2/17/2003	$0.16	$0.87	$0.33	$0.14	$0.18	$0.18	$1.86
2/24/2003	$0.18	$0.88	$0.36	$0.14	$0.18	$0.18	$1.92
3/3/2003	$0.14	$0.85	$0.51	$0.15	$0.18	$0.18	$2.01
3/10/2003	$0.13	$0.88	$0.55	$0.15	$0.18	$0.18	$2.08
3/17/2003	$0.15	$0.82	$0.65	$0.16	$0.18	$0.18	$2.14
3/24/2003	$0.20	$0.63	$0.79	$0.16	$0.18	$0.18	$2.14
3/31/2003	$0.26	$0.69	$0.66	$0.16	$0.18	$0.18	$2.13
4/7/2003	$0.29	$0.60	$0.70	$0.16	$0.18	$0.18	$2.11
4/14/2003	$0.29	$0.62	$0.66	$0.15	$0.18	$0.18	$2.08
4/21/2003	$0.29	$0.67	$0.57	$0.15	$0.18	$0.18	$2.01
4/28/2003	$0.25	$0.54	$0.67	$0.15	$0.18	$0.18	$1.98
5/5/2003	$0.26	$0.58	$0.57	$0.14	$0.18	$0.18	$1.93
5/12/2003	$0.33	$0.60	$0.43	$0.14	$0.18	$0.18	$1.87
5/19/2003	$0.28	$0.64	$0.39	$0.13	$0.18	$0.18	$1.81
5/28/2003	$0.23	$0.66	$0.38	$0.13	$0.18	$0.18	$1.76
6/2/2003	$0.20	$0.70	$0.34	$0.13	$0.18	$0.18	$1.73
6/9/2003	$0.14	$0.72	$0.34	$0.13	$0.18	$0.18	$1.70
6/16/2003	$0.05	$0.71	$0.53	$0.13	$0.18	$0.18	$1.79
6/23/2003	$0.03	$0.71	$0.57	$0.13	$0.18	$0.18	$1.80
6/30/2003	$0.05	$0.88	$0.57	$0.13	$0.18	$0.18	$1.80
7/7/2003	$0.08	$0.68	$0.53	$0.13	$0.18	$0.18	$1.79
7/14/2003	$0.11	$0.71	$0.44	$0.13	$0.18	$0.18	$1.76
7/21/2003	$0.11	$0.72	$0.40	$0.13	$0.18	$0.18	$1.73
7/28/2003	$0.11	$0.68	$0.43	$0.13	$0.18	$0.18	$1.71
8/4/2003	$0.08	$0.72	$0.41	$0.13	$0.18	$0.18	$1.70
8/11/2003	$0.07	$0.73	$0.45	$0.13	$0.18	$0.18	$1.74
8/18/2003	$0.00	$0.70	$0.71	$0.14	$0.18	$0.18	$1.92
8/25/2003	$0.05	$0.72	$0.81	$0.16	$0.18	$0.18	$2.10
9/1/2003	$0.16	$0.72	$0.71	$0.16	$0.18	$0.18	$2.10
9/8/2003	$0.22	$0.66	$0.69	$0.15	$0.18	$0.18	$2.08
9/15/2003	$0.26	$0.64	$0.58	$0.15	$0.18	$0.18	$2.03
9/22/2003	$0.33	$0.62	$0.52	$0.15	Excise	Excise	Retail
9/29/2003	$0.33	$0.65	$0.43	$0.14	$0.18	$0.18	$1.91
10/6/2003	$0.26	$0.69	$0.41	$0.14	$0.18	$0.18	$1.85
10/13/2003	$0.19	$0.72	$0.40	$0.13	$0.18	$0.18	$1.81
10/20/2003	$0.19	$0.68	$0.40	$0.13	$0.18	$0.18	$1.81
10/27/2003	$0.15	$0.67	$0.42	$0.13	$0.18	$0.18	$1.74

Date	Distribution Margin	Crude Oil Cost	Processing Margin	State/ Local Sales Tax	State Excise Tax	Federal Excise Tax	Retail Price
11/3/2003	$0.13	$0.65	$0.44	$0.13	$0.18	$0.18	$1.71
11/10/2003	$0.11	$0.69	$0.40	$0.13	$0.18	$0.18	$1.69
11/17/2003	$0.07	$0.71	$0.42	$0.12	$0.18	$0.18	$1.68
11/24/2003	$0.13	$0.67	$0.40	$0.13	$0.18	$0.18	$1.69
12/1/2003	$0.14	$0.67	$0.39	$0.12	$0.18	$0.18	$1.68
12/8/2003	$0.14	$0.72	$0.31	$0.12	$0.18	$0.18	$1.65
12/15/2003	$0.13	$0.76	$0.25	$0.12	$0.18	$0.18	$1.62
12/22/2003	$0.12	$0.73	$0.28	$0.12	$0.18	$0.18	$1.61
12/29/2003	$0.08	$0.74	$0.29	$0.12	$0.18	$0.18	$1.59
1/5/2004	$0.13	$0.78	$0.28	$0.12	$0.18	$0.15	$1.62
1/12/2004	$0.17	$0.80	$0.25	$0.12	$0.18	$0.15	$1.67
1/19/2004	$0.10	$0.84	$0.29	$0.13	$0.18	$0.15	$1.69
1/26/2004	$0.13	$0.79	$0.35	$0.13	$0.18	$0.15	$1.73
2/2/2004	$0.12	$0.81	$0.36	$0.13	$0.18	$0.15	$1.75
2/9/2004	$0.14	$0.76	$0.46	$0.13	$0.18	$0.15	$1.82
2/16/2004	$0.15	$0.80	$0.45	$0.14	$0.18	$0.15	$1.87
2/23/2004	$0.09	$0.79	$0.67	$0.15	$0.18	$0.15	$2.03
3/1/2004	$0.14	$0.85	$0.63	$0.16	$0.18	$0.15	$2.11
3/8/2004	$0.16	$0.84	$0.62	$0.16	$0.18	$0.15	$2.11
3/15/2004	$0.19	$0.86	$0.56	$0.16	$0.18	$0.15	$2.10
3/22/2004	$0.18	$0.85	$0.57	$0.15	$0.18	$0.15	$2.08
3/29/2004	$0.16	$0.81	$0.63	$0.15	$0.18	$0.15	$2.08
4/5/2004	$0.12	$0.79	$0.73	$0.16	$0.18	$0.15	$2.13
4/12/2004	$0.16	$0.87	$0.64	$0.16	$0.18	$0.15	$2.16
4/19/2004	$0.16	$0.86	$0.64	$0.16	$0.18	$0.15	$2.15
4/26/2004	$0.15	$0.85	$0.63	$0.16	$0.18	$0.15	$2.12
5/3/2004	$0.10	$0.88	$0.64	$0.16	$0.18	$0.15	$2.11
5/10/2004	$0.09	$0.90	$0.74	$0.16	$0.18	$0.15	$2.22
5/17/2004	$0.11	$0.96	$0.70	$0.17	$0.18	$0.15	$2.27
5/24/2004	$0.13	$0.97	$0.72	$0.17	$0.18	$0.15	$2.32
5/31/2004	$0.18	$0.99	$0.66	$0.17	$0.18	$0.15	$2.33
6/7/2004	$0.19	$0.89	$0.74	$0.17	$0.18	$0.15	$2.32
6/14/2004	$0.20	$0.86	$0.73	$0.17	$0.18	$0.15	$2.29
6/21/2004	$0.25	$0.86	$0.85	$0.17	$0.18	$0.15	$2.26
6/28/2004	$0.21	$0.83	$0.70	$0.17	$0.18	$0.15	$2.24
7/5/2004	$0.20	$0.88	$0.63	$0.16	$0.18	$0.15	$2.20
7/12/2004	$0.17	$0.91	$0.62	$0.16	$0.18	$0.15	$2.19
7/19/2004	$0.16	$0.95	$0.59	$0.16	$0.18	$0.15	$2.19
7/26/2004	$0.18	$0.96	$0.53	$0.16	$0.18	$0.15	$2.16
8/2/2004	$0.18	$1.01	$0.45	$0.16	$0.18	$0.15	$2.13

(*continued*)

Date	Distribution Margin	Crude Oil Cost	Processing Margin	State/Local Sales Tax	State Excise Tax	Federal Excise Tax	Retail Price
8/9/2004	$0.18	$1.04	$0.39	$0.15	$0.18	$0.15	$2.09
8/16/2004	$0.12	$1.06	$0.39	$0.15	$0.18	$0.15	$2.05
8/23/2004	$0.10	$1.06	$0.41	$0.15	$0.18	$0.15	$2.05
8/30/2004	$0.18	$0.94	$0.49	$0.15	$0.18	$0.15	$2.10
9/6/2004	$0.16	$0.97	$0.46	$0.15	$0.18	$0.15	$207.00
9/13/2004	$0.15	$0.97	$0.47	$0.15	$0.18	$0.15	$2.05
9/21/2004	$0.11	$1.03	$0.44	$0.15	$0.18	$0.15	$2.05
9/27/2004	$0.06	$1.10	$0.44	$0.16	$0.18	$0.15	$2.09
10/4/2004	$0.09	$1.11	$0.51	$0.16	$0.18	$0.15	$2.20
10/11/2004	$0.08	$1.17	$0.58	$0.17	$0.18	$0.15	$2.33
10/18/2004	$0.09	$1.18	$0.62	$0.18	$0.18	$0.15	$2.40
10/25/2004	$0.14	$1.16	$0.58	$0.18	$0.18	$0.15	$2.39
11/1/2004	$0.17	$1.09	$0.60	$0.18	$0.18	$0.15	$2.37
11/8/2004	$0.22	$1.02	$0.60	$0.17	$0.18	$0.15	$2.34
11/15/2004	$0.22	$0.98	$0.61	$0.17	$0.18	$0.15	$2.31
11/22/2004	$0.25	$1.00	$0.51	$0.17	$0.18	$0.15	$2.26
11/29/2004	$0.24	$1.18	$0.32	$0.17	$0.18	$0.15	$2.24
12/6/2004	$0.32	$0.86	$0.52	$0.16	$0.18	$0.15	$2.19
12/13/2004	$0.46	$0.81	$0.38	$0.16	$0.18	$0.15	$2.14
12/20/2004	$0.32	$0.93	$0.32	$0.15	$0.18	$0.15	$2.05
12/27/2004	$0.27	$0.82	$0.44	$0.15	$0.18	$0.15	$2.01
1/3/2005	$0.22	$0.84	$0.41	$0.15	$0.18	$0.18	$1.98
1/10/2005	$0.17	$0.93	$0.33	$0.14	$0.18	$0.18	$1.93
1/17/2005	$0.13	$1.04	$0.26	$0.14	$0.18	$0.18	$1.93
1/24/2005	$0.08	$1.03	$0.34	$0.15	$0.18	$0.18	$1.96
1/31/2005	$0.12	$1.04	$0.36	$0.15	$0.18	$0.18	$2.03
2/7/2005	$0.11	$1.00	$0.43	$0.15	$0.18	$0.18	$2.05
2/14/2005	$0.09	$1.02	$0.47	$0.15	$0.18	$0.18	$2.09
2/21/2005	$0.11	$1.12	$0.40	$0.16	$0.18	$0.18	$2.15
2/28/2005	$0.07	$1.12	$0.47	$0.16	$0.18	$0.18	$2.18
3/7/2005	$0.07	$1.19	$0.44	$0.17	$0.18	$0.18	$2.23
3/14/2005	$0.08	$1.21	$0.47	$0.17	$0.18	$0.18	$2.29
3/21/2005	$0.09	$1.26	$0.43	$0.17	$0.18	$0.18	$2.10
3/28/2005	$0.06	$1.21	$0.57	$0.18	$0.18	$0.18	$2.38
4/4/2005	$0.00	$1.28	$0.64	$0.18	Excise	Excise	$2.46
4/11/2005	$0.04	$1.20	$0.80	$0.19	$0.18	$0.18	$2.59
4/18/2005	$0.04	$1.12	$0.87	$0.19	$0.18	$0.18	$2.58
4/25/2005	$0.09	$1.22	$0.71	$0.19	$0.18	$0.18	$2.57
5/2/2005	$0.15	$1.14	$0.72	$0.19	$0.18	$0.18	$2.56
5/9/2005	$0.19	$1.17	$0.61	$0.19	$0.18	$0.18	$2.52

Date	Distribution Margin	Crude Oil Cost	Processing Margin	State/ Local Sales Tax	State Excise Tax	Federal Excise Tax	Retail Price
5/16/2005	$0.30	$1.08	$0.55	$0.18	$0.18	$0.18	$2.47
5/23/2005	$0.29	$1.12	$0.48	$0.18	$0.18	$0.18	$2.43
5/30/2005	$0.27	$1.17	$0.41	$0.18	$0.18	$0.18	$2.39
6/6/2005	$0.21	$1.31	$0.31	$0.17	$0.18	$0.18	$2.36
6/13/2005	$0.14	$1.26	$0.40	$0.17	$0.18	$0.18	$2.33
6/20/2005	$0.10	$1.35	$0.37	$0.17	$0.18	$0.18	$2.35
6/27/2005	$0.06	$1.38	$0.43	$0.18	$0.18	$0.18	$2.41
7/4/2005	$0.07	$1.34	$0.51	$0.18	$0.18	$0.18	$2.46
7/11/2005	$0.10	$1.35	$0.53	$0.19	$0.18	$0.18	$2.53
7/18/2005	$0.22	$1.32	$0.45	$0.19	$0.18	$0.18	$2.54
7/25/2005	$0.12	$1.31	$0.56	$0.19	$0.18	$0.18	$2.54
8/1/2005	$0.07	$1.42	$0.51	$0.19	$0.18	$0.18	$2.55
8/8/2005	−$0.03	$1.47	$0.61	$0.19	$0.18	$0.18	$2.60
8/15/2005	$0.04	$1.51	$0.61	$0.20	$0.18	$0.18	$2.72
8/22/2005	$0.14	$1.49	$0.56	$0.20	$0.18	$0.18	$2.75
8/29/2005	−$0.15	$1.53	$0.82	$0.21	$0.18	$0.18	$2.77
9/5/2005	−$0.10	$1.54	$1.03	$0.23	$0.18	$0.18	$3.06
9/15/2005	$0.26	$1.46	$0.70	$0.22	$0.18	$0.18	$3.00
9/19/2005	$0.18	$1.56	$0.63	$0.22	$0.18	$0.18	$2.95
9/26/2005	$0.16	$1.52	$0.69	$0.22	$0.18	$0.18	$2.95
10/3/2005	$0.04	$1.51	$0.84	$0.22	$0.18	$0.18	$2.97
10/10/2005	$0.37	$1.43	$0.58	$0.22	$0.18	$0.18	$2.96
10/17/2005	$0.40	$1.49	$0.44	$0.21	$0.18	$0.18	$2.90
10/24/2005	$0.45	$1.41	$0.40	$0.21	$0.18	$0.18	$2.83
10/31/2005	$0.39	$1.38	$0.42	$0.20	$0.18	$0.18	$2.75
11/7/2005	$0.29	$1.35	$0.46	$0.20	$0.18	$0.18	$2.66
11/14/2005	$0.30	$1.32	$0.41	$0.19	$0.18	$0.18	$2.58
11/21/2005	$0.19	$1.32	$0.40	$0.18	$0.18	$0.18	$2.45
11/28/2005	$0.16	$1.32	$0.39	$0.18	$0.18	$0.18	$2.41
12/5/2005	$0.15	$1.32	$0.28	$0.17	$0.18	$0.18	$2.34
12/12/2005	$0.12	$1.41	$0.22	$0.17	$0.18	$0.18	$2.27
12/19/2005	$0.04	$1.31	$0.36	$0.17	$0.18	$0.18	$2.25
12/26/2005	$0.04	$1.33	$0.33	$0.17	$0.18	$0.18	$2.23
1/2/2006	−$0.04	$1.43	$0.30	$0.16	$0.18	$0.18	$2.21
1/9/2006	−$0.03	$1.45	$0.37	$0.17	$0.18	$0.18	$2.33
1/16/2006	$0.05	$1.51	$0.31	$0.18	$0.18	$0.18	$2.42
1/26/2006	−$0.03	$1.58	$0.33	$0.18	$0.18	$0.18	$2.42
1/30/2006	$0.03	$1.56	$0.47	$0.19	$0.18	$0.18	$2.51
2/6/2006	$0.02	$1.50	$0.47	$0.19	$0.18	$0.18	$2.54
2/13/2006	$0.15	$1.40	$0.41	$0.19	$0.18	$0.18	$2.52

(*continued*)

Date	Distribution Margin	Crude Oil Cost	Processing Margin	State / Local Sales Tax	State Excise Tax	Federal Excise Tax	Retail Price
2/20/2006	$0.12	$1.40	$0.40	$0.18	$0.18	$0.18	$2.47
2/27/2006	$0.09	$1.40	$0.41	$0.18	$0.18	$0.18	$2.44
3/6/2006	−$0.03	$1.43	$0.54	$0.18	$0.18	$0.18	$2.48
3/13/2006	$0.05	$1.42	$0.51	$0.19	$0.18	$0.18	$2.53
3/20/2006	$0.04	$1.39	$0.64	$0.20	$0.18	$0.18	$2.64
3/27/2006	$0.03	$1.48	$0.59	$0.20	$0.18	$0.18	$2.67
4/3/2006	$0.02	$1.54	$0.62	$0.20	$0.18	$0.18	$2.74
4/10/2006	−$0.03	$1.59	$0.67	$0.21	$0.18	$0.18	$2.81
4/17/2006	−$0.07	$1.63	$0.76	$0.21	$0.18	$0.18	$2.90
4/24/2006	−$0.07	$1.65	$0.90	$0.23	$0.18	$0.18	$3.07
5/1/2006	$0.02	$1.71	$0.87	$0.24	$0.18	$0.18	$3.20
5/8/2006	$0.04	$1.62	$1.06	$0.25	$0.18	$0.18	$3.33
5/15/2006	$0.02	$1.61	$1.08	$0.25	$0.18	$0.18	$3.33
5/22/2006	$0.02	$1.61	$1.02	$0.24	$0.18	$0.18	$3.25
5/29/2006	$0.04	$1.68	$0.94	$0.24	$0.18	$0.18	$3.27
6/5/2006	$0.04	$1.69	$0.92	$0.24	$0.18	$0.18	$3.27
6/12/2006	$0.15	$1.64	$0.82	$0.24	$0.18	$0.18	$3.23
6/19/2006	$0.19	$1.61	$0.78	$0.24	$0.18	$0.18	$3.20
6/26/2006	$0.16	$1.68	$0.71	$0.24	$0.18	$0.18	$3.16
7/3/2006	$0.07	$1.73	$0.77	$0.24	$0.18	$0.18	$3.19
7/10/2006	$0.09	$1.72	$0.80	$0.24	$0.18	$0.18	$3.19
7/17/2006	$0.11	$1.76	$0.76	$0.24	$0.18	$0.18	$3.24
7/24/2006	$0.10	$1.75	$0.76	$0.24	$0.18	$0.18	$3.22
7/31/2006	$0.10	$1.74	$0.74	$0.24	$0.18	$0.18	$3.20
8/7/2006	$0.09	$1.80	$0.68	$0.24	$0.18	$0.18	$3.19
8/14/2006	$0.14	$1.72	$0.73	$0.24	$0.18	$0.18	$3.21
8/21/2006	$0.20	$1.69	$0.66	$0.23	$0.18	$0.18	$3.16
8/28/2006	$0.25	$1.65	$0.59	$0.23	$0.18	$0.18	$3.10
9/4/2006	$0.23	$1.60	$0.59	$0.22	$0.18	$0.18	$3.01
9/11/2006	$0.26	$1.53	$0.57	$0.22	$0.18	$0.18	$2.95
9/18/2006	$0.31	$1.49	$0.46	$0.21	$0.18	$0.18	$2.85
9/25/2006	$0.31	$1.41	$0.46	$0.20	$0.18	$0.18	$2.76
10/2/2006	$0.25	$1.42	$0.43	$0.20	$0.18	$0.18	$2.68
10/9/2006	$0.22	$1.30	$0.51	$0.19	$0.18	$0.18	$2.60
10/16/2006	$0.20	$1.29	$0.48	$0.19	$0.18	$0.18	$2.54
10/23/2006	$0.16	$1.25	$0.51	$0.18	$0.18	$0.18	$2.48
10/30/2006	$0.15	$1.27	$0.46	$0.18	$0.18	$0.18	$2.43
11/6/2006	$0.06	$1.32	$0.46	$0.18	$0.18	$0.18	$2.40
11/13/2006	$0.05	$1.28	$0.58	$0.18	$0.18	$0.18	$2.46
11/20/2006	$0.06	$1.23	$0.65	$0.18	$0.18	$0.18	$2.50

Date	Distribution Margin	Crude Oil Cost	Processing Margin	State / Local Sales Tax	State Excise Tax	Federal Excise Tax	Retail Price
11/27/2006	$0.06	$1.32	$0.55	$0.18	$0.18	$0.18	$2.49
12/4/2006	$0.05	$1.37	$0.52	$0.18	$0.18	$0.18	$2.50
12/11/2006	$0.06	$1.37	$0.50	$0.19	$0.18	$0.18	$2.50
12/18/2006	$0.09	$1.39	$0.51	$0.19	$0.18	$0.18	$2.56
12/25/2006	$0.14	$1.40	$0.51	$0.19	$0.18	$0.18	$2.61
1/1/2007	$0.13	$1.32	$0.59	$0.19	$0.18	$0.18	$2.61
1/8/2007	$0.17	$1.27	$0.62	$0.19	$0.18	$0.18	$2.63
1/15/2007	$0.17	$1.15	$0.69	$0.19	$0.18	$0.18	$2.58
1/22/2007	$0.19	$1.19	$0.59	$0.19	$0.18	$0.18	$2.54
1/29/2007	$0.12	$1.22	$0.60	$0.18	$0.18	$0.18	$2.49
2/5/2007	$0.07	$1.35	$0.54	$0.19	$0.18	$0.18	$2.54
2/12/2007	$0.03	$1.32	$0.71	$0.19	$0.18	$0.18	$2.63
2/19/2007	$0.07	$1.36	$0.70	$0.20	$0.18	$0.18	$2.71
2/26/2007	$0.05	$1.41	$0.75	$0.21	$0.18	$0.18	$2.80
3/5/2007	$0.07	$1.38	$0.86	$0.21	$0.18	$0.18	$2.90
3/12/2007	$0.06	$1.36	$1.04	$0.23	$0.18	$0.18	$3.07
3/19/2007	$0.03	$1.32	$1.12	$0.23	$0.18	$0.18	$3.08
3/26/2007	$0.07	$1.47	$1.00	$0.23	$0.18	$0.18	$3.15
4/2/2007	$0.06	$1.55	$1.00	$0.24	$0.18	$0.18	$3.23
4/9/2007	$0.08	$1.40	$1.11	$0.24	$0.18	$0.18	$3.25
4/16/2007	$0.03	$1.52	$1.14	$0.24	$0.18	$0.18	$3.31
4/23/2007	$0.09	$1.56	$1.04	$0.25	$0.18	$0.18	$3.32
4/30/2007	$0.03	$1.59	$1.11	$0.25	$0.18	$0.18	$3.36
5/7/2007	$0.06	$1.50	$1.26	$0.26	$0.18	$0.18	$3.46
5/14/2007	$0.13	$1.52	$1.17	$0.26	$0.18	$0.18	$3.45
5/21/2007	$0.17	$1.61	$1.03	$0.25	$0.18	$0.18	$3.44
5/28/2007	$0.21	$1.58	$0.99	$0.25	$0.18	$0.18	$3.41
6/4/2007	$0.31	$1.61	$0.82	$0.25	$0.18	$0.18	$3.37
6/11/2007	$0.35	$1.61	$0.74	$0.25	$0.18	$0.18	$3.32
6/18/2007	$0.25	$1.68	$0.69	$0.24	$0.18	$0.18	$3.24
6/25/2007	$0.14	$1.69	$0.74	$0.24	$0.18	$0.18	$3.19
7/2/2007	$0.07	$1.73	$0.77	$0.24	$0.18	$0.18	$3.19
7/9/2007	$0.12	$1.76	$0.65	$0.23	$0.18	$0.18	$3.14
7/16/2007	$0.14	$1.81	$0.60	$0.23	$0.18	$0.18	$3.16
7/23/2007	$0.21	$1.82	$0.48	$0.23	$0.18	$0.18	$3.12
7/30/2007	$0.23	$1.87	$0.35	$0.23	$0.18	$0.18	$3.06
8/6/2007	$0.27	$1.76	$0.39	$0.22	$0.18	$0.18	$3.02
8/13/2007	$0.24	$1.74	$0.35	$0.22	$0.18	$0.18	$2.93
8/20/2007	$0.17	$1.73	$0.37	$0.21	$0.18	$0.18	$2.86
8/27/2007	$0.14	$1.75	$0.31	$0.21	$0.18	$0.18	$2.79

(continued)

Date	Distribution Margin	Crude Oil Cost	Processing Margin	State/ Local Sales Tax	State Excise Tax	Federal Excise Tax	Retail Price
9/3/2007	$0.10	$1.80	$0.30	$0.21	$0.18	$0.18	$2.79
9/10/2007	$0.10	$1.86	$0.30	$0.21	$0.18	$0.18	$2.84
9/17/2007	$0.08	$1.91	$0.32	$0.22	$0.18	$0.18	$2.90
9/24/2007	$0.08	$1.96	$0.34	$0.22	$0.18	$0.18	$2.96
10/1/2007	$0.06	$1.89	$0.43	$0.22	$0.18	$0.18	$2.97
10/8/2007	$0.07	$1.86	$0.47	$0.22	$0.18	$0.18	$3.00
10/15/2007	$0.05	$2.03	$0.37	$0.23	$0.18	$0.18	$3.05
10/22/2007	$0.09	$2.05	$0.40	$0.23	$0.18	$0.18	$3.14
10/29/2007	$0.06	$2.20	$0.29	$0.23	$0.18	$0.18	$3.16
11/5/2007	$0.03	$2.20	$0.39	$0.24	$0.18	$0.18	$3.23
11/12/2007	$0.09	$2.22	$0.43	$0.25	$0.18	$0.18	$3.37
11/19/2007	$0.14	$2.21	$0.42	$0.25	$0.18	$0.18	$3.40
11/26/2007	$0.15	$2.28	$0.34	$0.25	$0.18	$0.18	$3.40
12/3/2007	$0.21	$2.07	$0.45	$0.25	$0.18	$0.18	$3.36
12/10/2007	$0.23	$2.01	$0.47	$0.25	$0.18	$0.18	$3.33
12/17/2007	$0.17	$2.09	$0.41	$0.24	$0.18	$0.18	$3.29
12/24/2007	$0.14	$2.16	$0.34	$0.24	$0.18	$0.18	$3.26
12/31/2007	$0.11	$2.23	$0.34	$0.24	$0.18	$0.18	$3.30

SOURCE: Author's calculations.

Appendix G

BP ARM per Gallon (January 3, 2000 to December 31, 2007)

Date	Distribution Margin	Crude Oil Cost	Discount to CARM Crude Oil Cost	Processing Margin	Premium to CARM Proc. Margin	Swap/ Hedge Spread	State/ Local Sales Tax	State Excise Tax	Federal Excise Tax	Excess Profit	Excess Profit %
1/3/2000	−$0.09	0.55	94.8%	0.25	104.2%	$0.07	$0.10	$0.18	$0.18	$0.11	8.1%
1/10/2000	$0.08	0.57	96.6%	0.24	104.3%	$0.07	$0.10	$0.18	$0.18	$0.10	7.5%
1/17/2000	$0.06	0.60	96.8%	0.19	105.6%	$0.07	$0.10	$0.18	$0.18	$0.08	6.3%
1/24/2000	$0.07	0.65	98.5%	0.17	113.3%	$0.08	$0.10	$0.18	$0.18	$0.10	7.3%
1/31/2000	$0.06	0.58	93.5%	0.24	104.3%	$0.07	$0.10	$0.18	$0.18	$0.11	8.3%
2/7/2000	$0.05	0.61	98.4%	0.26	108.3%	$0.07	$0.10	$0.18	$0.18	$0.07	5.5%
2/14/2000	$0.05	0.65	95.6%	0.23	109.5%	$0.08	$0.10	$0.18	$0.18	$0.13	9.4%
2/21/2000	−$0.01	0.63	95.5%	0.33	106.5%	$0.08	$0.11	$0.18	$0.18	$0.10	6.9%
2/28/2000	−$0.02	0.65	95.6%	0.42	105.0%	$0.08	$0.11	$0.18	$0.18	$0.14	9.3%
3/6/2000	−$0.01	0.65	91.5%	0.48	102.1%	$0.09	$0.12	$0.18	$0.18	$0.18	10.7%
3/13/2000	$0.00	0.66	91.7%	0.58	105.5%	$0.09	$0.13	$0.18	$0.18	$0.18	10.1%
3/20/2000	$0.05	0.61	98.4%	0.70	106.1%	$0.07	$0.13	$0.18	$0.18	$0.12	6.9%
3/27/2000	$0.18	0.62	100.0%	0.54	108.0%	$0.07	$0.13	$0.18	$0.18	$0.09	5.3%
4/3/2000	$0.17	0.59	101.7%	0.56	107.7%	$0.07	$0.13	$0.18	$0.18	$0.08	4.5%
4/10/2000	$0.26	0.52	94.5%	0.48	106.7%	$0.07	$0.13	$0.18	$0.18	$0.10	5.5%
4/17/2000	$0.33	0.51	89.5%	0.37	105.7%	$0.07	$0.13	$0.18	$0.18	$0.14	8.0%
4/24/2000	$0.31	0.54	93.1%	0.32	100.0%	$0.07	$0.13	$0.18	$0.18	$0.10	5.9%
5/1/2000	$0.25	0.53	91.4%	0.41	107.9%	$0.07	$0.12	$0.18	$0.18	$0.15	9.0%
5/8/2000	$0.16	0.59	93.7%	0.43	107.5%	$0.08	$0.12	$0.18	$0.18	$0.14	8.2%
5/15/2000	$0.13	0.64	95.5%	0.35	106.1%	$0.08	$0.12	$0.18	$0.18	$0.10	6.2%
5/22/2000	$0.09	0.60	93.8%	0.42	107.7%	$0.08	$0.12	$0.18	$0.18	$0.12	7.3%
5/29/2000	$0.09	0.65	97.0%	0.42	110.5%	$0.08	$0.12	$0.18	$0.18	$0.13	8.1%
6/5/2000	$0.08	0.60	92.3%	0.43	107.5%	$0.08	$0.12	$0.18	$0.18	$0.15	9.2%
6/12/2000	$0.09	0.66	94.3%	0.41	107.9%	$0.08	$0.12	$0.18	$0.18	$0.13	8.3%

Date	Distribution Margin	Crude Oil Cost	Discount to CARM Crude Oil Cost	Processing Margin	Premium to CARM Proc. Margin	Swap/Hedge Spread	State/Local Sales Tax	State Excise Tax	Federal Excise Tax	Excess Profit	Excess Profit %
6/19/2000	$0.06	0.64	91.4%	0.40	108.1%	$0.08	$0.12	$0.18	$0.18	$0.14	8.9%
6/26/2000	$0.03	0.72	93.5%	0.41	113.9%	$0.09	$0.12	$0.18	$0.18	$0.18	11.1%
7/3/2000	$0.00	0.64	94.1%	0.60	105.3%	$0.08	$0.13	$0.18	$0.18	$0.13	7.7%
7/10/2000	$0.01	0.63	95.5%	0.63	108.6%	$0.08	$0.13	$0.18	$0.18	$0.13	7.5%
7/17/2000	$0.08	0.65	94.2%	0.52	110.6%	$0.08	$0.13	$0.18	$0.18	$0.13	7.7%
7/24/2000	$0.13	0.59	95.2%	0.54	110.2%	$0.07	$0.13	$0.18	$0.18	$0.11	6.7%
7/31/2000	$0.13	0.57	95.0%	0.53	110.4%	$0.07	$0.12	$0.18	$0.18	$0.14	8.5%
8/7/2000	$0.07	0.61	95.3%	0.53	108.2%	$0.08	$0.12	$0.18	$0.18	$0.14	8.2%
8/14/2000	–$0.03	0.68	94.4%	0.54	105.9%	$0.09	$0.12	$0.18	$0.18	$0.15	8.8%
8/21/2000	–$0.02	0.66	91.7%	0.52	106.1%	$0.09	$0.12	$0.18	$0.18	$0.16	9.4%
8/28/2000	–$0.05	0.70	94.6%	0.57	105.6%	$0.09	$0.13	$0.18	$0.18	$0.15	8.8%
9/5/2000	–$0.10	0.73	94.8%	0.71	106.0%	$0.09	$0.13	$0.18	$0.18	$0.19	10.7%
9/11/2000	–$0.11	0.75	93.8%	0.71	107.6%	$0.10	$0.13	$0.18	$0.18	$0.15	7.9%
9/18/2000	$0.04	0.80	95.2%	0.49	111.4%	$0.10	$0.14	$0.18	$0.18	$0.16	8.8%
9/25/2000	$0.09	0.66	94.3%	0.62	106.9%	$0.08	$0.14	$0.18	$0.18	$0.26	14.4%
10/2/2000	$0.12	0.69	94.5%	0.55	105.8%	$0.09	$0.14	$0.18	$0.18	$0.16	8.6%
10/9/2000	$0.15	0.67	93.1%	0.49	106.5%	$0.09	$0.14	$0.18	$0.18	$0.15	8.0%
10/16/2000	$0.07	0.71	94.7%	0.52	106.1%	$0.09	$0.13	$0.18	$0.18	$0.13	7.2%
10/23/2000	$0.05	0.72	93.5%	0.50	106.4%	$0.09	$0.13	$0.18	$0.18	$0.13	7.4%
10/30/2000	$0.03	0.71	94.7%	0.57	105.6%	$0.09	$0.13	$0.18	$0.18	$0.15	8.3%
11/6/2000	$0.01	0.70	94.6%	0.61	107.0%	$0.09	$0.13	$0.18	$0.18	$0.17	9.4%
11/13/2000	$0.12	0.72	92.3%	0.43	107.5%	$0.09	$0.13	$0.18	$0.18	$0.18	10.3%
11/20/2000	$0.18	0.75	92.6%	0.32	114.3%	$0.10	$0.13	$0.18	$0.18	$0.18	10.1%

(continued)

Date	Distribution Margin	Crude Oil Cost	Discount to CARM Crude Oil Cost	Processing Margin	Premium to CARM Proc. Margin	Swap/ Hedge Spread	State/ Local Sales Tax	State Excise Tax	Federal Excise Tax	Excess Profit	Excess Profit %
11/27/2000	$0.16	0.72	90.0%	0.33	110.0%	$0.10	$0.13	$0.18	$0.18	$0.20	11.3%
12/4/2000	$0.17	0.66	98.5%	0.43	107.5%	$0.08	$0.13	$0.18	$0.18	$0.11	6.4%
12/11/2000	$0.29	0.56	94.9%	0.39	108.3%	$0.07	$0.13	$0.18	$0.18	$0.12	7.1%
12/18/2000	$0.27	0.54	91.5%	0.36	109.1%	$0.07	$0.12	$0.18	$0.18	$0.14	8.4%
12/26/2000	$0.24	0.55	93.2%	0.47	106.8%	$0.07	$0.12	$0.18	$0.18	$0.12	7.3%
1/2/2001	$0.18	0.48	94.1%	0.50	108.7%	$0.06	$0.12	$0.18	$0.18	$0.11	6.8%
1/8/2001	$0.16	0.49	94.2%	0.51	108.5%	$0.06	$0.12	$0.18	$0.18	$0.11	6.9%
1/15/2001	$0.19	0.58	96.7%	0.37	108.8%	$0.07	$0.12	$0.18	$0.18	$0.10	6.4%
1/22/2001	$0.15	0.63	96.9%	0.34	109.7%	$0.08	$0.12	$0.18	$0.18	$0.12	7.5%
1/29/2001	$0.13	0.55	93.2%	0.41	107.9%	$0.07	$0.12	$0.18	$0.18	$0.11	7.1%
2/5/2001	$0.09	0.58	90.6%	0.42	107.7%	$0.08	$0.12	$0.18	$0.18	$0.15	9.2%
2/12/2001	$0.04	0.60	92.3%	0.52	108.3%	$0.08	$0.12	$0.18	$0.18	$0.15	9.0%
2/19/2001	$0.04	0.55	90.2%	0.57	107.5%	$0.07	$0.12	$0.18	$0.18	$0.15	9.2%
2/26/2001	$0.02	0.54	90.0%	0.61	107.0%	$0.07	$0.12	$0.18	$0.18	$0.15	9.2%
3/5/2001	$0.02	0.58	93.5%	0.62	106.9%	$0.07	$0.13	$0.18	$0.18	$0.12	7.3%
3/12/2001	$0.03	0.51	94.4%	0.72	107.5%	$0.06	$0.13	$0.18	$0.18	$0.12	7.3%
3/19/2001	$0.04	0.52	92.9%	0.65	106.6%	$0.07	$0.13	$0.18	$0.18	$0.12	6.9%
3/26/2001	$0.01	0.55	93.2%	0.65	106.6%	$0.07	$0.12	$0.18	$0.18	$0.13	7.8%
4/2/2001	–$0.04	0.50	90.9%	0.77	106.9%	$0.07	$0.13	$0.18	$0.18	$0.14	7.9%
4/9/2001	–$0.05	0.57	93.4%	0.80	106.7%	$0.07	$0.13	$0.18	$0.18	$0.16	9.3%
4/16/2001	–$0.07	0.59	92.2%	0.81	108.0%	$0.08	$0.13	$0.18	$0.18	$0.17	9.3%
4/23/2001	$0.01	0.54	90.0%	0.82	107.9%	$0.07	$0.14	$0.18	$0.18	$0.19	10.5%
4/30/2001	$0.01	0.59	93.7%	0.81	108.0%	$0.08	$0.14	$0.18	$0.18	$0.15	7.8%
5/7/2001	$0.09	0.57	91.9%	0.83	112.2%	$0.07	$0.14	$0.18	$0.18	$0.17	9.0%

Date	Distribution Margin	Crude Oil Cost	Discount to CARM Crude Oil Cost	Processing Margin	Premium to CARM Proc. Margin	Swap/ Hedge Spread	State/ Local Sales Tax	State Excise Tax	Federal Excise Tax	Excess Profit	Excess Profit %
5/14/2001	$0.15	0.59	92.2%	0.72	110.8%	$0.08	$0.14	$0.18	$0.18	$0.15	7.5%
5/21/2001	$0.17	0.60	93.8%	0.73	112.3%	$0.08	$0.14	$0.18	$0.18	$0.17	8.6%
5/28/2001	$0.21	0.59	92.2%	0.65	108.3%	$0.08	$0.14	$0.18	$0.18	$0.14	7.0%
6/4/2001	$0.22	0.59	93.7%	0.66	110.0%	$0.08	$0.14	$0.18	$0.18	$0.16	8.1%
6/11/2011	$0.31	0.60	92.3%	0.52	110.6%	$0.08	$0.14	$0.18	$0.18	$0.13	6.6%
6/18/2001	$0.36	0.55	88.7%	0.53	115.2%	$0.08	$0.14	$0.18	$0.18	$0.19	10.1%
6/25/2001	$0.39	0.56	93.3%	0.46	109.5%	$0.07	$0.14	$0.18	$0.18	$0.13	6.9%
7/2/2001	$0.40	0.54	93.1%	0.41	110.8%	$0.07	$0.14	$0.18	$0.18	$0.10	5.4%
7/9/2001	$0.43	0.58	93.5%	0.34	117.2%	$0.07	$0.14	$0.18	$0.18	$0.15	8.5%
7/16/2001	$0.42	0.53	93.0%	0.31	119.2%	$0.07	$0.13	$0.18	$0.18	$0.11	6.1%
7/23/2001	$0.50	0.52	91.2%	0.18	120.0%	$0.07	$0.13	$0.18	$0.18	$0.11	6.3%
7/30/2001	$0.36	0.53	93.0%	0.31	114.8%	$0.07	$0.12	$0.18	$0.18	$0.15	8.9%
8/6/2001	$0.28	0.54	93.1%	0.33	117.9%	$0.07	$0.12	$0.18	$0.18	$0.14	8.6%
8/13/2001	$0.21	0.55	93.2%	0.35	112.9%	$0.07	$0.12	$0.18	$0.18	$0.15	9.7%
8/20/2001	$0.11	0.53	93.0%	0.42	105.0%	$0.07	$0.11	$0.18	$0.18	$0.12	7.8%
8/27/2001	$0.08	0.54	96.4%	0.37	105.7%	$0.07	$0.11	$0.18	$0.18	$0.11	7.1%
9/3/2001	–$0.08	0.52	91.2%	0.75	105.6%	$0.07	$0.12	$0.18	$0.18	$0.16	9.7%
9/10/2001	$0.01	0.55	93.2%	0.67	108.1%	$0.07	$0.12	$0.18	$0.18	$0.15	9.0%
9/17/2001	$0.02	0.57	93.4%	0.62	108.8%	$0.07	$0.12	$0.18	$0.18	$0.14	8.6%
9/24/2001	$0.12	0.40	90.9%	0.66	103.1%	$0.05	$0.12	$0.18	$0.18	$0.10	6.2%
10/1/2001	$0.22	0.45	91.8%	0.51	110.9%	$0.06	$0.12	$0.18	$0.18	$0.15	9.2%
10/8/2001	$0.19	0.44	93.6%	0.48	109.1%	$0.06	$0.12	$0.18	$0.18	$0.10	6.2%
10/15/2001	$0.21	0.42	89.4%	0.44	107.3%	$0.06	$0.11	$0.18	$0.18	$0.12	7.5%

(continued)

Date	Distribution Margin	Crude Oil Cost	Discount to CARM Crude Oil Cost	Processing Margin	Premium to CARM Proc. Margin	Swap/ Hedge Spread	State/ Local Sales Tax	State Excise Tax	Federal Excise Tax	Excess Profit	Excess Profit %
10/22/2001	$0.14	0.41	89.1%	0.49	108.9%	$0.06	$0.11	$0.18	$0.18	$0.14	9.0%
10/29/2001	$0.08	0.44	93.6%	0.51	108.5%	$0.06	$0.11	$0.18	$0.18	$0.11	7.2%
11/5/2001	$0.11	0.39	91.8%	0.49	108.9%	$0.05	$0.11	$0.18	$0.18	$0.12	8.2%
11/12/2001	$0.15	0.40	88.9%	0.36	109.1%	$0.05	$0.10	$0.18	$0.18	$0.12	9.0%
11/19/2001	$0.19	0.33	89.2%	0.37	112.1%	$0.04	$0.10	$0.18	$0.18	$0.10	7.8%
11/26/2001	$0.18	0.33	84.6%	0.31	114.8%	$0.05	$0.10	$0.18	$0.18	$0.12	9.1%
12/3/2001	$0.15	0.38	90.5%	0.26	113.0%	$0.05	$0.08	$0.18	$0.18	$0.10	8.1%
12/10/2001	$0.16	0.33	86.8%	0.27	117.4%	$0.05	$0.09	$0.18	$0.18	$0.14	11.3%
12/17/2001	$0.09	0.36	92.3%	0.25	113.6%	$0.05	$0.08	$0.18	$0.18	$0.10	8.5%
12/24/2001	$0.00	0.41	93.2%	0.26	113.0%	$0.05	$0.08	$0.18	$0.18	$0.09	8.4%
12/31/2001	–$0.05	0.37	90.2%	0.35	112.9%	$0.05	$0.08	$0.18	$0.18	$0.13	11.7%
1/7/2002	–$0.06	0.40	88.9%	0.32	114.3%	$0.05	$0.08	$0.18	$0.18	$0.09	8.3%
1/14/2002	$0.02	0.33	82.5%	0.34	113.3%	$0.05	$0.09	$0.18	$0.18	$0.11	9.2%
1/21/2002	$0.09	0.32	82.1%	0.35	116.7%	$0.05	$0.09	$0.18	$0.18	$0.13	10.5%
1/28/2002	$0.00	0.35	81.4%	0.40	117.6%	$0.05	$0.09	$0.18	$0.18	$0.15	12.4%
2/4/2002	$0.01	0.38	88.4%	0.41	117.1%	$0.05	$0.09	$0.18	$0.18	$0.12	9.7%
2/11/2002	$0.02	0.42	87.5%	0.36	116.1%	$0.06	$0.09	$0.18	$0.18	$0.13	10.2%
2/19/2002	$0.02	0.39	86.7%	0.43	113.2%	$0.05	$0.10	$0.18	$0.18	$0.11	8.8%
2/25/2002	$0.03	0.40	88.9%	0.42	113.5%	$0.05	$0.10	$0.18	$0.18	$0.10	7.5%
3/4/2002	$0.02	0.44	88.0%	0.43	116.2%	$0.06	$0.10	$0.18	$0.18	$0.13	9.8%
3/11/2002	$0.01	0.47	87.0%	0.52	110.6%	$0.06	$0.11	$0.18	$0.18	$0.15	10.7%
3/18/2002	$0.00	0.51	87.9%	0.57	114.0%	$0.07	$0.11	$0.18	$0.18	$0.18	12.0%
3/25/2002	$0.02	0.49	89.1%	0.60	113.2%	$0.07	$0.12	$0.18	$0.18	$0.17	10.6%
4/1/2002	$0.04	0.55	90.2%	0.50	111.1%	$0.07	$0.12	$0.18	$0.18	$0.11	7.1%

Date	Distribution Margin	Crude Oil Cost	Discount to CARM Crude Oil Cost	Processing Margin	Premium to CARM Proc. Margin	Swap/Hedge Spread	State/Local Sales Tax	State Excise Tax	Federal Excise Tax	Excess Profit	Excess Profit %
4/8/2002	$0.06	0.54	90.0%	0.53	112.8%	$0.07	$0.12	$0.18	$0.18	$0.15	9.4%
4/15/2002	$0.15	0.49	87.5%	0.52	115.6%	$0.07	$0.12	$0.18	$0.18	$0.15	9.1%
4/22/2002	$0.11	0.55	88.7%	0.47	117.5%	$0.07	$0.12	$0.18	$0.18	$0.16	10.2%
4/29/2002	$0.13	0.57	90.5%	0.45	115.4%	$0.08	$0.12	$0.18	$0.18	$0.17	10.3%
5/6/2002	$0.14	0.54	90.0%	0.44	112.8%	$0.07	$0.12	$0.18	$0.18	$0.15	9.6%
5/13/2002	$0.13	0.58	89.2%	0.37	115.6%	$0.08	$0.12	$0.18	$0.18	$0.17	10.7%
5/20/2002	$0.11	0.56	87.5%	0.41	117.1%	$0.08	$0.12	$0.18	$0.18	$0.18	11.3%
5/27/2002	$0.08	0.50	87.7%	0.50	113.6%	$0.07	$0.12	$0.18	$0.18	$0.16	10.2%
6/3/2002	$0.19	0.47	83.9%	0.51	113.3%	$0.07	$0.12	$0.18	$0.18	$0.18	11.4%
6/10/2002	$0.05	0.46	85.2%	0.58	116.0%	$0.06	$0.12	$0.18	$0.18	$0.16	10.6%
6/17/2002	$0.02	0.52	88.1%	0.59	115.7%	$0.07	$0.12	$0.18	$0.18	$0.16	10.1%
6/24/2002	$0.09	0.51	85.0%	0.52	115.6%	$0.07	$0.12	$0.18	$0.18	$0.18	11.2%
7/1/2002	$0.11	0.54	88.5%	0.51	115.9%	$0.07	$0.12	$0.18	$0.18	$0.18	11.3%
7/8/2002	$0.08	0.51	85.0%	0.53	115.2%	$0.07	$0.12	$0.18	$0.18	$0.18	11.3%
7/15/2002	$0.10	0.50	80.6%	0.51	118.6%	$0.07	$0.12	$0.18	$0.18	$0.24	15.3%
7/22/2002	$0.07	0.55	90.2%	0.50	113.6%	$0.07	$0.12	$0.18	$0.18	$0.14	9.0%
7/29/2002	$0.05	0.54	88.5%	0.51	113.3%	$0.07	$0.12	$0.18	$0.18	$0.15	9.7%
8/5/2002	$0.07	0.52	85.2%	0.52	115.6%	$0.07	$0.12	$0.18	$0.18	$0.18	11.5%
8/12/2002	$0.04	0.56	87.5%	0.49	114.0%	$0.08	$0.12	$0.18	$0.18	$0.16	9.9%
8/19/2002	$0.01	0.61	88.4%	0.44	112.8%	$0.08	$0.12	$0.18	$0.18	$0.15	9.7%
8/26/2002	$0.02	0.59	88.1%	0.47	117.5%	$0.08	$0.12	$0.18	$0.18	$0.15	9.5%
9/2/2002	$0.03	0.56	87.5%	0.52	115.6%	$0.08	$0.12	$0.18	$0.18	$0.17	10.4%
9/9/2002	$0.01	0.64	92.8%	0.48	114.3%	$0.08	$0.12	$0.18	$0.18	$0.15	9.6%

(continued)

Date	Distribution Margin	Crude Oil Cost	Discount to CARM Crude Oil Cost	Processing Margin	Premium to CARM Proc. Margin	Swap/ Hedge Spread	State/ Local Sales Tax	State Excise Tax	Federal Excise Tax	Excess Profit	Excess Profit %
9/16/2002	−$0.01	0.61	89.7%	0.49	116.7%	$0.08	$0.12	$0.18	$0.18	$0.15	9.6%
9/23/2002	$0.00	0.64	90.1%	0.44	112.8%	$0.09	$0.12	$0.18	$0.18	$0.18	11.2%
9/30/2002	$0.01	0.64	91.4%	0.45	115.4%	$0.08	$0.12	$0.18	$0.18	$0.17	11.2%
10/7/2002	$0.00	0.63	92.6%	0.46	115.0%	$0.08	$0.11	$0.18	$0.18	$0.15	9.8%
10/14/2002	$0.01	0.62	91.2%	0.47	114.6%	$0.08	$0.11	$0.18	$0.18	$0.18	11.9%
10/21/2002	−$0.01	0.55	85.9%	0.51	113.3%	$0.08	$0.11	$0.18	$0.18	$0.20	12.9%
10/28/2002	−$0.02	0.78	96.3%	0.56	114.3%	$0.10	$0.11	$0.18	$0.18	$0.16	10.3%
11/4/2002	$0.01	0.53	88.3%	0.57	116.3%	$0.07	$0.12	$0.18	$0.18	$0.16	10.4%
11/11/2002	$0.03	0.51	87.9%	0.56	109.8%	$0.07	$0.12	$0.18	$0.18	$0.13	8.2%
11/18/2002	$0.05	0.53	88.3%	0.53	112.8%	$0.07	$0.12	$0.18	$0.18	$0.15	9.6%
11/25/2002	$0.09	0.54	88.5%	0.46	115.0%	$0.07	$0.12	$0.18	$0.18	$0.15	9.8%
12/2/2002	$0.14	0.54	88.5%	0.39	114.7%	$0.07	$0.12	$0.18	$0.18	$0.15	9.8%
12/9/2002	$0.16	0.54	88.5%	0.34	113.3%	$0.07	$0.11	$0.18	$0.18	$0.15	9.9%
12/16/2002	$0.11	0.58	87.9%	0.31	119.2%	$0.08	$0.11	$0.18	$0.18	$0.17	11.1%
12/23/2002	$0.10	0.66	90.4%	0.28	121.7%	$0.09	$0.11	$0.18	$0.18	$0.18	11.7%
12/30/2002	$0.07	0.65	90.3%	0.32	114.3%	$0.09	$0.11	$0.18	$0.18	$0.17	10.9%
1/6/2003	$0.11	0.61	83.6%	0.33	122.2%	$0.09	$0.12	$0.18	$0.18	$0.23	14.4%
1/13/2003	$0.12	0.62	83.8%	0.34	121.4%	$0.09	$0.12	$0.18	$0.18	$0.24	15.0%
1/20/2003	$0.11	0.67	83.8%	0.31	124.0%	$0.10	$0.12	$0.18	$0.18	$0.24	14.5%
1/27/2003	$0.12	0.62	83.8%	0.38	118.8%	$0.09	$0.12	$0.18	$0.18	$0.23	13.9%
2/3/2003	$0.11	0.64	84.2%	0.42	120.0%	$0.09	$0.12	$0.18	$0.18	$0.27	16.1%
2/10/2003	$0.08	0.68	84.0%	0.45	118.4%	$0.10	$0.13	$0.18	$0.18	$0.27	15.3%
2/17/2003	$0.17	0.73	83.9%	0.39	118.2%	$0.10	$0.14	$0.18	$0.18	$0.25	13.7%
2/24/2003	$0.19	0.72	81.8%	0.43	119.4%	$0.11	$0.14	$0.18	$0.18	$0.30	15.4%

Date	Distribution Margin	Crude Oil Cost	Discount to CARM Crude Oil Cost	Processing Margin	Premium to CARM Proc. Margin	Swap/ Hedge Spread	State/ Local Sales Tax	State Excise Tax	Federal Excise Tax	Excess Profit	Excess Profit %
3/3/2003	$0.15	0.71	83.5%	0.60	117.6%	$0.10	$0.15	$0.18	$0.18	$0.27	13.5%
3/10/2003	$0.14	0.73	83.0%	0.65	118.2%	$0.11	$0.15	$0.18	$0.18	$0.30	14.2%
3/17/2003	$0.17	0.68	82.9%	0.77	118.5%	$0.10	$0.16	$0.18	$0.18	$0.29	13.5%
3/24/2003	$0.20	0.52	82.5%	0.92	116.5%	$0.08	$0.16	$0.18	$0.18	$0.19	8.7%
3/31/2003	$0.28	0.57	82.6%	0.93	140.9%	$0.08	$0.16	$0.18	$0.18	$0.38	18.0%
4/7/2003	$0.31	0.51	85.0%	0.82	117.1%	$0.07	$0.16	$0.18	$0.18	$0.19	9.1%
4/14/2003	$0.32	0.52	83.9%	0.79	119.7%	$0.07	$0.15	$0.18	$0.18	$0.17	8.4%
4/21/2003	$0.31	0.51	76.1%	0.79	117.5%	$0.08	$0.15	$0.18	$0.18	$0.28	14.0%
4/28/2003	$0.26	0.45	83.3%	0.79	117.9%	$0.06	$0.15	$0.18	$0.18	$0.17	8.8%
5/5/2003	$0.28	0.51	87.9%	0.68	119.3%	$0.07	$0.14	$0.18	$0.18	$0.17	8.8%
5/12/2003	$0.34	0.50	83.3%	0.51	118.6%	$0.07	$0.14	$0.18	$0.18	$0.18	9.7%
5/19/2003	$0.29	0.53	82.8%	0.46	117.9%	$0.08	$0.13	$0.18	$0.18	$0.20	10.9%
5/28/2003	$0.24	0.54	81.8%	0.45	118.4%	$0.08	$0.13	$0.18	$0.18	$0.21	11.9%
6/2/2003	$0.21	0.57	81.4%	0.44	129.4%	$0.08	$0.13	$0.18	$0.18	$0.26	15.3%
6/9/2003	$0.16	0.60	83.3%	0.39	114.7%	$0.09	$0.13	$0.18	$0.18	$0.25	14.5%
6/16/2003	$0.08	0.59	83.1%	0.63	118.9%	$0.09	$0.13	$0.18	$0.18	$0.27	14.8%
6/23/2003	$0.05	0.59	83.1%	0.67	117.5%	$0.09	$0.13	$0.18	$0.18	$0.23	12.5%
6/30/2003	$0.06	0.73	83.0%	0.68	119.3%	$0.11	$0.13	$0.18	$0.18	$0.30	16.4%
7/7/2003	$0.09	0.59	86.8%	0.62	117.0%	$0.08	$0.13	$0.18	$0.18	$0.18	10.1%
7/14/2003	$0.14	0.61	85.9%	0.52	118.2%	$0.09	$0.13	$0.18	$0.18	$0.22	12.2%
7/21/2003	$0.13	0.60	83.3%	0.48	120.0%	$0.09	$0.13	$0.18	$0.18	$0.24	13.7%
7/28/2003	$0.12	0.57	83.8%	0.51	118.6%	$0.08	$0.13	$0.18	$0.18	$0.20	11.8%
8/4/2003	$0.09	0.60	83.3%	0.49	119.5%	$0.09	$0.13	$0.18	$0.18	$0.23	13.3%

(continued)

293

Date	Distribution Margin	Crude Oil Cost	Discount to CARM Crude Oil Cost	Processing Margin	Premium to CARM Proc. Margin	Swap/ Hedge Spread	State/ Local Sales Tax	State Excise Tax	Federal Excise Tax	Excess Profit	Excess Profit %
8/11/2003	$0.08	0.60	82.2%	0.53	117.8%	$0.09	$0.13	$0.18	$0.18	$0.23	13.1%
8/18/2003	$0.02	0.57	81.4%	0.84	118.3%	$0.08	$0.14	$0.18	$0.18	$0.24	12.7%
8/25/2003	$0.04	0.60	83.3%	0.94	116.0%	$0.09	$0.16	$0.18	$0.18	$0.20	9.4%
9/1/2003	$0.16	0.60	83.3%	0.91	128.2%	$0.09	$0.16	$0.18	$0.18	$0.29	13.6%
9/8/2003	$0.23	0.55	83.3%	0.81	117.4%	$0.08	$0.15	$0.18	$0.18	$0.20	9.6%
9/15/2003	$0.28	0.53	82.8%	0.69	119.0%	$0.08	$0.15	$0.18	$0.18	$0.22	10.7%
9/22/2003	$0.35	0.51	82.3%	0.62	119.2%	$0.07	$0.15	$0.18	$0.18	$0.21	10.8%
9/29/2003	$0.34	0.54	83.1%	0.51	118.6%	$0.08	$0.14	$0.18	$0.18	$0.20	10.4%
10/6/2003	$0.27	0.57	82.6%	0.49	119.5%	$0.08	$0.14	$0.18	$0.18	$0.22	12.0%
10/13/2003	$0.21	0.60	83.3%	0.49	122.5%	$0.09	$0.13	$0.18	$0.18	$0.25	13.6%
10/20/2003	$0.22	0.57	83.8%	0.48	120.0%	$0.08	$0.13	$0.18	$0.18	$0.23	12.8%
10/27/2003	$0.16	0.56	83.6%	0.49	116.7%	$0.08	$0.13	$0.18	$0.18	$0.20	11.5%
11/3/2003	$0.15	0.54	83.1%	0.51	115.9%	$0.08	$0.13	$0.18	$0.18	$0.20	11.6%
11/10/2003	$0.12	0.57	82.6%	0.48	120.0%	$0.08	$0.13	$0.18	$0.18	$0.22	13.2%
11/17/2003	$0.09	0.59	83.1%	0.50	119.0%	$0.09	$0.12	$0.18	$0.18	$0.24	14.0%
11/24/2003	$0.14	0.58	86.6%	0.48	120.0%	$0.08	$0.13	$0.18	$0.18	$0.19	11.3%
12/1/2003	$0.15	0.56	83.6%	0.46	117.9%	$0.08	$0.12	$0.18	$0.18	$0.20	11.9%
12/8/2003	$0.16	0.59	81.9%	0.38	122.6%	$0.09	$0.12	$0.18	$0.18	$0.25	14.9%
12/15/2003	$0.14	0.63	82.9%	0.31	124.0%	$0.09	$0.12	$0.18	$0.18	$0.24	14.9%
12/22/2003	$0.13	0.61	83.6%	0.34	121.4%	$0.09	$0.12	$0.18	$0.18	$0.23	14.1%
12/29/2003	$0.09	0.62	83.8%	0.35	120.7%	$0.09	$0.12	$0.18	$0.18	$0.23	14.4%
1/5/2004	$0.14	0.64	82.1%	0.34	121.4%	$0.09	$0.12	$0.18	$0.15	$0.24	15.0%
1/12/2004	$0.18	0.66	82.5%	0.31	124.0%	$0.10	$0.12	$0.18	$0.15	$0.25	14.7%
1/19/2004	$0.11	0.69	82.1%	0.35	120.7%	$0.10	$0.13	$0.18	$0.15	$0.26	15.4%

Date	Distribution Margin	Crude Oil Cost	Discount to CARM Crude Oil Cost	Processing Margin	Premium to CARM Proc. Margin	Swap/ Hedge Spread	State/ Local Sales Tax	State Excise Tax	Federal Excise Tax	Excess Profit	Excess Profit %
1/26/2004	$0.14	0.65	82.3%	0.42	120.0%	$0.09	$0.13	$0.18	$0.15	$0.24	14.2%
2/2/2004	$0.13	0.66	81.5%	0.43	119.4%	$0.10	$0.13	$0.18	$0.15	$0.26	14.7%
2/9/2004	$0.15	0.61	80.3%	0.55	119.6%	$0.09	$0.13	$0.18	$0.15	$0.25	13.8%
2/16/2004	$0.16	0.66	82.5%	0.54	120.0%	$0.10	$0.14	$0.18	$0.15	$0.25	13.2%
2/23/2004	$0.10	0.65	82.3%	0.80	119.4%	$0.09	$0.15	$0.18	$0.15	$0.24	12.1%
3/1/2004	$0.15	0.70	82.4%	0.75	119.0%	$0.10	$0.16	$0.18	$0.15	$0.26	12.4%
3/8/2004	$0.17	0.69	82.1%	0.74	119.4%	$0.10	$0.16	$0.18	$0.15	$0.26	12.4%
3/15/2004	$0.18	0.71	82.6%	0.67	119.6%	$0.10	$0.16	$0.18	$0.15	$0.24	11.6%
3/22/2004	$0.17	0.71	83.5%	0.68	119.3%	$0.10	$0.15	$0.18	$0.15	$0.23	11.2%
3/29/2004	$0.16	0.66	81.5%	0.76	120.6%	$0.10	$0.15	$0.18	$0.15	$0.26	12.4%
4/5/2004	$0.13	0.65	82.3%	0.88	120.5%	$0.09	$0.16	$0.18	$0.15	$0.25	12.0%
4/12/2004	$0.17	0.71	81.6%	0.79	123.4%	$0.10	$0.16	$0.18	$0.15	$0.30	14.1%
4/19/2004	$0.17	0.71	82.6%	0.77	120.3%	$0.10	$0.16	$0.18	$0.15	$0.26	12.2%
4/26/2004	$0.16	0.70	82.4%	0.75	119.0%	$0.10	$0.16	$0.18	$0.15	$0.26	12.4%
5/3/2004	$0.11	0.72	81.8%	0.76	118.8%	$0.11	$0.16	$0.18	$0.15	$0.28	13.1%
5/10/2004	$0.10	0.74	82.2%	0.88	118.9%	$0.11	$0.16	$0.18	$0.15	$0.28	12.5%
5/17/2004	$0.12	0.80	83.3%	0.83	118.6%	$0.12	$0.17	$0.18	$0.15	$0.29	12.6%
5/24/2004	$0.14	0.79	81.4%	0.86	119.4%	$0.12	$0.17	$0.18	$0.15	$0.32	13.6%
5/31/2004	$0.19	0.83	83.8%	0.79	119.7%	$0.12	$0.17	$0.18	$0.15	$0.30	12.8%
6/7/2004	$0.21	0.73	82.0%	0.88	118.9%	$0.11	$0.17	$0.18	$0.15	$0.29	12.4%
6/14/2004	$0.22	0.71	82.6%	0.87	119.2%	$0.10	$0.17	$0.18	$0.15	$0.27	11.9%
6/21/2004	$0.26	0.69	80.2%	1.01	118.8%	$0.10	$0.17	$0.18	$0.15	$0.27	12.1%
6/28/2004	$0.22	0.68	81.9%	0.84	120.0%	$0.10	$0.17	$0.18	$0.15	$0.26	11.6%

(continued)

Date	Distribution Margin	Crude Oil Cost	Discount to CARM Crude Oil Cost	Processing Margin	Premium to CARM Proc. Margin	Swap/ Hedge Spread	State/ Local Sales Tax	State Excise Tax	Federal Excise Tax	Excess Profit	Excess Profit %
7/5/2004	$0.22	0.72	81.8%	0.75	119.0%	$0.11	$0.16	$0.18	$0.15	$0.29	13.0%
7/12/2004	$0.18	0.75	82.4%	0.74	119.4%	$0.11	$0.16	$0.18	$0.15	$0.28	12.7%
7/19/2004	$0.17	0.78	82.1%	0.71	120.3%	$0.11	$0.16	$0.18	$0.15	$0.30	13.9%
7/26/2004	$0.19	0.79	82.3%	0.64	120.8%	$0.12	$0.16	$0.18	$0.15	$0.31	14.1%
8/2/2004	$0.20	0.83	82.2%	0.54	120.0%	$0.12	$0.16	$0.18	$0.15	$0.32	15.1%
8/9/2004	$0.21	0.86	82.7%	0.47	120.5%	$0.12	$0.15	$0.18	$0.15	$0.33	16.0%
8/16/2004	$0.13	0.87	82.1%	0.48	123.1%	$0.13	$0.15	$0.18	$0.15	$0.34	16.4%
8/23/2004	$0.11	0.86	81.1%	0.50	122.0%	$0.13	$0.15	$0.18	$0.15	$0.35	16.9%
8/30/2004	$0.19	0.77	81.9%	0.59	120.4%	$0.11	$0.15	$0.18	$0.15	$0.30	14.4%
9/6/2004	$0.17	0.80	82.5%	0.55	119.6%	$0.12	$0.15	$0.18	$0.15	$0.30	0.1%
9/13/2004	$0.16	0.79	81.4%	0.56	119.1%	$0.12	$0.15	$0.18	$0.15	$0.31	14.9%
9/21/2004	$0.12	0.85	82.5%	0.54	122.7%	$0.12	$0.15	$0.18	$0.15	$0.32	15.8%
9/27/2004	$0.08	0.92	83.6%	0.54	122.7%	$0.13	$0.16	$0.18	$0.15	$0.34	16.4%
10/4/2004	$0.09	0.93	83.8%	0.61	119.6%	$0.13	$0.16	$0.18	$0.15	$0.31	14.2%
10/11/2004	$0.07	0.12	9.8%	0.69	119.0%	$0.14	$0.17	$0.18	$0.15	$1.19	50.9%
10/18/2004	$0.10	1.15	97.5%	0.74	119.4%	$0.14	$0.18	$0.18	$0.15	$0.18	7.6%
10/25/2004	$0.15	0.96	82.8%	0.69	119.0%	$0.14	$0.18	$0.18	$0.15	$0.35	14.6%
11/1/2004	$0.18	0.89	81.7%	0.72	120.0%	$0.13	$0.18	$0.18	$0.15	$0.35	14.8%
11/8/2004	$0.24	0.84	82.4%	0.73	121.7%	$0.12	$0.17	$0.18	$0.15	$0.33	14.2%
11/15/2004	$0.22	0.81	82.7%	0.74	121.3%	$0.12	$0.17	$0.18	$0.15	$0.30	12.9%
11/22/2004	$0.26	0.81	81.0%	0.61	119.6%	$0.12	$0.17	$0.18	$0.15	$0.32	14.2%
11/29/2004	$0.22	0.97	82.2%	0.39	121.9%	$0.14	$0.17	$0.18	$0.15	$0.33	14.8%
12/6/2004	$0.34	0.71	82.6%	0.62	119.2%	$0.10	$0.16	$0.18	$0.15	$0.27	12.5%
12/13/2004	$0.48	0.66	81.5%	0.46	121.1%	$0.10	$0.16	$0.18	$0.15	$0.27	12.5%

Date	Distribution Margin	Crude Oil Cost	Discount to CARM Crude Oil Cost	Processing Margin	Premium to CARM Proc. Margin	Swap/ Hedge Spread	State/ Local Sales Tax	State Excise Tax	Federal Excise Tax	Excess Profit	Excess Profit %
12/20/2004	$0.33	0.78	83.9%	0.41	128.1%	$0.11	$0.15	$0.18	$0.15	$0.29	14.2%
12/27/2004	$0.28	0.66	80.5%	0.54	122.7%	$0.10	$0.15	$0.18	$0.15	$0.28	13.9%
1/3/2005	$0.23	0.65	77.4%	0.52	126.8%	$0.10	$0.15	$0.18	$0.18	$0.31	15.7%
1/10/2005	$0.18	0.73	78.5%	0.41	124.2%	$0.11	$0.14	$0.18	$0.18	$0.32	16.7%
1/17/2005	$0.15	0.81	77.9%	0.33	126.9%	$0.12	$0.14	$0.18	$0.18	$0.37	19.4%
1/24/2005	$0.09	0.80	77.7%	0.43	126.5%	$0.12	$0.15	$0.18	$0.18	$0.36	18.6%
1/31/2005	$0.13	0.84	80.8%	0.45	125.0%	$0.12	$0.15	$0.18	$0.18	$0.33	16.5%
2/7/2005	$0.12	0.79	79.0%	0.53	123.3%	$0.12	$0.15	$0.18	$0.18	$0.33	16.1%
2/14/2005	$0.10	0.81	79.4%	0.58	123.4%	$0.12	$0.15	$0.18	$0.18	$0.34	16.4%
2/21/2005	$0.12	0.88	78.6%	0.59	147.5%	$0.13	$0.16	$0.18	$0.18	$0.47	22.1%
2/28/2005	$0.08	0.87	77.7%	0.60	127.7%	$0.13	$0.16	$0.18	$0.18	$0.41	19.0%
3/7/2005	$0.09	0.94	79.0%	0.55	125.0%	$0.14	$0.17	$0.18	$0.18	$0.41	18.5%
3/14/2005	$0.10	0.96	79.3%	0.59	125.5%	$0.15	$0.17	$0.18	$0.18	$0.43	18.6%
3/21/2005	$0.11	0.99	78.6%	0.54	125.6%	$0.15	$0.17	$0.18	$0.18	$0.44	21.0%
3/28/2005	$0.07	0.95	78.5%	0.71	124.6%	$0.15	$0.18	$0.18	$0.18	$0.42	17.4%
4/4/2005	$0.01	1.01	78.9%	0.79	123.4%	$0.15	$0.18	$0.18	$0.18	$0.44	18.0%
4/11/2005	$0.05	0.95	79.2%	0.99	123.8%	$0.14	$0.19	$0.18	$0.18	$0.40	15.6%
4/18/2005	$0.05	0.88	78.6%	0.11	12.4%	$0.13	$0.19	$0.18	$0.18	-$0.58	-22.4%
4/25/2005	$0.11	0.96	78.7%	0.88	123.9%	$0.15	$0.19	$0.18	$0.18	$0.43	16.6%
5/2/2005	$0.16	0.90	78.9%	0.89	123.6%	$0.14	$0.19	$0.18	$0.18	$0.39	15.1%
5/9/2005	$0.20	0.92	78.6%	0.76	124.6%	$0.14	$0.19	$0.18	$0.18	$0.40	15.9%
5/16/2005	$0.31	0.85	78.7%	0.68	123.6%	$0.13	$0.18	$0.18	$0.18	$0.37	15.0%
5/23/2005	$0.31	0.88	78.6%	0.60	125.0%	$0.13	$0.18	$0.18	$0.18	$0.37	15.4%

(continued)

Date	Distribution Margin	Crude Oil Cost	Discount to CARM Crude Oil Cost	Processing Margin	Premium to CARM Proc. Margin	Swap/ Hedge Spread	State/ Local Sales Tax	State Excise Tax	Federal Excise Tax	Excess Profit	Excess Profit %
5/30/2005	$0.29	0.92	78.6%	0.52	126.8%	$0.14	$0.18	$0.18	$0.18	$0.41	17.2%
6/6/2005	$0.25	0.11	8.0%	0.38	122.6%	$0.16	$0.17	$0.18	$0.18	$1.39	59.0%
6/13/2005	$0.16	1.00	79.4%	0.49	122.5%	$0.15	$0.17	$0.18	$0.18	$0.42	18.1%
6/20/2005	$0.11	1.07	79.3%	0.47	127.0%	$0.16	$0.17	$0.18	$0.18	$0.46	19.7%
6/27/2005	$0.08	1.08	78.3%	0.54	125.6%	$0.17	$0.18	$0.18	$0.18	$0.49	20.1%
7/4/2005	$0.09	1.06	79.1%	0.64	125.5%	$0.16	$0.18	$0.18	$0.18	$0.47	19.1%
7/11/2005	$0.12	1.07	79.3%	0.66	124.5%	$0.16	$0.19	$0.18	$0.18	$0.47	18.7%
7/18/2005	$0.23	1.04	78.8%	0.56	124.4%	$0.16	$0.19	$0.18	$0.18	$0.45	17.7%
7/25/2005	$0.13	1.03	78.6%	0.71	126.8%	$0.16	$0.19	$0.18	$0.18	$0.47	18.4%
8/1/2005	$0.09	1.14	80.3%	0.64	125.5%	$0.17	$0.19	$0.18	$0.18	$0.48	18.8%
8/8/2005	$0.00	1.16	78.9%	0.76	124.6%	$0.18	$0.19	$0.18	$0.18	$0.52	19.9%
8/15/2005	$0.05	1.21	80.1%	0.76	124.6%	$0.18	$0.20	$0.18	$0.18	$0.48	17.7%
8/22/2005	$0.16	1.19	79.9%	0.71	126.8%	$0.18	$0.20	$0.18	$0.18	$0.52	18.9%
8/29/2005	-$0.16	1.21	79.1%	1.03	125.6%	$0.18	$0.21	$0.18	$0.18	$0.51	18.5%
9/5/2005	-$0.09	1.25	81.2%	1.21	117.5%	$0.18	$0.23	$0.18	$0.18	$0.42	13.9%
9/15/2005	$0.25	1.18	80.8%	0.84	120.0%	$0.18	$0.22	$0.18	$0.18	$0.42	13.8%
9/19/2005	$0.19	1.25	80.1%	0.78	123.8%	$0.19	$0.22	$0.18	$0.18	$0.51	17.2%
9/26/2005	$0.18	1.22	80.3%	0.86	124.6%	$0.18	$0.22	$0.18	$0.18	$0.51	17.4%
10/3/2005	$0.05	1.20	79.5%	1.04	123.8%	$0.18	$0.22	$0.18	$0.18	$0.52	17.5%
10/10/2005	$0.38	1.15	80.4%	0.72	124.1%	$0.17	$0.22	$0.18	$0.18	$0.45	15.3%
10/17/2005	$0.41	1.27	85.2%	0.55	125.0%	$0.18	$0.21	$0.18	$0.18	$0.40	13.8%
10/24/2005	$0.46	1.12	79.4%	0.50	125.0%	$0.17	$0.21	$0.18	$0.18	$0.46	16.2%
10/31/2005	$0.41	1.08	78.3%	0.52	123.8%	$0.17	$0.20	$0.18	$0.18	$0.49	17.7%
11/7/2005	$0.31	1.06	78.5%	0.56	121.7%	$0.16	$0.20	$0.18	$0.18	$0.46	17.4%

Date	Distribution Margin	Crude Oil Cost	Discount to CARM Crude Oil Cost	Processing Margin	Premium to CARM Proc. Margin	Swap/ Hedge Spread	State/ Local Sales Tax	State Excise Tax	Federal Excise Tax	Excess Profit	Excess Profit %
11/14/2005	$0.32	1.03	78.0%	0.57	139.0%	$0.16	$0.19	$0.18	$0.18	$0.50	19.3%
11/21/2005	$0.21	1.04	78.8%	0.50	125.0%	$0.16	$0.18	$0.18	$0.18	$0.46	18.7%
11/28/2005	$0.18	1.01	76.5%	0.49	125.6%	$0.16	$0.18	$0.18	$0.18	$0.49	20.3%
12/5/2005	$0.16	1.09	82.6%	0.35	125.0%	$0.16	$0.17	$0.18	$0.18	$0.40	17.0%
12/12/2005	$0.13	1.08	76.6%	0.28	127.3%	$0.17	$0.17	$0.18	$0.18	$0.51	22.4%
12/19/2005	$0.05	1.06	80.9%	0.43	119.4%	$0.16	$0.17	$0.18	$0.18	$0.42	18.5%
12/26/2005	$0.06	1.04	78.2%	0.42	127.3%	$0.16	$0.17	$0.18	$0.18	$0.50	22.4%
1/2/2006	–$0.01	1.09	76.2%	0.39	130.0%	$0.17	$0.16	$0.18	$0.18	$0.56	25.4%
1/9/2006	–$0.01	1.08	74.5%	0.46	124.3%	$0.17	$0.17	$0.18	$0.18	$0.56	24.2%
1/16/2006	$0.06	1.15	76.2%	0.39	125.8%	$0.18	$0.18	$0.18	$0.18	$0.55	22.8%
1/26/2006	–$0.02	1.21	76.6%	0.40	121.2%	$0.19	$0.18	$0.18	$0.18	$0.56	23.1%
1/30/2006	$0.03	1.20	76.9%	0.58	123.4%	$0.19	$0.19	$0.18	$0.18	$0.55	21.8%
2/6/2006	$0.03	1.17	78.0%	0.59	125.5%	$0.18	$0.19	$0.18	$0.18	$0.52	20.5%
2/13/2006	$0.16	1.08	77.1%	0.51	124.4%	$0.17	$0.19	$0.18	$0.18	$0.50	19.8%
2/20/2006	$0.13	1.07	76.4%	0.50	125.0%	$0.17	$0.19	$0.18	$0.18	$0.51	20.6%
2/27/2006	$0.10	1.05	75.0%	0.51	124.4%	$0.17	$0.18	$0.18	$0.18	$0.53	21.6%
3/6/2006	$0.00	1.10	76.9%	0.69	127.8%	$0.17	$0.18	$0.18	$0.18	$0.55	22.2%
3/13/2006	$0.06	1.11	78.2%	0.63	123.5%	$0.17	$0.19	$0.18	$0.18	$0.48	19.0%
3/20/2006	$0.05	1.06	76.3%	0.78	121.9%	$0.17	$0.20	$0.18	$0.18	$0.50	18.8%
3/27/2006	$0.06	1.13	76.4%	0.75	127.1%	$0.18	$0.20	$0.18	$0.18	$0.58	21.6%
4/3/2006	$0.04	1.18	76.6%	0.79	127.4%	$0.18	$0.20	$0.18	$0.18	$0.58	21.3%
4/10/2006	$0.00	1.20	75.5%	0.85	126.9%	$0.19	$0.21	$0.18	$0.18	$0.63	22.4%
4/17/2006	–$0.05	1.25	76.7%	0.96	126.3%	$0.20	$0.21	$0.18	$0.18	$0.62	21.2%

(continued)

Date	Distribution Margin	Crude Oil Cost	Discount to CARM Crude Oil Cost	Processing Margin	Premium to CARM Proc. Margin	Swap/Hedge Spread	State/Local Sales Tax	State Excise Tax	Federal Excise Tax	Excess Profit	Excess Profit %
4/24/2006	−$0.05	1.25	75.8%	1.12	124.4%	$0.20	$0.23	$0.18	$0.18	$0.62	20.1%
5/1/2006	$0.03	1.31	76.6%	1.10	126.4%	$0.21	$0.24	$0.18	$0.18	$0.64	19.9%
5/8/2006	$0.05	1.25	77.2%	1.34	126.4%	$0.19	$0.25	$0.18	$0.18	$0.60	18.2%
5/15/2006	$0.03	1.24	77.0%	1.36	125.9%	$0.19	$0.25	$0.18	$0.18	$0.59	17.8%
5/22/2006	$0.03	1.23	76.4%	1.29	126.5%	$0.19	$0.24	$0.18	$0.18	$0.60	18.6%
5/29/2006	$0.06	1.22	72.6%	1.19	126.6%	$0.20	$0.24	$0.18	$0.18	$0.69	21.1%
6/5/2006	$0.05	1.30	76.9%	1.17	127.2%	$0.20	$0.24	$0.18	$0.18	$0.62	19.0%
6/12/2006	$0.18	1.25	76.2%	1.04	126.8%	$0.20	$0.24	$0.18	$0.18	$0.62	19.1%
6/19/2006	$0.21	1.24	77.0%	0.99	126.9%	$0.19	$0.24	$0.18	$0.18	$0.58	18.2%
6/26/2006	$0.18	1.29	76.8%	0.90	126.8%	$0.20	$0.24	$0.18	$0.18	$0.60	19.0%
7/3/2006	$0.09	1.33	76.9%	0.98	127.3%	$0.21	$0.24	$0.18	$0.18	$0.65	20.3%
7/10/2006	$0.11	1.32	76.7%	1.02	127.5%	$0.21	$0.24	$0.18	$0.18	$0.66	20.6%
7/17/2006	$0.12	1.35	76.7%	0.96	126.3%	$0.21	$0.24	$0.18	$0.18	$0.63	19.5%
7/24/2006	$0.12	1.34	76.6%	0.96	126.3%	$0.21	$0.24	$0.18	$0.18	$0.63	19.6%
7/31/2006	$0.11	1.33	76.4%	0.94	127.0%	$0.21	$0.24	$0.18	$0.18	$0.62	19.3%
8/7/2006	$0.12	1.38	76.7%	0.86	126.5%	$0.22	$0.24	$0.18	$0.18	$0.67	20.9%
8/14/2006	$0.16	1.33	77.3%	0.93	127.4%	$0.21	$0.24	$0.18	$0.18	$0.63	19.5%
8/21/2006	$0.21	1.30	76.9%	0.84	127.3%	$0.20	$0.23	$0.18	$0.18	$0.60	19.1%
8/28/2006	$0.26	1.27	77.0%	0.75	127.1%	$0.20	$0.23	$0.18	$0.18	$0.59	19.0%
9/4/2006	$0.25	1.23	76.9%	0.74	125.4%	$0.19	$0.22	$0.18	$0.18	$0.58	19.3%
9/11/2006	$0.27	1.18	77.1%	0.73	128.1%	$0.18	$0.22	$0.18	$0.18	$0.55	18.8%
9/18/2006	$0.32	1.15	77.2%	0.59	128.3%	$0.18	$0.21	$0.18	$0.18	$0.53	18.6%
9/25/2006	$0.33	1.08	76.6%	0.57	123.9%	$0.17	$0.20	$0.18	$0.18	$0.48	17.4%
10/2/2006	$0.26	1.09	76.8%	0.55	127.9%	$0.17	$0.20	$0.18	$0.18	$0.50	18.7%

Date	Distribution Margin	Crude Oil Cost	Discount to CARM Crude Oil Cost	Processing Margin	Premium to CARM Proc. Margin	Swap/ Hedge Spread	State/ Local Sales Tax	State Excise Tax	Federal Excise Tax	Excess Profit	Excess Profit %
10/9/2006	$0.23	0.99	76.2%	0.65	127.5%	$0.16	$0.19	$0.18	$0.18	$0.50	19.1%
10/16/2006	$0.21	0.98	76.0%	0.61	127.1%	$0.15	$0.19	$0.18	$0.18	$0.47	18.7%
10/23/2006	$0.18	0.96	76.8%	0.65	127.5%	$0.15	$0.18	$0.18	$0.18	$0.48	19.4%
10/30/2006	$0.17	0.97	76.4%	0.59	128.3%	$0.15	$0.18	$0.18	$0.18	$0.49	20.3%
11/6/2006	$0.09	1.01	76.5%	0.60	130.4%	$0.16	$0.18	$0.18	$0.18	$0.53	22.0%
11/13/2006	$0.06	0.98	76.6%	0.74	127.6%	$0.15	$0.18	$0.18	$0.18	$0.48	19.7%
11/20/2006	$0.06	0.94	76.4%	0.83	127.7%	$0.15	$0.18	$0.18	$0.18	$0.46	18.3%
11/27/2006	$0.05	1.01	76.5%	0.70	127.3%	$0.16	$0.18	$0.18	$0.18	$0.47	18.8%
12/4/2006	$0.06	1.05	76.6%	0.66	126.9%	$0.16	$0.18	$0.18	$0.18	$0.49	19.8%
12/11/2006	$0.07	1.04	75.9%	0.64	128.0%	$0.16	$0.19	$0.18	$0.18	$0.52	21.0%
12/18/2006	$0.10	1.07	77.0%	0.66	129.4%	$0.17	$0.19	$0.18	$0.18	$0.52	20.2%
12/25/2006	$0.15	1.08	77.1%	0.64	125.5%	$0.17	$0.19	$0.18	$0.18	$0.50	19.1%
1/1/2007	$0.14	1.00	75.8%	0.63	106.8%	$0.16	$0.19	$0.18	$0.18	$0.38	14.5%
1/8/2007	$0.18	0.96	75.6%	0.77	124.2%	$0.15	$0.19	$0.18	$0.18	$0.46	17.6%
1/15/2007	$0.19	0.85	73.9%	0.85	123.2%	$0.14	$0.19	$0.18	$0.18	$0.45	17.4%
1/22/2007	$0.21	0.89	74.8%	0.74	125.4%	$0.14	$0.19	$0.18	$0.18	$0.46	18.2%
1/29/2007	$0.15	0.92	75.4%	0.74	123.3%	$0.15	$0.18	$0.18	$0.18	$0.47	18.7%
2/5/2007	$0.09	1.02	75.6%	0.67	124.1%	$0.16	$0.19	$0.18	$0.18	$0.50	19.8%
2/12/2007	$0.04	0.98	74.2%	0.87	122.5%	$0.16	$0.19	$0.18	$0.18	$0.49	18.6%
2/19/2007	$0.08	1.01	74.3%	0.88	125.7%	$0.16	$0.20	$0.18	$0.18	$0.52	19.3%
2/26/2007	$0.06	1.05	74.5%	0.94	125.3%	$0.17	$0.21	$0.18	$0.18	$0.53	18.9%
3/5/2007	$0.08	1.04	75.4%	1.05	122.1%	$0.17	$0.21	$0.18	$0.18	$0.49	16.7%
3/12/2007	$0.07	1.02	75.0%	1.27	122.1%	$0.16	$0.23	$0.18	$0.18	$0.49	16.1%

(continued)

Date	Distribution Margin	Crude Oil Cost	Discount to CARM Crude Oil Cost	Processing Margin	Premium to CARM Proc. Margin	Swap/ Hedge Spread	State/ Local Sales Tax	State Excise Tax	Federal Excise Tax	Excess Profit	Excess Profit %
3/19/2007	$0.05	0.98	74.2%	1.37	122.3%	$0.16	$0.23	$0.18	$0.18	$0.50	16.2%
3/26/2007	$0.08	1.11	75.5%	1.27	127.0%	$0.18	$0.23	$0.18	$0.18	$0.56	17.7%
4/2/2007	$0.07	1.16	74.8%	1.23	123.0%	$0.19	$0.24	$0.18	$0.18	$0.55	16.9%
4/9/2007	$0.09	1.05	75.0%	1.36	122.5%	$0.17	$0.24	$0.18	$0.18	$0.51	15.6%
4/16/2007	$0.05	1.14	75.0%	1.41	123.7%	$0.18	$0.24	$0.18	$0.18	$0.51	17.3%
4/23/2007	$0.11	1.16	74.4%	1.28	123.1%	$0.19	$0.25	$0.18	$0.18	$0.60	18.0%
4/30/2007	$0.05	1.19	74.8%	1.36	122.5%	$0.19	$0.25	$0.18	$0.18	$0.59	17.6%
5/7/2007	$0.07	1.13	75.3%	1.54	122.2%	$0.18	$0.26	$0.18	$0.18	$0.52	15.0%
5/14/2007	$0.14	1.15	75.7%	1.41	120.5%	$0.18	$0.26	$0.18	$0.18	$0.51	14.9%
5/21/2007	$0.18	1.21	75.2%	1.26	122.3%	$0.19	$0.25	$0.18	$0.18	$0.55	16.1%
5/28/2007	$0.22	1.19	75.3%	1.19	120.2%	$0.19	$0.25	$0.18	$0.18	$0.52	15.2%
6/4/2007	$0.32	1.21	75.2%	1.02	124.4%	$0.19	$0.25	$0.18	$0.18	$0.57	17.0%
6/11/2007	$0.36	1.21	75.2%	0.90	122.3%	$0.19	$0.25	$0.18	$0.18	$0.52	15.8%
6/18/2007	$0.26	1.27	75.6%	0.85	123.2%	$0.20	$0.24	$0.18	$0.18	$0.52	16.1%
6/25/2007	$0.15	1.28	75.7%	0.91	123.0%	$0.20	$0.24	$0.18	$0.18	$0.61	19.2%
7/2/2007	$0.08	1.30	75.1%	0.95	123.4%	$0.21	$0.24	$0.18	$0.18	$0.63	19.7%
7/9/2007	$0.13	1.33	75.6%	0.81	124.6%	$0.21	$0.23	$0.18	$0.18	$0.65	20.7%
7/16/2007	$0.15	1.37	75.7%	0.74	123.3%	$0.22	$0.23	$0.18	$0.18	$0.66	20.8%
7/23/2007	$0.22	1.36	74.7%	0.59	122.9%	$0.22	$0.23	$0.18	$0.18	$0.68	21.7%
7/30/2007	$0.25	1.41	75.4%	0.44	125.7%	$0.22	$0.23	$0.18	$0.18	$0.70	23.0%
8/6/2007	$0.30	1.32	75.0%	0.48	123.1%	$0.21	$0.22	$0.18	$0.18	$0.67	22.2%
8/13/2007	$0.26	1.30	74.7%	0.44	125.7%	$0.21	$0.22	$0.18	$0.18	$0.67	22.8%
8/20/2007	$0.18	1.29	74.6%	0.46	124.3%	$0.21	$0.21	$0.18	$0.18	$0.64	22.3%
8/27/2007	$0.14	1.32	75.4%	0.39	125.8%	$0.21	$0.21	$0.18	$0.18	$0.64	22.9%

Date	Distribution Margin	Crude Oil Cost	Discount to CARM Crude Oil Cost	Processing Margin	Premium to CARM Proc. Margin	Swap/ Hedge Spread	State/ Local Sales Tax	State Excise Tax	Federal Excise Tax	Excess Profit	Excess Profit %
9/3/2007	$0.09	1.36	75.6%	0.38	126.7%	$0.22	$0.21	$0.18	$0.18	$0.62	22.1%
9/10/2007	$0.10	1.40	75.3%	0.39	130.0%	$0.22	$0.21	$0.18	$0.18	$0.69	24.4%
9/17/2007	$0.09	1.44	75.4%	0.38	118.8%	$0.23	$0.22	$0.18	$0.18	$0.68	23.4%
9/24/2007	$0.10	1.48	75.5%	0.42	123.5%	$0.24	$0.22	$0.18	$0.18	$0.74	24.8%
10/1/2007	$0.08	1.43	75.7%	0.53	123.3%	$0.23	$0.22	$0.18	$0.18	$0.81	27.2%
10/8/2007	$0.09	1.40	75.3%	0.58	123.4%	$0.22	$0.22	$0.18	$0.18	$0.69	23.1%
10/15/2007	$0.06	1.52	74.9%	0.46	124.3%	$0.24	$0.23	$0.18	$0.18	$0.75	24.7%
10/22/2007	$0.11	1.55	75.6%	0.51	127.5%	$0.25	$0.23	$0.18	$0.18	$0.78	24.7%
10/29/2007	$0.06	1.66	75.5%	0.36	124.1%	$0.26	$0.23	$0.18	$0.18	$0.79	25.1%
11/5/2007	$0.04	1.65	75.0%	0.48	123.1%	$0.26	$0.24	$0.18	$0.18	$0.81	25.2%
11/12/2007	$0.10	1.68	75.7%	0.53	123.3%	$0.27	$0.25	$0.18	$0.18	$0.81	23.9%
11/19/2007	$0.15	1.67	75.6%	0.52	123.8%	$0.27	$0.25	$0.18	$0.18	$0.81	23.7%
11/26/2007	$0.16	1.72	75.4%	0.42	123.5%	$0.27	$0.25	$0.18	$0.18	$0.83	24.5%
12/3/2007	$0.22	1.55	74.9%	0.56	124.4%	$0.25	$0.25	$0.18	$0.18	$0.77	22.9%
12/10/2007	$0.25	1.52	75.6%	0.58	123.4%	$0.24	$0.25	$0.18	$0.18	$0.74	22.3%
12/17/2007	$0.19	1.58	75.6%	0.51	124.4%	$0.25	$0.24	$0.18	$0.18	$0.77	23.4%
12/24/2007	$0.15	1.62	75.0%	0.42	123.5%	$0.26	$0.24	$0.18	$0.18	$0.80	24.5%
12/31/2007	$0.12	1.67	74.9%	0.43	126.5%	$0.27	$0.24	$0.18	$0.18	$0.83	25.1%

SOURCE: Author's calculations.

Notes

Chapter 1

1. An option is a contract providing a trader the right, but not the obligation, to buy (call) or sell (put) a security or commodity contract at a determined price for a designated period of time. Options are used to offset exposure to cash risk with futures contracts (which provide the requirement that a given contract be purchased at a determined price at a designated time). Employing options to lessen the forward risk of contracts is a standard ingredient in hedging.

2. For a good (readable) introduction to all of this, see Peter C. Fusaro's *Energy Risk Management: Hedging Strategies and Instruments for the International Energy Markets* (New York: McGraw-Hill, 1998), and his edited *The Professional Risk Manager's Guide to the Energy Market* (New York: McGraw-Hill, 2008).

3. All of the "Greeks" comprise what amounts to a set of risk variables used by option traders. *Delta* measures the amount of change in the price of an option for each dollar change in the underlying futures contract. In addition to *vega*, other major "Greeks" are *gamma* (a measure of the degree to which delta changes related to the change in the price of the underlying contract—a delta derivative, if you will, providing what some call "the delta of the delta"), *theta* (a measurement of the time decay in a position—it reflects the expected change in the option's premium, that is, the price an option buyer must pay to the option seller, given a change in the option's term of expiration, all other things remaining constant) and *rho* (the rate of change in the value of an option relative to a change in the interest rate). An excellent introduction to the entire subject of Greeks is Dan Passarelli, *Trading Greek Options: How Time, Volatility, and Other Pricing Factors Drive Profit* (New York: Bloomberg Press, 2008).

4. We shall have occasion to consider the "peak oil" debate further on.

5. The EIA is a division of the U.S. Department of Energy and provides the official statistics from the department. Anybody can access the extensive EIA data bank via www.eia.doe.gov/. The EIA usually releases its *Weekly Petroleum Status Report (WPSR)* at 10:30 A.M. Eastern time on Wednesday, comprising the condition of the market as of the previous Friday. Occasionally due to holidays, the EIA releases the figures on Thursday.

6. Given that the *WPSR* depends upon figures provided by the companies themselves, critics have often noted the potential skewing of the data provided. See, for example, Peter J. McCabe, "Energy Resources—Cornucopia or Empty Barrel?" *AAPG Bulletin* 82 (1998), 2110–2134; and Daniel Goldstein, "U.S. Oil Demand May Be Flat for Decades—EIA," *Platts Oilgram Price Report* (December 19, 2008).

7. The IEA was the product of the 28-member Organization for Economic Cooperation and Development (OECD) in the aftermath of the 1973 Arab oil embargo. Located in Paris, its publications can be accessed at www.iea .org/index.asp.

8. See the comments of IEA chief economist Fatih Birol, "How Sustainable Is Russia's Current Energy Boom?" and my response, "Risk Assessment and Currency Stabilization Factors in Russian Oil and Gas Projects," *Proceedings of the Oil and Gas Congress Russia 2008* (December 2008). Dr. Birol, and the IEA in general, later admitted revised approaches to both demand and extraction figures were required, acknowledging the problem was worse than anticipated. The widely commented upon change in emphasis first emerged in an interview with the U.K. newspaper *The Independent*. See Steve Connor, "Warning: Oil Supplies Are Running Out Fast," *The Independent* (August 3, 2009).

9. See http://tonto.eia.doe.gov/oog/info/twip/twip.asp and note 2 in this chapter.

10. Fischer Black and Myron Scholes, "The Pricing of Options and Corporate Liabilities," *Journal of Political Economy* 81 (1973), 637–654.

11. On Black's commodity option-pricing model, see Fischer Black, "The Pricing of Commodity Contracts," *Journal of Financial Economics* 3 (1976), 167–179. The model is used in the pricing of European-style options on futures or forward priced assets. European-style options can only be exercised at expiration, unlike American-style options allowing exercise at any time up to and including expiry. Hybrids exist between the two.

12. Good accessible treatments of the ongoing debates occasioned by the Black-Scholes approach are: Paul Wilmott, "Science in Finance IX: In Defense of Black, Scholes, and Merton," (April 29, 2008), found at www.wilmott .com/blogs/paul/index.cfm/2008/4/29/Science-in-Finance-IX-In-defence -of-Black-Scholes-and-Merton; and Dimitris N. Chorafas, *Introduction to Derivative Financial Instruments: Options, Futures, Forwards, Swaps, and Hedging*

(New York: McGraw-Hill, 2008), 194ff. A particularly good paper addressing some of the enduring challenges in applying the Black-Scholes-Merton approach to pricing options in the valuation of several different underlying (and liquid assets) is René Carmona and Valdo Durrleman, "Pricing and Hedging Spread Options," *SIAM Review* 45 (2003), 627–685.

13. Loc. cit., note 9 in this chapter.

14. See, for example, "Oil Sustainability in a Volatile Market," Keynote Address to the Global Business Forum, Banff, Alberta (September 2007); "Changing Risk Dynamics in the International Oil Market," *ENAEP Distinguished Lecture Series*, Quito, Ecuador (September 2008); "Assessing Risk in Estimating Dimensions and Impact of Oil Sands Project Growth," *Canadian Institute Seventh Annual Oil Sands Conference Proceedings*, Calgary (November 2008); and "The Energy Debate," Keynote Address before the Public Affairs Council's *2009 Public Affairs Institute*, Laguna Beach, CA (January 2009).

15. There were a number of indications pointing toward a direct negative effect upon productivity and economic indicators. See, for example, David Furceri, "Fiscal Convergence, Business Cycle Volatility and Growth," *OECD Economics Department Working Papers* No. 674 (2009); available at: www.oecd -ilibrary.org/docserver/download/fulltext/5ksnkl6cz6wh.pdf?expires=1 280955140&id=0000&accname=guest&checksum=0EFABA36D0DD1 FF08B9BBF26AD9A3EC7; Lutz Kilian, "Not All Oil Price Shocks Are Alike: Disentangling Demand and Supply Shocks in the Crude Oil Market," *American Economic Review* 99 (2009), 1053–1069; Ernest Gnan, "Energy, Commodity, and Food Price Volatility: What Policy Responses?" *CESifo Forum* 10 (2009), 21–28; and Ana Maria Herrera and Elena Pesavento, "Oil Price Shocks, Systematic Monetary Policy, and the 'Great Moderation,'" *Macroeconomic Dynamics* 13 (2009), 107–137(a useful caution against the temptation of viewing all pricing cycles as having the same market impact).

16. On the relationship between the rate of oil price volatility and economic impact, see Chia-Lin Chang, Michael McAleer, and Roengchal Tansuchat, "Forecasting Volatility and Spillovers in Crude Oil Spot, Forward and Futures Markets, *Center for International Research on the Japanese Economy (CIRJE)* Discussion Paper CIRJE-F-641 (2009), available at: www.e.u-tokyo .ac.jp/cirje/research/dp/2009/2009cf641.pdf; Shawkat Hammoudeh, H. Li, and B. Jeon, "Causality and Volatility Spillovers among Petroleum Prices of WTI, Gasoline and Heating Oil," *North American Journal of Economics and Finance* 14 (2003), 89–114; and Bradely T. Ewing, Farooq Malik, and Ozkan Ozfidan, "Volatility Transmission in the Oil and Natural Gas Markets," *Energy Economics* 24 (2002), 525–538.

17. James L. Smith, "World Oil: Market of Mayhem?" *Journal of Economic Perspectives* 23 (2009), 145–164; International Monetary Fund, *World Economic Outlook: Sustaining the Recovery* (October 2009), 33ff; and Julia

Devlin, "Managing Oil Price Risk in Developing Countries," *The World Bank Research Observer* 19 (2004), 119–139. A good recent case study is Shuddhasawtta Rafiq, Ruhul Salim, and Harry Bloch, "Impact of Crude Oil Price Volatility on Economic Activities: An Empirical Investigation in the Thai Economy," *Resources Policy* 34 (2009), 121–132.

18. Compare the regional consumption figures for 1998–2008 found in *BP Statistical Review of World Energy* (June 2009) at 12–14 with the import-export figures located at 20–22. On the overall trend, see Steve Arnold and Alistair Hunt, "National and EU Estimates of Energy Externalities," *CEPS Policy Brief* No. 186 (2009); William C. Ramsay, "Asian Oil Outlook and Challenges," *New Delhi Roundtable Conference on Regional Cooperation: Key to Energy Security* (2005), available at: www.iea.org/textbase/speech/2005/ramsay/asianoil.pdf; Mamdouh G. Salameh, "Quest for Middle East Oil: The U.S. Versus the Asia-Pacific Region," *Energy Policy* 31 (2003), 1085–1091; and Dermot Gately and Shane S. Streifel, "The Demand for Oil Products in Developing Countries," *World Bank Discussion Papers* No. 359 (1997), available at: www-wds.worldbank.org/external/default/WDSContentServer/WDSP/IB/1997/02/01/000009265_3970716145222/Rendered/PDF/multi_page.pdf.

19. EIA, "How Dependent Are We on Foreign Oil?" (updated April 23, 2009), available at: http://tonto.eia.doe.gov/energy_in_brief/foreign_oil_dependence.cfm. See also Keith Crane et al., *Imported Oil and U.S. National Security* (Santa Monica: Rand, 2009).

20. See, for example, Anthony H. Cordesman and Khalid Al-Rodhan, *The Global Oil Market: Risks and Uncertainties* (Washington, CSIS Press, 2006), especially 42–58; James Zucchetto, *Trends in Oil Supply and Demand, the Potential for Peaking of Conventional Oil Production, and Possible Mitigation Options* (Washington: National Academies Press, 2006); Zha Daojiong, "Energy Interdependence," *China Security* (2006), 2–16; Roger D. Blanchard, *The Future of Oil Production: Facts, Figures, Trends and Projections, by Region* (London: McFarland, 2005), especially 267ff; Susanne Peters, "Courting Future Resource Conflict: The Shortcomings of Western Response Strategies to New Energy Vulnerabilities," *Energy Exploration & Exploitation* 21 (2003), 29–60; Noureddine Krichene, "World Crude Oil and Natural Gas: A Demand and Supply Model," *Energy Economics* 24 (2002), 557–576; Edward L. Morse, "A New Political Economy of Oil?" *Journal of International Affairs* 53 (1999); and Marcello Colitti and Claudio Simeoni, *Perspectives of Oil and Gas: The Road to Interdependence* (Dordrecht: Kluwer, 1999), especially 125ff.

21. We consider the issue of pricing in Chapter 3.

22. NYMEX prices utilize West Texas Intermediate (WTI, also known as Texas Light Sweet) as the benchmark crude to establish pricing on future contracts. The oil hub at Cushing, Oklahoma, is the price settlement point for NYMEX trades in WTI future contracts. There are almost 400 benchmark

crude rates worldwide, many representing production for a single deposit or field system. Each of these establishes a grade of oil allowing for trade among crude volumes of different consistencies. Only a few, however, represent rates setting prices for appreciable international trading. The other primary benchmark rate most important in determining global pricing is Brent Crude (Dubai Crude and the OPEC Reference Basket would be the remaining benchmarks of significant cross-border consequence).

Brent Crude (also called Brent Blend) originates from the North Sea and obtained its name from a policy used by Shell UK Exploration & Development to name offshore fields after birds (in this case, the Brent Goose). Originally traded on the open outcry International Petroleum Exchange (IPE) in London, Brent trades since 2005 have been on the electronic IntercontinentalExchange (ICE). Brent contracts are denominated in U.S. dollars and actually represent over 65 percent of the internationally traded oil volume. NYMEX also offers Brent future contracts. Brent is light sweet crude but is a little heavier and has slightly higher sulfur content (is less sweet) than WTI.

23. I examine these relationships in Chapter 4.

24. Also reflecting one of the major assumptions by two of the greatest petroleum economists of the twentieth century, whose work largely defined the approach to how market dynamics determine the supply, demand, and pricing of crude oil—Paul Frankel and Morris Adelman. These two figures largely defined the nature of market research on oil for over two generations. See P. H. Frankel, *Essentials of Petroleum: A Key to Oil Economics* (London: Frank Cass, 1949); and M. A. Adelman, *The Economics of Petroleum Supply* (Cambridge: MIT, 1993). This latter volume comprises Adelman's most important papers from 1962 to 1993. When Frankel's volume was finally reprinted in 1969, Adelman wrote the Foreword.

25. The relational exchange between oil and oil product prices and usage has been the subject of much comment and debate. See, for example, Cutler J. Cleveland et al., eds., *Encyclopedia of Energy* 2 (Amsterdam: Elsevier, 2004); 67, 77; Dermot Gately and Hillard G. Huntington, "The Asymmetric Effects of Changes in Price and Income on Energy and Oil Demand," *C. V. Starr Center for Applied Economics Research Papers* No. 2001–01 (2001), available at: http://econ.as.nyu.edu/docs/IO/9187/RR01–01.PDF, along with Gately's earlier "Imperfect Price-Reversibility of U.S. Gas Demand: Asymmetric Reponses to Price Increase and Decreases," *The Energy Journal* 13 (1992), 179–208; Lorna A. Greening, David L. Greene, and Carmen Difiglio, "Energy Efficiency and Consumption—the Rebound Effect—A Survey," *Energy Policy* 28 (2000), 389–401; Horace Herring, "Does Energy Efficiency Save Energy? The Debate and Its Consequences," *Applied Energy* 63 (1999), 2009–2026; and Reinhard Haas and Lee Schipper, "Residential Energy Demand in OECD Countries and the Role of Irreversible Efficiency Improvements," *Energy Economics* 20 (1998), 421–442.

26. There are 11 components in the Index of Leading Indicators published monthly by the Bureau of Economic Analysis (BEA) at the U.S. Department of Commerce: average workweek of production workers, average weekly claims for state unemployment insurance, manufacturers' new orders for consumer goods and materials, vendor performance (measures lower deliveries to companies from suppliers), contracts and orders for plants and equipment, building permits, change in manufacturers' unfilled orders for durable goods, changes in sensitive materials prices, stock prices, M-2 money supply, and the index of consumer expectations.

27. There are six components in the Index of Lagging Indicators published monthly by the BEA: the unemployment rate, business spending, unit labor costs, bank loans outstanding, bank interest rates, and the book value of manufacturing and trade inventories. The BEA also publishes monthly an Index of Coincident Indicators, designed to provide a picture of current economic activity, which includes four components: the number of nonfarm payroll workers (actually released by the Department of Labor), aggregate personal income less transfer payments, industrial production, and manufacturing and trade sales.

28. Heading this list remains Daniel Yergin's Pulitzer Prize–winning *The Prize: The Epic Quest for Oil, Money, and Power* (New York: Simon & Schuster, 1991, reissued in 2008 with a "New Epilogue"), remaining the best single book ever written on the history of oil. From the hundreds of other volumes available, I would suggest Anthony Sampson's famous treatment of the great twentieth century oil majors *The Seven Sisters: The Great Oil Companies and the World They Shaped* (New York: Viking, 1975); Terry Lynn Karl, *The Paradox of Plenty: Oil Booms and Petro-States* (Berkeley: University of California, 1997); Anthony Cave Brown, *Oil, God, and Gold* (New York: Houghton Mifflin, 1999); Dag Harald Claes, *The Politics of Oil-Producer Cooperation* (Boulder: Westview, 2001); Francisco Parra, *Oil Politics: A Modern History of Petroleum* (London: I. B. Taurus, 2004); Aileen Keating, *Mirage: Power. Politics, and the Hidden History of Arabian Oil* (Amherst: Prometheus Books, 2005); Steve Levine, *The Oil and the Glory: The Pursuit of Empire and Fortune on the Caspian Sea* (New York: Random House, 2007); and Mahmoud A. El-Gamal and Amy Myers Jaffe, *Oil, Dollars, Debt, and Crises: The Global Curse of Black Gold* (Cambridge: Cambridge University, 2010).

29. I regularly comment on the geopolitical dimensions of the current oil market as a contributing editor to *Russian Petroleum Investor* and *Caspian Investor*, as well as in my advisory publications *Oil and Energy Investor* and *Energy Advantage*.

Chapter 2

1. Burton G. Malkiel is probably the best-known defender of the efficient market hypothesis. See, for example, his *A Random Walk Down Wall Street* (New York: Norton, 1973); "The Efficient Market Hypothesis and Its Critics,"

Journal of Economic Perspectives 17 (2003), 59–82; and "Reflections on the Efficient Market: 30 Years Later," *Financial Review* 40 (2005), 1–9. See also Eugene Farma, "Market Efficiency, Long-Term Returns, and Behavioral Finance," *Journal of Financial Economics* 49 (1998), 283–306, Gary S. Becker, "Irrational Behavior and Economic Theory," *Journal of Political Economy* 70 (1962), 1–13; and Franco Modigliani and Richard A. Cohn, "Inflation, Rational Valuation, and the Market," *Financial Analysts Journal*, 35 (1979), 24–44. Lawrence H. Summers, until his decision in late 2010 to step down, served as Director of the White House National Economic Council, provided some significant criticism of statistical methods used to measure the efficiency of speculative markets in "Does the Stock Market Rationally Reflect Fundamental Values?" *Journal of Finance* 41 (1986), 591–601.

2. Two highly provocative works on the subject have emerged recently. See George A. Akerlof and Robert J. Shiller, *Animal Spirits: How Human Psychology Drives the Economy, and Why It Matters for Global Capitalism* (Princeton: Princeton University, 2009); and Justin Fox, *The Myth of the Rational Market: A History of Risk, Reward, and Delusion on Wall Street* (New York: HarperCollins, 2009). See also Shiller's well-known *Irrational Exuberance* (Princeton: Princeton University, 2000); Werner F. M. De Bondt and Richard Thaler, "Does the Stock Market Overreact?" *Journal of Finance* 40 (1985), 793–805; id., "Further Evidence on Investor Overreaction and Stock Market Seasonality," *Journal of Finance* 42 (1987), 557–581; Allen M. Poteshman and Vitaly Serbin, "Clearly Irrational Financial Market Behavior: Evidence from the Early Exercise of Exchange Traded Stock Options," *Journal of Finance* 58 (2003), 37–70; and M. C. Findlay and E. E. Williams, "A Fresh Look at the Efficient Market Hypothesis: How the Intellectual History of Finance Encouraged a Real 'Fraud on the Market,'" *Journal of Post-Keynesian Economics* 23 (2000–2001), 181–199, in which the authors conclude (ibid., 181) that:

> [T]he "evidence" supporting the efficient market hypothesis (EMH) was never very strong, and that most of the arguments have been basically a manifestation of presumptions rather than something normal people might view as proof. Hence, the entire chain of logic supporting the efficient market position has always been based on a mountain of presumptions.

Dragan Milijkovic arrives at a similar highly critical conclusion in "Rational Choice and Irrational Individuals or Simply an Irrational Theory: A Critical Review of the Hypothesis of Perfect Rationality," *Journal of Socio-Economics* 34 (2005), 621–634.

3. See Michael D. Bordo, "The Crisis of 2007: The Same Old Story: Only the Players Have Changed," in Douglas D. Evanoff, David S. Hoelscher, and George G. Kaufman, eds. *Globalization and Systemic Risk* (Hackensack: World

Scientific, 2009), 39–50; Roy E. Allen and Donald Snyder, "New Thinking on the Financial Crisis," *Critical Perspectives on International Business* 5 (2009), 36–55; Norbert Walter, "Understanding the Financial Crisis: Roots and Developments in the Financial Sector," *European View* 8 (2009), 97–103; and Samuel Knafo, "Liberalisation and the Political Economy of Financial Bubbles," *Competition and Change* 13 (2009), 128–144.

This reflection is hardly unique to the current crisis. See, for example, David Hirshleifer and Siew Hong Teoh, "Thought and Behavior Contagion in Capital Markets," in Thorsten Hens and Klaus Reiner Schenk-Hoppé, eds., *Handbook of Financial Markets* (Maryland Heights: Elsevier, 2009), 1–56; Frederic S. Mishkin, "Anatomy of a Financial Crisis," *Journal of Evolutionary Economics* 2 (1992), 115–130; Jianping Mei and Limin Guo, "Political Uncertainty, Financial Crisis and Market Volatility," *European Financial Management* 10 (2004), 639–657 (conduct by investment managers); Franklin Allen, "Financial Structure and Financial Crisis," *International Review of Finance* 2 (2001), 1–19 (East Asian crisis); id. and Douglas Gale, "Bubbles and Crises," *The Economic Journal* 110 (2000), 236–255; and Tony Lawson, "Uncertainty and Economic Analysis," *The Economic Journal* 95 (1985), 909–927.

4. See Charles Freedman, Michael Kumhof, Douglas Laxton, and Jaewoo Lee, "The Case for Global Fiscal Stimulus," *IMF Staff Position Notes* SPN/09/03 (2009), available at: www. perjacobsson.org/external/pubs/ft/spn/2009/spn0903.pdf; Phillip Swagel, "The Financial Crisis: An Inside View," *Brookings Papers on Economic Activity* No. 1(2009), 1–63, available at: www .brookings.edu/economics/bpea/~/media/Files/Programs/ES/BPEA /2009_spring_bpea_papers/2009_spring_bpea_swagel.pdf (Swagel was Treasury Assistant Secretary for Economic Policy from December 2006 until the end of the Bush Administration in January 2009); and Dirk Willem te Velde, "The Global Financial Crisis and Developing Countries: An Update of the Monitoring Work," *Overseas Development Institute* (2009), available at: www .odi.org.uk/resources/download/4051.pdf.

At least one analyst is prepared to allow governments significant new powers in the aftermath of the crisis. See Randall Wray, "Minsky, the Global Financial Crisis, and the Prospects before the U.S.," *Development* 52 (2009), pp. 302–307.

5. On implied volatility, see the discussion in Chapter 1 above. An excellent overall introduction to the relationship between market behavior and volatility is Murray Gunn, *Trading Regime Analysis: The Probability of Volatility* (Hoboken, NJ: John Wiley & Sons, 2009). See also Adam Warner, *Options Volatility Trading* (New York: McGraw-Hill, 2010); Jeff Augen, *The Volatility Edge in Options Trading: New Technical Strategies for Investing in Unstable Markets* (Upper Saddle River: FT Press, 2008); Costas Siriopoulos and Athanasios

Fassas, "Implied Volatility Indices—A Review," *Social Science Research Network Working Papers*, No. 1421202 (2009), available at: http://papers.ssrn .com/sol3//cf_dev/AbsByAuth.cfm?per_id=341482, discussing the indices to be considered shortly below; Sheldon Natenberg, *Option Volatility Trading Strategies* (Columbia: Marketplace, 2007); and Andrew Szakmary, Evren Ors, and Jin Kyoumg Kim, "The Predictive Power of Implied Volatility: Evidence from 35 Futures Markets," *Journal of Banking & Finance* 27 (2003), 2151–2175.

6. The CBOE (pronounced "see-bo") is the largest U.S. options exchange, having founded the listed options business in 1973. For 2009, the CBOE posted annual trading volume of 1.135 billion option contracts with a notional value (i.e., the unrealized paper value of derivatives, based upon the value of the underlying security; this represents balance sheet value when accounting for derivatives) of about $24 trillion. It offers options on over 2,200 companies, 22 stock indexes, and 140 exchange-traded funds (ETFs). See *CBOE 2009 Annual Report*, available at: www.cboe.com/AboutCBOE/ AnnualReportArchive/AnnualReport2009.pdf.

An ETF is a mutual fund-like instrument traded on an exchange and investing in a diversified securities portfolio representing market indices. "Spiders" (Standard & Poor's Depository Receipts or SPDRS), "Dow Diamonds" (tracking the Dow Jones Industrial Average) and "WEBS" (World Equity Benchmark Shares, now known as "iShares"—for MSCI Index Fund Shares—tracking MSCI country indices) are well-known examples of an ETF. Unlike a normal mutual fund, however, an ETF can be traded throughout the day, traded at margin, sold short and bought or sold at limit. Institutional investors can also exchange the ETFs for the underlying stock. The best introduction is Richard A Ferri, *The ETF Book: All You Need to Know about Exchange-Traded Funds* (Hoboken, NJ: John Wiley & Sons, 2009).

7. The VIX was first proposed in a paper by Robert E. Whaley, "Derivatives on Market Volatility: Hedging Tools Long Overdue," *Journal of Derivatives* 1 (1993), 71–84. See also Whaley, "The Investor Fear Gauge," *Journal of Portfolio Management* 26 (2000), 12–17; and "Understanding the VIX," *Journal of Portfolio Management* 35 (2009), 98–105. It is the expression of a risk-neutral expectation of S&P volatility over the next 30 calendar days, quoted in percentage points on an annualized variance basis. See Ralf Becker, Adam E. Clements, and Andrew McClelland. "The Jump Component of S&P 500 Volatility and the VIX Index," *Journal of Banking & Finance 33* (2009), 1033–1038 (the "jump component" refers to a discontinuity in price or rate as a result of extreme market conditions); Yueh-Neng Lin, "Pricing VIX Futures: Evidence from Integrated Physical and Risk-Neutral Probability Measures," *Journal of Futures Markets* 27 (2007), 1175–1217; and Markus Leippold, Liuren Wu, and Daniel Egloff, "Variance Risk Dynamics,

Variance Risk Premia and Optimal Variance Swap Investments," paper presented at the *EFA 2006 Zurich Meetings*, available at: www3.imperial.ac.uk/portal/pls/portallive/docs/1/10869700.PDF.

8. An ETN is a debt issuance by an underwriting bank, unsecured by collateral, but taking precedence over other unsecured debt (i.e., the ETN is senior and unsubordinated debt). An ETN has a maturity date but is backed only by the credit of the issuer. Returns are generally tied to market benchmark or strategy performance, minus fees. That means at maturity the issuer agrees to pay the amount specified by the underlying indicator. As with an ETF (see note 6 to this chapter), an ETN trades on an exchange, can be traded at margin, sold short, and bought or sold at limit. However, an ETN carries additional risk beyond that of an ETF. If the underwriting institution suffers a credit reduction, the value of the ETN declines. Given that this is debt, the holder also does not own any asset as such. See Dean Diavatopoulos, James Felton, and Colbrin Wright, "Exchange Trades Notes: An Introduction," *Social Science Research Network Working Papers*, No. 1408173 (2009), available at: http://papers.ssrn.com/sol3/cf_dev/AbsByAuth.cfm?per_id=1089993#reg; and Leonard Kostovetsky, "Index Mutual Funds and Exchange-Traded Funds," *The Journal of Portfolio Management* 1 (2005), 88–99. The usage in conjunction with an ETF was a quick development. See Tom Haines, "The ETN Wrapper: Access to New Exposure," *ETF and Indexing* 1 (2008), 95–100.

9. See, for example, Edward Szado, "VIX Futures and Options—A Case Study of Portfolio Diversification during the 2008 Financial Crisis," *University of Massachusetts (Amherst) Center for International Securities and Derivatives Markets* (2009), working paper, summary available at www.cboe.com/micro/vix/VIXFuturesOptionsUMassSummary.pdf; Keith H. Black, "Improving Hedge Fund Risk Exposures by Hedging Equity Market Volatility, or How the VIX Ate My Kurtosis," *The Journal of Trading* 1 (2006), 6–15 (kurtosis is from probability theory and measures peaks in the probability distribution of a real-valued random variable; a higher kurtosis means a greater portion of variance resulting from infrequent but extreme variations, rather than more frequently occurring moderately sized deviations; we discuss this notion in Chapter 7); Jonathan Mun, *Modeling Risk: Applying Monte Carlo Simulation, Real Options Analysis, Forecasting, and Optimization Techniques* (Hoboken, NJ: John Wiley & Sons, 2006), 39–48; Dimitris N. Chorafas, *Introduction to Derivative Financial Instruments: Options, Futures, Forwards, Swaps, and Hedging* (New York: McGraw Hill, 2008), 246ff.; and John Marthinesen, *Risk Takers: Uses and Abuses of Financial Derivatives* (Boston: Pearson Prentice Hall, 2009).

10. See Nassim Taleb, *Dynamic Hedging: Managing Vanilla and Exotic Options* (New York: John Wiley & Sons, 1997); K. Demeterfi, E. Derman, M. Kamal, and J. Zhou, "A Guide to Volatility and Variance Swaps," *The Journal*

of Derivatives 6 (1999), 9–32; and O. Brockhaus and D. Long, "Volatility Swaps Made Simple," *Risk* 1 (1999), 92–95. On American and European options, vega and gamma, see the discussion contained in Chapter 1.

11. See www.cboe.com/micro/oilvix/introduction.aspx. For a complete overview of OVX, including methodology and historical prices dating back to May 10, 2007, see www.cboe.com/OilVIX.

12. USO is an exchange-traded security designed to track changes in crude oil prices. By holding near-term futures contracts and cash, USO performance is intended to mirror the spot price of West Texas Intermediate (WTI) crude oil, less fees (since this is a traded security and it will have brokerage fees).

13. See Christiane Baumeister and Gert Peersman, "Sources of the Volatility Puzzle in the Crude Oil Market," *Social Science Research Network Working Papers*, No. 1471388 (2009), available at: http://papers.ssrn.com/sol3/cf_dev/AbsByAuth.cfm?per_id=948547#show1471388; and Ahmad R. Jalali-Naini and Maryam Kazemi Manesh, "Price Volatility, Hedging, and Variable Risk in the Crude Oil Market," *OPEC Review* 30 (2006), 55–70.

14. See the charting results at http://revver.com/video/1107262/using-the-oil-vix-to-forecast-energy-prices/.

15. The way in which a commodity operates in the market introduces a range of other considerations. See, for example, James S. Doran, "Computing the Market Price of Volatility Risk in the Energy Commodity Markets," *Journal of Banking & Finance* 32 (2008), 2541–2552; Robert S. Pindyck, "Volatility and Commodity Price Dynamics," *Journal of Futures Markets* 24 (2004), 1029–1047; Eva Regnier, "Oil and Energy Price Volatility," *Energy Economics* 29 (2007), 405–427; Jian Yang, R. Brian Balyeat, and David Leatham, "Futures Trading Activity and Commodity Cash Price Volatility," *Journal of Business Finance & Accounting* 32 (2005), 297–323; Eduardo Schwartz and James E. Smith, "Short-Term Variations and Long-Term Dynamics in Commodity Prices," *Management Science* 46 (2000), 893–911; Bryan R. Routledge, Duane J. Seppi and Chester S. Spatt, "Equilibrium Forward Curves for Commodities," *The Journal of Finance* 55 (2000), 1297–1338; and, more generally, Neil C. Schofield, *Commodity Derivatives: Market and Applications* (Hoboken, NJ: John Wiley & Sons, 2007).

16. ETFs are often criticized for not being particularly successful in replicating the underlying assets. USO is hardly immune from this charge, one well known to the financial blogging community. See, for example, Charles Armstrong, "Energy RTFs: The Tracking Problem," *Seeking Alpha* (February 24, 2010), available at: http://seekingalpha.com/article/190477-energy-etfs-the-tracking-problem; "How Contango Affects Crude Oil ETFs and ETNs (USO, OIL, DBO)," *Marketfolly.com* (January 20, 2009), available at: www.marketfolly.com/2009/01/how-contango-affects-crude-oil-etfs-and.html;

and Ron Rowland, All Crude Oil is Similar, but Crude Oil ETFs are Not," *Daily Markets* (May 21, 2010), available at: www.dailymarkets.com/stock/2010/05/20/all-crude-oil-is-similar-but-crude-oil-etfs-are-not/. See also Victor Lin and Phil Mackintosh, "ETF Mythbuster: Tracking Down the Truth," *Journal of Index Investing* 1 (2010), 95–106; and Pankaj Agrrawai and Doug Waggle, "The Dispersion of ERF Betas on Financial Websites," *Journal of Investing* 19 (2010), 13–24.

17. Forward contracts have been around for more than two centuries. Historians point to the Dojime Rice Exchange in Japan established in the early 1730s as the first modern example, although the classical Greek philosopher Thales "cornered" the olive oil market more than two millennia ago by correctly forecasting future prices. While the terms "forward" and "future" refer to the same type of transaction—agreeing to sell a commodity for a specific price at a designated time—there is a very important difference. Futures trade on an exchange and are subject to standardized rules of operation, while forwards trade over-the-counter (OTC) and are ad hoc in nature. Forwards require nothing more than a signed contract between two parties. Because futures are exchange-traded, they are subject to a margin. That means traders are posting what amounts to a performance bond corresponding to a percentage of the trade's value with a clearinghouse guaranteeing the trade. That reduces counterparty risk and provides a distinct advantage for futures over forward contracts.

18. See Ronald D. Ripple and Imad A. Moosa, "Futures Maturity and Hedging Effectiveness: The Case of Oil Futures," Macquarie *University, Department of Economics Research Papers*, No. 0513 (2005), available at: www.econ.mq.edu.au/research/2005/HedgingEffectiveness.pdf.; and Richard Deaves and Itzhak Krinsky, "Risk Premiums and Efficiency in the Market for Crude Oil Futures," *The Energy Journal* 13 (1992), 93–117.

19. See, for example, G. David Haushalter, "Financing Policy, Basis Risk, and Corporate Hedging: Evidence from Oil and Gas Producers," *The Journal of Finance* 55 (2000), 107–152; Arkadej Pongsakdi, Pramoch Rangsunvigit, Kitipat Siemanond, and Miguel J. Bagajewicz, "Financial Risk Management in the Planning of Refinery Operations," *International Journal of Production Economics* 103 (2006), 64–86; and T. N. Sear, "Logistics Planning in the Downstream Oil Industry," *Journal of the Operational Research Society* 44 (1993), 9–17. Governments must also attend to the basis risk problem, whether they export or import oil. See James Daniel, "Hedging Government Oil Price Risk, *IMF Working Papers*, No. 01/185 (2001), available at: www.imf.org/external/pubs/ft/wp/2001/wp01185.pdf.

20. See, for example, Viral V. Acharya and Lasse Heje Pedersen, "Asset Pricing with Liquidity Risk," *Journal of Financial Economics* 77 (2005), 375–410. On the issue of how liquidity reflects the underlying dynamics of an exchange-based

transaction, see S. Kerry Cooper, John C. Groth, and William E. Avera, "Liquidity, Exchange Listing, and Common Stock Performance," *Journal of Economics and Business* 37 (1985), 19–33, Weimin Liu, "A Liquidity-Augmented Capital Asset Pricing Model," *Journal of Financial Economics* 82 (2006), 631–671; Gady Jacoby, David J. Fowler, and Aron A. Gottesman, "The Capital Asset Pricing Model and the Liquidity Effect: A Theoretical Approach," *Journal of Financial Markets* 3 (2000), 69–81; Timothy C. Johnson, "Volume, Liquidity, and Liquidity Risk," *Journal of Financial Economics* 87 (2008), 388–417; and Chitru S. Fernando, "Commonality in Liquidity: Transmission of Liquidity Shocks Across Investors and Securities," *Journal of Financial Intermediation* 12 (2003), 233–254.

21. See, for example, Jon Danielsson and Casper G. De Vries, "Value-at-Risk and Extreme Returns," *Annales d'Économiqueet de Statistique* No. 60 (2000), 239–270; Charles M. Jones and Gautam Kaul, "Oil and the Stock Markets," *Journal of Finance* 51 (1996), 463–491; and Gary B. Gorton, Fumio Hayashi, and K. Geert Rouwenhorst, "The Fundamentals of Commodity Futures Returns," *National Bureau of Economic Research Working Papers*, No. W13249 (2007), available at: www.nber.org/tmp/46297-w13249.pdf.

22. See Qin Lei, "Flight to Liquidity Due to Heterogeneity in Investment Horizon," *Social Science Research Network Working Paper*, No. 676100 (2009), available at: http://papers.ssrn.com/sol3/cf_dev/AbsByAuth.cfm?per_id=292899; and Alessandro Beber, Michael W. Brandt, and Kenneth A. Kavajecz, "Flight-to -Quality or Flight-to-Liquidity" Evidence from the Euro-Area Bond Market," *Review of Financial Studies* 22 (2009), 925–957.

23. See Louis Ederington and Jae Ha Lee, "Who Trades Futures and How: Evidence from the Heating Oil Futures Market," *Journal of Business* 75 (2002), 353–374; Jeff Fleming and Barbara Ostdiek, "The Impact of Energy Derivatives on the Crude Oil Market," *Energy Economics* 21 (1999), 135–167; and Spyros I. Spyrou, "Index Futures Trading and Spot Price Volatility," *Journal of Emerging Markets Finance* 4 (2005), 151–167.

24. See, for example, Emmanuel Farhi, Mikhail Golosov, and Aleh Tsyvinski, "A Theory of Liquidity and Regulation of Financial Intermediation," *Review of Economic Studies* 76 (2009), 973–992; Falko Fecht, Kevin X. D. Huang, and Antoine Martin, "Financial Intermediaries, Markets, and Growth," *Journal of Money, Credit and Banking* 40 (2008), 701–720; and Jon Daníelsson and Jean-Pierre Zigrand, "Equilibrium Asset Pricing with Systemic Risk," *Economic Theory* 35 (2008), 293–319.

25. An extremely interesting treatment in this regard is Markus K. Brunnermeier, "Deciphering the Liquidity and Credit Crunch 2007–2008," *Journal of Economic Perspectives* 23 (2009), 77–100. See also, id. and Motohiro Yogo, "A Note on Liquidity Risk Management," *The American Economic Review* 99 (2009), 578–583; Hyun Song Shin, "Reflections on Northern Rock: The

Bank Run that Heralded the Global Financial Crisis," *Journal of Economic Perspectives* 23 (2009), 101–119; Douglas W. Diamond and Raghuram G. Rajan, "The Credit Crisis: Conjectures about Causes and Remedies," *The American Economic Review* 99 (2009), 606–610; and John B. Taylor, "The Financial Crisis and the Policy Responses: An Empirical Analysis of What Went Wrong," *National Bureau of Economic Research Working Papers*, No. W14631 (2009), available at: www.nber.org/tmp/94053-w14631.pdf. It is also instructive to recognize the current Federal Reserve Chairman's earlier views on the subject. See Ben S. Bernanke, "Nonmonetary Effects of the Financial Crisis in the Propagation of the Great Depression," *The American Economic Review* 73 (1983), 257–276.

26. See, for example, Daniel O'Sullivan, *Petromania: Black Gold, Paper Barrels, and Oil Price Bubbles* (Petersfield: Harriman House, 2009); and Yelena Kalyuzhnova and Christian Nygaard, "Resource Nationalism and Credit Growth in FSU Countries," *Energy Policy* 37 (2009), 4700–4710.

27. See, for example, T. A. Edison, J. V. Sengers, J. Fleming, and B. Ostdiek, "The Impact of Energy Derivatives on the Crude Oil Market," *Energy Economics* 21 (1999), 135–167; and Kit Pong Wong, "Liquidity Constraints and the Hedging Role of Futures Spreads," *Journal of Futures Markets* 24 (2004), 909–921.

28. OPEC first determines global crude oil demand and then subtracts non-OPEC production before determining the "call on OPEC." OPEC officials maintained the position consistently throughout the period. See, for example, "OPEC Possible Production Cuts," *Middle East Oil & Gas News Wire* (December 27, 2005); Matt Piotrowski, "Study Finds OPEC Unlikely to Follow Through with Oil Cuts," *Oil Daily* (December 20, 2006); "The Background & Future of the Energy Demand Insecurity—of The Third Logic," *APS Review Downstream Trends*, 69 (December 24, 2007); and Kate Dourian, "OPEC Sees No Need to for More Crude in 2008: Research Head Hasan Qabazard Says Stocks Above Five-Year Average," *Platts Oilgram News*, 86 (May 20, 2008).

29. See the work of Paul J. Stevens: "The Prospects for Oil Prices: The Dangers of Wet Barrels Chasing Paper Barrels," *Oil, Gas & Energy Law* 3 (2004); "The Coming Oil Supply Crunch," *Chatham House Reports* (2009); and "Oil Markets," *Oxford Review of Economic Policy* 21 (2005), 19–42. See also Salah Abosedra and Hamid Baghestani, "On the Predictive Accuracy of Crude Oil Futures Prices," *Energy Policy* 32 (2004), 1389–1393; Imad A. Moosa, Param Silvapulle, and Mervyn Silvapule, "Testing for Temporal Asymmetry in the Price-Volume Relationship," *Bulletin of Economic Research* 55 (2003), 373–389; and Stelios D. Bekiros and Cees G. H. Diks, "The Relationship Between Crude Oil Spot and Futures Prices: Cointegration, Linear, and Nonlinear Causality," *Energy Economics* 30 (2008), 2673–2685.

30. See, for example, Michael S. Haigh, Jana Hranalova, and James A. Overdahl, "Hedge Funds, Volatility, and Liquidity Provision in Energy Futures Markets," *Journal of Alternative Investments* 9 (2007), 10–28; V. E. Putyatin and J. N. Dewynne, "Market Liquidity and Its Effect on Options Valuation and Hedging," *Royal Society Philosophical Transactions: Mathematical, Physical and Engineering Sciences* 2357 (1999), 2093–2108; and Gordon Hanka, "Simple Limits on Liquidity Hedging with Futures," working paper (2002), available at: www2.owen.vanderbilt.edu/fmrc/pdf /wp2002–15.pdf.

31. As noted earlier in this chapter, implied volatility is essential in deriving option values. Volatility is likewise pervasive in forex trading. See Debra Glassman, "Exchange Rate Risk and Transaction Costs: Evidence from Bid-Ask Spreads," *Journal of International Money and Finance* 6 (1987), 479–490; Phillipe Jorion, "Predicting Volatility in the Foreign Exchange Market," *Journal of Finance* 50 (1995), 507–528; and Christopher J. Neely, "Forecasting Foreign Exchange Volatility: Why Is Implied Volatility Biased and Inefficient? And Does it Matter?" *Journal of International Financial Markets, Institutions, and Money* 19 (2009), 188–205. This is a cross-border concern. See Ángeles Fernández-Izquierdo and Juan Angel Lefuente, "International Transmission of Stock Exchange Volatility: Empirical Evidence from the Asian Crisis," *Global Finance Journal* 15 (2004), 125–137.

32. This is a revised version of the definition offered in Mun, loc. cit, 33. Mun's approach is limited to the application of the concept to applied business risk modeling and analysis.

33. This likelihood can be either positive or negative, although risk is normally associated with the downside potential while opportunity is used to express the upside. Both are imperfect calculations. See James G. March and Zur Shapira, "Managerial Perspectives on Risk and Risk Taking," *Management Science* 33 (1987), 1404–1418; and Michael Frenkel, Ulrich Hommel, Gunter Dufey, and Markus Rudolf, eds. *Rick Management: Challenge and Opportunity* 2d ed. (New York: Springer-Verlag, 2005), especially Part 3.

34. See Frank J. Fabozzi, Henry A. Davis, and Moorad Choudhry, *Introduction to Structured Finance* (Hoboken, NJ: John Wiley & Sons, 2006), chap. 7, Olivier Renault, "Cash and Synthetic Collateral Debt Obligations: Motivations and Investment Strategies," in Arnaud de Servigny and Josef Jobst Norbert, eds. *The Handbook of Structured Finance* (New York: McGraw-Hill, 2007), 373–396; and generally, Janet M. Tavakoli, *Credit Derivatives & Synthetic Structures: A Guide to Instruments and Applications* (New York: John Wiley & Sons, 2001).

35. See, for example, Eugene A. Rosa, "White, Black, and Gray: Critical Dialogue with the International Risk Governance Council's Framework for Risk Governance," in Ortwin Renn and Katherine D. Walker, eds. *Global Risk Governance: Concept and Practice Using the IRGC Framework* (New York: Springer,

2008), 101–118; and Jonathan Baron, *Thinking and Deciding,* 4th ed. (Cambridge: Cambridge University, 2008), 497–525.

36. See, for example, Andrew M. Pettigrew, "Strategy Formulation as a Political Process," *International Studies of Management and Organization* 17 (1977), 78–87; Charles R. Schwenk, *The Essence of Strategic Decision Making* (New York: Free Press, 1988); Amos Tversky and Daniel Kahneman, "Rational Choice and the Framing of Decisions," *Journal of Business* (1986), 251–278; Inga Skromme Baird and Howard Thomas, "Toward a Contingency Model of Strategic Risk Taking," *Academy of Management Review* 10 (1985), 230–243; the work of K. M. Eisenhardt: Kathleen M. Eisenhardt, "Strategy as Strategic Decision Making," *Sloane Management Review* (1999), 1–13, available at: http://classes.bus.oregonstate.edu/spring-05/ba/350/ REQUIRED%READINGS/G-Strategy.doc; "Making Fast Strategic Decisions in High-Velocity Environments," *Academy of Management Journal* 32 (1989), 543–576; id. and L. J. Bourgeois III, "Politics of Strategic Decisions in High-Velocity Environments: Toward a Midrange Theory," *Academy of Management Journal* 31 (1988), 737–770; and id. and Mark J. Zbaracki, "Strategic Decision Making, *Strategic Management Journal* 13 (1992), 17–37.

37. See, for example, K. J. Radford, *Strategic and Tactical Decisions,* 2d ed. (New York: Springer-Verlag, 1988); and Kenneth J. Meier and Laurence J. O'Toole, Jr., "Strategic Management and the Performance of Public Organizations: Testing Venerable Ideas against Recent Theories," *Journal of Public Administration Research and Theory* 17 (2007), 357–377.

38. See Michael E. Porter, *The Competitive Advantage of Nations: With a New Introduction* (New York: Simon & Schuster, 1998), especially 69–130 and 482–542; Thomas C. Powell, "Strategic Planning as Competitive Advantage," *Strategic Management Journal* 13 (1992), 551–558; and Laura D'Andrea Tyson, "Creating Advantage: Strategic Policy for National Competitiveness," *Berkeley Roundtable on the International Economy*, Working Paper No. 23 (1987), available at: http://escholarship.org/uc/item/9b38c3p1.

39. Using the approach of Thomas C. Shelling in his classic *The Strategy of Conflict,* 2d ed. (Cambridge: Harvard University, 1980). Strategy is considered the best course of action based upon what others do. "The term is intended to focus on the interdependence of the adversaries' decisions and on their expectations about each other's behavior." ibid., 3, note 1.

40. See, for example, Janice A. Black and Kimberley B. Boal, "Strategic Resources: Traits, Configurations, and Paths to Sustainable Competitive Advantage," *Strategic Management Journal* 15 (1994), 131–148; Avi Fiegenbaum and Howard Thomas, "Strategic Risk and Competitive Advantage: An Integrative Perspective," *European Management Review* 1 (2004), 84–95; and Robert M. Grant, "The Resource-Based Theory of Competitive Advantage: Implications for Strategy Formulation," *California Management Review* 33 (1991), 114–135.

41. See, for example, Stephen P. Robbins and Timothy A. Judge, *Essentials of Organizational Behavior* (Upper Saddle River: Prentice Hall, 2009), chap. 5–7; Don Knight, Cathy C. Durham, and Edwin A. Locke, "The Relationship of Team Goals, Incentives, and Efficacy to Strategic Risk, Tactical Implementation, and Performance," *Academy of Management Journal* 44 (2001), 326–338; and Mark Harrison Moore, *Creating Public Value: Strategic Management in Government* (Cambridge: Harvard University, 1995), especially 27–56 and 239–292.

42. On this important distinction between rationalist assumptions and perception in strategic risk estimations, see James M. Collins and Timothy W. Rueffi, *Strategic Risk: A State-Defined Approach* (Norwell: Kluwer, 1995), 23ff and 16–182; and the classic treatments provided by S. Waite Charles III and Charles W. Smithson, *Managing Financial Risk* (New York: Harper & Row, 1990), and id., "Strategic Risk Management," *Journal of Applied Corporate Finance* 2 (2005), 6–18; Sim B. Sitkin and Amy L. Pablo, "Reconceptualizing the Determinants of Risk Behavior," *Academy of Management Review* 17 (1992), 9–38; James H. Barnes, Jr., "Cognitive Biases and Their Impact on Strategic Planning," *Strategic Management Journal* 5 (1984), 129–137; and Paul Slovic, Baruch Fischoff, and Sarah Lichtenstein, "Why Study Risk Perception?" *Risk Analysis* 2 (1982), 83–93.

43. See the summaries of developments contained in Aswath Damodaran, *Strategic Risk Taking: A Framework for Risk Management* (Philadelphia: Wharton, 2007), chaps. 10–12; James M. Collins and Timothy W. Ruefli, "Strategic Risk: An Ordinal Approach," *Management Science* 38 (1992), 1707–1731; and P. J. Eylon, "Avoid the Seven Deadly Sins of Strategic Risk Analysis," *Journal of Business Strategy* 9 (1988), 18–22.

44. Kent D. Miller finds the concept in use by the eighteenth century. See his "Organizational Risk after Modernism," *Organization Studies* 30 (2009), 157–180. However, the relationship of strategic advantage, and risk found in the classical Chinese doctrine of *Shih* may be the earliest example. Its application in the *Art of Rulership* (Book Nine of the *Huai Nan Tzu*) would place the concept of strategic risk as early as 140 B.C. See Roger T. Ames, *The Art of Rulership: A Study of Ancient Political Thought* (Albany: SUNY Press, 1994), chap. 3.

45. See the references cited in note 18 in this chapter.

46. See Paul Slovic and Robin Gregory, "Risk Analysis, Decision Analysis, and the Social Context for Risk Decision Making," in James Shanteau, David A. Shum, and Barbara A. Mellers, eds., *Decision Science and Technology: Reflections on the Contributions of Ward Edwards* (New York: Springer-Verlag, 1999), 353–366; and Mary Kay Stevenson, "The Impact of Temporal Context and Risk on the Judged Value of Future Outcomes," *Organizational Behavior and Human Decision Processes* 52 (1992), 455–491.

47. Low-intensity decisions are often less possible in politically charged situations. See Arild Underdal, "Issues Determine Politics Determine Policies: The Case for a 'Rationalistic' Approach to the Study of Foreign Policy Decision-Making," *Cooperation and Conflict* 14 (1979), 1–9; and Paul Slovic, "Perceived Risk, Trust, and Democracy," *Risk Analysis* 13 (1993), 675–682. On the similar phenomenon in markets, see Keith C. Brown and W. V. Harlow, "Market Overreaction: Magnitude and Intensity," *Journal of Portfolio Management* 14 (1988), 6–13.

48. Frank H. Knight, *Risk, Uncertainty, and Profit* (Boston: Houghton Mifflin, 1921).

49. See, for example, John McKinney, "Frank H. Knight on Uncertainty and Rational Action," *Southern Economic Journal* 43 (1977), 1438–1452; Stephen F. LeRoy and Larry D. Singell, Jr., "Knight on Risk and Uncertainty," *Journal of Political Economy* 95 (1987), 394–406; and Richard N. Langlois and Metin M. Cogsel, "Frank Knight on Risk, Uncertainty and the Firm: A New Interpretation," *Economic Inquiry* 31 (1993), 456–465; and Edward M. Miller, "Risk, Uncertainty, and Divergence of Opinion," *Journal of Finance* 32 (1977), 1151–1168.

50. See Robert G. Chambers, *Applied Production Analysis: A Dual Approach* (Cambridge: Cambridge University Press, 1988), 20ff; Akira Takayama, "On a Two-Sector Model of Economic Growth—A Comparative Analysis," *Review of Economic Studies* 30 (1963), 95–104; W. David Maxwell, "Short-Run Returns to Scale and the Production of Services," *Southern Economic Journal* 32 (1965), 1–14; and Nicholas Kaldor, "What Is Wrong with Economic Theory?" *Quarterly Journal of Economics* 89 (1975), 347–357.

51. See, for example, G. Hanock and H. Levy, "The Efficiency Analysis of Choices Involving Risk," *Review of Economic Studies* 36 (1969), 35–46; V. Kerry Smith and William H. Desvousges, "An Empirical Analysis of the Economic Value of Risk Changes," *Journal of Political Economy* 95 (1987), 89–114; Robert T. Clemen and Robert W. Winkler, "Combining Probability Distributions from Experts in Risk Analysis," *Risk Analysis* 19 (1999), 187–203; and Jean-Paul Chavas, *Risk Analysis in Theory and Practice* (London, Elsevier, 2004), chap. 1.

52. Harry Markowitz, "Portfolio Selection," *Journal of Finance* 7 (1952), 77–91; id, "The Utility of Wealth," *Journal of Political Economy* 60 (1952), 151–158; id., *Portfolio Selection: Efficient Diversification of Investments* (New York: John Wiley & Sons, 1959); and id., *Harry Markowitz: Selected Works* (Hackensack: World Scientific, 2009).

53. Among the pioneering works here are those of Jack L. Treynor, William F. Sharpe, John Lintner, and Jan Mossin. Treynor's contribution was early based upon two unpublished papers—"Market Value, Time, and Risk" (1961) and

"Toward a Theory of Market Value of Risky Assets," (1962)—subsequently revised and published, "Toward a Theory of Market Value of Risky Assets," in Robert A. Korajczyk, ed., *Asset Pricing and Portfolio Performance: Models, Strategy, and Performance Metrics* (London: Risk Books, 1999), 15–22; also, id., "How to Rate Management of Investment Funds," *Harvard Business Review* 43 (1965), 131–136; id. and Fischer Black, "Corporate Investment Decisions," in Stewart C. Myers, ed., *Modern Developments in Financial Management* (Hinsdale: Dryden Press, 1976), 310–327; on Treynor's contributions, see Craig W. French, "The Treynor Capital Asset Pricing Model," *Journal of Investment Management* 1 (2003), 60–72; William F. Sharpe, "A Simplified Model for Portfolio Analysis," *Management Science* 9 (1963), 277–293; id., "Capital Asset Prices—A Theory of Market Equilibrium Under Conditions of Risk," *Journal of Finance* 19 (1964), 425–442; id., *Portfolio Theory and Capital Markets*, 2d ed. (New York: McGraw-Hill, 2000); John Litner, "The Valuation of Risk Assets and the Selection of Risky Investments in Stock Portfolios and Capital Budgets," *Review of Economics and Statistics*, 47 (1965), 13–37; id., "Securities Prices, Risks and Maximal Gains from Diversification," *Journal of Finance* 20 (1965), 587–615; id., "The Aggregation of Investors' Diverse Judgments and Preferences in Purely Competitive Securities Markets," *Journal of Financial and Quantitative Analysis* 4 (1969), 347–400; id., *Finance and Capital Markets* (New York: National Bureau of Economic Research, 1972); Jan Mossin, "Equilibrium in a Capital Asset Market," *Econometrica* 34 (1966), 768–783; and Sayan Chatterjee, Michael H. Lubatkin and William S. Schulze, "Toward a Strategic Theory of Risk Premium: Moving Beyond CAPM," *Academy of Management Review* 24 (1999), 556–567.

54. See the discussion on variance in this chapter, along with the works cited in note 10 to this chapter.

55. That is, the volatility measurement as a standard deviation from a known index. See note 3 in Chapter 1.

56. See Josef Lakonishok and Alan C. Shapiro, "Systematic Risk, Total Risk, and Size as Determinants of Stock Market Returns," *Journal of Banking and Finance* 10 (1986), 115–132; and Hendrik Bessembinder, "Systematic Risk, Hedging Pressure, and Risk Premiums in Futures Markets," *Review of Financial Studies* 5 (1992), 637–667.

Chapter 3

1. With oil, as with most other attempts to forecast prices, there are really only two ways of approaching the subject—chartism or technical analysis (backward looking) and fundamental analysis (forward looking). Using the first (technical analysis), a price forecaster would look over a recent period (say

two or more decades), identify a median price, determine a volatility range, and then establish standard deviations from that mean. This makes a lot of sense in the oil industry, since it takes primary parts of this methodology from what reservoir engineers do regularly in extrapolating the productivity decline curve of a well. In the case of the second (fundamental analysis), the forecaster would accumulate all available (and hopefully relevant) data, information, opinions, polite guesses and the like, attempt to estimate future supply and demand, and then employ a price mechanism as a way of balancing what supply and demand levels result.

The first approach is safe but makes no allowance for a wealth of changes in the market and the industry over the period under consideration. The second will always lean too heavily on the continuation of current trends, volumes of supply, reserve levels, extraction flows, and so on. All fundamental analysts provide some credence to historical price levels, while all technical analysts recognize the need to extrapolate from current trends into forecasts of future levels. What is going to happen, after all, is what both kinds of analysts are trying to identify. Both cannot predict the exogenous factor (a war, earthquake, revolution, significant change in government policy, temperature variations) and, aside from unusually stable markets, both usually get the prediction wrong.

2. Uranium is a good example, and it is not unusual to find oil analysts drawing upon research about the uranium market in an attempt to draw conclusions about the expected movement of oil prices. See, for example, Thomas Neff, *The International Uranium Market* (Cambridge: Ballinger, 1984), 16f. Certain recent price rises in both crude oil and uranium have exhibited similar tendencies, but as Neff and others point out, uranium does not have the cartel element that is present in oil debates—The Organization of Petroleum Exporting Countries (OPEC).

3. That the U.S. will remain a net importer of oil is hardly open to dispute. Imports are estimated to represent about 58 percent of the American market, according to the Energy Information Administration (EIA). See EIA, "How Dependent Are We on Imported Oil?" available at http://tonto.eia.doe.gov/energy_in_brief/foreign_oil_dependence.cfm.

Even overlooking the substantial price differentials between the high lifting costs of American-based crude and the low cost of Saudi, Kuwaiti, or (following the lifting of sanctions) Libyan production, there are simply insufficient domestic exploitable reserves to reverse the trend. Placing the only major untapped onshore reserve remaining on line—the highly controversial and politically charged Arctic National Wildlife Refuge [ANWR}—would still result in imports representing 60 percent of total crude needs, rather than the projected 62 percent, by 2020, according to an EIA senatorial response memo in late 2003. Gerald Karey, "Ethanol Provision to Hike RFG Price: EIA,"

Platt's Oilgram News (October 1, 2003), 3. About six months later, a second EIA report, also resulting from a congressional request, indicated ANWR by 2025 would provide more of the domestic market demand, but in what is still estimated to be an increasingly import-dependent environment. The second EIA report ran three scenarios, concluding that ANWR production would reduce American dependence on imports from 70 percent to between 64 percent (best scenario) and 66 percent (worst) of domestic market crude oil requirements. See Jessica Marron, "ANWR Development Would Have Minimal Influence on Energy Market, EIA Finds," *Inside F.E.R.C.'s Gas Market Report* (March 26, 2004), 12.

4. The term "known" is used here to mean only "proven reserves," namely those that are commercially retrievable under virtually any market conditions (i.e., would not require a high per barrel market price increase to justify the extraction of the crude). The variations in reserve terminology will be discussed later in this chapter.

5. Combining separate surveys compiled by the U.S. Department of Energy, British engineering (this refers in the oil business to field services) consultant Wood MacKenzie and *Oil & Gas Journal*, veteran Venezuelan analyst Rafael Sandrea concluded that worldwide proven reserves of crude oil amount to 1.032 trillion barrels (bbl). Of that total, seven Persian Gulf countries account for 65.6 percent of the total—Saudi Arabia (25.1 percent), Iraq (12 percent), Iran (9.5 percent), Kuwait (9 percent), United Arab Emirates (8 percent), Qatar (1.5 percent), and Oman (0.5 percent). The first four alone accounted for 55.6 percent of all reserves worldwide, according to Sandrea's calculations. In contrast, U.S. domestic proven reserves account for 2.1 percent of the word total. Rafael Sandrea, "Imbalances among Oil Demand, Reserves, Alternatives Define Energy Dilemma Today," *Oil & Gas Journal* (July 12, 2004), 34ff. The 12-nation Organization of the Petroleum Exporting Countries (OPEC) has estimated worldwide reserves at 1.295 billion barrels and its own (including non-Gulf producing countries Venezuela, Nigeria, Libya, Algeria, Angola, and Ecuador) total portion at 79.3 percent, with the six OPEC Gulf states (Oman is not an OPEC member) accounting for 57.3 percent of the world totals. *OPEC Annual Statistical Bulletin* (Vienna: OPEC, 2009), 17–18.

Figures garnered from the *BP Statistical Review, Oil & Gas Journal*, and *World Oil* (as contained in Appendix A) estimate the overall "Middle East" portion of global proved reserves at 61 percent, 55.6 percent and 61.4 percent, respectively.

6. Daniel Yergin, *The Prize: The Epic Quest for Oil, Money & Power* (New York: Simon & Schuster, 1991), 567.

7. M. King Hubbert, "Nuclear Energy and the Fossil Fuels," *American Petroleum Institute Drilling and Production Practice, Proceedings of Spring Meeting, San Antonio* (1956), 7–25. Two excellent general treatments of the implications

flowing from Hubbert's approach are Kenneth S. Deffeyes, *Hubbert's Peak: The Impending World Oil Shortage* (Princeton: Princeton University, 2001); and David Goodstein, *Out of Gas: The End of the Age of Oil* (New York: W.W. Norton, 2004).

8. See M. King Hubbert, "Energy Resources," *National Academy of Sciences—National Research Council* Publication 1000-D (1962) and id., "Degree of Advancement of Petroleum Exploration in the United States," *American Association of Petroleum Geologists Bulletin* 51 (1967), 207–227.

9. See, for example, James E. Akins, "The Oil Crisis: This Time the Wolf Is Here," *Foreign Affairs* 51 (1973), 462–490; L. F. Ivanhoe, "Updated Hubbert Curves Analyze World Oil Supply," *World Oil* 72 (1996), 91–94; Colin J. Campbell, *The Coming Oil Crisis* (Brentwood: Multi-Science Publishing and Petroconsultants, 1997); and Craig Bond Hatfield, "Oil Back on the Global Agenda," 387 *Nature* (1997), 121. Ivanhoe is coordinator of the Hubbert Center at the Colorado School of Mines. Petroconsultants, now called IHS Energy, is a global consulting agency based in Geneva, Switzerland. The 1996 petroleum exploration and production data base published by Petroconsultants/IHS Energy remains an industry standard. Washington, D.C.–based consultant PFC Energy issued a report in September of 2004 which suggested that non OPEC global production would begin to decline in 2010, absent any major new discoveries. See "Demand to Exceed Supply: PFC," *International Oil Daily* (September 13, 2004). The 2010 decline, based upon what was termed "natural depletion" of global crude oil production, had earlier been advanced by Colin J. Campbell, *The Essence of Oil and Gas Depletion* (Brentwood, UK: Multi-Science Publishing and Petroconsultants, 2002).

Perhaps the first "peak energy" argument is found in William Stanley Jevrons' classic work *The Coal Question: An Inquiry Concerning the Progress of the Nation, and the Probable Exhaustion of Our Coal Mines* (London: Macmillan, 1865), especially Ch. 12.

10. See, for example, the 2000 U.S. Geological Survey report that estimated a peak in world production in 2015–2018, USGS World Energy Assessment Team, *U.S. Geological Survey World Petroleum Assessment 2000—Description and Results*, USGS Digital Data Series DDS-60 (an executive summary of which can be obtained in the "USGS Fact Sheet" 062–03) and the EIA estimates made in Jay Hakes, "Long-Term World Oil Supply: A Resource Base/Production Analysis," *Meetings of the American Association of Petroleum Geologists* (New Orleans, 2000). The EIA team surveyed 12 separate scenarios, resulting in peak world crude oil production emerging between 2021 to 2112, depending upon increases in extraction schedules and additions to reserves. The scenarios resulting in a peak hitting in 2026, 2037, and 2047 are most likely, given the data. The data slides for this presentation are available

at: http://eia.doe.gov/pub/oil_gas/petroleum/presentations/2000/long_term_ supply/sld001.html.

11. See, for example, M. A. Adelman, "Is the Oil Shortage Real? Oil Companies as OPEC Tax Collectors," *Foreign Affairs* 9 (1973), 69–107; id., "Mineral Depletion, with Special Reference to Petroleum," *Review of Economics & Statistics* 72 (1990), 1–10; and id., *The Economics of Petroleum Supply 1962–1993* (Cambridge: MIT, 1993).

12. Even the strongest proponents of renewable energy admit the amount of market need that could be reasonably filled from these sources would not be sufficient to meet the minimum market demands for most elements in a modern economy. The EIA has estimated that, by 2025, renewable energy sources would provide 9.00 quadrillion BTUs (British thermal units; a BTU is a traditional unit of energy equivalent to the heat required to heat one pound of water one degree Fahrenheit) out of a total expected U.S. energy production of 136.48 quadrillion BTUs—about 6.6 percent. In contrast, petroleum would account for 54.99 quadrillion BTUs (40.3 percent) and natural gas would provide 29.66 quadrillion BTUs (21.7 percent). Energy Information Administration, *Annual Energy Outlook 2004 with Projections to 2025*, Appendix A: Reference Case Forecast (2001–2025), Table 2: Energy Consumption by Sector and Source, available at: www.eia.doe.gov/oiaf/aeo/aeoref_tab.html.

    Critics counter that the EIA does not factor in as yet unknown technological developments and breakthroughs. Additionally, the EIA has been challenged in the past for overly optimistic hydrocarbon estimates while lowballing nontraditional sources. See Paul P. Craig, Ashok Gadgil, and Jonathan G. Koomey, "What Can History Teach Us? A Retrospective Examination of Long-Term Energy Forecasts for the United States," *Annual Review of Energy and the Environment* 27 (1992), 83–118.

    For a general overview of the "alternative sources" approach, see Leonardo Maugeri, *Beyond the Age of Oil: The Myths, Realities, and Future of Fossil Fuels and Their Alternatives*, Jonathan T, Hine, Jr., translator (Santa Barbara: Praeger, 2010); Paul Roberts, *The End of Oil: On the Edge of a Perilous New World* (Boston: Houghton Mifflin, 2004); Richard Heinberg, *The Party's Over: Oil, War, and the Fate of Industrial Societies* (Gabriola Island: New Society, 2003); Howard Geller, *Energy Revolution: Policies for a Sustainable Future* (Washington: Island Press, 2003); and F. E. Trainer, "Can Renewable Energy Sources Sustain Affluent Society?" *Energy Policy* 23 (1995), 1009–1025. Some positions in this debate require rather pronounced revisions in lifestyle. See, for example, Katie Alvord, *Divorce Your Car: Ending the Love Affair with the Automobile* (Gabriola Island: New Society, 2000).

13. There is, however, a price caveat in the discussion of energy replacement. See William D. Nordhaus, "The Allocation of Energy Resources," *Brookings Papers on Economic Activity* 3 (1973), 529–576. Nordhaus states that alternative energy

sources come into play when what he calls a "switch point to a backstop technology" is reached. This refers to the crude-oil pricing level at which the cost of research and production of alternative energy (Nordhaus primarily considers synthetic energy sources in this paper) is no longer regarded as prohibitive. David E. Spiro well summarizes the Nordhaus hypothesis as follows: "At this point increasing demand for energy and decreasing supply of oil do not lead to rises in the price of oil. And because the price trajectory of oil reaches a plateau, the present discounted price for future sales of oil decreases." David E. Spiro, *The Hidden Hand of American Hegemony: Petrodollar Recycling and International Markets* (Ithaca, NY: Cornell University, 1999), p. 27. Spiro adds: "Given the possibility of alternative energy sources in the future, oil sold now will result in cash that increases in value faster than oil not sold now." Ibid. On the calculation of the "switch point," see also Geoffrey Heal, "The Relationship between Price and Extraction Cost for a Resource with a Backstop Technology," *Bell Journal of Economics* 4 (1976), 371–378.

14. Øystein Noreng, *Crude Power: Politics and the Oil Market* (London: I. B. Taurus, 2002), 8. Bernard C. Beaudreau, an excellent contemporary commentator on the relationship between energy issues and the social sciences, begins his benchmark work by declaring bluntly: "[T]he study of political economy by moral philosophers was, in large measure, the result of an energy shock, namely the introduction of inanimate power sources . . . in late eighteenth/ early nineteenth century manufacturing. . . ." Bernard C. Beaudreau, *Energy and the Rise and Fall of Political Economy* (Westport, CT: Greenwood, 1999), 7. For Beaudreau, as for several other commentators, it is not accidental that the writer of *An Inquiry into the Nature and Causes of the Wealth of Nations* (Adam Smith) was also the author of *A Theory of Moral Sentiments*. The best treatment of "energy shock" as the foundation for the study of modern political economy is Maxine Berg, *The Machinery Question and the Making of Political Economy* (Cambridge: Cambridge University Press, 1980).

15. In classical economic thinking, production (and therefore the creation of value) resulted from the application of three things—capital, labor, and land.

16. Important contributing works to the pricing theory were Alfred Marshall, *Principles of Economics* (London: Macmillan, the eighth and last edition appearing in 1890); William Stanley Jevons, *The Theory of Political Economy* (London: Pelican, 1871); and Leon Walras, *Eléments d'Économie Politique Pure*, written in two volumes between 1844 and 1877. A complete translation into English of this last work did not take place until the mid-twentieth century—Leon Walras, *Elements of Pure Economics*, trans. William Jaffe (Cambridge: Harvard University, 1954).

17. See, for example, D.M.G. Newberry, "Oil Prices, Cartels, and the Problem of Dynamic Inconsistency," *The Economic Journal* 91 (1981), 617–646; Mark A. Hooker, "What Happened to the Oil Price-Macroeconomy Relationship?"

Journal of Monetary Economics 38 (1996), 195–213; J. Peter Federer, "Oil Price Volatility and the Macroeconomy," *Journal of Macroeconomics* 18 (1996), 1–26; Charles T. Carlstrom and Timothy Stephen Fuerst, "Oil Prices, Monetary Policy and Counterfactual Experiments," *Journal of Money, Credit, and Banking* 38 (2006), 1945–1958; and James D. Hamilton, "Understanding Crude Oil Prices," *National Bureau of Economic Research Working Papers,* No. W14492 (2008), available at: http://papers.ssrn.com/sol3/cf_dev/AbsByAuth .cfm?per_id=16249.

18. Rognvaldur Hannesson, *Petroleum Economics: Issues and Strategies of Oil and Natural Gas Production* (Westport: Greenwood, 1998), 85. The traditional application of scarcity considerations to the availability and pricing of a given product, thereby attempting to establish an overall rationing of supply in the market and equilibrium in pricing, has significant difficulties when applied to oil. See Ricardo Hausmann and Roberto Rigobon, "An Alternative Interpretation of the 'Resource Curse:' Theory and Policy Implications," in J. M. Davism, R. Ossowski, and A. Fedeline, eds. *Fiscal Policy Formulation and Implementation in Oil-Producing Countries* (Washington: International Monetary Fund, 2003), 13–44; Manmohan S. Kumar, "Forecasting Accuracy of Crude Oil Futures Prices," *International Monetary Fund Staff Papers* 39 (1992), 432–461; and Georg Koopmann, Klaus Matthies, and Beate Reszat, *Oil and the International Economy: Lessons from Two Price Shocks* (New Brunswick: Transaction Books, 1989), 225ff.

19. Price elasticity registers the relationship between the amounts spent on a good relative to the price of that good, expressed as the percentage change in quantity divided by the percentage change in price. Price decreases resulting in increases in spending, or price increases resulting in decreases in spending, mean that the good in question is price elastic. If, on the other hand, a decrease in price results in either no change or a decrease in spending, or conversely an increase in price results in either no change or an increase in spending, the good is price inelastic.

20. See A. J. Alhajji and Davie Huettner, "The Target Revenue Model and the World Oil Market: Empirical Evidence from 1971 to 1994," *The Energy Journal* 21 (2000), 121–140; Walter J. Mead, "An Economic Analysis of Crude Oil Price Behavior in the 1970s," *Journal of Energy and Development* 9 (1979), 1–25; and Noreng, loc. cit., 9.

21. As Adelman notes, "Oil development consists of spending large sums of money to build a shelf inventory, proved reserves. No manufacturer or shopkeeper will give away his wares because his stock-in-trade is a sunk cost. What he sells he must replace. . . . For oil, too, the true price floor includes replacement cost." Adelman, *Economics of Petroleum Supply,* 171.

22. A "discount rate" is an interest rate used to estimate future cash flows at present value, with the result called a "discounted cash flow." It is a common consideration in making virtually any investment decision and allows

for an investment to be compared to other usages of the same funds. In oil investment decisions, however, the discount rate employed is a very closely guarded figure. Given that 70 percent or more of all field expenses are accounted for by the work required to establish a field for development, including infrastructure and secondary service, discount rates applied to that stage are different from those applied to calculating how long a field should remain open. In the latter case, operating costs, which are fairly constant once a wellhead is producing, must be equated to the future expected price of the oil produced. See Charles R. Blitzer, Donald M. Lessard, and James L. Paddock, "Risk-Bearing and the Choice of Contract Forms for Oil Exploration and Development," *The Energy Journal*, 5 (1984), 1–28; R. C. Lind, ed., *Discounting for Time and Risk in Energy Policy* (Washington: Resources for the Future, 1982); and Paul M. Romer, "Increasing Returns and Long-Run Growth," *Journal of Political Economy*, 94 (1986), 1002–1037.

Crude oil and natural gas producers also have another option in determining discount rates that is unavailable to most other commodity-based investment decisions. They can leave it in the ground, if they conclude that the value of the reserves will increase by so doing. This introduces the famous Hotelling Rule and the variant Hotelling Valuation Principle, to be discussed later in this chapter.

23. Sliding scales are employed by producers in determining the payment of royalties, taxes and other fees, primarily in foreign projects. These are, therefore, payments made to the home government of the country in which the field is being developed. Yet they are also occasionally a matter of some dispute, and alternative calculations can result in increasing or reducing company proceeds. Usually the approach is to use an incremental sliding scale based on average daily production. But the production levels in sliding scale systems must be carefully chosen. Rates that are too high cease to be flexible (which is the essential rationale for a sliding scale). Those too low tend to disappoint local finance ministers.

It is important to remember that the calculation of royalties always includes the recovery of development and operational costs (either called "deductions" in a concessionary approach or "cost recovery" on a contractual basis). And the methodology used in calculating the scale, combined with occasional creative ways of determining costs, will sometimes produce results that enrage local governments or (more to our point here) distort actual cost ingredients in the determination of product price. For a general overview, see Daniel Johnston, *International Petroleum Fiscal Systems and Production Sharing Contracts* (Tulsa: PennWell, 1999), 53–63. A good overall view of the contractual implications is found in Daniel Johnston, "Production Sharing Contracts," *Petroleum Accounting and Financial Management Journal* 13 (1993), 24–75; and id., "Current Developments in Production Sharing Contracts and International

Petroleum Concerns," *Petroleum Accounting and Financial Management Journal*, 20 (2001), 90–100.

24. In fact, there has been a trend in the oil industry for decades, what some refer to as a built in bias, to overestimate prices, underestimate costs, and overestimate actual reserve potential. See Daniel Johnston, *International Exploration Economic, Risk, and Contract Analysis* (Tulsa: PennWell, 2003), 222–223.

25. A word about the terms designating where one finds oil. "A *reservoir* can be rigorously defined as a closed hydrodynamic system with precise limits in which fluid pressure (gas, oil, water) is balanced by the strength of the containment materials. Changes in pressure at any one place produce changes in pressure everywhere else." Adelman, *Economics of Petroleum Supply*, 133. A *field* refers to adjacent (and often overlapping) reservoirs sharing some common geological structure. Adjacent fields sharing the same geological event or cause are called a *trend*. Two or more trends comprise a *basin*. Ibid., 133–134. The use of the term *deposit* can refer to any accumulation of hydrocarbons considered sufficient to justify commercial development.

26. Gravity is the weight of a compound, which is then translated into something called specific gravity (the weight of the compound divided by the weight of water, with the weight of water being equal to 1). Oil folks, however, decided to complicate things by coming up with a unit of measurement for oil in degrees API [American Petroleum Institute] that, while providing a uniform standard, is actually an arbitrary scale. Degrees API express the gravity or density of liquid petroleum products. It is calculated using the following formula: API = (141.5/specific gravity) − 131.5. Two general conclusions flow from this. First, water has a specific gravity of 1 but a measurement of 10 degrees API. Second, the lighter the compound, the higher the API gravity. Light crudes generally exceed 35 degrees API and heavy crudes, often labeled "all crudes," have 25 degree API gravity or below. Intermediate crudes are usually placed between these two poles. Asphalt has a gravity of 11 degrees API. There are even heavier concentrations beyond asphalt, and they provide an important exception to the general proposition that oil floats on water. Recall that water measures 10 degrees API. As one professional tells the tale (and there are many versions of this one): "Industry lore has stories of barge operators who assumed that all oils are lighter than water. To their horror, as they filled their barge with heavy fuel oil, it sank before their eyes. After the fact, they learned they were loading 9 degree API fuel oil." William L. Leffler, *Petroleum Refining in Nontechnical Language*, 3rd ed. (Tulsa: PennWell, 2000), 16.

27. Viscosity is that physical property of crude oil impacting its flow. It is a property oil shares with other liquids. The higher is the viscosity, the greater is the impediment to flow. The greater is the impediment, the more expensive it is to provide external stimulus (usually hot water or natural gas injection) to keep the oil coming.

The impact of viscosity is well known to owners of automobiles, who must select a grade of motor oil based on viscosity. SAE (Society of Automotive Engineers) 10 weight motor oil, for example, flows easier than SAE 20 weight. With crude oil, viscosity is measured by an SSU (Seconds Saybolt Universal) number. A measured quantity of oil, usually 60 cubic centimeters, is put into a piece of equipment called a Saybolt viscosimeter and allowed to flow through a hole in the bottom of the device at a specified temperature. The number of seconds required for the flow-through is the oil's SSU number. The SSU approach is used more often with "light" oils (those whose chemical compositions are closer to the light distillate fraction of the distillation curve—gasoline and kerosene primarily) than with heavier oils (whose flow rates can be impacted by other factors, since it is already highly viscous oil). The approach usually translates into a "light" having gravity of degrees 35 API or above and a "heavy" coming in at degrees 25 API or below.

28. This refers to the encroachment of water into a well bore (the actual "hole" drilled from which the oil emerges). Given the degrees API discussion above, all but the heaviest of oil ends up "floating" on water, and water is almost always present in an oil reservoir. When coning takes place, the water below the oil moves upward to the well bore through venues which allow the water to bypass the oil. That water must be extracted and separated from the oil below it. This can rapidly become a prohibitively expensive proposition.

29. Prior to the mid-nineteenth century, however, collection of crude oil was dependent upon the forces of nature alone. Later, even after the advent of technology, the decision by developers to extract only the most easily obtainable (and least expensive to produce) crude from a deposit, leaving the remainder, was a standard practice. The practice is often called "creaming," and was a major problem in Soviet oil field development. On this issue, see, for examples, Leslie Dienes, "Observations on the Problematic Potential of Russian Oil and the Complexities of Siberia," *Eurasian Geography and Economics* 45 (2004), 319–345; and N. A. Krylov, A. A. Bokserman, and E. R. Stavrovsky, *The Oil Industry of the Former Soviet Union: Reserves and Prospects, Extraction, Transportation* (Amsterdam: Overseas Publishers Association, 1998), 63ff.

30. A step-out well is one drilled adjacent to a known location, but one for which the exact extraction level is unknown. They are often drilled to determine the extent and configuration of a reservoir.

31. Well logging is a standard field practice involving very sophisticated techniques to determine extraction factors, flow rate, and other elements. Logging constitutes the overwhelming amount of evaluation data compiled on a well. A log is usually conducted on an open bore hole prior to running the casing, since the pipe interferes with most measurements. Multiple open bore tests are run on all wells.

32. Harold Hotelling, "The Economics of Exhaustible Resources," *Journal of Political Economy*, 39 (1931), 137–175. The theory has engendered a prolonged debate. See, for example, Shantayanan Devarajan and Anthony C. Fischer, "Hotelling's Economics of Exhaustible Resources: Fifty Years Later," *Journal of Economic Literature* 19 (1981), 65–73; Stephen L. McDonald, "The Hotelling Principle and In-Ground Values of Oil Reserves: Why the Principle Over-Predicts Actual Values," *The Energy Journal* 15 (1994), 1–17; Lacombe Bell and May Ryan, "An Empirical Re-Examination of the Hotelling Valuation Principle," *Journal of Economic Research* 5 (2000), 1–15; and Andrew C. Thompson, "The Hotelling Principle, Backwardation of Futures Prices and the Values of Developed Petroleum Reserves: The Production of Constraint Hypothesis," *Resource and Energy Economics* 23 (2001), 133–156.

33. Dag Harald Claes, *The Politics of Oil-Producer Cooperation* (Boulder: Westview, 2001), 21.

34. That is, net of cost.

35. This is the version of the Hotelling rule most often applied, and follows the restatement of the thesis presented by Geoffrey M. Heal and Partha Dasgupta, *Economic Theory and Exhaustible Resources* (Cambridge: Cambridge University, 1979), 158, which sought to provide a direct equality between the annual growth in the price of the oil in the market and the interest rate. Discount rate considerations need to be added (at an equivalence to interest rates) to explain the motives of the oil producer. There were a number of attempts to validate the relationship, thereby validating the rule. Miller and Upton showed that the data results were inadequate from which to draw a firm conclusion. Therefore, they posited what they called the Hotelling Valuation Principle, which held that the in-ground unit value of the oil had to equal the net price for the rule to hold. Merton H. Miller and Charles W. Upton, "A Test of the Hotelling Valuation Principle," *Journal of Political Economy* 93 (1985), 1–25.

36. See Hannesson, *Petroleum Economics*, 96–97; and Margaret Slade, "Trends in Natural-Resource Commodity Prices: An Analysis of the Time Domain," *Journal of Environmental Economics and Management* 9 (1982), 122–137.

37. See Dermot Gately and Hillard G. Huntington, "The Asymmetric Effects of Changes in Price and Income on Energy and Oil Demand," *The Energy Journal* 23 (2002), 19–56; and Robert S. Pindyck, "Uncertainty and Exhaustible Resource Markets, *Journal of Political Economy* 99 (1980), 681–721.

38. Marginal cost specifies the increase or decrease in expenses attending the adding or subtracting of a single unit from the marketplace. It is a fundamental consideration in determining levels of production for virtually any product, also referred to as *differential* or *incremental* cost. When applied to oil, the rise may reflect a number of factors—increasing development expenses, rising

lifting costs at the wellhead, shipping or transport levels, and stockpiling, among others. Marginal cost is a crucial variable in determining production rises even during a period in which the market price of oil is increasing, and may even largely neutralize what might otherwise appear to be increasing returns from oil product sales. See, for example, "E&P Companies See Returns Stagnate Despite High Prices," *Oil Daily* (June 21, 2004).

U.S. independent producers' return on capital employed (ROCE) has been remarkably steady in recent years as rising costs neutralized the effect of high commodity prices. . . . The oil and gas business is characterized by a tug-of-war between growth and returns, where the pursuit of high rates of growth typically means sacrificing returns. While ROCE is a far from perfect metric, the report said, it does capture trends in noncash costs, which have been rising and which are largely absent from alternative performance measures that are based more on cash flow.

39. See, for example, Hilliard G. Huntington, "Crude Oil Prices and U.S. Economic Performance: Where Does the Asymmetry Reside?" *The Energy Journal* 19 (1998), 197–232; Nathan S. Balke, Stephen P. A. Brown, and Mine K. Yucel, "Oil Price Shocks and the U.S. Economy: Where Does the Asymmetry Originate? *The Energy Journal* 23 (2002), 27–52; and Noreng, loc. cit, 155.

40. See ibid., 52; and Adelman, *Economics of Petroleum Supply*, 308.

41. See Richard Barry, *The Management of International Oil Operations* (Tulsa: PennWell, 1993), 86–90; and Paul H. Frankel, *Essentials of Petroleum*, 2d ed. (London: Frank Cass, 1969), 18–22.

42. See, for example, Merton H. Miller and Charles W. Upton, "The Pricing of Oil and Gas: Some Further Considerations," *Journal of Finance* 40 (1985), 1009–1020; and A. F. Alhaji and David Huettner, "The Target Revenue Model and the World Oil Market: Empirical Evidence from 1971 to 1994," *The Energy Journal* 20 (2000), 121–144.

43. A project manager provides a certain amount for exploration and initial field development, the largest amount for field operations (including site preparation and extraction), and additional expenses for transportation, storage, and so on. This results in most of the budgeted expenses taking place early in a project (front loaded, in other words), with operating costs tending to decline per unit extracted as a well reaches maximum production. Unlike the consumer's interest in the price of each unit purchased in the market, the oil manager has a quite different view. Exploration, site development, operations, and others expenses must be regarded as sunk costs. It makes little difference whether these outlays can be charged against extraction proceeds in a lease or PSA agreement, or whether they constitute completely depreciable costs prior to calculating profits.

Variable costs, therefore, are low relative to the unit costs calculated for a multiyear project as a whole. But those unit costs become a concern when extractions begin to decline and new expansion of production capacity becomes necessary (either through drilling additional wells or increasing the secondary recovery at existing wells).

44. Adelman, *Economics of Petroleum Supply*, 220. Adelman is here specifically rejecting the idea advanced by Joseph Stiglitz that the acceptable initial premise in the equation is to cast a fixed stock of an exhaustible oil supply as a division between or among identifiable periods in the market. Joseph E. Stiglitz, "Monopoly and the Rate of Extraction of Exhaustible Resources," *American Economic Review* 66 (1976), 655–661.

45. Adelman, *Economics of Petroleum Supply*, 220. On the inability of "saving" the notion of a fixed stock of resources by establishing it as an actual economic portion of a price and cost dynamic, see Devarajan and Fischer, loc. cit., and Pindyck, loc. cit.

46. See note 35 to this chapter.

47. Adelman, *Economics of Petroleum Supply*, 275. See also id., "Modeling World Oil Supply," *The Energy Journal* 14 (1993), 8.

48. Shortly after Miller and Upton provided their revision of the *r* principle, data were compiled indicating less than a correlation between the in-ground unit value of the oil and the net price (as indicated in note 35 above, the equality necessary for the principle to hold). It was, in fact, a follow-up study by Miller and Upton that began the rethinking. See Miller and Upton, "The Pricing of Oil and Gas," loc. cit. See also Adelman's summary of later findings from several sources—Morris A. Adelman, Harindar de Silva, and Michael F. Koehn, "Unit Costs in Oil Production," *Resources & Energy* 13 (1991), 217–240; Morris A. Adelman and G. Campbell Watkins, "Reserve Asset Values and the 'Hotelling Valuation Principle,'" *Center for Energy and Environmental Policy Research, Massachusetts Institute of Technology*, Working Paper 92–004 (1992); ibid., "Reserve Asset Values and the Hotelling Valuation Principle: Further Evidence," *Southern Economic Journal* 61 (1995), 664–673; Adelman, *The Economics of Petroleum Supply*, 275; and G. Campbell Watkins, "The Hotelling Principle: Autobahn or Cul de Sac?" *The Energy Journal* 13 (1992), 1–24.

49. Adelman, Economics of Petroleum Supply, 275.

50. Ibid. (italics in original).

51. This is even the case when one considers a frequently observed element in positions advancing the "Hubbert's peak" approach to declining oil. A normal assumption in the argument contends that "cheaper" fields are developed first, with activities moving on to more "expensive" fields later. See, for example, Roberts, loc. cit., 44ff. There may well be a rise in costs as some

reservoirs become more expensive to develop. But an adherent to Adelman's approach would say it is the market that determines the price, not the oil field. If the price required to justify field expenses cannot be met, investment is curtailed.

There is also another reason why a field manager would deliberately move to market more expensive oil before releasing less expensive oil already in reserves—increasing the price (and thereby the profit) that cheaper oil would command. Additionally, one should remember that the production flow and the expected total oil recovery from a reservoir are functions of the number of wells extracting (and/or which have previously been extracting) from that reservoir. Changing the number of wells (operating or capped) has an impact on extraction, and therefore price. The very determination of whether oil is "cheap" or "expensive" may be less a reflection of geology and more a reflection of field management. *Lazier curves* (the technical name is actually *Dimensionless Average Well Rate versus Dimensionless Recovery curves*) are utilized to calculate such impact on production rates. See Barry, loc. cit., 242–250.

52. That is, buyers do not respond to changes in the price of a commodity by revising the demand for that commodity. Demand remains constant, even though a product may be increasing or decreasing in price. Elasticity (or inelasticity) of demand is expressed as the percentage change in the quantity demanded divided by the percentage change in the price.

53. The dramatic increases in prices for oil products following upon the 1973–1974 Arab oil embargo did translate into a decline in demand and some substitution of energy sources. But the termination of the embargo and the stabilizing of prices that followed reversed some of that trend. Most of the demand reduction occurred as a shock reaction to the dramatic increase in prices and was not sustained for long in the market. A similar, though less dramatic and sustained, decline in demand took place after the overthrow of the shah and the Iranian Revolution of 1979. A price spike in 1979–1981 following the events in Iran had a similar though less-pronounced effect upon demand levels than those having taken place in 1973–1974. See Georg Koopmann et al., loc. cit., 25–56. In both cases, demand returned to precrisis levels and even increased in the late 1980s and early 1990s due to increasing energy requirements in East Asia.

The decline in demand occurring along with the retreat of prices from the record high levels in July of 2008 was less a factor of reaction to pump prices as it was to an economic crisis, loss of employment, and a collapse in the housing market.

54. Francisco Parra, *Oil Politics: A Modern History of Petroleum* (London: I. B. Taurus, 2004), 189f. Panic buying was certainly supplemented by short-term demand inelasticity (i.e., low price elasticity of demand). See Hannesson, loc. cit,, 6; and Theodore Moran, "Modeling OPEC Behavior: Economic and

Political Alternatives," in James D. Griffin and David J. Teece, eds. *OPEC Behavior and World Prices* (London: Allen & Unwin, 1982), 102.

55. Robert L. Bradley, Jr., *Oil, Gas and Government: The U.S. Experience*, Vol. 1 (Lanham: Rowman & Littlefield, 1996), 487; and William Lane, *The Mandatory Price Controls and Allocation Regulations: A History and Analysis* (Washington: American Petroleum Institute, 1981), 31.

56. See Roberts, loc. cit., 193–194.

57. A significant (and sustainable) demand increase should also prompt new exploration and development. This does seem to be the reason for massive post–World War II exploration programs, for example.

58. Hong Kong's Hang Seng Stock Exchange lost 25 percent of its market value between October 20 and October 23, 1997. This was the last in a series of tumultuous events that began with attacks on the Thai baht currency in late 1995. Throughout the period, however, a rapid industrial expansion across East Asia resulted in significant increases in demand for crude oil and oil products. See Ray Tyson and James Norman, "Majors Still Waiting for Bargains in Ravaged Asia," *Platt's Oilgram News* 76 (February 11, 1998), 1.

59. The Arab oil embargo in 1973–1974, the fall of the Shah of Iran in 1979, initial reaction to the outbreak of the Iran–Iraq War in 1981, the Saudi refinery netback contracts beginning in 1986, and the First Gulf War in 1990–1991. Of these five developments, only the netback arrangements resulted in lower prices (and that was the Saudi intent). The other four sent prices higher.

60. "Supply/Demand: Shortage Amid Plenty," *Oil Market Intelligence* (October 19, 2004), 16:

> The traditional signposts are not much help in making sense of this oil market. Global supplies continued to exceed demand. . . but that did not hold back oil prices from hitting new record levels. Oil is abundant by traditional standards despite strong demand growth. . . . This contradiction between high prices and a relatively comfortable global supply-demand balance underscores the complexity and multi-faceted nature of the upward oil price "shock" that is upon us.

The strong supply indicator persisted despite significant political instability in Venezuela and Nigeria, an oil workers strike and lockout in Norway, a U.S.-led invasion of Iraq, and rising terrorism concerns in Russia. All of these events should have provided ample downward pressure on oil supplies. They did not.

61. The high taxes provide a certain domestic market "sterilization" of the oil price impact by having already occasioned a reduction in anticipated levels of consumption. In monetary terms, one normally associates the concept of

sterilization with a concerted attempt to insulate a domestic money supply from the effects of international forces. This is certainly true in any currency exchange scenario where an outflow of foreign currency reserves threaten to drive down the exchange value of the local currency. In such a situation, a central bank might constrict monetary emissions or increase interest rates. Neither would help domestic investment, but they would serve to segment the exogenous threat. Of course, they also could lead to a painful currency devaluation. See William C. Gruben, "Mexico: The Trajectory to the 1994 Devaluation," in Leslie Elliott Armijo, ed., *Financial Globalization and Democracy in Emerging Markets* (New York: Palgrave, 2001), 122–125.

Sterilization likewise has a primary role to play for emerging nations dependent upon the export of hydrocarbons for the bulk of foreign exchange earnings. The creation of oil stabilization funds serves to keep rising export earnings in exchange-denominated accounts, usually domiciled and/or invested out of the country, to prevent pressure on the local currency. That pressure develops when large amounts of foreign exchange earnings are converted, resulting in an increased demand for local currency and a corresponding rise in the exchange rate. This, in turn, produces the complete opposite of what the home government intends—imports become cheaper for local consumers, while exports become more expensive (and less competitive) for foreign purchasers.

62. See David Fyfe, "Oil Market Overview," a presentation before the Committee on Non-Member Countries of the International Energy Agency, Paris, October 7, 2004; and *Oil Information, 2004* (Paris: International Energy Agency, 2004), Part II, 8–22.

63. The discussion is taken from the textbook for a widely used industry "short course" on the subject, often taught to nonspecialists. Charles F. Conaway, *The Petroleum Industry: A Nontechnical Guide* (Tulsa: PenWell, 1999), 92ff. The most used definitional structure for the various reserve categories is "Oil and Gas Reserve Definitions," adopted by the World Petroleum Congress (WPC) in October of 1996 and by the Society of Petroleum Engineers (SPE) on March 7, 1997. The WPC/SPE definitions are available at http://spec.org/spedefinitions.htm.

64. Often, this classification is further divided into primary and secondary proved reserves. Primary proved reserves encompass reserves recoverable commercially at current prices and costs by conventional methods and equipment as a result of the natural energy (i.e., pressure) inherent in the reservoir. Secondary proved reserves would include the price and cost caveats advanced by the definition of primary proved preserves but require the supplemental application of artificial means in addition to that provided by the natural energy of the reservoir. Primary examples here would be the injection of pressurized water or natural gas, or the use of chemical additives. Secondary

proved reserves often will require developmental additions that significantly change the physical characteristics of the reservoir fluids. Secondary proved reserves are always more expensive to extract than primary proved reserves. See Jan J. Apps, "Estimation of Primary Oil and Gas Reserves," in Thomas C. Frick and R. William Taylor, eds., *Petroleum Production Handbook*, Vol. 2 (New York: McGraw Hill, 1962); and Chapman Conquest, *Estimation and Classification of Resources of Crude Oil, Natural Gas, and Condensate* (Paris: Editions Technip, 2001), Ch. 9.

65. Electric logging involves determining the resistance to electric current of the rock strata surrounding the well bore hole. Such surveying provides the well geologist with a way to determine the nature of the rock penetrated by the initial drilling as well as an indication of the strata's permeability. On well logging, see note 31 to this chapter. Electric logging was first developed by Conrad and Marcel Schlumberger in the early 1920s. The company which bears their name is today the largest oil field service provider in the world.

66. Otherwise, it is impossible to ascertain whether reserve additions are significant.

67. The WPC/SPE definitions (see note 63 to this chapter) describe probable reserves as follows:

> Probable reserves are those unproved reserves which analysis of geological and engineering data suggests are more likely than not to be recoverable. In this context, when probabilistic methods are used, there should be at least a 50 percent probability that the quantities actually recovered will equal or exceed the sum of estimated proved plus probable reserves. In general, probable reserves may include (1) reserves anticipated to be proved by normal step-out drilling where sub-surface control is inadequate to classify these reserves as proved, (2) reserves in formations that appear to be productive based on well log characteristics but lack core data or definitive tests and which are not analogous to producing or proved reservoirs in the area, (3) incremental reserves attributable to infill drilling that could have been classified as proved if closer statutory spacing had been approved at the time of the estimate, (4) reserves attributable to improved recovery methods that have been established by repeated commercially successful applications when (a) a project or pilot is planned but not in operation and (b) rock, fluid, and reservoir characteristics appear favorable for commercial application, (5) reserves in an area of the formation that appears to be separated from the proved area by faulting and the geologic interpretation indicates the subject area is structurally higher than the proved area, (6) reserves attributable to a future workover, treatment, re-treatment, change of equipment, or other mechanical procedures, where such procedure has not been proved successful in wells which exhibit similar

behavior in analogous reservoirs, and (7) incremental reserves in proved reservoirs where an alternative interpretation of performance or volumetric data indicates more reserves than can be classified as proved.

On step-out wells, see note 30 to this chapter.

68. The WPC/SPE definitions define possible reserves as follows:

> Possible reserves are those unproved reserves which analysis of geological and engineering data suggests are less likely to be recoverable than probable reserves.
>
> In this context, when probabilistic methods are used, there should be at least a 10 percent probability that the quantities actually recovered will equal or exceed the sum of estimated proved plus probable plus possible reserves. In general, possible reserves may include (1) reserves which, based on geological interpretations, could possibly exist beyond areas classified as probable, (2) reserves in formations that appear to be petroleum bearing based on log and core analysis but may not be productive at commercial rates, (3) incremental reserves attributed to infill drilling that are subject to technical uncertainty, (4) reserves attributed to improved recovery methods when (a) a project or pilot is planned but not in operation and (b) rock, fluid, and reservoir characteristics are such that a reasonable doubt exists that the project will be commercial, and (5) reserves in an area of the formation that appears to be separated from the proved area by faulting and geological interpretation which indicates the subject area is structurally lower than the proved area.

Infill drilling refers to wells drilled to "fill in" between already producing wells, usually part of an overall drilling program designed to reduce the spacing between wells in order to increase production from the field. When the field is a land lease of defined dimensions, the relationship governing the spacing between wells and productivity becomes all the more important.

69. The Canadian Petroleum Association approach is often cited in this regard. "Probable reserves are a realistic assessment of the reserves that will be recovered from known oil or gas fields based on the estimated ultimate size and reservoir characteristics of such fields." American Petroleum Institute— American Gas Association—Canadian Petroleum Association [API-AGA-CPA], *Reserves of Crude Oil, Natural Gas Liquids, and Natural Gas in the United States* (Washington: API-AGA, 1978), 263. As Adelman notes, the CPA definition is then revised "to denote amounts in known fields not now in proved reserves; the term 'proved plus probable' is their sum." See Adelman, *Economics of Petroleum Supply*, 134.

70. Book value refers to the overall worth of an oil company, including properties, leases, oil stock and all facilities, less depreciation.

71. Michael Economides and Ronald Oligney, *The Color of Oil: The History, the Money, and the Politics of the World's Biggest Business* (Katy: Round Oak, 2000), 166.

72. Robert Gilpin, *Global Political Economy: Understanding the International Economic Order* (Princeton: Princeton University, 2001), 18.

73. This is Kenneth Waltz's well-known phrase. See Kenneth N. Walz, *Theory of International Politics* (Reading: Addison-Wesley, 1979).

74. Gilpin, *Global Political Economy*, 18–19.

Chapter 4

1. Free-market capitalism provides what customers think they want. Despite a wide range of commentary (bordering on proselytizing reflective of the religious revivalist tradition) from members of the Chicago School and their progeny, capitalism makes no judgments about propriety or rationality. Therefore, in the pursuit of profit, the drive of participants focused only on return always provides room for the unscrupulous. It is not that the investor deserves what she gets. It is, however, an almost inevitable result of pursuing the new shortcut to wealth. As Akerlof and Schiller wryly put it, "Capitalism fills the supermarkets with thousands of items that meet our fancy. But if our fancy is for snake oil, it will produce that too." George A. Akerlof and Robert J. Shiller, *Animal Spirits: How Human Psychology Drives the Economy, and Why It Matters for Global Capitalism* (Princeton: Princeton University, 2009), 146.

2. John Cassidy, *How Markets Fail: The Logic of Economic Calamities* (New York: Farrar, Straus and Giroux, 2009). Rational irrationality is "a situation in which the application of rational self-interest in the marketplace leads to an inferior and socially irrational outcome." Ibid, 142. Cassidy's objective in this highly readable volume "is to explore the underlying economics of the crisis and to explain how the rational pursuit of self-interest, which is the basis of free-market economics, created and prolonged it." Ibid, 6.

3. See John B. Taylor, "The Financial Crisis and the Policy Responses: An Empirical Analysis of What Went Wrong," *National Bureau of Economic Research Working Papers Series*, Paper 14631 (2009), available at: www.nber .org/papers/w14631. Taylor's conclusion is "that government actions and interventions caused, prolonged, and worsened the financial crisis. They caused it by deviating from historical precedents and principles for setting interest rates, which had worked well for 20 years. They prolonged it by misdiagnosing the problems in the bank credit markets and thereby responding inappropriately by focusing on liquidity rather than risk." Ibid, 29. The liquidity-risk tradeoff is a matter I shall comment upon below. On which, see also Franklin Allen and Elena Carletti, "The Role of Liquidity in Financial Crises," *Jackson Hole Conference Proceedings* (2008), available at: www.kc.frb .org/publicat/sympos/2008/AllenandCarletti.08.04.08.pdf.

4. General equilibrium theory, usually considered to have originated with Leon Walras' *Eléments d'Économie Pure*, written between 1844 and 1877 (see note 16, Chapter 3 above), attempts to explain the relationship among factors of pricing, supply, and demand by specifying that equilibrium prices for all goods exist and all prices are subject to a movement toward reflecting market equilibrium. Broadly speaking, the approach overviews the economy as a whole from the "bottom up," usually beginning with analysis of individual markets and players. Hence, until recently (and the introduction of more complex applications), general equilibrium theory was included in the field of microeconomic neoliberal approaches, in contrast to the macroeconomic aggregate approach of the Keynesians.

5. Moral hazard arises in situations where a party not exposed to the risk manifestations implicit in an action would be likely to act differently if exposed to the risk. Essentially, it arises because the removal of risk allows one party to act less carefully than it would have otherwise, correspondingly transferring the risk exposure to the counterparty. As such, there is often included a factor of uneven information (information asymmetry), given that one party to a transaction may be in possession of relevant information not possessed by the other. Moral hazard in this instance provides an incentive toward action benefitting the party having the informational advantage.

   Our primary interest in this concept flows from the credit/risk separation introduced by the securitization process—where the originators of mortgages no longer had to carry the risk of default. Researchers had recognized this problem well before the current crisis. See, for example, Igawa Kazuhiro and George Kanatas, "Asymmetric Information, Collateral, and Moral Hazard," *Journal of Financial and Quantitative Analysis* 25 (1990), 469–490; Arnoud W. A. Boot and Anjan V. Thakor, "Moral Hazard and Secured Lending in an Infinitely Repeated Credit Market Game," *International Economic Review* 35 (1994), 899–920; Jerry L. Jordan, "Effective Supervision and the Evolving Financial Services Industry," *Federal Reserve Bank of Cleveland Economic Commentary* (2001), available at: www.clevelandfed.org/research/Commentary/2001/06.htm; Darrell Duffie and Kenneth J. Singleton, *Credit Risk: Pricing, Measurement, and Management* (Princeton: Princeton University, 2003), 33ff.; and Steven L. Schwarcz, "Protecting Financial Markets: Lessons from the Subprime Mortgage Meltdown," *American Law & Economics Association Annual Meetings* Paper 19 (2008), available at: http://law.bepress.com/cgi/viewcontent.cgi?article=2664&context=alea.

6. See Albert M. Wojnilower, Benjamin M. Friedman and Franco Modigliani, "The Central Role of Financial Crunches in Recent Financial History," *Brookings Papers on Economic Activity* (1980), 277–339.

7. Asset securitization refers to a process of structuring finance in which risk is distributed by bundling usually debt instruments and then issuing new

securities with the collected debt serving as collateral. All classes and types of assets can be securitized as long as they have a relationship to cash flow. Because of this, the paper resulting is called an asset-backed security (ABS).

8. See Karl E. Case and Robert J. Shiller, "Is There a Bubble in the Housing Market?" *Brookings Papers on Economic Activity* (2003), 299–362; and Richard Herring and Susan Wachter, "Bubbles in Real Estate Markets," in William C. Hunter, George G. Kaufman, and Michael Pomerleano, eds. *Asset Price Bubbles: The Implications for Monetary, Regulatory, and International Policies* (Cambridge: MIT, 2005), 217–230.

9. Interestingly, Alan Greenspan made a similar observation in 2002. See Alan Greenspan, "Monetary Policy and the Economic Outlook," prepared comments delivered before the Joint Economic Committee, House of Representatives, April 17, 2002. Available at: www.federalreserve.gov/boarddocs/testimony/2002/20020417/default.htm

10. Recalling Adam Smith's famous "coach and six" example of what is not effective demand: "A very poor man may be said in some sense to have a demand for a coach and six; he might like to have it; but his demand is not an effectual demand, as the commodity can never be brought to market in order to satisfy it." Adam Smith, *An Inquiry into the Nature and Causes of the Wealth of Nations* (London: Adam Smith Institute, 2001 on line edition), Book 1, ch. 7, par 8, available at: www.adamsmith.org/smith/won-b1-c7.htm.

11. The term refers to securities whose values have fallen precipitously and for which there is no longer a functioning market. Angelo Mozilo, the besieged former CEO of Countrywide Financial, usually receives the credit for coining the term. See www.ehsportal.com/ehs-daily-journal/toxic-assets.php.

12. The exact percentage is difficult to determine, given the intensely nontransparent nature of the market. However, with about 80 percent of the $2.5 trillion of subprime mortgages issued between 2000 and early 2008 ending up in securitization, and at least 40 percent of those effectively categorized as in default by June 2008, that would provide a (very) provisional baseline aggregate of at least $800 billion in "toxic assets." Hyun Song Shin has estimated, by the second quarter of 2008, the total asset pool comprising U.S. market securitizations had reached $17.6 trillion. See Hyun Song Shin, "Leverage, Securitization and Global Imbalances." *Hong Kong Institute for Monetary Research Occasional Papers* No. 5 (2009), available at: www.hkimr.org/cms/upload/publication_app/pub_full_0_1_216_HKIMR%20Occ%20Paper%20No5.pdf. That would put the percentage of toxic assets to overall securitized paper at less than 5 percent.

The overall impact to the broader global aggregate securitization market was even less pronounced. The Basel-based Bank for International Settlements (the effective central bank for the world's central banks) estimated that the face-value (notional) amount of credit default swaps (CDSs), used to hedge bank exposure to a wide range of loan, bond, and related paper defaults, had reached $42.6 trillion by the end of 2007. Bank of International Settlements, *Triennial Central Bank Survey of Foreign Exchange and Derivative Market Activity in 2007* (2008), 21. CDSs were attractive swing leverage between various exposures, made all the more enticing by the fact they were not regulated. This paper had no relationship to the issuer of the underlying debt. As Cassidy succinctly puts it:

> For example, Citigroup could agree to provide protection to Goldman Sachs on some mortgage bonds issued by Merrill Lynch. In this case, Goldman would pay premiums to Citigroup, and if the Merrill bonds get downgraded, say, Citigroup would pay Goldman an agreed sum of money. There was almost nothing to prevent the issuance of two or more CDCs on the same bond or loan. If Bank A had some loans it wanted to insure, it could buy protection from Bank B, which could lay off some of the risk on Bank C, which could buy protection from Hedge Fund Z, and so on.

Loc. cit., 281. Such approaches are what really caused the spread of the credit freeze occasioned by toxic assets, rather than the overall volume of the suspect assets themselves. See Rene M. Stulz, "Credit Default Swaps and the Credit Crisis," *European Corporate Governance Research Institute Finance Research Paper Series*, No. 264 (2009), available for download from: http://papers.ssrn.com/sol3/cf_dev/AbsByAuth.cfm?per_id=17753#.

13. See Jagadeesh Gokhale, "Financial Crisis and Public Policy," *Policy Analysis* No. 634 (2009), available at: www.cato.org/pubs/pas/pa634.pdf; Bryan R. Routledge and Stanley E. Zin, "Model Uncertainty and Liquidity," *Review of Economic Dynamics* 12 (2009), 543–566; Arvind Krishnamurthy, "The Financial Meltdown: Data and Diagnosis," paper prepared for the Credit Crisis Meeting of the National Bureau of Economic Research Corporate Finance Group (November 20, 2008), available at: www.kellogg.northwestern.edu/faculty/krisharvind/papers/diagnosis.pdf; and Mike Whitney, "Trouble in Banktopia: The Financial System Is Blowing Up," *Global Research* (September 28, 2008), available at: www.globalresearch.ca/index.php?context=va&aid=10355.

14. See note 5 to this chapter.

15. There are hundreds. A very good read is *And Then the Roof Caved In* (Hoboken, NJ: John Wiley & Sons, 2009) by CNBC's David Faber. Others worthy of note are: Charles Gasparino (also an on-air analyst at CNBC), *The Sellout: How Three Decades of Wall Street Greed and Government Mismanagement Destroyed the Global Financial System* (New York: HarperCollins, 2009);

Henry M. Paulson, Jr., *On the Brink: Inside the Race to Stop the Collapse of the Global Financial System* (New York: Grand Central, 2010); William D. Cohan, *House of Cards: A Tale of Hubris and Wretched Excess on Wall Street* (New York: Doubleday, 2009); Hal Schott, *The Global Financial Crisis* (St. Paul: Foundation Press, 2009); Mark Zandi, *Financial Shock: A 360° Look at the Subprime Mortgage Implosion, and How to Avoid the Next Financial Crisis* (Upper Saddle River: FT Press, 2009); Cassidy, loc. cit.; Robert J. Shiller, *The Subprime Solution: How Today's Global Financial Crisis Happened, and What to Do about It* (Princeton: Princeton University, 2008); Paul Muolo and Mathew Padilla, *Chain of Blame: How Wall Street Caused the Mortgage and Credit Crisis* (Hoboken, NJ: John Wiley & Sons, 2008); and Bill Bamber and Andrew Spencer, *Bear Trap: The Fall of Bear Stearns and the Panic of 2008* (New York: Brick Tower, 2008). On the other side of the equation is John Paulson and what stands as the greatest contrarian play in the history of Wall Street. See Gregory Zuckerman, *The Greatest Trade Ever: The Behind the Scenes Story of How John Paulson Defied Wall Street and Made Financial History* (New York: Broadway, 2009).

16. See, for example, Stephan Schulmeister, "Globalization without Global Money: The Double Role of the Dollar as National Currency and World Currency," *Journal of Post-Keynesian Economics* 22 (2000), 365–395.

17. Technically, the term refers to the profit resulting from the difference between the cost of printing money and the face value of that money. In international exchange, that becomes essentially an interest-free loan to the issuing nation. On this, see Stanley Fisher's seminal "Seiniorage and the Case for a National Money," *Journal of Political Economy* 90 (1982), 295–313.

18. SAMA received from the arrangement the three things the Saudi government wanted most: price, secrecy, and limited market movement. Washington, on the other hand, received a noninflationary way to deal with the current accounts deficit. See David E. Spiro, *The Hidden Hand of American Hegemony: Petrodollar Recycling and International Markets* (Ithaca, NY: Cornell University, 1999), 105ff. This work is one of the first analytical treatments of the petro-dollar problem confronting U.S. monetary policy to suggest that the market was not actually the agent cycling oil sale proceeds.

The central element was an add-on arrangement. This allowed SAMA "to buy securities at the average price (as determined by the competitive tranche), but outside of the auction. These issues of securities were sup-plemental to the normal parcel of debt offered at auction. The Treasury was therefore able to lower the amount of debt it put up for sale at auc-tion. . . ." Ibid., 109. See also Richard P. Mattione, *OPEC's Investments and the International Financial System* (Washington: Brookings, 1985), 68f; David F. Lomax, "The Oil-Finance Cycle Revisited," *National Westminster Bank Quarterly Review* (November 1982), 21–29; and Jan Tumlir, "Oil Payments and Oil Debt in the World Economy," *Lloyds Bank Review* 113 (1974), 1–15. Initially a secret deal, Congress in 1981 published the memorandum to Kissinger describing the arrangement. U.S. Congress, Committee on Government Operations, Subcommittee on Commerce, Consumer, and Monetary Affairs, *Federal Response to OPEC Country Investments in the United States (Part 1— Overview): Hearings Before a Subcommittee of the Committee on Government Operations*, 97th Congress, First Session (September 22–23, 1981), 467–468.

19. Soviet trade always labored under having to pay a premium, essentially the extra step of having to accumulate hard currency through the usage of raw materials, oil, gas, or gold exchange. As a "back door" fallback position, a de facto artificial ruble-Finnish markka convertibility was established. This resulted in some advantage in orchestrating trade with the Soviet Union in the 1970s, the 1980s, and in the early period of an independent Russia. Those connections, however, led to a rapid collapse of the Finnish banking sector following the Russian financial crisis of late 1998. See Tuomas Komulainen and Lauri Taro, "The 1998 Economic Crisis in Russia and Finland's Financial Trade," *Bank of Finland Institute for Economics in Transition*, No. 3 (1999), available at: http://finlandsbank.fi/NR/rdonlyres/598BBFFA-2B87–4F93-A63F-468E8F90AC89/0/bon0399.pdf.

   Much of that rapid collapse resulted from the Finnish banks occupying an intermediary position in issuing forward currency contracts for Russian foreign trade. With the ruble losing over 70 percent of its value against the dollar in six months, the massive calls resulting from the currency contracts (designed to insure trading partners against ruble depreciation) wiped out the Russian banking sector and the Finns right along with it.

20. Effectively, seiniorage exports inflationary pressure, since it facilitates the issuing of additional currency used outside the economy in which it is printed. So long as there is no repatriation and circulation, the inflationary impact hits elsewhere.

21. See, for example, Catherine L. Mann, *Is the U.S. Trade Deficit Sustainable?* (Washington: Institute for International Economics, 1999), especially, 149ff.; id., "Perspectives on the U.S. Current Account Deficit and Sustainability," *Journal of Economic Perspectives* 16 (2002), 131–152; Schulmeister, loc. cit.; and Phillip R. Lane and Gian Marian Milesi-Ferretti, "Financial Globalization and Exchange Rates," *International Monetary Fund Working Papers*, No. 05–3 (2005), available at: www.listweb.bilkent.edu.tr/bsb/x2005/Jan/att-0019/01-IMFwp0503_FinGlobal_ExRates_2005.pdf.

22. In short, Hume demonstrated that "any attempt to have a permanent trade/payments surplus is self-defeating." Robert Gilpin, *Global Political Economy: Understanding the International Political Order* (Princeton: Princeton University, 2001), 78, n. 4. The process itself undermines the sustainability of the surplus.

Hume had articulated the Quantity Theory and the price-specie flow mechanism as a response to mercantilism and its reliance in retaining a trade surplus. See David Hume, *Essays, Moral, Political, and Literary*, T. H. Green and T. H. Grouse, eds. (New York: Longman, 1898), Vol. 1, 312f. On the historical importance of the price-specie flow mechanism, and its direct connection to contemporary views, see Dietrich K. Fausten, "The Humean Origin of the Contemporary Monetary Approach to the Balance of Payments," *Quarterly Journal of Economics* 93 (1979), 655–673, especially 663f.

Current oil revenue flows operate quite similarly to Hume's gold and silver. There is a considerable body of evidence showing a clear relationship between oil export sales revenues on the one hand and overall domestic economic activity and inflation rates on the other. See, for example, Alan Gelb and associates, *Oil Windfalls: Blessing or Curse* (New York: Oxford University, 1988); Eduardo Engel and Patricio Meller, "Review of Stabilization Mechanisms for Primary Commodity Exporters," in Eduardo Engel and Patricio Meller, eds. *External Shocks and Stabilization Mechanisms* (Washington: Inter-American Development Bank, 1993), Ch. 1; Panayotis Varangis, Takamasa Akiyama, and Donald Mitchell, *Managing Commodity Booms—and Busts* (Washington: World Bank, 1995); C. Emre Alper, "Business Cycles, Excess Volatility, and Capital Flows: Evidence from Mexico and Turkey," *Russian and East European Finance and Trade* 38 (2002), 22–54; Julia Devlin, "Managing Oil Price Risk in Developing Countries," *World Bank Research Observer* 19 (2004), 119–139; Paulo Drummond, "Implications of Oil Inflows for Savings and Reserve Management in the CEMAC," *IMF Working Papers*, No. 243 (2007), available at: www.imf.org/external/pubs/ft/wp/2007/wp07243.pdf.; and C. Emre Alper and Orhan Torul, "Oil Prices. Aggregate Economic Activity and Global Liquidity Conditions: Evidence from Turkey," *Economics Bulletin* 17 (2008), 1–8.

23. For example, SOFAR, the Azerbaijani oil fund (perhaps the most transparent among developing countries) would annually fund the obligation of the country's state-run oil company (SOCAR) for the construction of the Baku-Tbilisi-Ceyhan (BTC) export crude oil pipeline. The BP-run project is vital to allow exports to international markets from Azerbaijan's largest fields (the offshore Azeri-Chyrag-Guneshli deposits). Since SOFAR incurred virtually all of these expenses abroad, the completion of an essential infrastructure project did not incur substantial inflation. The other mandated primary usage of SOFAR funds, however, is quite inflationary. This involves assistance to internally displaced persons (IDPs) from the Nagorno-Karabakh conflict with Armenia. The overwhelming majority of the national population approves of this expenditure, regardless of its economic impact. This is also a good example of how decisions do not always confirm to the efficient choice assumptions contained in the still-dominant views of free market economics.

A very useful comparison of transparent and nontransparent sovereign oil funds is Norio Usui, "How Effective Are Oil Funds? Managing Resource Windfalls in Azerbaijan and Kazakhstan," *Economics and Research Department [ERD] Policy Brief Series, Asian Development Bank*, No. 50 (2007), available at: www.adb.org/Documents/ EDRC/Policy_Briefs/PB050.pdf. See also, for example, Jeffry Davis, Rolando Ossowksi, James Daniel and Steve Barnett, "Oil Funds: Problems Posing as Solutions?" *Finance & Development (International Monetary Fund)* 38 (2001), available at: www.imf.org/external/pubs/ft/ fandd/2001/12/ davis.htm; and Fasano's study of raw material funds in Norway, Chile, Alaska, Venezuela, Kuwait and Oman—Ugo Fasano, "Review of the Experience with Oil Stabilization and Savings Funds in Selected Countries," *IMF Working Papers*, No. 112 (2000), available at: www .imf.org/external/pubs/ft/wp/2000/wp00112.pdf.

24. Resulting from a merger of two state-controlled energy majors, Statoil and Norsk Hydro.

25. See note 23 to this chapter. Another example would be the Turkish use of hydrocarbon transportation proceeds to fund its national obligations for additional pipeline extensions, terminals, and related infrastructure. See Alper and Torkul, loc. cit., for some of the implications arising from such usage. Turkey is positioning to become a major transit country for oil and gas from the Caspian basin, Russia, and Central Asia. The overall plan is to turn Samson on the north central Black Sea coast and Ceyhan on the Aegean into major hubs, with Ceyhan likely to become a new Rotterdam for the region. Turkey will not receive significant revenue from additional local production and export. However, it will be gaining considerable proceeds from the throughput of oil and gas. Turkey is now the major focus for considerable volume moving to the European and wider global markets. Turkish policy has already become a central issue in the ongoing Russian-European Union energy dispute.

26. See M. Baquer Namazi, "Nongovernmental Organizations in the Islamic Republic of Iran: A Situation Analysis," *United Nations Development Programme-Iran Technical Papers*, No. 1 (2000), available at: www.undp .org.ir/DocCenter/REPORTS/NGO-IR.pdf; and Hadi Salehi Esfahani, "Alternative Public Service Delivery Mechanisms in Iran," Quarterly *Review of Economics and Finance* 45 (2005), 497–525. Major charities allow conservative clerics and the Revolutionary Guard to exert extensive control over the Iranian society and wider region. See Kent F. Moors, "Iranian Insider: Control over Oil and Gas Revenues at Center of Latest Political Dispute," *Caspian Investor* 11 (July 2008), 18–21; Ted Galen Carpenter and Malou Innocent, "The Iraq War and Iranian Power," *Survival* 49 (2007–2008), 67–82; and Barbara Slavin, "Mullahs, Money, and Militia," *United States Institute of Peace Special Reports*, No. 206 (2008), available at: http://kms1.isn.ethz.ch/

serviceengine/Files/ISN/57476/ ipublicationdocument_singledocument/
037B80DD-D830 – 4525 – 8B3B-8499FDAC49A7/en/sr206.pdf.

27. Pension supplements and subsidies for selected domestic industrial and hydrocarbon projects receive injections from Russia's Stabilization Fund, often prior to elections. My preliminary estimate after the 2008 presidential election put the net add-on to the annualized Russian inflation rate at 2.5–2.8 percent from the injection of fund proceeds directly into the economy in the form of development grants or additions to social welfare programs. See Kent F. Moors, "Utilization of Oil Proceeds Adding to Inflation," *Russian Petroleum Investor Update* (March 3, 2008), on line edition.

28. Both the Alaska Permanent Fund and the Venezuelan Oil Stabilization Fund allow the legislature to determine how fund proceeds are spent. In the latter case, those decisions are in actuality made by the president's office. An October 2009 decision by the Nigerian government to inject $2 billion in oil sales proceeds directly into the economy in an attempt to stimulate economic recovery is a parallel example.

29. Some major crude producers also need to import oil products. Nigeria is a prime example, as noted in the anecdote that opens this chapter. Despite being a major crude oil producer, the nation has insufficient refinery capacity.

30. See, for example, Sarah Abdullah, "Saudi-CPI Shows Concern over Rising Prices," *Arab News* (December 20, 2009).

31. See Peter L. Swan, "The Political Economy of the Subprime Crisis: Why Subprime Was So Attractive to its Creator," *Social Science Working Papers*, No. 320783 (2009), available at: http://papers.ssrn.com/sol3/papers.cfrm_id=320783. An excellent treatment of the rising preponderance of subprime mortgages in securitized obligations is Adam B. Aschraft and Til Schuermann, "Understanding the Securitization of Subprime Mortgage Credits," *Federal Reserve Bank of New York Staff Reports*, No. 318 (2008), available at: www.newyorkfed .org/research/staff_reports/sr318.pdf. See also Souphala Chomsisengphet and Anthony Pennington-Cross, "The Evolution of the Subprime Mortgage Market," *Federal Reserve Bank of St. Louis Review* (2008), 37f.

32. Andrew Ross Sorkin, *Too Big to Fail: The Inside Story of How Wall Street and Washington Fought to Save the Financial System from Crisis—and Themselves* (New York: Viking, 2009), 88.

33. The ratings agencies became, in effect, a captive of the dynamics unfolding in the very market they were supposed to oversee. Analysts also relied heavily on Value at Risk (VaR) models in determining the overall risk exposure. On the process, see Linda Allen, Jacob Boudoukh, and Anthony Saunders, *Understanding Market, Credit, and Operational Risk: The Value at Risk Approach* (Hoboken, NJ: John Wiley & Sons, 2004); and Phillipe Jorion, *Value at Risk: The New Benchmark for Managing Financial Risk,* 2d ed. (New York: McGraw-Hill, 2000).

While of some benefit as an element in a broader approach to markets, VaR actually can only provide an analyst with a rough expectation of how securitized assets operate in a market containing little significant variation, as well as the capital commitment implied by those expectations. VaR does not, and cannot, provide any significant read on a market in which assets values are rapidly changing. This was of primary consequence in the MBO crisis. Markets in such a situation will exhibit very excessive changes in securitized assets, especially wide swings of value changes between types of assets. VaR is of no use in estimating what those rapid changes mean to holdings. As such, while the analysis continued to indicate there was adequate diversification to counter risk (a main concern), the market reality was moving quite in the opposite direction. For a broader application to energy budgets, see Jerry Jackson, *Energy Budgets at Risk (EBaR): A Risk Management Approach to Energy Purchase and Efficiency Choices* (Hoboken, NJ: John Wiley & Sons, 2008).

Of equal concern were the disconcerting actions of some governments. Despite the clear signals that the securitization process was in serious disarray, sovereign examples of such activity continued unabated. On the continuing U.K. usage, see Kevin Ingram, "If Securitization Is Dead, Why Do So Many Government Schemes Use It?" *Capital Markets Law Journal* 4 (2009), 462–476.

34. This is a developmental or project finance application of the approach behind the Hotelling rule discussed in Chapter 3. Producing countries are also turning to structured finance as a supplement or alternative to Oil Funds as a way of managing oil assets. See Julia Devlin, "Managing Oil Price Risk in Developing Countries," *World Bank Research Observer* 19 (2004), 119–139.

35. For a good overall treatment of the financing options utilized in the current market, see Jeffrey Munoz, "Financing of Oil and Gas Transactions," *Texas Journal of Oil, Gas and Energy Law* 4 (2009), 223–267.

36. See Andreas A. Jobst, "Sovereign Securitization in Emerging Markets," *Journal of Structured Finance* 12 (2006), 2–13, especially 6f; Suhas Ketkar and Dilip Ratha, "Recent Advances in Future-Flow Securitization," *The Financier* 11/12 (2004–2005), 1–14; and Charles E. Harrell, James L. Rice III, and W. Robert Shearer, "Securitization of Oil, Gas and Other Natural Resource Assets: Emerging Financing Techniques," *Business Lawyer* 52 (1997), 885–946.

37. "Synthetic" in this sense refers to instruments created artificially through the use of two or more underlying papers with the intention of imitating the movement of an existing vehicle or instrument. The design of the created synthetic issuance is to mimic the assets, debt, proceeds, interest, and so forth, upon which it is based to form a security traded or sold that mimics the movement of the underlying paper.

38. A good readable introduction to what is admittedly a very complicated subject matter is found in Christopher L. Culp and J. Paul Forrester, "Structured

Financing Techniques in Oil & Gas Project Finance: Future Flow Securitizations, Prepaids, Volumetric Production Payments, and Project Collateralized Debt Obligations," in Andrea S. Kramer and Peter C. Fusaro, eds. *Energy and Environmetal Project Finance Law and Taxation: New Investment Techniques* (London: Oxford University, 2010), Ch. 21, upon which I base the preceding discussion.

39. Subordination refers to the seniority of paper. Most financial instruments of this type issue four classes of securities in a descending order of security: super senior, senior, mezzanine and junior. As defaults increase, the junior (generally referred to as the equity) class of paper is the first to experience loss, mezzanine second, and so on. That means junior paper carries the highest risk and super senior the least. In compensation, junior class paper receives a higher interest rate than mezzanine, mezzanine higher than senior, and senior higher than super senior (although the actual interest differential here is usually less pronounced than between earlier classes). In the pursuit of the highest returns from CMOs, investment houses and hedge funds invested heavily in junior paper. When the default rate among the underlying suspect mortgages increased, therefore, these investors were the first to experience the meltdown.

40. See Michael S. Gibson, "Understanding the Risk of Synthetic CDOs," *Federal Reserve Board Working Papers*, No. 36 (2004), available at: http://papers.ssrn.com/sol3/cf_dev/AbsByAuth.cfm?per_id=16307.

41. Spreads refer to the difference between returns on securities identical in all respects except for quality rating. The average coupon would be the gross interest rates of CDOs underlying a pool as of the pool issue date; the balance of each CDO is used as the weighting factor.

42. Christopher L. Culp and J. Paul Forrester, "Structured Financing Techniques in Oil & Gas Project Finance: Future Flow Securitizations, Prepaids, Volumetric Production Payments, and Project Collateralized Debt Obligations," in Andrea S. Kramer and Peter C. Fusaro, eds. *Energy and Environmetal Project Finance Law and Taxation: New Investment Techniques* (London: Oxford University, 2010), Ch. 21.

43. All project-based synthetic debt will have one or more equivalent corporate debt issues constituting close comparisons (much as international syndicated debt has a comparison to corresponding sovereign treasury debt paper or interbank rates). Both project and corporate debt contain similar forward-looking considerations and can be compared using a number of differing "opportunity cost" approaches.

44. Both of these essentially result from the fact that fully funded project debt requires less access to additional credit (in market parlance, "credit enhancement") to receive the same credit rating as usual corresponding corporate debt.

The increasing arbitrage reflects a higher level of flexibility in possible applications. Oversimplifying somewhat, this results from the higher expected recovery rates and shorter assumed periods in which that recovery should occur. Such considerations, in turn, largely result from tighter covenants and specifications of default events contained in typical project finance contracts and supporting documentation. Ratings agencies view these as acceptable, regarding such elements as a more workable way of gauging overall risk. However, as noted above, in unusual market conditions, such agency assumptions may not be justified.

45. A current account deficit or surplus refers to a country's net income from foreign trade. It is one of the two main factors in the balance of payments. The other factor is the capital account measuring the net change in asset ownership.

46. A noticeable exception during this entire period was Richard Duncan. See his *The Dollar Crisis: Causes, Consequences, Cures,* rev. ed. (Hoboken, NJ: John Wiley & Sons, 2005).

47. See, for example, Joseph W. Gruber and Steven B. Kamin, "Explaining the Global Pattern of Current Account Imbalances," *Journal of International Money and Finance* 26 (2007), 500–522; and Sebastian Edwards, "Is the U.S. Current Account Deficit Sustainable? If Not, How Costly is Adjustment Likely to Be?" *Brookings Papers on Economic Activity* (2005), 211–271.

48. See William A. Allen and Richhild Meossner, "Central Bank Co-operation and International Liquidity in the Financial Crisis of 2008–9," *Bank for International Settlements Working Papers*, No. 310 (2010), available at: www.bis .org/publ/work310.pdf?noframes=1; Linda S. Goldberg, Craig Kennedy and Jason Miu, "Central Bank Dollar Swap Lines and Overseas Dollar Funding Costs," *Federal Bank of New York Staff Reports*, No. 429 (2010); available at: www.ny.frb.org/research/staff_reports/sr429.pdf; and Damien Cleusix's periodically updated *Global Tactical Asset Allocation [GATT]*, available on a number of Web sites. The second quarter 2010 edition, for example, can be found at: www.ritholtz.com/blog/2010/03/global-tactical-asset-allocation-q2–2010/.

49. See, for example, Paul Krugman, "Oil Shocks and Exchange Rate Dynamics," in J. A. Frankl, ed., *Exchange Rates and International Macroeconomics* (Chicago: University of Chicago, 1983), 259–284; James D. Hamilton, "Oil and the Macroeconomy since World War II," *Journal of Political Economy* 91 (1983), 228–248; Anne K. McGuirk, "Oil Price Changes and Real Exchange Movements among Industrial Countries," *International Monetary Fund Staff Papers* 30 (1983), 843–883; P. Loungani, "Oil Price Shocks and the Dispersion Hypothesis," *Review of Economics and Statistics* 60 (1986), 536–539; Kenneth Rogoff, "Oil, Productivity, Government Spending and the Real Yen–Dollar Exchange Rate," *Federal Reserve Bank of San Francisco Pacific Basin*

Working Paper Series, No. 91–06 (1991), available at: http://ideas.repec.org/cgi-bin/ ref.cgi?handle=RePEc:fip:fedfpb:91–06; M. Dotsey and M. Reid, "Oil Shocks, Monetary Policy and Economic Activity," *Federal Reserve Bank of Richmond Economic Review* (1992), 14–27; Robert A. Amano and Simon van Norden, "Oil Prices and the Rise and Fall of the US Real Exchange Rate," *Journal of International Money and Finance* 17 (1998), 299–316; and id., "Exchange Rates and Oil Prices," *Review of International Economics* 6 (1998), 683–694.

50. See, for example, Dimitri Vayanos, "Transaction Costs and Asset Prices: A Dynamic Equilibrium Model," *Review of Financial Studies* 11(1998), 1–58; id., "Flight to Quality, Flight to Liquidity, and the Pricing of Risk," *National Bureau of Economic Research Working Papers*, No. 10327 (2004), available at: http://eprints.lse.ac.uk/456/1/ Tvliq3.pdf;; Joel Hasbrouck and Duane J. Seppi, 2001, "Common Factors in Prices, Order Flows, and Liquidity," *Journal of Financial Economics* 59 (2001), 383–411; Michael J. Fleming, "Measuring Treasury Market Liquidity, *Federal Reserve Bank of New York Economic Policy Review* 9 (2003), 83–108; Andrea L. Eisfeldt, "Endogenous Liquidity in Asset Markets," *Journal of Finance* 59 (2004), 1–30; Francis A. Longstaff, "The Flight to Liquidity Premium in U.S. Treasury Bond Prices," *Journal of Business* 77 (2004), 511–526; Viral V. Acharya and Lasse Pedersen, "Asset Pricing with Liquidity Risk," *Journal of Financial Economics* 77 (2005), 375–410; and Qin Lei, "Flight to Liquidity Due to Heterogeneity in Investment Horizon" (Edwin L. Cox School of Business, Southern Methodist University, 2009), unpublished paper available at: http://69.175.2.130/~finman/Reno/Papers/ FTLHET05full.pdf.

51. See Damir Tokic, "The 2008 Oil Bubble: Causes and Consequences," *Energy Policy* 38 (2010), 6009–6015; and Chia-lin Chang, Michael McAleer, and Roengchai Tansuchat, "Analyzing and Forecasting Volatility Spillovers, Asymmetries and Hedging in Major Oil Markets," *Energy Economics* 32 (2010), 1445–1455.

52. See Tigran Poghosyan and Heiko Hesse, "Oil Prices and Bank Profitability: Evidence from Major Oil-Exporting Countries in the Middle East and North Africa," *International Monetary Fund Working Papers*, No. 220 (2009), available at: www.imf.org/external/pubs/ft/wp/2009/wp09220.pdf,

53. See Thomas R. Michl, "Falling into the Liquidity Trap: Notes on the Global Economic Crisis," *University of Massachusetts Amherst Political Economy Research Institute Working Papers*, No. 215 (2010), available at: http://scholarworks .umass.edu/cgi/viewcontent.cgi?article=1182&context=peri_workingpapers; and Michael Devereux, "Fiscal Deficits, Debt, and Monetary Policy in a Liquidity Trap," *Central Bank of Chile Working Papers*, No. 581 (2010), available at: www.bcentral.cl/estudios/documentos-trabajo/pdf/dtbc581.pdf.

The "trap," while observed by Keynes and others, is best known in the version provided by Hyman Minsky. See Hyman Minsky, "Finance and Stability: The Limits of Capitalism," *The Jerome Levy Economics Institute of Bard College Working Papers*, No. 93 (1999); and id., *John Maynard Keynes* (New York: Columbia University, 1975), 35f.

54. Even the actual volume of available liquidity is often impossible to calculate with any firm confidence. See C. P. Chandrasekhar and Jayati Ghosh, "The Global Liquidity Paradox," (2008), unpublished paper, available at: www .networkideas.org/news/mar2008/Global_Liquidity.pdf.

55. The pivotal position of the broker dealer results from the need to offset risk. Obviously, a market would prefer to accomplish that by finding buyers and sellers. On the risk element attendant in this positioning, see Tobias Adrian and Joshua V. Rosenberg, "Stock Returns and Volatility: Pricing the Short-Run and Long-Run Components of Market Risk," *Federal Reserve Bank of New York Research Staff Reports, No.* 254 (2006); and Tobias Adrian and Michael J. Fleming "What Financing Data Reveal about Dealer Leverage," *Federal Reserve Bank of New York Current Issues in Economics and Finance* 11 (2005), both of the above available from: http://papers.ssrn.com/sol3/cf_ dev/AbsByAuth.cfm?per_id=93743.

56. Hyun Song Shin, loc. cit., p. 14. The downside for profitability was as precipitous. Between the second quarter of 2006 and the third quarter of 2008, issuers of ABS paper saw annual growth rates collapse from 29 percent to minus 8 percent. Broker dealers experienced a similar fall from 32 percent to minus 7 percent. Ibid.

57. See David Greenlaw, Jan Hatzius, Anil Kashyap, and Hyun Song Shin, "Leveraged Losses: Lessons from the Mortgage Market Meltdown," *Report of the U.S. Monetary Forum*, No. 2 (2008), available at: www.chicagogsb.edu/ usmpf/docs/usmpf2008confdraft.pdf.

58. The indicators for a longer-term impact have been developing for the last several years. The liquidity injections are merely going to accentuate the trajectory. See Anne-Marie Brook, Robert Price, Douglas Sutherland, Niels Westerlund, and Christophe André, "Oil Price Developments: Drivers, Economic Consequences and Policy Responses," *Organization for Economic Co-Operation and Development Economics Department Working Papers*, No. 412 (2004), available at: www.olis.oecd.org/olis/2004doc.nsf/linkto/eco-wkp(2004)35; Toni Johnson, "Oil Market Volatility," *Council on Foreign Relations Backgrounder* (September 24, 2008), available at: www.cfr.org/publication/15017/; and Barbara Ostdiek and Jeff Fleming, "The Impact of Energy Derivatives on the Crude Oil Market," *Energy Economics* 21 (1999), 135–167.

59. See Tobias Adrian and Hyun Song Shin, "Liquidity and Leverage, "*Federal Reserve Bank of New York Staff Reports*, No. 318 (2008); available at: http://qed .econ.queensu.ca/pub/faculty/milne/872/Adrian%20and%20Shin%202008.pdf.

60. James D. Hamilton, "Understanding Crude Oil Prices," *University of California Energy Institute's Energy Policy and Economics Working Papers* No. 23 (2008), especially 6 and 37, available at: http://escholarship.org/uc/item/3fg2r29s.

61. Imad A. Moosa and Param Silvapulle, "The Price-Volume Relationship in the Crude Oil Futures Market: Some Results Based on Linear and Nonlinear Causality Testing," *International Review of Economics & Finance* 9 (2000), 11–30.

62. See James L. Smith, "World Oil: Market or Mayhem?" *Journal of Economic Perspectives* 23 (2009), 145–164; and Imad A. Moosa and Nabeel E. Al-Loughani, "The Effectiveness of Arbitrage and Speculation in the Crude Oil Futures Market," *Journal of Futures Markets* 15 (2006), 167–186.

63. That is, a contango market.

64. See Anthony Sampson's *The Seven Sisters: The Great Oil Companies and the World They Shaped* (New York: Viking, 1975), one of the most famous books ever written on the age of big oil. The "sisters," so named because the companies were "related" via previous holdings, controlled the international crude oil market until the rise of producing countries coming to have more than 50 percent of joint operating companies in the 1960s. The seven companies were: (1) Standard Oil of New Jersey (Esso) and (2) Standard Oil of New York (Socony, later Mobil), which later merged to form ExxonMobil; (3) Standard Oil of California (Socal, later Chevron) and (4) Texaco (later merging with Chevron); (5) Anglo-Persian Oil (later Anglo-Iranian Oil and now BP); (6) Gulf Oil (most of which later becoming part of Chevron, some of the remainder moving to BP); and (7) Royal Dutch (now Royal Dutch/Shell).

65. See the discussion in Chapter 2.

66. F. William Engdahl, "Perhaps 60% of Today's Oil Price is Pure Speculation," *Darululoom-Newcastle Centre for Research on Globalisation* (2008), available at: http://darululoom-newcastle.co.za/index.php/news/9-news/52-perhaps-60-of-todays-oil-price-is-pure-speculation.pdf. See also James L. Smith, op. cit.; and David Pais, "'Liquidity' and Oil Don't Mix," *Indian.express.com* (October 28, 2009), available at: www.indianexpress.com/news/liquidity-and-oil-dont-mix/534221/.

67. The T index approach, developed by Holbrook Working in 1960, measures the balance between hedging and speculation in commodity markets. Commodity markets operate to hedge and satisfy risk management needs. Therefore, implicit in the T index approach is the assumption that there is an essential position for speculation because there often is not a complete balance between short and long hedgers at any one time. As a result, speculation provides the necessary market balancing. See Holbrook Working, "Speculation on Hedging Markets," *Food Research Institute Studies* 1 (1960), 185–220.

68. Following Working, analysts have regarded agricultural futures as a good surrogate for oil prices, given their tendency to react in similar ways to

changing market conditions. They are likewise more transparent in operations and provide a far more detailed data history. Working's T index has also been successfully applied to agricultural futures, allowing some extrapolation of market trend projections. See Dwight R. Saunders, Scott. H. Irwin, and Robert P. Merrin, "The Adequacy of Speculation in Agricultural Futures Markets: Too Much of a Good Thing? *University of Illinois Department of Agricultural and Consumer Economics Marketing and Outlook Research Reports*, No. 2 (2008), available from: http://papers.ssrn.com/sol3/cf_dev/AbsByAuth.cfm?per_id=15146.

69. Hilary Till, "Has There Been Excessive Speculation in the U.S. Oil Futures Markets? What Can We (Carefully) Conclude from the New CFTC Data?" *EDHEC-Risk Institute Publications* (2009), 14, available at: www.edhec-risk.com/Interview/RISKArticle.2009-11-27.0901/attachments/EDHEC-Risk%20Position%20Paper%20Speculation%20US%20Oil%20Futures.pdf. See also Till's earlier analysis "The Oil Markets: Let the Data Speak for Itself," *EDHEC-Risk Institute Publications* (2008), available at: http://faculty-research.edhec.com/jsp/fiche_document.jsp?CODE =1228207209363&LANGUE=1.

70. See Holbrook Working, "New Concepts Concerning Futures Markets and Prices," *American Economic Review* 52 (1962), 431–459; id., "Speculation on Hedging Markets," loc. cit.; id., "Futures Trading and Hedging," *American Economic Review* 43 (1953), 314–353; id., "Theory of Inverse Carrying Charge in Futures Markets," *Journal of Farm Economics* 30 (1948), 1–28; and note 67 in this chapter. See also Paul H. Cootner, "Returns to Speculators: Telser versus Keynes," *Journal of Political Economy* 68 (1960), 398–404.

71. Saunders et al., loc. cit. Once again, the need for the balancing factor is a need for the counter positioning of liquidity in determining asset prices. See, for example, Markus K. Brunnermeier and Lasse Heje Pedersen, "Market Liquidity and Funding Liquidity," *Review of Financial Studies* 22 (2009), 2201–2238; and Nobuhiro Kiyotaki and John Moore, "Liquidity and Asset Prices," *International Economic Review* 46 (2005), 317–349.

72. See, for example, Rama Cont and Thomas Kokholm, "A Consistent Pricing Model for Index Options and Volatility Derivatives," *Finance Working Group Working Papers*, Paper F-2009–05 (2009), available at: www.hha.dk/afl/wp/fin/F_2009_05.pdf; Mark Broadie and Ashish Jain, "Pricing and Hedging Volatility Derivatives," *Journal of Derivatives* 15 (2008), 7–24; Yunbi An, Ata Assaf, and Jun Yang, "Hedging Volatility Risk: The Effectiveness of Volatility Options," *International Journal of Theoretical and Applied Finance* 10 (2007), 517–534; Lorne N. Switzer and Mario El-Khoury, "Extreme Volatility, Speculative Efficiency, and the Hedging Effectiveness of the Oil Futures Markets," (2006), unpublished paper available at: www.iae.univ-poitiers.fr/affi2006/Coms/073.pdf; Andrew Ang, Robert J. Hodrick, Yuhang Xing, and Xiaoyan Zhang (2006), "The Cross-Section of Volatility and Expected

Returns," *Journal of Finance* 61 (2006), 259–299; and Sanford Grossman's seminal paper—Sanford J. Grossman, "An Analysis of the Implications for Stock and Futures Price Volatility of Program Trading and Dynamic Hedging Strategies," *National Bureau of Economic Research Working Papers*, No. 2357 (1987), available at: www.nber.org/papers/w2357.pdf.

73. Fran Tonkiss, "Trust, Confidence and Economic Crisis," *Intereconomics* 44 (2009), 196–202; Felix Roth, "The Effect of the Financial Crisis on Systemic Trust," *Intereconomics* 44 (2009), 203–208; and Timothy C. Earle, "Trust Confidence, and the 2008 Global Financial Crisis," *Risk Analysis* 29 (2009), 785–792. On the implications of trust/confidence applied to broader markets, see Sjoerd Beugelsdijk, "A Note on the Theory and Measurement of Trust in Explaining Differences in Economic Growth," *Cambridge Journal of Economics* 30 (2006), 371–387.

Chapter 5

1. This remains the primary assumption in any traditional approach to the oil market. See, for example, Henning Bohn and Robert T. Deacon, "Ownership Risk, Investment, and the Use of Natural Resources, *American Economic Review* 90 (2000), 526–549; Noureddine Krichene, "World Crude Oil and Natural Gas: A Demand and Supply Model," *Energy Economics* 24 (2002), 557–76; Bassam Fattouh, "The Drivers of Oil Prices: The Usefulness and Limitations of Non-Structural Model, the Demand-Supply Framework and Informal Approaches," *Centre for Financial and Management Studies*, Discussion Paper No. 71 (2007), available at: www.cefims.ac.uk/documents/research-64.pdf; and Jan Kjärstad and Filip Johnsson, "Resources and Future Supply of Oil," *Energy Policy* 37 (2009), 441–464.

2. "Upstream" refers to any operation taking place prior to a reference point, while "downstream" considers any after. Traditionally in oil, the reference point has been a refinery. That would position wellhead production as an upstream activity, while marketing oil products would be downstream. Earlier usage also included a "midstream" component, considering essentially shipping crude from field to refinery. Given that refineries are generally close to the end-user markets serviced, the refinery is now considered a downstream element. The clear point with VIOCs is that they are involved in the production of crude, as well as the refining and distribution of oil products—although, as noted in a moment, an oil major is no longer present in both upstream and downstream segments equally.

3. It is certainly possible for a VIOC not to be international in its operations. However, for our purposes, I propose to use the term only for companies working both upstream and downstream, while also having cross-border impact in those operations.

4. See http://tonto.eia.doe.gov/energy_in_brief/world_oil_market.cfm.

5. Seehttp://tonto.eia.doe.gov/cfapps/ipdbproject/IEDIndex3.cfm?tid=5&pid=53&aid=1.

6. This figure would be higher if state company holdings in joint ventures and international consortia were considered. The EIA puts Russian average daily production at 9,931,915 bpd, displacing Saudi Arabia as the world's largest producer. However, in the estimated 2009 percentage figure offered, I have included only 3,041,300 bpd in Russian production reported by majority-state controlled Rosneft and Gazprom Neft (the crude oil unit of natural gas giant Gazprom), along with that of Tomskneft (controlled at parity by the two companies).

7. From the standpoint of reserves, PetroStrategies has calculated that companies either completely or majority owned by the state hold down the top 14 slots worldwide, along with 16 of the first 20 and half of the leading 50. See www.petrostrategies.org/Links/worlds_largest_oil_and_gas_companies.htm. At number 15, Russian LUKOIL is the highest-ranked private VIOC, while ExxonMobil comes in at 17, BP at 19 and Petrobras at number 20 (but is also one-third owned by the Brazilian government). At 28, ENI is at least 30 percent controlled by the Italian state. The actual reserves held, however, show a disproportionate NOC control. Combining the NOCs with the state-controlled percentage of reserves in Petrobras and ENI results in aggregate reserves of 1.6 trillion barrels, which is *12.7 times* more than the aggregate reserves of 126 billion barrels in private company hands among the top 50.

   The most recent annual *Petroleum Intelligence Weekly* listing of the top global companies, widely considered an industry standard, shows a similar finding. In that survey, containing factors including production, sales, and asset value, NOCs take four of the top five rankings (ExxonMobil comes in third) and 16 of the top 25. See "Supplement: *PIW* Ranks the World's Top 50 Oil Companies," *Petroleum Intelligence Weekly* (November 30, 2009).

   In both the PetroStrategies and *PIW* studies, Saudi Aramco leads the list and the National Iranian Oil Co. (NIOC) comes in second.

8. However, this transformation in upstream control has also significantly changed the NOCs and, as we shall see later, provided some significant problems in the rentier countries. On the change, see Ann Myers Jaffe and Ronald Soligo, "The International Oil Companies," in *The Changing Role of National Oil Companies in International Energy Markets* (a joint Baker Institute/Japanese Petroleum Energy Center Policy Report, 2007), available at: www.bakerinstitute.org/programs/energy-forum/publications/energy-studies/docs/NOCs/Papers/NOC_IOCs_Jaffe-Soligo.pdf.; and Majed A. Al-Moneef, "Vertical Integration Strategies of the National Oil Companies," *The Developing Economies* 36 (1998), 203–222.

9. The full list is available at: http://money.cnn.com/magazines/fortune/ global500/2009/full_list/. Royal Dutch/Shell is number1 with a revenue total of $458.4 billion. ExxonMobil is second with $442.9 billion. By contrast, Sinopec, the highest ranked NOC has $207.8 billion in revenues while CNPC is at $181.1 billion. Of course, the top two producers and holders of reserves— Saudi Aramco and NIOC—do not list revenues. According to the *FT Non-Public 150*, however the estimated market value of Aramco assets is $781 billion, while that of NIOC is $220 billion. See www.ft.com/cms/s/2/5de6ef96 −8b95−11db-a61f-0000779e2340.html. In contrast, According to ExxonMobil's *2009 Financial and Operating Review*, the company's market assets are valued at about $233.3 billion. See http://thomson.mobular.net/thomson/7/2946/4183/ document_0/XOM_2009F&O.pdf. Having an asset base almost three and a half times greater would seem to suggest that Saudi Aramco should have a competitive revenue flow. Yet the *MOJ News Agency* has estimated Aramco annual revenues at $216 billion, NIOC at $101 billion. "Aramco Top, NIOC Second Among Major Islamic Companies," *MOJ News Agency* (February 14, 2009).

10. See Daniel Johnston, "Changing Fiscal Landscape," *Journal of World Energy Law & Business* 1 (2008), 31–54; Marcos Singer and Patricio Donoso, "Upstream or Downstream in the Value Chain?" *Journal of Business Research* 61 (2008), 669−677; Christian Wolf, "Does Ownership Matter? The Performance and Efficiency of State Oil versus Private Oil (1987–2006)," *Energy Policy* 37 (2009), 2642–52; and Biplab Dasgupta, "Large International Firms in the Oil Industry," *Institute of Development Studies Bulletin* 6 (2009), 46−67.

VIOCs have several advantages resulting from their ability to operate in a number of different tax and regulatory jurisdictions worldwide. Research has recently indicated how this contributes to project profitability. See Axel Perrou and Denis Babusiaux, "Valuation of Investment Projects by an International Company: A New Proof of a Straightforward, Rigorous Method," *Institut Francais du Pétrole, Série Recherche, Le Cahiers de l'Économie*, No. 72 (2009), available at: www.ifp.com/layout/set/print/content/download/68897/1490023/ version/3/file/ECO72_PIERRU-BABUSIAUX_FEV_2009-VA.pdf. See also Richard C. Levin, "Vertical Integration and Profitability in the Oil Industry," *Journal of Economic Behavior and Organization* 2 (1981), 215–35. However, there does seem to be a limit to VIOC efficiency advantages in so doing when field assets are at issue. See Gavin L. Kretzschmar and Lilya Sharitzyanova, "Limits to International Diversification in Oil & Gas—Domestic vs. Foreign Asset Control," *Energy* 35 (2010), 468−477.

On the other hand, Hartley and Medlock have identified nonmarket inefficiencies besetting NOCs. Their government owners often apply priorities to company operations that do not arise from commercial considerations. See Peter Hartley and Kenneth B. Medlock III, "A Model of the Operation and Development of a National Oil Company," *Energy Economics* 30

(2008), 2459–2485; and Peter Hartley, Kenneth B. Medlock III, and Stacy Elder, "Empirical Evidence on the Operational Efficiency of National Oil Companies," *Empirical Economics* 38 (2011), forthcoming. An earlier version of this paper is located at: https://netfiles.uiuc.edu/skarimi2/www/MEEA/Paper%20Eller,%20Baker,%20Hartly,%20and%20Medlock.doc. See also Robert Pirog, "The Role of National Oil Companies in the International Oil Market," *Congressional Research Service Reports*, RL 34127 (August 21, 2007), available at: http://relooney.fatcow.com/0_New_2276.pdf.

11. A demand curve is usually the way of depicting demand in economics. It actually refers to the graphic representation of a *demand schedule*—that is, a table illustrating the connection between the price and the quantity of a good. The graph plots price vertically and quantity horizontally. A demand curve usually slopes downward from left to right, representing higher quantities demanded at lower prices. The *demand price* represents what consumers would offer for a given quantity of a commodity at a given point in the curve.

12. See, for example, Lutz Kilian and Robert Vigfusson, "Pitfalls in Estimating Asymmetric Effects of Energy Price Shocks," *Federal Reserve Bank International Finance Discussion Papers*, No. 970 (2009), available at: www.federalreserve.gov/Pubs/ifdp/2009/970/ifdp970.pdf; and Olutomi I. Adeyemi, David C. Broadstock, Mona Chitnis, Lester C. Hunt, and Guy Judge, "Asymmetric Price Responses and the Underlying Energy Demand Trend: Are They Substitutes or Complements? Evidence from Modeling OECD Aggregate Energy Demand," *Surrey Energy Economics Discussion Series (SEEDS)*, Paper No. 121 (2008), available at: www.seec.surrey.ac.uk/Research/SEEDS/SEEDS121.pdf.

That uncertainty is also reflected on the supply side in estimations of oil, gasoline, and distillate inventories, as well as refinery usage. Both *Platt's* and the American Petroleum Institute provide surveys of market analysts prior to the Energy Information Administration (EIA) release of weekly data (usually on Wednesday, unless a holiday intervenes delaying it to Thursday; the figures tell us what the market looked like the previous Friday). For the period between October 1, 2009, and April 1, 2010, the "experts" were wrong six weeks out of ten on the direction of inventories and refinery usage (up or down) and/or volumes within 25 percent. Overall EIA projections (as contained in the *Annual Energy Outlook*) have been suspect for some time. See, for example, "What the US Government (the EIA) Is Forecasting with Respect to U.S. Oil Production and Renewable Energy," *The Oil Drum* (June 1, 2010), available at: www.theoildrum.com/node/6535; Kristofer Jakobsson, Bengt Soderbergh, Mikael Höök, and Kjell Aleklett, "How Reasonable Are Oil Production Scenarios from Public Agencies?" *Energy Policy* 37 (2009), 4809–4818; and J. T. Hwang, "Multiplicative Errors in Variable Models with Applications to Recent Data Released by the U.S. Department of Energy," *Journal of the American Statistical Association* 81 (1986), 680–688.

13. The term *demand destruction* has experienced wide usage in explanations for the decline in crude oil and oil product demand during the global recession and credit crunch. The term usually stands for a decline in demand, primarily of a commodity, resulting from a period of tight supply or rising prices. Some would suggest that genuine demand destruction requires a permanent or long-term downward trend in the demand curve (see note 11 to this chapter), while others (including myself) would utilize the term more as a response to an acute *demand shock*. Compare Leonardo Maugeri, "Understanding Oil Price Behavior through an Analysis of a Crisis," *Review of Environmental Economics and Policy* 3 (2009), 147–166; Elliott Gue, "Defining Demand Destruction," *The Energy Letter* (August 1, 2008), available at: www.kciinvesting.com/articles/9196/1/Defining-Demand-Destruction /Page1.html; Jeffrey Currie, Allison Nathan, David Greeley and Damian Courvalin, "Commodity Prices and Volatility: Old Answers to New Questions," *Goldman Sachs Global Economic Papers*, No. 194 (2010), available at: http://gsfacts.com/ideas/global-economic-outlook/commodity-prices -doc.pdf.; and "Oil Demand & Brittle Systems," *The Oil Drum* (August 20, 2008), available at: www.theoildrum.com/node/4411.

Emphasizing *demand shock* has the advantage of encompassing an acute and sudden disturbance in an economic system that has an adverse impact on demand, especially that occasioned by rapid changes having a direct impact on energy pricing, without requiring that such a disturbance has any permanent character. See Lutz Kilian, "Not All Oil Price Shocks Are Alike: Disentangling Demand and Supply Shocks in the Crude Oil Market," *American Economic Review* 99 (2009), 1953–1969; and James D. Hamilton, "Causes and Consequences of the Oil Shock of 2007–2008," *Brookings Papers on Economic Activity* No. 1 (2009), 215–261.

14. See the discussion in Chapter 3.

15. Estimates of current excess global capacity range from 2 to 6 million bpd. The former figure appears too low. According to Saudi Aramco CEO Khalid al-Falih, Saudi Arabia alone could put 4 million bpd on line in a matter of hours and, at government projections, keep the flow at that level. See "Official: Saudis Have Plenty of Oil Capacity as Demand Returns," *Bloomberg News* (March 9, 2010). Keep in mind, however, that this excess capacity is based upon a Saudi export of some 8.25 million bpd, itself almost 4 million barrels below the country's daily export during the 2008 summer price spikes. In short, a return to that level would again press the ability of OPEC to provide additional volume, as was the case then. See "Gulf Oil Producers Say 'No Excess Capacity,'" *CNN Marketplace Middle East* (May 16, 2008), available at: http://edition.cnn .com/2008/BUSINESS/05/13/oilcapacity.mme/index.html.

On the other hand, the latter figure (6 million bpd) seems only possible during the depths of the recession in oil prices (and demand) brought about by the credit meltdown—when a good portion of the excess capacity was accounted for by supply withdrawn from a depressed market. See, for example, "OPEC's Spare Capacity Ignored by Crude Oil Market," *Trader's Narrative* (August 17, 2009), available at: www.tradersnarrative.com/opecs-spare -capacity-ignored-by-crude-oil-market-2853.html; and "Saudi Arabia's Oil Capacity and Copenhagen," ft.com/energysource (July 29, 2009), available at: http://blogs.ft.com/energy-source/2009/07/29/saudi-arabias-oil-capacity -and-copenhagen/.

16. A brown field refers to a previously producing field or one on which an operator has already conducted activities and has placed facilities, now subject to reworking to be brought back into production. A green field is new, requiring completely new infrastructure and support facilities.

17. Those downstream (i.e., refineries in this case) end-users without their own upstream production fields would augment the problems by having to agree with virtually whatever pricing producing countries would establish. That simply increased the overall price in the market for all crude users, including the VIOCs. While the majors would still have access under such conditions to producing fields under their control (or at least in which they controlled a percentage of the volume), their own refining needs would require volume greater than they could provide for themselves. See Gavin Bridge and Andrew Wood, "Less Is More: Spectres of Scarcity and the Politics of Resource Access in the Upstream Oil Sector," *Geoforum* (2011, forthcoming)—revised version of a paper by the same title delivered before the 2008 Association of American Geographers Annual Meeting; and Wouter Pieterse and Aad Correljé, "Crude Oil Demand, Refinery Capacity, and the Product Market: Refining as a Bottleneck in the Petroleum Industry," *Clingendael International Energy Programme Papers* (2008), available at: www.nbiz.nl/publications/2008/ 20080400_ciep_energy_crudeoil.pdf.

18. VIOCs still have a smattering of exploration and production (E&P) projects spread out over the globe, but these projects must be integrated into where each company receives its primary return on investment. See Gizatulla Aibassov, *Optimization of Petroleum Producing Assets Portfolio* (Saarbrücken: Lambert Academic Publishing AG & Co. KG, 2010).

    The process whereby a producing unit of a VIOC would sell lifted volume to any refinery (rather than those connected to the parent company) is an application of *vertical deintegration* or *diversification* (widely practiced in other industries), introduced by Royal Dutch/Shell and thereafter adopted by other international majors. See Stephen Howarth, Joost Jonker, and Keetie Sluyterman, *The History of Royal Dutch Shell* (New York: Oxford University, 2007), Vol. 3, Sec. 2: "Mixed Results of the Diversification Strategy, 1973– 2000; Daniel Yergin, *The Prize: The Epic Quest for Oil, Money, & Power* (New York: Simon & Schuster, 1991), 721–724; Robert M. Grant and Renato

Cibin, "Strategy Structure and Market Turbulence: The International Oil Majors, 1970–1991," *Scandinavian Journal of Management* 12 (1996), 165–188; Walter Adams, "Vertical Divestiture of the Petroleum Majors: An Affirmative Case," *Vanderbilt Law Review* 30 (1977), 1115–1147; also David J. Teece, *Vertical Integration and Vertical Divesture in the U.S. Oil Industry: Economic Analysis and Policy Implications* (Stanford: Institute for Energy Studies, 1976); See also Walter S. Measday's well-known defense of the approach in his paper "The Case for Vertical Divesture," presented before *Capitalism and Competition: Oil Industry Divestiture and the Public Interest, Proceedings of the Johns Hopkins University Conference on Divestiture* (1976), available at: www .geonius.com/family/dad/vertical.html; against which, compare Arthur M. Johnson, "Lessons of the Standard Oil Divestiture," in Edward J. Mitchell, ed., *Vertical Integration in the Oil Industry* (Washington: American Enterprise Institute, 1976), 191–214.

19. Bleakley, Gee, and Hulme coined the phrase "Petropreneurs" in reference to those taking over the pricing in the market (and the creation of most market value) from the vertical majors. See Timothy Bleakley, David S. Gee, and Ron Hulme, "The Atomization of Big Oil," *The McKinsey Quarterly* (1997), 122–142.

20. See Grant and Cibin, loc. cit.; Robert M. Grant, "Strategic Planning in a Turbulent Environment: Evidence from the Oil Majors," *Strategic Management Journal* 24 (2003), 491–517; and Hossein Askari and Noureddine Kruchene, "Oil Price Dynamics (2002–2006)," *Energy Economics* 30 (2008), 2134–2153. The resulting explosion in futures contracts and the replacement of wet barrels by paper barrels as the driving force in the determination of market pricing have introduced a new volatility of concern to the traditional majors. As I have noted throughout this book, that volatility prompts an accentuating inability to determine an accepted actual market price for the underlying wet barrel. VIOCs have been increasingly seeing this difficulty in the spreads realized. Put simply, the futures contract pricing does not correlate well with spot market pricing. See Ron Alquist and Lutz Kilian, "What Do We Learn about the Price of Crude Oil Futures?" *Journal of Applied Econometrics* 25 (2010), 539–573. On the restructured approach required by such market dynamics, see also Svetlana Maslyuk and Russel Smyth, "Cointegration between Oil Spot and Future Prices of the Same and Different Grades in the Presence of Structural Change," *Energy Policy* 37 (2009), 1687–1693.

21. As (then) BP Amoco vice president and chief economist Peter Davies noted in his paper "The Changing World Petroleum Industry—Bigger Fish in a Large Pond?" delivered before the British Institute of Energy Economics Conference (St. John's College, Oxford, 1999), available at: www.dundee .ac.uk/cepmlp/journal/html/vol6/article6–14.html.

22. See, for example, Paul Paine, *Oil Property Valuation* (New York: John Wiley & Sons, 1942), 109f.; M. A. Adelman, *The Economics of Petroleum Supply* (Cambridge: MIT, 1993), 226ff.; Dimitrios Ghicas and Victor Pastena, "The Acquisition Value of Oil and Gas Firms: The Role of Historical Costs, Reserve Recognition Accounting, and Analysts' Appraisals," *Contemporary Accounting Research* 6 (1989), 125–142; Andrei Shleif and Robert W. Vishny, "Value Maximization and the Acquisition Process," *The Journal of Economic Perspectives*, 2 (1988), 7–20; S. R. Horn, "Analysis of Oil and Gas Reserve Acquisition Costs in Corporate and Property Purchases," paper delivered at the *Society of Petroleum Engineers Annual Technical Conference* (New Orleans, 1986), abstract available at: www.onepetro.org/mslib/servlet/onepetropreview ?id=00015353&soc=SPE; Jim Haag, *The Acquisition and Divestiture of Petroleum Property* (Tulsa: PennWell, 2005), 55ff; and Charlotte J. Wright and Rebecca A. Gallun, *Fundamentals of Oil & Gas Accounting*, 5th ed. (Tulsa: PennWell, 2008), 719f.

23. See, for example, M. Feygin and R. Satkin, "The Oil Reserves-to-Production Ratio and Its Proper Interpretation," *Natural Resources Research* 13 (2004), 57–60; the exchange between Matthew Berman and Bradford Tuck, "New Crude Oil Reserve Formation: Responsiveness to Changes in Real Prices and the Reserves-to-Production Ratio, *OPEC Review* 18 (1994), 413–430, and Mamdouh G. Salameh, "Technology, Oil Reserve Depletion, and the Myth of the Reserves-to-Production Ratio," *OPEC Review* 23 (1999), 113–125; Ian Lerche and Sheila Noeth, *Economics of Petroleum Production: A Compendium*, Vol. 2: *Value and Worth* (Brentwood, UK: Multi-Science Publishing, 2004), 149ff; Fattouh, loc. cit.; and Arthur C. Thompson, "The Hotelling Principle, Backwardation of Future Prices and the Values of Developed Petroleum Reserves—The Production Constraint Hypothesis," *Resource and Energy Economics* 23 (2001), 133–56. On the Hotelling Principle, see the discussion in Chapter 3.

24. Mark L. Sirower, *The Synergy Trap: How Companies Lose the Acquisition Game* (New York: The Free Press, 2000), 18ff; David Wood, "More Aspects of E&P Asset and Portfolio Risk Analysis," *Oil & Gas Journal* (October 6, 2003), 28–33; Reider B. Bratvold and Steve H. Begg, "I Would Rather Be Vaguely Right Than Precisely Wrong: A New Approach to Decision Making in the Petroleum Exploration and Production Industry," *AAPG Bulletin* 92 (2008), 1373–1392; and J. Myles Shaver, "A Paradox of Synergy: Contagion and Capacity Effects in Mergers and Acquisitions," *Academy of Management Review* 31 (2008), 962–976.

25. See note 18 to this chapter.

26. On which, see Nicholas Argyres, "Evidence on the Role of Firm Capabilities in Vertical Integration Decisions," *Strategic Management Journal* 17 (1998), 129–150; V. Kasturi Rangan, E. Raymone Corey, and Frank Cespedes,

"Transaction Cost Theory: Inferences from Clinical Field Research on Downstream Vertical Integration," *Organization Science* 4 (1993), 454–477; and Stefan Buehler and Armin Schmutzler, "Intimidating Competitors— Endogenous Vertical Integration and Downstream Investment in Successive Oligopoly," *International Journal of Industrial Organization* 26 (2008), 247–265.

27. Peter Osmundsen, Klaus Mohn, Magne Emhjellen and Flemming Helgeland, "Size and Profitability in the International Oil and Gas Industry," in Jerome Davis, ed., *The Changing World of Oil: An Analysis of Corporate Change and Adaption* (Aldershot: Ashgate, 2006), 13–28; John Hayes, Carl Shapiro and Robert J. Town, "Market Definition in Crude Oil: Estimating the Effects of the BP/ARCO Merger," *The Antitrust Bulletin* 52 (2007), 179–197, available at: www.ftc.gov/bc/gasconf/comments2/oilpaperjohnhayesetal.pdf; and Perry Sadorsky, "Assessing the Impact of Oil Prices on Firms of Different Sizes: It's Tough Being in the Middle," *Energy Policy* 36 (2008), 3854–61.

28. See, for example, Charles McPherson, "National Oil Companies: Evolution, Issues, Outlook," in J. M. David, R.Ossowski, and A. Fedelino, eds. *Fiscal Policy Formulation and Implementing in Oil-Producing Countries* (Washington: International Monetary Fund, 2003), 184–203; David Lertzman, Percy Garcia and Harrie Vredenburg, "A National Oil Company as Social Development Agent," *International Review of Business Research Papers* 5, No. 5 (2009), available at: www.bizresearchpapers.com/1.David.pdf; Gavin L. Kretzschmar and Liliya Sharifzyanova, "Limits to International Diversification in Oil & Gas—Domestic vs. Foreign Asset Control," *Energy* 35 (2010), 468–477; and Ryan J. Orr and Jeremy R. Kennedy, "Highlights of Recent Trends in Global Infrastructure: New Players and Revised Game Rules," *Transnational Corporations* 17 (2008), 95–129.

29. See generally, Vlado Vivoda, "Resource Nationalism, Bargaining and International Oil Companies: Challenges and Change in the New Millennium," *New Political Economy* 14 (2009), 517–534, and his larger work, *The Return of the Obsolescing Bargain and the Decline of Big Oil: A Study of Bargaining in the Contemporary Oil Industry* (Saarbrücken: VDM Verlag, 2008); Roland Brown, "The Relationship between the State and the Multinational Corporation in the Exploitation of Resources," *International and Comparative Law Quarterly* 33 (1984), 218–229; and Christian Wolf, "Does Ownership Matter? The Performance and Efficiency of State Oil vs. Private Oil (1987–2006)," *Energy Policy* 37 (2009), 2642–2652.

30. Friess, Baumgartner, and Bauer have suggested that a company's size may also affect internal perceptions of what projects and objectives are acceptable. See Bernhard Friess, Rupert J. Baumgartner, and Gerhard Bauer, "Success Factors of Petroleum Exploration and Production Companies," *International Journal of Services and Operations Management* 4 (2008), 145–164. The authors identify size as a variable in such estimates. As such, the results correspond

to studies completed in other market sectors. See, for example, Jeffry S. Hornsby, Donald F. Kuratko, Dean A. Shepherd, and Jennifer P. Bolt, "Managers' Corporate Entrepreneurial Actions: Examining Perception and Position," *Journal of Business Venturing* 24 (2009), 236–247; Simon Veenker, Peter van der Sijde, Wim During, and Andre Nijhof, "Organisational Conditions for Corporate Entrepreneurship in Dutch Organisations," *The Journal of Entrepreneurship* 17 (2008), 49–58; and David Offenberg, "Firm Size and the Effectiveness of the Market for Corporate Control," *Journal of Corporate Finance* 15 (2009), 66–79.

31. See, for example, Kent Moors, "The 'Grandaddy' of Shale Formations Just Got Profitable Again," *Oil and Energy Investor* (June 11, 2010), available at: http://oilandenergyinvestor.com/2010/06/shale-formations/; William Patalon III, "The 'New' Energy Sector," *Money Morning* (July 1, 2010), available at: http://moneymorning.com/2010/07/01/energy-sector/; and "John Simpson, Do the Major Oil Companies Anticipate Production Allocations? An Examination of Oil and Financial Market Data for Arbitrage Investment Opportunities," *The Journal of Wealth Management* 12 (2010), 101–118.

32. See Sheila McNulty, "Wildcatters: Minnows Lead the Way on Lucrative Frontiers," *Ft.com* (June 17, 2010), available at: www.ft.com/cms/s/0/dfca8c3a-78da-11df-a312-00144feabdc0,dwp_uuid=39fbcb54-78dd-11df-a312-00144feabdc0.html; and "Energy: Hitch Your Wagon to a Wildcatter," *Bloomberg Businessweek* (June 27, 2005), available at: www.businessweek.com/magazine/content/05_26/b3939622.htm.

The history here remains one of the more colorful parts of oil lore. See Roger M. Olien and Diana Davids Hinton, *Wildcatters: Texas Independent Oilmen* (College Station: Texas A&M University, 2007); Samuel W. Taft, Jr., *The Wildcatters: An Informal History of Oil-Hunting in America* (Princeton, NJ: Princeton University, 1946); and Brad Reagan, "Modern-Day Wildcatters," *WSJ.com* (May 27, 2008), available at: www.smartmoney.com/investing/economy/modern-day-wildcatters-23130/.

33. See, for example, Omowumi O. Iledare, "Worldwide Deepwater Petroleum Exploration and Development Prospectivity: Comparative Analysis of Efforts and Outcomes," paper delivered at the *Society of Petroleum Engineers Annual Technical Conference* (New Orleans, 2009), abstract available at: www.onepetro.org/mslib/servlet/onepetropreview?id=SPE-125085-MS&soc=SPE; V. I. Khain and I. D. Polyakova, "Large and Giant Hydrocarbon Accumulations in the Transitional Continent-Ocean Zone," *Geotechtonics* 42 (2008), 163–75; Steven Mufson, "Trend toward Deep-Water Drilling Likely to Continue," *Washington Post* (June 22, 2010), available at: www.washingtonpost.com/wp-dyn/content/article/2010/06/21/AR2010062104744.html; and Toni Johnson, "U.S. Deepwater Drilling's Future," *Council on Foreign Relations*

Backgrounder (May 27, 2010), available at: www.cfr.org/publication/22204/us_deepwater_drillings_future.html.

The competition for Arctic raw materials will heat up as the climactic conditions lead to further melting of the Arctic Ocean's ice cap. Russia has issued an intention to claim much of the waters as territorial, filing with the United Nations a conclusion that an extension of the Lomonosov Ridge and its connection with the Laptev and East Siberian Sea shelves justifies the bulk of Arctic reserves as Russian. See Vladimir Baidashin, "Russia Seeks to Obtain the Arctic Shelf," *Russian Petroleum Investor* 17, No. 6 (June–July 2008), 5–10. The reserves could be considerable. See A. E. Kontorovich, et al., "Geology and Hydrocarbon Resources of the Continental Shelf in Russian Arctic Seas and the Prospects for Their Development," *Russian Geology and Geophysics* 51 (2010), 3–11; and Victor Kaminsky, Oleg Suprunenko, and Victoria Suslova, "Russian Arctic Shelf Resources: Estimations and Problems," *Russian Petroleum Investor* 18, No. 5 (May 2009), 40–45. Moscow's intentions notwithstanding, as of the beginning of 2010, over 80 countries had claimed Arctic territory. Many have no territorial waters bordering on the Arctic.

34. Definitions of deep water drilling vary but 1,000 feet is an often-accepted minimum. Of course, this is referring only to the water depth. The production casing will extend far below the seabed. The Macondo-1 well that ruptured in the Gulf of Mexico had been drilled to a total depth of 18,360 feet—over 5,000 below the water surface and some 13,000 feet below the seabed.

35. "Oil Industry Faces 'Three Mile Island' Moment," *Oil Daily* (June 25, 2010), available at: www.energyintel.com/DocumentDetail.asp?document_id=675800.

36. Neil Hume, "Deep Waters Obscure Case for Oil Investment," *FT.com* (June 25, 2010), available at: www.ft.com/cms/s/0/f9d987ca-807d-11df-be5a-00144feabdc0.html.

37. See "The Disconnect between Oil Reserves and Production," *The Oil Drum* (March 6, 2008), available at: www.theoildrum.com/node/3664. Feygin and Satkin, loc. cit., point out that the actual ratio may include volumes unavailable because of reservoir deterioration or other factors, resulting in an increased figure without any genuine opportunity to enhance actual production levels. Others regard the calculations themselves as having intrinsic inaccuracies. For example, Owen, Inderwild, and King note that the ratio makes no allowances for a distinction among oil grades, types or reporting methods. Nick A. Owen, Oliver R. Inderwild, and David A. King, "The Status of Conventional World Oil Reserves—Hype or Cause for Concern?" *Energy Policy* 38 (2010), 4743–4749.

It may appear axiomatic, but a company's oil price risk is positively impacted by increases in oil production. Oil price risk is more sensitive to changes in production rates than to changes in reserve addition rates. See Perry Sadorsky, "The Oil Price Exposure of Global Oil Companies," *Applied Financial Economics Letters* 4 (2008), 93–96. An interesting methodological treatment of why the reserve availability windows should be more rigorously reevaluated is found in Shahriar Shafiee and Erkan Topol, "An Overview of Fossil Fuel Reserve Depletion Time," paper presented at the *31st IAEE International Conference* (Istanbul, 2008), available at: http://74.125.155.132/scholar?q=cache:HPrdlN1H4l8J:scholar.google .com/&hl=en&as_sdt=800000000000&as_ylo=2009.

Reserve figures and the reserve to production ratio are also subject to considerable manipulation for political reasons, an element increasing of late. See Oded Balaban and Alexander Tsatskin, "The Paradox of Oil Reserve Forecasts: The Political Implications of Predicting Oil Reserves and Oil Consumption," *Energy Policy* 38 (2010), 1340–1344; and Reid W. Click and Robert J. Weiner, "Resource Nationalism Meets the Market: Political Risk and the Value of Petroleum Reserves," *Journal of International Business Studies* 41 (2010), 783–803.

38. In fact, the body of literature on this relationship is increasing, and from a widening range of analysts. See, for example, Steve Sorrell, Jamie Speirs, Roger Bentley, Adam Brandt, and Richard Miller, "Global Oil Depletion: A Review of the Evidence," *Energy Policy* 38 (2010), 5290–5295; Kristofer Jakobson, "Modeling Oil Exploration and Production: Resource-Constrained and Agent-Based Approaches," Licentiate Thesis, Uppsala University (2010), available at: www.tsl.uu.se/uhdsg/Publications/Jakobsson_Lic_Thesis.pdf; Philip Suaré, "Overreporting Oil Reserves," *Swiss National Bank Working Papers*, No. 2010–7 (2010), available at: www.snb.ch/n/mmr/reference/ working_paper_2010_07/source; A. E. Kontorovich, "Estimate of Global Oil Resource and the Forecast for Global Oil Production in the 21st Century," *Russian Geology and Geophysics* 50 (2009), 237–242; and Mazen Labban, "Oil in Parallax: Scarcity, Markets, and the Financialization of Accumulation," *Geoforum* 41 (2010), 541–552. A good overview of primary implications is found in William Nordhaus, "The Economics of an Integrated World Oil Market," Keynote Address, International Energy Workshop (Venice, 2009), available at: http://aida.econ.yale.edu/~nordhaus/homepage/documents/ iew_052909.pdf.

39. I have suggested that the top 15 global producers have replaced only about 70 percent of extractable reserves lifted over the past 10 years. See Kent Moors, "Despite Meager Demand, Oil Companies to Boost Spending," *Oil and Energy Investor* (June 30, 1020), available at: http://oilandenergyinvestor .com/2010/06/oil-companies/. Some estimates are even steeper. See, for example, Mikael Höök, Robert Hirsch, and Kjell Aleklett, "Giant Oil Field Decline Rates and Their Influence on World Oil Production," *Energy*

Policy 37 (2009), 2262–2272; "Why You Should Worry about Big Oil," *Bloomberg Businessweek* (March 15, 2006), available at: www.businessweek .com/magazine/content/06_20/b3984001.htm; Okullo Samuel Jovan and Frédéric Reynès, "Can Reserve Additions in Mature Crude Oil Provinces Attenuate Peak Oil?" unpublished paper, Institute for Environmental Studies (IVM), Amsterdam (2010), available at: www.cer.ethz.ch/sured_2010/ programme/SURED-10_127_Okullo_Reynes.pdf; and Clifford G. Gaddy and Barry W. Ickes, "Russia's Declining Oil Production: Managing Price Risk and Rent Addiction," *Eurasian Geography and Economics* 50 (2009), 1–13.

40. See note 11 to this chapter, and the accompanying discussion in the text.

41. See, for example, Kilian, "Not All Oil Price Shocks"; Marc de Wit, Martin Junginger, Sander Lensink, Marc Londo, and André Faaij, "Competition between Biofuels: Modeling Technological Learning and Cost Reductions over Time," *Biomass and Bioenergy* 34 (2010), 203–217; Robert K. Kaufmann and Laura D. Shiers, "Alternatives to Conventional Crude Oil: When, How Quickly, and Market Driven? *Ecological Economics* 67 (2007), 405–411; and generally, Karl-Johan Lundquist, Lars-Olof Olander and Martin Svensson Henning, "Producer Services: Growth and Roles in Long-Term Economic Development," *Service Industries Journal* 28 (2008), 463–477; Stacy Barlow Hills and Kenneth R. Bartkus, "Market-Driven versus Market-Driving Behaviours: Preliminary Evidence for Developing Competitive Advantage in High-Technology Markets," *International Journal of Technology Marketing* 2 (2007), 140–156; and Per Hilletofth, Dag Ericsson, Martin Christopher, "Demand Chain Management: a Swedish Industrial Case Study," *Industrial Management & Data Systems,*109 (2009), 1179–1196.

42. Daniel O'Sulllivan, *Petromania: Black Gold, Paper Barrels, and Oil Price Bubbles* (Petersfield, Hampshire, UK: Harriman House, 2009). O'Sullivan's usage of the term "petromania" should be distinguished from another broader usage of the same term—referring to the mind set resulting from dependence upon the sale of oil. See Simen Saetre, *Petromania: A Journey through the Richest Oil Countries of the World* (Oslo: J. M. Stenersens Forlag, 2009).

43. On the overall analytical treatment of speculation in oil trading and its relationship to market pricing, see, for example, Giulio Cifarelli, and Giovanna Paladino, "Oil Price Dynamics and Speculation: A Multivariate Financial Approach," *Energy Economics* 32 (2010), 363–371; Hillary Till, "Has There Been Excessive Speculation in the U.S. Oil Futures Markets? What Can We (Carefully) Conclude from New CFTC Data?" *EDHEC-Risk Institute Position Papers* (2009), available at: www.iamgroup.ca/doc_bin/EDHEC-Risk _Position_Paper_Speculation_US_Oil_Futures.pdf; Damir Tokic, "The 2008 Oil Bubble: Causes and Consequences," 38 *Energy Policy* (2010), 6009–15; E. Mamatzakis and P. Remoundos, "Threshold Cointegration in BRENT Crude Futures Market" (2010), unpublished paper available at: http://mpra

.ub.uni-muenchen.de/19978/1/thresholdCI-BRENT-MPRA.pdf;and
Guglielmo Maria Caporate, Davide Ciferri, and Alesandro Girardi, "Time-
Varying Spot and Futures Oil Price Dynamics," *DIW Berlin Discussion Papers*,
No. 988 (2010), available at: http://papers.ssrn.com/sol3/cf_dev/AbsByAuth
.cfm?per_id=953767.

44. This anticipated market reaction to increasing price is tempered in the case
of oil by the presence of demand inelasticity. This posits that demand does
not decline when pricing increases; that is, there remains need for a product that cannot be offset. Significant price increases, however, will lead to a
decline in oil usage, although how extensive is the resulting demand destruction remains a subject of debate. See Hillard G. Huntington, "Short- and
Long-Run Adjustments in U.S. Petroleum Consumption," *Energy Economics*
32 (2010), 63–72; Michael A. Levi, "Energy Security," *Council on Foreign
Relations Working Papers* (2010), 14f, available at: http://74.125.155.132/
scholar?q=cache:xNL1KHibTvwJ:scholar.google.com/+%22oil+
demand+elasticity%22&hl=en&as_sdt=800000000001&as_ylo=2010; and
Mark A. Bernstein and James Griffin, *Regional Differences in the Price-Elasticity
of Demand for Energy* (Santa Monica: Rand, 2005), available at: www.rand
.org/pubs/technical_reports/2005/RAND_TR292.pdf.

45. See Dalton Garis, "The Behavior of Petroleum Markets: Fundamentals
and Psychologicals in Price Discovery and Formation," in Joanne Evans and
Lester C. Hunt, eds., *International Handbook on the Economics of Energy*
(Cheltenham: Edward Elgar, 2009), 420–440.

46. About 75 percent of all Mexican production comes from the Bay of
Campeche. See Roger D. Blanchard, *The Future of Global Oil Production*
(London: McFarland, 2005), 74f.; and "A Primer on Oil & Gas in Mexico,"
Simmons & Co. International Energy Industry Research (June 6, 2003), available at: www.simmonsco-intl.com/files/060603.pdf. However, production there has been steadily collapsing, largely as a result of poor planning
by the national oil company Pemex, following the introduction of a nitro-
gen injection process in 1999–2002. The crown jewel of the structure is
the Cantarell offshore field. Discovered in 1974 and put on line in 1978, it
reached a staggering 2.1 million barrels a day by 2004. From a still robust
daily production figure of over 1.2 million barrels at the outset of 2008, the
field has declined rapidly to 499,286 barrels by January 2010. See "Cantarell
Finally Slips to Below 500 kbpd," *Gregor.us* (June 28, 2010), available at:
http://gregor.us/oil/cantarell-finally-slips-below-500-kbpd/. The decline is
likely to extend, and with it any genuine prospects that Mexico will continue to provide significant import volume to the U.S. market. Much of the
analytical community, including the EIA, was caught flat-footed by the collapse. Unfortunately, Cantarell is not the only major Mexican source under
decline pressure. The Chicontepec basin and Ku-Maloob-Zaap, the two

fields comprising about 72 percent of all non-Cantarell proved reserves, are experiencing significant problems in maintaining production levels. See Jude Clemente, "Cantarell Is Not Mexico's Only Oil Production Problem," *Pipeline & Gas Journal* 235, No. 10 (2008), 52–54.

47. See Kathleen L. Abdalla, "The Changing Structure of the International Oil Industry: Implications for OPEC," Energy Policy 23 (1995), 871–877; Raymond Li, "The Role of OPEC in the World Oil Market," *International Journal of Business and Economics* 9 (2010), 83–85; Robert K. Kaufmann, Andrew Bradford, Laura H. Belanger, John P. Mclaughlin, and Yosuke Miki, "Determinants of OPEC Production: Implications for OPEC Behavior," 30 *Energy Economics* (2008), 333–351; and Sharon Xiaowen Lin and Michael Tamvakis, "OPEC Announcements and Their Effects on Crude Oil Prices," *Energy Policy* 38 (2010), 1010–1016.

48. That is, related to such sourcing as Canadian oil sands, bitumen, or North American and (to a much lesser extent, European and Chinese) oil shale. The argument in favor of these sources as a counterpoint to conventional crude production in general, and OPEC control in particular, is usually undermined by the actual practice. In addition, given the greater expense in developing unconventional sourcing, it falls prey first to downward cycles in the economy as a whole. See Richard Jones, "The Emerging Petroleum and Natural Gas Economy," presented before the *Energy Symposium: A Global Challenge* (Institute for National Strategic Studies, 2009), available at: www.dtic.mil/cgi-bin/GetTRDoc?AD=ADA509187&Location=U2&doc =GetTRDoc.pdf; Larry Hughes and Jacinda Rudolph, "Future World Oil Production: Growth, Plateau, or Peak?" *Current Opinions in Environmental Sustainability* (2011, forthcoming), paper available at: http://dclh.electrical andcomputerengineering.dal.ca/enen/2010/ERG201005.pdf; and R. W. Bentley, "The Expected Dates of Resource-Limited Maxima in the Global Production of Oil and Gas," *Energy Efficiency* 3 (2010), 115–122.

49. The merger of such majors, occurring during a period of low oil prices, accentuates the focus on downstream assets and concentration of market share. Hendricks and McAfee suggest in their analysis of the Exxon and Mobil merger that the more inelastic is downstream demand, the more captive production and consumption (i.e., that not traded in the interme-diate market) would affect price-cost margins. Kenneth Hendricks and R. Preston McAfee, "A Theory of Bilateral Oligopoly," *Economic Inquiry* 48 (2009), 391–414. See also Michael Kendix and W. D. Walls, "Oil Industry Consolidation and Refined Product Prices: Evidence from the US Wholesale Gasoline Terminals," *Energy Policy* 38 (2010), 3498–3507; Hayes et al., loc. cit.; Ben Worthen, "Drilling for Every Drop of Value," *CIO Magazine* (June 1, 2002), available at: http://massbal.com/publication_files/CIO6–1–02.pdf (on the Chevron Texaco merger); and J. Fred Weston, Brian A. Johnson, and

Juan A. Siu, "Mergers and Restructuring in the World Oil Industry," *Journal of Energy Finance & Development* 4 (1999), 149–183.

50. See, for example, Richard B. Mancke, "Interfirm Profitability Differences: A Reinterpretation of the Evidence," *Quarterly Journal of Economics* 98 (1974), 181–193; id, "Competition in the Oil Industry," in Mitchell, op cit., 35–72; K. Binderman, "Vertical Integration in the Oil Industry: A Review of the Literature," *Journal of Energy Literature* 5 (1999), 3–26; and Paul Stevens, "Economics and the Oil Industry: Facts versus Analysis, the Case of Vertical Integration," in Lester S. Hunt, ed., *Energy in a Competitive Market: Essays in Honour of Colin Robinson* (Cheltenham: Edgar Elgar, 2003), 95–101.

51. See Bard Misund, Petter Osmundsen, and Frank Asche, "The Pricing of International Oil and Gas Companies 1990–2003—A Structural Shift in the Equity Valuation Process," (2003), unpublished paper, available at: www1 .uis.no/vit/sv/tveteras/Structural%20shift.pdf; id., "Industry Upheaval and Valuation: Empirical Evidence from the International Oil and Gas Industry," *The International Journal of Accounting* 43 (2008), 398–424; and Fehmi Bouguezzi and Moez El-Elj, "Vertical Integration and Patent Licensing in Upstream and Downstream Markets," (2009), unpublished paper, available at: http://mpra.ub.uni-muenchen.de/22212/1/MPRA_paper_22212.pdf.

52. See Levin, loc. cit.; and Luis M. B. Cabral, "Horizontal Mergers with Free-Entry: Why Cost Efficiencies May Be a Weak Defense and Asset Sales a Poor Remedy," *International Journal of Industrial Organization* 21 (2003), 607–623.

53. See note 18 to this chapter.

54. See Purvez Captain, "The Smart Approach to Transfer Pricing," *Oil & Gas Financial Journal* 5, 8 (August 1, 2008), available at: www.ogfj.com/index /article-display/336434/articles/oil-gas-financial-journal/volume-5/issue-8 /capital-perspectives/the-smart-approach-to-transfer-pricing.html; Thomas A. Gresik and Petter Osmundsen, "Transfer Pricing in Vertically Integrated Industries," *International Tax and Public Finance* 15 (2007), 231–255; and Brent Neiman, "Stickiness, Synchronization, and Passthrough in Intrafirm Trade Prices," *Journal of Monetary Economics* 57 (2010), 295–308.

55. See, for example, Prem Sikka and Hugh Willmott, "The Dark Side of Transfer Pricing: Its Role in Tax Avoidance and Wealth Retentiveness," *Critical Perspectives on Accounting* 21 (2010), 342–356; and Muhammad Khalid Malik, "Tax Avoidance by Multinational Enterprises through Transfer Pricing," dissertation, International Economic Law, University of Warwick (2006), available at: http://dgtrdt.gov.pk/Research/TAX%20AVOIDANCE.pdf.

56. On the relationship between strike and spot pricing in an accelerating environment of oil volatility, see Chia-Lin Chang, Michael McAleer and Roengchai Tansuchat, "Analyzing Volatility Spillovers, Asymmetries, and Hedging on Major Oil Markets," *Energy Economics* 32 (2010), 1445–1455;

J. Glenn Andrews and Ehud I. Ronn, "The Valuation and Information Content of Options on Crude-Oil Futures Contracts," unpublished paper, Department of Finance, University of Texas-Austin (2010), available at: www.centerforpbbefr.rutgers.edu/20thFEA/FinancePapers/Session7/Andrews%20and%20Ronn.pdf; and Ryan Kellogg, "The Effect of Uncertainty on Investment: Evidence from Texas Oil Drilling," unpublished paper, Department of Economics, University of Michigan (2010), available at: www-personal.umich.edu/~kelloggr/Kellogg_UncertaintyAndDrilling.pdf.

57. Fractals are recurring mathematical patterns in nature. Recently, they have been applied in a number of ways to suggest that similar recurring patterns occur even in apparently random events. For some, a "fractal approach" is the parallel view to chaos theory and surfaces in both physical nature and human events. One short piece that has received wide play in this regard is Yonathan Shapir, Subhadip Raychaudhuri, David G. Foster, and Jacob Jorne, "Scaling Behavior of Cyclical Surface Growth, *Physical Review Letters* 84 (2000), 3029–3032, on which see "Nature's Cycles in a Fractal State of Mind," *ScienceDaily* (April 21, 2000), available at: www.sciencedaily.com/releases/2000/04/000421083242.htm. See also Glenn Borchardt and Stephen J. Puetz, "Unified Cycle Theory: Integration toward a Cause," unpublished paper (2010), available at: www.worldsci.org/pdf/abstracts/abstracts_5229.pdf. On the biological approach, see David Lloyd, "Biological Time is Fractal," *Journal of Biosciences* 33 (2008), 9–19. Jackson Pollock's "drip painting" has a particular fascination for fractal theorists. See, for example, Francis Halsall, "Chaos, Fractals, and the Pedagogical Challenge of Jackson Pollock's 'All-Over' Paintings," *Journal of Aesthetic Education* 42 (2008), 1–16.

58. See Shahriar Yousefi, Ilona Weinreich, and Dominik Reinarz, "Wavelet-Based Prediction of Oil Prices," *Chaos, Solutions, and Fractals* 25 (2005), 265–75; Ling-Yun He and Shu-Peng Chen, "Are Crude Oil Markets Multifractal? Evidence from MF-DFA and MF-SSA Perspectvies," *Physica A: Statistcial Mechanics and its Applications* 389 (2010), 3218–3229, Xiucheng Dong, Junchen Li, and Jian Gao, "Multi-fractal Analysis of World Crude Oil Prices," *2009 International Joint Conference on Computational Sciences and Optimization,* Vol. 2, 489–93; Ling-Yun He, Ying Fan, and Yi-Ming Wei, "The Empirical Analysis for Fractal Features and Long-Run Memory Mechanism in Petroleum Pricing Systems," *International Journal of Global Energy Issues* 27 (2007), 492–502; and the intriguing interpretation of both natural resource and human life by Nate Hagens, "Fractal Adaptive Cycles in Natural and Human Systems," *The Oil Drum* (January 7, 2010), available at: www.theoildrum.com/node/6099.

59. See, for example, Edgar E. Peters, *Fractal Market Analysis: Applying Chaos Theory to Investment & Economics* (Hoboken, NJ: John Wiley & Sons, 1994); Bikas K. Chakrabart, Arnab Chatterjee, and Pratip Bhattacharyya, "Two-fractal

Overlap Time Series: Earthquakes and Market Crashes," *Pramana* 71 (2008), 20310; and Wei Sun et al., "Fractals in Trade Duration: Capturing Long-Range Dependence and Heavy Tailedness in Modeling Trade Duration," *Annals of Finance* 4 (2007), 217–241.

60. This distinction is increasing. The International Energy Agency (IEA) estimated in its *Oil Market Report* of July 13, 2010, that 2009–2011 over-all world oil demand would increase 3.7 percent, from 84.7 to 87.8 million barrels per day (mbd). See the IEA's "World Oil Balance Charts" at http://omrpublic.iea.org/balances.asp. This location provides regularly updated figures as IEA revises its revisions in 36 specific categories. Each edition of *Oil Market Report* is found at www.oilmarketreport.org. However, the IEA sees the combined Organization for Economic Cooperation and Development (OECD, the body representing the developed countries and the founder of the IEA) demand as flat; actually declining marginally during the three-year period (by 0.02 percent, from 45.4 to 45.3 mbd), while North American (the United States and Canada) will increase by only 1.3 percent (23.3 to 23.6 mbd). On the other hand, non-OECD demand will jump 8.1 percent (from 39.3 to 42.5 mbd), which Chinese demand rises 14.3 percent (from 8.4 to 9.6 mbd).

61. The "Asian premium" comprises an increased cost associated with importing crude oil into Asia over the price commanded by the same grade of crude if sold to Europe. See, for example, Battam Fattouh, "The Dynamics of Crude Oil Price Differentials," *Energy Economics* 32 (2010), 332–342, and Mohna Nandha and Robert Brooks, "Oil Prices and Transport Sector Returns: An International Analysis," *Review of Quantitative Finance and Accounting* 33 (2009), 393–409. The introduction of a new Russian ESPO benchmark grade (representing the export oil to move through the now-under-construction East Siberia–Pacific Ocean pipeline) may lessen the current regional premium. The new grade actually has a better overall quality than the Oman/Dubai blends against which the Asian premium is calculated. See Victoria Nezhina and Elena Kirillova, "ESPO Prepares to Move Crude to China," *Russian Petroleum Investor* 19, No. 6 (June–July 2010), 21–26.

62. According to Cushing, Oklahoma West Texas Intermediate (WTI) FOB spot prices, as reported by the EIA, prices increased from $30.81 per barrel on December 22, 2008, to $80 on July 31, 2010. See the entire Cushing WTI spot price archive from December 1985 at: http://tonto.eia.doe.gov/dnav/pet/hist/LeafHandler.ashx?n=PET&s=RWTC&f=D.

63. According to the EIA's Europe Brent Spot Price FOB London (Dollars per Barrel), prices rose from $34.16 on December 29, 2008 to $78 on July 31, 2010. See the entire Europe Brent spot price archive from May 1987 at: http://tonto.eia.doe.gov/dnav/pet/hist/LeafHandler.ashx?n=PET&s=RBRT mE&f=D.

64. See Nelson D. Schwartz, "BP Loses Trading-Floor Swagger in Energy Market," *The New York Times* (June 27, 2010), A1, available at: www .nytimes.com/2010/06/28/business/global/28bptrade.html?_r=1&dbk.

65. See Paul Davidson, "Crude Oil Prices: 'Market Fundamentals' or Speculation?" *Challenge* 51 (2008), 110–18. BP, ExxonMobil, Royal Dutch / Shell, CITGO, and Marathon, collectively controlling (directly or indirectly) more than 58 percent of the access to aggregate gasoline sales in the United States have all put greater reliance upon trading units since 2007. See Kent F. Moors, Affidavit of March 10, 2008, *Siegel v. Shell et al.* (U.S. District Court for the Eastern District of Illinois, Docket 06 D 0035), §35.

66. See Alex Lawler, "BP's Oil Trading Profit Weakens as Contango Eases," *Reuters* (April 27, 2010), available at: www.reuters.com/article/idUSLDE63Q 19B20100427. See also, for example, Fabian Kesicki, "The Third Oil Price Surge—What's Different This Time?" *Energy Policy* 38 (2010), 1596–1606; Takashi Kanamura, Svetlozar T. Rachve, and Frank J. Fabozzi, "A Profit Model for Spread Trading with an Application to Energy Futures," *The Journal of Trading* 5 (2010), 48–62; and "What Do We Learn from the Price of Crude Oil Futures?" *Journal of Applied Econometrics* 25 (2010), 539–573.

67. Moors, Affidavit, *Siegel*, loc it, §45.

68. See, for example, Robert Campbell, "Conoco Aims for Global Trading Role with Revamp," *Reuters* (January 28, 2010), available at: www.reuters .com/article/idUSN2811790020100128; Tom Grieder, "Prime Minister of Singapore Vows to Protect Oil Companies' Interests," *Global Insight* (July 15, 2010)—Exxon Shell and PetroChina expanding trading from the Singapore exchange; and Paul Young and Jorge Montepeque," Saudi Aramco Plans to Start Oil Trading Firm," *Platt's Oilgram News* 88 (May 4, 2010), 6.

69. Technically in the futures markets, a crack spread is simultaneously buying and selling contracts for crude oil and oil products coming out of a refinery process, usually gasoline and heating oil. In point of fact, however, the transactions can involve a number of other products—diesel (the most-often seen additional element on the distilled side of a crack spread), kerosene, jet fuel (actually high end kerosene), and naphtha (a group of light-end distillation cuts used as feeder stock for high octane gasoline or other applications in refining and the production of petrochemicals). Gasoline (or RBOB, the "reformulated gasoline blendstock for oxygen blending," now the traded NYMEX gasoline contract) and low sulfur-content heating oil remain the most used due to the close pricing connection between their contracts in the trading process.

70. The optimal production mix is the most efficient and highest returning selection of production segments, given the refinery's capacity, complexity, how high a percentage of the crude oil throughput can be processed, and wholesale market requirements, among other factors. It is the point at which

net profits from sales are maximized, that is, the refinery margin is at its greatest. See Wafa B. E. Al-Othman, Haitham M. S. Lababidi, Imad M, Alayiqi, and Khawla Al-Shayji, "Supply Chain Optimization of Petroleum Organization under Uncertainty in Market Demands and Prices," *European Journal of Operational Research* 189 (2008), 822–840; Lee Ying Koo, Arief Aditha, Rajagopalan Srinivasan, and I. A. Karimi, "Decision Support for Integrated Refinery Supply Chains," *Computers & Chemical Engineering* 32 (2008) 2787–2800; and Tsiakis Panagiolis and Lazaros G. Papageorgiou, "Optimal Production Allocation and Distribution Supply Chain Networks," *International Journal of Production Economics* 111 (2008), 468–483.

The optimum production mix cannot be determined without knowing the actual running distillation capacity of the refinery. There are two standards applied here. The first is *barrels per stream day* (BPSD) and the second is *barrels per calendar day* (BPCD). The former is always a few percent higher, thereby providing a temptation to use it. However, BPSD measures the maximum number of input barrels a facility can process when running at maximum capacity under optimal crude and processed product market and sale conditions without providing for any down time. BPCD calculates under normal conditions with down time—more realistic, but providing less pop in the figures. See James G. Gary, Glenn E. Handwerk and Mark J. Kaiser, *Petroleum Refining: Technology and Economics*, 5th ed. (Boca Raton, FL: CRC, 2007), 2.

71. See, for example, Atilim Murat and Ekin Tokat, "Forecasting Price Movements with Crack Spread Futures," *Energy Economics* 31 (2009), 95–90; Paul Berhanu Girma and Albert S. Paulson, "Risk Arbitrage Opportunities in Petroleum Futures Spreads," *Journal of Futures Markets* 19 (1999), 931–955; and Andres Garcia Mirantes, Javiar Poblacion, and Gregorio Serna, "Hedging Refining Margin with Crack Spread Options: A Common Long-Term Trend Model from Crude Oil and Refined Products," (2010), unpublished paper available at: www.pfn2010.org/papers/1268391500.pdf.

72. For an overview of NYMEX crack spread futures and options, see New York Mercantile Exchange, *Crack Spread Handbook*, available at: http://offers .quote.com/marketcenter/pdfs/crack.pdf.

73. See, for example, Matthew Chesnes, "Capacity and Utilization Choice in the U.S. Refinery Industry," (2009), unpublished paper, available at: www .chesnes.com/docs/oil.pdf.; and Carlos Tolmasky and Dmitry Hindanov, "Principal Components Analysis for Correlated Curves and Seasonal Commodities: The Case of the Petroleum Market," *Journal of Futures Markets* 27 (2002), 1019–1035.

74. According to the EIA (www.eia.doe.gov/glossary/index.cfm?id=O), the operable utilization rate "represents the use of the atmospheric crude oil distillation units. The rate is calculated by dividing the gross input to these units

by the operable refining capacity of the units." Operable capacity is a bit more difficult to express. Remember, this is a government agency talking. EIA defines it as "the amount of capacity that, at the beginning of the period, is in operation; not in operation and not under active repair, but capable of being placed in operation within 30 days; or not in operation but under active repair that can be completed within 90 days. Operable capacity is the sum of the operating and idle capacity and is measured in barrels per calendar day or barrels per stream day." On the latter two terms, see note 70 to this chapter. Atmospheric crude oil distillation is how a normal refinery operates. The process involves separating the ingredients in crude oil by heating the oil (distillation) and then condensing the fractions (separate components vaporizing at different temperatures) that result.

75. Figures from the EIA "U.S. Percent Utilization of Refinery Operable Capacity" tables available at: www.eia.gov/dnav/pet/hist/LeafHandler .ashx?n=PET&s=MOPUEUS2&f=M.

76. From 254 operating refineries on January 1, 1982 (the first year EIA published figures) to 137 on January 1, 2010. See EIA, "U.S. Number of Operating Refineries as of January 1," table available at: www.eia.gov/dnav/pet/hist/ LeafHandler.ashx?n=PET&s=8_NA_8OO_NUS_C&f=A.

77. From 13.2 mbd in January 1988 (when EIA begin compiling these statistics) to 15.5 mbd by May 2010. See EIA, "U.S. Gross Input to Refineries" tables available at: www.eia.gov/dnav/pet/hist/LeafHandler .ashx?n=PET&s=MGIRIUS2&f=M.

78. From 15.6 mbd in January 1985 (when EIA began compiling these statistics) to 17.6 mbd by May 2010. See EIA, "U.S. Operable Crude Oil Distillation Capacity," tables available at: www.eia.gov/dnav/pet/hist/LeafHandler.ashx?n =PET&s=MOCLEUS2&f=M.

The EIA assembles refinery capacity and use figures as part of its monthly petroleum supply report. The data then appear in the *Petroleum Supply Monthly* (*PSM*) and the *Weekly Petroleum Status Report* (*WPSR*). Recall, the base for refinery capacity figures is actually crude oil distillation capacity (on which see note 74 to this chapter). Operable capacity includes both refineries operating and capacity available but idle—that is, where start up is possible within 30 days (according to the definition also contained in note 74 to this chapter). Capacity permanently shut is removed from the calculations.

As several commentators have noted, there is a timing delay in the EIA figures that upon occasion makes interpretation difficult. See, for example, Chesnes, loc. cit; Robert K. Kaufmann and Laura D. Shiers, "Alternatives to Conventional Crude: When, How Quickly, and Market Driven?" *Ecological Economics* 67 (2008), 405–411; and Timothy Dunne and Xiaoyi Mu, "Investment Spikes and Uncertainty in the Petroleum Refining Industry,"

Journal of Industrial Economics 58 (2010), 190–213. The problem involves the time lag for the figures reported. The operable capacity totals reported in the *WPSR*, and used to calculate the weekly utilization rate, are updated when the *WPSR* is benchmarked to the latest monthly data, which occurs more than two months after the reporting month, and at least three months after the effective refinery capacity update. This is compounded by a further delay—the EIA requests that respondents (the EIA relies upon data supplied on a voluntary basis by the refineries; there is no independent way of verifying the numbers) report capacity as of the beginning of the reporting month. That can effectively add another month to the time lag once the figures are released.

79. See note 65 to this chapter.

80. At one point in 2005–2006, the average rise in gasoline prices exceeded the average cost of crude oil by as much as 54 percent. See Tim Hamilton, *U.S. Motorists Subsidize French, German, British Drivers"* (Santa Monica, CA: The Foundation for Taxpayer and Consumer Rights, 2006), available at: http://cwd.grassroots.com/energy/rp/6775.pdf.

81. See note 67 to this chapter.

82. Initial rises in gasoline prices may be tempered by company concerns over public reaction or local competition among various providers. However, neither of these ultimately prevents the increase. The dynamics of enhancing profit margins is the controlling factor. The overall issue of gauging retail prices against the cost of crude has held a pivotal position for some time in determining utilization of refinery capacity. See, for example, L. Horn, "Refinery Margin Risk Management," *Petroleum Review*, 50 (1996), 323–325; Severin Borenstein, A. Colin Cameron, and Richard Gilbert, "Do Gasoline Prices Respond Asymmetrically to Crude Oil Price Changes?" *The Quarterly Journal of Economics*, 112 (1997), 305–339; Nathan S. Balke, Stephen P. A. Brown, and Mine Y. Yucel, "Crude Oil and Gasoline Prices: An Asymmetric Relationship?" *Federal Reserve Bank of Dallas Economic Review* (First Quarter 1998), 2–11; Szymon Wlazlowski, "Petrol and Crude Oil Prices: Asymmetric Price Transmission," unpublished paper (2001), available at: http://mpra.ub.uni-muenchen.de/1486/; Matt Lewis, "Asymmetric Price Adjustment and Consumer Search: An Examination of the Retail Gasoline Market," *University of California Energy Institute Center for the Study of Energy Markets Working Papers*, No. 120 (2003), available at: www.escholarship.org /uc/item/6266b54f?display=all#page-1; Robert K. Kaufmann and Cheryl Laskowski, "Causes for an Asymmetric Relation between the Price of Crude Oil and Refined Petroleum Products," *Energy Policy* 33(2005), 1587–1596; Robert K. Kaufmann and Ben Ullman, "Oil Prices, Speculation, and Fundamentals: Interpreting Casual Relations among Spot and Futures Prices," *Energy Economics* 31 (2009), 550–558; Michael Kendrix and W. D. Walls, "Oil Industry Consolidation and Refined Product Prices: Evidence from US

Wholesale Gasoline Terminals," *Energy Policy* 38 (2010), 3498–3507; and Fattouh, loc. cit.

83. CARM provides a profit level for refining utilizing the 2000 margin adjusted for the average cost of crude oil, expenses for refinery maintenance, and inflation. ARM represents the actual refining margin—the difference between actual costs incurred and prices charged. CARM indicates the anticipated profit resulting from a cost-adjusted application of the normal refinery margin applied by the companies themselves prior to 2001. ARM illustrates the actual profitability resulting from an accelerated usage of a rising refinery margin. The difference is pure profit resulting from a greater control over both process and market. The Government Accounting Office (GAO) detected a parallel trend resulting from consolidation in the oil sector, utilizing a very different methodology. See GAO, *Effects of Mergers and Market Concentration in the U.S. Petroleum Industry*, Publication GAO-04–96 (2004), available at: www.gao.gove/sgi-bin/getrpt?GAO-04–96.

84. The study utilized the following refineries: Exxon–Baytown (562,500 bpd; weighted .432), Baton Rouge (503,000 bpd; weighted .386), Joliet (236,600 bpd; weighted .182); Shell–Anacortes (145,000 bpd; weighted .229), Deer Park (333,700 bpd; weighted .526), Martinez (155,600 bpd; weighted .245); BP–Cherry Point (225,000 bpd; weighted .205), Texas City (460,000 bpd; weighted .420), Whiting (410,000 bpd; weighted .375); CITGO–Corpus Christi (156,000 bpd; weighted .207), Lake Charles (429,500 bpd; weighted .571), Lemont (167,000 bpd, weighted: .222); Marathon: Garyville (245,000 bpd; weighted: .481), Robinson (192,000 bpd; weighted: .377), Texas City (72,000 bpd; weighted: .142).

85. OPIS provides daily multiple retail sales readings at over 125,000 locations nationwide.

86. The following eight-step methodology was applied for each daily station reading: (1) data located in the OPIS data base for each retail location utilizing that station's unique OPIS ID number; (2) last retail sales price (LRP) for regular grade gasoline identified for that day's transactions at that location; (3) daily volume sales (in gallons) identified for location; (4) sales volume aggregate for the company on that day calculated by combining location specific volume figures for all 50 locations; (5) each location sales volume divided by aggregate—resulting in a composite sales factor (CSF) for each location; (6) each location's CSF would be multiplied by the LRP figure at that location—resulting in that location's retail price contribution (RPC); (7) All 50 location RPCs are combined; (8) resulting in a retail sales price weighted for actual sales volume at these locations for that company on that date.

The following hypothetical provides an example of how this works. Company 1 location 1 (1.1) had an LRP of $2.00 and a CSF of .1 (representing 10 percent of the aggregate sales at all 50 locations). The RPC for

1.1 would then be $0.20. Company 1 location 2 (1.2) had an LRP of $2.05 and a CSF of .05. The RPC for 1.2 would be $0.1025. The process would be repeated for all 50 locations for that company on that date. The CSF always totals 1 for all 50 locations (or 100 percent of total volume), but the CSF composite provides a more accurate view of actual company revenue.

87. This process involves a modern refinery "cracking" heavy hydrocarbon molecules into lighter ones by a variety of thermal, catalytic hydrocracking and other techniques. This results in a greater volume of product coming out than raw material going in—a sort of bonus from Mother Nature.

88. Moors, Affidavit of February 2, 2008, §8 and Affidavit of March 10, 2008, §38, *Siegel,* loc cit.

89. Compare the tables at www.eia.gov/dnav/pet/hist/LeafHandler.ashx?n= PET&s=RCLC1&f=D and www.eia.gov/dnav/pet/hist/LeafHandler.ashx?n= PET&s=MG_TT_US&f=W.

90. See note 76 to this chapter.

91. See John Porretto, "Exxon Mobil to Sell Stations to Distributors," *New York Sun* (June 3, 2008), available at: www.nysun.com/business/exxon-mobil -to-sell-stations-to-distributors/79934/; and Elizabeth Souder, "Exxon Selling Service Stations, but Brand Isn't Going Away," *Dallas Morning News* (June 13, 2008), available at: www.dallasnews.com/sharedcontent/dws/dn/ latestnews/stories/061308dnbusexxonstatons.263f5e44.html.

92. Among the considerable body of research on this subject, see, for example, Paul R. Zimmerman, "The Competitive Impact of Hypermarket Retailers on Gasoline Prices," unpublished paper (2009), available at: mpra.ub .uni-muenchen.de/20248/1/MPRA_paper_20248.pdf; Justine Hastings, "Wholesale Price Discrimination and Regulation: Implications for Retail Gasoline Prices," unpublished paper (2009), available at: www.econ.brown.edu/ econ/events/Hastings_WPD_Draft200910.pdf; id, "Vertical Relationships and Competition in Retail Gasoline Markets: Empirical Evidence from Contract Changes in Southern California," *American Economic Review*, 94 (2004), 317–328 and the response by Christopher T. Taylor, Nicholas M. Kreisle, and Paul R. Zimmerman, "Vertical Relationships and Competition in Retail Gasoline Markets: Empirical Evidence for Contract Changes in Southern California: Comment," *American Economic Review* 100 (2010), 1269–1276; Justine Hastings and Richard J. Gilbert, "Vertical Integration in Gasoline Supply: An Empirical Test of Raising Rivals' Costs," *Journal of Industrial Economics*, 53 (2005), 437–571; Mark D. Manusziak, "Predicting the Impact of Upstream Mergers on Downstream Markets with an Application to the Retail Gasoline Industry," *International Journal of Industrial Organization* 28 (2010), 99–111; Michael D. Nowl, "Edgeworth Price Cycles: Evidence from the Toronto Retail Gasoline Market," *Journal of Industrial Economics*

55 (2007), 69–92; Severin Borenstein and Andria Shepard, "Sticky Prices, Inventories, and Market Power in Wholesale Gasoline Markets," *RAND Journal of Economics*, 33 (2002), 116–139; Justine Hastings and R. Gilbert, "Vertical Integration in Gasoline Supply: An Empirical Test of Raising Rivals' Costs," *Journal of Industrial Economics*, 53 (2005), 437–571; and S. B. Villas-Boas and R. Hellerstein, "Identification of Supply Models of Retailer and Manufacturer Oligopoly Pricing," *Economics Letters* 90 (2006), 132–140. A version of this argument written for general audiences can be found in Richard Clough, *The Truth behind High Fuel Prices* (Fort Worth: Fullness Publishing, 2006).

93. On the debate, see Kenneth S. Deffeyes, *When Oil Peaked* (New York: Farrar, Straus and Giroux, 2010); id., *Hubbert's Peak: The Impending World Oil Shortage* (Princeton: Princeton University, 2001); id., *Beyond Oil: The View from Hubbert's Peak* (New York: Hill and Wang, 2005); Robert L. Hirsh, Roger Bezdek, and Robert Wendling, *Peaking of World Oil Production: Impacts, Mitigation, and Risk Management* (New York: Novinka, 2007); Colin J. Campbell, *Oil Crisis* (Brentwood: Multi-Science, 2005); David Doostein, *Out of Gas: The End of the Age of Oil* (New York: W. W. Norton, 2004); Duncan Clarke, *The Battle for Barrels: Peak Oil Myths & World Oil Futures* (London: Profile, 2007); Robin M. Mills, *The Myth of the Oil Crisis: Overcoming the Challenges of Depletion, Geopolitics, and Global Warming* (Westport: Prager, 2008); as well as the discussion of Hubbert's approach and its usage in Chapter 3. As should hardly be surprising, the peak oil discussion also morphs into advice on how to survive the end of oil. See, for example, Stephen Leeb with Glen Strathy, *The Coming Economic Collapse: How You Can Thrive When Oil Costs $200 a Barrel* (New York: Warner, 2006) and Brian Hicks and Chris Nelder, *Profit from the Peak: The End of Oil and the Greatest Event of the Century* (Hoboken, NJ: John Wiley & Sons, 2008).

94. This is because volatility is actually measuring standard deviations and in so doing all differentials are squared—no distinction between actual positive and negative numbers, no direction.

95. And that places a significant limitation on the use of the Black–Scholes equation as well as options price forecasting based upon it and its applications in an attempt to limit range. The equation requires constant volatility, something foreign to what markets actually do. See the discussion on Black-Scholes in Chapter 2, the treatment upcoming in Chapter 7 and EIA, "Energy Price Volatility and Forecast Uncertainty," updated monthly at: www.eia.doe.gov/steo/uncertainty.html.

96. See, for example, Richard Barry, *The Management of International Oil Operations* (Tulsa: PennWell, 1993), 129ff.; and Gerard H. Kuper, "Measuring Oil Price Volatility," *University of Groningen, CCSO Centre for Economic Research Working Papers*, No. 200208 (1992), available at: http://ccso.eldoc.ub.rug.nl/FILES/root/2002/200208/200208.pdf.

97. According to the overly limited view practiced by many companies, risk assesses the likelihood or threat of loss from operations or reduced return from investment, and nothing more. Risk in this approach is *managed*. On the other hand, *volatility* extends no further that assessing change from a common standard (still regarded as a norm of stability). Volatility is *offset* or *weathered*. Of course, there is a usage of both terms together in considering options on futures contracts. There, *volatility risk* refers to the risk exposure of an option holder based upon the volatility of the underlying security and/or the view held by a market as a whole that a currently experienced volatility will change. Compare the discussion in Chapter 2.

Chapter 6

1. Neorealism stresses that relations among nations are defined by a distribution of capabilities such that the overall system lacks central authority (i.e., exhibits anarchy), provides structural constraints over objectives and methods, and is characterized by the operations of a number of great powers within it. Nations are formally equal in their sovereign capacities and are essentially equal in needs and desires, but have decidedly asymmetrical capabilities to achieve objectives. Nonetheless, all nations pursue their own interests above those of others and will apply the doctrine of self-help as the underlying premise of action; survival is the driving force. Cooperation among nations is tempered by concerns over the gains made by some states relative to others, with the individual attempts to maximize power providing for the development of balances of power that shape the dimensions of international relations. Kenneth Waltz is best known as a proponent of neorealism (which he refers to as structural realism). See Kenneth Neal Waltz, *Theory of International Politics* (New York McGraw Hill, 1979); id., *Man, the State and War* (New York: Columbia University, 1959); id., "The Emerging Structure of International Politics," *International Security* 18 (1993), 44–79; id., "Structural Realism After the Cold War," *International Security* 25 (2000), 5–41; id., "Realist Thought and Neorealist Theory," *Journal of International Affairs* 44 (1991), 21–37; id., *Realism and International Politics: The Essays of Kenneth Waltz* (New York: Taylor & Francis, 2008); and his five essays contained in Robert O. Keohane, ed., *Neorealism and Its Critics* (New York: Columbia University, 1986). On some of the aspects and criticisms of the approach, see, for example, Robert Powell, "Anarchy in International Relations Theory: The Neorealist-Neoliberal Debate," *International Organization* 48 (1994), 313–344; Harmut Behr and Amelia Heath, "Misreading in IR Theory and Ideology Critique: Morgenthau, Waltz and Neo-Liberalism," *Review of International Studies* 35 (2009), 327–349; Charles L. Glasser, *Rational Theory of International Politics: The Logic of Competition and Cooperation* (Princeton: Princeton University, 2010); and J. Samuel Barkin, *Realist Constructivism: Rethinking International Relations Theory* (New York: Cambridge University, 2010).

2. Robert Gilpin, Global Political Economy: Understanding the International Economic Order (Princeton, NJ: Princeton University, 2001), 15–23.

3. See Paul Stephen Dempsey, "Economic Aggression & Self-Defense in International Law: The Arab Oil Weapon and Alternative American Responses Thereto," Case Western Reserve Journal of International Law 9 (1977), 253–273; and Robert Slater, Seizing Power: The Grab for Global Oil Wealth (Hoboken, NJ: John Wiley & Sons, 2010), 49–61. While providing their share of belligerent rhetoric, Iranian President Mahmoud Ahmadinejad and Venezuelan head of state Huge Chavez are actually limited in delivering on the their threats. Tehran needs to sell crude to the West whether it likes Washington and Brussels or not. It needs to generate hard currency (through oil sales) to offset the rising economic price of sanctions against its nuclear program. Meanwhile, while Chavez continues to rant against the United States, Venezuela must still sell its crude to American refineries, while at the same time providing adequate volume for its own CITGO refinery and retail network in the U.S. CITGO is owned by Petróleos de Venezuela, S.A. (PDVSA), the state oil company. Neither can actually deliver on his threats without putting his domestic economy into significant difficulty.

4. The most comprehensive treatment remains Robert L. Bradley, Jr., Oil, Gas, and Government: The U.S. Experience, 2 Vols. (Lanham: Rowman and Littlefield, 1996). See also, Norman Nordhauser, "Origins of Federal Oil Regulation in the 1920s," Business History Review 47 (1973), 53–71; Douglas R. Bohi and Milton Russell, Limiting Oil Imports: An Economic History and Analysis (Baltimore, MD: The Johns Hopkins University, 1978); Gary D. Libecap, "The Political Economy of Oil Cartelization in the United States, 1933–1972," Journal of Economic History 49 (1989), 833–855; John M. Blair, The Control of Oil (New York: Pantheon, 1976) and Walter J. Mead, "The Performance of Government in Energy Regulations," The American Economic Review 69 (1979), 52–56.

5. Released on November 10, 2010; see the "Executive Summary" at: www.worldenergyoutlook.org/docs/weo2010/WEO2010_es_english.pdf.

6. Organization for Economic Cooperation and Development, the 28 most developed nations globally and the founders of the IEA back during the Arab oil embargo of 1973–1974.

7. See www.basel-iii-accord.com/. According to the Bank for International Settlements (BIS), Basel III is a comprehensive set of reform measures, developed by The Basel Committee on Banking Supervision, to strengthen the regulation, supervision and risk management of the banking sector. These measures aim to: improve the banking sector's ability to absorb shocks arising from financial and economic stress, whatever the source; improve risk management and governance; while strengthening banks' transparency and disclosures. Meanwhile, the reforms target bank-level, or microprudential, regulation, which will help raise the resilience of individual banking institutions

to periods of stress, macroprudential, system wide risks that can build up across the banking sector as well as the procyclical amplification of these risks over time. See www.bis.org/bcbs/basel3.htm.

8. The Fund for Peace provides the following definition of a failed state:

> A state that is failing has several attributes. One of the most common is the loss of physical control of its territory or a monopoly on the legitimate use of force. Other attributes of state failure include the erosion of legitimate authority to make collective decisions, an inability to provide reasonable public services, and the inability to interact with other states as a full member of the international community. The 12 indicators cover a wide range of state failure risk elements such as extensive corruption and criminal behavior, inability to collect taxes or otherwise draw on citizen support, large-scale involuntary dislocation of the population, sharp economic decline, group-based inequality, institutionalized persecution or discrimination, severe demographic pressures, brain drain, and environmental decay. States can fail at varying rates through explosion, implosion, erosion, or invasion over different time periods.

   See www.fundforpeace.org/web/index.php?option=com_content&task=view&id=102&Itemid=327#3. Some have suggested that the concept is now out of date and needs to be replaced with a more realistic approach to addressing internal instability in developing countries. See, for example, Charles T. Call, "Beyond the 'Failed State': Toward Conceptual Alternatives," *European Journal of International Relations* 17 (2011), forthcoming; and id., "The Fallacy of the 'Failed State," *Third World Quarterly* 29 (2008), 1491–1507.

9. This interchange between the developed (North) and developing (South) has often been characterized by a more concerted attack from the developing against some of the fundamental market assumptions accepted by the developed countries. The rancor tends to become increasingly prevalent with each international financial or economic crisis. This has been the case, for example, in "Southern" reactions to the aftermath of the subprime mortgage crisis, the resulting credit constriction and the decline in dollar-denominated asset value. The South in these cases holds the North responsible. See, for example, Yilmaz Akyüz, "Policy Response to the Global Financial Crisis: Key Issues for Developing Countries," *South Centre Research Papers* 24 (2009), available at: www.southcentre.org/index.php?option=com_docman&task=doc_view&gid=1376&tmpl=component&format=raw&Itemid=99999999&lang=en; Joseph Nathan Cohen, "Neoliberalism's Relationship with Economic Growth in the Developing World: Was It the Power of the Market or the Resolution of Financial Crisis?" (2010), unpublished

paper, available at: http://mpra.ub.uni-muenchen.de/24399/1/Joe_Cohen -Lib_Periodicity.pdf; and Barry K. Gills, "The Return of Crisis in the Era of Globalization: One Crisis, or Many?" *Globalizations* 7 (2010), 1, 3–8.

10. See the discussion in Chapter 2.

11. Kent Moors, "The New Oil Strategy," *MarketWatch* (November 1, 2010), available at: www.marketwatch.com/story/oil-investing-in-heavy-volatility -2010–11–01;l; id., "What Crude Oil Prices Are Telling Us," *Oil and Energy Investor* (October 1, 2010), available at: http://oilandenergyinvestor .com/2010/10/what-crude-oil-prices-are-telling-us/; id., "What Is (and Isn't) Driving Oil Prices," *Oil and Energy Investor* (November 5, 2010), available at: http://oilandenergyinvestor.com/2010/11/what-is-and-isnt -driving-oil-prices/; and id., "How Energy Plays in a Volatile Market," *Energy Advantage Portfolio Update* (August 18, 2010), available at: http:// moneymappress.com/2010/08/18/how-energy-plays-in-a-volatile -market/. See also, Chia-Lin Chang, Michael McAleer and Roengchai Tansuchat, "Forecasting Volatility and Spillovers in Crude Oil Spot, Forward and Futures Markets" (2009), unpublished paper, available at: http://publishing .eur.nl/ir/repub/asset/16107/EI2009–12.pdf.

12. There is a developing body of scholarly literature relating economic consequences of oil production or dependence and the form of government experienced. See, for example, Merrie Gilbert Klapp, *The Sovereign Entrepreneur: Oil Policies in Advanced and Less Developed Capitalist Countries* (Ithaca, NY: Cornell University, 1987); Michael Ross, "Does Oil Hinder Democracy?" *World Politics* 53 (2001), 325–361; Benn Eifert, Alan Gelb, and Nils Borje Tallroth, "The Political Economy of Fiscal Policy and Economic Management in Oil-Exporting Countries," *World Bank Policy Research Papers* No. 2899 (2002), available at: www-wds.worldbank.org/servlet/ WDSContentServer/WDSP/IB/2002/11/01/000094946_0210180511040/ Rendered/PDF/multi0page.pdf; Rudger Ahrend and William Tompson, "Realizing the Oil Supply Potential of the CIS: The Impact of Institutions and Policies," *OECD Economics Department Working Paper* No. 484 (2006), available at: www.oecd.org/officialdocuments/ displaydocumentpdf/?cote= ECO/WKP(2006)12&doclanguage=en; and Oksan Bayulgen, *Foreign Investment and Political Regimes: The Oil Sector in Azerbaijan, Russia, and Norway* (Cambridge: Cambridge University, 2010).

13. See John Hofmeister, *Why We Hate the Oil Companies: Straight Talk from an Energy Insider* (New York: Palgrave Macmillan, 2010); Gene L. Theodori and Douglas Jackson-Smith, "Public Perception of the Oil and Gas Industry: The Good, The Bad, and the Ugly," *SPE Annual Technical Conference* (2010), abstract available at: www.spe.org/atce/2010/pages/schedule/tech_program/documents/ spe1342531.pdf; and Toby Bolsen and Fay Lomax Cook, "Public Opinion on Energy Policy: 1974–2006," *Public Opinion Quarterly* 72 (2008), 364–388.

14. The most direct parallel in recent U.S. history was the reaction to the China National Offshore Oil Corp. (CNOOC) attempted takeover of California-based Unocal in 2005. Congress stepped in to prevent the acquisition, despite the CNOOC bid being higher than the eventual winner Chevron. The result was the erection of a de facto political barrier to foreign acquisition of controlling interest in major American oil companies. See, for example, Kam-Ming Wan and Ka-fu Wong, "Economic Impact of Political Barriers to Cross-Border Acquisitions: An Empirical Study of CNOOC's Unsuccessful Takeover of Unocal," *Journal of Corporate Finance* 15 (2009), 447–468; Kevin McGill, "Selling Away Our Oil: Protectionism and the True Threat Raised by CNOOC's Attempted Acquisition of Unocal," *Georgia State University Law Review* 23 (2007), 657–680; and James A. Dorn, "An Abuse of the Free Market," *South China Morning Post* (August 5, 2005), reprinted at: www.cato .org/pub_display.php?pub_id=4062.

15. See, for example, Robert Pirog, "The Role of National Oil Companies in the International Oil Market," *Congressional Research Service Report to Congress*, RL34137 (2007), available at: http://assets.opencrs.com/rpts/RL34137_ 20070821.pdf; David Lertzman, Percy Garcia, and Harrie Vredenburg, "A National Oil Company as Social Development Agent," *International Review of Business Research Papers* 5 (2009), 1–15; and Paul Stevens, "National Oil Companies and International Oil Companies in the Middle East: Under the Shadow of Government and the Resource Nationalism Cycle," *Journal of World Energy Law & Business* 1 (2008), 5–30.

　　Focus is often directed to Chinese companies, especially in their dealings in Africa and the Caspian basin. See Matthew E. Chen, "Chinese National Oil Companies and Human Rights," *Orbis* 51 (2007), 41–57; Charles E. Ziegler, "Competing for Markets and Influence: Asian National Oil Companies in Eurasia," *Asian Perspective* 32 (2008), 129–163; and Erica S. Downs, "The Fact and Fiction of Sino-African Energy Relations," *China Security* 3 (2007), 42–68. See also, Steven W. Lewis, "Chinese NOCs and World Energy Markets: CNPC, Sinopec and CNOOC," *Baker Institute-Japan Petroleum Energy Center Papers* (2007), available at: www.bakerinstitute.org/programs/ energy-forum/publications/docs/NOCs/Papers/NOC_CNOOC_Lewis .pdf; and Shaofeng Chen, "Motivations behind China's Foreign Oil Quest: A Perspective from the Chinese Government and the Oil Companies," *Journal of Chinese Political Science* 13 (2008), 79–104.

16. See David K. Backus and Mario J. Crucini, "Oil Prices and the Terms of Trade," *Journal of International Economics* 50 (2000), 185–213; David A. Deese, "The Future of World Oil Exports: Assessing Saudi and Gulf State Interests and Strategies," *International Studies Association Annual Meetings* (2008), available at: www.allacademic.com//meta/p_mla_apa_research_ citation/2/5/4/1/7/pages254175/p254175-1.php; and Vlado Vivoda,

"Diversification of Oil Import Sources and Energy Security: A Key Strategy or an Elusive Objective?" *Energy Policy* 37 (2009), 4615–4623.

17. The basis of the economic rent concept used in oil essentially still comes from David Ricardo. As summarized by John Warnock, it translates into the following:

> Within the oil and gas industry today, economic rent is generally defined as the difference between the cost of exploration, field development and extraction and the market price. These costs include a normal rate of return on investment. . . . Economic rent is the surplus that is created by the use of natural resources *over and above* what is necessary to keep labour and capital on the land and producing products.
>
> It is most important to remember that these costs include a normal profit. Economic rent therefore is created when the exploitation of natural resources like oil and gas produce a return that is *over and above* the normal rate of return. Economic rent is a *monopoly profit* or an *excess profit*.

John W. Warnock, *Selling the Family Silver: Oil and Gas Royalties, Corporate Profits, and the Disregarded Public* (Regina: Parkland Institute/Canadian Centre for Policy Alternatives, 2006), 26–27. The entire report is available at: http://parklandinstitute.ca/downloads/reports/FamSilverreport.pdf.
Warnock's analysis emerged during a protracted debate in Alberta over the proper level for oil and gas company royalty taxes, an issue in which I had some direct involvement as an advisor to the provincial government. One of the conclusions drawn by most participants in the debate was the admission that economic rent *as it affects policy outcomes* is very difficult to measure. Dam had early suggested that the size of economic rent is directly related to the size of the field. Kennneth W. Dam, *Oil Resources* (Chicago: University of Chicago, 1976). Such rent is actually passed on to the consumer in the form of increased prices. See Benn Eifert, Alan Gelb, and Nils Borje Tallorth, "Managing Oil Wealth," *Finance & Development: A Quarterly Journal of the IMF* 40 (2003), available at: www.imf.org/external/pubs/ft/fandd/2003/03/eife.htm.

18. Introducing a major ingredient in the so-called "resource curse." See, for example, Terry Lynn Karl, *The Paradox of Plenty: Oil Booms and Petro-States* (Berkeley: University of California, 1997); Michael Ross, "The Political Economy of the Resource Curse," *World Politics* 51 (1999), 297–322; Macartan Humphreys, Jeffery D. Sachs, and Joseph E. Stiglitz, eds. *Escaping the Resource Curse* (New York: Columbia University, 2007); Michael Alexeev and Robert Conrad, "The Elusive Curse of Oil," *Review of Economics & Statistics* 91 (2009), 586–598; Mohsen Mehrara, "Reconsidering the Resource Curse in Oil-Exporting Countries," *Energy Policy* 37 (2009), 1165–1169; and

Gilbert E. Metcalf and Catherine Wolfram, "Cursed Resources? Political Conditions and Oil Market Volatility," (2010), unpublished paper, available at: http://erbdev.bus.umich.edu/Research/Initiatives/colloquiaPapers/Metcalf-WolframOilMarch.pdf.

19. A good statement of the price maker/price taker distinction is found in M. A. Adelman and H. D. Jacoby, "Alternative Methods of Oil Supply Forecasting," *M.I.T. World Oil Project Working Papers*, No. MIT-EL-77–023WP (1977), available at: http://dspace.mit.edu/bitstream/ handle/1721.1/31271/MIT -EL-77–023WP-04140305.pdf?sequence=1. See also M. A. Alderman, *The Economics of Petroleum Supply* (Cambridge: M.I.T., 1993), 145–165; and James L. Smith, "World Oil: Market or Mayhem?" *Journal of Economic Perspectives* 23 (2009), 145–164.

While there are a number of approaches to articulating how one determines a price maker, one good approach is to equate whether decisions on volume released to the market and/or field capacity utilization impact the prices recognized by the price-takers. OPEC by this measure certainly qualifies; the cartel's volume/capacity decisions have such an impact, despite production available from other non-OPEC sources. See Stéphane Dées, Pavlos Karadeloglou, Robert K. Kaufmann, and Marcelo Sánchez, "Modeling the World Oil Market: Assessment of a Quarterly Econometric Model," *Energy Policy* 35 (2007), 178–191.

20. Aside from desiring a stable market providing a reasonable transparent pricing model, the general perception is to regard exporters (price makers) and importers (price-takers) as approaching markets with quite different perspectives. OPEC is certainly the dominant price maker in the global oil market, with the concomitant assumption that cartel members would prefer to maximize the price commanded by the market.

Yet dominant producer Saudi Arabia has had a more temperate view of pricing levels than other members of OPEC, for example Venezuela or Iran, and does regard high price as encouraging alternative energy development and demand destruction. Riyadh has traditionally regarded both as self-defeating to OPEC objectives and production targets. See Roberto A. De Santis, "Crude Oil Price Fluctuations and Saudi Arabia's Behaviour," *Energy Economics* 25 (2003), 155–173.

The disadvantage of being a primary price-taker in this market is found in the dependence required of a domestic economy on the sourcing of an essential component abroad. The full range of national security debates in the United States is a striking testimonial to the mind-set established in such an environment. However, there is a downside as severe on the price-maker side, given the living off revenues without a corresponding investment. See Øystein Noreng, *Crude Power: Politics and the Oil Market* (London: I. B. Taurus, 2002), 118.

It is useful to remember that this distinction does not merely reflect whether a nation provides or consumes oil. It just as fundamentally addresses the primary economic vulnerability presented by that position.

21. An illustrative case in point is the premise of some American as well as other developed nation opposition to the Kyoto Protocol and the attempt to reduce greenhouse gas emissions. What is the point of entering into difficult and sometimes painful attempts to limit emissions if other nations will continue to spew toxins into the atmosphere, and are even permitted to do so by the same international standards that hold the industrialized nations responsible? On the issue, see David G. Victor, *The Collapse of the Kyoto Protocol and the Struggle to Slow Global Warming* (Princeton: Princeton University, 2001); William D. Nordhaus and Joseph G. Boyer, "Requiem for Kyoto: An Economic Analysis of the Kyoto Protocol," *Yale University, Cowles Foundation for Research in Economics*, Discussion Paper No. 1201 (1998), available at: http://cowles.econ.yale.edu/P/cd/d12a/d1201.pdf; and Christoph Bohringer, "The Kyoto Protocol: A Review and Perspectives," *Oxford Review of Economics Policy* 19 (2003), 451–466.

   This is hardly the occasion to debate the merits of such an opinion. However, judging by the tenor this conversation often takes (at least in my experience), it is yet another example of the "In politics, it is often less important what is true as what is believed to be true" approach. See Matthew Parris' well-known missive "The Sad Truth: Appearance Is the New Reality," *The Sunday Times* (July 21, 2007), available at www.timeson line.co.uk/tol/comment/columnists/matthew_parris/article2112757.ece

22. The functionalist school of thought has its base in the European post-war integration experience, but it was presented early on as an alternative to political and constitutional forms of integration. Rather, it posited (at least initially) that cooperation should begin with defined cross-border problems that emphasized the ability to apply technical knowledge and the utilization of ad hoc or problem specific arrangements. As success resulted from these approaches, the assumption is that they could expand into others. See David Mitrany, *Functional Theory of Politics* (New York: St. Martin's, 1975); id., *A Working Peace System: An Argument for the Functional Development of International Organization* (London: Royal Institute of International Affairs, 1944); and id., "The Functional Approach in Historical Perspective," *International Affairs* 47 (1971), 532–543. See also Peter Wolf, "International Organization and Attitude Change: A Re-Examination of the Functionalist Approach," *International Organization* 27 (1973), 347–371; and Lucian M. Ashworth and David Long, eds., *New Perspectives on International Functionalism* (New York: St. Martin's, 1999).

   I must admit there is an ancillary reason for mentioning this school of thought. The dynamics of the way in which international politics treats oil is about as far removed from the functionalist agenda as from any.

23. See Michael Brecher, Johnathan Wilkenfeld, and Patrick James, *Crisis, Conflict, and Instability* (Oxford, UK: Pergamon, 1989); and Arjen Boin, Paul Hart, Eric Stern, and Bengt Sundelius, *The Politics of Crisis Management: Public Leadership under Pressure* (New York: Cambridge University, 2005).

24. Charles P. Kindleberger, *Manias, Panics, and Crashes: A History of Financial Crises*, 5th ed. (Hoboken, NJ: John Wiley & Sons, 2005). Kindleberger approaches a crisis as a brief, ultra-cyclical deterioration of all or most of a group of financial indicators, including short-term interest rates, asset (stock, real estate, land) prices, commercial insolvencies, and failures of financial institutions. See ibid., 1–8.

    Kindleberger's "crisis model" owes heavily to the work of contrarian economic theorist Hyman Minsky. See ibid., 25 f.; Hyman Minsky, "Finance and Stability: The Limits of Capitalism," *The Jerome Levy Economics Institute of Bard College Working Papers*, No. 93 (1999); id., "The Financial Instability Hypothesis: Capitalistic Processes and the Behavior of the Economy," in Charles P. Kindleberger and Jan-Pierre Laffargue, eds., *Financial Crises: Theory, History, and Policy* (Cambridge: Cambridge University, 1982), 13–29; id., *Stabilizing an Unstable Economy*, rep. ed. (New York: McGraw Hill 2008), especially 77ff.; and his well-known *John Maynard Keynes* (New York: Columbia University, 1975), especially 35f. See also Lance Taylor and Stephan A. O'Connell, "A Minsky Crisis," *Quarterly Journal of Economics* 100 Supp. (1985), 871–885; Randall Wray, "Minsky, the Global Financial Crisis, and the Prospects before the U.S.," *Development* 52 (2009), 302–307; Perry Mehrling, "The Vision of Hymn P. Minsky," *Journal of Economic Behavior & Organization* 39 (1999), 129–58; and John Cassidy, *How Markets Fail: The Logic of Economic Calamities* (New York: Farrar, Strauss and Giroux, 2009), 205–217.

25. See Charles P. Kindleberger, *The World in Depression 1929–1939*, rev. ed. (Berkeley: University of California, 1986); id., *Keynesianism vs. Monetarism: And Other Essays in Financial History*, rev. ed. (Milton Park, UK: Routledge, 2006), especially the still-prescient comments "1929 Ten Lessons for Today," 314–320. See also his comments in the 1985 Marshall Lectures published as *International Capital Movements* (Cambridge: Cambridge University Press, 1987). As Kindleberger notes (1–2), the lectures provided an occasion for a rethinking of his 1937 dissertation at Columbia, published as *International Short-Term Capital Movements* (New York: Columbia University, 1937).

    The attempt to define the "crisis" element in the Great Depression has fascinated and perplexed two generations of scholars. Clearly, the crisis included uncertainty and instability, but what constitutes causality remains debated. See, for example, the current head of the Federal Reserve Ben S. Bernanke, "Nonmonetary Effects of the Financial Crisis in the Propagation of the Great Depression," *American Economics Review* 73 (1983), 257–276; id., "The Macroeconomics of the Great Depression: A Comparative Approach,"

Journal of Money. Credit, and Banking 27 (1995), 1–28; and Ben Bernanke and Harold James, "The Gold Standard, Deflation, and Financial Crises in the Great Depression: An International Comparison," in R. Glenn Hubbard, ed., *Financial Markets and Financial Crises.* (Chicago: University of Chicago, 1991), 33–68. See also, for example, Elmus Wicker, *The Banking Panics of the Great Depression* (Cambridge: Cambridge University, 1996), especially 46 ff.; and Maurice Obstfeld and Alan M. Taylor, "The Great Depression as a Watershed: International Capital Mobility over the Long Run," in Michael D. Bordio, Claudia Goldin, and Eugene N. White, eds., *The Defining Moment: The Great Depression and the American Economy in the Twentieth Century* (Chicago: University of Chicago, 1998), 353–402; and Patrick J. Coe, "Financial Crisis and the Great Depression: A Regime-Switching Approach," *Journal of Money, Credit, and Banking* 34 (2002), 76–93.

26. See Kindleberger, *International Capital Movements*, 2.

27. Black defines sovereignty as follows:

> The supreme, absolute and uncontrollable power by which any independent state is governed; supreme political authority; paramount control of the constitution, the self-sufficient source of political power, from which all specific political powers are derived; the international independence of a state, combined with the right and power of regulating its internal affairs without foreign dictation; also a political society, or state, which is sovereign and independent. (Henry Campbell Black, *Black's Law Dictionary*, 5th ed. by the Publisher's Editorial Staff, Joseph R. Nolan, and M. J. Connolly, contributing authors [St. Paul: West Publishing, 1979], 1252).

The doctrine of sovereignty has come under increasing pressure. The rise of multinational corporations, cross-border banking transactions, and international dependence on oil and other raw materials have led to a range of revisions in its meaning and impact. See, for example, Saskia Sassen, *Losing Control? Sovereignty in an Age of Globalization* (New York: Columbia University, 1996); Paul Haslam, "Globalization and Effective Sovereignty: A Theoretical Approach to the State in International Political Economy," *Studies in Political Economy* 58 (1999), 41–68; William Rasch, *Sovereignty and Its Discontents: On the Primacy of Conflict and the Structure of the Political* (London: Birbeck Law, 2004); Tina Hunter and Thomas Storey, "Oil and Political Apparently Do Mix: The Role of Multinational Resource Corporations in National Sovereignty," *Asia Pacific Law Review* 16 (2008), 111–131; John Gledhill, "'The People's Oil': Nationalism, Globalization, and the Possibility of Another Country in Brazil, Mexico, and Venezuela," *Focaal* 52 (2008), 57–74; Klaus Dodds, "A Polar Mediterranean? Accessibility, Resources, and Sovereignty in the Arctic Ocean," *Global Policy* 1 (2010),

303–311; and Rachel Denae Thrasher and Kevin P. Gallagher, "21st Century Trade Agreements: Implications for Development Sovereignty," *Denver Journal of International Law & Policy* 38 (2010), 313–350.

Carmody suggests that the contemporary revisions in how developed national ideas of sovereignty counteract with those in the developing world, viewed from the standpoint of the "North-South" debate with particular reference to oil, has perpetuated endemic problems while producing a "cruciform" structure of sovereignty. Pádraig Carmody, "Matrix Governance, Cruciform Sovereignty and the Poverty Regime in Africa," *Institute for International Integration Studies Discussion Papers*, No. 267 (2008), available at: www.tcd.ie/iiis/documents/discussion/pdfs/iiisdp267.pdf.

> Structurally, matrix governance represents a horizontal sharing of Northern countries' sovereignty and power, which is then projected southwards to ensure vertical sovereignty sharing and continued resource extraction; giving sovereignty a global cruciform structure.
>
> This undemocratic structure of global governance, and the transnational contract of extroversion between corporations and state elites which underpins it, paradoxically, helps to produce conditions conducive to conflict and corruption, recreating the conditions for its own perpetuation. (Id., 4)

Overall in the case of oil, the rise of IOCs and the global oil market has complicated the doctrine of sovereignty when applied to extraction and sale. While the land remains under the jurisdiction of the home government, and thereby within the purview of a traditional application of sovereignty, the production is now at least partially under the control of a foreign major, especially if the contract for development is a concession. See Michael Klein, "Bidding for Concessions," *Revista de análisis económico* 13 (1998), 35–50. Even when the arrangement is a production sharing agreement (PSA), in which the state typically does not relinquish formal ownership but rather allows the operating company to recover expenses and profit from the sale of the oil, the *de facto* contractual provisions for such compensation places the ownership of at least that part of production in question. In most cases, it effectively segregates a factor of extraction from the exercise of sovereignty. This is hardly a recent issue. See the interesting study by Marcelo Bucheli, "Multinational Corporations and Business Negotiations under the Monroe Doctrine: Lord Cowdray and Oil Policies in Columbia," (2007), working paper available at: www.business .illinois.edu/working_papers/papers/07–0115.pdf.

The pressures put on sovereignty by the rise of multinational corporations and cross-border investment has led to a call for transnational regulation to augment the traditional position of sovereignty in addressing impact. See, for example, Larry Catá Backer, "Multinational Corporations as Objects and Sources of Transnational Regulation," *ILSA Journal of International and Comparative Law* 14 (2008), 499–523; and Jonathan Crystal, "Sovereignty, Bargaining and the International Regulation of Foreign Direct Investment," *Global Society* 23 (2009) 225–243.

28. There is a pervasive relationship between power (both its application and perception) and the exercise of national interest across borders. See Freeman's well-known definition:

> Power is the capacity to direct the decisions and actions of others. Power derives from strength and will. Strength comes from the transformation of resources into capabilities. Will infuses objectives with resolve. Strategy marshals capabilities and brings them to bear with precision. Statecraft seeks through strategy to magnify the mass, relevance, impact, and irresistibility of power. It guides the ways the state deploys and applies its power abroad. These ways embrace the arts of war, espionage, and diplomacy. The practitioners of these three arts are the paladins of statecraft. (Charles W. Freeman, Jr., *Arts of Power: Statecraft and Diplomacy* [Washington: United States Institute of Peace, 1997], 3. See also Talcott Parsons, "On the Concept of Political Power," *Proceedings of the American Philosophical Society* 107 [1963], 232–262; and Michael Barnett and Raymond Duvall, "Power in International Politics," *International Organization* 59 [2005], 39–75)

29. The utilization of power arises from asymmetrical relationships between and among nations. It is, therefore, always perceived in relative terms. See Herbert A. Simon, "Notes on the Observation and Measurement of Political Power," *Journal of Politics* 15 (1953), 500–516; James A. Caporaso, "Dependence, Dependency, and Power in the Global System: A Structural and Behavioral Analysis," *International Organization* 32 (1978), 13–43; and Robert O. Keohane and Joseph S. Nye, Jr., "Power and Interdependence Revisited," *International Organization* 41 (1987), 725–753.

30. Rapid changes in volatility will affect the total marginal cost of production as well as the marginal value of storage. See Robert S. Pindyck, "Volatility and Commodity Price Dynamics," *Journal of Futures Markets* 24 (2004), 1029–1047.

31. See Frederick van der Ploeg, "Aggressive Oil Extraction and Precautionary Saving: Coping with Volatility," *Journal of Public Economics* 94 (2010), 421–433.

32. See, for example, Mohsen Mehrara, "Energy Consumption and Economic Growth: The Case of Oil Exporting Countries," *Energy Policy* 35 (2007), 2939–2945; M. Hakan Berument, Nildag Basat Ceylan, and Nukhet Dogan, "The Impact of Oil Price Shocks on the Economic Growth of Selected MENA Countries," *Energy Journal* 31 (2010), 149–176; Olivier

J. Blanchard, Mitali Dias and Hamid Faruqee, "The Initial Impact of the Crisis in Emerging Market Countries," David E. Romer and Justin Wolfers, eds., *Brookings Papers on Economic Activity* (Spring 2010), 263–307; Subhes C. Bhattacharyya and Andon Blake, "Analysis of Oil Export Dependency of MENA Countries: Drivers, Trends and Prospects," *Energy Policy* 38 (2010), 1098–1107; and Mohsen Mehrara, "Effects of Oil Price Shocks on Industrial Production: Evidence from Some Oil-Exporting Countries," *OPEC Energy Review* 33 (2009), 170–183.

33. That is, regard the volatility as comprising one or more shocks. The shocks, in turn, are held to be unpredictable and largely caused by exogenous factors; but often shocks exhibiting genuinely different causalities are not adequately differentiated. See Lutz Kilian, "Not All Oil Price Shocks Are Alike: Disentangling Demand and Supply Shocks in the Crude Oil Market," *American Economic Review* 99 (2009), 1953–1969; and the more expansive working paper version (2006), available at: www.vanderbilt.edu/econ/sempapers/Kilian.pdf; Gert Peersman and Arnoud Stevens, "Oil Demand and Supply Shocks: An Analysis in an Estimated DSGE-Model," (2010), working paper, available at: www.qass.org.uk/2010-May_Brunel-conference/Stevens.pdf.; and Prakash Loungani, "Oil Price Shocks and the Dispersion Hypothesis," *Review of Economics and Statistics* 68 (1986), 546–539. DSGE stands for "dynamic stochastic general equilibrium."

34. A price maker gains in a volatile market to the extent that it is able to use its production to generate higher prices without cutting demand. See, for example, Rudolfs Bems and Irineu de Carvalho Filho, "Exchange Rate Assessments: Methodologies for Oil Exporting Countries," *International Monetary Fund Working Papers*, No. WP/09/281 (2009); available at: www.imf.org/external/pubs/ft/wp/2009/wp09281.pdf. It must also pay particular attention to the domestic fiscal policy implications of the policy. See Zeljko Bogetic, Karlils Smits, Nina Budina and Sweder van Wijnbergen, "Long-Term Fiscal Risks and Sustainability in an Oil-Rich Country: The Case of Russia," *World Bank Policy Research Paper,* No.5240 (2010), available at: http://elibrary.worldbank.org/docserver/5240.pdf.

35. The OPEC Secretariat in Vienna first determines the overall global demand. It then deducts from that figure the production estimated from non-OPEC countries. The remainder is the "call on OPEC." That is then fulfilled by applying the members' monthly quotas. The quotas are evaded by individual cartel states, but are also acceded to about 55 percent of the time.

On the overall determination of the call on OPEC and the production implications, see, for example, Robert K. Kaufmann, Andrew Bradford, Laura H. Belanger, John P. Mclaughlin and Yosule Miki, "Determinants of OPEC Production: Implications for OPEC Behavior," *Energy Economics* 30 (2008), 333–351; James A. Griffin and David J. Teece, eds., *OPEC Behaviour and*

World Oil Prices (London: Allen & Unwin, 1982); and Finn Roar Aune, Klaus Mohn, Petter Osmundsen and Knut Einar Rosendahl, "Industry Upheaval, OPEC Response—and Oil Price Formation" (2007), unpublished paper, available at: www.uis.no/getfile.php/Forskning/Vedlegg/09%20%C3%98konomi/KM0705_FRI.pdf.

On the membership adherence to quotas, see Douglas B. Reynolds and Michael K. Pippenger, "OPEC and Venezuelan Oil Production: Evidence against a Cartel Hypothesis," Sel Dibooglu and Salim N. Al Gudhea, "All Time Cheaters versus Cheaters in Distress: An Examination of Cheating and Oil Prices in OPEC," *Economic Systems* 31 (2007), 292–310; and Dag Harald Claes, *The Politics of Oil-Producer Cooperation* (Boulder, CO: Westview, 2001), one of the best analytic works on OPEC ever written. Claes suggests that:

> The OPEC members can be assumed to know that their relationship will prevail in the foreseeable future and that the basis for the collective action, the quotas, can be changed in a few months' time. The quotas are in principle open for renegotiation at every OPEC meeting. In such iterated games . . . the strategy of noncooperation can no longer be a dominant strategy. . . . The higher the discount factor—that is, the more value the players can attach to future gains—the lower the subset of cooperators . . . needed in this equilibrium.

Id., 261–262. On the background Claes uses to establish the parameters of choice, see Robert Axelrod, *The Evolution of Cooperation* (New York; Basic Books, 1984), especially 3–26; Robert Axelrod and Robert O. Keohane, "Achieving Cooperation under Anarchy: Strategies and Interpretations," in Kenneth A. Oye, ed., *Cooperation under Anarchy* (Princeton: Princeton University, 1986), 226–246; and Thomas Schelling, *Micromotives and Macrobehavior* (New York: W. W. Norton, 1978), especially 9–44.

Barros, Gil-Alana, and Payne have advanced an interesting analysis using a fractional integration modeling framework to study structural breaks and outliers in OPEC member production between January 1973 and October 2008. They conclude that, ". . . shocks affecting the structure of OPEC oil production will have persistent effects in the long run for all countries, and in some cases the effects are expected to be permanent." Carlos Pestana Barros, Luis A. Gil-Alana, and James E. Payne, "An Analysis of Oil Production by OPEC Countries: Persistence, Breaks and Outliers," *Energy Policy* 39 (2011), forthcoming.

36. See the discussion in Chapter 5. The notion of demand destruction remains one in flux. Certainly, rapidly accelerating prices will constrain economic development and result in a decline in demand. Yet, the nature of that "destruction" remains under some doubt. See note 13 in Chapter 5; also

Battam Fattouh, "The Drivers of Oil Prices: The Usefulness and Limitations of Non-Structural Model, the Demand-Supply Framework and Informal Approaches," *Centre for Financial and Management Studies Discussion Papers,* No. 71 (2007), available at: www.cefims.ac.uk/documents/research-64.pdf; Leonardo Maugeri, "Understanding Oil Price Behavior through an Analysis of a Crisis," *Review of Environmental Ethics and Policy* 3 (2009), 147–166; Antonio Merino and Rebeca Albacete, "Econometric Modeling for Short-Term Oil Prime Forecasting," *OPEC Energy Review* 34 (2010), 25–41; "Demand Destruction from Peak Oil," *Peak Oil Proof* (November 9, 2010), available at: www.peakoilproof.com/2010/11/demand-destruction-from -peak-oil.html; and Tony Allison, "The Coming Oil Train Wreck," *Financial Sense Observations* (December 12, 2008), available at: www.financialsensearchive .com/Market/allison/2008/1222.html.

37. Where volatility is intensifying and the presumption is for prices to be increasing—the current scenario—an increase in aggregate supply on the market is the almost inevitable result. Producing countries have little recourse in an attempt to maintain effective revenue flow. See Leonid Kogan, Dmitry Livdan, and Amir Yaron, "Oil Futures Prices in a Production Economy with Investment Constraints," *Journal of Finance* 64 (2009), 1345–1375; Andres Gallo, Paul Mason, Steve Shapiro, and Michael Fabritius, "What Is behind the Increase in Oil Prices? Analyzing Oil Consumption and Supply Relationship with Price," *Energy* 35 (2010), 416–41; and Lutz Kilian, "Oil Price Volatility: Origins and Effects," *World Trade Organization, Economic Research and Statistics Division Staff Working Papers,* No. ERSD-2010–2 (2010), available at: www.wto.int/english/res_e/reser_e/ersd201002_e.pdf.

38. See the discussion in Chapters 1 and 2 above, as well as Svetlana Borovkova and Ferry J. Permana, "Implied Volatility in Oil Markets," *Computational Statistics & Data Analysis* 53 (2009), 2022–2039; Bradley T. Ewing and Farooq Malik, "Estimating Volatility Persistence in Oil Prices under Structural Breaks," *Financial Review* 45 (2010), 1011–1023; Ron Alquist and Lutz Kilian, "What Do We Learn from the Price of Crude Oil Futures?" *Journal of Applied Econometrics* 25 (2010), 539–573; Ying Fan and Lei Zhu, "A Real Options Based Model and Its Application to China's Overseas Oil Investment Decisions," *Energy Economics* 32 (2010), 627–637; and J. Glenn Andrews and Ehud I. Ronn, "Content of Options on Crude-Oil Futures Contracts," (2009), working paper, available at: www.wsuc3m.com/2/ Ehud-Ronn_ValInfoOpts1.pdf.

39. Although, crude oil prices are not necessarily the primary ingredient in determining overall VIOC profit spreads. See the discussion of refinery margins in Chapter 5 above.

40. In normal market situations, conservation makes sense only to the point that it begins adversely impacting productivity. When it moves beyond

that benchmark, it is in reaction to a crisis environment and will almost always result in a contraction of economic activity. See, for example, Jason E. Bordoff and Gilbert E. Metcalf, "Breaking the Boom-Bust Oil Cycle," *The New Republic* (January 2009), available at: www.brookings.edu/opinions/2009/0106_oil_cycle_bordoff.aspx; Ted Robert Gurr, "On the Political Consequences of Scarcity and Economic Decline," *International Studies Quarterly* 29 (1985), 51–75; and Jörg Friderichs, "Global Energy Crunch: How Different Parts of the World Would React to a Peak Oil Scenario," 38 *Energy Policy* (2010), 4562–4569.

41. Research consistently indicates a correlation between lowering oil prices resulting in an increase in consumption. Absent significant exogenous factors (such as the current ebbing financial crisis), conservation declines in impact once the prices of crude oil and oil products reverse. See, for example, Dermot Gately, "The Imperfect Price-Reversibility of World Oil Demand," *C. V. Starr Center for Applied Economics Research Reports*, No. 92–21 (1992), available at: http://econ.as.nyu.edu/docs/IO/9391/RR92-21.pdf; Eva Regnier, "Oil and Energy Price Volatility," *Energy Economics* 29 (2007), 405–427; Hillard G. Huntington, "Short- and Long-Run Adjustments in U.S. Petroleum Consumption," *Energy Economics* 32 (2010), 63–72; and Olivier J. Blanchard and Marianna Riggi, "Why Are the 2000s So Different from the 1990s? A Structural Interpretation of Change in the Macroeconomic Effects of Oil Prices," *National Bureau of Economic Research Paper*, No. w15467 (2009), available at: http://phdschool-economics.dse.uniroma1.it/website/workshop/RIGGIW09.pdf.

42. See, for example, Stefan F. Schubert and Stephen J. Turnovsky, "The Impact of Oil Prices on an Oil-Importing Developing Economy," *Journal of Development Economics* 94 (2011), 18–29; Syed A. Basher and Perry Sadorsky, "Oil Price Risk and Emerging Stock Markets," *Global Finance Journal* 17 (2006), 224–251; H. Günsel Doğrul and Ugur Soytas, "Relationship between Oil Prices, Interest Rate, and Unemployment: Evidence from an Emerging Market," *Energy Economics* 32 (2010), 1523–1528 (a study of the Turkish market); Paresh Kumar Narayan and Seema Narayan, "Modeling the Impact of Oil Prices on Vietnam's Stock Prices," *Applied Energy* 87 (2010), 356–361; and the comments by Bank of Chile Governor José De Gregario, "Recent Challenges of Inflation Targeting," *Bank for International Settlements Papers*, No. 51 (2010), available at: www.bis.org/publ/bppdf/bispap51c.pdf?frames=0.

43. See, for example, Matt Elbeck, "Advancing the Design of a Dynamic Petro-Dollar Currency Basket," *Energy Policy* 38 (2010), 1938–1945; Michael B. Devereux, Kang Shi, and Juanyi Xu, "Oil Currency and the Dollar Standard: A Simple Analytical Model of an International Trading Currency," *Journal of Money, Credit, and Banking* 42 (2010), 521–550; Mohamed El Hedi Arouri

ad Christophe Rault, "Oil Prices and Stock Markets: What Drives What in the Gulf Corporation Council Countries?" *CESinfo Working Papers*, No. 2934 (2010), available at: www.cesifo-group.de/pls/guestci/download/CESifo%20Working%20Papers%202010/CESifo%20Working%20Papers%20January%202010/cesifo1_wp2934.pdf; and José De Gregario, "Implementation of Inflation Targets," in Gill Hammond, Ravi Kanbur and Eswar Prasad, eds. *Monetary Frameworks for Emerging Markets* (Cheltenham: Edward Elgar, 2009), 40–58.

44. One of the ways an industrializing country can offset a dollar-adjusted rise in the price of oil imports, especially when those dollars are worth less than in the past, is to develop advancing production positions expanding proceeds from export markets. This has certainly allowed China to offset an increasing need for energy without generating significant inflationary pressure. See Weiqi Tang, Libo Wu, and Zhong Xiang Zhang, "Oil Price Shocks and Their Short- and Long-Term Effects on the Chinese Economy," *Energy Economics* 32, Supplement 1 (2010), S3–S14; João Ricardo Faria, André Varella Mollick, Pedro H. Albuquerque, and Miguel A. Léon-Ledesma, "The Effect of Oil Price on China's Exports," *China Economic Review* 20 (2009), 793–805; and Saang Joon Baak, "The Bilateral Real Exchange Rates and Trade between China and the U.S.," *China Economic Review* 19 (2008), 117–127.

45. The Asian premium is the best known. Up until 2009, Asian importing countries would have expected to pay as much as $6 more per barrel for Arab Light benchmark crude than would European or American importers. That premium has averaged $1.20 since 1988. Now, however, the premium is averaging less than $1 a barrel and has even moved into a *discount* upon occasion. There are some crack spreads (differentials in the pricing of refined oil products) that create variations, but the balance is shifting price advantages to Asian demand. See Carolyn Cui and Liam Pleven, "Economic Clout Earns Asia a Discount," *The Wall Street Journal Asia* (May 25, 2010); available at: http://online.wsj.com/article/SB10001424052748703341904575266913913683300.html; also, Ian Coxhead and Sisira Jayasuriya, "China, India, and the Commodity Boom: Economics and Environmental Implications for Low-Income Countries," *The World Economy* 33 (2010), 525–551.

46. See, for example, Théo Naccache, "Slow Oil Shocks and the Weakening of the Oil Price-Macroeconomy Relationship," *Energy Policy* 38 (2010), 2340–2345; Michael Alexeev and Robert Conrad, Babatunde Olatunji Odusami, "To Consume or Not: How Oil Prices Affect the Co-Movement of Consumption and Aggregate Wealth," *Energy Economics* 32 (2010), 857–867; "The Elusive Curse of Oil," *Review of Economics & Statistics* 91 (2009), 586–598; Akira Maeda, "On the Oil Price-GDP Relationship," *Japanese Economy* 35

(2008), 99–127; and Rebeca Jiménez-Rodriquez and Marcelo Sánchez, "Oil Price Shocks and Real GDP Growth: Empirical Evidence for Some OECD Countries," *Applied Economics* 37 (2005), 201–228.

47. The most visible proponent of this view is the contrarian analyst Robert Bryce. See his *Gusher of Lies: The Dangerous Delusions of "Energy Independence"* (New York: Public Affairs, 2008); and id., *Power Hungry: The Myths of "Green" Energy and the Real Fuels of the Future* (New York: Public Affairs, 2010).

48. There are four major uses of crude oil. Significant alternative applications have emerged in three—petrochemicals, electricity generation, and industrial purposes. It is the fourth and largest, as a transport fuel, that continues to require massive reliance on oil. The transition to natural gas-powered vehicles would seem the most immediate possibility, given the additional expense and technical development required to bring alternatives on line. However, some interesting progress has been made on the margins. See, for example, Kent Moors, "The Prototype for a Major New Energy Industry," *Oil and Energy Investor* (July 12, 2010), available at: http://oilandenergyinvestor .com/2010/07/new-energy-industry/. On the transition in transport fuels, see, for example, Eric Spiegel and Neil McArthur with Rob Norton, *Energy Shift: Game-Changing Options for Fueling the Future* (New York: McGraw Hill, 2009); Leonardo Maugeri, *Beyond the Age of Oil: The Myths, Realities, and Future of Fossil Fuels and Their Alternatives* (Santa Barbara: Praeger, 2010), Jonathan T. Hine, Jr., trans; and Thomas Homer-Dixon, eds., *Carbon Shift: How the Twin Crises of Oil Depletion and Climate Change Will Define the Future* (Toronto: Random House of Canada, 2009). On natural gas, compressed natural gas (CNG) and bio-gas, see R. S. Taylor, P. Tertzakian, T. Wall, J. Wilkinson, M. Graham, P. J. Young and S. W. Harbinson, "Natural Gas: The Green Fuel of the Future," *Canadian Unconventional Resources and International Petroleum Conference/Society of Petroleum Engineers*, Paper No. 136-MS (2010), abstract available at: www.onepetro.org/mslib/servlet/ onepetropreview?id=SPE-136866-MS&soc=SPE; Fearghal Ryan and Brian Cauldfield, "Examining the Benefits of Using Bio-CNG in Urban Bus Operations," *Transportation Research: Part D: Transport and Environment* 15 (2010), 362–365; Andrea Stoccheti and Giuseppe Volpato, "In Quest for a Sustainable Motorisation: The CNG Opportunity," *International Journal of Automotive Technology and Management* 10 (2010), 13–36; and Paul Jarod Murphy, "The Role of Natural Gas as a Vehicle Transportation Fuel," M.S. Thesis in Technology and Policy, M.I.T. (2010), available at: http://dspace .mit.edu/handle/1721.1/59773. On biofuels, see also note 53 in this chapter.

49. The energy independence debate has been perhaps the most disingenuous discussion in recent U.S. policy history. It often includes patently incorrect assumptions and the idea that, if a solution is theoretically possible, it must therefore be a practical solution. Genuinely removing the nation

from dependence on foreign oil is not possible. Period. The solution is, of course, to wean ourselves from crude oil and move into another energy source altogether. But that is an enormous undertaking. And all the rhetoric aside, we have no clue how this is to be done. On the side of advocating oil independence, we have such works as: Jay Hakes, *A Declaration of Energy Independence: How Freedom from Foreign Oil Can Improve National Security, Our Economy, and the Environment* (Hoboken, NJ: John Wiley & Sons, 2008); Davis Sandalow, *Freedom from Oil: How the Next President Can End the United States' Oil Addiction* (New York: McGraw Hill, 2008); Alfred Theurich, *Independence Day 2030: Freedom from Foreign Oil* (Frederick: Publish America, 2009); Newt Gingrich, *Drill Here, Drill Now, Pay Less: A Handbook for Slashing Gas Prices and Solving Our Energy Crisis* (Washington: Regnery, 2008); Ian Rutledge, *Addicted to Oil: America's Relentless Drive for Energy Security* (London: I. B. Taurus, 2008); Gordon H. Dahle, *Energy Independence* (Parker: Outskirts Press, 2007); Paul Bures, *America: The Oil Hostage* (College Station: Virtualbookworm.com, 2006); Robert Zubrin, *Energy Victory: Winning The War on Terror by Breaking Free of Oil* (Amherst: Prometheus, 2007); Terry Tamminen, *Lives Per Gallon: The True Cost of Our Oil Addiction* (Washington: Island Press, 2006); and Raymond J. Learsey, *Over a Barrel: Breaking the Middle East Oil Cartel* (Nashville: Nelson Current, 2005). The most adamant figure rejecting the possibility of energy independence is Robert Bryce. See the works cited in note 47 to this chapter; also, Pietro S. Nivola, "Rethinking 'Energy Independence,'" *Governance Studies at Brookings* (December 30, 2008), available at: www.brookings.edu/~/media/Files/rc/papers/2008/1230_energy_nivola/1230_energy_nivola.pdf; David L. Greene, "Measuring Energy Security: Can the United States Achieve Oil Independence?" *Energy Policy* 38 (2010), 1614–1621; and Robin M. Mills, *The Myth of the Oil Crisis: Overcoming the Challenges of Depletion, Geopolitics, and Global Warming* (Westport: Praeger, 2008).

50. U.S. production has declined from 3.52 billion barrels in 1970 to 1.96 billion barrels in 2009, a decline of 56 percent. Energy Information Administration, "U.S. Field Production of Crude Oil," available at: www.eia.gov/dnav/pet/hist/LeafHandler.ashx?n=PET&s=MCRFPUS1&f=A.

51. See Editorial Staff, "Is the North Sea Oil Production Bonanza Approaching Twilight?" *Oil Price* (February 24, 2010), available at: http://oilprice.com/Energy/Crude-Oil/Is-the-North-Sea-Oil-Production-Bonanza-Approaching-Twilight.html; see the U.K. Department of Energy and Climate Change (DECC) figures compiled by Mike Earp at: www.og.decc.gov.uk/information/bb_updates/chapters/production_projections.pdf

52. Unconventional oil refers to sources that can be liquefied like conventional crude, but are extracted by methods other than a traditional oil well.

53. Ethanol was at one point hailed as a solution to the gasoline problem but has since witnessed a decline in enthusiasm for two reasons: (1) the dislocation

caused to the corn-based food and product cycle, leading to increases in food and related expenses; and (2) the problem in generating sufficient energy to offset the energy expended in its production. Alternative sourcing for ethanol production, other than corn, has shown some prospects, but the problem remains from committing a large amount of growing acreage only for the production of fuel. In addition, the energy achieved is on average only 75−84 percent of that found in gasoline, requiring either a greater amount of ethanol or a preferred ethanol-gasoline mix.

According to Peter Hubbard, first-generation biofuels are produced by fermenting plant-derived sugars from such crops as corn and sugar beets. Second generation biofuels make use of the residual nonfood parts of plants, commonly called cellulose, which contains complex carbohydrates that require advanced methods to extract before fermentation. Third-generation biofuels are derived from algae and have a theoretical yield up to 30 times that of traditional biofuels. See Peter Hubbard, "Biofuels and the Developing World," *Bologna Center Journal of International Affairs*, Special Volume (2008), available at: http://bcjournal.org/2008/biofuels-and-the-developing-world/.

On the broader issues regarding ethanol, see, for example, Régis Rathmann, Alexandre Szklo, and Roberto Schaeffer, "Land Use Competition for Production of Food and Liquid Biofuels: An Analysis of the Arguments in the Current Debate," *Renewable Energy* 35 (2010), 14−22; Paul C. Westcott, "Ethanol Expansion in the U.S.: How Will the Agricultural Sector Adjust? *United States Department of Agriculture, Economic Research Service Reports*, FDS-07D-01 (2007), available at: www.ers.usda.gov/Publications/FDS/2007/05May/FDS07D01/fds07D01.pdf; David Pimentel, Tad Patzek, and Gerald Cecil, "Ethanol Production: Energy, Economic, and Environmental Losses," *Review of Environmental Contamination and Toxicology* 189 (2007), 25−41; Olga V. Naidenko, "Ethanol-Gasoline Fuel Blends May Cause Human Health Risks and Engine Issues," *Environmental Working Group* (May 18, 2009), available at: www.ewg.org/files/2009/ethanol-gasoline-white-paper.pdf; and C. Ford Runge and Benjamin Senauer, "How Biofuels Could Starve the Poor, *Foreign Affairs* 86 (2007), 41−53.

54. See Lester G. Telser, "A Theory of Speculation Relating Profitability and Stability," *Review of Economics and Statistics* 41(1959), 295−301; John A Carlson and Carol L. Osler, "Rational Speculators and Exchange Rate Volatility," *European Economic Review* 44 (2000), 231−253; T. Klitgaard and L. Weir, "Exchange Rate Changes and Net Positions of Speculators in the Futures Market," *Federal Reserve Bank of New York Economic Policy Review* 10 (2004), 17−28; and Robert K. Kaufmann, "The Role of Market Fundamentals and Speculation in Recent Price Changes for Crude Oil," *Energy Policy* 39 (2011) forthcoming.

55. In commodities markets, speculators decidedly favor being short while hedgers prefer going long. In rising markets, such as the market currently

experienced, speculators tend to be net buyers while hedgers are generally net sellers. See Stephen Fagan and Ramazan Gençay, "Liquidity-Induced Dynamics in Futures Markets," (2008), unpublished paper, available at: http:// mpra.ub.uni-muenchen.de/6677/1/MPRA_paper_6677.pdf. See, generally, Markus K. Brunnemeier and Lasse Heje Pedersen, "Market Liquidity and Funding Liquidity," *Review of Financial Studies* 22 (2009), 2201–2238; Dan Bernhardt, P. Seiler and B. Taub, "Speculative Dynamics," *Economic Theory* 44 (2010), 1–52; and Ronel Elul, "Liquidity Crises," *Philadelphia Fed Business Review* (2008), available at: www.philadelphiafed.org/research-and-data/ publications/business-review/2008/q2/elul_liquidity-crises.pdf.

56. John Maynard Keynes, *The General Theory of Employment, Interest, and Money* (New York: Harcourt Brace, 1936), 159.

57. Minsky, *Stabilizing an Unstable Economy*, 230. Minsky distinguishes among hedge financing—in which "cash flow from operating capital assets . . . [are] more than sufficient to meet contractual payment commitments now and in the future . . . " (ibid)—and speculative financing (as per above), and Ponzi financing—where "financing costs are greater than income, so that the face amount of outstanding debt increases: Ponzi units capitalize interest into their liability structure" (ibid, 231).

58. Ibid. See also, Markus Hockradl and Christian Wagner, "Trading the Forward Bias: Are There Limits to Speculation?" *Journal of International Money and Finance* 29 (2010), 423–441. This is of particular note in crude oil futures trading. See Axel Pierru and Denis Babusiaux, "Speculation without Oil Stockpiling as a Signature: A Dynamic Perspective," *M.I.T. Center for Energy and Environmental Policy Research*, No. 10–004 (2010), available at: http://mit.dspace.org/bitstream/handle/1721.1/54754/2010–004 .pdf?sequence=1.

59. However, the idea of the "Minksy moment" gains even greater weight in the age of synthetic debt. This is the point at which cash flow problems, resulting from overextension caused by increasing debt incurred in speculative investment moves, results in the necessity to sell otherwise solid assets. Given the inability to attract buyers for overinflated asset prices and the declining leverage of the asset holder, both market prices and market liquidity collapse. According to the concept, the longer the speculation lasts, the worse is the market result.

The term was coined by Paul McCulley of Pacific Investment in 1998 when discussing the Asian and Russian debt crises of 1997–1998. See Justin Lahart, "In Time of Tumult, Obscure Economist Gains Currency," *Wall Street Journal* (August 18, 2007), available at: http://online.wsj.com/public /article/SB118736585456901047.html. On the concept, see, for example, David L. Prychtko, "Competing Explanations of the Minsky Moment: The Financial Instability Hypothesis in Light of Austrian Theory," *Review of Austrian Economics* 23 (2009), 199–121; John Cassidy, "The Minsky Moment," *The New Yorker* (February 4, 2008), available at: http://bss.sfsu .edu/jmoss/PDF/MinskyMomentNewYorker.pdf; id, *How Market Fail*, 209; and Charles Whalen, "Understanding the Credit Crunch as a Minsky Moment," *Challenge* 51 (2008), 91–109.

60. Dimitris N. Chorafas, *Introduction to Derivative Financial Instruments* (New York: McGraw Hill, 2008), 113. See also Harrison Hong, "Asset Float and Speculative Bubbles," *Journal of Finance* 61 (2006), 1073–1117; Mitchell Y. Abolafia, "Can Speculative Bubbles Be Managed? An Institutional Approach," *Strategic Organization* 8 (2010), 93–100; and Carlos J. Pérez, "Bubble and Manias," (2010), working paper, available at: http://zoltar2 .uc3m.es/temp/Perez.pdf.

61. See, for example, R. S. Eckaus, "The Oil Price Really is a Speculative Bubble," *M.I.T. Center for Energy and Environmental Policy Research*, No. 08–007 (2008), available at: http://dspace.mit.edu/bitstream/handle/1721.1/45521/ 2008–007.pdf?sequence=1; Giulio Cifarelli and Giovanna Paladino, "Oil Price Dynamics and Speculation: A Multivariate Financial Approach," *Energy Economics* 32 (2010), 363–372; Didier Sornette, Ryan Woodward, and Wei-Xing Zhou, "The 2006–2008 Oil Bubble: Evidence of Speculation, and Prediction," *Physica A: Statistics Mechanics and its Applications* 388 (2009), 1571–1576; Xun Zhang, Kin Keung Lai, and Shouyang Wang, "Did Speculative Activities Contribute to High Crude Oil Prices during 1993 to 2008?" *Journal of Systems Science and Complexity* 22 (2009), 636–646; and Pierru and Babusiaux, loc. cit.

62. See, for example, Michael W. Brandt, Alton Brav, John R. Graham, and Alok Kumar, "The Idiosyncratic Puzzle: Time Trend or Speculative Episodes?" *Review of Financial Studies* 23 (2010), 863–889; and Korkut Erturk, "Macroeconomics of Speculation," *Levy Economics Institute Working Papers*, No. 464 (2005), available at: www.levyinstitute.org/pubs/wp_424.pdf.

63. See, for example, Robert K. Kaufmann and Ben Ullman, "Oil Prices, Speculation, and Fundamentals: Interpreting Causal Relations among Spot and Futures Prices," *Energy Economics* 31 (2009), 550–558; James D. Hamilton, "Causes and Consequences of the Oil Shock of 2007–2008," *Brookings Papers on Economic Activity* (Spring 2009), 215–61; available at: http://muse.jhu.edu/journals/brookings_papers_on_economic_activity/ v2009/2009.1.hamilton.pdf; Stelios D. Bekiros and Cees G. H. Diks, "The Relationship between Crude Oil Spot Prices and Futures Prices: Cointegration, Linear and Nonlinear Causality," *Energy Economics* 30 (2008), 2673–2685; Bahattin Büyükşahin, "The Role of Speculators in the Crude Oil Futures Markets," (2009), unpublished papers, available at: www.tinber gen.nl/~NYSEEuronext/ TIWorkshop2009/Papers/BuyuksahinHarris2009 .pdf; and Ronald D. Ripple and Imad A. Moosa, "Futures Maturity and

Hedging Effectiveness: The Case of Oil Futures" (2005), unpublished paper, available at: www.econ.mq.edu.au/research/2005/HedgingEffectiveness.pdf.

64. See Peter Y. Malyshev, "Comprehensive Re-Regulation of U.S. Commodities and OTC Derivatives Industry—Back to the Futures and Beyond," *Futures & Derivatives Law Report* 29, 6 (2009), 1–13; David R. Just and Richard E. Just, "Monopoly Power, Futures Market Manipulation, and the Oil Price Bubble," *Journal of Agricultural & Food Industrial Organization* 6 (2008), Issue 2, Article 2, electronic publication, abstract available at: www.bepress.com/jafio/vol6/iss2/art2/; L. Randall Wray, "The Commodities Market Bubble: Money Manager Capitalism and the Financialization of Commodities," (2008), unpublished policy brief, available at: http://accidentalhuntbrothers.com/wp-content/uploads/2008/09/commodities-brief-9–11–08-updated.pdf; "The Role of Market Speculation in Rising Oil and Gas Prices: A Need to Put the Cop Back on the Beat," *Staff Report of the Permanent Subcommittee on Investigations of the Committee on Homeland Security and Governmental Affairs, United States Senate* (June 27, 2006), available at: http://hsgac.senate.gov/public/_files/SenatePrint10965MarketSpecReportFINAL.pdf; Edward N. Krapels, "Financial Energy Markets and the Bubble in Energy Prices: Does the Increase in Energy Trading by Index and Hedge Funds Affect Energy Prices?" *Testimony before a Joint Hearing of the Permanent Subcommittee on Investigations of the Committee on Homeland Security and Governmental Affairs and the Subcommittee on Energy and Natural Resources, United States Senate* (December 11, 2007), available at: http://hsgac.senate.gov/public/index.cfm?FuseAction=Hearings.Hearing&Hearing_id=dc7368c2–0ea1–4151–9fc5–06317a5bba79; Diana B. Henriques, "Regulators Say Company Manipulated Oil Market," *New York Times* (July 25, 2008), available at: www.nytimes.com/2008/07/25/business/25cftc.html; David Goldman, "Oil Speculation: What Congress Wants," *CNNMoney.com* (June 24, 2008), available at: http://money.cnn.com/2008/06/24/news/economy/oil_legislation/; and Jad Mouawad, "Congress Looks for a Culprit for Rising Oil Prices," *New York Times* (June 25, 2008), available at: www.nytimes.com/2008/06/25/business/25oil.html.

65. See, for example, Henriques, loc. cit.; Elison Elliott, "Price Manipulation in Global Energy Markets," *ForeignPolicyBlogs.com* (June 30, 2010), available at: http://globaleconomy.foreignpolicyblogs.com/2009/06/30/price-manipulation-in-global-energy-markets/; Kenneth B. Medlock III and Amy Myers Jaffe, "Who is in the Oil Futures Market and How Has It Changed?" *James A Baker III Institute for Public Policy* (2009), working paper, available at: www-local.bakerinstitute.org/publications/EF-pub-MedlockJaffeOilFuturesMarket-082609.pdf; and Rachel McCulloch, "The International Trading System and Its Future "(2010) working paper, available at: http://people.brandeis.edu/~rmccullo/wp/WorldTradingSystem0610.pdf.

66. Oil, however certainly remains a weapon in general conflict. Here, we speak not of some nefarious plot to destabilize a national market by manipulating the instability in oil trade. Rather, this is the presence of oil as a factor in flat out cross-border or internal military and political combat. See, for example, Michael T. Klare, *Blood and Oil: The Dangers and Consequences of America's Growing Dependence in Imported Petroleum* (New York: Henry Holt, 2004); id., *Resource Wars: The New Landscape of Global Conflict* (New York: Henry Holt, 2001); Dilip Hiro, *Blood of the Earth: The Battle for the World's Vanishing Oil Resources* (New York: Avalon, 2007); Richard Heinberg, *The Party's Over: Oil, War, and the Fate of Industrial Societies*, 2d ed. (Gabriola Island: New Society, 2005); Kevin M. Morrison, "Oil, Conflict and Stability" (2010), unpublished paper, available at: http://politics.as.nyu.edu/docs/IO/14563/ Morrison.pdf; Clayton K. S. Chun, "Do Oil Exports Fuel Defense Spending?" (Carlyle Barracks: Army War College Strategic Studies Institute 2010), monograph is available at: www.dtic.mil/cgi-bin/GetTRDoc?AD= ADA514758&Location=U2&doc=GetTRDoc.pdf; Freedom C. Onuoha, "The Geo-Strategy of Oil in the Gulf of Guinea: Implications for Regional Stability," *Journal of Asian and African Studies* 45 (2010), 369–84; Luke A. Patey, "Crude Days Ahead? Oil and the Resource Curse in Sudan," *African Affairs* 109 (2010), 617–636; and Miriam Shabafrouz, "Oil and the Eruption of the Algerian Civil War: A Context-Sensitive Analysis of the Ambivalent Impact of Resource Abundance," *German Institute of Global and Area Studies Working Papers*, No. 118 (2010), available at: http://edoc.bibliothek.uni-halle .de:8080/servlets/MCRFileNodeServlet/HALCoRe_derivate_00003970/ wp118_shabafrouz.pdf.

67. See the discussion in Chapter 2 above.

68. See the discussion of the more traditional wet barrel/paper barrel distinction centered about the loading date of a crude shipment, as discussed in Chapter 2, as well as the discussion of forward contracts in note 17, Chapter 2.

69. SWFs have been around for some time, but have become a factor in international trade and finance only in the past decade or so. The term appears to first have been used in 2005 by Andrew Rosanov of State Street Global Advisors, who has since become a fixture in the debate over the use and structure of such funds. See Andrew Rosanov, "Who Holds the Wealth of Nations?" *Central Bank Journal* 15 (2005), 52–57; reprinted in *State Street Global Advisors* (August 2005), 1–4, available at: http://web.archive.org/ web/20080529122341/www.ssga.com/library/esps/Who_Holds_Wealth_ of_Nations_Andrew_Rozanov_8.15.05REVCCRI1145995576.pdf; id., "The Sovereign Wealth Funds Debate," *State Street Global Advisors* (January 2008), 1–2, available at: www.ssga.com/library/esps/The_SWF_Debate_Andrew_ Rozanof_1.8.08CCRI1200431495.pdf; and id., "Long-Term Consequences of the Financial Crisis for Sovereign Wealth Funds," *Vision* 4 (2009), 13–19.

70. See, for example, Donghyun Park and Andrew Rozanov, "Asia's Sovereign Wealth Funds and Reform of the Global Reserve System," *Economic Growth Centre Working Papers Series*, No. 2010/03 (2010), available at: www.ntu.edu .sg/hss2/egc/wp/2010/2010−03.pdf; Vidhi Chhaochharia and Luc Lavern, "Sovereign Wealth Funds: Their Investment Strategies and Performance," (2008), working paper, available at: www.isb.edu/EMFConference/File/ Sovereignwealthfunds.pdf; Joshua Aizenman and Reuven Glick, "Asset Class Diversification and Delegation of Responsibilities between Central Banks and Sovereign Wealth Funds," *Federal Reserve Bank of San Francisco Working Paper Series*, Paper 2010−20 (2010), available at: www.frbsf.org/publications/ economics/papers/2010/wp10−20bk.pdf; and Raphael W. Lam and Marco Rossi, "Sovereign Wealth Funds—Investment Strategies and Financial Distress," *Journal of Derivatives & Hedge Funds* 15 (2010), 304−322.

71. See the discussion in Chapter 4 above.

72. The term first appeared in 1977 to label the internal dislocation resulting from discoveries of natural gas off the coast of the Netherlands. See "The Dutch Disease," *The Economist* (November 26, 1977), 82−83. The concept, however, has been recognized for some time. Development of the current approach is usually ascribed to W. Max Corden, "Booming Sector and Dutch Disease Economics: Survey and Consolidation," *Oxford Economic Papers* 36 (1984), 359−380, as well as W. Max Corden and J. Peter Neary, "Booming Sector and De-Industrialisation in a Small Open Economy," *Economic Journal* 92 (1982), 825−848. The approach posits that a "boom" in resources, usually but not always the result of extractions of raw materials (primarily oil and gas), will result in a further resource movement into the advancing (or booming) sector at the expense of lagging (non-booming) sectors. The Cordon-Neary approach studied the manufacturing sector as the lagging example, although in many countries agriculture would also be a good example. Labor will also move from the lagging to the booming sectors, with prices increasing for nontraded goods, while traded goods (the prices of which are determined by the international market) cannot compensate with similar rises, further exacerbating the imbalance. A good recent statement of the current dominant approach can be found in Kareem Ismail, "The Structural Manifestation of the 'Dutch Disease:' The Case of Oil Exporting Countries," *International Monetary Fund Working Papers*, No. 10/103 (2010), available at: www.imf.org/ external/pubs/ft/wp/2010/wp10103.pdf.

   See also Norio Usui, "Dutch Disease and Policy Adjustments to the Oil Boom: A Comparative Study of Indonesia and Mexico," *Resources Policy* 23 (1997), 151−162; Michael Bruno and Jeffrey Sachs, "Energy and Resource Allocation: A Dynamic Model of the 'Dutch Disease,'" *Review of Economic Studies* 49 (1982), 845−859; Mouhamadou Sy and Hamidreza Tabarraei, "Capital Inflows and Exchange Rate in LDC: The Dutch Disease Problem Revisited,"

(2009), working paper, available at: www.dsg.ae/oxcarre/conference%20papers/ Tabarraei.pdf; and Julien Daubanes, "Taxation of Oil Products and GDP Dynamics of Oil-Rich Countries," *Center of Economic Research at ETH-Zurich Working Papers*, No. 09/102 (2009), available at: http://e-collection.ethbib.ethz .ch/eserv.php?pid=eth:41360&dsID=eth-41360−01.pdf.

73. See, for example, Paul Rose, "Sovereign Wealth Fund Investment in the Shadow of Regulation and Politics," *Georgetown Journal of International Law* 40 (2009), available at: www.thefreelibrary.com/Sovereign+Wealth+Fund +investment+in+the+shadow+of+regulation+and. . .-a0215514217; Paul Collier, "Natural Resources, Development and Conflict: Channels of Causation and Policy Interventions," in François Bourguignon, Pierre Jacquet and Boris Pleskovic, eds., *Economic Integration and Social Responsibility* (Washington: The World Bank, 2007), 323–335; Harry G. Broadman, "The Social Cost of Imported Oil," *Energy Policy* 14 (1986), 242–252; Lutz Kilian, Alessandro Rebucci and Nikola Spatafora, "Oil Shocks and External Balances," *Journal of International Economics* 77 (2009), 181–194; Larry Catá Backer, "Sovereign Investing in Times of Crisis: Global Regulation of Sovereign Wealth Funds, State-Owned Enterprises and the Chinese Experience," *Transnational Law and Contemporary Problems* 19 (2009), 5–144; Simone Mezzacapo, "The So-Called 'Sovereign Wealth Funds;' Regulatory Issues, Financial Stability and Prudential Supervision," *European Economy: Economic Papers*, No. 378 (2009), available at: http://ec.europa.eu/economy_ finance/publications/publication15064_en.pdf; and Benjamin J. Cohen, "Sovereign Wealth Funds and National Security: The Great Tradeoff," *International Affairs* 85 (2009), 713–731.

74. This is certainly not to say they are without significance. Such acquisitions may rise to a bona fide national security issue. See Edwin M. Truman, "Sovereign Wealth Fund Acquisitions and Other Foreign Government Investments in the United States: Assessing the Economics and National Security Implications," *Testimony before the Committee on Banking, Housing, and Urban Affairs, United States Senate* (November 14, 2007), available at: www.peterson-institute.org/publications/papers/truman1107.pdf.

75. See Bernardo Bortolotti, Veljko Fotak, William L. Megginson and William F. Miracky, "Quiet Leviathans: Sovereign Wealth Fund Investment, Passivity, and the Value of the Firm," (2010), working paper, available at: http:// ec.europa.eu/economy_finance/publications/publication15064_en.pdf; Gawdat Bahgat, "Oil Funds: Perils and Opportunities," *Middle Eastern Studies* 45 (2009), 283–293; and Stefano Curto, "Sovereign Wealth Funds in the Next Decade," in Otaviano Canuto and Marcelo Guigale, eds., *The Day After Tomorrow: A Handbook on the Future of Economic Policy in the Developing World* (Washington: The World Bank, 2010), 239–249.

76. See Farouk El-Kharouf, Sulayman Al-Qudsi and Shifa Obeid, "The Gulf Cooperation Council Sovereign Wealth Funds: Are They Instruments for Economic Diversification or Political Tools?" *Asian Economic Papers* 9 (2010), 124–151; and April Knill, Bong-Soo Lee, and Nathan Mauck, "Bilateral Political Relations and the Impact of Sovereign Wealth Fund Investment," (2010), working paper, available at: www.peterson-institute.org/publications/papers/truman1107.pdf.

77. There may also be another motive for acquiring access to extractions elsewhere. The SWF-sponsoring country may prefer to withhold some of that volume to maintain wider pricing levels. This concern is already surfacing in advance of significantly greater Iraqi volume coming on line in the next several years. See Kent Moors, "Iraqi Oil May Finally Be Open for Business," *Oil and Energy Investor* (November 12, 2010), available at: http://oilandenergy investor.com/2010/11/iraqi-oil-finally-open-for-business/. That volume, which the Iraqi Oil Ministry claim could shoot up to 12 million barrels a day, would tear apart the current OPEC members' quota structure. Concerns have also been advanced by non-OPEC country producers in Iraq, such as Russian LUKOIL and Italian ENI. To what extent could the largess coming from Iraq undermine the pricing of company volume extracted elsewhere? See id., "Commentary: Oil Reserves Rise, But Iraqi Development Remains Challenged," *Caspian Investor* 13, 8 (2010), 1, 8–10.

78. See Kent Moors, "Nobody's Covering the *Other* Oil Story in the Gulf," *Oil and Energy Investor* (May 19, 2010), available at: http://oilandenergy investor.com/2010/05/oil-spill-2/; Martin Kronicle, "How Venezuela Can Have Their $80–$100 Crude Oil Price Band," *Insight from a Commodity Trader* (April 6, 2010), available at: http://martinkronicle.com/2010/04/06/how-venezuela-can-have-their-80–100-crude-oil-price-band/; and Mark Weisbrot and Rebecca Ray, "Oil Prices and Venezuela's Economy," *Center for Economic and Policy Research* (2008), available at: www.cepr.net/documents/publications/venezuela_2008_11.pdf.

79. See Kent Moors, "Analysis: Tehran Again Attacks Petrodollar System: Euro Central to New Strategy," *Caspian Investor* 11, 1 (2008), 1, 9–10; Ali Sheikhholeslami and Nandini Sukumar, "Tehran Exchange Trades Futures to Attract Investors," *Bloomberg Businessweek* (January 26, 2010), available at: www.businessweek.com/news/2010–07–26/tehran-exchange-trades -futures-to-attract-investors.html; and Cyrus Bina, "Petroleum and Energy Policy in Iran," *Economic and Political Weekly* (January 3, 2009), available at: www.urpe.org/ec/Iran/Bina09Energy.pdf.

80. The Saudis have had a traditional reticence to spike the price of crude oil and have regarded volatility in pricing as a disadvantage to balancing production and demand. See, for example, "Saudis Support Stable Oil Price," *VOANews.com* (November 22, 2010), available at: www.voanews.com/

english/news/economy-and-business/Saudis-Support-Stable-Oil-Price-107546808.html; Jad Mouawad, "Saudi Officials Seek to Temper the Price of Oil," *New York Times* (January 28, 2007), available at: www.t4engr.com/Clients_Only/NYTimes/Saudi%20Officials%20Seek%20to%20Temper%20the%20Price%20of%20Oil%20-%20New%20York%20Times.pdf; Albert Bressand, "The Future of Producer-Consumer Cooperation: A Policy Perspective," Andreas Goldthau and Jan Martin Witte, eds., *Global Energy Governance: The New Rules of the Game* (Berlin: Global Public Policy Institute, 2010), 269–285; Abdul Ruff, "Saudi Oil Price Summit," *Global Politician* (June 27, 2008), available at: www.globalpolitician.com/24949-saudi-arabia-oil; and Claes, loc. cit., 231 ff.

81. See Kent Moors, "New Turn in Iranian Sanctions," *Caspian Investor* 13, 8 (2010), 2–6; and id., "Commentary: Iranian Fuel Situation Deteriorates," *Caspian Investor* 13, 6 (2010), 1, 8–10. Beginning in July of 2010, the U.S. and EU sanctions make it more difficult for Iran to import gasoline and heating oil. Iran produces considerable crude oil but has insufficient refinery capacity. The UN sanctions prevent Iran from utilizing normal banking venues for foreign exchange transactions. That requires the usage of inefficient and expensive alternatives.

82. The retention of petrodollars abroad has been the primary reason why running expanding trade deficits has not resulted in accelerating inflationary pressures in the U.S. market.

    For an excellent treatment of the rise and implications of the petrodollar system, see David E. Spiro, *The Hidden Hand of American Hegemony: Petrodollar Recycling and International Markets* (Ithaca, NY: Cornell University Press, 1999). See, also Matthew Higgins, Thomas Klitgaard, and Robert Lerman, "Recycling Petrodollars," *Federal Reserve Bank of New York Current Issues in Economics and Finance* 12 (2006), available at: www.newyorkfed.org/research/current_issues/ci12–9.pdf; Ravi Balakrishnan, Tamim Bayoumi, and Volodymyr Tulin, "Rhyme or Reason: What Explains the Easy Financing of the U.S. Current Account Deficit?" *International Monetary Fund Staff Papers* 56 (2009), 410–445; and Tahereh Alavi Hojjat and Bhagyavati Bhagyavati, "Petrodollars, Globalization and U.S. Inflation," *Global Journal of Business Research* 3 (2009), 49–63.

83. See the discussion in Chapter 4 above, as well as, for example, Linda S. Goldberg, "Is the International Role of the Dollar Changing?" *Federal Reserve Bank of New York Current Issues in Economics and Finance* (2010), available at: www.newyorkfed.org/research/current_issues/ci16–1.pdf; Maria N. Ivanova, "Hegemony and Seigniorage: The Planned Spontaneity of the U.S. Current Account Deficit," *International Journal of Political Economy* 39 (2010), 93–130; and Ari Aisen and Francisco José Veiga, "The Political Economy of Seigniorage," *Journal of Development Economics* 87 (2008), 29–50.

84. See the discussion in Chapter 4 above, as well as Lawrence E. Mitchell, *The Speculation Economy: How Finance Triumphed over Industry* (San Francisco: Berrett-Koehler, 2009), especially 192ff.; Cetin Ciner, "Hedging or Speculation in Derivatives Markets: The Case of Energy Futures Markets," *Applied Financial Economics Letters* 2 (2006), 189–192; Mark Jickling, "Primer on Energy Derivatives and Their Regulation," *CRS Report for Congress*, RS22918 (2008), available at: http://fpc.state.gov/documents/organization /108322.pdf; id. and Lynn J. Cunningham, "Speculation and Energy Prices: Legislative Responses," *CRS Report for Congress*, RL34555 (2008), available at: http://fpc.state.gov/documents/organization/107210.pdf; and Damir Tokic, "The 2008 Oil Bubble: Causes and Consequences." *Energy Policy* 38 (2010), 6009–6015.

85. This discussion draws on Jickling, Primer, loc. cit. See also, Mazan Labban, "Oil in Parallax: Scarcity, Markets, and the Financialization of Accumulation," *Geoforum* 41 (2010), 541–552; Bassam Fattouh, "The Dynamics of Crude Oil Price Differentials," *Energy Economics* 32 (2010), 334–352; and Medlock and Jaffe, loc. cit.

86. Swaps are a frequently used approach in which parties exchange aspects of their financial instruments. The International Swaps and Derivatives Association (ISDA) put the mid-year 2010 swaps total at over $466 trillion, with the top 14 derivatives dealers accounting for 82 percent of interest rate derivatives, 90 percent of credit default swaps, and 86 percent of equity derivatives. See David Mengle, "Concentration of OTC Derivatives among Major Dealers," *ISDA Research Notes*, 4 (2010), available at: http://isda.org/ researchnotes/pdf/ConcentrationRN_4–10.pdf. Diego Valiante puts the total amount of OTC derivatives at $604 trillion. Diego Valiante, "Shaping Reforms and Business Models for the OTC Derivatives Market: Quo Vadis? *ECMI Research Reports*, No. 5 (2010), available at: www.ceps.eu/system/ files/book/2010/04/ECMI%20RR5%20Valiante%20on%20Derivatives.pdf.

87. The usage of options on swaps has produced something called a swaption— providing the right but not the obligation to enter into a swap. See Richard Flavell, *Swaps and Other Derivatives*, 2d ed. (Hoboken, NJ: John Wiley & Sons, 2010), 214ff. These are having an impact in futures, especially oil, because they increase the flexibility of entering into a range of operations beyond merely a volume of crude at a stated contract price. However, they are also instruments that increase volatility. See Damiano Brigo, Kyriakos Courdakis, and Imane Bakkar, "Counterparty Risk Valuation for Energy-Commodity Swaps: Impacts of Volatility and Correlation," (2008), working paper, available at: www.damianobrigo.it/commoditiescr_fs.pdf; and Söhnke M. Bartram, Gregory W. Brown, and Frank R. Fehle, "International Evidence on Financial Derivatives Usage," *Financial Management* 38 (2009), 185–206.

88. 7 USC §1 et seq. CEA replaced the Grain Futures Act of 1923.

89. The Commodity Futures Trading Commission Act of 1974 (P.L. 93–463) created the CFTC to replace the U.S. Department of Agriculture's Commodity Exchange Authority.

90. Both agencies oversee exchange markets having self-regulating responsibilities. Exchanges are required to set and enforce rules providing for a number of things, including the protection of customers, prevention of fraud and manipulation, as well as maintaining orderly and fair markets. In this structure, regulators have the power to modify exchange rules, in addition to issuing their own rules and regulations.

91. §4(a) defines it as "undue burden on interstate commerce."

92. On which, see note 2, Chapter 2 and associated text.

93. This had led some commentators to suspect that court action might declare OTC trading illegal, thereby invalidating the contracts. On that discussion, see, for example, Graham Purcell and Abelardo Lopez Valdez, "The Commodity Futures Trading Commission Act of 1974: Regulatory Legislation for Commodity Futures Trading in a Market-Oriented Economy," *South Dakota Law Review* 21 (1976), 555–590; and Frank D'Souza, Nan S. Ellis, and Lisa M. Fairchild, "Illuminating the Need for Regulation in Dark Markets: Proposed Regulation of the OTC Derivatives Market," *University of Pennsylvania Journal of Business Law* 12 (2010), 473–516.

94. P.L. 106–554.

95. The CFTC can issue a specific exemption after a finding that a proposed OTC agricultural contract would be consistent with the public interest.

96. Still unknown is the extent to which the legislation can effectively force OTC into regulated markets. The requirement that banks must spin-off oil trading to subsidiaries may increase transparency. The imposition of position limits across markets should greatly restrict manipulative activities. Key elements of the law include:

Position limits: The bill empowers the CFTC to establish position limits on traders to keep them from manipulating prices. However, the new law also requires the CFTC to study and report to Congress the effects of position limits on excessive speculation and the possible movement of transactions from U.S. to foreign exchanges. In January 2010, the CFTC laid out some seemingly mild directions on positions, but there is likelihood the commission will revisit the issue. Strict limits could remove the ability to influence prices, but might hit liquidity and the maneuverability of the largest players, whether they are servicing commercial clients, making bets on short-term volatility, or taking passive long positions.

Proprietary trading: Federally insured banks are prohibited from trading for their own accounts. However, these banks may invest up to 3 percent of their tangible equity into hedge or private equity funds to engage indirectly in proprietary trading. Separating proprietary trading from commercial hedging at banks managing more global books allows for greater division between servicing clients and betting on prices, but again could hurt liquidity, a mechanism for reducing volatility, and the hedging services of these institutions as they will be constrained in taking an effective counter-position. The banks most affected by this rule are Goldman Sachs, JPMorgan, Bank of America, Citigroup, and Morgan Stanley, which all have lucrative energy trading practices and are among the leading providers of tailored OTC instruments.

Regulating derivatives: The law requires more standardized OTC derivative transactions to be moved to regulated exchanges, while more exotic ones may be allowed to remain outside the regulated area. The objective in moving OTC transactions onto a clearinghouse is to increase transparency and prohibit excessive risk taking (see the discussion in Chapter 7). Oil end-users will be allowed to continue hedging on OTC markets to protect themselves against price fluctuations. However, the language of the exemption is narrow, which may cause some hedgers to be classified as "swap dealers" and thus subject to the clearing requirements. There is also the problem that some of the small exempt market players—especially wholesalers to limited markets—could be pushed out of the trade entirely because of greater margin requirements leading to increased transaction costs.

97. See, for example, Craig Pirrong, "Mutualization of Default Risk, Fungibility, and Moral Hazard: The Economics of Default Risk Sharing in Cleared and Bilateral Markets," (2010), working paper, available at: http://business .nd.edu/uploadedFiles/Academic_Centers/Study_of_Financial_Regulation/ pdf_and_documents/clearing_moral_hazard_1.pdf; id., "The Inefficiency of Clearing Mandates," *Policy Analysis*, No. 665 (July 21, 2010), available at: www.cato.org/pubs/pas/PA665.pdf; and Valiante, loc. cit.

98. Commodity Futures Trading Commission, *Report on the Oversight of Trading on Regulated Futures Exchanges and Exempt Commercial Markets* (2007), available at: www.cftc.gov/ucm/groups/public/@newsroom/documents/file/ pr5403–07_ecmreport.pdf; Government Accountability Office, *Commodity Futures Trading Commission: Trends in Energy Derivatives Markets Raise Questions about CFTC's Oversight*, GAO 08–25 (2007), available at: www.gao.gov/new .items/d0825.pdf; Interagency Task Force on Commodity Markets, *Interim Report on Crude Oil* (2008), available at: www.cftc.gov/ucm/groups/public /@newsroom/documents/file/itfinterimreportoncrudeoil0708.pdf; and Commodity Futures Trading Commission, *Staff Report on Commodity Swap Dealers & Index Traders with Commission Recommendations* (2008), available at: www.cftc.gov/ucm/groups/public/@newsroom/documents/file/cftcstaff reportonswapdealers09.pdf.

99. Daniel O'Sullivan, *Petromania: Black Gold, Paper Barrels and Oil Price Bubbles* (Petersfield, Hampshire, UK: Harriman House, 2009), 191–192; see also 102–105.

100. See Kent Moors, "The New Oil Index Is about to Create Even More Opportunity for Investors," *Oil and Energy Investor* (January 12, 2010), available at: http://oilandenergyinvestor.com/2010/01/new-oil-investments/.

Chapter 7

1. The company could be a VIOC, in which case it is usually "selling" its production to itself and applying transfer pricing between subsidiary units rather than actual market prices. Transfer pricing always is substantially less than a sale completed between separate companies (an arm's-length transaction), since the object is to maximize the overall profitability to the VIOC by booking a cost that reflects the minimum amount required to cover the needs of the subsidiaries while charging the maximum market price when the crude or processed product is sold to a party not part of the VIOC. Transfer pricing is a primary source of disagreement between a foreign VIOC and a rentier state, since the home country receives royalties and taxes, not on the fair market value of the production, but on an amount that is substantially less. See, for example, Thad Dunning, "Endogenous Oil Rents," *Comparative Political Studies* 43 (2010), 379–410; Neil Dias Karunaratne, "Regulation of Transnational Corporations (TNCs) by Host Developing Countries (HDCs)," *International Journal of Social Economics* 9 (1993), 72–89; Prem Sikka and Hugh Willmott, "The Dark Side of Transfer Pricing: Its Role in Tax Avoidance and Wealth Retentiveness," *Critical Perspectives in Accounting* 21 (2010), 342–356; Prem Sikka and Colin Haslam, "Transfer Pricing and Its Role in Tax Avoidance and Flight of Capital: Some Theory and Evidence" (2007), working papers, available at: http://jppsg .ac.uk/carbs/news_events/events/past/conferences/ipa/ipa_papers/00267 .pdf; and Connie R. Bateman, "Minimizing Risk of Transfer Pricing Audit and Awakening the Giant of Corporate Stewardship: An Ethical Decision Making Model (EDMM) for Multinational Enterprise (MNE) Transfer Pricing," *Journal of Legal, Ethical, and Regulatory Issues* 10 (2007), 109–127. The most recent example of developing the guidelines for cross-border transfer pricing is Organisation for Economic Cooperation and Development (OECD), *OECD Transfer Pricing Guidelines for Multinational Corporations and Tax Administrations* (Paris: OECD, 2010), available at: http://browse.oecd bookshop.org/oecd/pdfs/browseit/2310091E.PDF

   However, in the case of syndicated finance, the preferable approach for both the company and the bank will be to utilize the price expected from a first instance "arm's-length" sale transaction. That would be at the wellhead, marking the transfer at the point the extraction leaves the well.

2. London Interbank Offered Rate. LIBOR is the most widely used benchmark interest rate for global financial transactions. It is calculated by

the British Banking Association (BBA) each day by 11:00 A.M. London time and published by *Thomson Reuters*. It reflects the offer rate between banks. As the BBA describes it, LIBOR is a trimmed average of inter-bank deposit rates offered by designated contributor banks, for maturities ranging from overnight to one year. LIBOR is calculated for 10 curren-cies. There are either eight, twelve, or sixteen contributor banks on each currency panel and the reported interest is the mean of the middle val-ues (technically, the interquartile mean). The rates are a benchmark rather than a tradable rate; the actual rate at which banks will lend to one another continues to vary throughout the day. See http://bbalibor.bladonmore .com/bbalibor-explained/the-basics.

3. August 2009. See the discussion in Chapter 1.

4. See Chapter 2, note 9.

5. The standard deviation is a way of looking at the distribution of data about a mean point. Robert Niles has a good (largely painless) explanation as follows:

> The standard deviation is kind of the "mean of the mean," and often can help you find the story behind the data. To understand this concept, it can help to learn about what statisticians call normal distribution of data.

> A normal distribution of data means that most of the examples in a set of data are close to the "average," while relatively few examples tend to one extreme or the other. . . . The standard deviation is a statistic that tells you how tightly all the various examples are clustered around the mean in a set of data. When the examples are pretty tightly bunched together and the bell-shaped curve is steep, the standard deviation is small. When the examples are spread apart and the bell curve is relatively flat, that tells you taht you have a relatively large standard deviation. (See www.robertniles.com/stats/stdev.shtml.)

6. As Vineer Bhansali well reminds us, tail risk is a significant problem in highly volatile investment markets.

> Tail risk can be defined as the risk posed by events that are relatively rare, but that can have substantial impact on a portfolio. These rare events can cause outsized gains or losses for investors. . . . Tail risk refers to the risk of potential investment outcomes on the edges of sta-tistical return distributions. In a typical bell curve, the tallest areas near the center represent the more likely outcomes. The "tails" are where the bell curve tapers down toward the edges. Of course, there are both left tails and right tails, but having a long-term view requires special attention to the avoidance of catastrophic losses, or left tails. Because real markets don't neatly follow the bell curve, underestimating the

likelihood and severity of events on the tails can result in extreme losses. Traditional risk management and pricing tools often underestimate the frequency and severity of these left tail events and, by extension, their detrimental effect on returns. (Vineer Bhansali, "Tail Risk Management: Why Investors Should Be Chasing Their Tails," *Viewpoints* [December 2008], available at: www.pimco.com/Pages/ Spotlight_%20Bhansali%20Tail%20Risk%2012−08%20US.aspx)

7. See, for example, "Get Ready for Tail Hedging: PIMCO," *Canadian Investment Review* (August 9, 2010), available at: www.investmentreview .com/expert-opinion/get-ready-for-tail-hedging-pimco-4643; "Uncertainty, Distribution, and Fat-Tails," *Reuters* (August 6, 2010), available at: http:// blogs.reuters.com/great-debate/2010/08/06/uncertainty-distributions -and-fat-tails/; Stefan Thurner, J. Doyne Farmer, and John Geanakopolos, "Leverage Causes Fat Tails and Clustered Volatility," *Yale University, Cowles Foundation for Research in Economics Discussion Papers*, No. 1745 (2010), available at: http://dido.econ.yale.edu/P/cd/d17a/d1745.pdf; Zhiguang Wang and Prasad V. Bidarkota, "A Long-Run Risks Model of Asset Pricing with Fat Tails," *Review of Finance* 14 (2010), 409−449; and Carolyn Kousky and Roger Cooke, "Adapting to Extreme Events: Managing Fat Tails," *Resources for the Future*, Issue Brief 10−12 (2010), available at: www.rff .org/rff/documents/RFF-IB-10−12.pdf.

8. See, for example, Antonio Mele, "Asymmetric Stock Market Volatility and the Cyclical Behavior of Expected Returns," *Journal of Financial Economics* 86 (2007), 446−78; Jennifer Huang and Jiang Wang, "Liquidity and Market Crashes," *Review of Financial Studies* 22 (2009), 2607−2643; and Louis H. Ederington and Wei Guan, "How Asymmetric Is U.S. Stock Market Volatility?" *Journal of Financial Markets* 13 (2010), 225−248.

9. See, for example, Lorne N. Switzer and Mario El-Khoury, "Extreme Volatility, Speculative Efficiency and the Hedging Effectiveness of the Oil Futures Markets," *Journal of Futures Markets* 27 (2007), 61−84; Tao Wang, Jingtao Wu, and Jian Yang, "Realized Volatility and Correlation in Energy Futures Markets," *Journal of Futures Markets* 28 (2008), 993−1011; and Chia-Lin Chang, Michael McAleer and Roengchai Tansuchat, "Analyzing and Forecasting Volatility Spillovers, Asymmetries, and Hedging in Major Oil Markets," *Energy Economics* 32 (2010), 1445−1455.

10. Referred to as OTM, this occurs when a call option's strike (or exercise) price is higher than the market price of the underlying asset or a put option's strike price is lower than the underlying asset. Essentially, an OTM option is considered worthless if it would expire in either condition. On the

Black-Scholes problem, see Espen Gaarder Haug and Nassim Nicholas Taleb, "Options Traders Use (Very) Sophisticated Heuristics, Never the Black-Scholes-Merton Formula," *Journal of Economics Behavior & Organization* 77 (2011), forthcoming; Vladimir G. Ivancevic, "Adaptive-Wave Alternative for the Black-Scholes Option Pricing Model," *Cognitive Computation* 2 (2010), 17–30; Shalom Benaim, Peter Friz, and Roger Lee, "On the Black-Scholes Implied Volatility at Extreme Strikes," (2008), working paper, available at: http://math.uchicago.edu/~rl/BFL2008v5.pdf; and L.C.G. Rogers and Surbjeet Singh, "The Cost of Illiquidity and Its Effects on Hedging," *Mathematical Finance* 20 (2010), 597–615.

11. See Rachel A. J. Campbell, Catherine S. Forbes, Kees G. Koedijk, and Paul Kofman, "Increasing Correlations or Just Fail Tails? *Journal of Empirical Finance* 15 (2008), 287–309; and Bhansali, loc. cit.

12. See, for example, Olivier J. Blanchard and Jordi Gali, "The Macrocosmic Effects of Oil Price Shocks: Why Are the 2000s So Different from the 1970s?" in Jordi Gali and Mark Gertler, eds., *International Dimensions of Monetary Policy* (Chicago: University of Chicago, 2009), 373–428; Jer-Shiou Chiou and Yen-Hsien Lee, "Jump Dynamics and Volatility: Oil and the Stock Markets," *Energy* 34 (788–796); and Giulio Cifarelli and Giovanna Paladino, "Oil Price Dynamics and Speculation: A Multivariate Financial Approach," *Energy Economics* 32 (2010), 363–372.

13. By taking the trading in forward supply out of the hands of a few major oil companies, futures contracts provided a major stimulus to regularizing the market and increasing participation. Prior to futures, the trading was oligopsonistic—too few buyers (the major VIOCs) controlled the posted price system. See Paul Davidson, "Public Policy Problems of the Domestic Crude Oil Industry," *American Economic Review* 53 (1963), 85–108. On the broad implications, see, for example, Ron Alquist and Lutz Kilian, "What Do We Learn from the Price of Oil Futures?" *Journal of Applied Econometrics* 25 (2010), 539–573; James L. Smith, "World Oil: Market or Mayhem?" *Journal of Economic Perspectives* 23 (2009), 145–164; and Tao Wu and Andrew McCallum, "Do Oil Futures Prices Help Predict Future Oil Prices?" *FRBSF Economic Letter*, No. 2005–38 (December 30, 2005), available at: www.frbsf.org/publications/economics/letter/2005/el2005–38.pdf.

14. On which, see, for example, Peregrine Financial Group, "Futures Spread Trading: A Time-Tested Strategy," (2005), available at: www.pfgwest.com/media/Futures_spreads.pdf; Alquist and Kilian, loc, cit; Michael Yee, John Zyren, Joanne Shore, and Thomas Lee, "Crude Oil Futures as an Indicator of Market Changes," *International Advances in Economic Research* 16 (2010), 257–268; Atilim Murat and Ekin Tokat, "Forecasting Oil Price Movements with Crack Spread Futures," *Energy Economics* 31 (2009), 85–90; and Thalia Chantziara and George Skiadopoulos, "Can the Dynamics of the

Term Structure of Petroleum Futures Be Forecasted? Evidence from Major Markets," *Energy Economics* 30 (2008) 962–985.

15. "Today, although many oil supply contracts specify spot or 'prompt' prices for Brent, Dubai, and other crudes traded in open markets, the markets involved are mostly concerned with prices agreed upon in futures or other 'forward' contracts." J. E. Hartshorn, *Oil Trade: Politics and Prospects* (Cambridge: Cambridge University, 1993), 206.

16. This remains all about the flow of liquidity. See the discussion in Chapter 4 above. On the liquidity function of futures contracts, see, for example, C. J. Cuny, "The Role of Liquidity in Futures Market Innovations," *Review of Financial Studies* 6 (1993), 57–78; Stephen Fagan and Ramazan Gencay, "Liquidity-Induced Dynamics in Futures Markets," (2008), unpublished paper, available at: http://mpra.ub.uni-muenchen.de/6677/1/MPRA_paper_6677.pdf; Kit Pong Wong, "Production, Liquidity, and Futures Price Dynamics," *Journal of Futures Markets* 28 (2008), 749–762; and Alex Frino, Elvis Jarnecic, and Roger Feletto, "Local Trader Profitability in Futures Markets: Liquidity and Position Taking Profits," *Journal of Futures Markets* 30 (210), 1–24.

17. In a very basic sense, futures contracts and related derivatives serve a necessary function to the hedging process. If they are not present, the underlying contract can often be struck only in a more inefficient and unstable manner. This is another view of the liquidity function served by the futures contract (or, for that matter, the speculator).

18. Yanbo Yin and Phillipe Jorion, "Firm Value and Hedging: Evidence from U.S. Oil and Gas Producers," *Journal of Finance* 61 (2006), 893–919; Chaio-Yi Chang, Jin-Yi Lai, and I-Yuan Chunag, "Futures Hedging Effectiveness under the Segmentation of Bear/Bull Energy Markets," *Energy Economics* 32 (2010), 442–449; and Won Cheol-Yun and Hyun Jae Kim, "Hedging Strategy for Crude Oil Trading and the Factors Influencing Hedging Effectiveness," *Energy Policy* 38 (2010), 2404–2408.

19. The concept implies that the level of counterparty risk can be reduced if there is a good credit (or liquid) third party acting as an intermediary in the transaction. See, for example, Rüdiger Frey and Jochen Bauckhaus, "Pricing and Hedging of Portfolio Derivatives with Interacting Default Intensities," *International Journal of Theoretical and Applied Finance* 11 (2208), 611–634; Olivier Mahul and J. David Cummins, "Hedging under Counterparty Credit Uncertainty," *Journal of Futures Markets* 28 (2008), 248–263; Damiano Brigo, Kyriakos Courdakis, and Imane Bakkar, "Counterparty Risk Valuation for Energy-Commodity Swaps: Impacts of Volatility and Correlation" (2008), working paper, available at: www.damianobrigo.it/commoditiescr_fs.pdf; Viral Acharya and Alberto Bisin, "Counterparty Risk Externality: Centralized

versus Over-the-Counter Markets" (2010), working paper, available at: www.econ.nyu.edu/user/bisina/OTC24.pdf; and Stephen G. Cecchetti, Jacob Gyntelberg, and Marc Hollanders, "Central Counterparties for Over-the-Counter Derivatives," *BIS Quarterly Review* (2009), available at: www .elpoderdelaetica.com/spip/IMG/r_qt0909.pdf#page=49.

20. See, for example, Martin F. Hellwig, "Systemic Risk in the Financial Sector: An Analysis of the Subprime-Mortgage Financial Crisis," *De Economist* 157 (2009), 129–207; Steven L. Schwarcz, "Systemic Risk," *Georgetown Law Journal* 97 (2008), 193–249; and Viral V. Acharya, Lasse H. Pedersen, Thomas Phillipon, and Matthew Richardson, "Regulating Systemic Risk," in Viral V. Acharya and Matthew Richardson, eds., *Restoring Financial Stability: How to Restore a Failed System* (Hoboken, NJ: John Wiley & Sons, 2009), 283–304.

21. The master-swap agreements usually follow the standards set by the International Swaps and Derivatives Association (ISDA). See www.isda .org/. Credit support annexes of these master-swap agreements govern collateral requirements as well as the obligations of the two counterparties in the event that one of them cannot perform. As the market values of the derivatives contracts between two counterparties fluctuate, the collateral required is recalculated, normally on a daily basis.

22. Most of this discussion focuses on the cutting of oil use in society as a whole, not as a weapon to offset oil vega by lessening the volume of crude available for futures contracts. But see William J. Antholis and Charles K. Ebinger, "Message to the President: Build a Secure Energy Future," *Brookings Memos to the President*, No. 2 (November 11, 2009), available at: www.brookings.edu/opinions/ 2010/~/link.aspx?_id=4B86E817F31E489AB8850D53C5B69133&_z=z.

23. The more extreme wings of the environmentalist movement may be in support of reducing the footprint of society, reversing technological development, and hurling ourselves back to a more rustic and simpler time. But the population as a whole is not in support of this. Robin Mills refers to these approaches as "neo-Luddite," an unflattering reference to the nineteenth-century British textile workers' movement that protested modernization by destroying machines. Robin E. Mills, *The Myth of the Oil Crisis: Overcoming the Challenge of Depletion, Geopolitics, and Global Warming* (Westport: Praeger, 2008), 19–20. Among current writers, Mills includes in this camp Richard Heinberg, *The Party's Over: Oil, War, and the Fate of Industrial Societies* (Gabriola Island: New Society, 2003); and Julian Darley, *High Noon for Natural Gas: The New Energy Crisis* (White River Junction, VT: Chelsea Green, 2004).

24. Electric vehicles (EVs) would be a case in point. In addition to the product line improving, infrastructure needs are quickly giving way to some interesting developments. See Kent Moors, "NRG Moves into the Electric Car Market," *Energy Advantage Portfolio Update* (November 24, 2010), available at: http:// moneymappress.com/2010/11/24/nrg-moves-into-the-electric-car-market/.

25. See Chapter 6, note 98 and associated text.

26. In August 2006, the Amaranth hedge fund lost $2 billion in natural gas derivatives, subsequently liquidating its entire $8 billion portfolio. A staff report from the Senate Permanent Subcommittee on Investigations determined that the fund's collapse precipitated a deep and unexpected decline in gas prices, concluding that the large positions held by Amaranth were also the cause for significant market price movements in gas prior to the fund's failure. "Excessive Speculation in the Natural Gas Market," *Staff Report of the Permanent Subcommittee on Investigations, United States Senate* (June 25 and July 9, 2007), available at: http://hsgac.senate.gov/public/_files/REPORTExces siveSpeculationintheNaturalGasMarket.pdf. The report also concluded that the fund evaded limits on the size of speculative positions by moving from NYMEX to exempt and unregulated markets. This is the swap dealer loophole. See Chapter 6, note 99 and associated text.

     On Amaranth, see, for example, Roger T. Cole, Greg Feldberg, and David Lynch, "Hedge Funds, Credit Risk Transfer, and Financial Stability," *Banque de France Financial Stability Review Special Issue on Hedge Funds*, No. 10 (2007), 7–17; Hillary Till, "The Amaranth Collapse: What Happened and What Have We Learned Thus Far," *EDHEC Risk and Asset Management Centre* (2007), available at: www.premiacap.com/publications/EDHEC_Amaranth_Collapse. pdf; id., "Amaranth Lessons Thus Far," *Journal of Alternative Investments* 10 (2008), 82–98; and Wouter van Eechoud, Wybe Hamersma, Arnd Sieling, and David Young, "Future Regulation of Hedge Funds—A Systematic Risk Perspective," *Financial Markers, Institutions & Instruments* 19 (2010), 269–353.

27. The classic treatment of the LTCM collapse remains Roger Lowenstein, *When Genius Failed: The Rise and Fall of Long-Term Capital Management* (New York: Random House, 2000). The fate of LTCM is all the more intriguing given two of its partners—Myron Scholes of the Black-Scholes model and Robert Merton, whose application of the model to price European options (options than can only be exercised at maturity) produced the Black-Scholes-Merton model. The two were awarded the 1997 Nobel Prize in Economics (Fischer Black was deceased by that time and the Swedish Academy does not award the prize posthumously). Less than a year later, LTCM lost $4.6 billion in four months and closed in 2000. This maybe the most spectacular example of what fat tails can do to an investment strategy.

28. See the discussion in Chapter 6.

29. Darrell Duffie, "How Should We Regulative Derivatives Markets?" *The PEW Financial Reform Project*, Briefing Paper No. 5 (2009), available at: www.pewfr .org/admin/project_reports/files/Pew_Duffie_Derivatives_Paper_FINAL -TF-Correction.pdf.

30. See note 21 to this chapter.

31. Such a normal commoditized instrument would be considered a "vanilla" derivative. Most pure credit derivatives, such as a straightforward CDS, are considered vanilla. On the overall structure, see Antonio Nicolò and Loriana Pelizzon, "Credit Derivatives: Capital Requirements and Strategic Contracting" (2006), working paper, available at: www.biz.org/bcbs/events/rtf06nicolo_etc.pdf.

32. The best history of the SPR is Bruce A. Beaubouef, *The Strategic Petroleum Reserve: U.S. Energy Security and Oil Politics, 1975–2005* (College Station: Texas A&M University, 2007).

33. See note 1 to this chapter.

34. As of November 24, 2010, USO has net assets in excess of $1.9 billion.

35. See Kent Moors, "How the Little Guy Will Fix Oil Futures and Get in on the Profits," *Oil and Energy Investor* (March 16, 2010), available at: http://oiland energyinvestor.com/2010/03/oil-futures/.

36. Friedman uses this on several occasions. See, for example, Thomas Friedman, *The World Is Flat: A Brief History of the Twenty-First Century* (New York: Farrar, Straus and Giroux, 2005), 114. The quotation is of unknown origin. It does, however, have a universe of its own, appearing in thousands of locations on the Web, has its own sites, and is frequently used by supporters of everything from long-distance running to motivational speaking.

About the Author

Kent Moors is a Professor in the Department of Political Science and the Graduate Center for Social and Public Policy at Duquesne University, where he also directs the Energy Policy Research Group.

An internationally recognized expert in oil and gas policy/finance and risk assessment, Kent is also president of the oil and gas consulting firm ASIDA, Inc., advising companies, financial institutions, law firms, and governments worldwide. He authors the *Oil and Energy Investor,* a twice-weekly advisory, the monthly *Energy Advantage*, and the investment alert service *The Energy Inner Circle*, and is a frequent contributor to *Money Morning* and contributing editor to the two leading post–Soviet Union oil and gas publications *Russian Petroleum Investor* and *Caspian Investor.* Through an agreement with DeMatteo Monness, he provides specialized advisories to a broad range of Wall Street analysts, as well as investment, hedge fund, capital, and asset managers.

Index